Spectrum Guide to
KENYA

Facts On File
New York • Oxford

Spectrum Guide to Kenya

©1989 Camerapix

First published 1989 by
Facts on File, Inc.,
460 Park Avenue South,
New York, NY 10016,
USA

Library of Congress
Catalog Card Number 89-045758.
CIP data available on request from the
publisher

ISBN 0-8160-2129-5

This book was designed and produced by
Camerapix Publishers International,
P.O. Box 45048,
Nairobi, Kenya

Facts on File books are available at special
discounts when purchased in bulk
quantities for businesses, associations,
institutions or sales promotion. Please
contact the Special Sales Department of our
New York office at 212/683-2244 (dial 800/
322-8755 except in NY, AK, or HI).

The **Spectrum Guides** series provide a
comprehensive and detailed description of
each country they cover together with all
the essential data that tourists, business
visitors, or potential investors are likely to
require.

Publisher and Chief Executive:
Mohamed Amin
Editorial Director: Brian Tetley
Art Director: Duncan Willetts
International Projects Manager: Debbie Gaiger
Editors: Marti Colley and Jack Crowther
Editorial Consultants: Chege Mbituru and
Bob Smith
Co-ordinator: Nazma Rawji
Production Assistant: Kimberly Davis
Photographic Research: Abdul Rehman
Editorial Assistant: Mary-Anne Muigari
Design Consultant: Craig Dodd

Printed and bound in Hong Kong

This book is printed on acid-free paper.

TABLE OF CONTENTS

PART FOUR: BUSINESS KENYA

PART FIVE
FACTS AT YOUR FINGERTIPS

IN BRIEF

LISTINGS

MAPS

Half-title: Vasco da Gama monument, Malindi. Title Page: Elephant beneath Mount Kilimanjaro in Amboseli. Previous pages: Tiwi Beach on Kenya's south coast.

Editorial Board

Spectrum Guide to Kenya is one of a series of high-quality, lavishly and colourfully illustrated international *Spectrum Guides* to exotic and exciting countries, cultures, flora, and fauna.

The idea behind the series came from the three-man travel book team of **Mohamed Amin, Duncan Willetts,** and **Brian Tetley,** whose *Journey through* series on various countries have been published in many languages.

Too often they were unable to find the answers to questions — not always about guide book "places" — that would help them to complete their work. They felt that there was need for a guide that not only lavished space on detail, descriptions, and photographs of tourist "destinations" but tried to answer all the questions a traveller or resident might ask. They soon discovered that such a concept involved a massive amount of research to uncover information about the other areas of a country — and its institutions and systems.

All the photographs in this guide were taken by Kenyan-born Amin and his English colleague and friend, Willetts, who is equally renowned for his superb photography.

Research and writing were assigned by Tetley, an English-born Kenyan with forty years of editorial experience in Europe and Africa. His knowledgeable team — each an authority on some aspect of Kenya — contributed information and helped verify facts.

For all three, Kenya is their home so *Spectrum Guide to Kenya* holds a special place in their affections.

Text editing was the responsibility of **Marti Colley,** an English journalist, and **Jack Crowther,** an Australian editor based in Kenya, was responsible for maintaining *Spectrum Guide* in-house style and copy editing. Both relative newcomers to Kenya, but much-experienced independent travellers, their enthusiasm and eye for detail added much to this publication.

Kenyan **Nazma Rawji** was responsible for the complex co-ordination and design was by **Craig Dodd,** one of Europe's leading graphic designers, based in London.

Editorial assistant **Mary-Anne Muiruri** and **Peris Oweggi**, an experienced publishing executive, both Kenyans, undertook the task of preparing and revising the many draft manuscripts while Nairobi-born Abdul Rehman spent long hours on photographic research.

Together, the diverse cultural backgrounds of the *Spectrum Guide to Kenya* team have created a guide book that seeks to answer virtually any question that any traveller or resident might ask — together with quirky stories about the early settlers, and suggested alternatives to the established tourist circuits.

With detailed route descriptions, maps, gazeteer, and address listings, *Spectrum Guide to Kenya* contains all the practical advice needed to plan and make your holiday a truly original and memorable experience.

Opposite: Burji farmers sifting chaff near Moyale on the Kenyan-Ethiopian border.

Overleaf: Oxbow lake in Pokomo country on the lower reaches of the Tana River.

Following pages: Flamingo spectacle at Lake Bogoria in the Rift Valley.

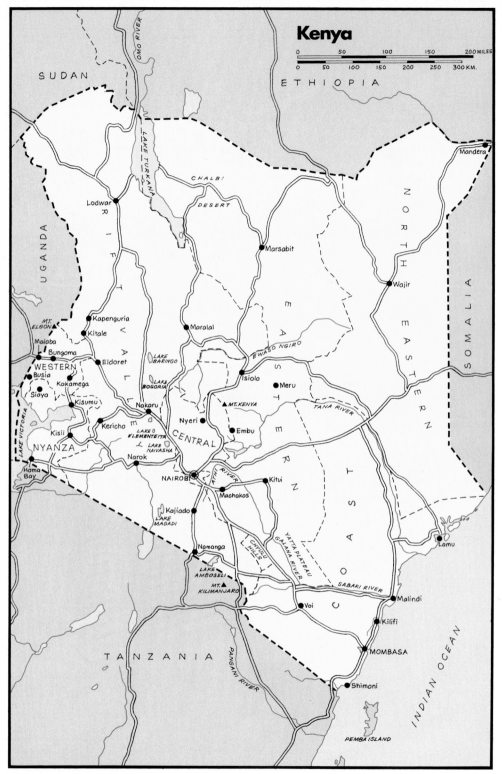

Kenya

SUDAN

ETHIOPIA

50   100   150   200 MILES
50   100   150   200   250   300 KM.

OMO RIVER

LAKE TURKANA

CHALBI

DESERT

Lodwar

UGANDA

MT. ELGON ▲

Kapenguria

Kitale

Malaba

Bungoma

WESTERN

Eldoret

Busia

Kakamega

Siaya

Kisumu

Kericho

Kisii

NYANZA

Homa Bay

LAKE VICTORIA

Nakuru

Narok

LAKE BARINGO

LAKE BOGORIA

LAKE ELEMENTEITA

LAKE NAIVASHA

Nyeri

CENTRAL

Marsabit

Maralal

EWASO NGIRO

Isiolo

Meru

MT. KENYA ▲

Embu

NAIROBI

Machakos

ATHI RIVER

Kajiado

LAKE MAGADI

Namanga

LAKE AMBOSELI

MT. ▲ KILIMANJARO

CHYULU HILLS

TANZANIA

PANGANI RIVER

Kitui

Wajir

Mandera

NORTH EASTERN

SOMALIA

EASTERN

TANA RIVER

COAST

YATTA PLATEAU

GALANA RIVER

SABAKI RIVER

Lamu

Voi

Malindi

Kilifi

MOMBASA

Shimoni

INDIAN OCEAN

PEMBA ISLAND

R I F T   V A L L E Y

The Kenya Experience

A Welcome

The suddenness of dawn in Kenya brings a quickening of the pulse. Now lambent dawn floods the plains and the light flushes the shadows of night from the thickets, along the hidden rills, and chases them across the tawny grasslands as the sun climbs, agile, over the curve of the Equator.

The pink sky begins to dissolve into a flawless blue and the faint breath of the day's first thermal stirs the still, chill air.

To experience first light in Kenya is to be overwhelmed with a feeling of the world new-born. Across savannah plains, forest-cloaked mountains, and lakes and rivers flashing silver in the sun, the land reflects an incredible freshness.

Yet, many millions of years ago, long before our earliest ancestors evolved in the Great Rift Valley, Kenya was a flat and sterile country. It was dramatically refashioned by tumultuous forces deep inside the earth.

Intense pressures, from between 160 and 250 kilometres (100-150 miles) below the surface, forced ancient foundation strata upwards.

Nascent streams of molten rock burst forth through flaws in the earth's crust as incandescent fingers of magma and fire. As the extensive lava flowed through these fissures, it slowly cooled to form the dome-shaped volcanic plateaux of central Ethiopia, Kenya, and western Uganda.

Over the aeons, with each new explosion, great cones of rock were thrust skywards. Layer upon layer, each intermittent explosion built up Mount Kenya until it stood between 7,000 and 8,300 metres (23,000-27,000 feet) above the Equator.

As the wrack and warp slowly abated, one last spasm gave birth to the Rift Valley which runs the length of much of East Africa.

When the ashes and the dust settled, the rain and sun gave flesh to Kenya's bare lava bones, leaving a sensuous skin of rich, loamy soil where lush forests of podocarpus, cedar, hagenia, and bamboo thrived. A mantle of peat, bog, and strange exotic plants grew over the mountain skeletons, and a veneer of grass spread across the plains. The new earth was rich and fertile.

It was to become an Eden, where massive elephants, sabre-toothed tigers, giant pigs, rhinoceros, and crocodiles roamed. It was also to be the home of mankind's ancestors, for as far as we know it was in ancient Kenya that man learned to stand upright and take his first faltering footsteps.

Yet even as the early hominids began leaving the shores of Lake Turkana to explore the new-born fertile plains, the dying forces that gave birth to Mount Kenya were still at work.

As recently as 40,000 years ago they burst forth once more, creating the Nyambeni hills on its north-eastern flank.

Thirty thousand years later, immigrants began moving down from the north to colonise this new land. The first outsiders venturing into Kenya, ancestors of today's indigenous populations, were nomads, warriors, craftsmen, and farmers. For over 10,000 years, they moved south along the mighty Nile culminating with the arrival of the Maasai and the Kikuyu during the last 1,000 years.

Later came the Persians, Arabs, Europeans, and Asians with new-found faiths in their blood.

More than forty different ethnic groups make up the mosaic of modern Kenya. Today, they're united under the national green, black, and red flag — green representing the land, black for the people, and red for the blood shed in the fight for freedom — and their unity is expressed in the national motto *Harambee*, meaning "Let's all pull together".

Together, they make a land of harmonious contrasts.

As much as the animals and landscapes, it is these people who, each year, draw more and more visitors to this great, natural paradise. This land, where mankind took his first steps has always invited discovery — now as much as ever before.

Today, Kenya's greeting is warmer and more generous than at any time in its history.

So, *Karibu* — welcome.

Previous pages: Aerial view of Nairobi with the railway station in foreground right.

Travel Brief and Social Advisory

Some dos and don'ts to make your visit more enjoyable.

Adventure in comfort

Almost no other resort destination in the world offers the potential for so much adventure in such safety — and comfort — as Kenya.

Visitors can spend days and nights in the wilderness at close quarters with the greatest and most ferocious natural predators on earth — apart from mankind — but with all the luxuries of civilization on hand and nothing to fear.

The luxuries include self-contained suites with private bathrooms, air-conditioning, well-stocked cocktail bars, crackling log fires, and five-course gourmet dinners.

Wherever you go in Kenya, no matter how remote or rugged, you'll find full accommodation of at least three- and often four- or five-star comfort.

With all this, and given the climate and natural spectacle, a Kenya holiday is certain to be the adventure of a lifetime. Nonetheless, particularly in the towns and cities, unforeseen problems may arise. This section focuses on both the benefits and the potential pitfalls.

GETTING AROUND

By Road

Road maps of Kenya vary in accuracy. The main problem is the speed at which new roads are built and deteriorate so that gradings are misleading. Unfortunately, the best maps, produced by the Survey of Kenya, are often out of print.

Similarly, there are good street maps of the major towns and cities but since these areas are also developing — and degrading — at a tremendous rate, the information is often out of date.

The A-Z guides of Nairobi and Mombasa by Kenway Publications are revised regularly, however, and though somewhat confusing in layout, are informative and clear enough to enable anyone to find their way around.

Driving in Kenya is for the fatalistic and suicidal. Too many drivers have a blatant disregard for speed limits or traffic laws. Besides a good map, essential equipment for visitors who wish to drive is a large supply of sedatives.

Trucks, lorries, buses and the ubiquitous *matatus* — private freelance commuter vehicles ranging from hotrod Peugeot 504s through minibuses down to dilapidated pickups — and darkness are the real enemies. Wherever you're going it's best to aim to arrive before sundown.

Additional hazards include potholes the size of frontline shell craters, *kamikaze* cyclists, pedestrians, cattle, goats, sheep, speed bumps that weren't there the week before, unmarked sharp bends, unannounced roadworks, and slow moving — sometimes stationary — traffic without lights.

Signposts do exist but have often been mangled in an accident or uprooted for use as building or fencing material.

Although the Mombasa to Uganda road is the main artery for much of eastern and central Africa — South Sudan, Uganda, Rwanda, Burundi, and Eastern Zaire — it should be used as little as possible, especially at night.

The top speed in unrestricted areas on main roads is limited to 100 kilometres (seventy miles) an hour. In urban areas this varies between fifty and eighty kilometres (30-50 miles) an hour. These limits are rarely observed or enforced, except through an occasional speed trap.

This guide gives approximate distances in kilometres and miles, verified by the Automobile Association of Kenya.

Remember that for off-the-road driving, particularly in game sanctuaries and the north, especially during the rains, often only 4WD is suitable — and, even then, not infallible.

Most tour groups travel in the privacy of well-maintained, reasonably new minibuses with drivers who, for the most part, are cautious and experienced.

For the independent traveller, major towns are linked by reasonably comfortable, frequent, and — by western standards — extremely cheap scheduled coach services.

The cheapest, most uncomfortable, but certainly the most colourful and most intimate means of travel is by country bus or *matatu*. Shoulder to shoulder, rib-to-rib, "there's always

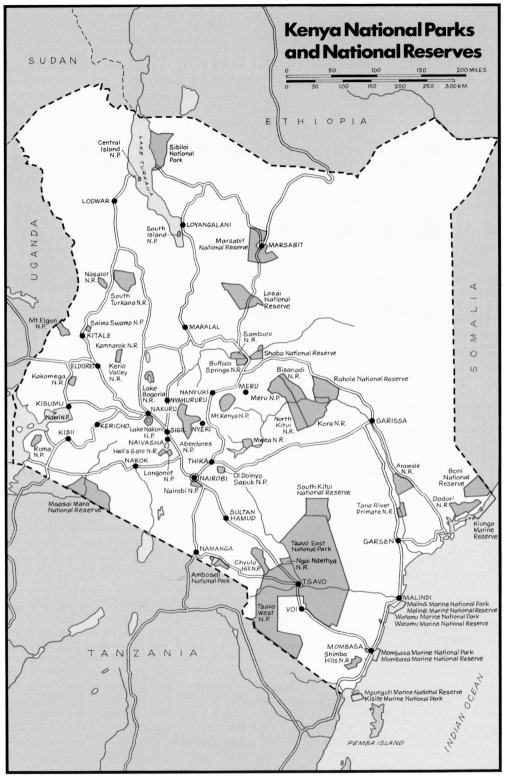

Kenya National Parks and National Reserves

SUDAN

ETHIOPIA

UGANDA

SOMALIA

TANZANIA

INDIAN OCEAN

Central Island N.P.

Sibiloi National Park

Lake Turkana

LODWAR

South Island N.P.

LOYANGALANI

Marsabit National Reserve

MARSABIT

Nasalot N.R.

South Turkana N.R.

Losai National Reserve

Mt. Elgon N.P.

Saiwa Swamp N.P.

KITALE

Kamnarok N.R.

MARALAL

Samburu N.R.

Shaba National Reserve

Buffalo Springs N.R.

ELDORET

Kerio Valley N.R.

Bisanadi N.R.

Rahole National Reserve

Kokomega N.R.

Lake Bogoria N.R.

NANYUKI

MERU

Meru N.P.

KISUMU

Nderi N.P.

NAKURU

NYAHURURU

North Kitui N.R.

Kora N.R.

GARISSA

KERICHO

Lake Nakuru N.P.

Mt. Kenya N.P.

KISII

GIGIL

NYERI

Ruma N.P.

NAIVASHA

Aberdares N.P.

Mwea N.R.

Hell's Gate N.R.

NAROK

THIKA

Arawale N.R.

Boni National Reserve

Longonot N.P.

Ol Doinyo Sapuk N.P.

NAIROBI

Nairobi N.P.

South Kitui National Reserve

Dodori N.R.

Maasai Mara National Reserve

SULTAN HAMUD

Tana River Primate N.R.

Kiunga Marine Reserve

GARSEN

NAMANGA

Tsavo East National Park

Amboseli National Park

Chyulu Hill N.P.

Ngai Ndethya N.R.

TSAVO

MALINDI

Malindi Marine National Park
Malindi Marine National Reserve
Watamu Marine National Park
Watamu Marine National Reserve

Tsavo West N.P.

VOI

MOMBASA

Shimba Hills N.R.

Mombasa Marine National Park
Mombasa Marine National Reserve

Mpunguti Marine National Reserve
Kisite Marine National Park

PEMBA ISLAND

0   50   100   150   200 MILES
0 50 100 150 200 250 300 KM.

room for one more", these vehicles are a certain way of getting close to your Kenyan neighbours, if not to understanding them altogether.

Unfortunately, some local *makoras* (villains) have discovered a new trick. The hospitable guy offering you a bun, sandwich, cup of tea, or soda may well have laced his offering with a knockout drug.

It's not unknown for passengers to wake up long after they reach their destination to find they have been robbed of everything. So the golden rule on *matatu*, bus, or train is "never take sweets — or anything else — from a stranger".

By Air

Kenya has the busiest domestic flight network in Africa with more than 200 scheduled flights a week to fifteen destinations. The national carrier, Kenya Airways, and its fleet of Airbuses, 707s, DC9s, and Fokkers, serves major destinations, with private schedule and charter services flying to the more remote areas.

From Nairobi there are forty-seven flights a week to Mombasa, and fifty in return to Nairobi; twenty-eight from Nairobi to Maasai Mara; fourteen to Lamu; eleven to Kisumu and Malindi; seven to Amboseli, Garissa, Kiwaiyu, Nanyuki, Nyeri, and Samburu, and four to Eldoret.

In addition there are two weekly flights from Mombasa to Lamu and eight from Mombasa to Malindi.

Although convenient, especially during the rains, air travel is much more expensive than ground transport.

By Train

Those who wish to travel by train in Kenya should be in no hurry. The "Lunatic Express" is still as slow as it was almost 100 years ago when the Mombasa to Lake Victoria line was built. The metre-gauge track and severe gradients—such as the Rift Valley escarpment — limit speed.

The overnight train from Nairobi to Mombasa is perfect for romantics who wish to travel like the pioneers for whom the railway was the only link between most towns and settlements.

There are two trains each night in both directions, the "express" leaving some ninety minutes after the "slow" train. It takes just under thirteen hours to cover the 500 kilometres (310 miles).

The highpoint of the journey is dinner in the dining car as the train passes herds of zebra grazing at sunset. The five course English cuisine is well-cooked and superbly served with a choice of wines by white coated waiters. And it costs little more than a beefburger in London or New York.

Accommodation is two to a compartment in first class. Second class is for four occupants and is clean, comfortable and functional. Bed linen, pillows and blankets are available for hire from the conductor.

Third-class offers only wooden benches and can be extremely uncomfortable.

Fares are extremely cheap by western standards but places should be reserved in advance because the train is generally full. Special discounts are available for group bookings.

Similar facilities are available on the twice-daily service between Nairobi-Nakuru-Kisumu and the thrice-weekly service from Nairobi to Malaba on the Uganda border.

By Foot

Vast open spaces, rolling hills and rugged mountain moorlands offer ideal walking country to those with time to spare.

Off the main tarmac highways, minor murram roads and cotton-soil byways pass through what are still known as the "reserves" which make up the true heart of Kenya. Much of this land is found in the central, western and north-western regions of the country and ranges between 1,200 and 2,750 metres (4,000-9,000 feet) in height. It's more strenuous than lowland walking in Europe or America, but rewarding. However, avoid cotton-soil roads during the rainy season when they become a glutinous morass.

Small hamlets and villages are sprinkled across these glorious farmlands which are tended by strong, thrifty, hardworking people with a sense of humour and always a warm welcome for passing strangers.

While much of Kenya has yet to be discovered by walkers, the main focus for trekkers and climbers is still Mount Kenya, although there are a wide range of alternatives such as Mount Elgon, the Cheranganis, the Aberdares, the Mau summit, the Chyulu Hills and many others (See "Kenya's Mountains").

The People

The spirit of Kenya is exemplified by its tradition of hospitality. Few people in the world are as welcoming. The peaceful stranger who visits an unknown village is greeted with an openness that many Westerners find overwhelming. And it often happens, paradoxically, that the poorer the home, the poorer the person, the richer the welcome.

In the metropolitan and municipal areas twenty-five years of urbanization and rural migration to fast-growing townships has eroded this spirit.

But, nonetheless, ninety-nine per cent of Kenyans demonstrate an open-handedness and willingness to help that is hard to find elsewhere.

In a land where much of the rural population has no access to electricity, life is tuned to the sun. Activity is at its height during the early hours and in the brief cool of the late afternoon.

It's as well to remember that less than a century ago only a handful of outsiders had visited the Kenya hinterland. The cash economy was unknown and there was no modern technology — just communities of proud, independent, hard-working farmfolk who traded on barter.

In a few short decades, Kenya has travelled far and fast. The immediate descendants of a society denied access to centuries of urban living, knowledge, and evolving technology, have adapted at every level to what is known as civilization.

Whatever you think of western civilization, the structures and values of Kenyan society that have enabled the people to adapt with such dynamic success must be respected.

Long before the western Bible or middle eastern Qur'an came to Kenya, people believed in God under a variety of names. Inherent in all Kenya cultures is a pure and simple vision of a creator who sanctifies life, predisposing no idols, totems, or rituals.

This unsullied reverence for a supreme being is reflected perhaps in the manner in which Kenyans took to Christianity and Islam, both orthodox and unorthodox. In the 1980s Kenya had more registered church organisations than any other country in the world. Well over 1,700 different non-secular societies were potent proof of Kenya's commitment to freedom of expression, association, choice, and worship.

As you travel around the country, you'll meet many Kenyans, most of whom speak good English. They have a tradition of oral communication, and delight in explaining the history, customs, and geography of their home. Through their eyes, their intricate social customs are woven into a rich cultural tapestry.

To enjoy your visit to the full, first familiarize yourself with some of the country's customs and taboos. Good manners aside, a knowledge and awareness of these will give you a greater insight into Kenyan culture.

The standard greeting, and always welcome to whomever it is addressed, is *jambo* — a kind of "hello" and "how are you?" — that should elicit the standard response, *mzuri,* meaning "all is well".

If however the reply is *mbaya,* meaning "not so good", a commiserative *pole* — "sorry" — will express your sympathy.

In Kenya physical contact is all-important. Everybody shakes hands upon meeting — even friends who last saw each other two hours ago. The proffered hand is only refused when an offence has been committed. The handshake is not just an introduction — it is a gesture of trust and peace.

Most important, "face" — respect — is everything. Kenyans are extremely proud of their country and it ill-behoves any passing stranger to offer gratuitous or condescending criticism or advice about national or local affairs. However, once you know a few Kenyans you may well become involved in animated but friendly discussions on the values of differing cultures; i.e., African culture as opposed to European culture.

It's considered gravely insulting to shout at anybody, even with words of praise, so whatever you have to say deliver it *sotto voce.*

Anything evocative of a colonial stance will provoke even the most gentle of these gentle folk so don't call the waiter, or anybody else over the age of sixteen, "boy". The normal address when calling for service in a restaurant or bar, is a less offensive colonial hangover — "steward" — a reminder that until the 1950s the main means of passage to Kenya was by sea.

Better still, use the standard *rafiki* — "friend" — or *bwana,* meaning "mister".

For anybody clearly over forty years of age, *Mzee* is a euphemistic form of address that expresses respect not only for the person but for his wisdom and experience. For women, the word *Mama* carries the same connotation.

The term *mwananchi* refers to a person — the plural, *wananchi*, covers the entire community — a word that denotes respect. The other collective for people, *watu*, has a sneering undertone.

Never use the collective "blacks" anymore than you would "honkies" to describe whites. The normal references are Africans, *wananchi*, Asians, *wahindi*, and Europeans, *wazungu*.

Always respect lawful authority. There's talk of corruption but most visitors find the established services, especially the police, exemplary — always polite, helpful, and considerate. Tourists who unwittingly commit minor infringements of traffic laws, for instance, are usually waved on with the words, "Enjoy your visit to our country".

In Africa, the head of the community traditionally enjoys a great deal more status and commands more obedience than in western cultures and this is transposed to the executive. The President is always treated with deference and you should not attempt to take his photograph unless you have permission from one of his entourage.

Since the opportunity to ask is unlikely to arise keep your camera packed away.

This sensitivity applies to the Presidential portrait on Kenyan currency. It is a criminal offence to deface, damage, or destroy Kenya currency. Some visitors, in a fit of annoyance at being asked to surrender their remaining Kenya currency on departure — its export is illegal — have destroyed it and found themselves in jail.

So take your currency form to an official bank and convert the balance to hard currency before you get to the departure lounge at the airport.

Always seek consent before you attempt to take anyone's photograph. In the most remote regions, where superstition still persists, it's thought you are attempting to steal their soul. In more sophisticated areas it's just regarded as downright rude not to ask first.

Apart from social customs, always respect the law. For tourists, the main hazards are black-market money street deals which infringe Kenya's strictly-enforced currency controls. In any case, you stand a good chance of being conned out of your money. The hiring of prostitutes, other sexual offences, and drug taking are other frequent infringements.

In its application to tourists, law-enforcement in Kenya is always understanding and reasonably mild, depending, of course, on which law has been transgressed and the degree of involvement.

The judicial system is based on the British model so bond or bail can be granted at the police or magistrate's discretion and all cases must be brought before a court. Kenya's judiciary has won high regard for its impartiality.

Safety

Since Kenyan society is less affluent than western society, never make an ostentatious show of wealth.

Nairobi is as safe as most capital cities; and Mombasa is a typical dock town. Apply common sense: muggings do take place after dark (usually unaccompanied singles or couples at most) and bag and watch-snatching occur even by day.

Safeguard money, passports, travellers' cheques, and airline tickets. Do not leave personal documents in your hotel room or luggage. Most hotels and lodges have safekeeping facilities. Ask at the desk for this facility and always insist on a receipt.

Never take out cameras or other valuables in public unless absolutely necessary. Do not tempt fate by carrying around your handbag loose and open or carry large amounts of cash.

If you are driving, do not leave anything of value in a locked car. In towns, there is usually someone who will volunteer to "guard" it for you for a few shillings.

Be careful of the "hustlers" in Nairobi. You may hear a hard luck story designed to get you to donate money to a "worthy" cause.

Beggars are common. Most are visibly destitute and many are cripples, lepers, or homeless mothers with children. Some have regular pitches, others keep on the move. They are often rounded up, but soon return.

Clothes

As Kenya rises from sea-level to more than 5,200 metres (17,000 feet), and much of the

Opposite: Tourists drift over Tsavo's savannah plains near Kilimanjaro.

country is between 1,500 and 2,100 metres (5,000-7,000 feet) visitors will experience contrasting climates and extremes of temperature.

Even at 3,000 metres (10,000 feet) on the Equator, the sun can be blistering — and the nights frozen.

For most of the year the standard Safari outfit — tailored shirt or top jacket and trousers — is ideal for bush travel. Carry a hat to avoid sunstroke.

At other times, shorts, casuals, and anything you require for sports and swimming should suffice, but bring along some woollens for those evenings at high-altitude.

In the cities and towns, western business convention prevails — tailored suit, shirt, and tie. Otherwise, smart casual wear is acceptable.

June to August can be overcast — cool in the daytime and chilly at nights — so include some warm cardigans and sweaters. Smart, medium-weight clothes will suffice for the evenings.

Women will probably find cotton dresses cooler and more comfortable than trousers, particularly for daytime wear. "Baggy" trousers rather than skin tight jeans are obviously better ventilated. For footwear, comfort should take precedence over style since many pavements are uneven in the cities and towns, and non-existent in the bush.

Specialized sports clothes, including swimwear, should be packed. Most items are available in Nairobi and Mombasa, but in a limited range and often more expensive than back home.

Drip dry clothing is ideal, although virtually all hotels and lodges offer same-day laundry services. Even so, in many places the dust may make two or three changes a day necessary for the more fastidious.

Safari clothes and boots for both men and women, reasonably-priced, are available in Nairobi and Mombasa. Tailor-made safari suits can be run up in a matter of hours and men, particularly, find them a valuable addition to their holiday wardrobe. They look smart, feel cool, and cost only a fraction of a regular suit, with the added bonus of being washable.

For women, the local *kitenge* dresses and loose blouses are a most attractive and popular wardrobe addition. These are available in an infinite variety of designs and at little cost. *Kangas* and *kikois* (simple wrap around sarongs) are also useful.

At the coast, shorts are acceptable — but bear in mind the Muslim ethic in dress. This, especially, forbids nude bathing on the beach.

What to take

Most essentials are available anywhere in Kenya. However, if you are on specific, prescribed drugs for prolonged periods, our advice is to carry adequate dosages to cover your safari as pharmaceutical products tend to be much more costly in Kenya.

It's also worth carrying a spare pair of eye glasses and, failing that, at least a prescription that would enable you to get another pair. However, like drugs, these too are inordinately expensive in Kenya. Contact lens solutions are available in Nairobi and Mombasa although occasionally supplies run out, so bring your own.

Laundry

Major hotels offer same day or twenty-four hour laundry and dry-cleaning service.

Elsewhere Kenya — unlike Asia, for example — is distinguished by its lack of laundry facilities. Economy travellers staying in lodging houses or camping will have no alternative but to do their own laundry.

Health

Doctors recommend all visitors have inoculations against tetanus, polio, cholera, typhoid, and paratyphoid. A gamma globulin injection provides some protection against hepatitis and it is well worth taking this precaution.

Malaria is endemic and all visitors should take an anti-malarial prophylactic beginning two weeks before their arrival and for six weeks after departure.

Kenya has excellent medical facilities, better than most African countries. There are first-rate private hospitals in Nairobi, Kisumu, and Mombasa, and there are a surprising number of specialist physicians and surgeons, many of international reputation. There are also excellent dentists and opticians. However, medical treatment is very expensive.

All visitors, therefore, should have medical insurance. It can be obtained in Kenya but usually at a higher premium than you would pay in Europe and North America for the same cover.

Temporary membership is available with

the East African Medical Research Foundation — AMREF — which operates the world-famous Flying Doctor service throughout Kenya and Tanzania. For a token payment, AMREF guarantees to fly patients to the nearest well-equipped hospital should they fall ill or suffer injury while on safari.

There is no shortage of chemists or drug stores in Kenya, all of them staffed with qualified pharmacists. Most drugs are available, although sometimes they may have unfamiliar brand names.

If your specific prescription is not available, the pharmacist will often prescribe a suitable alternative.

Most chemists close on Saturday afternoons, Sundays, and public holidays. When closed, the name and location of the duty chemist is usually posted on the shop door, or may be obtained at the nearest hospital. The list of roster chemists who open at weekends in Nairobi and Mombasa is also listed in the newspapers.

Photography

Colour and black and white film, sixty-minute, and one-day processing are readily available in all major centres. Camera equipment (tripods, lenses, flash etc) can be hired from camera shops in Nairobi and Mombasa.

It is forbidden to photograph State Houses and military installations.

When to Go

The tourist season extends all year round with "lows" during the two rainy seasons — which are often the best time to visit. The "long rains" normally fall between mid-March and the end of May, and the "short rains" from the end of October to early December. Nairobi and the Central Highlands are depressingly cold, grey and overcast on most days between June and August.

Although some areas may be closed because of road conditions, the advantages of a low-season visit are often stunningly-clear mornings and early afternoons, special hotel and lodge rates, and fewer visitors to scare off the wildlife.

The high seasons, when advance booking is mandatory, are from December to the end of March and from mid-September to the end of October, with a "shoulder" season at the coast and in the game reserves from the end of June to mid-September.

On Safari

Many view a Kenya safari as some kind of happy endurance test highlighted by glimpses of stunning scenery, colourful people, and herds of wild animals.

You'll enjoy Kenya all the more if you scrutinise your itinerary with care and insist on enough time in each place to enjoy it to the full. Be selective. If it means cutting down the number of parks and reserves, it also cuts down the number of jolting kilometres you travel each day.

Remember, too, that although some animals have become used to people, they are still wild animals. Do not feed monkeys or other primates — nor make excessive noise to attract their attention.

Do not leave the designated trails for that closer shot — and do not get out of your vehicle except at designated areas. Close all windows and zips when you leave your room or tent.

Many visitors believe success is related to the number of animals they check-off in the shortest possible time. But this is a sad way to enjoy the unprecedented opportunities for wildlife viewing.

Instead, read up on wildlife to help you identify the smaller creatures and the birds. Then, if something catches your eye, spend time observing it and learning its habits and characteristics first-hand.

Remember that the maximum speed limit is fifty kilometres (30 miles) an hour in the game reserves — and often slower.

Tell your guide that, despite the watch you wear, you are in no hurry. The slower you drive, the more you see; a lioness crouched in the grass, tail swishing and eyes alert, may be looking for supper.

Stop and wait. Before the hour is up you may well witness the unparalleled spectacle of a lioness bringing down a gazelle in full flight.

Always keep your camera loaded and ready for action. You never know when it's going to start. But do not stand or sit on top of the

Overleaf: Reticulated giraffe and zebra beneath Mount Kenya.

vehicles for a better view and do not forget to adhere to the park and game reserve visiting hours 06.30-18.30. The best time to see wildlife is early morning or late afternoon.

Money on safari

A good supply of travellers' cheques is essential for anyone travelling in Kenya, but they can remain mere pieces of paper once you get to remote places far from the banks.

This applies especially to almost the entire northern part of the country, where even in the larger townships the bank may only be an agency operating once or twice a week.

On the beaten track

The best way to travel is to take along enough cash to cover expenses *en route*, plus some extra for emergencies, say to buy that spare tyre or inner tube when you unexpectedly lose your tread.

Ideally, the rest should be in Kenya shillings travellers' cheques. These are available for a small charge and are cashed at face value, with no deductions, in any bank and most hotels.

Carrying Kenya shillings travellers' cheque eliminates any problem about fluctuating foreign exchange rates. If you do take travellers' cheques in "hard" foreign currencies, shop around for the most favourable rate.

Generally, banks give a much better rate than hotels, which often charge hefty commissions.

It's also worth noting that they charge for each cheque leaf — one charge for a single £100 cheque, but ten for ten £10 cheques.

Don't assume that large hotels with twenty-four hour cashier facilities will be prepared to cash your travellers' cheques unless you're staying there. If you don't have a room number they may decline to change your money on the grounds that they do not provide this facility for non-residents.

Smaller hotels tend to be more helpful, but often don't have enough cash on hand.

In Nairobi and Mombasa foreign exchange bureaux are open until 16.30 daily and also Saturdays and some Sundays and public holidays.

Credit cards are invaluable for settling bills. There are several local credit cards dealing in Kenya money, but American Express, Barclaycard, and Visa are widely accepted.

Off the beaten track

Most of northern Kenya, "game country" and other places with sparse population lack normal bank facilities.

The chances are that you will have problems changing large denomination bank notes, unless it is market-day in a sizable village or trading centre. One solution is to buy something useful from a remote petrol station then use the change as needed.

Never rely on changing travellers' cheques except at an overnight stop. Even then, if the travellers' cheques are in foreign currency, the hotel or lodge staff may not know the current exchange rate and be reluctant to take your word for it.

Ideally you should carry plenty of small denomination notes and always keep loose change for the "helpers" who appear out of nowhere if your vehicle has a flat tyre, or gets stuck in the mud.

At such times their muscle-power can be a blessing, since the alternative could mean being stranded for hours, or even days, especially if the track is soggy "black cotton soil" which takes ages to dry after a storm.

For lesser "favours", the odd cigarette is always appreciated. It's a good idea to keep a couple of packs in the glove compartment of your car.

Sweets are always useful for persuading children to be photographed and give away instant pictures are much appreciated.

Where to Stay

Kenya is Africa's number one tourist destination south of the Sahara, with an incredibly sophisticated tourist infrastructure and the best range of accommodation on the continent.

Other options include self-service lodges in national parks and reserves, campsites, and youth hostels (See Listings).

Standards at self-service lodges vary. For most, you should carry your own bedding, food, crockery, cutlery, and cooking utensils.

Camping

With more than 200 official campsites in well-chosen wilderness areas throughout the country, Kenya is ideal for those who enjoy the rugged, outdoor life.

Many people claim camping is the only

way to enjoy Kenya — an inexpensive and delightful do-it-yourself holiday offering a way of life you will never forget.

Wherever you camp, make sure you choose a spot to pitch your tent well before sundown. If possible, choose level ground with short grass and plenty of shade. But watch which tree you stay under.

Thorn trees provide good, safe shade because they discourage snakes and climbing creatures such as leopards but the thick canopy of thorns beneath them tends to make sleeping uncomfortable.

Other trees can exude unpleasant sap and birds nesting and monkeys romping can mean unpleasant droppings around the camp — and a nasty mess on the tents themselves.

Avoid dried-up river beds: sudden storms create flash floods that might even sweep you away, vehicles and all.

Where the climate is generally hot — in low country — pitch your tent with the largest windows facing the prevailing wind. Temperatures become unbearable without adequate ventilation.

Do not camp across or too near to game trails. Animals can be curious as well as dangerous.

Ensure adequate control of camp fires. If stones are available, place them around the fireplace — and clear all dry grass and leaves.

What you need

Tents of course — with sewn-in groundsheets and mosquito-net windows; camp beds, sleeping bags; folding chairs and table; pots and pans (sufurias, Kenya-made pots are ideal for camp fires); airtight containers for bread and biscuits, salt and sugar; at least one axe and panga (machete) for clearing camping sites and chopping firewood; metal bowl for washing; kettle if you prefer for tea and coffee; ideally, small camping gas lamps; spade (preferably the folding type); lots of water; plates, mugs, knives, forks and spoons; food. Binoculars will add to your enjoyment. You can hire tents and camping equipment in Kenya.

National Anthem

O God of all creation
  Bless this our land and nation.
Justice be our shield and defender
  May we dwell in unity
Peace and liberty
  Plenty be found within our borders.

Let one and all arise
  With hearts both strong and true.
Service be our earnest endeavour,
  And our Homeland of Kenya.
Heritage of Splendour,
  Firm may we stand to defend.

Let all with one accord
  In common bond united,
Build this our nation together
  And the glory of Kenya
The fruit of our labour
  Fill every heart with thanksgiving.

Failure to stand for the national anthem in a public place — cinemas, theatres — could result in your being asked to leave.

PART ONE : HISTORY, GEOGRAPHY, AND PEOPLE

Above: Fossil remains of elephant that lived on the shores of Lake Turkana 1.5 million years ago.
Opposite: Maasai girl with colourful-beaded jewellery.

Land of Adventure

Many millions of years ago Kenya's shape and form was dramatically remodelled — changed beyond recognition. Its ancient plateau, flat and monotonous, draining gently east to the Indian Ocean, was wrenched apart, and forced upwards in a series of massive earth movements and volcanic eruptions.

But just what caused all this violent movement is not exactly known.

The violent movements continued over millions of years, however, causing the earth to rise up in a dome and molten magma from deep beneath the surface to form huge volcanoes. Some, like Mount Kenya, have since been worn down to stumps by wind and rain erosion.

As it continued to swell, the land also split from north to south, forming a great depression in the west. This giant basin finally filled with water to become Lake Victoria.

Joined with other fissures, the main crack formed the Great Rift Valley, stretching from Jordan to Mozambique.

Thus in ancient times was Kenya transformed. Streams from the high ground on both sides of the fault began to flow into this great trough, forming a series of lakes which waxed and waned with the different levels of rainfall.

But these new highlands also created rain shadows on their leeward sides. As a result the forests in the lower and hotter sections of the valley floor began to disappear, their place taken by a new natural phenomenon — the most recent of all major environmental changes on planet earth — savannah grasslands.

Much later, some ape species on the fringes of these vanishing forests moved into the new rolling grasslands, adapting and learning to exploit their resources.

And, as the land changed, the family of apes made their home on the shores of the Rift Valley lakes and along the streams that poured down from the mountains.

In time, one of these ape species evolved into an early form of hominid — our ancestral apeman — and began to wreak far greater change on the environment than any other animal.

The record of evolution in the Kenyan Rift Valley stretches back twenty-five million years. Within that span virtually all stages of life's evolution are found in its fossil records.

Homo erectus was the first species of man to walk upright. But since those first faltering footsteps along the shores of Lake Turkana, perhaps a million years ago, the fascinating narrative is void of detail. Its blank pages echo only with an oral history enriched time and again in the telling.

When the Rift formed, Arabia was divided from Africa, leaving a legacy of migrant wildlife that mingled with endemic species. Like the people who were to follow, many animals also crossed the land bridge between East and West Africa when the great rain forests of western Africa extended to the shores of the Indian Ocean.

Between five and ten thousand years ago Kenya's original inhabitants included the ancestors of today's remnant groups of hunter-gatherers — the Boni, Wata, and Wariangulu wanderers of the forest and bush.

The pan-African transmigration started about 4,000 years ago — and has since brought successive waves to this land that has always lured migrants. Through most of the second millennium BC, crop-growing Cushites from southern Ethiopia and their domesticated animals were the major immigrants.

They were followed 1,000 years later by eastern Cushites. After them, between 500 BC and AD 500, came a floodtide of Cushitic, Nilotic, and Bantu groups — from all parts of the continent. These ancestors of today's Kenyans found the land and climate good and stayed to settle.

Smaller numbers continued to arrive until this century. They included the Arab and Persian traders who colonized the coast and, later, the Asians and Europeans.

Through this movement of people, which constantly shaped and reshaped cultures and communities, the land continued to remodel itself too. Although the immense and intense activity which created the Rift Valley slackened, it never ceased.

As recently as 40,000 years ago violent earth movements and volcanic forces gave birth to the Nyambeni Hills north-east of Mount Kenya. Between 400 and 500 years ago, similar volcanic frenzies sent great cones of lava spewing upwards to form the Chyulu Hills north of Kilimanjaro.

Out of all this violence came beauty. The landscapes, flora, and fauna are as diverse —

and as magnificent — as the people. One-third of Kenya is arid or semi-arid desert: barren, brown, burnt-out land which is hauntingly lovely.

One-third is highland, mountain, forest, lake, and farmland, much of it fertile and bountiful.

The remaining third is savannah grassland — home of the last remaining great wildlife spectacle in the world, where creatures such as the crocodile and rhinoceros, which evolved more than 100 million years ago, still survive.

The country's wildlife boasts more than eighty major mammal species including the Big Five — lion, leopard, elephant, buffalo, and rhino. And there are countless smaller animals, the richest birdlife on the African continent (and the third richest in the world), and a treasury of reptiles and insects so numerous and varied that they have not yet all been counted and identified (See In Brief).

A British protectorate for more than seventy years, a Crown colony for just forty-three years, Kenya's political stability and economic growth have become a benchmark for the African continent, and much of the developing world, since the country attained Indepedence on 12 December, 1963.

Concerned to improve the quality of life for all citizens, the pragmatic government has encouraged industrial development and initiated major social welfare schemes.

With its freedom and peace intact, Kenya has seen tourism grow from fewer than 100,000 visitors in 1963 to close to three-quarters-of-a-million in 1989. Now a major catalyst for growth and development, tourism offers holiday-makers the unforgettable magic of Kenya's panoramic vistas and untamed wildlife.

History

The Dust and the Ashes

Written in the rock of Kenya, amid the ashes of the fires which gave birth to the world, is the story of creation. And though the wind has stirred the dust and sent it eddying away, the geological notebooks remain an indelible confirmation of Kenya's claim as Cradle of Mankind.

Yet though Kenya boasts the world's oldest-known palaeontological record — and perhaps, therefore, the longest continuous testament to the history of life on earth — much of it remains undeciphered.

The story that is known has been uncovered, so far, with camel's hair brush, dental pick, and scrupulous research, then painstakingly pieced together, fragment by fragment.

The transcription of this unique archaeological narrative has been carried out over the last sixty years by a dynasty of peerless fossil hunters.

In 1926 an autocratic and eccentric Kenyan-born European, Louis Seymour Bazett Leakey, began to dig deep into the surface of East Africa. Five years later he married Mary Douglas Nicol and in the decades that followed, this fiery, iconoclastic man-and-wife team led several archaeological expeditions in Tanzania and Kenya. Together their research extended our understanding of mankind's beginnings by millions of years.

In the space of more than thirty years these unashamed Apostles of Adam uncovered an amazing collection of stone artefacts and hominid, ape, and animal fossils ranging across twenty-five million years of evolution.

Now, in the blink of a geological eyelid, the different layers of sediment and dust that were turned over when the East African Rift Valley was formed have become an open book documenting the prehistory and history of human evolution.

Each sentence is written in the fossil remains covered and preserved by calcium carbonate silts and sand — deposited from rising lake water, or volcanic ash, at early man's ancient campsites.

The most important work carried out by the Leakeys was at Olduvai Gorge in Tanzania in the 1950s and 1960s. From banded sediments in this deep fissure in the Serengeti

Below: Statue of Dr. Louis Leakey head of a peerless dynasty of fossil hunters.

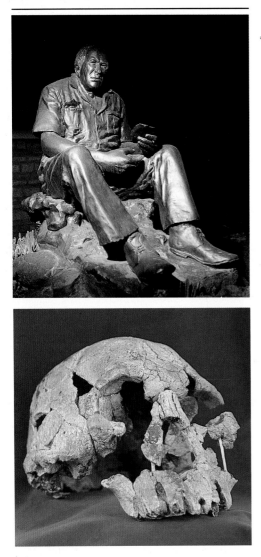

Above: Priceless clue to mankind's beginnings. This skull of an early hominid, KNM-ER 1470 is in Kenya's National Museum.

plain, they traced man's biological and cultural development back from about 50,000 years to 1.8 million years ago.

On 17 July, 1959, Mary Leakey found 400 fragments of the skull of *Zinjanthropus Boisei* "Zinj". The "Nutcracker Man" was an important early "apeman". Painstakingly reassembled — the reconstructed fossil is now in Tanzania's National Museum in Dar es Salaam — the skull was perhaps the beginning of a new Chapter of Revelations in the story of human evolution, one that has successfully established the East African Rift Valley — the Kenyan section, in particular — as a true Cradle of Mankind.

Some years later, in the early 1960s, the Leakeys discovered the skull and bones of a 10,000-to-12,000-year-old fossil which they named *Homo habilis*, "Handy man". Physiologically he was a contemporary of *Zinjanthropus*, but with a larger brain, and a gripping thumb.

Despite bitter opposition from other palaeontologists, the Leakeys considered their "handy man" a true ancestor of modern man. Their theory was seemingly confirmed when, in 1967, their son Richard investigated the bleak, arid shore at Koobi Fora on Lake Turkana in Kenya's far north and picked up a Stone-age tool similar to those that he had found as a youngster in Olduvai Gorge.

Since his father's death in 1972, Richard Leakey has made even more significant discoveries — and the shores all around Lake Turkana, where he has organised one of the greatest multi-disciplinary fossil hunts in the history of archaeology, have revealed more profound clues to mankind's origins than any other place in the world.

Fossil-bearing strata have preserved four million years of human and animal remains and tens of thousands of them have been studied at Kenya's National Museum. These studies have thrust back knowledge of life's beginnings on earth many millions of years before that deduced from previous evidence (See "Great Rift Valley: the land that was Eden", Part Two).

Other finds by American researchers in sections of the Rift in Ethiopia confirm that the beginnings of modern man go back at least 2.6 million years — and that "two, or even three, manlike creatures co-existed with the original *Homo* for more than a million years".

Above: Archaeological excavation on Hyrax Hill, Menengai, near Nakuru.

All these spectacular finds shifted the search for the crucible where mankind was first cast from Europe and Asia to the East African Rift Valley.

Soon after our ancestral *Homo erectus* stood upright and took his first faltering footsteps, his new-found mobility inspired him to move much further afield in the search for food and water. He became a wanderer and spread out across much of what is today Kenya and Tanzania. Fossil sites in the southern Rift show that *Homo erectus* and his descendants swiftly expanded their range.

But although little evidence of the intermediate milleniums has been uncovered, it is known that much more recently, between the last five and ten thousand years, Kenya was inhabited by the ancestors of today's remnant groups of hunter-gatherers — the Boni, Wata, and Wariangulu peoples.

These traditional wanderers of the forest and bush have a link with the "click-speaking" Khosian peoples of southern Africa, such as the Bushmen of the Kalahari desert, the San, and the Hottentots. Closer to home they are also related to the Sandawe and the Hadza, two small groups in Tanzania.

The immigrants

Later began the ancestral influx of today's ethnic groups in a long series of migrations that lasted well into the nineteenth century. The first wave came from Ethiopia when a group of tall, lean nomadic peoples speaking the Cushitic languages moved into Kenya in a series of gradual movements spaced over the second millennium BC.

These early southern Cushites adopted the peculiar dental clicks of the Khosian as a modulation of their own tongues. They also introduced new languages. And they kept domesticated cattle, which they milked and bled, along with goats and sheep. They tilled the soil and planted crops like sorghum.

Archaeological excavations have uncovered their stone bowls and earthenware pots, grindstones and pestles, as well as gourds, knives, spears, hoes, and basketwork.

They also left a more enduring legacy in the irrigation systems that still exist — and many of the deep wells and large dams found in remote, arid northern Kenyan were probably built by them. But when the climate changed and the lakes dried up these early settlers moved on again — south-west to the hills above Lake Victoria.

About 3,000 years ago they were followed by an eastern Cushitic pastoralist group, the Yaaku, which occupied much of central Kenya for several centuries. Even now, a small remnant group lives on, at the edge of the Laikipia escarpment, north-west of Mount Kenya.

Where the Yaaku settled, the hunter-gatherers who lived there adopted their language. Yaaku-speakers were also assimilated by other agricultural communities and spread across the land.

In the next millenium, between 500 BC and AD 500, the ancestors of the present-day Kenyan communities began to arrive from all over the continent. Nourished by the rich grazing and fine farmlands, well-watered by the streams and rivers that poured down from the forest-clad highlands, this tide of Cushitic, Nilotic, and Bantu groups stayed on.

The expansion of the smaller, darker, iron-making Bantu farmers which began 2,000 years ago in south-eastern Nigeria, was explosive. Today the Bantu, who only arrived at their present locations in the nineteenth century, occupy a great deal of central, southern, and eastern Africa — and continue to move into new lands.

Yet, even at the conclusion of these epochs of trans-African migration and internal tribe-state expansion, the Kenyan hinterland remained as mysterious to the rest of the world as the far side of the moon.

The Taru Desert on the first inland steppe served as a forbidding natural barrier that few were brave or foolhardy enough to tackle. The Rift Valley far beyond was another vast and natural impediment. Through successive milleniums, geographers and academics could only vaguely conjecture what lay inland.

But the Kenya Coast was already known. The first unequivocal description is in the log of the Greek, Diogenes, who returned to Egypt from a voyage of exploration around AD 110. His log lists the cloth, tools, glass, brass, copper, iron, olives, adzes, weapons, ivory, and rhinoceros horn loaded and unloaded at Mombasa, ruled by a King Muza.

Not much later the geographer, Ptolemy, another Greek living in Egypt, incorporated the same details in his "Map of the World", *circa* AD 150.

Island of war

Almost another millennium would pass before

Below: Portuguese navigator Vasco da Gama.

Above: Rusting anchor outside Mombasa's Fort Jesus.

Above: Shot and cannon at Mombasa's 16th-century Fort Jesus.

the arrival of Islam — and the dawn of the coast's golden age, around the ninth century, which gave rise to a glorious cultural and architectural heritage.

By the fourteenth century, a distinctive community — the Swahili — had emerged. The name Swahili derives from the Arabic plural of Sahel, meaning coast. The Islamic religion was the Arab legacy; the Kiswahili language the Bantu.

The Arabian and Persian settlers developed coastal and caravan trade, established commercial centres, and made great contributions to the new literature, arts, and crafts.

Their crude rag-and-coral homes gradually gave way to the architectural glories of fine houses, mosques, and monuments. Tall residences with elegantly-carved balconies overlooked each other, providing continuous shade in the narrow streets below, except when the sun was at its zenith.

From the outset Mombasa was rich in gold and ivory. Near the end of the fifteenth century these marked it out as a prize for the Portuguese fleets whose greatest navigator, Vasco da Gama, was ordered in 1497 by King John to round the Cape and find the sea route to India. When

the Portuguese fleet entered Mombasa harbour a year later, it was repulsed by the Arabs, who cut their anchor ropes.

Da Gama sailed on to a royal welcome in Malindi from the local sultan. But Mombasa suffered for its reprisal. Two years later Cabral sailed behind da Gama and sacked the town. Five years later, in 1505, another Portuguese mariner, Almeida, came to plunder, followed twenty-three years later by the pillaging sailors of Nuna da Cunha.

Finally, the Portuguese occupied Mombasa and, between 1593 to 1598, built the brooding bastion of Fort Jesus, overlooking the entrance to the old harbour. Its ramparts and battlements, weathered over 400 years, remain silent witness to the town's turbulent history. The stormy centuries that followed earned Mombasa its name as an "Island of War".

Arab resistance was strong. They attacked from sea and land but, even backed by the forces of the Turkish corsair, Ali Bey, were unable to shake off the tenacious Portuguese.

The first of Kenya's European colonizers remained for a century, defying siege and disease, surviving almost entirely off produce from convoys sailing from Goa in India where

they had established another enclave.

What finally brought about the Portuguese downfall was the siege of Fort Jesus which began on 15 March, 1696. Some fifty Portuguese, together with 2,500 locals, were barricaded inside the fort on short rations smuggled in at night for months.

The fort was relieved after eighteen months — in September 1697 — by 150 Portuguese and 300 Indian troops. But they did not break the siege which continued for another fifteen months until — with the help of a passing Welsh captain and crew — the Arabs finally scaled the fortress walls.

Plague, disease, and famine had taken a terrible toll. Inside the fort, only thirteen people survived — eleven men and two women. The merciless Arabs ran them through immediately. Finally, in 1720, the last Portuguese garrison left the Kenya Coast for good.

Within years it was almost as if they had never been, save for the maize, cassava, cashews, tomatoes, and tobacco that they had introduced from the Americas.

Arab renaissance

Once again the coastal towns were subject to the Arabs. But throughout the eighteenth century, the rival Omani dynasties reflected in their African territories the mutually destructive intrigues at home. Trade dwindled and the coast no longer prospered.

Then in 1805, Bey Saidi Sultan Sayyid Said, stabbed the incumbent ruler, and seized power in Oman. Seventeen years later, now secure upon his throne, he sent an army to quell the islands of Pate, Pemba, and Mombasa which were under the rule of the Mazruis.

When a British ship, HMS *Leven*, visited Mombasa, the embattled Mazruis begged its commander, Captain Owen, for British protection. And on 7 February, 1824, the British officer proclaimed Mombasa a British "protectorate". In return, the Mazruis agreed to abolish slavery.

Well pleased with his Christian crusade, Owen appointed his first officer, Lieutenant J. J. Reitz, as proconsul, together with an interpreter, four sailors, and four marines. Sending messages to London and India asking for ratification of the "treaty", he then set sail to continue his voyage.

This casual negotiation marked the beginning of British influence in East Africa. In the history of empire, there can be few instances to match such cursory presumption of imperial power but, ultimately, it led to Kenya's colonization.

Two months later, with Reitz dead of malaria, his deputy, a Lieutenant Emery, assumed the role of "Governor" — a function that lasted for three years — until Whitehall, which had sat on Owen's protectorate agreement, repudiated it.

So did Britain relinquish its first brief foothold in Kenya, not to return to lay its imprint, first on Mombasa and then remorselessly inland, until more than half a century later.

Those fifty years were a time of unparalleled prosperity for the Sultan. From Cape Guardafui to Cape Delgado, the East African coast was his acknowledged dominion and, as the slave trails ran up through the hinterland as far as Lake Victoria, his dreams of an African empire began to flower.

But, even as they did so, Sayyid Said who had moved the Omani government to Zanzibar, came under increasing pressure from Britain to halt the trade, and in 1845 he was forced into a treaty which severely restricted it.

In 1844, the year before the treaty, the German missionary Johan Ludwig Krapf had established a British Church Missionary Society mission at Rabai just a few kilometres from Mombasa on the mainland. In 1846 he was joined by Johanne Rebmann. Both men wanted to end the slave trade and convert Africa to Christianity — and to achieve their aims they travelled far inland, where few Europeans had ever ventured.

The Explorers

From the second half of the eighteenth century the question of East Africa aroused an unusual degree of passion, conscience, and diatribe within the British political parties and the ruling classes.

Legions of leaders, from Prime Minister Pitt's first term of office in 1783, sought by every means to evade British involvement in this unknown territory.

But in the end, the overwhelming force of Victorian puritanism and scientific curiosity — a mixture of empirical pride, the desire to explore, and Christian conscience — were

Opposite: Liberty Bell, Freretown, Mombasa.

enough to inspire the British to venture forth into the "Dark Continent".

In the middle of the nineteenth century, the anti-slavery campaign was at its height. Missionary and explorer became one in their endeavour to end the trade in human souls and, at the same time, chart the interior and discover the source of the Nile, long believed to be part of a great watershed in the East African interior.

Greater impetus was given to British curiosity by the discovery of a permanent layer of snow atop 5,985-metre-high (19,340-feet) Mount Kilimanjaro. Johanne Rebmann saw the mountain on 11 May, 1848, two years after he had arrived at Mombasa, during an upcountry evangelical mission to the Chagga people.

His report provoked outrage among the learned academics of London. Such statements, wrote Desborough Cooley, an important member of the Royal Geographical Society ". . . could not fail to awaken mistrust. . . . Those eternal snows . . . have so little shape . . . they take quite a spectral character".

Cooley's wrath must have been compounded some nineteen months later when Rebmann's colleague, Johan Ludwig Krapf, set out from his Rabai mission (See "The Road to Mombasa: highway to adventure", Part Two) on a visit to Ukamba, north-east of Kilimanjaro. From a hill close to Kitui, he saw the twin peaks of Mount Kenya, also snowclad straddled across the Equator some 160 kilometres (100 miles) away. It was 3 December, 1849.

Five years later Krapf produced a rough map of the interior showing the approximate locations of Kilimanjaro and "Kenia". It also showed a single inland sea — possibly Lake Victoria. It was largely to find out if this sea was the source of the Nile that Richard Burton and John Hanning Speke set out from Zanzibar in 1856.

British concern, and curiosity, over East Africa reached its peak in the 1880s when the Royal Geographical Society despatched Joseph Thomson to explore the region. In spite of Stanley's advice to "take a thousand men or die" in the warrior kingdoms of the Maasai, Thomson, then twenty-six, set forth in March 1883 with just 143 porters and commissaries, of which only a dozen could fire a rifle. His odyssey was as remarkable for its humour as its adventure. He charted virtually all of what

is today Kenya, with the exception of its great northern deserts.

Keeping a steady distance between himself and the following Maasai, Thomson marched on from the base of Kilimanjaro to Lake Naivasha, in the shadows of the extinct volcano Longonot. Then he continued up the eastern wall of the Rift Valley to the 3,650-metre (12,000-feet) heights of the Nyandarua (Aberdares) mountain massif.

It was there, as he crested the moorlands early one morning, that Mount Kenya (*Kirinyaga*, sacred peak and abode of the Kikuyu God, *Ngai*) shed its veils of mist and revealed the startling glory of its eternal necklace of ice: glistening glaciers astride the Equator beneath the twin peaks of Batian and Nelion which, at 5,199 metres (17,058 feet), is second in Africa only to Kilimanjaro (See "Heartland Kenya: magic mountains, moorlands wild", Part Two).

From there he ventured northward along the floor of the Rift to Lake Baringo and then up the precipitous Elgeyo escarpment, the western wall of the Rift. He crossed the moorlands of Mount Elgon — 4,320 metres (14,178 feet) high — and returned through the western plains of Kenya on the shores of Lake Victoria to the coast. By any standards, it was a monumental feat of endurance and enterprise.

Thomson, a genuinely modest man, was a hero back in England. His heady adventures in the wilds of Africa fired the Victorian imagination and, soon afterwards, other missions set off into the uncharted areas on either side of his route.

In 1885 James Hannington, an Anglican bishop, on his way to start a diocese in Uganda, found a lake Thomson had missed just above Baringo. But, as he went on towards the Nile, Hannington was murdered. The lake, which was named in his honour, is now Bogoria.

The following year, another monumental safari traversed the Kikuyu heartland and went on far north to discover a massive inland sea — Lake Turkana — which the local Samburu called, in the Maa language, *Embasso Narok* ("the Black Lake").

The leader of this 700-strong expedition was a rich Austro-Hungarian, Count Samuel Teleki von Szek. With him he took a meticulous biographer, Lieutenant Ludwig von Hohnel, who painstakingly recorded every step of the epic journey. The Austrians named the lake "Rudolf", after the crown prince of Austria

Above: Joseph Thomson on his *"Walk Through Masai Land"*.

who later shot himself, and his mistress, at Mayerling.

Finally, two Americans, Donaldson Smith and William Chanler, surveyed the Tana River and the featureless commiphora bush of the north-east and the main outline of the land and people that was to become Kenya was known to the outside world.

Throughout all this, in an atmosphere of intensifying international rivalry, the Germans also sought to impose their influence in East Africa, particularly in what became Tanganyika where the mercenary, Carl Peters, persuaded many unsuspecting and illiterate chiefs to "sign" Treaties of Friendship — treaties which they neither understood nor could ever dispute.

Now the British

Europe's political squabble for this land of stunning beauty astride the Equator had barely begun. Thomson's written account, *Through Masai Land*, was the final thrust needed to propel Britain's imperial instincts into an East African adventure. The white pioneers were drawn by the rich farmland in this land of eternal summer. To western eyes, unstructured and unhegemonic, Kenya promised

Above: Kenya's earliest Anglican church — St. Paul's built at Rabai in 1887 and still in use. At right is the house that Johanne Rebmann built.

SIR WILLIAM MACKINNON, BART.

SIR FREDERICK LUGARD, K.C.M.G.,
C.B., D.S.O.

Opposite top: Passengers on the "Central African Railway" — an 11-kilometre-long track on Mombasa Island.
Opposite: Remembrance Day parade in colonial Nairobi's Delamere Avenue, now Kenyatta Avenue.

only bountiful harvests and was there for the taking.

Thomson's journey had been across a loosely-defined land. As now, Kenya was then a kaleidoscope of people and cultures, but local boundaries were delineated in accordance with the traditional balance of power.

The Maasai had ascendancy over grazing grounds around Kilimanjaro, Naivasha, and the Mara. The Kikuyu were content to rule and cultivate on the fertile, higher grounds of the escarpments and mountains.

To the Luo, Akamba, Giriama, Turkana, Samburu, Abaluyia, Boran, Taita, Kalenjin, Maasai, Kikuyu, Meru, and Nandi peoples, the tribal territories were as well defined as the fiefdoms of Scotland and the shires of England.

Though Kenya's dynamics were tribal, its strengths were those of warriors whose history of battle honours dated back 1,000 years or more. Their characteristics of courage were noted by the incoming Europeans. There was about this yet-to-be defined nation and its people a character that set it apart from the rest of Africa.

In 1886, soon after Thomson's return, Britain and Germany agreed to the extent of the Zanzibar dominion. On the strength of Peters' treaties, what is today mainland Tanzania became the German colony of Tanganyika, and Kenya and Uganda were assigned to the British.

A fellow Scot of Thomson's, Sir William Mackinnon, was already established in East African trade and the anti-slavery campaign through his British India Steam Navigation Company's fleet which plied regularly between Zanzibar and British ports.

Even before Thomson's epic adventure, Mackinnon had been invited by the Sultan of Zanzibar to lay down proposals for a chartered trading company that would operate throughout East Africa.

Nothing came of it until 1887 when, with the backing of the Foreign Office, he founded the British East Africa Association. Within a year it had a capital of £240,000, a Royal Charter, and an appropriate name for such an enterprise: the Imperial British East Africa Company (IBEA).

IBEA built its headquarters — a crude shantytown of iron — at Mombasa. It coined its own money, printed its own postage stamps,

Above: Fort Smith, now a private residence, near Kabete, Nairobi.

and published its own treaty documents. These impressive forms carried the seal of Crown authority, if not the weight.

With these it set about establishing its presence in the interior. Its young officers carried the flag which encapsulated the anti-slavery convictions of its founder: it bore the motto, "Light and Liberty".

Between 1888 and 1890 the flag was hoisted over several IBEA upcountry outposts. A small contingent of British officials and soldiers carved a 500-kilometre-long (300-mile) dirt road to Machakos and beyond — to a flat, dank, foul-smelling swamp — called Nyrobi by the Maasai, meaning "place of the cold waters."

From this place, the small band cut through the forest for a few kilometres to Kabete, where in 1890 they built a fortress — naming it Fort Smith after the first commanding officer.

They lived under siege. Walk today a few hundred metres from Fort Smith, now aged and mellow, and you'll come across the marble headstones, untended and neglected in a fallow maize field, of three British: one the victim of the Kikuyu, another of a lioness, the third of a lion.

At the end of 1889 the company had recruited an ex-Indian Army officer, Frederick Dealtry (later Lord) Lugard, and assigned him the perilous task of surveying a new route to the company station at Machakos, run by John Ainsworth who was to play a major role in the early growth of Nairobi.

Returning to Mombasa five months later, Lugard was immediately ordered to march again, this time through Kikuyuland to Uganda. He was to make alliances but he preferred to negotiate with the tribes he encountered in simpler terms than those rendered on the regal-looking treaty forms that he carried.

He struck treaties with the Kikuyu and other people through their own unshakeable bond, that of blood brother. Lugard felt it more honourable and less demanding of African credibility.

One treaty he concluded was at Fort Smith with the Kikuyu chief Kinyanjui who planted a fig tree in the compound of the fort as a symbol of the new-found friendship between his people and the British.

Above: Britain's vice-consul in Zanzibar Sir Arthur Hardinge with the Maasai leader Lenana.

The Lunatic Express

The key to penetrating the interior, of course, was a railway to the great lake, Victoria — a thousand kilometres (620 miles) away across some of the most hostile terrain in the world.

Mackinnon originally conceived this idea as a weapon against slavery and sowed the seed with eleven kilometres (seven miles) of comic track on Mombasa Island which was called, grandiosely, the "Central African Railway".

It was later pulled up and relaid as a municipal tramway powered by Africans who pushed and pulled the little rickshaw-style tramcars. But the seed grew in others and now the seed blossomed into a magnificent obsession which found flower in two strange bed fellows — Lugard, and Sir Gerald Portal, Britain's Acting Consul in Zanzibar.

Lugard's experience had turned him into an evangelist for British annexation of Uganda as a Protectorate. The thirty-five-year-old Portal, who embarked with his brother on what for both of them was to be a fatal fact-finding mission to Uganda, was aghast at the behaviour of IBEA officers such as Lugard. "The combination of administration and

trading is fatal," he reported to the Foreign Office.

Certainly it was more than IBEA could sustain. Each post required over 2,000 manloads of between twenty-seven and thirty-one kilos (60-70 lbs) of supplies each year. Portal saw the impossible logistics of this. In his final recommendation, shortly before his death from fever, contracted at Mumias on his return journey, he wrote:

"To effect any real improvement in property or commerce, efficiently to reap the benefit of material progress that may be made, there is but one course open. . . . The only means of effectively doing this is by a railway."

Portal died and Lugard lived, to achieve great honours, but despite their differences both had the same ambition — to establish a permanent British presence in East Africa.

The idea of the railway aroused fervid opposition and ridicule on all sides. The loudest voice against was that of the radical Henry Labouchere who warned Parliament that whenever Britain "annexes some wretched, miserable jungle in the centre of Africa, we will be called upon to build a railroad to it".

But the Government of Lord Salisbury prevailed. The estimated cost, £3.6 million (it

Above: R. O. Preston's ramp railway that overcame the barrier of the great eastern wall of the Rift Valley when the railhead arrived there in 1900.

eventually exceeded £5 million) was phenomenal for those days. Britain's sense of imperial righteousness had never been greater.

But 1,000 kilometres (620 miles) of track — crossing a burnt-out desert, an infinite stretch of thorn and scrub savannah, climbing the walls of the Great Rift Valley, and down the almost sheer face for 600 metres (2,000 feet), ending with 160 kilometres (100 miles) across a spongelike morass of swamp and cotton soil plain — required an engineering miracle.

And along every mile lay in wait ferocious predators, both human and animal, little water, and endemic diseases for which no Empire had yet found the cures.

Why build it at all, notwithstanding the situation in Uganda? Why, indeed?

Nobody knew, not even Sir Charles Eliot, one of the first British administrators to serve in Nairobi, who wrote in 1904:

"It is a curious confession, but I do not know why the Uganda Railway was built, and

I think many people in East Africa share my ignorance."

Henry Labouchere anticipated him by nine years. After an acrimonious exchange during the Parliamentary debate on the Railway estimates, when George Curzon, Under-Secretary of State for Foreign Affairs, pronounced that without a railway to the coast a British Protectorate in Uganda would be absurd, Labouchere replied in satirical verse in the London magazine *Truth*:

What it will cost no words can express;
What is its object no brain can suppose;
Where it will start from no one can guess;
Where it is going to nobody knows;

What is the use of it none can conjecture;
What it will carry there's none can define;
And in spite of George Curzon's superior lecture,
It clearly is naught but a lunatic line.

Shanty Town

Lunatic or not, little under three years after the first rail was laid in place in Mombasa in August 1896, it had reached the railhead at Mile 327, where lion, cheetah, zebra, antelope, dik-dik, duiker, wart hog, and ostrich roamed in abundance.

Two or three lean-to shacks, stables for oxen and mule, an army telegraph office run by Sergeant George Ellis of the Royal Engineers, and a few tents were the only signs of human occupation.

At the end of May 1899, these crude shelters were swollen by a village of tents — a camp for thousands of workers brought in like flotsam on the irreversible tide of the railway which had now assumed a will of its own and swept all before it with a purpose and direction nothing could deflect.

So it was, by accident, in a miscarriage of circumstances and out of recrimination and chaos, that Nairobi was born.

Fifty-six kilometres (35 miles) behind, flanked by hills, and surrounded by blossoming trees, IBEA's former upcountry administrator and now Crown servant, John Ainsworth, delighted in his Machakos headquarters.

He had assumed, wrongly, that his chief engineer, George Whitehouse, would centralize his operations in this pleasant verdure but had watched in consternation as the railroad paused, then bypassed the ring of his beloved Iveti Hills to carve a straight scar through the Kapiti Plains, at the base of the eastern ramp of the Rift.

In three years and 530 kilometres (330 miles) the track had eased itself one-and-a-half kilometres (one mile) above sea level in a steady, equable ascent. Railhead would be at Nairobi for one reason only. There was no more flatland.

In the next fifty-six kilometres (35 miles) the railway would have to climb half its height again — 720 metres (2,200 feet) to the lip of the escarpment, a gradient averaging one-in-84.

Machakos and Kikuyu, pleasantly situated 300 metres (1,000 feet) higher than Nairobi, with rich, red soil and great forests, had both been suggested as tentative railheads.

Whitehouse had ignored the suggestions. Yet his decision to rebuild his resources and centralize the railroad's administration in Nairobi was made only in January 1899 — when he could prevaricate no longer.

It was an engineer's decision, without thought or consideration for the natural consequences he should have foreseen. Whitehouse's, blinkered eyes saw only track, and the long divide between Nairobi and Lake Victoria. His brilliance as an engineer was unquestionable but his vision of the future was myopic.

Blind to all but the immense requirements of manpower and material needed to achieve one of the most remarkable feats of engineering in the history of railway construction, Whitehouse unerringly chose the most unsuitable location within a radius of 160 kilometres (100 miles) as the site from which to direct his operations — the area around the papyrus swamp into which the Nairobi, Mathari, Masongawai, and Ngong streams drained.

And men and impedimenta settled remorselessly on the glutinous black soil like a swarm of flies on a carcass. As the sun drew the mists from the swamp, so the railhead drew the traders, prostitutes, gentlemen of fortune, and the swelling hordes of camp followers.

Ainsworth watched the birth of this instant slum, appalled. Whitehouse, he and others reasoned, should have chosen Machakos and failing Machakos, the administration should be moved up the hill to Kikuyu. Nairobi had neither drainage nor water supplies.

Within the next ten months more than 700 men died in the Nairobi railhead and a graveyard became the first permanent fixture of the unborn city. The little cemetery at the side of Nairobi's Uhuru Highway at the far end of the Railway Golf Course, remains the grim reminder (See "Nairobi, city in the sun", Part Two).

Thirty months after reaching Nairobi, on 20 December 1901, Florence Preston, wife of Ronald Preston, the engineer who had led the construction work all the way, hammered home the last key of the track overlooking Lake Victoria.

It was nothing short of a magnificent success and remains one of the great railways of the world. It climbs from sea-level through desert, grass plain, mountain, and forest to cross the Equator at 2,785 metres (9,136 feet) before heading down again to the humid 1,150-metre-altitude (3,760-feet) of Lake Victoria's shores. This unforgettable journey across almost 1,000 kilometres (620 miles), covers much of the

Above: The highest railway station in the Commonwealth: 2,656 metres high in the Timboroa highlands.

Opposite top: Steam train excursions through the Rift Valley in 1989 celebrated Kenya Railways colourful history.

Opposite: Nairobi's Railway Museum relives the days of the "Lunatic Line".

geographic and climatic range of Africa.

Whitehouse was honoured. He was made a Knight Commander of the Order of the Bath.

The "Lunatic Line" would, wrote best-selling novelist, Ronald Hardy, "open a wilderness to trade and cultivation. From that thin metal line a colony would grow and there would be settlers, towns and cities in the sun. . . . He had seen a vision. . . . His had been the burden, his the responsibility."

Eliot noted: "It is not an uncommon thing for a line to open up a country, but this line has literally created a country."

Certainly the railway was the catalyst that created a sense of nationalism, though never in the sense Eliot intended. Almost as soon as work started, Kenya's African communities served notice that they would not surrender their liberty or land freely.

Paradise found

The first decade and a half of British rule in Kenya, from 1895 to 1910, was marked by a series of uprisings, particularly in the fertile western highlands, which the British ruthlessly suppressed by massacre and betrayal.

Although the majority seemed to accept the takeover passively, certain groups, among them the Kamba, were not so supine. Their resistance resulted in the despatch of at least four heavy-duty punitive military expeditions before the Kamba, weakened by rinderpest and smallpox, succumbed to "Pax Britannica".

To counter the Kikuyu's highland forest activities the British established garrisons — at Fort Smith and near the Maasai *manyatta* on the Nairobi River at Ngong.

The Nandi tribe, too, were equally defiant. In 1895, from their verdant hills above Lake Victoria, they started the guerrilla resistance which lasted more than ten years. Eventually their leader, seer, and soothsayer, the *laibon*, Koitalel, was lured to peace talks under a flag of truce and then shot dead by a British officer, Captain Richard Meinertzhagen. Finally subjugated, but never acquiescent, on pain of death the Nandi were forced into compliance and by 1905 the Nandi Hills were quiet.

Through most of the first decade of this century, British punitive expeditions were also busy in the north, especially around Turkana where the Turkana warriors were never wholly subjugated. They faced similar resistance in Luyia territory, around Broderick Falls in north-west Kenya, and in the Kisii highlands of the Gusii in south-west Kenya.

Until the dawn of the century the renowned Maasai were among the most intractable of those who opposed the colonists. In 1895, when a passing caravan on the slave trail through the Kedong Valley made too many advances to the morans' girl friends, the Maasai warriors cut down at least 500 of the 1,100 strong party.

This brought a response from a European — Andrew "Trader" Dick — who happened to be nearby and decided to exact retribution on behalf of the Crown: something for which he had no authority or mandate. Attacking the Maasai and making off with a large number of their cattle he fled up the escarpment around the uplands. When the Maasai finally caught up with him Dick was added to the 452 Kikuyu and ninety-eight Swahili they had killed earlier.

An official Court of Inquiry found that the Maasai had been unjustly provoked and they were acquitted — but their cattle were seized as compensation.

Land was the lure that drew nearly every settler. In their minds Kenya, if not actually El Dorado, was the closest thing yet. The railway's objective was simple. It needed produce to carry to earn revenues — and farmers would provide that produce.

But in such a vast country there was no way of knowing who owned which land. The administration surveyed vast tracts of the fertile "White Highlands" which seemed to be unoccupied and sold them in parcels for settlement. Traditional tribal disputes over grazing and agricultural land paled in comparison with these massive territorial seizures.

One of the major players in this first decade was Hugh Cholmondeley, the aristocratic third Baron Delamere, who mortgaged his Vale Royal estates in Cheshire to establish large-scale mixed farming in the Rift Valley.

Another settler, "Pop" Binks, was also determined to have his share of this tropical paradise and scouted around Nairobi for his own Arcadia. Eventually Binks found fifty-seven hectares (160 acres) in the Kikuyu Forest. His experience casts some light on the difficulties the early settlers faced. The asking price from the Crown was two rupees an acre, together with 180 rupees for a Crown survey, the price payable in thirty-two annual instalments.

It worked out at about US$10 a year — and at the end of thirty-two years the settler was given the freehold title.

But Binks soon discovered that the "Promised Land" was not all it appeared to be. One condition of the lease was that he put at least six hectares (16 acres) a year under cultivation. Thus, at the end of ten years, the landholder would have the entire fifty-seven hectares under cultivation.

But, as Binks put it, it would be doubtful if he "could even sell a cabbage".

In his first year he paid five rupees in Nairobi for twenty-seven kilos (60 lbs) of potato seed but he was offered only one-and-half rupees for the entire crop.

Binks, however, lacked both Delamere's vision and determination. The Cheshire nobleman envisaged Kenya as the granary of Africa — and no matter the difficulties he encountered his faith never faltered. Within a year of Pop's failure, potatoes were being shipped by rail and sea, at the cost of £3-a-ton, to South Africa.

The bi-weekly rail service between Mombasa and Nairobi was already beginning to show a profit as new people and goods arrived with every ship that docked at Mombasa. Life for many in the new British Protectorate, despite the price of imported goods and hazards of farming, had its good side.

"My pay in India," Meinertzhagen noted on 25 July, 1902, "was exactly £108 a year and now I find myself with £400 a year under cheaper conditions for, outside luxuries such as cartridges, alcohol, etc., living is absurdly cheap. Eggs three a penny, sheep 3 rupees, a chicken half a rupee, and we grow our own vegetables. My daily expenditure on food is only about the equivalent of 2s. a day."

The army captain who arrived in Nairobi in 1902 without a penny left in 1906 with £3,000.

Land grab

Land sales were the great betrayal of African interests. The blame, however, was not altogether on the Crown's side for Lenana, the Maasai chief, had welcomed the Europeans warmly and was to agree to the disposal of their highland ranges.

The key to successful large-scale farming was adequate labour but Africans were reluctant to work for somebody else. By introducing hut taxes and other laws, however, the administration forced them into low-paid wage employment, introducing a cash economy in a land of barter.

The resentment went deep. But firm in his belief in the supremacy of white dominion, Eliot was untroubled by the prospect of the Africans giving way to the European. "There can be no doubt that the Maasai and many other tribes must go under. It is a prospect which I view with equanimity and clear conscience."

In an entry in his diary on 13 July, 1902, Meinertzhagen noted that Eliot was a "scholar, philosopher and a very able man with great vision".

But he disagreed with Eliot's vision of the day when the whole of Kenya would be a thriving European colony, the whole of the Rift Valley cultivated, and the entire country under white settlement.

"I suggested," recalls Meinertzhagen, "that the country belonged to Africans and that their interests must prevail over the interests of strangers. He would not have it . . . I said that some day the African would be educated and armed. Eliot thought that day was so far distant as not to matter . . . but I am convinced that in the end the Africans will win."

He had much the same argument with Delamere. "I take the view, with which Delamere has no patience, that in a hundred years time there may be 50,000 white settlers with flourishing farms and 5,000,000 discontented and envious natives; can the white man hold out against such numbers without terrible slaughter?"

In the euphoria of the new colony, however, Meinertzhagen was a voice out of tune. No realistic vision could be allowed to mar the joyous illusion of white supremacy that existed in those early days.

Meinertzhagen was not alone in his conviction. From the outset Whitehall maintained that the interests of the African were paramount in Kenya. Eliot resigned.

But almost immediately on taking office, his successor, the bucolic Sir Donald Stewart, presided over the Maasai "sellout" initialled by himself and Lenana, the Maasai leader. In this and a subsequent 1911 treaty, the Maasai surrendered all their grazing grounds in the fertile highlands in exchange for the fragile, arid pastures of south-western and southern Kenya.

Other areas, the most fertile in a country where about eighty per cent of the land is marginal, were also earmarked exclusively for European settlement.

Inevitably there was bitterness — a bitterness that came to be expressed in the African struggle for *Uhuru*, the Kiswahili word for freedom.

White settlers

Delamere, the extraordinary, titian-haired, leprechaun of an English Lord, tried — and more often failed — in many farming ventures that did much to sow the seeds for Kenya's farm industry of today.

With many experiments he lost a fortune. He imported high-grade Australian sheep but the land on which they grazed was mineral deficient. He ploughed in English clover, restocked with sheep, and watched the clover fail. The indigenous African bees were unable to pollinate it.

He imported English bees — and this worked. But with no dormant winter period to keep the crop down, and no frost to kill off the pests, the clover grew into a luxuriant, shin-high jungle. The sheep died of foot rot.

He tried cattle, mixing good beef stock from

his Cheshire estate with the long-horned, hump-backed Boran cattle of the northern tribes. The progeny were resistant to most local viruses — but not to a new East Coast fever which came up from German East Africa and wiped him out again.

The Maasai who had cynically watched the misfortunes of this eccentric Englishman, for some reason — perhaps admiration for the peer's tenacity, or for the new cattle breeds that he had introduced — now came to his rescue. They offered to manage Delamere's stock, and with the help of imported veterinary science, built up the cattle on those sections of the ranch where they knew the grazing could support the herds.

The Maasai had won a staunch supporter for their land battles with the British administration.

As his ranching ventures gathered momentum, after months of isolation on the farm Delamere earned a reputation as a "damned scallywag" for his party rampages through Nairobi with other fun-seeking settlers.

Their arrival in Nairobi was usually the start of a cavalry charge down Government Road (now Moi Avenue), often shooting out the glass oil lamps as they galloped past. Other "enjoyable" entertainment included disrupting chic garden parties and heavy drinking sprees in one of the clubs, usually Muthaiga, which Delamere often capped by riding his horse into the Norfolk Hotel to blast off his six-gun at the bottles behind the bar.

Throughout his life, this controversial character remained a vigorous protagonist of a white Kenya. But although he and the young Winston Churchill took a liking to each other when they enjoyed a day's pig-sticking on Delamere's Elmenteita ranch during the latter's 1907 visit, Churchill was against an autonomous white colony.

Subsequently Churchill wrote: "Just and honourable discipline, careful education, sympathetic comprehension are all that are needed to bring a very large proportion of the tribes of East Africa to a far higher social level than that at which they now stand.

"And it is, after all, their Africa."

Yet, despite Whitehall insistence that Kenya was a protectorate and therefore a "foreign country" where the British code of law did not apply, in August 1907 a seven-man Legislative Council (Legco) was established with Lord Delamere as one of the settler members.

The fact that four million Africans were without representation or that 600 or so settlers and the administration were the sole voice was not taken into consideration.

By 1912, however, the protectorate had begun to pay its way and the European population stood at 3,000. When the First World War ended in 1918, the most significant political consequence was the British Government's decision to offer war veterans land in the Kenya Highlands in a settlement scheme.

Farms were either given away to winners of a lottery or sold at nominal cost on long-term credit. The main objective was to increase the European settler population and therefore revenue.

The scheme was bitterly resented by the African community, not least by those who had fought alongside these same soldiers in the Great War in which many Africans died. Naturally they, too, looked for gains on account of their war efforts.

But nothing was forthcoming, neither for them nor for any other sections of the African and Asian communities. Thus the scheme was seen as an overt move to advance the objective of a permanent White Man's Kenya.

By 1922 the European population had risen to more than 10,000 and in the White Highlands the settlers had laid claim to the best 27,000 square kilometres (10,500 square miles) of the colony's 580,000 square kilometres (225,000 square miles).

Nevertheless, a 1923 government White Paper stated that the old principle of Africa for the Africans was to be revived and enforced: "Primarily, Kenya is an African country. H. M. Government think it necessary definitely to record their considered opinion that the interests of the African native must be paramount, and that if and when those interests and the interests of the immigrant races should conflict, then the former should prevail."

From then on, a succession of various governors — with or without personal conviction — were obliged to uphold the policy. By the 1920s, many Africans, principally the Kikuyu, had found work in the rapidly-growing capital of Nairobi — crossing the social and geographical divide from African bush to sophisticated, cosmopolitan town.

But their traditional lifelines remained firm. The *shamba* (farm) retained its quasi-religious significance in the lives of the new urban dwellers who left their senior wives behind to ensure its maintenance and prosperity.

Struggle for freedom

Some of these young Kikuyu formed urban community groups. Their fundamental concern was land, and these early associations in Nairobi orchestrated and articulated the demand for the return of the "alienated" Highlands.

Around this time, a former mission boy, Johnstone Kamau, took a job as a water meter inspector with the Nairobi Municipal Council. As his involvement in the political organisation of the Kikuyu increased, he changed his name to Jomo Kenyatta.

If the urban Kikuyu constituted the main political body in Kenya, then the Asians were the natural clients of a burgeoning civil service bureaucracy.

As Churchill had forecast, they worked long hours in closed, mutually-supportive communities to establish a near-monopoly in trade, light industry, and semi-professional services.

Some already had enough capital to fund local development projects in partnership with the Government. Others provided credit to the settlers between harvests. Most settlers saw this purely as an economic bridge between two socially distinct communities.

They reacted offensively, labelling the Asians "the Jews of East Africa". Others responded with resignation, bemused by the changed relationship between the Indian and the British Raj.

Essentially, Nairobi society was comprised of two upper levels: officers of the Crown and officers of the British Army commanding African infantry battalions.

Although some considered the white settlers socially agreeable, many found their aristocratic eccentricity and colonial attitudes too pretentious.

One officer, the Earl of Lytton, preferred the solitude of a command at Baragoi, in the desert of Samburu country, and the occasional company of the respected Baron von Otter who led a long British campaign against the dissident Turkana tribe, earning their respect and admiration.

Regardless of material substance, new immigrants automatically entered the upper social bracket. All were entrepreneurs of some sort — commercial speculators, professionals, skilled artisans, or remittance men and were allied to the administration since only a few could "make the settler grade".

In Nairobi, the Muthaiga Country Club served as the settlers hangout as well as an elegant venue for hunt balls, the occasional wild party and other revelry which, in the permissive scenario played out in the Wanjohi — "Happy" — Valley of the highlands, was said to include wife-swapping.

An acclaimed heroine of this period was Isaak Dinnesen, the first Baroness Blixen of *Out of Africa* fame, whose hunter husband, Bror, took off with another woman leaving her to go bankrupt on their Nairobi coffee farm under the Ngong Hills.

Among others, she entertained Edward, Prince of Wales, and her own tragic love story with Denys Finch-Hatton was made into an Oscar-winning film.

But looming over the early settlers eccentric — and debauched — gaiety were the Kikuyu woodsmen waiting to chop down their Elysian paradise.

In the next few years, as the settlers continued to press their claims for autonomy, this intensified African demands for the restoration of their liberty and the release of their lands.

They were supported by many of Kenya's Asian community who, like the Africans, were denied representation in Government, and placed in a social "ghetto" somewhere between the two communities.

Several factors militated against the settlers achieving autonomy. One was the founding of the East African Association, the first pan-Kenyan nationalist movement, led by Harry Thuku, which was supported by a number of influential and militant Asians. His subsequent arrest resulted in the massacre of twenty-three Kenyan Africans outside Nairobi's Central police station in March 1922 (Thuku was detained and remained incarcerated for seven years).

The incident welded Kenya's African communities firmly together in their demands for freedom which were given added impetus in the 1923 Devonshire White Paper "primarily Kenya is an African territory . . . [and] the interests of the African natives must be paramount".

Another boost came from Governor Sir Ormsby Gore who, in 1922, asserted that the

Above: Britain's future King George VI on a 1920s Kenyan safari with the future Queen Elizabeth the Queen Mother.

"ultimate object that I have in regard to Kenya Colony, namely, [is] that it should be regarded primarily as an African country . . . that we should be there for Africans first as we are in Nigeria, and that it should not become an Indian colony or a white English colony".

Gore's view was anathema to his successor Sir Robert — "Gentlemen, you may remember that I am South-African born" — Coryndon. So, too, was Thuku's organisation which, being open to all ethnic groups, represented a complete nullification of his administration's policy of divide-and-rule. Coryndon ordered the association to change its name to the Kikuyu Association.

Thus, the Association's complaints unheeded by the settler-dominated Legco, Kenyatta left for England in 1929 to present the Association case to the Colonial office, the British parliament and people. He returned in September 1930.

The following year Harry Thuku was released and the Carter Land Commission was convened to adjudicate on land interests in Kenya.

Once again Kenyatta sailed to Britain to present the African case — the start of many long and lonely years of self-imposed exile.

Although he gave evidence to the Commission in 1932, its findings — published in 1934 — exacerbated the ever-widening rift between African and European.

The commission delineated the permanent barriers between European-owned farms in the highlands and what it described as African Land Units, henceforth labelled, somewhat derogatorily, "reserves". Five years later, on the eve of the Second World War, Legco passed legislation confirming the barriers drawn in the Carter report.

As a result, the number of political organisations demanding greater African participation proliferated. But one immediate consequence of the war was that all African political associations were banned in 1940 and twenty-three of their leaders detained under new wartime defence regulations.

The despairing voice of the vast majority remained largely unheard, even though in 1944 Eliud Mathu, an early product of Balliol College, Oxford, became the first African to be nominated a member of the Legco.

Their voice was swollen by the clamour of thousands of veterans returning from the war theatres of Asia and Europe where, during the five-year-long conflict, they had been exposed to many fresh influences.

As discontent grew, the tide of freedom turned into a ground swell that swept across Africa. Two of its most articulate proponents were Kwame Nkrumah of what would become the first independent African state, Ghana, and Jomo Kenyatta.

Together they participated in the Fifth Pan-African Congress in Manchester in 1945. The following year, in September 1946, Kenyatta returned home from a self-imposed exile of fifteen years.

Meanwhile, well aware of his need for a base from which to speak in Legco, Mathu had formed the Kenya African Study Union. It attracted moderates such as Harry Thuku who became its first President, and more passionate advocates of freedom like James Gichuru, who replaced him within a few months. The Union's title was soon shortened to the more pragmatic Kenya African Union (KAU).

In 1947, Gichuru resigned to let Kenyatta, widely acknowledged as the one man who could unite the various African political and ethnic factions and give common voice to the aspirations of all, become President.

The colonial administration's response was to increase African participation in Legco to four — a token recognition of discontent that was far from enough to satisfy the forces of protest about to be unleashed.

Under Kenyatta, KAU grew swiftly. Political agitation spread throughout the country, and resulted in a hardening of the colonial Government's attitude.

When police suppressed strikes at Mombasa port and Uplands bacon factory on the Limuru escarpment by firing on demonstrators the stage was set for the long drawn-out battle for freedom.

Now the Kikuyu formed secret societies. New members were sworn in through ancient and traditional oathing ceremonies. Others, including two fanatical religious groups, and politically-conscious members of the Luo, Maasai, Luyia, Kamba, and Kipsigis followed suit.

The Kikuyu-dominated Mau Mau came into existence in 1948 as a natural consequence of the colonial authorities refusal to recognise African demands for the return of their land and proper representation in Legco. It was proscribed in 1950. Its aims were considered violent.

Not all saw violence as the solution. Many Kikuyu, including Kenyatta, still sought a middle road to political, economic, and social equality. Among these was Mbiyu Koinange, the son of a senior Kikuyu chief. Early in 1952 he and others formed the Kenya Citizens Association. They wanted peaceful change brought about by persuasion and conciliation rather than confrontation and violence.

But although the majority of victims in the Mau Mau struggle were Africans loyal to their Christian church or the authorities, Governor Sir Evelyn Baring had already demonstrated that his administration was unwilling to compromise the interests of Kenya's vociferous white minority in any way.

The final battle

At midnight on 20 October, 1952, one day after Sir Evelyn declared a State of Emergency and imposed martial law, Jomo Kenyatta and five colleagues — Paul Ngei, Achieng Oneko, Bildad Kaggia, Fred Kubai, and Kungu Karumba — were arrested. Sir Evelyn described Kenyatta as a "leader into darkness and death" — a slander that Kenyatta was to forgive but never forget.

The Mau Mau took to the forests to begin the war in earnest. Many innocent victims were caught in the middle, including at least ninety-seven so-called "loyalists" to the colonial administration who were brutally slaughtered.

While in custody awaiting trial on charges of organising the Mau Mau — a charge he always denied — Kenyatta and his arrested colleagues heard of this, the "Lari Massacre".

Later, after a rigged trial at remote Kapenguria, in the Cherangani Hills, Kenyatta and his colleagues were found guilty on the basis of perjured evidence. They were sentenced to seven years hard labour in the scorched wastes of remote Lokitaung on the far north-western shores of Lake Turkana, still known then as Lake Rudolf.

There, far removed from the mainstream of Kenya society, the administration perhaps hoped that the heat and dust of the semi-desert around Lokitaung, would finish off Kenyatta who was already in his fifties; and that, at least, his pervading personality would cease to exercise its powerful influence on events.

In 1954 the inmates were joined by one of

the Mau Mau's military leaders, General "China" Waruhui Itote, who was captured by colonial security forces in the highlands.

Now the repression began in earnest. During "Operation Anvil" carried out in Nairobi, almost 30,000 suspected Mau Mau sympathisers were rounded up and held in concentration camps.

In the months that followed, thousands more innocent men, women, and children throughout the country were also incarcerated, many losing their homes and their land.

Two years later, in 1956, another Mau Mau leader, Dedan Kimathi was trapped and wounded in an ambush. Brought to court, he was found guilty and later hanged — the first martyr to the cause of Kenya's freedom.

Yet even as the struggle escalated, the colonialists began to concede political ground. By 1959 twenty-five Africans were sitting in Legco together with fifteen Asians and five Arab members. But the minority Europeans still claimed forty-six seats.

Not all settlers were opposed to an independent Kenya. A minority of influential Europeans — Michael Blundell, Wilfred Havelock, and Derek Erskine among them — supported the campaign to free Kenyatta and the independence movement. Many members of the minority Asian community, long committed to the cause of a democratic and independent Kenya, reiterated their belief in the future of Kenya under a one-man, one-vote majority rule.

But even when Kenyatta and his colleagues completed their seven-year term, Kenyatta was immediately detained and held first at Lodwar and then moved to Maralal where he remained, virtually *incommunicado,* for another two years, although at this time, Rawson Macharia, the key witness at his Kapenguria trial, was jailed for twenty-one months for perjury.

The following year, though still detained at Maralal, Kenyatta was elected President *in absentia* of the newly-formed Kenya African National Union (KANU) which was the natural successor to KAU. Some months later another group formed the Kenya Africa Democratic Union (KADU).

Both were anticipating the inevitable elections to come. In August 1960, the same month that KADU came into being, the eight-year-old State of Emergency finally came to an end.

The force of the African majority had become irrepressible. Leaders of both KANU and KADU — except Kenyatta who remained in Maralal — were invited to the first of the constitutional talks to discuss Kenya's future as a free nation, at Lancaster House, London.

But if Kenyatta was unable to bring his incisive mind and forceful personality to bear on the talks, his influence was clearly felt. He commanded as much interest as the talks. Interviewed at his Maralal residence and asked when he would like Independence he replied, "Today".

And with the subsequent announcement — after the first Lancaster House talks — that Africans would participate fully in the general elections of February 1961, the path to full Independence was open.

KANU won eighteen of the thirty-three seats with an overwhelming majority of sixty-seven per cent, against KADU's sixteen per cent. Among the first African members of the pre-Independence Kenya Parliament were Daniel arap Toroitich Moi who succeeded Kenyatta as President, Tom Mboya (later assassinated), Ronald Ngala who died in a 1972 road accident, and Oginga Odinga, a colourful and controversial figure in the country's political history.

Nonetheless, unless Kenyatta was released, KANU, and the mainly Asian Kenya Freedom Party, together with independent European and Asian members, refused to participate in Government.

Then bitterness between the two African parties was fuelled by the administration's invitation to KADU to form a minority Government. Under increasing pressure, however, the authorities finally relented. On 15 August, 1961, Kenyatta was released. He was now free to pursue the struggle that he had begun so long ago. On 6 November he led a KANU delegation to London to discuss Kenya's future.

Soon after his return, in January 1962, Kariuki Njiri, the Member for Fort Hall (now Muranga) resigned his Legco seat in favour of Kenyatta who was returned unopposed.

The British Colonial Secretary returned Kenyatta's visit and during his stay announced the date for the second round of constitutional talks at Lancaster House.

Clear divisions now emerged between the two parties over the form of constitution they favoured. KADU sought a federal form of government, KANU opted for a strong central government.

But, on their return, ever the conciliator, Kenyatta agreed to form a coalition government with KADU until Independence which in May 1963, was augured by the first general elections ever held in Kenya on the universal franchise of one-man, one-vote. The result: a landslide triumph for KANU as Kenyatta swept in, unopposed, as the Member for Gatundu.

Thus, the first independent Government with a full mandate for *Madaraka* (internal self-rule) was formed on 1 June, 1963. Kenyatta was Prime Minister.

In his inaugural address he coined the word that has become Kenya's clarion call, an official motto now incorporated on the country's coat of arms. He invited all, minority Europeans and Asians as well as Africans, to work in the spirit of *Harambee* ("Pulling together") in nation-building.

A firm friend of both Kenyatta and the Kenyan people, Kenya's last Governor, Malcolm MacDonald, became the first and only Governor-General.

A world leader of immense stature, few statesmen of this century, or any other, could claim to be as charismatic, visionary, and pragmatic as Kenyatta. One of MacDonald's *Seven Titans,* he possessed what MacDonald described as the "great gift of magnaminity".

Though he suffered a long and lonely self-imposed exile in Britain, and years of incarceration, Kenyatta rose above all malice. His subsequent book, *Suffering Without Bitterness,* is testimony to the gift that MacDonald divined.

It is doubtful, however, whether he foresaw during his incarceration how soon Kenya would be free. In later years, he even confided to one friend that in his lifetime he had never expected to see India free.

But now that freedom had finally arrived he set about applying all his energy and vast intellect to cement it into a solid and unshakeable foundation.

Two months after taking office he invited the European farmers and entrepreneurs of the White Highlands to a Nakuru meeting to convince them of his faith in an undivided, non-racial Kenya. So evident was his sincerity and integrity that when he asked them to stay on to help build a Kenya in which all were equally free he won many over.

The following month, at the third and final round of talks at Lancaster House, the date of Kenya's Independence was set for 12 December under a constitution that abolished discrimination in all fields of life.

Three months later, at the stroke of midnight on the dawn of 12 December, 1963, the Union Jack was hauled down for the last time — and the new green, black, red, and white flag of Kenya raised in its place: green for the land, black for the people, and red for the blood shed in the fight for freedom.

With Independence, bitterness was laid aside in the joy of nationhood. The *mugumo* (fig tree), which Lugard and Kinyanjui had planted near the turn of the century at Fort Smith as a symbol of peace between the two peoples, still flourished, towering forty metres (130 feet) above the compound.

And now the villagers around Fort Smith, sons and daughters of those Kikuyu warriors, were ready to salute the European with a smile and a word of welcome.

The First Republic

Prime Minister Jomo Kenyatta inaugurated Kenya's birth as a member of the family of free nations — and the United Nations, Commonwealth, and Organization of African Unity — with an address to the State opening of Kenya's first parliament on 13 December, 1963.

As a new member of the Commonwealth, Kenya's first year was a period of intense restructuring and rebuilding. Supported by the British, the Government organised massive land purchases on a willing-seller, willing-buyer basis intended to settle many landless Africans on former European-owned farms. Funded by the British Government, the scheme continued for some years at a cost of many millions of pounds.

Social welfare and a better quality of life for all, particularly the low-income and subsistence groups, were the main aims of a pragmatic policy that encouraged foreign investment and sought to diversify from economic dependence on agriculture.

One of the main concerns was to maintain the economic market that had existed before Independence, the East African Common Services, as it was known, between Tanganyika — soon to become Tanzania — which had achieved Independence two years earlier, and Uganda, which had become independent on

Opposite: Mission-educated Johnstone Kamau who changed his name later to Jomo Kenyatta.

Opposite right: Jomo Kenyatta at the height of the Independence struggle.

Above: Mural at Kenyatta International Conference Centre depicting midnight arrest of Jomo Kenyatta on 20 October 1952.

Opposite: The cell at Kapenguria where Jomo Kenyatta was held during his trial.

9 October, 1962.

Now the market, which brought together thirty million people, became the East African Community. The main institutions were the East African Posts and Telecommunications Corporation, East African Railways and Harbours Corporation, and East African Airways. It was a bold and vigorous partnership yet, sadly, ideological differences and economic imbalances combined to work against it. Fourteen years after Kenya's Independence it collapsed.

Although Kenya was firmly non-aligned, its western-style Government and economy were a glaring contrast to the socialist policies of its two sister states, Uganda and Tanzania. Only the pragmatism of the three EAC leaders — Obote, Nyerere, and Kenyatta — held the federation together.

In November 1964, in the spirit of nationhood and pragmatic patriotism that had marked Kenya's first year, Ronald Ngala and his KADU colleagues, crossed the floor of parliament from the opposition benches to join KANU.

Effectively, Kenya became a one-party state. Kenya's first year of Independence was marked by many significant developments. The Kenya Air Force and Navy were formed, Parliament Buildings extended (the Speaker, Muinga Chokwe, laid an airtight cylinder containing the national flag, postage stamps, daily papers, and the names of all members of the first Parliament, in the concrete foundations), the last British troops departed, and it was announced that Kenya would become a Republic.

On 10 December, 1964, seventy-one years after Kenya became a protectorate and forty-four years after it was made a colony, reviewing the guard of honour formed by the last platoons of the departing British army the Prime Minister thanked the troops for their help in times of flood and famine.

The bonds that now united Britain and Kenya were those of admiration and affection — not colonial subjugation.

The following day Kenyatta gave Malcolm MacDonald a glowing valedictory on his departure for home leave at the end of his tenure as Governor-General. He achieved the unique distinction of serving in Kenya as Governor, Governor-General and, from 1965, as Britain's first High Commissioner to the former colony he had ostensibly ruled in the Queen's name.

Finally, on 12 December, 1964, Kenya became a Republic. Prime Minister Jomo Kenyatta was sworn in as the country's first President at a colourful ceremony in the Agricultural Society of Kenya's Mitchell Park showground, renamed Jamhuri (Independence) Park to mark this momentous step in national history. Oginga Odinga became the country's first Vice-President.

Harambee

Throughout, Kenyatta continually rallied the people to join together.

He pledged to accelerate land consolidation and speed up the issue of title deeds. Initiating such major development projects as the inauguration of the Seven Forks hydroelectric scheme at Kindaruma, in a major policy statement — "Sessional Paper No 10" — he also spelt out Kenya's blueprint for African socialism.

It was based on political democracy, mutual social responsibility and dependency, and equitable distribution of income and property.

With the purchase of three Super VC-10s for East African Airways — a firm sign of Kenya and its sister states own confidence in their future — foreign investment began to come into the country. Among new investors in 1965 were Philips, makers of light bulbs and electric appliances, and the Life Insurance Company of India.

Although severe famine struck Kenya's drought-prone Akambaland, the last edifices of colonial prejudice were removed. Free medical care for all children and adult outpatients became available at the former King George V Hospital, now Kenyatta National Hospital; racial discrimination was eliminated at Nairobi City primary schools, and free education for Form V and VI high school students was introduced.

In March 1965, under close scrutiny for alleged links with eastern bloc countries and China, Vice President Odinga complained of a systematic campaign by his Parliamentary colleagues to oust him. And at a subsequent conference in Limuru, intended to reorganise and streamline KANU, Odinga was replaced as the Party's Deputy Vice President.

Some days later, along with twenty-seven members of the National Assembly, Odinga resigned from KANU to form the breakaway opposition party, Kenya Peoples Union (KPU), which was registered on 23 May, 1966. A subsequent Parliamentary Bill, passed the same month, stripped the dissidents of their Parliamentary seats, except for twelve members who withdrew their support for Odinga.

But Kenyatta, wanting to avoid the divisions that had marred the progress and stability of other newly-independent African states, told KPU to seek a mandate at the polls. In what was described as a "little General Election", KPU won only nine seats.

Meanwhile, Kenyatta appointed a new Vice-President, Joseph Murumbi, and reshuffled the cabinet. At the same time, parliament endorsed the Preservation of National Security Act which allowed preventative detention.

Two other significant developments in 1966 were the Parliamentary merger of the lower house and the Senate into one common chamber; and the opening of the Central Bank which launched Kenya's first currency coins and notes — pegged to sterling at par value, twenty shillings to the £1.

Consolidation

Murumbi's tenure as Vice-President was brief. In failing health, he tendered his resignation and on 5 January, 1967, Daniel Toroitich arap Moi became the country's third Vice-President.

The years that followed were ones of consolidation for the new nation. In many ways, physical independence took much longer to achieve than political independence. Four years after the Kenya flag was raised many non-Kenyans were still living and working in Kenya.

Thus, from 2 November, 1967, all non-Kenyans working in Kenya had to obtain an official entry permit.

Together with the announcement — early in 1968 — of new regulations for Asian holders of British passports in Britain, this triggered a massive exodus of Asians from Kenya.

Other significant developments were the opening of the new Mombasa-Nairobi Highway in August and the appointment of Kitili Mwendwa as Kenya's first African Chief Justice.

The following month, Kenyans were given a new vision and sense of national destiny with the country's athletics triumph in the Mexico Olympics, winning three golds, three silvers, and two bronze medals to bring home a haul of eight — the highest athletic tally of any of the 118 nations competing, except for the USA.

In 1969 the prospect of the first post-Independence general elections became the main focus but, before these the country was stunned by the 5 July assassination of the Minister for Economic Planning, Tom Mboya. A charismatic and popular leader, he was one of the vanguard who had campaigned for Kenya's Independence.

In the political aftermath, there was confrontation between the Government and the KPU. The opposition party was subsequently banned and its leader, Odinga, and all KPU MPs, were detained. Using the December general election to bring many new faces into the Cabinet, Kenyatta gave a new sense of purpose and direction to the country.

But on 14 June, the first voice of Kenya's political consciousness, Harry Thuku, aged seventy-five, died. Nonetheless, the founder of the Kikuyu Central Association must have been a happy man at the progress he had seen during Kenya's first seven years of freedom.

Second decade

For Kenya, the second decade of Independence represented not only a period of unprecedented growth and development, but also a challenge to the management skills of its economists and administrators.

With the 1970 opening of its satellite ground station in the Rift Valley, extensions to Nairobi International Airport for the arrival of the first jumbo jet, the 1972 opening of the new Central Bank building and the completion of thirty-three-storey Kenyatta International Conference Centre, Kenya had solid physical testimonials to its progress.

In 1973, this progress was recognised when Nairobi was the first third-world capital to become a United Nations headquarters city — the home of the United Nations Environment Programme (UNEP).

That same year Kenya celebrated both ten years of Independence and a decade of Jomo Kenyatta's presidency. Achievements noted included a doubling of national income, free education up to the first four grades, school attendance increased by 150 per cent, a tripling of tea production and a fifty per cent growth in the coffee crop, the number one foreign exchange earner. But against this, the first oil price hike resulted in a twenty per cent inflation rate.

Above: The late President, Jomo Kenyatta, with his successor, Daniel arap Moi, then Vice-President.

Kenya-style democracy, based on choice of personalities not ideologies, continued to flourish. In the 1974 elections, more than half the sitting members lost their seats.

The following year was marked by the disappearance in March 1975 of J. M. Kariuki, a popular left-leaning Parliamentarian and former asssistant minister with considerable charisma and a strong following among the radical student community.

A subsequent inquiry by a Select Parliamentary Committee left many questions unanswered but as pressures from outside continued, particularly on Kenya's western borders with Idi Amin's Uganda, Kenya's solidarity and unity deepened.

The most significant outcome of Amin's dictatorial regime was the collapse of the East African Community — and the common market — in February 1977.

Within days Kenya launched its own national airline, transformed its share of the railways and harbours into a national corporation, and established the Kenya Post and Telecommunications Corporation.

In 1977, Kenyatta's rapidly-failing health caused the cancellation of KANU party elections in spite of the fact that none had been held for eleven years.

The "Mzee" had earned the trust and love of all Kenyans — and throughout the world he inspired respect and confidence for his statesmanship and humanity. His death on 22 August, 1978, heralded a period of intense mourning. Most Kenyans felt as if they had lost a father.

But as princes, presidents, statesmen, and world leaders arrived in Nairobi for his funeral on 31 August, 1978, the legacy of freedom and stability that he had created remained his enduring memorial.

Above: Ministers and Parliamentarians greet President Daniel arap Moi.

The Second Republic

The transition of leadership was smooth — and constitutional. Within hours, Vice President Daniel Toroitich arap Moi was sworn in as President. He marked his inauguration by exhorting all Kenyans to follow Mzee Kenyatta and his own footsteps. The *Nyayo* era had begun. In the subsequent general elections of November 1978 he was returned unopposed as President of both country and party. Finance Minister, Mwai Kibaki, was named Vice-President.

Moi made no major changes in the Cabinet, but ordered a major shake-up of the security services and Immigration Department. The new President also cracked-down on corruption, smuggling, and nepotism, and promised that political detention would only be used as "a last resort". He also dissolved all tribal organisations in the interests of national unity.

In his third year as President, he was made Chairman of the Organization of African Unity (OAU) during its 1981 summit in Nairobi, an office he held for an unprecedented two terms.

In August 1982 an abortive coup attempt by rebel junior Air Force personnel was swiftly crushed by the Kenya Army. Later, two self-confessed ringleaders were court-martialled and, with ten other airmen, sentenced to death for treason. Another ninety or so airmen received prison sentences for taking part in the coup, and the entire Kenya Air Force was immediately replaced by a new unit, '82 Air Force. Most coup members were given a presidential pardon.

When Minister for Constitutional Affairs, Charles Njonjo, was suspended from the Cabinet a year later, he resigned his seat in Parliament. General elections were held a year ahead of schedule in September 1983, in the words of President Moi, "to give the country time to clean up its house".

A judicial inquiry into allegations against Njonjo concluded on 12 December, 1984, that Njonjo had been involved in corruption, the illegal import of firearms into Kenya, and an attempt to topple the Government of the Seychelles. Although subsequently given a Presidential pardon, the sixty-four-year-old former Minister did not return to politics.

In 1987, Kenya staged the spectacular Fourth All Africa Games at Nairobi's 80,000-seat Moi International Stadium, one of the most modern sports complexes in Africa, built and designed

Above: Elite troops of the Kenya army.

by Chinese specialists with the aid of a Chinese loan.

In 1988 a new voting system to decide nominations for KANU candidates was introduced. Electors queued up behind the candidate of their choice. Those with more than seventy per cent support were elected unopposed. Where two or more candidates had less support they contested the election by secret ballot.

The first decade of Moi's leadership was marked with impressive achievements in education and social welfare. He introduced free education and free milk for all primary school students; *Nyayo* wards in hospitals throughout the country; the settlement of long-standing land disputes; and the issue of long-delayed land title deeds to smallholders and peasant farmers.

Except for farming, the mainstay of the economy, Kenya had few real economic resources at Independence. Change was swift and stunning. Inspired by the credo of nation building, major industrial and agricultural development continues. Tourism was the obvious avenue for development. Indeed, from fewer than 100,000 visitors in 1963,

twenty-five years later Kenya's visitors numbered three-quarters-of-a-million — and tourism had become the country's major foreign exchange earner and industry.

The traditional cash crop of coffee had moved into second place along with tea, another remarkable success story. The smallholder tea growing scheme launched at Independence had seen Kenya become the world's third-largest producer and second-largest exporter.

Kenya also produces what experts acclaim as the finest coffee in the world. It is also the world's third-largest producer of pineapples. From plantations around Thika this crop takes the taste of Kenya across the world.

Undoubtedly, however, Kenya's biggest success was in education and social welfare, now available to all. The number of primary schools doubled to accommodate more than five million pupils, with a sixfold increase in teachers to 150,000. Secondary schools have increased more than twelvefold to 2,500 with half a million students. There are now four universities with 30,000 undergraduates — and more institutes of further education are to be opened.

Above: Nairobi's Nyayo Monument erected in 1988 to honour a decade of President Moi's leadership.

The increase in health facilities is equally dramatic. In 1989, Kenya had 30,000 specialists, surgeons, doctors, trained nurses, and health workers, compared to only 4,000 in 1963. There were almost 2,000 hospitals, clinics, and health centres and 30,000 hospital beds. And the number is increasing all the time.

Kenya is the star sports nation of developing countries, with some of the world's greatest distance runners and finest boxers. At the 1988 Seoul Olympics, the team earned the nation its greatest medal haul — a fitting gift for Kenya's twenty-fifth anniversary.

Kenya is also the home of the greatest rally in the world motor sports calendar. The gruelling 4,000-kilometre-long (2,500-mile) Safari Rally continues as the ultimate test of man and machine.

Stability

Though the style of leadership remains traditionally African-patriarchal, rather than Western party-oriented, parliament still emulates the Westminster model. The bureaucracy and judiciary follow the English pattern.

Blessed with an abundance of decisive and incisive decision makers and administrators, both in public and private sectors, despite the enormous population growth, Kenya has made great economic and social progress.

When it celebrated its twenty-fifth anniversary on 12 December, 1988, Kenyans could look back with satisfaction on a quarter of a century of growth and prosperity. The fact that five successive Parliaments had been decided in the ballot box at five general elections was solid testimony to the strength of Kenyan democracy.

Indeed, arguably no other nation on the African continent has so emphatically maintained law and order or sustained the democracy so essential to the individual freedom that all Kenyans enjoy.

65

The Land: Ice and Fire, Wood and Water

Like its people, Kenya's landscapes are characterized by their diversity. Covering an area of 582,644 square kilometres (225,000 square miles) the country is a world in miniature. Almost every known type of landform, from snow mountain and glacier to true desert, exist within its boundaries.

Similarly, all stages of landscape evolution — from Africa's oldest eroded plains to its most recent volcanic, and tectonic, rifts and mountains — are clearly evident.

Kenya's different facets are reflected in the aureole of pink-shrouded mist that swirls among Mount Kenya's loftiest, ice-clad spires, and on the crystal clear waters of Naivasha. And in the bubbling vivacity of the 700-kilometre-long (435-mile) Tana River as it leaps, new-born, down the shoulders of Mount Kenya and the Aberdares on its long run to the Indian Ocean where it's whispered in the rustle of the monsoon winds through the palms along Kenya's Indian Ocean coast.

Kenya has twenty mountain peaks above 2,000 metres (6,500 feet) and five great massifs rising more than 3,000 metres (10,000 feet).

Its western borders fall in the waters of Africa's largest lake, Victoria, and its eight major rivers, all more than 200 kilometres (125 miles) long, feature many impressive waterfalls. Gura Falls, high in the Aberdare Mountains, is almost 300 metres (1,000 feet) deep.

Rising from sea level to 5,199 metres (17,058 feet) on the summit of Mount Kenya, this land of contrasts is dominated by several plateaux, leading up like a series of steps and creating an impression of extensive upland plains rather than mountainous terrain. It has given Kenya a unique landscape, with a beauty equalled or surpassed by few nations.

So diverse, in fact, that there are five distinct physiographic regions.

First, the low plateau of western Kenya, warm and fertile, enjoys year-round rain. Second, the central highlands, bisected by the Great Rift Valley, almost all above 1,500 metres (5,000 feet), although touched in some parts by rain shadow, form Kenya's most productive and scenic region, a land of fertile farms,

ancient forests, rivers, lakes, and mountains.

The vast semi-arid plains and deserts of the north, where little grows and few live, make up the third area. The foreland plateau, the immediate hinterland of the coast, which seems almost a continuation of the arid north, is the fourth region.

And the fifth is the semi-arid plain that runs parallel to the 480 kilometre-long (300-mile) palm-fringed coastline. Guarded by magnificent coral reefs, this has become one of the world's great holiday playgrounds.

All this beauty and grandeur were created by the tectonic disturbances spaced over many millions of years that forced Africa to arch its back, causing warps and fractures and explosive volcanoes. During the long dormant periods in between, wind and rain reshaped the lands and silt laid fresh flesh on the dry bones.

There were six vital periods of dormancy. The first one resulted in many of today's greatest land masses, usually more than 2,000 metres (6,500 feet) high — such as the Kisii Highlands and the high Cheranganis, including the Trans-Nzoia and the Elgeyo-Suk plateaux.

The second period created the landscape found between 1,800 and 2,000 metres (5,900-6,500 feet), including the Kilungu and Mbooni Hills in Ukambani, and the low bench of the Lerogi Hills near Maralal.

The third period formed the lands between 1,500 and 1,650 metres (5,000-5,450 feet) — the plains around Kajiado and Machakos.

During the fourth dormant era the land between 1,200 and 1,450 metres (3,000-3,900 feet), settled Siaya and Busia districts and large areas of Machakos and Kitui.

The last two periods resulted in the landscape between 900 and 1,200 metres (3,000-3,900 feet) and 300 and 750 metres (1,000-2,200 feet). These form the extremely extensive foreland plateau between the central highlands and the coast, and the coastal hinterland and littoral. Both are characterised by ubiquitous, marginal "islands of rock" — isolated inselbergs — for in this semi-arid land many scarps retreated and there was much long-

Opposite: Satellite picture of Kenya's Rift Valley — Lakes Turkana (top) and Victoria (left); Mounts Elgon (left of centre), Kenya (right of centre), and Kilimanjaro (bottom right). The blue lake (centre) is Baringo.

term erosion.

Undoubtedly the greatest outcome of all this geological rock and roll was the formation of the Rift Valley and its subsidiaries — the most dramatic landscape in Kenya with sheer walls of rock up to 3,000 metres (10,000 feet) high.

But although the forces that shaped the Rift are still not fully understood, clearly this — and other smaller but similar valleys — were the final result of extensive uplift as the arched land fell.

In Kenya, the greatest movements took place intermittently between five and twelve million years ago (during the mid-Miocene and late-Pliocene period) following a series of major earth movements at the close of the forty-five-million-year-long age of the dinosaurs (the Jurassic Period).

Subsequently, in the last million years, other minor grid faults have taken place in the floor of the central Rift Valley.

Earlier, beginning some seventeen million years ago (in mid-Miocene times), stunning eruptions spread lava over the Kapiti, Simbara, Samburu, and Kericho areas.

Although Kenya appears quiescent today, the forces that shaped the country are still at work. This is evident in the immense thermal activity beneath the Rift floor, and in the eruption of the Teleki volcano (and others) at the southern end of Lake Turkana as recently as 1899.

Indeed, in geologically-speaking recent times — say the last 400 to 600 years — this widespread activity manifested itself in eruptions in Menengai and Longonot and also created the Chyulu Hills.

The most dramatic eruptions in the Rift, however, took place long ago — many millions of years before the fractures that formed the present prominent scarps.

Drainage

All Kenya's main rivers were formed by the uplifting that created the great massif of the central highlands.

Spiralling down from these highlands is one of the greatest-known radial river systems. Ignoring the deep depression between the two highland blocks — normally a natural route for any major river — the drainage system instead took on its now familiar pattern, seen in the parallel streams that drain both the Aberdare and the Mau dip slopes, together with the low belt between the Galana and Tana Rivers. Minor radial streams also wash the main volcanic cones as well as the interior highlands.

But, except for the Nzoia, Yala, Mara, Galana and Tana, most rivers and tributaries are seasonal. Perennial water shortage remains one of Kenya's most pressing problems. And none of Kenya's rivers are navigable except in the lower reaches of the Tana and where the Athi-Galana becomes the Sabaki.

Ecological potential

Kenya's ecological value is affected by a wide range of conditions and a rapidly-growing population. Defined by climate, soil, and vegetation, Kenya has six broad ecological zones. The close relationship between climate and altitude is also reflected in the vegetation.

Where certain plant species and vegetation types occur it is possible to define climatic boundaries more accurately than by records from the relatively few "met" stations.

Central Kenya is dominated by the three great volcanic ranges of Mount Kenya, the Aberdares, and the Mau Hills, together with the massive trough of the Great Rift Valley which divides Kenya neatly in two.

A once dome-shaped volcanic pile, Mount Kenya, Africa's second-highest point, is the world's most perfect model of an Equatorial mountain. Both the Aberdares and the Mau Ranges are essentially the product of fissure volcanic eruptions. But their inner halves have been incorporated into the downthrown sides of the Rift Valley.

Between sixty and 100 kilometres (40-60 miles) wide, the Rift Valley floor is studded with a number of small, shallow salt lakes, of which Lake Magadi — a source of trona from which soda ash is extracted — has the greatest economic value. Many prominent volcanic cones, including Longonot, Susua, and Menengai, also rise above the Rift floor.

The main plateaux are either lava plains or denuded surfaces created by the long and continuous erosion characteristic of this area. By comparison, the lava plains are still fairly intact and young. The best-known examples

Opposite: Mountain Lodge in one of Mount Kenya's forest reserves.
Overleaf: Elephant on the banks of the Tana River.

are the Kaputei (Kapiti) Plains, the Athi Plains, and the Yatta Plateau. But the Laikipia Plateau is either a lava flow along a former pre-existing river valley, or an eroded remnant of lava outpouring reduced by scarp retreat. It remains a geological riddle.

The eroded plateaux are confined to the non-volcanic areas east of Athi River and south of Kajiado. The hill region of Ukambani is an old and dissected land with a number of plateaux plains that were levelled by erosion. While the Mbooni, Kilungu, Ol Doinyo Sapuk, and the Mau Hills, together with the hills around Kajiado, are the remnants of Africa's oldest erosion surface — generally regarded as late Jurassic.

Another intermediate plateau around Kajiado, Masii, Wamunyu, and between Kangondi and Kitui town, is a remnant of sub-Miocene landscapes.

The youngest surface, dominating the area east of Kitui town, is a low plateau littered with many inselbergs and rock outcrops of which Endau, Makongo, and Ithumba are examples. But the Taita Hills, and others south of Kilaguni in Tsavo West, resisted the erosion which levelled the plains.

In the volcanic south, between Sultan Hamud and Mtito Andei, the recently-formed Chyulu Hills, together with many small cones, should not be mistaken for inselbergs. You can also see one or two similar cones on the southern edge of the Yatta Plateau where the drainage system holds the headwaters of Kenya's two major rivers — the Tana and the Athi. The peculiar course of the Athi River in its upper section may have been caused by backtilting before the Aberdares burst out of the plains.

And the valley cut by the misfit Ol Keju Ado may be one of the oldest in the area — it once joined the Namanga river flowing south and eastwards before the birth of Mount Kilimanjaro.

But although there are many streams it does not mean that the area is any more well-watered than the rest of Kenya. Many of these streams are only seasonal. Indeed, water shortage is a major problem, not only in the eastern half of the area, but also in the Rift Valley.

The influence of these geophysical features on land routes is obvious. The greatest obstacle was the precipitous drop of the Rift Valley escarpment. Both the railway line and the road had to negotiate the sides of the escarpment. The Magadi railway took advantage of the smooth watershed between Konza and Kajiado, before finally dodging sinuously into the Rift.

And the natural gap between Mount Kenya and the Aberdares also served as an important gateway to the north. But a similarly well-suited gap, between the Aberdare and Kikuyu dip slopes, created difficulties. The closely-spaced parallel streams meant that there was no direct link between villages only sixteen kilometres (ten miles) apart.

Yet, even if it was unhealthy, Nairobi's open ground before the final climb to the Rift wall gave great scope for development. The flat Embakasi Plains proved ideal for airport development. Three airports within a radius of seven kilometres (four miles) of the City centre are something few cities can claim. Nairobi's well-known National Park, which marks its southern edge, also gives this "City in the Sun" an unrivalled charm and attraction.

Coast

Although much of the lush Kenya coast evolved in the last thirty million years, only a few kilometres inland, the land becomes barren and desolate *nyika* (scrub plain) sloping gently to the east.

Of the coastal region's three main land forms, the lowest is the coastal belt and plains that lie less than 150 metres (5,000 feet) above sea level. Above this, between 150 and 300 metres (500-1,000 feet), is the *nyika* proper, including the scorched Taru Desert which almost defeated the early European explorers and railway gangs — broken only by the Shimba, Jibana, and Kulalu hills, which defied erosion because of the different composition of their stones and rocks.

The third unit, part of the low foreland plateau, covers all the higher ground up to 900 metres (3,000 feet) above sea level where the slight eastward slope is typical of Eastern Africa's general tilt.

Extensive yearly floods on the lower Tana plain, which leave the rich highland silt behind, have also created many small oxbow lakes. But the lower reaches of the Athi-Galana-Sabaki still appear geologically young — partly

Opposite: Tour group on a game drive in one of Kenya's wildlife sanctuaries.
Overleaf: Passenger train on the "Lunatic Line" descends into the Rift Valley.

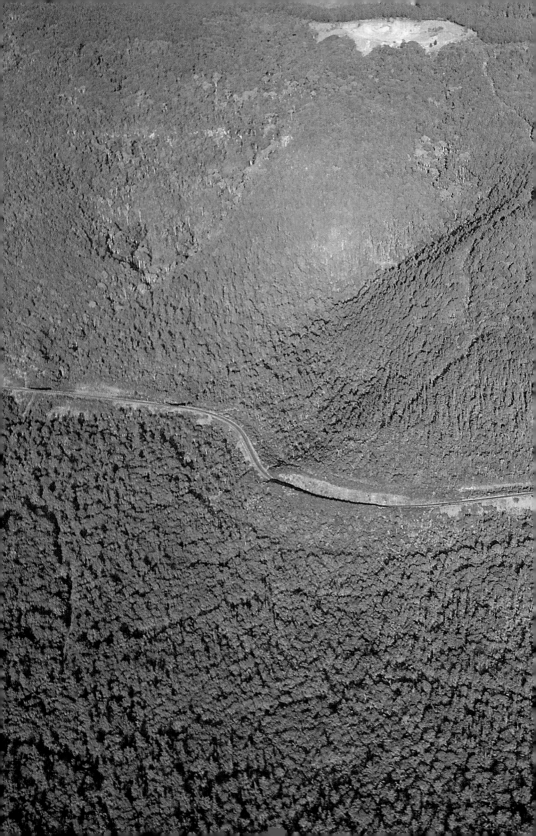

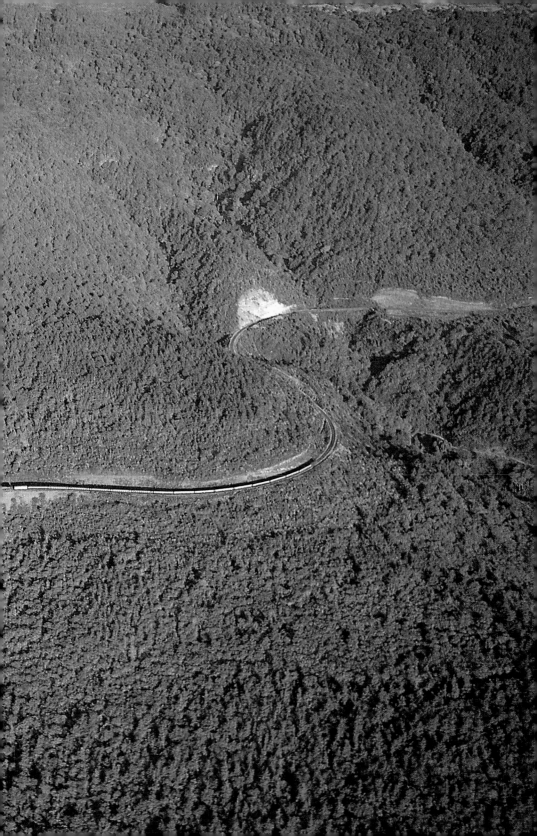

because of the dramatic changes that formed the 300-kilometre-long (185-mile) Yatta plateau.

On the slender coastal littoral many short parallel streams reach the ocean as creeks — testimony to the changes in sea level during the last million years. And where the parallel streams were closely spaced, and the hinterland was made of soft shales, following the rise in sea level which drowned the river valleys, different forms of erosion created such islands as Mombasa.

In other parts, the fluctuating sea level created different features, such as raised platforms at three distinct levels, which are clearly visible, especially around Mombasa Island. Elsewhere, raised beaches, degraded clifflines, stacks, et al, are also found.

The most outstanding feature, however, is the well-developed barrier reef that extends all the way from Shimoni in the south to Malindi in the north, without significant break — except at the mouths of rivers.

The Kenya coast has many features that make it an ideal holiday resort — beautiful, palm-fringed, white sand beaches and warm, safe lagoons and coral gardens.

Vegetation

Many forms of vegetation thrive in Kenya. But prolonged grazing, burning, shifting cultivation, or selective cutting has caused dramatic change.

Forests, for instance, have been reduced to bushland or grassland by cutting and burning — and overgrazing has turned grasslands to thicket or barren land. Kenya can also claim a rare if dubious distinction in having two sub-types of barren land — the ecological extremes of glacier and desert.

Annual rainfall

There are strong differences in Kenya's mean annual rainfall, ranging from less than 254 millimetres (10 inches) in the north-east to more than 2,030 millimetres (80 inches) on the high mountains.

A relatively wet belt extends along the Indian Ocean coast. Another wet area covers western Kenya just east of Lake Victoria. All the mountain ranges have high rainfall with dry tongues in the valleys and basins.

There are no absolutely dry seasons and rain may fall at any time in all areas. But generally rainfall follows strong seasonal patterns, most pronounced in the dry lowlands of the north and east and less apparent in the humid highlands of the central and Rift Valley areas.

Although these seasonal variations differ throughout the country, they can be classified under three main types.

Coastal area

The year starts dry and remains so until March, when rainfall gradually increases. A fairly rapid increase occurs through April and builds up to its maximum in May. After this it decreases steadily, although significant amounts are still recorded in October and November. During December it begins to fade away altogether, with minimal rainfall in January and February.

East, North-East, South-East, and Central

The two distinct rainy seasons — March-May and October-December — are separated by a minimum — June-September — which is most distinct in the lower areas of eastern Kenya.

April is generally the rainiest month but there have been years when exceptionally heavy rain gave record totals in October and November. The second minimal period — January-February — is again most pronounced in the low eastern regions.

Western Rift, Western, Lake Victoria

There is no real "dry season". But rainfall is highest between March and September and lowest during January and February.

The People: A Multi-Coloured Canvas Of Cultures

Kenya is a cultural microcosm of Africa. People from many parts of the continent have been migrating to Kenya for centuries, each bringing some distinctive feature of their own culture and language to create a colourful mosaic of mankind.

This melting-pot of peoples, a vibrant community of twenty-two million citizens, will reach almost forty million by the turn of the century.

Spread all across this vast land astride the Equator, many have had to adapt their cultures and customs to the terrain in which they live — sometimes green and fertile, often harsh and arid.

Ironically, the smallest group, the Cushitic-speaking Kenyans, occupy the largest area. These nomads of the north, who roam almost half the country, make up only three per cent of the population.

For two-thirds of all Kenyans, the common tongue is that of the Bantu languages. The remainder speak Nilotic languages. But these three language structures bind together a country of more than forty different ethnic groups.

All those who migrated here during the last 4,000 years assimilated something of those who were already here, including the earliest ancestors of modern man.

Over the centuries, before the arrival of Europeans, three great waves of migrants slowly moved into the area now defined as Kenya — the largely but not exclusively agricultural Bantu, the pastoral Cushitic speakers, and the pastoral-agricultural Nilotes.

The small groups of hunter-gatherers who lived in this then sparsely-populated region were swamped as the conflicting tides of people met, and out of the eddies and whirlpools of their intermingling, today's cultures developed.

Colonial rule drew rigid and distinct divisions between different ethnic groups who most early European administrators too readily identified as time-honoured tribes.

"Tribe", as defined by Professor P. H. Gulliver, means "any group . . . distinguished by its members . . . on the basis of cultural-regional criteria". Linguistic and anthropological studies continue to reveal that such European presumptions were far from true.

Populations are taken from the 1979 census.

Bajun, Swahili, and Shirazi (Bantu)

These people of the coast share a common language (Kiswahili), religion (Islam), and culture.

The Bajun people (population 37,000), who live on the Lamu archipelago and coastal strip to the north, believe they originally came from further north.

Centuries of immigration, conquest, transmigration, and miscegenation, resulted in the Bantu-speaking Swahili absorbing immigrants of Arabic and Persian descent.

The Shirazi (numbering, together with the Swahili, 5,500), who claim to come from Persia once made up the aristocratic families and dynasties of the Ozi kingdoms of Shaka, Mwana, Ungwana, Malindi, and Mombasa.

Many of these fishing and farmfolk are skilled craftsmen, their shipbuilding and woodwork being especially famous. Their ocean-going dhows, with their distinctive triangular sails, still ply between Arabia, the Persian Gulf, even Pakistan and India, and Lamu, Malindi, and Mombasa.

Boni, Wata, Yaaka and Dahalo (Cushitic)

These small groups of hunter-gatherers live in the coastal hinterland (Boni, Wata, and Dahalo) and on the Mukogodo massif, far inland north of Mount Kenya (Yaaka). Numbering some 4,200, they once traded ivory and honey, but have now become farmers and cattle herders. But they still gather wild fruits and honey and kill an occasional antelope for food.

Boran (Cushitic)

Numbering more than 70,000, of Ethiopian Oromo origin, the nomadic Boran live in the arid north-east of Kenya around Moyale, Marsabit, along the Ewaso Nyiro river, and in Isiolo district. They raise cattle, camels, sheep, and goats.

Right: Kipsisigis girl at initiation.

Middle: Luyia woman with farm produce.

Below: Boni girl carries home a pitcher of water.

Above: Gusii soapstone carver in the Kisii highlands.

Right: Maasai warriors with ostrich headdresses.

Above: El-Molo family at Loiyangalani, Lake Turkana.

Burji (Cushitic)

Settled farmfolk from Southern Ethiopia, the Burji are one of several Oromo-speaking communities which were displaced by the expansionist schemes of Emperor Menelik II in the last century and fled across the border into northern Kenya.

They grow maize, *teff* (a cereal), beans, pumpkins, coffee, cotton, tobacco, and bananas and claim never to have worn skins. They weave fine garments, *bado* and *kuta*, from the cotton they grow.

A law-abiding community, the Burji became farmworkers and road builders in the Moyale and Marsabit districts. Many have since moved into urban Kenya, mainly as traders.

Dassenich (Cushitic)

Only a few thousand Dassenich live in Kenya permanently — around Ileret, in Marsabit District, at the northern tip of Lake Turkana. The majority live in Ethiopia where, after the rains, they farm for five or six months. Then, during the dry season they make ritual sacrifices, feast, and celebrate their annual ceremonies.

In Kenya they fish instead, travelling down the eastern shore of Lake Turkana as far as Alia Bay and beyond in their dugout canoes, sun-drying their catch.

Their headdresses of coloured ochre and ostrich feathers testify to long hours of grooming. To avoid damage to their elaborate hair-styles, Dassenich men always carry a neck stool on which to sleep.

In raids against neighbouring tribes, killings were often cruel and deliberate. The Turkana, Gabbra, and Rendille bore the brunt of these attacks and retaliation resulted in periods of outright confrontation leaving villages and grazing grounds deserted.

El-Molo (Cushitic)

The el-Molo, once numbering fewer than 500 people, have abandoned their two small island-homes in Lake Turkana and now live at Loiyangalani, on the south-eastern shore, eking out a subsistence living by fishing from their doum palm rafts. Fresh or dried fish form their staple food, augmented by crocodile, turtle and hippopotamus meat. They also eat game and birds.

But life is changing rapidly. They have turned to cattle herding and some now work

Above: Colourful traditional Akamba dance group.

in tourism. Commercial fishing supplements their traditional subsistence. Larger, more permanent settlements have replaced their traditional homes of sticks covered with flimsy thatch and skins.

Embu (Bantu)

The Embu (population 180,500) who occupy the south-eastern slopes of Mount Kenya, are an assimilation of successive waves of immigrants from Meru to the north-east, Kikuyu to the west, and Mbeere to the south.

Although hunting and gathering now contribute little to their economy, the Embu remain notable bee-keepers. With well-distributed and abundant rainfall, the rich, fertile soil of their farmlands encourages many crops, such as coffee, tea, and pyrethrum that are marketed through co-operative societies. The Embu also keep cattle, sheep, and goats.

Gabbra (Cushitic)

The 30,000 camel-herding Gabbra of Marsabit District also keep cattle, goats, and sheep but in vastly different terrain. An Oromo group forced south-west from Ethiopia in the last century, the Gabbra are now under continuous pressure from the Somali for grazing and water along their eastern boundary.

Schools at Marsabit, Maikona, North Horr, Sololo and elsewhere have created a more settled life for many but the great majority of these handsome, thrifty people still roam the vast semi-arid deserts west and north of Marsabit with their herds and their way of life remains singularly unchanged.

Gusii (Bantu)

The Gusii, Kenya's sixth largest group (population 944,000), who live in the fertile Kisii highlands and parts of South Nyanza, claim kinship with the Kuria, Suba, and Luyia.

Under pressure from successive waves of Luo immigration, they migrated eastwards about 200 years ago to settle in the Kisii highlands subsisting on bananas, millet, eleusine, and maize. Now these hills are one of Kenya's prime tea, coffee, and pyrethrum-producing areas. Passion fruit, another exotic cash crop, grows prolifically.

More and more grade cattle are kept on the well-planned smallholdings around their neatly thatched homesteads. Traditionally, they have close trade ties with the Luo.

Above: A Bok group, of the Sabaot community, on the slopes of Mount Elgon.

Fine sculptors, too, the Gusii fashion the soft, pinkish-white soapstone, quarried locally in the Itumbe hills, into small animal statuettes, candlesticks, vases, and other *bric-a-brac* which are sold throughout Kenya in curio and handicraft shops.

And their traditional healers for centuries practised a primitive form of trepanning, successfully performing delicate hole-in-the-head brain surgery with crude surgical instruments and no anaesthetics.

The Gusii are also notable athletes. Several have won honours in the Commonwealth and Olympic Games.

Ilchamus (Nilotic)

Closely related to the Samburu and Maasai, the Ilchamus of Lake Baringo number only 7,500. But unlike their cattle-herding relatives, the Maa-speaking Ilchamus are settled farmers and fisherfolk, grazing their stock along the receding lake shoreline during the long dry seasons.

Now that the lake resort attracts increasing numbers of visitors, however, the Ilchamus's traditional way of life is changing rapidly.

But dancing is still a form of personal expression and celebration — and elevation to a new age-grade, circumcision, the birth of a baby, the onset of the rains, or a simply spontaneous need, are good enough reason to dance.

Iteso (Nilotic)

The Iteso, (population 132,500) of Busia and Bungoma in Western Province, belong to the *Ateker* — "people of one language" — family of tribes. They drifted eastwards from Uganda into Kenya between 1750 and 1850. Settling on the plains south of Mount Elgon, they came into conflict with the Luyia, especially the Bukusu, and laid waste vast stretches of country.

The aim of these raids was to rustle cattle. But although pastoralists, they were also cultivators, and as they began to barter produce for small stock, which in turn were exchanged for the cattle they coveted, the Iteso found stability.

Now they grow maize, cotton, sugarcane, and tobacco commercially and the pace of development throughout western Kenya has made them even more zealous farmers.

Iteso artisans are renowned potters and use

Above: Gabbra camel herd in northern Kenya's "Plains of Darkness".

their pots to store water, grain, and other foods — and to brew millet and honey beer.

Kamba (Bantu)

Occupying the Machakos and Kitui districts of Eastern Province, the 1.7 million Akamba are Kenya's fourth-largest ethnic group.

Originally hunters, the Kamba settled at Mbooni about four centuries ago, adopting a more sedentary life as farmers. As with most Bantu, political power lay with the clan elders who functioned as the "parliament".

From Mbooni they eventually colonised the whole area and began trading — at first with the neighbouring Kikuyu, Embu, Tharaka, and Mijikenda, and later the coast.

But late last century, rinderpest decimated their herds. And with the building of the Uganda Railway and the ban on expansion into the empty land around Ulu and Yatta, Kamba prosperity declined.

Drought and famine still plague the Kamba people, especially in the arid north-east around Kitui. Poor farm practices and severe deforestation from charcoal production hampers development.

Skilled metalworkers, potters, and basket-makers, their inlaid woodwork and carvings,

have become a major handicraft industry, with significant local and export sales.

Keiyo (Nilotic)

A Kalenjin group, the Keiyo — thought to have moved to their present homeland from around Mount Elgon some time in the late sixteenth and early seventeenth centuries — live on the almost inaccessible ledges of the precipitous Elgeyo Escarpment 700 metres (2,300 feet) or more above the sheer gorge of the river Kerio.

The Keiyo used to graze their stock on the rich grasslands of the eastern Uasin Gishu plateau but raids by Karamoja and others in the last century forced them to seek refuge on the cliffside. And although many are now farmers, cattle remain their first love.

Traditionally the Keiyo were courageous and adept hunters of elephant, buffalo, and rhinoceros which they took for meat.

Kikuyu (Bantu)

Largest of all Kenya's ethnic groups, the 3.2 million Kikuyu moved from Meru and Tharaka to their present homeland in the highlands between Kiambu, Nyeri, Muranga, and Kirinyaga on the south and south-west slopes of Mount Kenya, some 400 years ago.

Land, the dominant factor in the social, political, religious, and economic life of these farmers, soon brought them into conflict with the European settlers who seized Kikuyu land.

Yet, perhaps more successfully than any other tribe, the Kikuyu adapted to the challenge of Western culture, displaying an early political awareness. This resulted in the formation of a political association in 1920 which drew up a petition of grievances to present to the Chief Native Commissioner (See "The Dust and the Ashes", Part One).

Now these progressive farmers use modern methods and maintain fine livestock, benefitting from the growing markets of Nairobi and the thriving export trade in coffee, tea, pyrethrum, horticultural crops, vegetables, and flowers.

They have bought most of the former White Highlands farmlands and are active in business and commerce throughout Kenya. About 400,000 Kikuyu (forty per cent of the city population) make their home in Nairobi and they form a significant number of the citizens in other towns.

Kipsigis (Nilotic)

The Kipsigis, the largest group of Kalenjin people who number 1.5 million in the Rift Valley of Western Kenya, speak different dialects of the same language. Kericho is the administrative centre.

Other Kalenjin groups with common affinities and customs are the Nandi, Tugen, Marakwet, Keiyo, Pokot, Terik, and Sabaot.

The Kipsigis — once known as the Lumbwa — have a passionate love of cattle. Raids across their borders to rustle cattle from the Gusii, Luo, and Maasai were a constant source of friction. Increasing numbers of grade cattle graze the well-kept smallholdings of this leading farm community.

The Kipsigis also grow a number of cash crops, especially tea, pyrethrum, potatoes, maize, cabbage, tomatoes, onions, peas, and beans, as well as traditional crops such as bananas and sweet potatoes.

The Kalenjin, especially the Nandi and Kipsigis, are renowned athletes. Many of Kenya's track stars are Kipsigis.

Kuria (Bantu)

Astride the Kenya-Tanzania border on the cool, high ground south of Kisii and east of Lake Victoria, the Kuria (population 89,000) are separated from the lake by the Suba and the Luo communities.

Even now few roads lead into their South Nyanza highlands with deeply-cut valleys and fast-flowing streams.

Loamy soils combined with abundant and well-dispersed rainfall make for productive farming. Cash crops include pyrethrum, coffee and, more recently, tobacco.

Although they keep sheep and goats, dual-purpose cattle are the principal livestock. Newly-introduced Swahili bulls are upgrading the beef and dairy herds.

The majority live across the border in Tanzania, but those in Kenya have responded to the stimulus of education. There are many primary and secondary schools throughout their region.

In the last three decades a quiet revolution has also taken place in the development of their economy. The small townships of Ntimaru, Nyabasi, Taraganya, and Kihancha have become thriving markets and social venues — and are now also busy trade-centres for many diversified craft industries.

Luo (Nilotic)

Largest of Kenya's non-Bantu ethnic groups, the two million strong Luo of Central and South Nyanza districts, around the Kavirondo Gulf of Lake Victoria, were the most vigorous of the Nilotes who moved south from Sudan, arriving in Nyanza at least 500 years ago.

The acquisition of cattle and the constant search for pastures dominated the minds of the first Luo immigrants. But expansion eastwards was blocked by the barrier of the Mau and the Rift Valley, and the warlike Maasai.

Their herds decimated by rinderpest, the Luo became increasingly dependent on farming and fishing for subsistence. But these itinerant people of the lakes and rivers are still on the move.

The Luo say they are like the water which flows until it finds its own level. Indeed, tens of thousands have spread across the country into major towns, especially Nairobi and Mombasa, north to the shores of Lake Turkana and south to Lake Jipe.

Articulate and civic-minded, the Luo were prominent in the struggle for Independence. Many leading trade unionists and politicians, in particular the late Tom Mboya (assassi-

Above: Traditional Chuka dancers from Meru district.

nated in 1969) and former Vice-President, Oginga Odinga, fanned the flame of *Uhuru* (Independence) (See "The Dust and the Ashes").

Luyia (Bantu)

Seventeen groups make up the 2.1 million Abaluyia community of western Kenya. With more than 750 people to the square kilometre, the population density between Kisumu and Kakamega, their administrative centre, is one of the highest in rural Africa and their birth-rate one of the highest in the world.

The earliest Luyia probably settled in the area around the fourteenth century and arrivals continued into the seventeenth century. The Samia ironworkers were the most skilled of Luyia smelters, forging knives, hoes, and other implements which they used as a currency over a wide area.

Pottery and basket-making are still common crafts. Groundnuts, sim-sim, maize, and later cotton, were early cash crops.

Third largest of Kenya's ethnic groupings, the Luyia have two major recreational passions: music and soccer.

Maasai (Nilotic)

The pastoral and nomadic Maasai (population 241,500), who live in Narok and Kajiado districts, are a fusion of Nilotic and Cushitic peoples who lived north-west of Lake Turkana 1,000 years ago.

Then the Maasai began to move south, climbing the Laikipia and Cherangani escarpments out of the Rift Valley and in the ensuing centuries spreading out across the fertile grasslands of the central and southern Rift and surrounding uplands.

By the last century, the Maasai had earned a reputation as powerful and ferocious warriors who raided hundreds of kilometres into neighbouring territories to rustle cattle.

Their life, conditioned by the constant quest for water and grazing, remained unchanged for centuries. In the more arid areas, livestock is moved seasonally, often several hundred kilometres, to undergrazed areas or to new grass stimulated by local rain.

Fresh and curdled milk, carried and stored in long, decorated gourds, is the basic Maasai diet. Blood tapped from the jugular vein of a steer or cow is mixed with cattle urine to ferment it, making a potent stimulant.

Cattle are rarely slaughtered and then only for ceremonial purposes. Game meat, with

84

Right: Pokomo fisherman with basket trap.

Middle: Pokot warrior.

Below: Swahili woman in traditional veiled dress, *bui bui.*

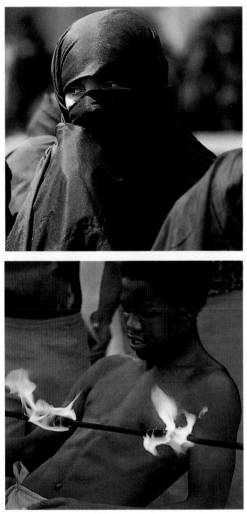

Above: Giriama limbo dancer entertains tourists.

Right: Turkana youngster collecting water from a desert wadi.

Overleaf: Colourfully-dressed Maasai women.

the exception of eland and buffalo, is forbidden.

In Kajiado, group ranching schemes have encouraged permanent settlement. In Narok, the fertile wheatlands on the slopes of the Mau, initially developed by entrepreneurs, are now being exploited by the Maasai themselves. Inevitably, change, long-resisted, is now reluctantly accepted.

Marakwet (Nilotic)

The Marakwet of the Kerio Valley and Cherangani Hills are another Kalenjin group. Their administrative centre is Iten.

As defence against disease and enemy (until recently, the Kerio Valley — rife with mosquitoes and tsetse fly — was a natural north-south route for raiding parties) the Marakwet built their houses on an escarpment that in the west rises to 3,370 metres (11,057 feet).

Such awesome terrain limits livestock, although cattle are increasing. Crops on the escarpment ledges and in the valley are irrigated by 400-year-old furrows running from the Arror, Embebut, and Embomen rivers. These furrows are still maintained and repaired by the community.

Eleusine and sorghum grown on tilled strips of land are traditional staples, together with bananas, cassava, and maize. Bee-keeping is also important.

Mbeere (Bantu)

The Mbeere (population 62,000) occupy 1,600 square kilometres (994 miles) of dry savannah, thorny acacia and commiphora bound by the Thika and Tana rivers south-east of Embu District. They share cultural and historical ties with the Embu and their administrative centre is Embu.

Skilled blacksmiths, the Mbeere obtain their iron-ore from alluvial sands in the Kithunthiiri area. In their workshops, equipped with simple skin bellows, crude hammers, chisels, and pliers, they fashioned spears, arrowheads, axes and knives, as well as fine chains, bells, and earrings for both men and women.

A musical people fond of songs, the Mbeere are skilled drummers and dancers.

Meru (Bantu)

Eight groups make up the Meru community (population 840,500) who live on the north-eastern slopes of Mount Kenya.

Only the arrival of Europeans at the turn of the century ended the frequent intertribal conflicts between these ethnically and culturally diverse people. The concept of one Meru group is recent.

The region's fertile soil and abundant rainfall have made it the richest farmland in Kenya. Tea, coffee, pyrethrum, maize, and potatoes all grow in the highland areas. Lower down, cotton and tobacco flourish.

Another profitable cash crop, *miraa* (khat), a mild stimulant much in demand in Somalia and Yemen, is grown in the Nyambeni mountains.

It is big business. Fast vehicles and light aircraft rush the bundles of fresh twigs and leaves to markets in Nairobi, Mombasa, and northern Kenya and across the border into Somalia.

Mijikenda (Bantu)

Nine Bantu groups of the coastal hinterland make up the Mijikenda, often referred to collectively as the Nyika. They are the Giriama, Digo, Duruma, Chonyi, Jibana, Ribe, Kambe, Rabai, and Kauma communities, totalling 733,000 people in all.

Tradition has it that an Oromo invasion from the north forced them out of the hinterland into fortified hilltop villages in the south-east, sometime between the late sixteenth and early seventeenth century.

Straddling the routes into the interior, the Mijikenda were able to dominate trade with their neighbours. But these links also influenced the movement of the Mijikenda from their traditional hilltop villages into the mainstream of coastal life.

Tourism has increased the tempo of coastal development. In the drier areas of the coastal hinterland co-operative ranches have been established to meet the demands for fresh produce from the hotels and Mombasa's burgeoning population.

Nandi (Nilotic)

Second-largest of the Kalenjin communities, the Nandi first settled in the beautiful Nandi Hills between the sixteenth and seventeenth century. They moved in successive waves from Mount Elgon and an earlier, still obscure, dispersal point much further north.

Agricultural skills and cattle were acquired from the neighbouring Luo and Luyia and, with economic prosperity, expansion to the north and east of the Nandi Escarpment became necessary. But their success was cut short with the arrival of the "Lunatic Line".

This earned the Nandi a reputation almost as formidable as that of the Zulu, when they defied the British for more than a decade.

From around 1895 until 1905, Nandi *esprit de corps* and military tactics were so tenacious they seriously held up the building of the Uganda Railway (See "The Dust and the Ashes").

They had a particular penchant for the copper telegraph wire which ran alongside the track and made excellent bracelets, armlets, and necklaces.

Even after an armistice was arranged following the killing of their Chief, Koitalel, the Nandi were unable to resist plundering the telegraph wires. For years after, communications in this part of Kenya were erratic.

The Nandi Hills are ideal for such cash crops as tea — many large and picturesque plantations roll from one hilltop to another — pyrethrum, tobacco, and coffee.

Okiek (Nilotic)

The Okiek, a small, diversified but culturally homogenous group of hunter-gathers, are scattered throughout the highland forests. Although only thirty Okiek communities have been positively identified in Kenya, the 1979 census figure of 7,200 is likely to be low.

The Okiek use different ecosystems in their high mountain retreats throughout the year, subsisting by hunting, gathering wild fruits and edible plants, and honey collecting. Occasional parties go down on to the plains with packs of dogs for hunting.

Until recently, these expert trackers hunted virtually every animal of the high forest for food.

Bark and log hives hung throughout the forest heights produce honey of different flavours as the bees collect pollen from many species of flowers and shrubs.

Orma (Cushitic)

The descendants of the once all-conquering Oromo who swept through north-east Kenya and beyond the Tana river several centuries ago, subsequently to come under pressure from the Somali, the Orma are also known as the Galla. They number 32,500.

They herd cattle along both banks of the Tana river — from Garissa downstream to Garsen where the delta drains into the Indian Ocean.

Renowned for their tall, slender physique and handsome, Cushitic features, the Orma pastoralists are also famous for their herds of white, long-horned Zebu-type cattle — among the finest in Africa. Other than a little sorghum, few crops are grown.

Pokomo (Bantu)

The thirteen sub-tribes which make up the Pokomo of the Tana river valley, numbering 40,000 people, are composite, like the Mijikenda, in origin, deriving traditionally from Bantu immigrants driven south by the Oromo.

Other than the immediate banks of the Tana, the Pokomo have no land. Farming is their main pursuit and maize and rice have long been their major crops.

They often harvest three crops a year from their silt-rich irrigated fields. They also grow tobacco for cash and hunt and fish to supplement their subsistence diet.

Crocodile and hippopotamus meat were once a regular part of their diet, along with fish, honey, and the fruit of the wild palm.

Expert swimmers and canoeists, the Pokomo use dugout canoes for fishing, lashing two canoes together with a platform of poles for longer journeys.

Pokot (Nilotic)

The militant pastoralists of the plains, and the less belligerent "corn people" of the hills, make up the Pokot.

Kalenjin by language, affinity, and traditions, they have adopted many of their neighbours' customs — the Turkana to the north and the Karamoja of Uganda to the west.

One bond with the Turkana is their willingness to eat virtually every kind of meat, except carrion-feeding hyena and jackal. Milk, blood drawn from cattle, and honey supplement their restricted diet.

The warriors also share the distinctive Turkana and Karamoja headdresses of painted clay which are protected by a wooden headrest when sleeping.

The pastoral Pokot herd their cattle and flocks across the waterless scrub north of Lake Baringo — from the Tiati Hills across the Kerio river to the Turkwel river and Karasuk

Above: Somali camelherd milks one of his beasts.

Hills that mark Kenya's border with Uganda.

Their aggressive search for water and grazing often brings them into conflict with the Turkana and the Karamoja. Even today, the constant raids by Turkana rustlers inevitably result in retaliation.

Millet, eleusine, and tobacco used to be the traditional crops of the Pokot hill farmers, who also kept a few cattle and smaller stock.

Crafts such as pottery, metalwork, and making snuff-boxes from small calabashes, ram or oryx horns are confined to the hill people.

Rendille (Cushitic)

The 22,000 camel-owning Rendille who roam the rocky wastes of the Kaisut Desert in Marsabit District, are north-eastern neighbours of the Samburu, with ties of kinship and economic co-operation that go back many generations, despite linguistic and cultural differences.

The Rendille live in large, semi-permanent settlements, using their camels as pack animals. Watered every ten to fourteen days, the camels give enough milk even in the dry season when other milk producers have stopped lactating.

Rendille mix camel's milk with blood, using a small knife or blunt arrow to open a vein in the camel's throat. After sufficient blood has been drawn off, the wound is closed with a mixture of hair and camel dung.

Following their centuries' old tradition, the Rendille herd their stock across the harsh semi-desert and scrub of the Korante Plains and Kaisut Desert, south-east of Lake Turkana.

Sabaot (Nilotic)

The Kalenjin-speaking Bok, Bongomek, Kony, and Sebei are known collectively as the Sabaot.

The Bok, Bongomek, and Sebei lived on the Uasin Gishu plateau before — their women and children stolen by the neighbouring Pokot, Karamajong, and Nandi — they were forced to move west on to the slopes of Mount Elgon.

Inevitably, farming replaced pastoralism, although they still own considerable numbers of cattle, sheep, and goats.

Not until modern times and the introduction of the ox-plough and maize did the Sabaot return to the fertile flatlands. In addition to their traditional crops of eleusine, millet, sorghum, and bananas, they now grow a wide range of other crops, including European vegetables, maize, cassava, and cash crops such as sugarcane, pyrethrum, and coffee.

The Sabaot have benefited from modern farm techniques and livestock development and from the improvement of communications in western Kenya. An inherited trait, shared with all other Kalenjin groups, is their outstanding athletic prowess.

Sakuye (Cushitic)

Today, most Oromo-speaking Sakuye (population 1,800), predominantly a camel-owning people from the desert areas north of Buna, live along the Ewaso Nyiro river in Isiolo District.

According to legend, their ancestors — who owned thousands of camels — were part of an original Oromo expansion from southern Ethiopia who settled initially at a placed called Saku (Marsabit) from which they took their name.

They moved into Isiolo District where they came into conflict with the Samburu and, more recently, the Somali.

Now, more than ever before, the Sakuye are curtailing their nomadic life. This was first forced upon them in the mid-1960s as a result of demands for closer administration during the campaign against the *shifta* (Somali bandits). Educational and health facilities are now available, and Sakuye life is changing .

Samburu (Nilotic)

A nomadic Maa-speaking people, the 73,000-strong Samburu who live in Maralal and northern Kenya between Lake Turkana and the Ewaso Nyiro river, are said to have migrated south, like the Maasai, to their present location from the north of Lake Turkana several centuries ago.

These cattle-owning pastoralists, who live mainly off their herds, have long resisted change. Milk is the principal food, supplemented with blood tapped from the veins of living cattle or from sheep and goats slaughtered for meat in the dry season. Certain roots and barks are added to Samburu soups for nutritional value.

Semi-desert land restricts farming in the lowlands, but on the Lorogi plateau and in the Karisia Hills, they grow maize, sorghum, and vegetables, and large tracts are now being leased to produce wheat seed.

Unlike the warlike Maasai, whose language and cultural heritage they share, the Samburu are tolerant of other groups and place a high value on social respect.

Segeju (Bantu)

The last descendants of a once numerous pastoral people, fewer than 1,000 Segeju remain in Kenya. Originally, they lived around the Mount Kenya area and four centuries ago they were warlike pastoralists, similar to the Maasai, owning large herds of cattle and living on a diet of blood and milk.

Top: Rendille matriarch grooming youngster.

Above: Pensive Samburu maiden.

Above: Traditional Taita musicians.

In 1592 the Segeju conquered Mombasa for their Malindi allies. Later, in the seventeenth century, the Segeju in turn were forced out of the Malindi area by Oromo pressure from the north and settled around Shimoni and Vanga at the extreme south of the Kenya coast.

During the last century the Segeju people drifted even further south. Today the majority live at Bwiti, near Tanga, in Tanzania.

Somali (Cushitic)

Occupying some 150,500 square kilometres (58,500 square miles) — a quarter of Kenya — of the arid North-Eastern Province, the nomadic Somali camel-herders number 381,000.

They crossed the Juba river about 140 years ago and arrived in Wajir in 1906. Subsequently, they settled the entire north-eastern area of Kenya, driving out or absorbing any minority hunter-gatherer groups and Bantu farmers in their path.

Pastoral nomads who own large camel herds, cattle, sheep, and goats, the Somali are entirely dependent on the precarious grazing and water in the semi-desert region where they live.

Highly articulate and politically aware, the Somali are united equally by family loyalty and formal political contracts.

Suba (Bantu)

Suba (population 59,500) are an agglomeration of sub-tribes closely allied to the Kuria, remnant groups of whom occupy the Lake Victoria islands of Rusinga and Mfangano.

Like other Bantu-speaking people of the Lake Victoria region, the Suba say they travelled to the area from Western Uganda, moving eastwards, then south around the shore.

Apart from a small group of farmers, the Suba were hunters and fisherfolk. They hunted hippo for meat and fat, and the killing was a time for celebration, for special songs and rites.

Hunters no more, the Suba concentrate on fishing, which provides a cash income that is often the envy of their farming neighbours.

Canoes play a prime role in their economy. The Suba are skilled boatbuilders and their craft are in great demand by the neighbouring Luo.

Taita/Taveta (Bantu)

The 16,000 people of the fertile Taita Hills and Taveta district include the Kasigau, Sagala, and Dabida. Divided into seven clans, they have long farmed the land: always with a great many spiritual preliminaries.

Cultivation requires authority from tribal elders, sacrifices, and supplications made to the collections of skulls kept in sacred caves, which contain the ancestral spirits. Before Christianity, the Taita believed in communion with the dead as a means of arbitration and future direction.

Traditional Taita crops include millet, beans, cow-peas, cassava, sweet potatoes, sugarcane, and maize — much of it grown under irrigation.

There are many banana, sugarcane, and mango plantations in Taveta, and the produce finds a ready market in Mombasa and along the coast. Other commercial crops include vegetables and coffee. Taita Hills was one of the first areas in Kenya where coffee was grown.

Traditionally, hunting and trapping game was linked to trade with coastal peoples. Meats and skins were bartered for simple manufactured goods which in turn were exchanged for livestock. Taita crafts include leatherwork, metalwork, basket-weaving, and woodwork.

Tharaka (Bantu)

The 10,000-strong Tharaka, the southernmost people of Meru District, occupy the low, hot plains east of Mount Kenya where there are few resources. Frequent droughts often threaten famine. Malaria and sleeping sickness are endemic.

The Tharaka were famed for witchcraft and are colourful drummers, and bee-keepers. Both drums and hives are made from hollowed logs. Some individuals may own a hundred or more hives. They trade in honey and grain. They also keep goats, sheep, cattle, and chickens and, along the Tana and Kizita rivers, supplement their meagre diet with fish.

Grain and threshed millet is stored in large wicker and plaited-grass granaries sealed by a slab of stone. They grow cotton and tobacco as cash crops.

Shopping baskets plaited from the leaves of the doum palm are one source of money to the many women and children who can be seen industrially weaving away at all times and places.

Tugen (Nilotic)

Third-largest of the Kalenjin-speaking groups, the semi-pastoral Tugen occupy a narrow rectangle of the Rift Valley floor, bound in the west by the Kerio river and in the east by the parallel ranges of the 2,500-metre-high (8,200-feet) Tugen and Kamasia hills.

The administrative centre is fast-developing Kabarnet. Other centres are Eldama Ravine and Kabartonjo. Like the other Kalenjin groups in the Kerio Valley, the Tugen claim to have come from the Mount Elgon region.

President Daniel Toroitich arap Moi, born in 1924 in the tiny village of Kurieng'wo in Sacho Location of Baringo District and educated at Kabartonjo and Kapsabet, is a Tugen.

Turkana (Nilotic)

The 210,000-strong Turkana inhabit the north-west of Kenya between Lake Turkana in the east and the escarpment marking the Uganda boundary in the west. The administrative centre is Lodwar.

Milk and blood are the main food. Men herd and water the cattle, sing and dance to them in the evening and rub their horns with fat. The horns are used for snuff containers.

Camels are also important and small girls or boys herd sheep and goats which are killed for guests or minor rituals. Donkeys are used solely as pack animals, the hides being cut into strips for panniers.

They make dried milk by boiling large quantities of fresh milk and drying it on skins. They also make cakes from wild berries which are crushed and mixed with blood.

Fishing in Lake Turkana plays little part in Turkana economics, but is practised during the dry season or famine.

Skilled herdsmen and fearless warriors, improved communications have eroded the Turkana's traditional insularity.

Settlement schemes along the Turkwel and Kerio rivers and fishing co-operatives along the western shore of Lake Turkana are being encouraged by hydroelectric schemes that will provide many thousands of hectares of irrigated land.

Paul Ereng, the 800 metres 1988 Olympic champion, is a Turkana.

PART TWO: PLACES AND TRAVEL

Above: Highland forest glade.
Opposite: One of the major hydroelectric schemes on the Tana River.

Nairobi: City in the Sun

If Nairobi was nothing more than a city that has grown in ninety years from zero population and two and a half square kilometres (one square mile) to more than two million people and 700 square kilometres (270 square miles) it would be remarkable.

But it's also a brawling, dynamic maelstrom of cultures and enterprises that reflects its melting-pot heritage.

If the city sometimes seems a little contradictory and eccentric, don't be too surprised. Less than a century ago it didn't exist. Indeed, Nairobi only arose as a secondary coincidence of one man's unwavering ambition and steely determination to build a railway line across Kenya.

George Whitehouse, general manager of the Uganda Railway, was no visionary in matters metropolitan. His single-minded intent was to complete one of the most audacious feats of civil engineering ever attempted in the Victorian era — the 1,000-kilometre-long (620 mile) "Lunatic Line" from Mombasa to Lake Victoria (See "The Dust and the Ashes", Part One).

Whitehouse chose Nyrobi (Maasai for "place of the cool waters") as his main upcountry railhead. Then just a bleak and disease-infested swamp, it was, in engineering terms, the last piece of totally flat ground before the hard climb up the eastern shoulders of the Great Rift Valley escarpment.

The thought that one day "Nyrobi" might be an important capital never crossed Whitehouse's mind, otherwise he might have chosen a more suitable location. The black cotton soil of the swamplands expands to become a sludge-like mass when wet, and contracts when dry. It's probably the worst imaginable foundation on which to build a city. But like so much in Kenya in the first fifty years of this century, Nairobi evolved spontaneously.

The first resident, apart from the itinerant Maasai who brought their herds to water, was Sergeant George Ellis, from the more sedate village of Newington Butts, Surrey, England, in 1896. He built stables and an office.

Then huts began to grow up around the railhead which settled, halfway between Mombasa and Victoria, with a belch of steam on 30 May, 1899.

Ten months after the railhead was established, Sir Arthur Hardinge, the British Consul-General based in Zanzibar, gave it township status on 16 April, 1900, when he published the first fifteen clauses of the Nairobi Municipal Regulations.

The first town clerk was appointed in 1904, by which time Nairobi was a municipality covering 104 square kilometres (40 square miles). It was invested as a city on 30 March, 1950, when the Duke of Gloucester presented a Royal charter on behalf of King George VI of England.

At Independence on 12 December, 1963, the population was about half a million people and it covered an area of 350 square kilometres (135 square miles). Twenty-five years later Nairobi's boundaries embraced 700 square kilometres (270 square miles) and its population, officially around one million, had in reality swollen to more than two million people.

Now a United Nations headquarters city, Nairobi is the economic, if not political, capital of much of east and central Africa as well as Kenya.

It continues to grow as it was conceived — at an astonishing speed and with great energy if, at times, seemingly without control. In some areas, Nairobi still looks and feels like an afterthought.

Despite its shantytown origins, to which many of its suburban areas seem to be reverting, Nairobi remains truly memorable — both in the contrasts and experiences it affords, and in its setting.

Situated 500 kilometres (300 miles) from the coast and 1,670 metres (5,500 feet) above sea level, the metropolitan area stretches from the Embakasi plains in the east up the once-wooded slopes of the eastern wall of the Great Rift Valley in the west, from the Ngong Hills in the south to the foothills of the Aberdares in the north.

When To Go

Nairobi is pleasant all year round but best in September when the jacaranda, bougainvillaea, and flame trees bloom, and worst between June and August when it's often overcast, miserable, and cold.

Opposite: Aerial view of the heart of bustling Nairobi.

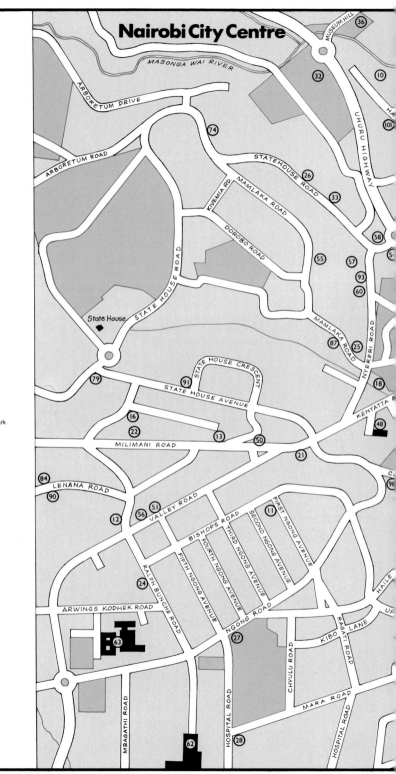

Nairobi City Centre

CINEMAS:
1 Cameo
2 20th Century
3 Embassy
4 Nairobi
5 Kenya
6 Odeon

THEATRES:
7 Pheonix Players
8 Kenya National

HOTELS:
9 Ambassadeur
10 Boulevard
11 Fairview
12 Grosvenor
13 Heron Court
14 Hilton
15 Inter Continental
16 Milimani
17 Nairobi Safari Club
18 Nairobi Serena
19 New Stanley
20 Norfolk
21 Panafric
22 Sagret
23 680

HOSTELS:
24 Youth Hostel
25 YWCA
26 YMCA

CLUBS & SPORTS GROUNDS:
27 Nairobi Club
28 Public Service Club
29 Railway Golf Club
30 Railway Sports Club
31 Sir Ali Sports Club
32 University Sports Ground
33 United Kenya Club

MUSEUMS AND LIBRARIES
34 Kenya Cultural Centre
35 MacMillan Library
36 National Museum & Snake Park
37 British Council
38 American Cultural Centre
39 French Cultural Centre
49 Goethe Institute
41 Italian
42 National Archives
43 Japanese Information Centre
45 Railway Museum

INFORMATION:
46 Public Maps Office
47 Tourist Information Centre

PLACES OF WORSHIP
48 All Saints Cathedral
49 Holy Family Cathedral
50 Seventh Day Adventist
51 Greek Orthodox
52 Jamia Mosque
53 Khoja Mosque
54 Lutheran Church
55 Nairobi Chapel
56 Pentecostal Church
57 St. Andrew's
58 St. Paul's
59 St. Peter Claver's
60 Christian Science Church

HOSPITALS AND CLINICS
61 Inoculation Centre
62 Kenyatta National Hospital
63 Nairobi Hospital

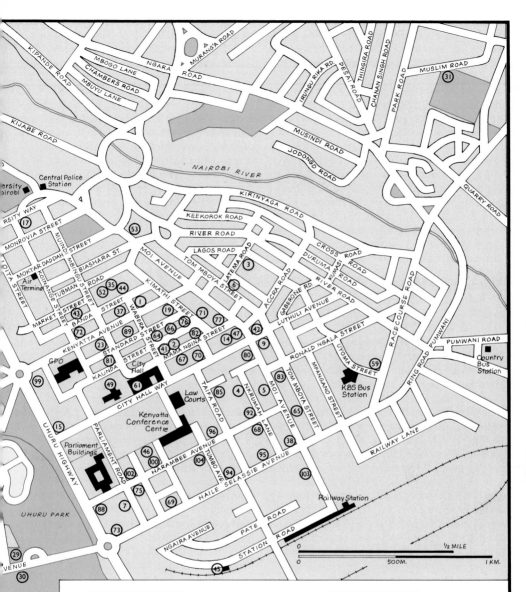

CONSULATES AND EMBASSIES

64 Argentine	78 Indonesia	70 Rwanda
65 Australia	79 Iran	70 Somalia
66 Austria	40 Ireland	81 Spain
67 Belgium	41 Italy	70 Sri Lanka
68 Brazil	37 Japan	87 Sudan
65 Burundi	80 Korea	67 Swaziland
69 Canada	76 Kuwait	70 Sweden
70 Chile	40 Lebanon	70 Switzerland
71 Cyprus	70 Lesotho	88 Tanzania
72 Denmark	81 Liberia	89 Uganda
69 Djibouti	70 Luxembourg	81 UK
73 Egypt	81 Malawi	90 USSR
74 Ethiopia	82 Mauritius	38 USA
70 Finland	83 Morocco	91 Yugoslavia
75 France	4 Netherlands	92 Zaire
75 Germany	84 Nigeria	93 Zambia
76 Greece	72 Norway	87 Zimbabwe
77 Iceland	85 Portugal	
68 India	86 Romania	

GOVERNMENT DEPARTMENTS
PUBLIC BUILDING &
PLACES OF INTEREST

94 Central Bank
95 Commerce
85 Culture & Social Services
96 Education
97 Forest Department
98 Health
96 Home Affairs & National Heritage
99 Immigration
95 Industry
96 Information & Broadcasting
100 President's Office
99 Nairobi PC
78 Tourism & Wildlife
99 Trade Licensing
101 VOK/KBC
102 A-G's Office
103 Railway HQ

Getting There

There are international flights daily from many centres in Europe and regular scheduled services via West Africa from America and from Asia. Gone are the days when passenger liners regularly plied their way to Mombasa and the passengers travelled upcountry on the Nairobi "Express". It's still possible to find passage on a cargo ship and when the trade winds are favourable it may also be possible to take a dhow from the Gulf or Mogadishu. From the west you can travel by road or railway from Kampala to Nairobi but it's a long way and, in 1989, hazardous on the Uganda side. Roads from North and West Africa were also uncertain but several overland companies out of London continue to cater for those with the spirit of adventure.

Where To Stay

Just a small cross selection: Devon Hotel (3-star), Uhuru Highway; Fairview Hotel (4-star), Bishop's Road; Nairobi Hilton International (5-star), Mama Ngina Street; Ambassadeur (4-star), Moi Avenue; Boulevard Hotel (4-star), Harry Thuku Road; Heron Court Hotel (3-star), Milimani Road; Nairobi Inter-Continental (5-star), City Hall Way-Uhuru Highway; Hurlingham Hotel (English rustic and fine home cooking), Argwings-Kodhek Road; Jacaranda Hotel (4-star), off Waiyaki Way, Westlands; PanAfric Hotel (4-star), Kenyatta Avenue; Meridien Court Hotel (4-star), Muranga Road; Safari Park Hotel (5-star), Thika Road; Nairobi Safari Club (5-star), Koinange Street-University Way; Nairobi Serena Hotel (5-star), Nyerere Road-Kenyatta Avenue; New Stanley (5-star), Kimathi Street; Norfolk Hotel (5-star), Harry Thuku Road.

There are many others. See Listings for "Hotels".

Sightseeing

Jomo Kenyatta International Airport, one of the busiest and most modern in Africa, lies to the east of Nairobi in the lee of the Lukenia Hills and Ol Doinyo Sapuk National Park. The glide path brings giant jetliners in over the Ngong Hills and Nairobi National Park in the south-west.

Named after Kenya's founding father, the airport was opened five months after his death by his successor, Kenya's second President, Daniel Toroitich arap Moi, on 8 December, 1978. In 1989 it was showing signs of neglect but still retained some hint of its early elegance.

Scheduled bus services costing a few "bob" (shillings), fairly expensive taxis at around Kshs 200/- (you can haggle, it's a way of life), and the Kenya Airways bus (Kshs 60/- one way in 1989) will take you the sixteen kilometres (10 miles) into the city. On your left, you pass **Nairobi National Park**, and in the distance Isaak Dinnesen's, alias Karen Blixen's, favourite African panorama, the misty, blue-grey knuckle profile of the **Ngong Hills**, made famous worldwide by the film, *Out of Africa*.

The broad, dual carriageway leading into town also slices through the nether end of the city's **industrial area** which houses Nairobi's inland port with its giant container terminal, the General Motors assembly plant and the Firestone tyre factory.

Hard to imagine that less than two kilometres (just over a mile) away from these mundane manufacturing units a pride of lion is roaming the still pristine national park, perhaps about to pounce on a young wildebeest, or gnu. An exotic first thought for travellers from less exceptional climes.

If you fly overnight on the red-eye from Europe, the chances are that you will arrive in Nairobi at the start of the morning rush hour. If you intend to hire your own vehicle this will serve as an appropriate introduction to Kenya's erratic and sometimes dangerously individualistic driving styles. Be warned.

The road from the airport leads to the intersection with the main Mombasa-Nairobi highway and **Langata Road** landmarked by the **Nyayo Sports Stadium**, one of the venues for the 1987 All Africa Games.

Travel the length of the stadium and you negotiate a roundabout that keeps, on your left, the city's first **cemetery**, a *potpourri* or, more accurately, posthumous enclave of Kenya's colonial history.

The central section is Jewish and the area around contains the remains of the first seven victims of lion and one of rhinoceros attacks.

Charles Ryall, one of history's more celebrated failures, is also buried here. He sat up all night in a railway coach, intending to ambush a maneating lion. But he fell asleep and the lion dragged him from the coach in which Ryall lay waiting and was able to enjoy yet another *Homo sapiens* supper.

The cemetery abuts on to the nine-hole **Railway Golf Club** (*circa* 1922) whose ninth

Above: Golden light illuminates Uhuru Fountain in Nairobi's Uhuru Park.

tee stands a two-wood drive from **Parliament Buildings**. Giant blue gums line the fairways. How many cities can boast such a sylvan recreation facility so close to their heart?

The Mombasa road now becomes **Uhuru Highway**, a celebration of Kenya's freedom. Taken from the Kiswahili, its name was changed from Queen Elizabeth Highway at Independence. In the twenty-five years since then virtually every city street and district nomenclature which reflected the colonial heritage, has been "Africanized". Good for national pride but difficult for those intent on tracking down Nairobi's historic landmarks.

Haile Selassie Avenue, for instance, which intersects with Uhuru Highway at the next roundabout after the railway bridge, was originally Ellis Avenue, named after the capital's founding citizen. Together with **Moi Avenue** (previously Government Road), these were Nairobi's first two public thoroughfares.

The Hill

If you turn left off Uhuru Highway along **Ngong Road** and up the hill, you pass the stone-built **Railway Club** where the first game of cricket was played in Nairobi in 1899.

The club's tin-and-timber predecessor also served as Kenya's first Parliament. When the Legislative Council (Legco) held its initial meeting on 17 August, 1907, one question the all-European, seven-member council debated was capital punishment, which was carried out by firing squad. Too often, the bullets spent themselves before they left the barrel of the old Henry-Martini rifles — salvaged from the bottom of Mombasa Harbour — and simply fell to the ground.

The general consensus was that this was hardly fair on the condemned, so a bill was enacted to replace the firing squad with the gallows. It subsequently transpired that there was no official hangman but, when the vacancy was advertised, an ex-Royal Navy Petty officer filled the post. He was previously a steam-roller driver who came to Kenya along with his vehicle to improve the roads after the Governor of the day muddied his shoes in Government Road during the rainy season. Hanging remains the official form of death penalty.

Higher up the hill, just past the **National Library**, to the right, is the mellow, creeper-woven stonework of the 1913 **Nairobi Club** on the left. It replaced the original building, established in 1901, which burnt down some

Above: Jomo Kenyatta International Airport, Nairobi.

time before.

It was Nairobi's first social institution and remains very much the preserve of the capital's elite. Since cash payments have always been disdained, bar chits are settled at the end of each month and members default at the peril of being blackballed.

Once an exemplary bastion of male chauvinism, feminism has struck telling blows at the club's infrastructures but, to the relief of many older members, its ruling hierarchy still manages to perpetuate one Men Only bar.

The sprawling grounds provide a wide range of leisure pursuits — swimming pool, bowling greens, cricket and hockey pitches, and tennis courts.

Next left, beyond the club, is the **Police Traffic Headquarters** followed by **Kenyatta National Hospital**, a free referral centre for Kenya citizens and an impressive demonstration of government commitment to social welfare. However, the neglected interior reveals the financial constraints which limit the staff's ability to care for both the institution and its patients.

Nairobi Hospital, opposite, (physically and in every sense), is a landmark of the private medical sector, employing dedicated staff and top grade specialists. Its contemporary equipment includes sophisticated intensive-care units.

Tucked away between Nairobi Club and the Police Traffic HQ is the highly social **Kenya Regiment Association**. A survivor of the old King's African Rifles that fought valiantly in East Africa during the two world wars, the regiment's history is recorded in *The Charging Buffalo*, by Leo Pardoe.

Beyond the next roundabout, take the first left and you arrive at the **Royal Nairobi Golf Club**, which was carved out of indigenous forest in 1904. In the past, its members were occasionally mauled by lion or gored by rhinoceros. It received its Royal accolade during the brief rule of Britain's King Edward VIII in 1936.

The forest has long gone and the course is now hemmed in on all sides by serried rows of suburban maisonettes and houses.

This entire hill area, dry and forested, was claimed by Whitehouse when the Railway arrived in Nairobi. Hearing of this, the first British administrator in Kenya, Manchester-born John Ainsworth, rode up from Machakos where he had established his headquarters and had expected Whitehouse to make the railhead (See "The Dust and the Ashes", Part One).

Ainsworth removed the stakes which had been hammered in on Whitehouse's instructions, much to Whitehouse's annoyance.

In the argument which ensued, Whitehouse claimed the hill was Railway land, Ainsworth that it was sovereign land: neither remembering it was African land. Announcing his intention to protect Crown interests, Ainsworth at once set up his administrative headquarters in Nairobi.

The City Centre

Nairobi's focal point is the attractively laid-out three-square-kilometre (just over a square mile) city centre, bound in the east by Haile Selassie Avenue, in the south by Parliament Buildings, in the north by Moi Avenue, and in the west by **University Way**.

The skyline is dominated by the thirty-three storey, 105-metre-high (344-feet) profile of the **Kenyatta International Conference Centre**, which draws its architectural inspiration from both rural Africa and ancient Rome.

At one side of the hexagonal tower is a well-appointed amphitheatre shaped like a *rondavel* (African hut), and the main plenary hall, a modern version of the Senate, can seat 4,000 delegates. The interior is laid out with indoor fountain pools and red-tiled promenades.

Approaching from the direction of the airport, you turn right off Uhuru Highway into Haile Selassie Avenue, the left-hand corner dominated by the impressive marble facade built by the Central Bank Co-operative Society.

The first left is **Parliament Way** where the small precinct that occupies the corner block houses the **Professional Centre**, offices for such professional bodies as Kenya's architectural and accountants associations.

The basement is home to Eastern Africa's only professional repertory company, the **Phoenix Players**, a generic successor to Kenya's founding repertory company that emerged out of the volatile dismemberment of the Donovan Maule Theatre. This stood on the corner opposite the Professional Centre but was demolished in 1988.

Continuing down Haile Selassie Avenue

you pass the **Central Bank of Kenya** and then arrive at the roundabout connecting it with Moi Avenue.

Turn right and you enter **Nairobi Railway Station**, where the city all began, flanked on the right by the neo-classical, colonial lines of the 1929 **Kenya Railways Headquarters**.

In the **Railway Museum**, located at the upcountry end of the station, are the glistening relics of old "Lunatic Express" trains, including ancient steam engines, and the coach from which Charles Ryall was dragged to his death.

In the housed section of the Museum other *bric-a-brac*, including the old cowcatcher on which former US President Theodore Roosevelt rode in 1909 during his grand hunting safari in Kenya, commemorate the five-year drama of the railway's construction.

In the middle of the sprawling marshalling yards, the **Railway Workshops**, founded by Whitehouse, still remain one of Kenya's biggest industrial undertakings, employing a large staff of skilled and highly-trained personnel.

Moi Avenue is a curious mixture of some of the capital's earliest buildings, still roofed with corrugated iron, juxtaposed among some of its most modern office blocks and hotels. It marks a unique division of the city — the boundary between upmarket and downmarket downtown Nairobi.

The north side of this divide endows the capital with its vibrant, colourful African character.

Above: Traditional handwoven baskets, *kiondos*, are popular buys for tourists.

TAKE A WALK ON THE "WILD" SIDE

Moi Avenue divides the smart, metropolitan, office blocks and colonial landmarks from what many consider the real Nairobi.

This begins with **Tom Mboya Street** (previously Victoria Street), renamed in memory of the slain Kenya political leader. Here, the first bazaar and shanty in Nairobi sprang up, soon to spread down to the Nairobi River.

This is where the capital's African ambience comes to vivid life. Open-fronted shops display colourful wares, and cupboard-size radio shops blare out the latest Swahili music hits night and day.

Continue along Moi Avenue and take the left turn at the **Khoja Mosque** and you come to the roundabout dominated, on the right as you enter the traffic stream, by **Nation House**. In 1989 this was home to the country's largest-selling newspaper but is soon to be replaced by a custom-built Nation House in Kimathi Street — on the smart side of the city.

If you keep left you descend to the **Globe roundabout**, Nairobi's biggest, dominated, at the left, on the corner of **Kijabe Street** which runs up to **Harry Thuku Way**, by the Globe Cinema (the old **Paramount Cinema**) now a victim of the video revolution, and used for offices and warehousing.

The roundabout is cut by Nairobi River, a seasonal stream born in the Ngong Hills which becomes a raging torrent during the rainy season. The roundabout, in fact, marks the head of the old swamp which gave the city its name.

Above: Tourist enthuses over authentic African woodcarvings.

Circle the roundabout and you return to Tom Mboya Street, passing on your left **Kirinyaga Road**, formerly Grogan Road after Colonel Ewart Grogan, an adventurer who made his fortune in colonial Kenya.

This is a street of frenetic enterprise marked by squalid lodgings and grease-stained workshops that specialise in motor vehicle parts and repairs. Its only landmark is the **colonial clock** at the far end just before it enters **Racecourse Road**.

Back at the Nation roundabout you leave **River Road**, Nairobi's most tireless commercial enterprise, to your left. This mixture of up-country *matatu* and bus operators, shops, and small-scale industrial enterprises is liberally scattered with lodging houses and cheap restaurants, both African and Asian, serving ethnic stews of *sukuma wiki* (kale or spinach) and beef and *matumbo* (tripe).

River Road operates round the clock, a vibrant, colourful high street where you can haggle with the shopkeepers and snap up bargains at half the price charged on the smart side of Moi Avenue.

Both here, and on the slightly more up-market Tom Mboya Street, which is lined with shops and office blocks until you reach its intersection, near the city bus station, with the tail end of Haile Selassie Avenue, you get a taste of Nairobi's inherent African character.

Turn left near the massive milling and warehouse facilities of the **Kenya Coffee Growers Co-operative Union**, into the one-way system which leads past **St Peter Claver's Church** into **Uyoma Street** with the 1963 **Siri Guru Singh Sabha Temple**, like an incongruous Earls Court of Nairobi.

Continue into **Racecourse Road**, which until the end of World War II was the road to the old racecourse at **Kariokor** (the Kiswahili phonetic for "Carrier Corps"). Here you'll find a colourful market popular for its *nyama choma* (roast meat), usually beef or goat, served with large helpings of delicious and nutritious *irio*, a Kikuyu vegetable mash of beans, peas, and potatoes (See "Tastes of Kenya", Part Three).

Beyond the market roundabout a faceless array of middle-income maisonettes occupies the level ground that served as the city's racecourse for more than half a century — from the first meeting in 1901, when pack horses were enlisted to enliven the event and make up a decent field. It became a twice-yearly gymkhana meeting, but on several occasions the start was delayed by wild game on the track — rhinoceros, lion, and others.

The course at Kariokor served until the **Jockey Club of Kenya** acquired the **Ngong Racecourse** to the west of the city, said by many to be the most beautiful race track in the Commonwealth. There are now about forty Sunday meetings a year, and the bloodstock has been refined over the years by imported thoroughbreds.

Complete a full circle of Kariokor and return to the roundabout that marks the inter-section of Racecourse Road with **Pumwani Ring Road**. Turn left into Ring Road and at the far end, leaving the mosque and police station on the left, turn left into **Landhies Road** for **Kamakunji**. This is the country bus terminal known affectionately to the city's

polyglot millions as **Machakos Airport**.

In one corner, hundreds of artisans convert scrap metal into *sufurias* (pots) and old tyres into sandals. These are especially favoured by the Maasai, who name them after the distance the shoes cover before wearing out, so favourites are known as "Loitokitok", far away on the slopes of Kilimanjaro, or perhaps as "Kajiado", the southern administrative capital of Maasailand.

Machakos airport is a riot of garish colours and noise: the vivid hues of cheap plastic and cloth items flood the pavements and stalls with brilliant splashes: blaring radios, record-players, and loud-hailers, complete with the raucous cries of sidewalk vendors and *manambas* (touts), luring passengers on to country buses and the ubiquitous freelance *matatus*, Kenya's version of West African "mammy wagons", which supplement the public transport system.

You can find almost anything you need here and at the back of Kamakunji, which leads into the squatter township of **Shauri Moyo** and to the **Hindu crematorium** and the headquarters of the Central Organisation of Trade Unions (**COTU**). Hundreds of craftsmen in this area work for a large **Kamba wood-carvers' co-operative,** turning out statues and figurines of Kenya's wildlife and people that are sold by curio vendors in almost every tourist centre of the country.

Fascinating to watch, these nimble-fingered and dexterous artists transform chunks and chips of mahogany and other wood into elephants, giraffes, and Maasai warriors in the space of minutes.

Past Kamakunji, at the roundabout marked on the right by the old **City Stadium**, until the 1980s the city's major sports arena, Landhies Road becomes **Jogoo Road**, the northern boundary of the industrial area, notable for its depressing and endless low-cost housing estates.

Return to Ring Road and cross over, via the Racecourse Road roundabout, into Pangani. This suburb was founded very early in the city's history by pioneer Asian traders and entrepreneurs and, for many, is still their inner suburban home. **Pangani** also embraces **Ngara**, with its many Asian shops selling textiles and confections.

Above: Jamia Mosque, Nairobi.

Mainstream Nairobi

The central point of Moi Avenue is dominated by the circular **Hilton Hotel** which faces the massive ramparts of **Kenya Commercial Bank**. This could have been designed by a frustrated Lancashire cotton mill architect, although some people consider it remarkably similar to the flagship of the American Sixth Fleet.

As the pivot around which all Nairobi seems to flow, the Hilton also faces the **National Archives**, repository of much treasured but faded paper relating to Kenya's recorded history. Judging by the amount of vetting a potential researcher undergoes, it may also store some state secrets.

The archives are housed in the refurbished old Bank of India building, (*circa* 1906), one of the city's oldest stone buildings.

New traffic lights were installed on this section of Moi Avenue in 1988 but did nothing to halt the roar and confusion of city traffic. At least now, however, you can drive straight along Moi Avenue to the next set of traffic lights and the intersection, left, with the city's grand mall, **Kenyatta Avenue**, which during its lifetime has also been known as Sixth Avenue and Delamere Avenue.

On the right is the rather scruffy **Imenti building**, another large island of offices, shops, and restaurants, around which the tide of Nairobi's traffic swirls day and night. In 1904, the previous building on this spot formed young Nairobi's first municipal offices and, later, the first law courts.

The large hole in the ground diagonally opposite Imenti building, at the corner of Moi Avenue and Kenyatta Avenue, used to be occupied by the capital's first stone building, **Nairobi House**, which was declared a protected edifice in the 1970s.

Unfortunately, it occupied prime real estate space and was levelled — illegally — by the wrecker's ball. Nothing can restore it but it also seems that nothing is to occupy the hole either. The vacant space has remained since 1983 and appears to testify to the planning authority's umbrage over the building's wanton destruction.

Beyond the intersection, halfway along the block, stands the old company office of the **Imperial British East Africa** company (IBEA) built in 1919. Early in the 1940s a French couple opened the **Sans Chique** which in those days occupied the niche now taken by the **Tamarind**, the City's top *cordon bleu* restaurant. Times change, however, and the Sans Chique, like the massage parlour and offices above, was depressingly seedy in 1989.

Just a few paces farther along, again on the right, is the Ismaili **Khoja Mosque**, the place of worship for followers of the Aga Khan, a small but devotedly patriotic section of the Kenyan community who make a large contribution, both socially and economically, to national development.

Opposite is **Jeevanjee Gardens**, the city's first recreational area, donated to the city after the bazaars that stood there were consumed in a tinder-brush fire, by the public benefactor and philanthropist, A. M. "Haj" Jeevanjee, who made his fortune as a railway contractor.

In March 1906, the Duke of Connaught unveiled a bust of his mother, Queen Victoria, which now watches over lunchtime crowds who come to listen to impromptu sermons by itinerant preachers with loud-hailers. Dr. Livingstone, one presumes, would be delighted to learn that evangelism appears to be Kenya's major social recreation.

Jeevanjee Gardens is close to **Biashara Street**, the city's first bazaar, and to **City Market**, Nairobi's fruit and vegetable market.

On the right of Moi Avenue, just beyond the gardens, where the road turns left to become **University Way**, some of the tin huts in which John Ainsworth, Nairobi's first administrator, shaped the outline of the city, still stand. Until recently they were the offices of the **Survey of Kenya**.

Turn into University Way and take the first turning right to come to the celebrated **Norfolk Hotel**. Not much remains of the old property, which opened on Christmas Day, 1904. Time and a terrorist bomb blast on New Year's Eve, 1980 finished off most of the original. But lovingly rebuilt, the Norfolk still wears its mock-Tudor front of red brick, and black-and-white timber.

The murals behind the Delamere bar, originally painted for the **New Stanley Hotel**, once owned by the same Block family, tell of early London scenes and old Nairobi. Inside the gardens an old motor car and oxwagon remind guests of the pioneering spirit in which the timbers of the Norfolk are steeped.

Few hotels in the world can boast its history, or its roll call of aristocratic and rich and famous guests, many of whom are recorded in colourful detail in Jan Hemsing's excellent book, *The Norfolk Hotel*.

Opposite is the **University** of Nairobi, **Cultural Centre** and **National Theatre**, built with a British Council grant of £50,000, the support of the great Shakespearean actor Sir Donald Wolfit, and opened by Sir Ralph Richardson in 1952. One of its building stones is from Shakespeare's birthplace in Stratford-upon-Avon and the rosemary tree outside came from Shakespeare's garden.

It occupies the spot where Nairobi's **Police Headquarters** once stood where, on 16 March, 1922, Kenya's first public demonstration against colonial rule took place.

The reason for the demonstration was the arrest of Harry Thuku. Still in his 20s, he was a £4-a-month telephone operator at the Treasury who lived in Pangani and was friendly with the leaders of the Indian Association which represented Indian interests in Legco. With their assistance he formed the East African Association.

On 14 March, 1922, as he addressed a fair-deal-for-real-Kenyans meeting in Pangani, he was arrested by Chief Inspector Satwant Bachan Singh, head of the Nairobi CID, who drove him away on the pillion of his motor cycle for interrogation by the Superintendent of Police.

Two days later the mobs outside the Police HQ demanding his release were swollen by thousands of strikers and sympathisers, Attempts to disperse the protesters failed and, when Captain G. S. Cary was knocked to the ground, Bachan Singh gave the order to open fire. At the end of the day twenty-one people, including several women and one fifteen-year-old youth, lay dead (See "The Dust and the Ashes", Part One).

Thuku was Kenya's first political hero and, after Independence, the road in which the

Above: Haunches of beef and venison broil at the Carnivore Restaurant.

Norfolk stands was renamed **Harry Thuku Road**.

The National Theatre is part of a cultural precinct occupied on one side by **Broadcasting House**, operated by the **Voice of Kenya**, and on the other by the **Kenya Cultural Centre**.

When you return to University Way turn right and continue past the elegant **Nairobi Safari Club**, on the left, to the roundabout on Uhuru Highway that marks the far end of the defined city centre.

Now turn left in the direction of the airport, remarking the major 1989 development taking place on the once vacant land to the left of the Highway, and **Central Park** to the right, with the children's traffic playground and the compact hexagonal-shaped **Nyayo Monument**, built late in 1988 to mark President Moi's first decade as Kenya's leader.

The dominant statue represents President Moi's raised hand, holding his familiar swagger stick, breaking out of Mount Kenya's twin peaks. Each of the four relief panels set in its side symbolises one of the major developments that took place during the first ten years of his administration.

Opposite, in **Uhuru Park**, work began in 1989 on the foundations of the sixty-storey *Kenya Times* "city in the sky" offices.

Street of History

Walk beyond the monument and you come to the lush gardens of another of Nairobi's major five-star hotels, the **Nairobi Serena**, which many green-eyed developers consider fortunate to have been allocated land on such a prime green belt site. At least the architect had the foresight to hide the building in landscaped gardens so it doesn't look in the least intrusive.

The next roundabout brings you to the intersection of **Kenyatta Avenue** and Uhuru Highway. Turn left and you're on the city's main street. First, on the corner, is the old Nairobi **Provincial Commission** office (*circa* 1913), a protected building that sits in the shadow of its twenty-storey successor, **Nyayo House**. This houses all manner of Government departments including the **Immigration Department**.

Kenya loves to welcome visitors — and to see them go. With an annual birthrate of

Opposite: Jacaranda bloom on Nairobi's Kenyatta Avenue.

Above: Kenya's colourful textiles.

around four per cent, and more than a million school leavers a year looking for work, there are major unemployment problems and the limited opportunities available are zealously guarded for Kenyan citizens.

A great many visitors fall in love with the country and devise all manner of means to prolong their stay or make it permanent. At the same time, the Immigration Department devises all manner of scrutiny to ensure that they don't succeed.

The next corner was occupied by the post-war, pre-independence **General Post Office** but in 1989 this was demolished for re-development.

Until 1955, the road that divides it from Nyayo House was the upcountry leg of the — Lunatic Line" — all the way to Lake Victoria or Uganda's far north — which crossed Kenyatta Avenue by courtesy of a barred, level crossing.

Opposite the GPO is **Kipande House**, another of the city's historical buildings where, both before and after Independence, citizens and residents were fingerprinted and issued with identity cards. Lovingly restored, Kipande House is now a busy branch of Kenya Commercial Bank.

On the opposite side of Kenyatta Avenue, at the intersection with Koinange Street, stands the memorial to the pioneering spirit of motoring enthusiast **Galton Fenzi**, founder of the Automobile Association of Kenya. He was the first man to drive from Nairobi to Mombasa over what was then trackless bush, thorn, *wadi*, ravine, and mountain. He also pioneered the Nairobi to Cape Town run.

The faraway places and vast mileages inscribed on his memorial read more like an aviation navigation chart than a monument to a pioneer of the motor age in Africa.

Two intersections further along Kenyatta Avenue are the **memorials** to Kenya's dead of two world wars: the valiant Africans of the Carrier Corps and King's African Rifles who sacrificed their lives for a monarch and an empire that had colonized them. One monument is a plain, sombre cenotaph: the other, sculpted by Myrander in 1924, depicts three *askaris*, (African soldiers).

Turn left into **Wabera Street** for **Macmillan Library**, donated to the city by Lady Macmillan as a memorial to her late husband,

Opposite: Kipande House, Nairobi: history in a living environment.

Above: Akamba arrowmaker displays his wares in market.

Sir Northrup Macmillan. An Anglicised American, he was knighted for his services in East Africa to Britain during World War I. Next to it, beautiful at night when it's lit by fairy lights, stands the city's main Muslim place of worship, the **Jamia Mosque**.

The next block along the left of Kenyatta Avenue contains two more historic buildings. The **Cameo Cinema**, which began its life before World War I as the **Theatre Royal**, was for many years the city's entertainment centre. Many ex-servicemen who spent time in East Africa during two world wars will remember the shows that were laid on for them at this venue.

Torr's Hotel, on the corner of the intersection with Kimathi Street, is an elegant redbrick building, built in the 1920s, and now converted into offices. Diagonally opposite is the **New Stanley Hotel**, whose **Thorn Tree Cafe** which fronts the street is arguably the capital's favourite meeting spot.

Built in the first decade of this century, twice razed by fire and redeveloped many times, the New Stanley, just like the Norfolk, has a guest register that reads like a celebrity Who's Who. The Thorn Tree cafe is domi-

nated by an acacia thorn planted two years before Independence, in 1961. A message board around its trunk is used by passing tourists and backpackers looking for companionship as they travel through Kenya and onwards — and by those seeking lost friends.

The Hilton dominates the intersection of Kimathi Street and **Mama Ngina Way**. Turn right and ahead of you, across Wabera Street, is **City Hall**, built in 1937. On the balcony at the front, overlooking the colonial Law Courts, built in the 1920s, and **Kenyatta International Conference Centre**, the Duke of Gloucester, on 30 March, 1950, presented Nairobi aldermen with the Royal Charter and letters patent proclaiming it a city.

On the same balcony, two years later, Prince Philip and Princess Elizabeth acknowledged the salute of Nairobi's citizens just a few days before the death of King George VI in February 1952. Princess Elizabeth was staying with her husband at Treetops in the Aberdare National Park.

The road below the balcony was for many years the start and finish of Kenya's world famous **Safari Rally**. It began in 1953 as the Coronation Safari: then in 1973 it moved to

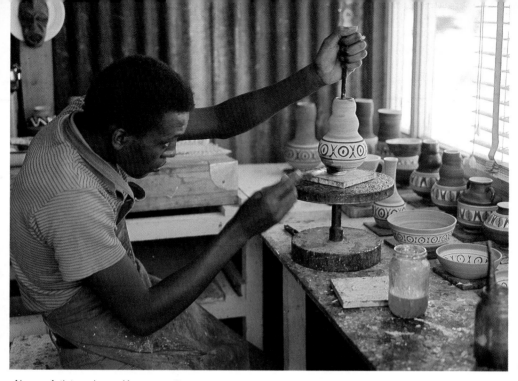

Above: Artist works on Kenyan pottery.

the ceremonial mall in the gardens of the Kenyatta International Conference Centre whose forecourt is dominated by a magnificent stone **statue** of Jomo Kenyatta, founding father of the Kenyan nation.

Directly facing the starting ramp are Kenya's **Parliament Buildings**, built in the 1930s, and focal point of the city's master plan which was drawn up in 1948. In its grounds is another prominent statue of Jomo Kenyatta whose remains are buried in the **mausoleum** in the west of **Parliament Gardens**. Lined by flags, the mausoleum is watched day and night by ceremonial guards.

Every five years Kenya elects 188 MPs who sit, together with twelve others nominated by the President, to decide the nation's legislation and debate its progress.

A tour of these historic buildings can be arranged through the Sergeant-at-Arms. It begins when you step through the splendid entrance of carved timber doors along a floor laid with Italian marble. Ten shields, one from each of Kenya's ten major tribes, line the entrance. On the left is the country's **Seal of Independence** and on the right the **Commonwealth Parliamentary Association**

Room with some fascinating antique wall hangings.

The old chamber that served from 1952 to 1954 now contains two despatch boxes, a gift from New Zealand to mark Kenya's Independence. The striking, wood panel on the landing was presented by Kabete School. Made at the end of the 1950s, each of its thirty-two pieces represents one of Kenya's indigenous hardwoods.

The **Long Gallery** houses a magnificent collection of forty-nine wool and canvas tapestries, made by members of the East African Women's League. The **tapestries** tell the picturesque, colonial history of Kenya and were presented to Parliament in 1968.

At the left, the gallery ends in the fine, blue mosaics that form the facade of the **New National Assembly Chamber** and were donated by the country's Ismaili community.

On the corner opposite Parliament Gardens is the Nairobi **Inter-Continental Hotel**, built in 1969. Facing it is the Catholic **Holy Family Cathedral**.

Turn left across Uhuru Highway for **Uhuru Park** with its tiered grass arena, behind the elegant **Uhuru Fountains** built to commemo-

113

Opposite: Moi International Stadium, Kenya's finest sports arena.
Top: Kenya schoolchildren spell out anniversary message in the Moi International Sports complex.
Above: Schoolchildren mark the 25th anniversary of Independence.

rate twenty years of Independence, and **VIP pavilion** where Kenya used to celebrate its significant anniversaries and where Pope John Paul conducted mass for more than half a million people in 1980.

Above the park is **The Hill**, prime real estate that houses many fine office buildings representing various government ministries. Right of the park is the Anglican **All Saints Cathedral**. Its foundation stone was laid in 1917 but work was not completed until its consecration in 1952. Inside, the stained glass windows, nave, transept, Gothic arches, and pews are reminiscent of ancient England recreated here in sentimental glory.

The **plaques** on the walls commemorate colonial pioneers like Northrup Macmillan and heroes like **Baden-Powell**. Some of the stones in the walls came from Lindisfarne, Canterbury, and St Paul's cathedrals.

In 1946 Britain's King George VI and Queen Elizabeth, now the Queen Mother, presented two Bibles, and two of the **cypress trees** outside grew from seeds taken from the Garden of the Tomb and Gethsemane in Israel.

The bridge that links the Cathedral grounds to Kenyatta Avenue commemorates Charles Ryall.

Just beyond the cathedral is the **Panafric Hotel**, built in anticipation of the tourist boom that came with Independence. Turn right into treelined **Nyerere Avenue** past the Serena and YWCA and you come to a cluster of churches — the Presbyterian **St Andrew's**, the **Lutheran Church**, and St Paul's Catholic Chapel.

Opposite, between Uhuru Highway and Nairobi University, is the Jewish **Synagogue**, formerly Vermont Hall, located next to the University campus which was upgraded after Independence from the Royal Technical College.

Cross over from Nyerere Avenue into **State House Road**, and continue past the University halls of residence and **Moi Girls High School** to the **Nairobi Arboretum Forest Reserve**, on the right. Little more than thirty-two hectares (80 acres) in extent, it contains some 270 species of indigenous and exotic trees — all labelled (See "Flora: forests of flame, streets of mauve", Part Three). It is not advisable to go here alone.

Further on are the extensive grounds of State House, the official residence of the President, where photography is strictly prohibited.

To get to the city centre's other forest reserve, return to the Globe roundabout and continue up the dual carriageway past the Ngara roundabout to the junction of Limuru Road with **Forest Road**, on the right. To the left is **St Francis of Xavier's Church**, built in 1933.

The land on either side of Forest Road is devoted to a multitude of sports clubs — **Nairobi Gymkhana**, **Premier Club**, and **Simba Union**, formerly Sikh Union until a government ordinance banned racial or tribally aligned organisations.

Between Forest Road and Limuru Road is **City Park**, a forest reserve excised by Ainsworth as early as 1904 as Nairobi's first recreational area. Its gardens are magnificent, with trees and shrubs and a city parks department **plant nursery**. Follow the path down into the **sunken gardens** where there's a **playground** for children and ponds containing frogs and fish.

Also on the left is the notable **Boscawen Memorial Collection** of orchids, donated in memory of Lt. Col. M. T. Boscawen, DSO, MC, by his sister.

Adjacent to the park area, within its 120 hectares (300 acres), is one of Kenya's many war **cemeteries** with the graves of ninety-seven men, most from World War II but some from 1950 and World War I.

Vervet monkeys gambol among the trees and picnickers, and the early twentieth-century **bandstand**, and **maze** remain an affectionate legacy of the colonial past.

Much of the forest remains pristine. Leopard were seen in City Park as recently as 1980 and some may still live there secretively.

If you continue along Limuru Road, instead of turning right into Forest Road, you arrive at the city's Nob Hill estate of **Muthaiga** known to all and sundry as Millionaire's Row. Carved out of an indigenous forest, it is the most exclusive suburb in Nairobi and a favoured area for diplomatic residences. The **Karura Forest Reserve** backs on to its manicured lawns and landscaped gardens.

On the other side of the forest, at **Gigiri** on the Limuru Road, are the headquarters of two world organisations — the **United Nations**

Opposite: Home of Kenyan democracy—Parliament Buildings in Nairobi.

Above: Young nation at play. More than half of Kenya's 22 million people are school age or under.

Environment Programme (UNEP) and Habitat, the United Nations Centre for Human Settlement.

If you turn into Forest Road it links up with Muranga Road at the Pangani roundabout, with Nairobi's second cemetery to the left. Follow Muranga Road to the Muthaiga roundabout.

First left leads to what may well be considered the ultimate, bastion of Kenya's colonial past, Muthaiga Country Club. In the closing stages of the twentieth century the rules of membership are as anachronistic today as feudal England would have been in the Britain of the 1950s.

In this conservative institution, the chef wears cotton gloves to carve the meat of the day, brought in on a trolley, and business talk over luncheon is prohibited. Featured in *Out of Africa*, Muthaiga's timbers and members are soaked in nostalgia.

An afternoon here may delight those who believe in an empire on which the sun never set, but it's definitely a bewildering time-warp for those involved in the daily struggle for existence in contemporary Kenya.

Framing the roundabout itself are the fairways of Muthaiga Golf Club, home to the Kenya Open Golf Tournament which features some of the great names of contemporary golf, such as Seve Ballesteros, on its roll of winners.

Muranga Road now becomes Thika Road, and passes to the left the other half of Muthaiga Golf Club and, to the right, Utali Hotel and training college — which provides graduates for Kenya's hotel and tourist industry. National Youth Service headquarters and Survey of Kenya are on the left and finally, to the right, the Fox Drive-In Cinema.

The Thika Road intersects here with Outer Ring Road, with the General Service Unit (GSU) headquarters at the left of the roundabout and the first of Kenya Breweries many brewing installations on the right.

Drive on past the Safari Park Hotel and Country Club, formerly the Spread Eagle, to the left, elegant in landscaped gardens with thorn, eucalyptus, and acacia trees.

On the right, the Moi International Sports Centre is Kenya's central motif as one of Africa's, and indeed the world's, great sporting nations. Built with Chinese expertise and finance, the centre is set around Africa's most modern sports stadium, a 60,000-seat arena that was the main venue of the 1987 All Africa Games.

Nairobi National Park

The best introduction to Kenya safaris is a visit to **Nairobi National Park**. To get there, follow **Uhuru Highway** to the roundabout where it intersects with **Lusaka Road** on the left, and **Langata Road** to the right. Keeping **Nyayo Stadium** on the right, carry on past **Wilson Airport** — one of Africa's busiest, which is named after Florrie Wilson who founded Kenya's pioneer domestic airline, Wilson Airways, in 1929. At the entrance is the **Dambusters** — a popular "pub" — and at the far end are the **Aero Club of East Africa** and, incongruously, the headquarters of the **Mountain Club of Kenya**. In between lie a host of enterprises, mainly concerned with aviation. Wilson Airport offers charter services throughout Kenya and eastern Africa.

On the left is **Nairobi Sailing Club**, built on the eastern bank of the **Nairobi Dam** which was hastily constructed after World War II to boost municipal water supplies, but is no longer used.

The Sailing Club's dinghies cruise on the dark waters of the dam, which is outlined, opposite, by the tin roofs, timber and mud shacks of **Kibera** shantytown. The land on which these stand was presented by the colonial authorities to the city's Nubian population in 1922 as a mark of appreciation for their service and loyalty in the 1914-18 war. Now Kibera is home for hundreds of thousands of urban poor.

Nonetheless, although they may seem out of place, both the Aero Club and the Sailing Club retain a particular ambience — the aviator and yachtsman's ideal leisure resorts. Both boast good, home cooking, and well-stocked bars which the Sailing Club shares with the **Kenya Sub Aqua Club**.

Left of Langata Road, opposite the Sailing Club entrance, the road leads to the **Carnivore**, formerly the Golf Range, now a Brazilian inspired restaurant-cum-nightclub. Here you can eat every imaginable exotic meat, from crocodile and zebra to eland and impala steaks, and countless others, at an all-inclusive price. Carnivore is also the capital's most popular disco, headquarters of the **East African Motor Sports Club** and **Nairobi's Motocross course**.

Next left from the Carnivore is **Uhuru Gardens**, where Kenya was delivered of colonial bondage at the stroke of midnight on 12 December, 1963. The Gardens were neglected for twenty years until 1983, when they were transformed into a national heritage centre.

The central motif, a slender, soaring granite and marble column on three curved legs, is almost twenty-four metres (80 feet) high. The monument's symbol is clasped hands adorned with a dove of peace: its outliers are Kenya's freedom fighters raising the national flag, and a sentinel in front of crossed spears and a shield.

All around are lush gardens, laid out in the map of Kenya with Mount Kenya at the centre and lakes Turkana and Victoria at the peripheries.

To mark twenty-five years of freedom, another **monument** and **musical fountains** were unveiled in 1988.

Further up the hill, past the **army barracks** at the left, and the serried, middle-income housing estates of **Langata** on the right, are the gates, left, of Nairobi National Park and the headquarters of Kenya's **Wildlife Conservation and Management Department**.

Inside the administration area is a **Wildlife Conservation Education Centre** with public film shows on set days of the week and a **library** and **museum**.

Nairobi Animal Orphanage, on the right as you approach the gates into the park, has suffered from the malady of planning schizophrenia. When it was founded in 1963, mainly with overseas financial support, it was declared that it would never be a zoo although it has all the appearances of one, including two tigers — gifted from overseas.

In 1989, however, it was being refurbished and was to reopen in April 1990 as sanctuary to the lame and the laggard, the sick and the orphaned, who are cared for until well and strong enough to be repatriated to the wild.

However, the most threatened species — orphaned elephants and rhinos — are cared for by Daphne Sheldrick, a famous author who lives in a compound in the west corner of the park. She is the linchpin of the **David Sheldrick Conservation Foundation**, founded in memory of her late husband who tended Tsavo National Park for many years.

Nairobi National Park was the first Kenya national park, gazetted in 1945 and opened in 1946. Covering only 117 square kilometres (46 square miles), it incorporates a surprising number of different environments and habitats.

Set at an altitude of between 1,533 and 1,760 metres (5,000-5,775 feet), only eight kilometres (five miles) south of Nairobi, the park forms a long, sloping plain of black cotton soil crossed by several deep river valleys. The **Athi river** forms part of the southern boundary.

Vegetation is mainly dry, transitional savannah with gallery forests in the valleys. This close proximity of forest cover, pasture, and permanent water makes it the focus of an animal migration area, particularly in drought years.

There are more than eighty recorded mammal species, and some 500 species of birdlife. Hippo and crocodile live in the various ponds, waterholes, and the Athi river.

The park was created out of what was once a Somali reserve, Nairobi Common, a World War I training ground, and a World War II firing range. But it's difficult to believe if you're lucky enough to experience one of those days when the lion pride has made a kill, the cubs are playful, the wildebeest are gathered *en masse*, the buffalo herds have moved in through their shrinking wildlife corridor, the giraffe are cropping the thorn, and the rhino are feeding against the silhouette of Kenyatta Conference Centre in the background.

Fenced in on only three sides, it is still not an artificial safari park, although squatters and homesteaders are swiftly shrinking the preserved "corridor" through the **Kitengela Conservation Area** along which most of the park species migrate.

With new factories rising directly on its northern perimeter, Athi River and its cement factory and abattoir at its eastern end, new housing estates to the west, and the noose tightening around its southern entrance, Nairobi Park may now be in its last vestiges as a natural ecosystem but still a rare legacy for any city, even one in wildlife Kenya, and worth protecting fiercely.

In the east, in a murky part of the Athi-Sabaki-Galana river, lies the **hippo pool**.

Signs warn you not to feed the monkeys, but take care — they will steal not only your picnic but anything else left loose in the car or held lightly in the hand.

There's no lodge in the park itself but the **Maasai Lodge** which sits on one side of the gorge that marks its western boundary is a pleasant place to spend the night.

Ngong Hills: The Giant's Knuckles

From Nairobi take the **Langata Road** past Wilson Airport and the National Park gates to the junction of **Magadi Road** and **Forest Edge Road**. Turn right into Forest Edge Road and first right again for the **Bomas of Kenya**, a parastatal entertainment centre.

The enclosed arena, held up with massive timber supports, is a giant auditorium where young, professional dance groups from many of Kenya's ethnic communities perform sophisticated, and choreographed, traditional dance routines.

Visitors can also tour ethnic villages and houses and buy traditional craftware. The auditorium restaurant serves ethnic food and has a well-stocked bar.

Forest Edge Road continues into a track that cuts through the thick, dark, indigenous **Ngong Forest**. Although the forest harbours an unknown number of leopards it is, nevertheless, popular with Hash House Harrier runners, and horse riders, in particular Ginger Bell's pink-coated hunt. The lure is aniseed sacks dragged along the trails by fast-running hunt servants.

The track exits on the other side of the forest on the **Ngong Road** near the Jockey Club of Kenya racecourse.

Follow Magadi Road, leaving the National Park fence on the left, and plush private estates on the right, including the famous **Banda Preparatory School**, and continue past the **Kenya Posts and Telecommunications Training College** on the right. Turn left for Maasai Lodge, or straight into fast-growing **Ongata Rongai**, an amazing complex of little suburban houses, basic shopping centres, and many bars and *nyama choma* eating places — all seemingly unplanned — and carry on to Kiserian, where the road to Magadi becomes the responsibility of the Soda Company.

Turn right at **Kiserian** for **Ngong Hills**, keeping them to your left as you drive to **Ngong Town**. Farms, smallholdings, and smart houses in landscaped gardens are set in the dimpled valleys on the eastern slopes of these lovely hills. Amid the maize stalks stands the simple **obelisk monument** that Karen Blixen built to the memory of Denys Finch Hatton.

Above: Start of one of the classic races run at Nairobi's Ngong Racecourse, Nairobi.

Drive through Ngong Town, an unkempt and undistinguished shopping centre, past the **Ngong Road** on the right, and turn left up the scenic dirt trail past the **police station** to the **communications antennae** where the track ends. Leave your car and walk uphill to look at the glorious views in any direction, particularly of Nairobi. Kajiado County Council have installed a toll gate — in your interest. It's to keep potential muggers off the hills.

It takes two hours to walk up and down these ridges. From the top you can gaze down the western slopes with almost sheer drops to the stark, volcanic tumult on the floor of the Great Rift Valley. From one end to the other — the highest point **Lamwia**, is 2,460 metres (8,070 feet) — these views are one of the delights of living in Nairobi (See "Kenya's Mountains").

Maasai legend claims that this range of folded hills, shaped like the knuckles of a clenched fist, were formed when a giant tripped over Kilimanjaro, more than 250 kilometres (155 miles) south-east, and clawed at the earth as he fell.

Look eastward to see the suburb of **Karen**

laid out beneath you. It was here that Karen Blixen settled in 1913 with her husband, Baron Bror Blixen, to establish a coffee farm, which she abandoned — penniless in the 1930s. Her experiences, and her love affair with Denys Finch Hatton, inspired the book *Out of Africa*, which she wrote under the pen name Isaak Dinnesen. In the book she expresses her love for these hills "that had not its like in all the world".

To reach Karen return to Ngong Town and turn left along Ngong Road. This takes you past a Voice of Kenya **transmitter**, and a popular **night club** to Karen shopping centre. Turn right into **Langata Road**, past a forest of radio masts on the left that denote the presence of the **BBC Monitoring Unit**, then turn first right into **Karen Road**.

A kilometre or so along here, the lush, treelined fairways of **Karen Golf and Country Club** are at the left. Just before the right turn into **Bogani Road** is Karen Blixen's old farmhouse, right, restored to the style in which she maintained it and now a **museum** in her honour.

The coffee estate that she developed on 144 hectares (360 acres) was a wedding present-cum-investment from her Danish family. Bror Blixen, also her cousin, wrote *African Hunter* and figured in the Hemingway classic, *The Short, Happy Life of Francis Macomber*. Also in the grounds is **Karen College** which was founded as a Danish gift following Karen Blixen's death in 1962.

At the junction with Bogani Road turn right into **Mbagathi Ridge** and drive along the back of the Blixen Museum. This takes you around what was her coffee *shamba*.

Turn right into **Forest Lane**, left into Karen Road, then cross Langata Road and continue to the junction with Ngong Road. Turn right and almost immediately on your right is Karen's Anglican **St Francis Church**, built in 1952, which lacks only a traditional English village church spire.

Follow the chicane as the road dips and winds through the Ngong Forest and then straightens out alongside **Lenana School**, left, formerly the Duke of York school, followed by **Ngong Racecourse**, right.

Regarded by many as the most beautiful racetrack in the Commonwealth, the Jockey Club of Kenya run an average of forty Sunday race meetings a year with bloodstock imported from Europe by, among others, the Aga Khan.

Opposite the grandstand on the far side of the track is the **Commonwealth War cemetery**, beautiful in its sylvan glades, where Queen Elizabeth II of Britain celebrated Remembrance Day in 1983 among the many graves of African and British soldiers who fell in the two world wars. To visit the graves, take the next right after the racecourse.

To return to the city centre take the next right turn through the forest, past the Agricultural Society of Kenya's **Jamhuri Park Showground** on the left, which annually hosts the Nairobi show, Kenya's farm and industrial trade fair. On the right is the **Rowallan Boy Scouts Camp**.

Olorgesailie and Magadi

By far the most dramatic excursion from the capital in a day is a visit to the Aechulian tool site of **Olorgesailie** and the soda lake **Magadi**, little more than 100 kilometres (60 miles) from Nairobi on a well-maintained metal road. But the land is 1,070 metres (3,500 feet) lower, and simmers in the merciless heat of the sump of the **The Great Rift Valley**. Be sure you have a full petrol tank or, better still, take a 4WD vehicle and also carry jerricans of both water and petrol.

You can also drive across the Magadi salt pans to camp or picnic around its many boiling springs or just to enjoy the incredible bird life and panoramas of this magnificent, but improbable, scenic backdrop so close to cosmopolitan Nairobi (See "Great Rift Valley: the land that was Eden").

The Escarpment: At the Edge of the Abyss

The **Uplands Escarpment**, near **Limuru**, cresting between 2,440 and 2,740 metres (8,000-9,000 feet) provides one of the most spectacular vantage points of the Great Rift Valley, and posed terrible problems for Robert Preston, the chief engineer of the Uganda Railway which reached this spot late in 1899.

Until the 1950s the track from Nairobi ran out of the city across what is now Kenyatta Avenue, through the Chiromo campus and up past the Italian mission of the **Consolata Fathers** and the **Lady Consolata Catholic Church**. It continued through **Westlands** along an alignment now occupied by Uhuru Highway and **Waiyaki Way**. The Italian ambience was extended in the Agip Motel now renamed the **Jacaranda**.

At the Westlands roundabout Uhuru Highway ends and becomes **Waiyaki Way**, formerly Sclaters Road after the commanding officer of the Royal Engineers squad who carved this trail when they surveyed the railway route.

For three kilometres (almost two miles), past the extant ruins of the unfinished **All Africa Conference of Churches** conference centre, the potholed road is an example of much of what is to be experienced in driving through Kenya. But at **James Gichuru Road**, on the left, it broadens out again into a smooth dual carriageway — part of the **Great North Road** that goes through Uganda to Rwanda, Burundi, and Zaire and is eventually planned to reach Lagos in Nigeria. Other spurs lead into south Sudan and, eventually it is hoped, on to Cairo.

If you turn left into **James Gichuru Road**, formerly St Austin's Road, you'll come across a little piece of the city's pioneering days. The **St Austin's Mission** to the left (now with convent school) was founded by the Irish **Holy Ghost Fathers** in the 1890s when they turned much of this land into Kenya's first coffee plantation. This was after the crop failed to take root at Kibwezi, much further back down the line between Mtito Andei and Sultan Hamud (See "Nairobi to Mombasa: highway to adventure").

The original coffee plantation is now largely upmarket, suburban **Muthangari**, still known by many as Lavington, complete with English village-green. But the devout continue to worship at St Austin's, as did Karen Blixen who wrote of it in *Out of Africa*.

You can drive on through Muthangari to **Dagoretti Corner**, a colourful, if somewhat disorganised ethnic market and shopping centre. Turn north at the roundabout along the **Naivasha Road** — through **Kawangare** shantytown to **Uthiru** and **Upper Kabete**, or return to Waiyaki Way which continues through the shantytown of **Kangemi**, largely hidden from sight, to link up with Naivasha Road at **Kabete**.

Located on the left off the Naivasha Road just before it rejoins Waiyaki Way is the headquarters of **ILRAD**. At this international livestock research organisation cattle graze lush fields but are also used as "test beds" — bitten by tsetse flies — in the battle to discover shields against the fatal trypanosomiasis (sleeping sickness).

Other veterinary and agriculturally orientated educational campuses are also here with, on the right of Waiyaki Way, the **University of Nairobi** and **Wellcome Foundation's** extensive veterinary laboratories and research institutions. Here, too, the rustic charms of the **Vet Labs Golf Club** can be enjoyed by all — membership is open to everyone.

Near this establishment, a few metres off the main road, is **Ndumbeini** — a small strip of ravaged tarmac laid on the original Sclaters's Road, and a stone block, frontier-style, shopping centre with bars, butcheries, and *dukas* (shops).

The road leads on to **Fort Smith**. This well-stockaded, timber fort, now a private residence, was built in the impenetrable forest of the Kikuyu in 1890 by Major Eric Smith, the first British commander (See "The Dust and the Ashes", Part One).

Naturally, the Kikuyu were hostile to this invasion and, across the road from the fort, a maize field contains the neglected **marble graves** of three Britons, one of them killed by Kikuyu who besieged the fort.

Also in Kabete is the site of the **Church Missionary Society**'s first upcountry station, established in 1901. It was here that Canon Harry Leakey arrived from Reading in 1902 to build a permanent Anglican church, spread the gospel, and found the remarkable dynasty that has done more to dissemble the Biblical theory of Genesis than any other family in the world — first through his son Louis and then through his grandson, Richard.

Return to Ndumbeini and turn left into **Kapenguria Road**, past the **University Farm** on the right, and the **Artificial Insemination Stud** to the left, and continue to the crossroads with **Lower Kabete Road**. Five hundred metres (a third of a mile) along on the right the former Kenya Institute of Administration is now part of the Nairobi University campus. The training centre for Kenya's administrative personnel such as district commissioners and officers has moved some distance away. To the left lie steep hills of rich, red soil and verdant crops of maize, banana trees, vegetables, and fruit.

Take this road and the departure from Nairobi's broken, potholed strip is felt when the surface suddenly becomes smooth Kiambu County Council maintained tarmac. After a few kilometres you come to **Wangige** where the Monday Market is a riot of farm-fresh produce and haggling vendors and buyers. Unsullied by tourists, here is a characteristic and authentic demonstration of the Kikuyu's lively entrepreneurial spirit.

Turn left at Wangige on to more smooth tarmac to rejoin the **Naivasha Road** at **Kikuyu**. In 1989 this was still the same road that was built around 1940 by Italian Prisoners of War, but it is scheduled to become a modern dual carriage highway by 1990-91.

THE CHURCH OF THE TORCH

If you cross the main road into **Kikuyu Road** it follows the course of the new rail alignment for some distance leaving **Kikuyu** town, with its homely, timbered, Anglo-Saxon style **Kikuyu Country Club**, on the right.

Under the rail bridge there are stunning views of Kikuyu farmlands, Nairobi, Ol Doinyo Sapuk and the Ngong Hills. After Kikuyu town, on the right, is **Alliance High School**, famous *alma mater* of Kenya's post-Independence decision makers and cabinet ministers. The **Alliance Girls High School**, close by on the right, was modelled on the same lofty, idealistic but pragmatic approach to education.

Also on the right is **Thogoto**, notable for its Presbyterian **Church of the Torch** which was established by Scottish missionaries in 1898 — two years ahead of the Anglicans — and is the beacon of the Presbyterian Church of East Africa. Jomo Kenyatta was baptized here and it still stands, well-preserved.

Monuments in the grounds of the succeeding 1928 **church** give you some sense of the loneliness and hazards experienced by these first evangelists of the Christian cause almost a century ago. And of the reciprocal kindness and affection that they were accorded by those they came to convert.

The Kikuyu are the largest ethnic group in Kenya, numbering about four million in 1987. The founding members of the kirk were quick to notice that there was much of the Scot about Kikuyu ways and character, finding them thrifty, industrious, and clever with their hands. They lived in round thatched huts which they share with their livestock — as the Scots did four centuries ago — and brewed a fine, colourless whisky, celebrated major occasions with the haggis (the boiled innards of goat or sheep stuffed in gut skin) and danced a passable Highland reel of their own (See "The People", Part One).

So given the mission's early start at Thogoto, it's not surprising that the kirk — founded in Scotland by John Knox — is the strongest of Kikuyuland's secular faiths.

Rhubarb and Rabbits

At Kikuyu, from Wangige, turn right on to the appalling potholes and switchbacks of the Great North Road which climbs steeply, leaving **Sigona Golf Club** — with its much-envied fairway panoramas of the Ngong Hills, Athi Plains, occasionally Kilimanjaro, Nairobi, and the Embakasi Plains — on the left, to the **Presbyterian Pastoral Institute** (formerly the Zambezi Motel), also on the left, with rich farmlands on either side.

Higher up, again on the left, is **Rironi**, a typical rural shopping centre, with the **Voice of Kenya**'s television transmitter to the right. Half a kilometre (a third of a mile) later the road broadens out into a smooth, modern freeway which leaves **Limuru** town on the right and swoops up and down through green meadowlands to **Uplands**, also to the right. It then follows a hard curve right and climbs steeply to emerge suddenly above the Great Rift Valley, hundreds of metres below.

This fine highway was constructed in 1973 by the Israeli Solel Boneh company. Almost immediately there's a **Viewing Spot** where you can pull in — if you feel up to beating off the vocal assault of vendors selling everything from giant rhubarb stems, to live rabbits, to sheepskin rugs, and, when in season, pears and plums.

Almost the entire roadside, from Rironi through to Naivasha, is lined with these mainly young entrepreneurs. On the downleg to Naivasha it's mostly Kikuyu mothers and daughters offering *debes* (tins) of wholesome potatoes, carrots, onions, and other vegetables and the sales pitch is more restrained (See "Tastes of Kenya", Part Three).

Most likely you'll be so overwhelmed by the views — a magnificent panorama over **Lake Naivasha** almost into the bowels of **Longonot** — that you'll buy something anyway. This view is as spectacular as that from the Ngong Hills *en route* to Magadi.

It's the same grandstand scenery and immensity of scale, but without the harshness of the southern valley landscape. Instead of serried scarps, the Rift above Naivasha drops down in a single sweep, leaving towering walls on either side, with distant blue-grey mountains forming the western wall almost 100 kilometres (60 miles) away.

With the white radial dishes of Kenya Posts and Telecommunications **Longonot Satellite Station** appearing minute in the foreground,

Mount Susua stands out in the middle of the valley and, more immediately ahead, clouds brim around the knife-edge rim of the tallest of the Rift Valley's volcanoes, 2,776-metres-high (9,107-feet) high **Longonot** (See "Great Rift Valley: the land that was Eden").

The alternative route, down into the Rift itself, is to turn left at Rironi on to the old Naivasha Road that juggernauts must use by law. This means braving the atrocious potholes and bumps to arrive at the escarpment edge through the **Ngubi Forest**. Until a few years ago it was the only route.

This road, with its precipitous edge, follows a series of terrifying hairpin bends along the course of the first railway alignment created at the turn of the century.

Halfway down, on the left, is a forestry **picnic site**, complete with tumbledown grandstand and trellised benches set on the edge of the cliff overlooking the Rift Valley. In this little-visited place the wind soughs through the trees and the lyrics of silence should inspire even the most jaded muse.

Further down, on the right, a dirt road leads to the African Inland Church mission town of **Kijabe**, Kenya's own version of Salt Lake City in Utah, USA, founded by missionaries of an evangelistic American sect under strict rules of abstinence but, like the Mormons, not celibacy. Their first converts were polygamous. Missionaries have always been careful first to catch their converts before reforming their traditional ways.

Kijabe's sleepy monastic community is ruled by a council of elders who still invoke the same ordinances that applied in the first decade. There's a model community hospital — funded by mission money and overseas donations — but no shop sells tobacco or liquor.

Former US President Theodore Roosevelt, in the course of his great African Safari of 1909, laid the church's foundation stone after an exhilarating train ride from Nairobi on the cowcatcher of the locomotive.

Though no more than sixty kilometres (37 miles) from the capital, in time and place Kijabe could be another world. When drought struck Kenya in 1984, its citizens were forced to remain indoors — or walk outside at their peril. Rampaging forest buffaloes moved down into the town in search of grazing and water. The **hospital** was kept busy with casualties who had been gored.

Above: Shade trees dot a tea plantation in the Tigoni Uplands near Nairobi.

Take the right turn under the **railway bridge** for the steep climb up the richly-forested wall of the Rift to return to the new Naivasha Road. Turn left for Naivasha (See "Great Rift Valley: the land that was Eden") or right for **Limuru town**, which is fifteen kilometres (10 miles) or so in the direction of Nairobi, with a left turn into Limuru itself.

Set 2,160 metres (7,300 feet) above sea level, Limuru's champagne air is turbocharged by the constant thermals that thunder up the eastern wall of the Rift and even during day-time, can carry a touch of ice in their breath.

In the past, many pointed to "Limoru", as an ideal site for a capital. If this had happened, its western suburbs would have run straight off the edge of the Escarpment down into the Rift — certainly a dramatic setting for any capital city.

As it is, Limuru is a bustling little farm capital of its own and houses the headquarters of the Bata shoe company's Kenya manu-facturing operations. With its more recent subsidiary at Voi, the company now turns out more than nine million pairs of shoes a year.

The old **Tigoni Road** leaves the town past **Loreto High School** on the left, and the lush

fairways of **Limuru Country Club** to the right. The golf course also hides Kenya's prettiest **cricket ground**, complete with shingle-roofed pavilion, and an antique racecourse where once a year — with boaters, strawberries, cream, and champagne — the Jockey Club stage a festive charity race meeting that is not just all thoroughbreds.

Continue along Tigoni Road through **Tigoni,** an imitation Surrey stockbroker village, with its fine houses cut off from view by tall, thickset, but well-manicured hedges. These were uprooted and transplanted in a kind of ersatz Hollywood image of an English land-scape — albeit with tea bushes and giant eucalyptus. Continue past Brooke Bond's **Mabroukie Tea Estate,** founded in 1903 when the first clippings of *Thea sinensis* were introduced from India.

They prospered well. Tea grows everywhere in the fertile, well-watered highlands and Kenya is now the world's third-largest pro-ducer and second-largest tea exporter — all premium grade.

As you descend from the tea belt, past the upmarket mock-Tudor, farmhouse style **Kentmere Club,** with one of Kenya's *haute*

Above: Kenya's prime Arabica coffee ripens in the Equatorial sun.

cuisine restaurants (a quality reflected in its prices), past Brooke Bond's **Kentmere Estate**, you soon begin to enter the coffee-rich plantations of **Kiambu** district. This crop, which flourishes best at a lower altitude than tea, is Kenya's largest single foreign exchange earner after tourism.

The country's *Arabica* is considered the *crême de la crême* of world coffees and generally fetches top prices, even when the market is in glut with Latin American *Arabicas.*

After lively **Banana Hill,** a rural metropolis, turn left by the speed bumps for **Chief Koinange High School**, at Kiambaa, where one of the ridges, known as millionaire's ridge, is at the right height with the right amount of sun and rain to produce the most perfect coffee ever grown.

Continue through a succession of small townships and shopping centres, all reminiscent of Wild West frontier towns (minus the stage coaches and hitching posts) into **Kiambu,** administrative capital of the district and surrounded by coffee plantations.

Turn left at the main junction for **Cianda, Githunguri,** and **Gatundu** — all beautifully rural — or right to go back to Nairobi.

Mountain of the Buffalo

Leave Nairobi along the **Thika Road** as far as the **Kasarani Roundabout,** then take the **Kasarani Road** past **Moi International Sports Centre** on the right. This leads past the **Casino de Paradise** to the **Kangundo Road.**

Turn left on to well-maintained tarmac — only small sections had potholes in 1989 — and ahead you will see the coffee hills of **Kangundo** and, to the left, the brooding hump of the Maasai's **Ol Doinyo Sapuk** which is the Kamba's **Mountain of the Buffalo, Kilimambogo.**

The road cuts through once semi-arid ranchland, now carved up into settler and co-operative smallholdings, and fifty-eight kilometres (36 miles) from Nairobi finally reaches **Tala** in the heart of Kambaland where the market is one of the most colourful in the country. **Kangundo**, seven kilometres (four miles) on from Tala, if nothing else, is a bustling, entrepreneurial trading town with lively bars, at the centre of a rich coffee area. Beyond Kangundo the road is all second grade to **Machakos.**

Above: Fourteen Falls, near Thika, send the Athi River cascading down to the Indian Ocean.

Instead turn left in Tala at the **BP station** and **Kwa Joe's Tourist Lodge** for **Kabaa** and **Yatta** which brings you out at the back of Del Monte's massive **pineapple plantation**, the largest in the world. Kenya is the world's third-largest producer of pineapples, nearly all grown on this single estate.

Back on what is sometimes defined as a grade one road — though weather and abuse have taken their toll — turn left for **Fourteen Falls** and the entrance to **Ol Doinyo Sapuk National Park** (one of only a few admission-free national parks in Kenya), covering just eighteen square kilometres (seven square miles).

The falls are less than a kilometre (two thirds of a mile) from the clearing where you park. Don't leave your car unattended: unfortunately there have been some nasty instances of muggings and robbery so it is best

to go in with an accompanied party or large group.

From the car park follow the path through the forest to the foot of the falls, pausing at a clearing halfway down for a splendid view of the twenty-seven-metre-deep (90-feet) cataracts, a magnificent feature of the Athi-Sabaki-Galana river.

Back in your car, drive across three bridges, turn right at a shantytown, and through the Del Monte **coffee plantation** for two kilometres (just over a mile) to the park gate. Although there's no admission charge, entrance is by vehicle only. The mountain is still home to large populations of unpredictable and bad-tempered Cape buffalo, one of Africa's Big Five animals, hence its Kamba name, *Kilimambogo*.

But it was for the wealth of birdlife that the humpbacked 2,146-metre-high (7,040-feet)

Above: Cattle meadow in the Limuru Uplands above Nairobi.

mountain was declared a national park in 1969.

Lying fifty kilometres (30 miles) north-east of Nairobi, the park's main feature is an inselberg rising from the surrounding plains. Its solitude is now slightly disfigured by the image of technology represented by the microwave **relay mast** on its summit.

Except for a small bare patch around the crest, the mountain is entirely covered with montane forest. Wildlife includes colobus monkey, leopard, black rhino, bushbuck, buffalo, duiker, impala, and numerous bird species. There are two campsites.

On a clear day, from its summit, lakes and ponds shimmer below like tiny jewels in a carpet of green, while the twin spires of Mount Kenya rise up in the distance.

From the entrance picnic site to the summit is nine kilometres (five and a half miles) through the thick, indigenous forest. Roughly halfway up the trail a bend gives way to a rugged bluff with panoramic views of the surrounding countryside — a vista beloved of Sir William Northrup Macmillan and his wife.

An American, Macmillan was one of the most outstanding — both mentally and physically — of Kenya's many colourful pioneer settlers. He owned much of Chiromo Forest, prime land in central Nairobi, and farmed the land beneath Kilimambogo, where he settled in 1905 and which he named after a mysterious encounter with West African witchcraft. The family's hospitality to friends on their 8,094-hectare (20,000-acre) **Juja Farm**, now a large co-operative, was legendary.

Macmillan is buried in the place he loved best, together with his wife and their faithful servant of more than seventy-five years, Louise Decker, who died on 1 December, 1938. The three simple **graves** are hewn out of mountain rock each set with a simple inscribed marble plaque.

From the national park it's only a few kilometres into Thika.

Nairobi-Thika

Most people drive direct from Nairobi to Thika along the new dual carriage highway which roughly follows the alignment of the railway that Sir Percy Girouard, an Anglo-French Governor initiated in the second decade of this century.

Before coming to Kenya, Sir Percy, a railway engineer, had been in charge of the construction of a major line from Kanó to Lagos in Nigeria. But still appalled by the cost of the "Lunatic Line" Whitehall were aghast at his suggestion that they should pay for another line.

Out jogging in Nairobi one morning Sir Percy was struck by the idea that he might win their approval for a low-cost tramway instead. His ruse worked. Built to the same gauge as the Mombasa-Kisumu line, for years afterwards the line to Thika was shown on all maps as the Thika Tramway.

But while the road journey takes only thirty minutes, it's more than ninety by rail. Queen Elizabeth II of Britain, on a sentimental return to the spot where she became Queen in 1952, rode this track on the Royal Train in 1983 — passing through **Kahawa,** the Kiswahili word for coffee, the military garrison built by the British.

Completed just before Independence, it was handed over to the Kenya Government by the departing colonialists and is now the **Kenyatta University** campus.

After this, the train wound through **Ruiru** which is the headquarters for Kenya's **Coffee Research Centre.** The **Ruiru river,** flowing off the **Aberdares,** brought Nairobi its first street lighting when it was harnessed as a source of power in 1913.

The Royal Train passed that first hydroelectric power plant and continued through the grounds of the **Ruiru Club** where hundreds of members — patriotic British expatriates — turned out on the club's **golf course** to greet their Majesty.

From there, the train travelled on to **Mangu** where one of Kenya's oldest schools was established long ago by an order of Catholic White Father missionaries. From here it's a short ride into Thika.

The railway established its prominence as a major town. Although within sight and earshot of some of the most fertile land in the country — rich volcanic soils where coffee and fruit burgeon with prolific ease — Thika, often described as the "Birmingham" of Kenya, now boasts tanneries, vehicle assembly plants, fruit processing factories, textile mills, grain mills, chemical factories, and packaging industries.

It's odd to think that just ninety years ago this area was as wild and thick with game as the Maasai Mara today.

Though unprepossessing as a community, Thika also has a **country club** to the west of the town, with rolling fairways and verdant greens for golf. In 1983, Queen Elizabeth II ate lunch here before driving on to Nyeri.

The club is not far from the **Blue Posts Hotel,** built in the first decade of the century, close to the **Chania waterfalls** where Churchill camped during his African journey in 1907. He had hoped to shoot a lion but, though he heard many, was frustrated.

Machakos: Hills and Orchards

Machakos is sixty-five kilometres (40 miles) from Nairobi. Follow **Uhuru Highway** out on to the **Mombasa Road,** past the Jomo Kenyatta Airport turnoff, and through Athi River. After forty-six kilometres (28 miles), just before the **toll station,** there's a left turn and then, sixteen kilometres (ten miles) on, **Machakos.** You can also make a circular excursion in either direction via Tala and Kangundo (See "Mountain of the Buffalo").

Ringed by the green and pleasant **Ukambani Hills,** it was at **Machakos** that Britain's first upcountry administrator in Kenya, Manchester-born John Ainsworth, made his headquarters in 1889.

The mudbrick fort that Ainsworth built in Machakos no longer exists. In fact, his request to build it was turned down but when the answer arrived he'd already completed the work.

The Machakos area is the capital of Kenya's Akambaland whose ethnic people have inhabited this region for at least the last five centuries. The town is named after the Akamba chief and seer, Masaku, who predicted the coming of the railway — "the iron snake"— and the pestilent plagues that followed. Smallpox and rinderpest decimated both human and animal populations throughout a large portion of the region. Masaku died in the first decade of this century.

In the hills above the town Kenya Orchards Mua Hills **jam factory** is the legacy of missionary Reverend Stuart Watt who, at the turn of the century, walked all the way from Mombasa with his wife. When he went lame she had to carry him for part of the journey.

Above: Colourful market at Tala, near Kangundo, in Kambaland.

Apart from fruit for making jam, the Reverend also introduced wattle and eucalyptus trees.

The Church Missionary Society arrived in 1895 to add wheat, and ten years later the South African Boers pioneered an ostrich farm. It was here that the Mackinnon's Imperial British East Africa Company established the first inland African Training Centre, taken over by the Protectorate government in 1914.

The **clock tower** put up to mark the visit of Britain's Princess Margaret in October 1956 during colonial times is the only monument of note. It still stands in the town centre at the main roundabout — though it always shows three o'clock in the afternoon whatever time you visit.

Nonetheless, the clock tower and the old **pre-Independence buildings** and tree-lined streets give Machakos a distinct rustic charm.

Centre of the town's social ambit is the long established **Machakos Sports Club,** though cricket no longer continues. The discovery of a box of cricket balls in the 1980s caused undue worry to non-cricketing members of the committee who thought they had stumbled upon a cache of revolutionary hand grenades left over from World War II.

Sisal basket weaving is a thriving cottage industry and the principal occupation for many of the local women. The **Machakos Handicrafts Centre** was set up by a self-help women's group. They work in a small shop full of finished and half-finished baskets, heaps of sisal and hand-made leather straps.

The **Mwangaza Gift Centre** is also worth visiting since it sells some splendid wood and goatskin drums, although these are not so easy to carry home.

From Machakos the road winds down the hills on to the dry, arid plain of the Akamba and continues through forlorn scrub and desperately poor smallholdings for 130 kilometres (80 miles) to **Kitui**, well off the tourist track, but an interesting and little-seen side of Kenya.

Kitui was the home town of Kivoi, the most celebrated Akamba trader. It was he who met the German Johann Krapf in Mombasa in the late 1840s and guided him back to Kitui where the missionary became the first European known to have seen Mount Kenya (See 'The Dust and the Ashes', Part One).

Heartland Kenya: Magic Mountains, Moorlands Wild

The central highlands of Kenya are crowned by 5,189-metre-high (17,058-feet) snowcapped, **Mount Kenya,** the glistening, frosted coronet astride the Equator that gave the country its name.

These intensively-farmed highlands support the country's highest rural population — on all the lower slopes and much of the high ground too.

Years ago, the majority of European settlers established their farms in these fertile "White Highlands" on land that for centuries had been cultivated by local communities. Suddenly the Kikuyu, Meru, and Embu farmers found themselves "squatters" on their own land.

Their smouldering dissatisfaction culminated in the freedom war which, for the most part, was carried out from the forests and moorlands of Mount Kenya and the **Aberdares** to the plains beneath.

In a loose circumference central Kenya embraces **Muranga** in the south, the Aberdares in the west, **Nyeri** in the centre, **Nyahururu** and **Nanyuki** in the north, and **Meru** and **Embu** in the east.

As you travel through the highlands, the tremendous panoramas and rapid changes of light and colour are both surprising and rewarding. Rainbows curve over the green sunlit land as black thunder clouds dance around the peaks of the mountains.

Dominating the landscape, Mount Kenya's twin spires thrust upwards through shrouds of mist and storm — which suddenly lift, exposing its dramatically-beautiful profile. With a base diameter of more than 200 kilometres (125 miles), it is one of the largest free-standing volcanic mountains in the world.

To the east and south, the mountain slopes slip steeply away to the **Tana River** basin and the broad arid plains that end in the Akamba's Ukambani hills. And in the north they drop even more precipitously to the desert floor.

Westward it drops more gently to the rolling uplands of **Laikipia,** which are even drier than the east and, for the most part, treeless.

The central highlands remain magically unspoilt — a pastoral idyll of small market

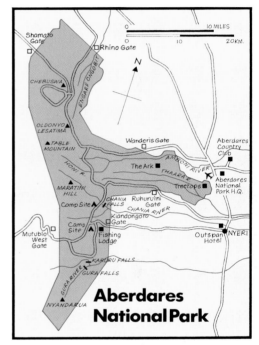

Overleaf: Giant groundsel in rare 20-year bloom above 11,000 feet on the Aberdares.

Opposite: 275-metre-drop (900-feet) Gura Falls, Aberdare National Park.

Above: Fly fishing in the Aberdares — a delight of trout streams.

towns and well-tended smallholdings. Indeed, after the game parks and the coast, this natural circuit is the most travelled in Kenya.

Where to stay

In Karatina, Mountain Lodge (5-star) (Mount Kenya Forest reserve), book through African Tours and Hotels, Utali House, Nairobi, Elephant and Castle (Budget), Karatina Tourist Lodge (2-star); New Karatina Lamu Lodge (Budget). In Nyeri, Greenhills Hotel (3-star), Outspan (4-star), White Rhino (3-star). In Mweiga, Aberdare Country Club (5-star). In Nyahururu, Thomson's Falls Lodge (homely 3-star). In Naro Moru, Naro Moru River Lodge (4-star). In Nanyuki, Mount Kenya Safari Club (5-star), Sportsman's Arms (Budget and rustic); In Meru Pig and Whistle (Budget). In Embu, Izaak Walton Inn (3-star). There are many others. See Listings for "Hotels".

National Parks and Reserves

In the Aberdares National Park, Treetops Hotel book through Block Hotels, Rehema House, Nairobi; and The Ark, book through Lonrho Hotels, Bruce House, Nairobi. In Meru National Park, Meru Mulika Lodge (4-star),

book through Msafiri Inns, Utali House, Nairobi; and Leopard Rock Safari Lodge (self-service), book through AA Travel, Union Towers, Nairobi.

Game sanctuaries

El Karama Ranch, book through AA Travel, Nairobi; Sweetwaters Tented Camp (5-star, *circa* Adnan Kashoggi), book through Lonrho Hotels, Bruce House, Nairobi.

Sightseeing

The main road from Nairobi runs through **Thika** and continues for a few kilometres, to **Kabete** where the old road, left, used mostly by buses and *matatus,* runs on to **Saba Saba** and Muranga.

A new road that starts here continues straight on to Sagana, past **Makuyu Country Club**, a legacy from the settlers who, far from the amenities of town life, had to make their own recreations. The club, one of three golf clubs in this region, set amid olive-green coffee plantations close to an abandoned sisal plantation, stands on the border between traditional Kikuyu and Kamba lands.

From here, a rough road, right, leads east to **Kandara Valley** in the northern lee of **Kilimambogo.** Ruggedly beautiful, the close-cropped crests of the once-forested hills combined with frequent drought, indicate why this potentially productive area is now marginal land. The dirt road is made of deep, fine-grained sand — a finger of the northern deserts only an hour's journey from the Kenya capital.

Straight on from Makuyu, eighty-seven kilometres (54 miles) from Nairobi and forty-five kilometres (28 miles) from Thika, Muranga was established in 1900 as Fort Hall, a British administrative outpost, which consisted initially of "two grass huts within a stone wall and a ditch".

Today it is growing swiftly as a farm entrepôt. It sits on the brow of a cliff above the **Tana River.** A new road cuts along the lower part of the cliff, through countryside fat with farms, to Nyeri.

Perched on a hillside above the bustling town, the **Memorial Cathedral Church** of St James was consecrated by the Archbishop of Canterbury on 18 May, 1955, as a memorial to the thousands of Kikuyu who died during the fight for Independence. The church has a fascinating mural by the artist, Elimu Njau.

It depicts the Nativity, Last Supper and Crucifixion — with a black Christ in a typical Muranga landscape. The Nativity scene shows a Kikuyu manger with African shepherds and womenfolk bearing gifts. The Last Supper is set in a *banda* with giraffe and acacia trees beside it — and Kikuyu villages straggle up Golgotha's slopes.

The Kikuyu consider Muranga their homeland, principally because between Muranga and Nyeri on a minor switchback road at **Mugeka** lies Mukuruene wa Nya-Gathanga — the "tree of the building site" — which, according to Kikuyu legend, is the Garden of Eden.

In this grove of wild fig trees the Kikuyu god, *Ngei*, commanded Gikuyu and Mumbi, the father and mother of all **Kikuyu**, to make their home. Here **Mumbi** raised nine daughters who later became the founding matriarchs of the nine Kikuyu clans. Both fig trees and Mount Kenya (known as *Kirinyaga*, the home of *Ngei*) are still considered sacred by the Kikuyu.

To get to Mukuruene wa Nya-Gathanga, you drive eighteen kilometres (11 miles) to Mugeka. The fig grove is just beyond the village and although there is no longer a museum, the original fig tree, which was split by lightning, has been replaced.

It could, indeed, be Eden for here on the slopes of the Aberdares, the land is bountiful. The mountain massif falls steeply away to the many enchanting valleys which have been cultivated by smallholders.

Lured by the crisp air, open moorlands, and gushing streams with trout, the Europeans were quick to settle these mountains. The scene is just as pastoral today — rugged rock outcrops interspersed with green meadows stocked with herds of grazing sheep and cattle.

Out on the other side of Muranga, the old road and railway head towards **Sagana** where there is a colourful **market, leather tannery, fish farm** and **railway warehouses** for coffee and grain crops.

Turn left on to the main Nairobi-Nyeri road that clings to the north-west foothills of Mount Kenya as it climbs up the steep *Pole Pole* "slowly slowly" hill — to **Karatina** in Nyeri district. Fertile farms, lush with groves of banana palms, vegetables, fruit, tea, coffee, and flowers, all stepping down the hillsides in neat terraces, are irrigated year-round by the swift waters of the Sagana River and its tributaries.

Karatina, 128 kilometres (80 miles) from Nairobi and forty-one kilometres (25 miles) from Muranga, is an unkempt town whose only interest is as the major stronghold of the Mau Mau movement during the freedom battle, and the threshold to what is arguably Kenya's most magnificent country.

Here, the rounded foothills of the Aberdares and Mount Kenya merge in a cluster of domed crowns, many of them now cleared of forest and turned into tidy farms.

During the dry season, Karatina is a swirl of dust: during the rains, it becomes a mud bath. But its **market** is one of the most colourful in Kenya — a brilliant mixture of cloths, grains, utensils, vivacious traders, and argumentative buyers.

To the east, in the forest reserve of the Mount Kenya foothills behind Karatina, lies **Mountain Lodge,** signposted by an ancient tree at the roadside, with a cleft in its bole, which was used as a Mau Mau mailbox. Urgent messages with notice of British troop movements were left in the cleft to be picked up by other guerilla forest units.

Not far from the lodge, in a forest glade, is **Sagana State Lodge** (photography prohibited) which was given to Princess Elizabeth by the colonial government when she visited Kenya with Prince Philip in 1952. It was on the lawns of this lodge, after a night spent watching game at Treetops, that she was told of the death of her father, King George VI.

West of this lodge lies Kiganjo, the closest that the railway came to Nyeri, although for decades it was called Nyeri Station. Today,

Above: Fading blooms of lobelia on Kenya's high moorlands.

Kiganjo is the base for **Kenya's Police Training College,** where many of the country's award-winning athletes first spring to prominence.

From Karatina, the road rolls on another twenty-seven kilometres (17 miles), following the hills like a gigantic roller-coaster, alongside fast-flowing streams, into **Nyeri.** Where it enters the town, 155 kilometres (96 miles) from Nairobi, an avenue of jacaranda trees sends blossoms cascading like confetti in late September and October to carpet the road a rich purple.

Home to the **administrative headquarters** of Kenya's Central Province, which occupy the former cricket ground where once a brilliant mass of blazing flame trees grew, Nyeri has expanded over the year into a sprawling and dynamic commercial capital.

Nestling in the middle of a broad vale, embraced by the green hills of Mount Kenya and the Aberdares, Nyeri's many **markets, shopping centres** and *jua kali* (self-employed) mechanics and woodworkers clearly define its entrepreneurial spirit.

It was the frontline town during the war for Independence and the main street, **Kimathi Way,** commemorates the memory of the famous Kikuyu freedom fighter, Dedan Kimathi. A simple **stone cenotaph** has been erected "To the Memory of the Members of the Kikuyu Tribe who Died in the Fight for Freedom 1951-1957".

At the far end of Kimathi Way there is also a **monument** from the colonial days — a now useless **clock** and a dry **fountain** "erected by the People of Kenya in memory of His Majesty George V".

To the right stands **St. Cuthbert's Presbyterian Church,** built in 1926, but since fallen into decay.

White Rhino

The **Outspan** and **White Rhino** were originally two **settler hotels,** now owned by indigenous business men and still flourishing after more than sixty years.

The Outspan, headquarters for **Treetops,** was built by Eric and Betty Sherbrooke-Walker who bought the land on which it stands when it was a patch of bare scrub above the **Chania River** facing Mount Kenya.

To the west stood the Aberdares, and to the north the land plunged into the fern-shrouded gorge where the Chania River boiled over the rocks. The Sherbrooke-Walkers could hardly

Above: Baden-Powell's last home, Paxtu, in the grounds of Nyeri's Outspan Hotel.

believe their good fortune.

"The more we looked at it, the more strongly we felt it was the only place for our hotel."

They bought twenty-eight hectares (70 acres) of land from the colonial government and set about building. The **clubhouse,** made of cedar bark shingles, and the **golf course** — facing Mount Kenya's glistening glaciers — already existed. All around the countryside was being transformed into coffee plantations, farmlands, and sawmills.

A neighbouring sawmiller, Grace Berry, won the Sherbrooke-Walker's competition to find a name for their hotel receiving a bottle of champagne for suggesting "The Outspan" — where, "at the end of the day's journey, the traveller outspans the weary oxen".

The White Rhino, built by a trio of aristocrats — Berkeley Cole, Lord Cranworth, and Sandy Herd — is sometimes known as "the hotel which charges on sight".

Sherbrooke-Walker, had been private secretary to the founder of the World Scout Movement and hero of Mafeking, Lord Baden Powell, who visited Kenya in 1935. He also fell in love with "the wonderful views over the plains to the bold snow peaks of Mount Kenya. . . . The nearer to Nyeri, the nearer to bliss", he noted.

Three years later, in October 1938, he retired to **Paxtu,** the cottage that the Sherbrooke-Walkers built within the hotel grounds for him and his wife, Chief Girl Guide, Lady Olave Baden Powell.

When Baden Powell died on 8 January, 1941, he was buried, amidst British civilian and military graves, in the graveyard of **St. Peter's** Anglican church, facing the mountain. Inscribed on his tomb is the Boy Scout's "Gone Home" sign — a circle and dot. Lady Baden Powell is buried besides him and today their graves serve as a pilgrimage shrine for scouts and guides worldwide.

From Nyeri one road travels west up into the **Aberdares** to the two eastern gates of the **Aberdare National Park,** a second north to **Naro Moru** and **Nanyuki,** and another northwest past the tracks to **Treetops** and **The Ark,** each on separate salients of the Aberdare National Park, then through **Mweiga,** and on over the flanks of the Aberdares, across lonely forested ridges and wide savannahs, to **Nyahururu** (Thomson's Falls) on the northern fringes of the Highlands.

The Aberdares: The Queen's Cave and Happy Valley

The road west out of Nyeri leads up into the **Aberdare National Park.** Established as a 767-square-kilometre (311-square-mile) sanctuary in 1948, this isolated volcanic massif forms part of the eastern wall of the Rift Valley. The mountain is ringed by one of Kenya's largest forest reserves, covering more than 1,000 square kilometres (386 square miles).

The Kikuyu call this compact mountain range **Nyandarua** ("drying hide") after the shape of its silhouette. Joseph Thomson came upon the range on his wandering *Through Masai Land* in 1883, and renamed them after Lord Aberdare, president of the Royal Geographical Society.

Steeper, starker, and with denser rain-forest, the Aberdares are neither as densely-settled or as extensively-farmed as Mount Kenya, except in the south.

Though scaling their heights demands little mountaineering skill, it requires monumental stamina to reach the crown: the rarefied air sucks the breath from the lungs with every stride.

But the views over the Rift Valley are spectacular. The clouds curl around the 3,968-metre-high (13,020-feet) bluff of **Lesatima**, the highest point. From here, the ground falls quickly away to the broad moorland plateau which stretches south forty-six kilometres (28 miles) to the second-highest and slightly more precipitous point of **Kinangop** at 3,906 metres (12,815 feet). A **stone cairn** commemorates the first ascent by a European early in the century. These two peaks and the moorlands between them offer trekkers some magnificent walks.

In the west, above the Wanjohi — "Happy" — Valley, are the peaks of Kipipiri around 3,350 metres (11,000 feet) and, somewhat lower, **"The Elephant"**. All are relatively easy to climb, given good weather (See "Kenya's Mountains"), but remember that you can only walk in the park with the approval of the Park Warden at Mweiga.

Vegetation varies with altitude. The lush, well-tended vegetable, tea, and coffee smallholdings give way to the bamboo-belt between the 2,100 and 2,400 metre (7,000-8,000 feet) contours. The forests belt begins around 3,000 metres (10,000 feet).

Here are some of Kenya's most ancient trees, cedar and hagenia, whose gnarled and rheumy limbs are reminiscent of Tolkien fantasies, with treetops often shrouded in clammy fingers of mist and entwined with Old Man's Beard (Spanish moss) whose wispy festoons dangle from every branch and leaf.

Higher up, the forest gives way to alpine oddities, including giant heather, tussock grass sometimes a metre or two deep, St John's wort, lobelia and groundsel, which grows to astonishing heights at this altitude under the ultra-violet glare on the Equator.

Heavy rain falls through most of the year, filling the many clear streams and waterfalls that are etched in deep ravines on the eastern and western flanks of the mountain.

The roaring waters of **Queen's Cave Waterfall** — so called because Queen Elizabeth of Britain lunched there and the remains of the wooden pavilion testify to her visit — cascade into a small ravine resembling a fairy glade. You reach it by climbing down the cliff.

Another spectacular fall, Kenya's deepest, is the **Gura**. It plummets more than 300 metres (1,000 feet) into an impenetrable ravine opposite the **Karura Falls,** which drop almost 275 metres (900 feet) to merge downstream into the **Chania River.**

These waters, rippling like a pliant ribbon in the strong winds that gust along the gorge, were filmed for the scenic aerial essay in *Out of Africa.*

All these natural wonders occur well above the Aberdare forest belt where the wildlife is fascinating (See "National Parks", In Brief). Birdlife is abundant and varied, with more than 200 recorded species. Trout can be caught in the moorland streams.

During the 1950s the high moorlands above the 3,000 metres (10,000 feet) contour were the strategic hideout of Mau Mau freedom fighters. When the British tried to flush them out with bombing runs over the plateau, many a cave and impenetrable forest served as a shelter.

The moorlands have some rare melanistic leopard, serval, and genets. The high altitude and closeness to the Equator have turned their coats black. There are some mythical beasts, too, including a spotted lion which has never been seen.

Game here is little used to humans. The

Above: Queen Elizabeth II of Britain on her return to Treetops.

lion in particular have a well-earned reputation for ferocity. At one time, after campers had been held in terror through the night, camping in the park was suspended. One beast even attacked a Land Rover, shredding the tyres while the terrified passengers cowered inside.

To the frustration of visitors — but to the benefit of the beasts and plants — the park is often inaccessible during the rains. Even in the dry season, the high altitude and rough trails make 4WD vehicles mandatory.

One gate from Naivasha lies above 3,000 metre (10,000 feet) — up a rough, rocky road that amazingly turns into tarmac near the top. It was laid in 1959 for the visit of Britain's Queen Mother. Several other gates lead from Nyeri, Mweiga, and Pesi on the eastern face (See "Kenya's Mountains").

Near one of the gates from Nyeri, there's a **fishing camp** with log cabin at around 3,000 metres (10,000 feet). Both brown and rainbow trout flourish in the icy streams and some have weighed in at seven kilos (15 lbs).

The park is a delight of rolling downs, open vistas, little dells, icy tarns, bubbling streams and waterfalls. With Mount Kenya, eighty kilometres (50 miles) away across the

Laikipia plateau, it forms Kenya's major watershed.

To the west, the steep Rift wall deters game, but it was here, in the high Wanjohi Valley, that divides the Kipipiri peak from the main massif, that a concentration of settlers in the 1920s and 1930s created the myth of "Happy Valley". This lush, forested region became a *nirvana* for the titled and aristocratic whites who settled in Kenya between the World Wars.

Some were black sheep, pensioned off by their lordly families to enjoy their frolics without shaming the ancestral home. They built great feudal manors and wooden chateaux, reminiscent of the Middle Ages, tended graceful gardens, and farmed.

In their spare time they held champagne parties which ended with keys thrown on the table and spouses departing with somebody else's husband or wife. These and similar antics earned Wanjohi its "Happy Valley" nickname.

Its greatest notoriety came in the 1940s with the murder of Lord "Joss" Errol, a story that became a best-selling book and film, *White Mischief,* made on location in Kenya.

Today, the manors and chateaux have collapsed or fallen into shambling disrepair and are used as cowsheds and chicken houses. Kikuyu smallholders and peasant farmers tend the valley lands where little evidence remains of the antics of former days, except for entertaining legends told by the few remaining veteran white settlers.

The House that Peter Pan Built

The road from Nyeri to Nyahururu switchbacks out of the town over a series of steep hills cut through coffee plantations and then arrives at a T-junction. Straight on is **Kiganjo** and the main **Nanyuki** road. Left is the **Nyahururu** (Thomson's Falls) road.

Just a few kilometres along this, left, is the turn along a track through more coffee plantations to the **Treetops** gate of the Aberdare National Park.

Perhaps the most famous hotel in Africa, it was Eric Sherbrooke-Walker's brainchild after his wife Betty's whimsical hankerings for a Wendy-style tree house (inspired by J. M. Barrie's play, *Peter Pan*).

The first recorded visitors in the two-room tree house, perched precariously in the fork of a fig tree, spent a night there in November 1932.

Twenty years later, when Princess Elizabeth was escorted through the game-filled forest to climb the ladder into the tree and to return a queen, she followed a distinguished list of royalty and celebrities — Tsar Ferdinand of Bulgaria, the Duke and Duchess of Gloucester, Mr. and Mrs. Neville Chamberlain, and Earl Mountbatten. By then the treehouse had expanded to four rooms, but in 1954 it was burned down by the Mau Mau.

Its replacement was finished in 1957 — on a site opposite the original fig tree — with "seven wash basins and water closets". Since then, it has grown considerably and now accommodates almost eighty guests.

As darkness descends, the floodlights bathe the salt lick and waterhole below, where elephants amble in to drink.

For many, this lodge offers the definitive Kenya experience, even though the forest in which the treehouse once stood has vanished and the settlement has moved up close to the boundary fence.

But Treetops remains unique and was given the royal accolade in November 1983 by the Queen's sentimental homecoming to the spot where she became Queen. The fact that it's always booked up, and not just by safari-suited package-tourists, affirms its attraction.

Twelve kilometres (seven miles) from Nyeri, **Mweiga** town serves as trade centre for a large area spread out over the **Laikipia** plains between the Aberdares and Naro Moru. Its principal distinction is as the headquarters of the Aberdare and Mount Kenya National Parks.

Close by is the **Aberdare Country Club,** an elegant baronial style country home set in sprawling and superbly-landscaped gardens on the side of Mweiga hill. It's also the departure base for the third of central Kenya's three forest lodges, **The Ark.**

Aberdare Country Club is worth a visit in its own right. The grounds are immaculate and colourful, with excellent golfing and horse-riding.

Some eighteen kilometres (11 miles) from the club and 370 metres (1,200 feet) higher, you enter the **Ark Gate** in the Aberdare National Park to arrive soon after at The Ark, built at the end of the 1960s in the shape of an ark, in an open glade with a natural waterhole.

A drawbridge opens on to a wooden catwalk that leads to a fine twentieth-century replica of what Noah used to escape the flood, with comforts he could never have dreamed of — comfortable beds, hot showers, gourmet food, and piping hot cups of tea.

Once the guests are "aboard" for the night they are truly a captive audience because the drawbridge is drawn up until next morning.

As darkness falls, visitors take their place in front of the large, panoramic window and wait to see which forest inhabitants will appear first. Every dawn the hunter records the number and species of animals seen in the Ark's log book.

Elephant, rhino, and bongo — rare nocturnal antelope with bold black stripes on chestnut flanks — are the star players in the Ark's nightly pageant of wildlife (See "Great and small, wild and wonderful", Part Three).

Should something spectacular appear at the waterhole and salt lick in the middle of the night, true-grit nocturnal enthusiasts are woken by an alarm. Old hands switch it off — content to slumber in the wild.

Beyond Mweiga the road rides high over the flanks of the Aberdares with fantastic views over the Laikipia plateau far below and Mount Kenya rising on the other side.

Above: Thompson's Fall's Nyahururu.

Some forty kilometres (30 miles) beyond Nyeri, there's a right turn to **Ngobit.** The main road continues past the link fence that guards the western perimeter of the vast **Solio Ranch** for many years a successful private sanctuary for Kenya's imperilled rhino population.

It was so successful that, in 1987, Kenya's Wildlife Conservation and Management Department began a major translocation operation — removing many rhino to specially-created sanctuaries within national parks and reserves. Indeed, the Solio stock may well provide the breeding nucleus that will revitalise Kenya's rhino population.

Ol Pejeta, another nearby private reserve on the Laikipia, covers 6,500 hectares (16,000 acres) of scrub savannah and thorn. In 1984, film star Brooke Shields spent an idyllic day there among the ranch's elephant and lion. Her memorable moment came when a pride feasted on cattle meat in the back of the pick-up she was driving.

For many years Ol Pejeta was the Kenya playground of armaments billionaire Adnan Kashoggi, but in the wake of the Iran arms deal it was seized by the Kenya subsidiary of the giant Lonrho group in settlement of debts Kashoggi owed the conglomerate. He had already transferred the Mount Kenya Safari Club to them.

Lonrho have turned Ol Pejeta into a luxurious holiday resort. Guests are accommodated at Kashoggi's Italian-style ranch house with its gold-tapped bathrooms, or in the ranch's luxury tented camp, **Sweet Waters.**

Beyond Solio, the road continues through **Ndaragwa,** past a right turn along a dirt trail to **Nanyuki** and **Rumuruti,** and a dirt trail leading to the **Pesi gate**, the northern extension of the Aberdare National Park, then on to Nyahururu, 100 kilometres (60 miles) from Nyeri.

Pesi lies just beneath Lesatima's eastern face. In the 1960s it was pure forest, but it has since been carved out as smallholdings and medium-size farms that are fertile and productive except during the periodic droughts that grip Kenya.

The rolling fields of lush green grass and herds of dairy cattle which suddenly appear after the steep drive through the forest and bamboo are reminiscent of European meadowland. It's hard to imagine anything could trouble the peaceful atmosphere.

But in 1985 lion and elephant came rampaging down from their lofty forest sanctuary. The elephant pillaged maize and vegetables, and the lion killed cattle. Forest wardens and villagers dug a deep moat, but still the cats came in the night to take the herds.

This incident symbolizes the increasing conflict which preoccupies Kenya; wildlife versus people and the demand by both for living space.

Thomson's Falls

Nyahururu, one of Kenya's youngest and highest towns, sits at 2,360 metres (7,743 feet). It's name in Maa means "where waters run deep" but it is still better known outside Kenya as Thomson's Falls — named by Joseph Thomson in 1883 in honour of his father.

In the 1920s, it was nothing much more than a log cabin for a settler angling club. But with the arrival of the railway in 1929, Thomson's Falls proper was born.

The town nestles against the sweep of the great **Marmanet Forest**, from the base of which the Laikipia Plains stretch all the way to the black pyramid of Mount Kenya. Sleepy and undisturbed, Thomson's Falls reflects the pace of the agricultural communities it serves.

It earned brief fame as the high-altitude training camp where Kenya's Olympic medallists prepared for their trial in Mexico. But it's the seventy-two-metre-deep (237-feet) falls which Thomson came across on his trek north that give the town its atmosphere.

In spate, the waters of the **Ewaso Narok River,** born on the slopes of Lesatima, gather themselves in the hippo-infested marsh and bogland that lie atop the falls and then thunder over the narrow lip in a cascade that amounts to around a million litres (220,000 gallons) a minute.

In too-frequently dry Kenya, Nyahururu's planners have finally succumbed temptation, and at one side of the falls there is now an obtrusive waterworks, which supplies the town's growing population.

Nonetheless, this is a popular tourist stop-over and picnic spot, especially for those *en route* between Samburu and the Maasai Mara Game Reserve.

The path leading to the bottom of the falls is dangerous when wet. However, don't attempt to climb up again by any other route

— the cliffs are extremely loose.

If you have several hours to spare, you might perhaps enjoy a longer walk. Go out of the lodge entrance gate, left over the bridge and left again down the other side of the forested valley, following the Ewaso Narok river.

If you're lucky, you might see troops of colobus monkeys jostling the branches of over-hanging trees. A few kilometres downstream you come to a point where you can cross the river on a fallen tree or boulder and return to the lodge.

To Rumuruti

From Nyahururu, a fine new road leads thirty-four kilometres (21 miles) northward down the steep gradient of the Marmanet Forest to the ranching town of Rumuruti, a major gateway to the northern deserts.

Headquarters of the district administration for a large area of the Laikipia, the tarmac sweeps into the dusty one-street town and out again along a gravel dirt road that eventually lands up on the shores of Lake Turkana (See "Great Rift Valley: the land that was Eden").

The tarmac road has brought Rumuruti into mainstream Kenya but watching the Samburu and Maasai idling around the bars and *dukas* on the one street, and the relaxed indolence of everybody else, you get a sense of the isolation it once enjoyed as a cattle town where European settlers, raising their beef herds in the arid savannah around these parts, met and quaffed ales in the town's old club. Most have gone now.

The **District Commissioner's office**, with the Kenya flag flying, is at the far end of the street, just past the **post office**, where the tarmac ends and the gravel begins.

To Gilgil

Heading west out of Nyahururu, the road to **Ol Kalau** and **Gilgil** takes you through **Ol Joro Orok,** under the shadow of the northern wall of the Aberdares and Lesatima where the hippo-infested waterbird sanctuary of **Lake Ilpolosat**, dreams on, unvisited by any tourists — a hauntingly-lovely sheet of water. It's some kilometres to the left of the main road on a bumpy farm track, midway between Joro Orok and Ol Kalau.

This wildfowl paradise is virtually undisturbed by duck hunters, but many of the peasant farmers have to keep a wary eye on the hippo which tumble out of its water at night to raid their *shambas* (farms).

Ol Kalau, fifty-two kilometres (32 miles) from Nyahururu, is a rapidly-growing farm and trade centre, the moorlands around it intensively cultivated on fair-sized holdings.

Until the 1970s the only tarmac between Gilgil and Nyahururu was sixteen kilometres (10 miles) stretching from one side of the town to the other. Some kilometres beyond Ol Kalau on the thirty-kilometre (19-mile) stretch to Gilgil there's a left turn along a dirt road that takes you into the high valley between the main Aberdare massive and Kipipiri. This is Wanjohi Valley — the "Happy Valley" of *White Mischief* fame.

You can also drive in reverse direction — Gilgil-Nyahururu (See "Great Rift Valley: the land that was Eden").

To Subukia

A new highway from Nyahururu down the eastern wall of the Rift, built in the 1980s, makes a scenically dramatic route to **Nakuru** via **Subukia**.

As you leave Nyahururu, the new highway plunges down a series of faults in the scarp to a series of breathtaking hairpin bends which wind into an African Shangri-la, Subukia.

Already the cool highland air has begun to change to the sweltering heat of the Rift Valley: sugar, coffee, and bananas burgeon in this hothouse environment which remains as remote as the world of the Middle Ages.

Even the little Anglican church that was built in 1951 reflects the feeling of time and setting removed. With its Norman architecture, it could have stood in its colourful gardens — overlooking the great divide of the Rift and the faraway lakes scintillating in the noonday sun — for a thousand years.

For the Maasai, these lush pastures were their secret retreat from the drylands when they occupied the Laikipia. They called it *Ol Momoi Sidai*, (the "Beautiful Place").

But in 1911 the Maasai were evicted and the land was opened up to settler families. Looking around at the soft, Arcadian beauty of this high valley, it's not hard to understand why they chose this spot.

Subukia itself has a small number of **hotels** as well as a helpful **police post** where you can obtain up-to-date road and route information. For the cross-country shortcut to **Lake Bogoria** you can drive several kilometres past

the quaint, Anglican **St Peter's Church**, (visible on the road before you reach Subukia) to the signposted **Nakuru/Bogoria** fork. Although rough in parts, the road down is normally quite passable — and incredibly dramatic.

This will give you a special feel for the Rift Valley's striking topography as it drops from one monumental block of land to another, with dramatic changes of climate and scenery.

When you reach the plain at the bottom, you'll have an indelible impression of the way the earth split apart and sank to form the Rift.

At the bottom look out for landmarks such as a disused railway line, which you cross at a place called **Milton's Sidings. Kisanana** is a useful night stop, and **Mugurin**, an almost-imperceptible village, is a good place for a refreshing cup of tea and *chapatis*.

Mount Kenya: On God's Mountain

With its many ridges and valleys, radiating like the spokes of a wheel, the bulk of Mount Kenya straddles the Equator. Though its highest point lies seventeen kilometres (10 miles) to the south, the Equator cuts across the northern shoulders at a height of 3,350 metres (11,000 feet).

The mountain lies 193 kilometres (120 miles) north-east of Nairobi and 480 kilometres (300 miles) west of the Kenya coast. It is regarded as the perfect model of an Equatorial mountain.

Soon after his colleague Johanne Rebmann had caught that first tantalizing glimpse of the snows of Kilimanjaro, missionary Johann Krapf saw the glaciers of Mount Kenya, on 3 December, 1849, from Kitui, nearly 160 kilometres (100 miles) away.

Nineteenth-century European geographers dismissed the idea of snow on the Equator as ridiculous. But forty years after Krapf's first sighting Thomson's delight at his discovery was lyrical.

"Through a rugged and picturesque depression in the range [Aberdares] rose a gleaming snow-white peak with sparkling facets which scintillated with the superb beauty of a colossal diamond. It was in fact the very image of a great crystal or sugar loaf."

The twin peaks of **Batian** and **Nelion** crown

Above: Metal cross, a gift of Pope Pius XI to Nyeri's Consolata Mission, was set in place on Point Lenana, Mount Kenya, on 31 January 1933.

Mount Kenya National Park. It is one of the world's highest national parks, with 704 square kilometres (286 square miles) of forest, moorland, rock, and ice.

The mountain slopes above 3,100 metres (10,170 feet), with their two salients, **Naro Moru** and the **Sirimon**, down to approximately 2,600 metres (8,530 feet), were declared a National Park in 1949. The lower area, between 1,600 and 3,100 metres (5,250 and 1,020 feet), constitutes **Mount Kenya Forest Reserve.**

The park became a 717-square-kilometre (277-square-mile) UNESCO Biosphere Reserve in April 1978, along with 1,420 square kilometres (548 square miles) of the Mount Kenya forest reserve. The upper base of the mountain is close to 100 kilometres (60 miles) across.

Batian, 5,199 metres (17,058 feet), and Nelion, 5,192 metres (17,036 feet), are the remains of a gigantic eroded plug that once thrust another 3,000 metres (10,000 feet) and more into the sky. Its Kikuyu name, *Kirinyaga*, is derived from *Kere Nyaga* ("White Mountain").

The first Europeans to venture to any heights on the mountain were Count Samuel Teleki von Szek and Ludwig von Hohnel from Austria who followed much of Thomson's epic route

in their 1887 travels. They explored the moorlands 900 metres (3,000 feet) beneath the peaks and went on to discover Lake Turkana, which they named Rudolf (See "The Dust and the Ashes", Part One).

Two or three years later, an expedition led by Captain F. G. Dundas with Bird Thompson and C. W. Hobley, made an attempt on the southern slopes but failed to penetrate the forest belt. In 1893, J. W. Gregory ascended the glacier zone to about 4,725 metres (15,500 feet). In 1897, George Kolb reached the moorland from the east.

Twelve years later, the great Victorian alpinist, Sir Halford Mackinder, made it to the summit with two Courmayeur guides, Joseph Brocherel and Cesar Ollier, but in those days Kenya was so remote that the significance of this achievement was underrated. In 1929, Eric Shipton, who later became one of Britain's greatest Himalayan specialists, made the second recorded ascent.

The same year, **Carr's Road** from the **Chogoria Gate,** became the highest motor track in Africa when Ernest Carr drove a Model T-Ford up the trail to a height of more than 4,260 metres (14,000 feet).

Perhaps the most unusual assault, however, was the one made by three Italian prisoners of war interned at Nanyuki during the 1940s. They broke out of the camp to climb the mountain equipped with a label from a tin of canned meat—showing an artist's painting of the mountain's twin peaks — as their only map.

Hunger and the alpine weather overcame the runaways, whose failed attempt is recounted in the book *No Picnic on Mount Kenya*. Their exploit over, they returned to camp to resume their confinement.

With two major peaks above 5,180 metres (17,000 feet), Mount Kenya has many jewel-like lakes, including the **Curling Pond** beneath the **Lewis Glacier** and **Lake Michaelson.**

One was the location for what may well have been the highest underwater exploration ever undertaken, when a group of aqualung *aficionados* lugged their oxygen cylinders up the shores and plunged to the bottom.

Mount Kenya plays a crucial role in the life of the country. It is Kenya's single, most important permanent watershed and its largest forest reserve. The fertile loams of its lower slopes, particularly in the north-east, sustain the growth of the nation's richest farmlands.

Much of the vegetation is unique and there are thirteen species endemic to the mountain. Vegetation varies with altitude and rainfall and includes rich alpine and sub-alpine flora with montane and bamboo forests, moorlands, and tundra.

The **forest reserve** covers more than 2,000 square kilometres (770 square miles) and contains Kenya's greatest trees (See "Flora: forests of flame, streets of mauve", Part Three). In the east and to the south, where the rains are frequent and heavy, the forests are thick and rich, particularly in the number of species of indigenous trees.

Their great trunks, thrusting high into the canopy, are carved by age and parasites into exotic, fluted shapes, and knitted together with lianas and vines. Camphor (*Ocotea usambarensis*), one of Kenya's most valuable indigenous trees, which flourishes here, rises up to forty-six metres (150 feet) high.

In the drier parts below 2,500 metres (8,200 feet), with average annual rainfall of between 875 and 1,400 millimetres (35-55 inches), juniper and podocarpus are the giants of the forest.

African olives, (*Olea hochstetteri*), smooth and straight-limbed, rise eighteen metres (60 feet) high and wear a dense crown of olive-green leaves, ferns, mosses, and "Old Man's Beard" (Spanish moss).

Higher up, where annual rainfall is more than 2,000 millimetres (78 inches), bamboo dominates the belt between 2,600-2,800 metres (8,500-9,200 feet), buffered between 2,500-2,600 metres (8,200-8,500 feet) and 2,800-3,000 metres (9,200-9,900 feet) by stands of podocarpus. Towards the west and north, the bamboo is smaller and less dominant.

Between 2,000 and 3,500 metres (6,562-11,480 feet) where annual rainfall is up to 2,400 millimetres (95 inches), long-living Hagenia is the dominant tree.

Beyond 3,000 metres (9,900 feet), where the cold is more extreme, hypericum with its more open canopy and more developed understorey replaces podocarpus. Now grassy glades are common, especially on ridges.

In the glades beneath the middle canopy the profusion of shrubs, including some members of the coffee family, *Rubicae*, is thick and tangled. They rise as high as nine-twelve metres (30-40 feet) and the air is filled with the sweet, fragrant breath of their flowers.

The trees are host to flowering climbers such as a rare begonia (*Begonia meyeri-johannis*) with its striking, asymmetric leaves and delicate-white flowers that glow a soft pink.

Underfoot, the forest floor is deep with rotting leaves, ferns and occasional plants, including the balsam "touch-me-not" (*Impatieus fisheri*). In bloom. this plant bears remarkable scarlet flowers with spurred edges.

Among the ferns on the valley floor and by the banks of streams, where the forest is wettest, you may chance across the tall, prickly-stemmed tree fern (*Cyathea manniana*) and a smaller fern (*Asplenium hypomelas*) found in leaf scars and also around the base of the forest giants, which is closely associated with *Cyathea*.

The western forests are comparatively dry and less prolific and the north is virtually devoid of any forest.

Red Hot Pokers

The high moorlands start at around 3,350 metres (11,000 feet) with a heath zone of *Erica arborea*, a weirdly-shaped bush, often as large as a tree and covered with moss and lichen. This gives way higher up to tussock grass and a rich profusion of everlasting helichrysums, gladioli, delphiniums, and "red-hot pokers" — a riot of unusual flora.

In the high valleys, some of the world's most spectacular mountain plants flourish.

"Water-holding cabbages" or "ostrich plume plants" are actually a giant mutation of the tiny alpine groundsel, here growing up to six metres (20 feet). When the leaves die they remain attached to the plant and help to keep out much of the cold like an overcoat.

Lobelias grow even higher than the groundsel — up to eight metres (27 feet) — its hairy, grey leaves, dotted with tiny blue flowers, it looks like a grotesque furry giant. This wrapping seals out the frost at night.

Another plant, in the shape of a huge rosette filled with water, grows closer to the ground. At night this water freezes over and the ice acts as insulation so protecting the central bud.

These plants mark the extreme range of wildlife. The only permanent residents at this altitude are rock hyrax which feed off lobelia leaves (See "Wildlife: Great and small, wild and wonderful", Part Three).

At higher altitudes, endemic mole-rat are common and there have been rare sightings of a mysterious "golden cat". Eland and zebra have been seen occasionally at the base of the peaks, around 4,300 metres (14,000 feet).

Moorland mammals, found lower down, include rock hyrax, Mount Kenya mouse shrew and common duiker. Buffalo and elephant sometimes roam here, and lion are permanent residents.

In the mountain's thick and ancient forests black and white colobus monkeys leap from one branch to another in the canopy trees. Few sights are more graceful than the colobus in flight.

Wildlife in the lower forest and bamboo zone includes giant forest hog, tree hyrax, white-tailed mongoose, black rhino, suni, and leopard.

Forest birds include an endemic race of green ibis, Ayre's hawk eagle, threatened Abyssinian long-eared owl, scaly francolin, Ruppell's robin-chat, and many beautiful sunbirds.

Moorland birds include scarlet-tufted malachite sunbirds, montane francolin, Mackinder's eagle owl, and a rare, endangered swift.

Vegetation and wildlife aside, it's for the climbs on its ice-cliffs and rock faces that Mount Kenya is renowned. Much exploration was done after World War I, but it was not until 1929 that P. Wyn Harris and Eric Shipton ascended Nelion, the second-highest peak, 5,192 metres (17,036 feet) for the first time,

and also made the second ascent of Batian.

Anyone moderately fit can attempt the third-highest peak, **Point Lenana**, 4,985 metres (15,193 feet), although its reputation as a relatively easy walk is somewhat misleading.

Above: *Kniphofia thomsoni* — afro-alpine versions of Europe's "red hot pokers".

Opposite: Spanish moss festoons hagenia tree in mountain forest.

In all, there are now thirty-four difficult, technical routes to the summits which, though much lower, many experienced climbers claim to be as testing as the major Himalayan climbs, offering a challenge of couloirs, ice-cliffs, secondary peaks, cornices, and sheer rock walls.

Kenya's location on the Equator has given it a unique seasonal characteristic. Between June and October the sun is on its north face, while the south experiences its "winter" and is covered in snow and ice.

At this time the mountain's ice climbs are magnificent. But between December and March when the sun is on the south face the rock climbs are more popular, while snow and ice prevail during the north face's "winter".

For this reason it is best to climb in the two dry seasons — January to early March and July to early October. The east face is generally clear of ice and snow for most of the year due to the morning sun, but the west face does not enjoy this advantage.

At the top of the mountain, even during the dry season, it usually rains at some time of the day. The air is thin and wickedly cold.

Anywhere above 3,350 metres (11,000 feet) you notice the effects of altitude. But in spite of warnings, many people set off up the mountain quite unprepared for high-altitude living.

Even more important than physical fitness is the need to acclimatise so that your body has a chance to produce extra oxygen-supplying red blood cells (See "Trekking Advisory", In Brief).

More than half the world's recorded cases of pulmonary oedema — about fifty a year — occur on Mount Kenya. Without exception, the cause is climbing too high, too quickly, without pausing for acclimatisation.

All those who climb Mount Kenya should be aware of the dangers. If you suffer the symptoms of mountain sickness, stubborn insistence on continuing the ascent is suicidal.

Accidents are almost inevitably the result of human error. The most common mishap involves people getting confused by mist and cloud, getting lost on the way down or losing the trail through the forest.

Despite the large number of climbers, however, fatalities on Mount Kenya are surprisingly rare — around twenty-five people in the last fifty years. In nearly all cases the victims were climbers abseiling down.

As more and more people enter the national park to enjoy Mount Kenya's moorland peaks and climbs, its continued protection is vital.

Trail proliferation along the Naro Moru Track has already resulted in muddy swathes up to 100 metres (330 feet) wide in the lower alpine zone, and the destruction of an estimated ten per cent of the entire valley-bottom habitat in the upper Teleki Valley.

Initial attempts to redesign the trail system have met with limited success. Fire from humans and lightning are other threats in the dry, lower forest although recovery takes place through natural recolonization.

Getting there

Leave Nyeri and pass through Kiganjo to arrive on the main Nairobi-Nanyuki road. Turn left for **Naro Moru** and Nanyuki. This road was being rebuilt in early 1989.

Naro Moru, the most popular base from which to prepare for climbing Mount Kenya, lies in the mountain's western rain shadow some twenty-five kilometres (15 miles) south of Nanyuki.

The tiny town is built around the railway station which frequently wins the Kenya Railways award for the nation's best kept station. No doubt one factor in this must be the efforts of the staff who have plenty of time to tend to the station since there are only two trains a week.

There are few facilities apart from a **sub-post office** and a few unstocked shops, with little more than bread and milk for sale. If you plan on spending some days on the mountain, you'd be well advised to stock up with food and other essentials in Nairobi or Nyeri.

The Routes

There are six main routes up Mount Kenya. On the western side, these include the **Naro Moru** track, the **Burguret** trail, just north of Naro Moru and, beyond Nanyuki, the **Sirimon** and **Timau** tracks.

But arguably the most beautiful, enjoyable, and dramatic of all the approaches to the peaks is from **Chogoria**, on the eastern side of mountain, following **Carr's Road**.

And perhaps the toughest and most demanding, cutting as it does through the thickest and oldest of Mount Kenya's forests, is the **Kamweti** trail from the south.

Of the six, the Sirimon trail is the driest, Chogoria the wettest, demonstrating the predominant pattern of the rainfall, since the north-western slopes lie in an almost permanent rain shadow.

The Naro Moru Route

The main gate is reached along a track from Naro Moru that crosses over the railway and then the main road. Climbing gradually at first, through grasslands and smallholdings, the trail cuts through a forest reserve, climbing more steeply to the gate.

This is set at around 2,430 metres (8,000 feet) on a ridge with deep valleys on either side that plunge down to the humid bamboo belt.

Beyond the forest, above 3,000 metres (9,900 feet), the road ends at the **Meteorological Station,** leaping-off point for moorland walks and climbing expeditions.

From the village it's seventeen kilometres (10 miles) to a comfortable and economic **Youth Hostel.** From here it's another four-hour walk to the **airstrip** and the **park gate.**

Park fees are calculated according to the number of guides and porters who accompany you or your party and how many days you intend to stay in the park.

From the gate, the road twists and climbs through a thick and ancient indigenous forest up into the bamboo zone. Beware of buffalo and elephant — they are totally unpredictable and potentially lethal.

The forests here are as old as in the south of the mountain but of more temperate stock, with robust cedars.

The final three kilometres (less than two miles) to the Met station winds up a series of steep hairpin bends, usually surmountable only in 4WD. The track then crosses **Percival's Bridge** which was built many years ago by British army engineers to honour an officer who died attempting to climb the twin peaks.

This apt memorial commands a view over the Laikipia Plains to the north-west and the panorama tells you how far and how high you have climbed. Close by is the southern ridge of the **Teleki Valley** along which the aristocrat made his way up the mountain.

At the Met station it's best to take things gently and accustom yourself to the 3,050-metre (10,000-feet) altitude. Either take a stroll a little higher or, if camping, take your tent an extra hour's climb up to the treeline, and rest there.

Standing tents can be rented at the Met station if you find the basic timber *bandas* too costly.

Another good reason for making a night stop at this point is the mountain weather. After midday, it's generally miserable — foggy, heavy drizzle, and almost zero visibility.

With an early start from Naro Moru it's quite possible for the superfit to reach **Mackinder's Camp** at 4,200 metres (14,000-feet) in one day. But unless you're already acclimatised you'll probably feel more than just a little jaded by the time you reach the Met station. If you overnight, however, an early start in the morning should see you to Mackinder's just after lunchtime — before the clouds start rolling down.

From the Met station the trail passes through a barrier and climbs steeply up through the last of the 300-year-old forest trees. By the roadside are many rare and beautiful flowers. The delicate-pink, exquisitely-shaped blossoms with stamens like a filament of fire are known as bottle flush.

The gnarled limbs of the hagenia testify to their ancient existence, sentinels long before man ventured along these trails, carved over the aeons by buffalo, elephant, rhino, and forest hog.

The made road ends at the **radio station** and afterwards deteriorates into a narrow foot trail through dwarf hagenia to emerge on the moorland where the forest ends as neatly as if divided by a knife.

Almost immediately the hagenia is replaced by *Erica arborea* — a giant mutation of small alpine heather shrubs — endemic only to Mount Kenya. Ahead, appallingly steep and forbidding, rises the Vertical Bog — 300 metres (1,000 feet) of treachery, a massive and sullen rampart that hides the peaks.

At the start of the rainy season water cascades down this 55° incline like whitewater rapids. Later, as the rains continue and its level rises, it becomes a waist-deep, swirling torrent, rushing soundlessly down the steep-pitched slope. For the inexperienced, what in the dry season may take anything from ninety minutes to three hours to traverse, now becomes a day-long battle.

Here the *Erica arborea* is intermingled with lobelias and groundsels, and other strange and unworldly plant forms. Enormous tussock grass, clovers, irises, larkspurs, and helichrysums of many different structures grow in unique form on the flanks of the high valleys.

Perhaps the most remarkable of all the world's alpine flora, many bloom only once every two decades when they adorn the entire moorlands with a glorious burst of colour, luring beautiful malachite sunbirds and others into their branches. At this altitude you may also see a rare Lammergeier eagle on one of its forays from its cliffside eyrie.

Near the crest of the Vertical Bog the incline slackens — still steep but not so severe. Just a few more hundred metres to a small rock bluff — and there is the south wall of Teleki Valley, the crest of a long radial ridge, with the peaks and their grand west-facing amphitheatre visible in all their glory — no more than five kilometres (three miles) away.

But by the time you cross the fast-flowing **Naro Moru stream** to the other side of the valley and hike the final kilometre to **Teleki Lodge** the mists will have already begun to swirl and boil around the many peaks.

Batian and Nelion tower majestically over the valley and a third pinnacle, **Point John,** looms even closer.

Everywhere you'll see a ubiquitous species of fat, bloated rock hyrax (*Procavia johnstoni mackinderi*), endemic only to this mountain. They thrive on scraps from **Mackinder Lodge,** run by the Naro Moru River Lodge.

This recent addition to the **radio station**, **ranger's post**, and **Mountain Club** buildings in the valley, is a simple concrete-slab and tin-roof barrack room. It is the most common departure point for the severe walk, up the steep-pitched scree alongside the **Lewis Glacier,** to **Point Lenana.**

Certainly no five-star hotel, it does at least provide some warmth and the company of fellow climbers, Kikuyu guides, and porters. Although there's usually a fresh covering of snow every morning, the early morning sunlight melts most by midday.

If you want to climb direct to Point Lenana you are likely to find at least one group leaving early the following morning, usually around 03.00 with a guide. However, it's not difficult to find your own way, especially if there is a moon.

By leaving this early, you can get to the top for a breathtaking dawn view (sometimes) all the way across to **Kilimanjaro**. And if you

want, you can descend to the Met station or even Naro Moru the same day.

Many climbers just head straight up to Point Lenana and back down. However, trekking around the peaks, with the added chance to explore some of the tarns and glacial valleys on the north side is far more exhilarating.

One word of warning. Nights in these huts are more often than not shared with large numbers of hyrax and resident rodents so remember to protect your food supplies.

The Chogoria Route

Scenically, the Chogoria track is superior to all the others. It's also much longer than the Naro Moru route and it takes about three days to hike to the top.

From **Chogoria village**, the hamlet of **Mutindwa,** where you can hire guides and porters, is four kilometres (2.5 miles) up the mountain. If you are alone you will definitely need to hire a guide as you are not allowed into the park unaccompanied.

From Mutindwa it's about twenty-six kilometres (16 miles) to the **park gate.** If you intend to exit from the park by another gate make sure you keep your receipts to show the rangers at the other gates.

Inside the park, close by the entrance, is **Meru Mount Kenya Lodge,** which offers comfortable, reasonably priced, self-service bandas with roaring log fires and hot showers. Run by Meru County Council, it is the best value in accommodation anywhere on the mountain.

Some sixty minutes walk from the gate, the Mountain Club of Kenya's **Urumandi Hut** offers an alternative to the lodge.

The joy of all this for those sufficiently acclimatized is that both the lodge and the hut are on Carr's Road which continues up even higher from the Urumandi Hut — a forty-five minute walk if you've no wheels — to a parking lot.

This road was pioneered by Ernest Carr in the 1920s. With two missionaries, the Reverends Dr J. W. Arthur, and A. R. Barlow sent to establish a mission at Chogoria on the eastern slopes of Mount Kenya, he was among the most dedicated of the many attempting to succeed Sir Halford Mackinder's as the second team to stand on the summit of Mount Kenya.

Arthur and Carr established the first two climbers' huts on the mountain — Urumandi at 3,050 metres (10,000 feet) and **Top Hut** at 4,790 metres (15,715 feet), on the Lewis Glacier besides the frozen pool known as the Curling Pond — in January 1922.

During the course of this expedition they came across the source of the **Ruguti River**, a tributary of the Tana, which is born in a steaming, boiling hot spring at 3,600 metres (11,800 feet). Arthur thought that "here there might be formed later a health camp".

From Urumandi the landscape is spectacular. The trail to **Minto's hut**, a stiff six-hour walk, follows the crest of a long ascending ridge to the rim of the precipice that plunges sheer to the floor of the **Gorges valley**, 300 metres (1,000 feet) below.

The first man to conquer Mount Kenya, Sir Halford Mackinder named the valley after Captain (later Brigadier-General) Gorges who came to the expedition's rescue from Naivasha when their base camp was raided by Kikuyu.

On the other side of these sheer cliffs is another smaller sheet of water, **Hall Tarn**, which Mackinder named after Major Hall, the British officer in command of Fort Hall (now Muranga) at the turn of the century.

It's a giddying but exhilarating experience to follow the trail along the edge of this stunning escarpment overlooking the valley that was scoured out by Mount Kenya's ancient glaciers. Ahead, the twin peaks beckon you forward.

Most people spend the night at Minto's Hut, perched above the head of the Gorges valley by three glittering tarns that overlook the sparkling jade waters of **Lake Michaelson**, surrounded by remarkable specimens of giant groundsel and lobelia, which spawns the Nithi River. Mackinder named the lake after one of his closest friends.

From this spot to Point Lenana takes between three and four hours of laborious climbing. There are two routes to choose from: one leads up a ridge west to **Simba Tarn**, and then south around the peaks, passing **Square Tarn**, and climbing steeply up to the **Austrian Hut**, by the Curling Pond.

This tarn was "discovered" by Arthur in 1919, when the Scotsman gave his friend, Jack Melhuish, his first and only lessons in the ancient Scottish sport of curling, thus earning the tarn its curious name.

In 1922, when they planned to build the

Top Hut, the climbers carried some skates with them and one fine morning skated for some time — at an altitude of around 4,880 metres (16,000 feet) — gliding and waltzing among the clouds that drifted over the glacier, much to the delight of the African members of the party, who were no doubt amused by the curious behaviour of the *wazungu* (white men).

The second route from Minto's leads up a slope of loose, savage scree in the south, over a saddle, to **Two Tarns** at the head of the Hobley Valley. Another hour of hard walking from this point takes you to the base of a ridge descending from Point Lenana, at the side of which are the **Austrian** and Top huts.

Many prefer to spend the night here and then make the climb to Lenana next morning to watch the sunrise.

The Austrian hut was built in 1973, as a gesture of appreciation from Austria for the efforts of European and Kenya climbers in attempting to save the life of Gerd Judmaier, a young Austrian who fell off Batian in September 1970. Unable to move because of a broken leg, he was trapped on a narrow ledge, set in a sheer cliff, for seven days and eight nights — surely one of the most dramatic rescues in climbing history.

The Burguret Route

This follows the course of the **Burguret river** from **Bantu Lodge**, some eight kilometres (five miles) north of Naro Moru on the Nanyuki road, through thick bamboo forest to the moorland.

It's possible to take a 4WD vehicle up to around 3,000 metres (10,000 feet), passing some caves that were used as a battle headquarters by the Mau Mau freedom fighters.

The main blessing of this route is that it is drier than the Naro Moru trail — and avoids anything like a Vertical Bog.

The Lodge management has built two huts on the mountainside — one near a natural salt lick at 3,000 metres (10,000 feet) which is known as **Bantu Secret Valley Camp.** The other at 4,000 metres (11,500 feet) is known as the **Highland Castle.**

The Burguret route ends at **Two Tarn Hut** in the valley.

The Sirimon Route

Driest of all the major routes, after the first

Overleaf: One of the many gemlike tarns that nestle at the throat of Mount Kenya.

nine kilometres (five and a half miles) through the forest reserve to the park gate at 2,640 metres (8,650 feet), the Sirimon route is virtually all pure moorland.

The trail starts fourteen kilometres (eight and a half miles) north of Nanyuki, by the **Sirimon river bridge** on the Nanyuki-Meru road.

In such open country the wildlife is more visible and there are fantastic panoramas over the northern deserts.

This approach also provides perhaps the most stunning and least seen perspectives of Batian and Nelion — all the grandeur of their northern face, and their smaller, but no less dramatic minions, 4,714-metre-high (15,466-feet) **Terere** and 4,704-metre-high (15,433-feet) **Sendeyo,** named after nineteenth-century Maasai leaders.

Nanyuki-Meru: Across the Equator

Although somnolent Nanyuki is only twenty-three kilometres (14 miles) from Naro Moru you could say it lies half a world away in one sense. For, just before you enter the town, the road crosses the **Equator** from southern to northern hemisphere.

The Equator is marked by two signs less than a kilometre apart — one official, the other unofficial. It has been set up by a rival group of souvenir curio sellers eager to steal a march on those on the proper Equator.

Nanyuki's metamorphosis from a handful of Maasai *manyattas*, and "a great deal of game and nothing else", began with the arrival of the railhead at the end of the 1920s. Before that it was just a shopping centre for the largely white-farming population on the Laikipia Plains and the slopes of the mountain, who arrived as settlers.

Nanyuki lies on the banks of the Maasai's Ngare Nanyuki ("Red River"). Today it serves as a major Kenya air force base — as well as a training centre for men of the British army under an Anglo-Kenya treaty.

Set at a height of 1,950 metres (6,400 feet), the climate is temperate and the air bracing. The wide, tree-lined main street and relic monuments, such as the small **clock tower,** do little to reduce Nanyuki's frontier town ambience.

The **Nanyuki Spinners and Weavers workshop,** just out of town on the **Nyahururu road,** opposite the **District Hospital,** is well worth a visit. Run by a women's co-operative, it produces splendid rugs and other traditional hand-woven items.

Probably the most famous of the main street shops is **Settlers' Stores.** Almost an institution, this shop has been on the map since 1938 and many a white hunter and movie star have passed through it.

They were probably guests at what has been described as the world's most exclusive resort — a millionaire's retreat, a few kilometres east of town, on the shoulders of the mountain.

The **Mount Kenya Safari Club,** the brainchild of an oil baron, a Swiss financier, and the late film star, William Holden, is set in thirty-seven hectares (91 acres) of manicured lawns, bowling greens, flowerbeds and ornamental ponds, with an immaculately-kept golf course.

It also boasts the only heated swimming pool on the Equator, horse-back riding, tennis, and wildlife safaris to the northern deserts. Sixty-seven species of birds inhabit the gardens, many of them imported exotics, such as peacocks.

The service is impeccable, the food ambrosial, and the atmosphere rich — opulent contrast to the harshness of the surrounding African wilderness. But you need only step outside the club gates to return to reality.

On three sides the Club is surrounded by 492 hectares (1,216 acres) of African bush that were transformed into the **Mount Kenya Game Ranch,** founded and funded by William Holden and his old friends, Don and Iris Hunt, who still run it.

Among the species kept within the sanctuary is a thriving herd of bongo, as well as the rare albino zebra, eland, oryx, and gazelle. Attached to the ranch, and open to Club visitors is an Animal Orphanage, home to a variety of orphaned species including cheetah, lion, chimpanzee, and camel.

Also on the ranch, set in its own six-hectare (15-acre) reserve is the **William Holden Wildlife Education Center,** established as a memorial to the film star by the William Holden Foundation with the aim of promoting knowledge and understanding of Kenya's unique wildlife legacy.

Film star Stefanie Powers was the major fund-raiser, and other donations came from

Above: Exotic swans grace one of Mount Kenya Safari Club's ponds.

such people as ex-American president, Ronald Reagan.

Another conservation project in the area is the private **Ngare Sergoi Rhino Sanctuary** on **Lewa Downs Ranch** north of Nanyuki on the Laikipia. If successful, it is possible that the rhino may have a chance of survival in Kenya. There are several other game ranches in the wide country that stretches out north and west of Nanyuki towards the desert.

Desert Panorama

From Nanyuki, on the ninety-kilometre (55-mile) drive to **Meru,** you first cross the **Sirimon Bridge** (turn right for the Sirimon trail up the mountain), and then drive on to **Timau** where staff at a trout farm restaurant pull the fish of your choice out of the tank and cook it before your eyes.

Not long after this, high on the shoulders of Mount Kenya, the horizon suddenly drops down to the burning wastes of the northern semi-deserts far below that seem to roll on into infinity.

This expanse of warm, arid plains and volcanic hills includes the dramatic mesa of **Lololokwe** almost 100 kilometres (60 miles)

away (See "Kenya's Mountains"). Covering one-third of Kenya, this region was first crossed by Chanler, the explorer, in 1892, and it was through these deserts, from Somalia in the north-east, that Delamere first travelled to Kenya in 1897.

To reach Meru, however, the road veers south-east around the shoulders of the mountain — with another dramatic change of scenery. This time the vista is of fertile, verdant farms, profuse with lush, green banana palms. North-east across the plains stands the rugged profile of the volcanic **Nyambeni Hills.**

Though a survey was carried out, plans to extend the railway line from Nanyuki to Meru, on the eastern slopes of Mount Kenya, have never materialised. Nonetheless, this bustling town is one of Kenya's fastest-growing.

On the mountain slopes high above the town are forests and lakes sacred to the Meru, close kin of the Embu and Kikuyu (See "The People", Part One). Beneath it, the fertile lands proliferate with agricultural produce.

Forest still comes right to the town's edge. Against the evergreen backdrop of a seemingly West African landscape, wood smoke spirals into the azure sky from thatched and tin-

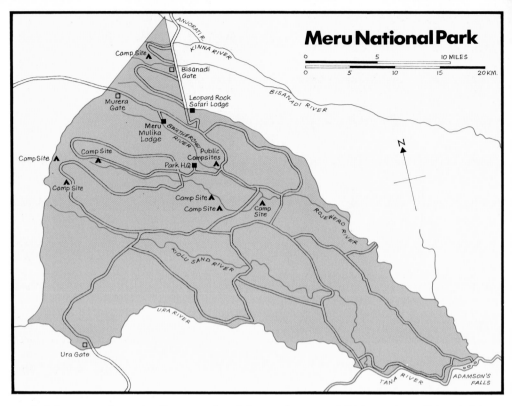

roofed homesteads and offers a colourful contrast to the rolling, dun-coloured, semi-arid grasslands on the north-west side of the mountain.

Meru, an unusual town, was founded on timber. Its first enterprises were the timber yards that exploited the indigenous Meru oak now, like Kenya's wildlife, an endangered species through over-exploitation.

Since then, coffee and tea have become important cash crops in this region. Others are pyrethrum, cotton, tobacco, bananas — and *miraa*, the leaf of a small tree which contains a mild amphetamine. This acts as a stimulant and also kills the appetite. The thin, freshly-plucked stems are chewed monotonously by addicts through the day and often the night. Though frequently denounced, it is not prohibited by law.

Miraa grows wild around Meru but so great is demand that it is now cultivated.

Meru's **National Museum** has an interesting exhibition of Meru prehistory, tribal life, and beekeeping, a traditional agricultural idiom of the indigenous people.

Outside the museum, housed in Meru's oldest stone building — the former DC's office

— is an exhibition of traditional Meru homesteads and plots filled with typical crops and herbs of the region, including an unusual plant, *mimosa pudica*, which shuts tight when it is touched. The authentic homestead comes to throbbing life when traditional Meru dances and plays are enacted.

The colourful **market** is another lively place, where stallholders offer a wide range of wares, including traditional domestic utensils, baskets, *miraa*, and farm produce.

Meru National Park

Meru, of course, is the base from which to visit **Meru National Park.** The new road swoops down Mount Kenya's north-eastern slopes to **Maua**, in the **Nyambeni Hills**, and on along a murram track another thirty kilometres (18 miles) to the **Murera Gate**.

Set beneath the slopes of Mount Kenya and covering a total of 870 square kilometres (143 square miles) of contrasting landscapes, wildlife rehabilitation was Meru's main *raison d'étre*. Founded as a reserve in 1959 by the Meru District Council, it became a National Park in the late 1960s. The park, one of Kenya's loveliest, is where George and Joy Adamson brought Boy, son of Elsa, to rehabilitate him to the wild and hunting. Here, too, Joy trained Pippah the cheetah back to her wild ways.

The park lies east-north-east of Mount Kenya at an altitude between 366 and 914 metres (1,200-3,000 feet). The wooded western grasslands form a hilly upland of volcanic rocks drained by fifteen permanent streams. The east is an open grassland plain of red lateritic soils drained by three rivers, with considerable sections drying out seasonally.

So great is the contrast between these two areas that rainfall in the west of the park is almost double that in the east (See "National Parks" In Brief, for wildlife and vegetation).

One area of the park has been designated a wilderness area; no tourists are allowed to enter nor are there any trails to follow.

Pippah's grave is marked by a simple cairn in the riverine forest near the **Rojewero confluence** where the mighty **Tana** boils and bubbles over **Adamson's Falls**, the last of the major rapids and cataracts it encounters before broadening out on its stately journey to the Indian Ocean.

Adamson's Camp

The Tana River some kilometres downstream, divides Meru National Park from the **Kora Game Reserve,** home to George Adamson, 83, murdered on 20 August 1989.

Leonine in aspect and character, Adamson relished his isolated refuge from the hectic pressures of twentieth-century life, a benign and lively old man who looked twenty years younger than his age. He shared his existence with his brother until Terence's death in 1986, and a younger disciple, Tony Fitzjohn.

Kora lies at an altitude of between 250 and 440 metres (820-1,445 feet), 125 kilometres (78 miles) east of Mount Kenya, and covers 1,787 square kilometres (690 square miles) of acacia bushlands from whose alluvial plains rise granite inselbergs and low hills.

Bordered to the south-east by the **Mwitamisyi River**, it was established in 1973 (see "National Parks", In Brief, for wildlife and vegetation). The rivers support a wide range of amphibians, lizards, snakes, tortoise, and crocodile.

A joint Royal Geographical Society and National Museums of Kenya expedition spent 1983 and 1984 studying the flora, fauna, and soils of what turned out to be a remarkable ecosystem. Out of this came *Islands in the Bush*

written by expedition leader Malcolm Coe.

When the expedition was about to end, the safari firm of Ker and Downey in Nairobi — founded by the late Syd Downey and the late Donald Ker, two famous white hunters turned conservationists — appealed for funds to help protect Kora.

The organisers also placed a brass **memorial plaque** in one of the inselbergs near a water-hole to commemorate the founding partners and their friend, the late Kenya hotelier Jack Block. In 1989 building was going ahead on a new tourist lodge in the reserve.

Adjacent to Meru's north-east boundary is **Bisanadi National Reserve,** 606 square kilometres (233 square miles) of dry, open plain dissected by seasonally dry luggas, set between an altitude of 320 and 660 metres (1,050-3,165 feet).

This mainly thorny bushland and thicket merges into wooded grasslands with dense riverine forests of doum and raffia palm along the watercourses.

During the rains, Bisanadi serves as a vital dispersal area for wildlife from Meru National Park, primarily elephant and buffalo. There are no visitor facilities.

The reserve's eastern boundary is joined to Kora National Reserve, while Kora's boundary in the south is formed by the **North Kitui National Reserve** and in the north-east by **Rahole National Reserve.**

Rahole, a lowland sanctuary, covers 1,270 square kilometres (490 square miles) of as yet unsurveyed dry thorn bushland frequented by elephant, Grevy's zebra, and beisa oryx.

North Kitui National Reserve covers 745 square kilometres (290 square miles) of dense bushland, with low hills and seasonal water-courses, along the south bank of the Tana River, which demarcates twenty kilometres (twelve miles) of the northern boundary.

From **Meru** to **Embu,** the new road swoops over one green-and-tan gorge after another, on the eastern slopes of Mount Kenya. Completed in 1983 by British engineers, this highway links Meru to mainstream Kenya.

The innumerable streams that cut deep into the volcanic soil of this eastern flank are the runoff from the luxuriant rainfall blown in by the south-east monsoon.

Above Embu, flashing through the thick forest in their haste to greet the Tana, are some of Kenya's finest fly-fishing rivers. Not for nothing is Embu's timbered, cottage-style

Above: Combine harvesters reaping wheat near Timau on the shoulders of Mount Kenya.

hostelry known as the **Isaak Walton Inn**, named after the grand seventeenth-century patron of English anglers who wrote *The Compleat Angler*. He would have delighted in the fat river bounty and forest landscapes above Embu.

There's not much in the town, however, to excite the visitor, although an avenue of jacaranda beautifies the road between the **Institute of Agriculture** and the Inn, and the **District Hospital** and Catholic **Church of St Mary Assumption.** The main road drops between Embu's **State House** and the **Police** and **Eastern Province Headquarters,** in front of which is a flat-topped pyramid, the town's **Uhuru Monument** complete with *bas-relief.*

Some distance beyond Embu a smooth new road leads south-west towards Nairobi, cutting through the 68-square-kilometre (26-square-mile) **Mwea National Reserve**, a flush of brilliant-green rice paddies, irrigated by the waters of the Tana, where wildfowling is allowed by permit, before joining the Nyeri-Nairobi road just after Sagana.

Only 100 kilometres (60 miles) north-east of Nairobi, at an altitude of around 1,000 metres (3,300 feet), Mwea's southern border is formed by the **Kamburu reservoir** on the Tana River.

No other river in the world has been quite so exploited for hydroelectric power as the Tana. Work was recently completely on the seventh project along its upper reaches.

The previous scheme — on the Sagana road — created a lake forty kilometres (25 miles) long, which is already used for fish farming and a waterfowl reserve and is to be developed as a marina.

The first hydroelectric plant, at **Kindaruma,** destroyed forever the spectacle of Seven Forks — named after the seven rivers which merged into the Tana — that plunged 137 metres (450 feet) in a roaring torrent of untapped power.

Western Kenya: The Source of the Nile

Western Kenya is the most populous and productive region of Kenya and the least visited. Yet were it not for the allure of "easy option, pre-arranged package safaris" to the coral coast and the game-rich savannahs in the north and south, it undoubtedly would be a prime tourist destination.

It contains remarkable and contrasting landscapes: dense farmlands, rolling green valleys, pockets of thick jungle, semi-desert, the only tropical rain forest in East Africa, with endemic bird and animal species, and the eastern waters and shores of Africa's largest lake.

Few inland seas measure up to Lake Victoria's proportions. Its 68,800-square-kilometre (26,563-square-mile) surface — of which Kenya claims only 3,785 square kilometres (1,461 square miles) — makes it the world's second largest freshwater lake, and the third largest of all lakes, exceeded in size only by Russia's Caspian Sea and Canada's Lake Superior.

It creates a unique local climate. As the sun sucks out the water, the clouds that form meet the cold air streaming from the mountain ramparts that surround the lake, resulting in heavy and consistent rainfall — particularly on the **Mau** massif that lies on its eastern shores and is the centre of Kenya's tea-growing industry.

Ethnically, the densely-populated region is dominated by the Luo on the lakeshore lowlands, the Bantu-speaking Luyia on the sugarlands north of Kisumu, and the Gusii in the fertile Kisii hills, south-east of Kisumu.

Travel is easy: well-surfaced roads service this region — and public transport, by road, rail, and water, is frequent.

Getting there

As the fish eagle flies, it's just ninety-five kilometres (60 miles) from the Mau, the region's eastern border massif that rises up to 3,098 metres (10,165 feet) above sea level, to **Kisumu** on the shores of a deep gulf of Lake Victoria. This may seem brief in distance but in terms of contrasting landscapes, it's a long journey through many different worlds.

Where to stay

In Kericho, Tea Hotel (4-star). In Kisii, Kisii Hotel (2-star), Riverside Tourist Resort (Budget). In Homa Bay, Homa Bay Hotel (3-star). In Kisumu Hotel Cassanova (Budget), Imperial Hotel (2-star), Lake View Hotel (Budget), New Kisumu Hotel (not visited), Sunset Hotel (5-star). In Kapsabet, Kapsabet Hotel (rustic charm, comfortable). In Kakamega, Golf Hotel (4-star). In Bungoma, Bungoma Tourist Hotel (4-star). There are others. See Listings for "Hotels".

Sightseeing

Today, a new highway from **Nakuru** rolls up the hills towards the **Uasin Gishu Plateau** with a left turn to **Molo** and **Londiani**. From here it continues for 110 kilometres (68 miles) up through the rolling swathe of tea bushes and over the crest of the delightful **Mau Summit,** to **Kericho**, the tea capital of Kenya and the world's third-largest tea producer.

At first the road climbs about 910 metres (3,000 feet) in just sixty kilometres (40 miles) through fertile hills, where the land is ideal for farming and sheep rearing.

The first place you pass is the handsome pasture-land around **Njoro**, the rambling farm town where Delamere established his first Kenya estate, some eighteen kilometres (11 miles) from Nakuru. This region is noted for its excellent cheeses.

A left fork at Njoro leads across the **Nderit River** and up the south-eastern face of the Mau Escarpment. The road follows a route often blazed by the drivers in the Safari Rally, above Lake Nakuru National Park and Naivasha, on to the summit's highest point, 3,098-metre-high (10,164 feet), **Melily,** to the capital of **Mau Narok** in the south-west.

In the 1950s Mau Narok was the focus of a European settlement scheme that has since been taken over by indigenous Kenyans. Smallholdings have sprung up everywhere. The dirt road then winds on through thick forest to **Enangipiri.** Many narrow forest trails and byways lead off the road along this massif including one steep, precipitous path to the ridge of brooding **Opuru** that rises 2,854 metres

(9,365 feet) above sea level, and looks down on Lake Naivasha.

Settlement and development are taking their toll on the primal forests clothing these heights. Where ancient podocarpus and cedar once spread their roots beneath the rich forest floor, now wheat and barley stretch as far as the eye can see.

Above the wheat fields, more forest has been cleared for potatoes. The damp chill mists and rich soil nourish their growth. Large tracts of forest still remain, however. The foot trails wind beneath cathedral-like arches of tall branches as sunbeams stream through the canopy and warm the occasional glades cleared by peasant farmers for their thatched homesteads and subsistence smallholdings.

For thousands of years these forests have been home to the Okiek, a small group of hunter-gatherers, known to the Maasai as the *il Torrobo*, anglicised into Dorobo (see "The People", Part One). The Okiek claim ancestral ownership of much of the Mau forest.

At the escarpment's edge, the forest stops and the walls plunge down — as does the boneshaking murram trail — past **Mathera** with its very English-style church. Southward, the Mau slopes down to **Narok,** gateway to Maasai Mara and district headquarters of this area of Maasailand (See "Southern Kenya: theatres of the wild").

West from Njoro, the main road follows the folds and contours of the gentle hills, through dales and downs, to **Elburgon**, thirty-eight kilometres (24 miles) from Nakuru. Another thirteen kilometres (eight miles) from Elburgon is **Molo,** where the evergreen grass feeds the finest sheep and lamb in the country. Molo lamb is the quintessence of Kenya's home-cooking.

A timbered **roundhouse theatre** marks the brief tenancy of European settlers, who shaped the highest **golf course** in the Commonwealth — 2,440-2,590 metres (8,000-8,500 feet) — at the Highlands Hotel.

Nothing exemplifies the British capacity for nostalgia better than this half-timbered rustic hostelry complete with skittle alley. It could have been transposed straight from a fifteenth-century Elizabethan English village. Only the crackling log fires and crisp night air betray its Highland location.

A few kilometres beyond Molo, the road crests 2,650 metres (8,700 feet) at its highest point. All along the great ridge, the landscape

and climate is temperate and gentle — idyllic counterpoint to the harsh heat and wildlife of the faraway savannahs and deserts.

From the summit, this great massif slopes gently down 1,830 metres (6,000 feet) to the lush, humid shores of Lake Victoria. The road bypasses **Londiani**, just twelve kilometres (7.5 miles) beyond Molo, where straggling streets of timber and stone houses, rolling fields, and wooded copses, make up this sleepy rural retreat of less than 4,000 inhabitants. Far from the hectic bustle and noise of Nairobi, the air here is cool and exhilarating as a glass of champagne.

When the railway was built at the turn of the century it required twenty-seven viaducts to ascend the east face of the Mau. The construction chief, Ronald Preston built them of timber until steel arrived from the American Bridge Company in the USA.

They curve and twist in a riotous elegance of trellises that span sparkling streams, deep ravines, and gentle valleys, enhancing rather than detracting from the beauty of the landscapes. So pure is the air of the Mau highlands that the first lick of paint on these viaducts weathered until 1967 before, finally, they needed another coat.

In 1899, Sir Harry Johnston, a Special Commissioner for Uganda, visited the Mau's tranquil meadows and forests. So entranced was he that, with the same kind of nostalgia so evident at Molo, he declared Londiani the future capital of British East Africa — which then included Uganda.

Later, however, it was discovered that the site was liable to flooding, and so another site, Njoro, was chosen. That, too, never came into existence.

Johnston's announcement coincided with the first wave of Voertrekkers — South African Europeans of Dutch descent — to Kenya. Their eyes were set covetously on the fertile lands atop the Uasin Gishu plateau across rugged unmarked country. Along the top of the escarpment, trails had to be hacked out of the thick forest and their ox-wagons (outspans) soon became bogged down in torrential rains.

The town they built, Eldoret, was for many years called simply "Sixty-Four" — which was the distance in miles from Londiani (See "North-Western Kenya: enchanted mountains, unspoilt vistas").

The Mau summit is alive with movement

Above: sheep on Kenya's highland meadowlands.

as the great canopy of forest giants sways and bends in a choreography of restless stillness. The cedars, blue gums, conifers, olives, and oaks are an ocean of motion.

The Mau range forms part of the great mountain amphitheatre that steps down, in a series of tiers, to the lush fertile plains of Kenya's western sugarbowl and the shores of Lake Victoria.

The old trail from Londiani, the nearest station to Kericho, cuts through what were the thick forest lands of the Okiek hunter-gatherers. During the first two decades of this century, the ancient forests were felled and the hardy tea bush took firm root in their place.

The Londiani trail more or less follows the railway's circuitous descent to the Nyondo Plains, cutting through **Fort Ternan** where a European farmer experimented successfully with bio-gas during the late 1930s. So successful was he that, during World War II, he converted his car to methane gas.

Fort Ternan was founded by a European pioneer in 1897. It is a rich fossil site first excavated in 1961, when animal fossils fourteen-million years old were revealed.

Beyond is **Muhoroni,** sugar capital of western Kenya, where Lord Kitchener retired to farm in 1910 and where Kenya's 1988 Olympic team manager Joshua Okuthe has a farm. Beyond that, well past **Kericho,** the road rejoins the main Nakuru-Kericho-Kisumu road.

Above the western Mau, Kericho, forty kilometres (25 miles) from Londiani, is almost always marked by bright, sunny mornings but nearly every day in the late afternoon lightning flashes and thunder rumbles.

Such equal amounts of rain and sunshine combine with the rich loams of these hills to make Kericho, Kisii, and the Nandi Hills the most perfect tea growing region in the world.

Kericho's high plateau and gentle hills are covered with a mantle of brilliant green. Plantations established as long ago as the 1920s still yield prolific, high quality harvests.

Kenya tea has earned a reputation as the *crème de la crème* of all teas, and fetches premium prices at the regular Mombasa tea auctions.

To the harvests that are culled from plantations around Limuru, Kericho and the Nandi Hills, has been added the leaf produced through Kenya's unique smallholder scheme begun at Independence in 1963.

Immaculately maintained, the curves, rhomboids, cubes, and triangles of these plantations, intercut with roads, create an astonishing panorama of manicured nature.

Unlike coffee, which left wild is a tree that grows to giant heights and soon becomes jungle, tea is a bush. But it also flourishes if neglected and becomes tangled and unkempt. Like coffee, it demands constant attention and pruning.

But the strong roots serve the same purpose as the forests, binding the precious soil together and their thick green foliage encourages similar levels of precipitation, so helping the environment to remain stable.

Westward Ho!

As befits the country's tea capital, Kericho, one of the tidiest towns in Kenya, is laid out around a compact square in neat patterns that reflect the ordered geometry of the tea plantations.

Two of the town's landmarks were built in 1952: the **Tea Hotel** and the **Holy Trinity Church,** complete with clinging ivy on the tower, which looks like an import from the English shires.

The Tea Hotel is happy to organise three-hour tours of the surrounding nurseries, plantations, and **Tea Research Institute** for interested guests. There's a first-class company-run **hospital,** a company-run **airstrip,** one of Kenya's loveliest golf courses at the **Kericho Club,** and a **Kericho-Sotik Fishing Association.**

The forest streams in the Mau offer some of Kenya's finest, and least exploited, fly-fishing, and in the comfortable **Tea Hotel** a river map highlights the best beats.

Kericho also has a **village green** and **war memorial,** inscribed in the vernacular for "We Will Remember Them", that commemorates the Kipsigis who fell in two world wars in service to a King and Empire that held them in bondage.

Behind the Tea Hotel, down in the **Kiptariet Valley,** you get an idea of what the land was like before the settlers arrived. The valley is a tangle of sprawling trees and undergrowth, with shafts of sunlight picking out clouds of butterflies.

Aside from tea, you can also visit a Trappist monk community at **Lumbwa Monastery** near **Kipkelion,** some forty kilometres (25 miles) from Kericho.

South-west of Kericho the road drops down the escarpment as it rises and falls over the hills, to curve south, around great bends that sweep through rich and fertile farmland lush with sugarcane, maize, and banana groves for ninety-eight kilometres (60 miles) to **Kisii.** This landscape is a living, pastoral canvas, worthy of the great masters.

After passing through **Kapsuser, Chemosit,** and **Litein,** just beyond **Kapkatet** the road forks. The fork is south-east along a rough and rugged trail that heads around the southern slopes of the Mau to the bustling farm town of **Bomet.** Finally it crosses over the barrier of the **Soit Olol Escarpment** and drops down to **Ngorengore** and **Ewaso Ngiro,** whence you can either travel on to Narok or turn on to the Maasai Mara trail.

Back on the Kisii road, a few kilometres beyond this fork, is **Sotik,** fifty-three kilometres (33 miles) from Kericho. The area around this small, sleepy town, which is set at an altitude of 1,830 metres (6,000 feet) and has a **hospital** and **petrol station,** must be among the most beautiful and least visited in Kenya.

Soapstone cultures

Forty-five kilometres (28 miles) beyond Sotik, the road veers west into **Kisii,** centre of the Gusii people, Kenya's most fecund community, who are as fertile as the lands they till for bananas, vegetables, and fruit.

Along with the Luyia, their Bantu kin who occupy the lower slopes of the Nandi Hills, the Gusii's rapidly-increasing population promises to break all known birthrate statistics.

With 700 people to the square kilometre (about 1,800 to the square mile), the community has one of the highest population densities in Kenya — and the highest birthrate in the world. It's well above the national average of four per cent. Indeed, from a figure of one million in the 1979 population census, their numbers had increased dramatically by 1989.

A sadder statistic is the price the Gusii pay for living where they do. No region in Africa is so prone to lightning strike as these seemingly innocent hills.

Opposite: Tobacco grows well in the Kenya sunshine.

Indiscriminately, periodic thunderbolts strike tree, house, school, and farm building during the afternoon storms. In the 1980s more than twenty school children were killed after a lightning flash struck the tin roof of their classroom.

At the turn of the century, European administrators and settlers, with their alien ideas of law and order, enraged the Gusii community (See "The Dust and the Ashes", Part One). Defying British imperial might, they massed an army of spearsmen to defend their interests — only to hurl themselves at the rotating barrels of a lone Gatling gun. They were scythed down in their hundreds.

In 1908, after a British official was speared, more massacres took place. As the Gusii fled, they were mown down ruthlessly, and their villages and fields razed. The punitive British spared none.

Fresh from his African journey Churchill was appalled. He cabled from Whitehall questioning the need to kill defenceless people on such "an enormous scale".

Capital of south-western Kenya, close to the Tanzanian border, Kisii was established as a British administrative base for the area in 1907 and seven years later became a strategic area headquarters during World War I when German troops raided from Tanzania.

Perhaps the least-known incident of the East African campaign was the taking of Kisii by the Germans during a thrust into Kenya. The British commander had withdrawn hours earlier, leaving behind his well-stocked cocktail cabinet and a note of welcome to the German commander.

When the British retook the town the English officer found his cocktail cabinet somewhat diminished — and a note of thanks from his departing German counterpart.

Although the British behaviour left Gusii society in shreds, no traces of bitterness remain. The Gusii surely rank among the friendliest of people and that in a country where every community accords stranger and guest an equal measure of friendship and hospitality.

The Gusii have long been the most artistic of Kenyan ethnic groups. The sculptor Elkana Ongesa's modern masterpiece, carved from the malleable pink and white soapstone quarried out of these hills adorn the UNESCO headquarters in Paris.

Sightseeing

Kisii is ninety-eight kilometres (60 miles) from Kericho and straggles down a steep hillside. It is a bustling, entrepreneurial town where trader and farmer vie with each other in their nonstop enterprise.

It boasts many **hotels,** a **hospital, sports stadium, light industrial estate,** and continues to develop at an astonishing pace.

A few kilometres south of Kisii, the soapstone quarries around the village of **Tabaka** provide almost the entire world with this fine, elegant, delicately-hued sculpting material.

Above: Masterpiece in soapstone — by Elkana Ongesa.

Previous pages: Fishing canoes on a Lake Victoria shore.

White is the softest stone, rich roseate the hardest. Wherever you go around Tabaka, families are busy crafting chess pieces, eggs, bowls, ashtrays, wine glasses, candlesticks and more (See "The People", Part One).

Just five kilometres (three miles) out of town, along a road north-west from the main road, stands **Manga Ridge,** a sheer escarpment that falls almost 305 metres (1,000 feet) and offers breathtaking views of Lake Victoria.

To the south of Kisii you will find some of Kenya's most rewarding but least-visited landscapes and cultures.

For the adventurous, the winding road south-east leads some fifty kilometres (30 miles) to **Kilkoris,** at the base of 2,060 metres (6,760 feet) high **Olasaayiet.** From this point, intrepid travellers may try the often impassable dirt road over the **Soit Olol Escarpment** to **Lolgorien** and then on to the Maasai Mara.

Most people, however, remain on the main road to fast-developing **Migori.** From Migori (all bustle and touts) a good road leads through the Kenya-Tanzania **border post** at **Isebania,** the least fussy crossing point between the two countries, to **Mwanza.**

In 1989, Migori was the scene of a human drama when a semi-tame crocodile escaped from its owner and became a maneater. It killed one person and maimed five others during its three-week reign of terror.

In one incident a man leaped into the river to save a child who was being dragged away, wounding the reptile. It was shot days later by administration police and its body dragged through the streets of the town to the cheers of a jubilant crowd.

In the high hills around these parts live the Kuria community made up of seventeen clans (See "The People", Part One). Their lands, like so many, were divided during colonial times by the unconcerned bureaucrats in Europe who sliced up Africa like a loaf of bread.

Their closest kin, the Suba fisherfolk, live beneath the Kuria Hills on the shores and islands of Lake Victoria.

Many dusty trails around here lead to remote, unspoilt beaches and fishing villages on the south-eastern shores of Lake Victoria.

Kehancha, one of the "undiscovered" pearls of Lake Victoria, is reached either from Homa Bay in the north or along the road from Migori to **Suna,** forking right at **Masara** to **Karungu,** a total of about fifty kilometres (30 miles).

Situated on the wide sweep of **Karungu Bay**, this delightful fishing village has real atmosphere and a fine beach, although like everywhere else around Lake Victoria, it can be humid and malarial.

Rising from **Mungeri Bay**, the 2,270 metres (7,450-feet) **Gwasi Hills,** the highest point in this region, form the western boundary of the little-known **Ruma (Lambwe Valley) National Park**.

Ruma National Park

Bound in the north by the volcanic plugs of the **Ruri Hills**, and to the north-west by the **Gembe Hills,** the eastern border of this 120-square-kilometre (46-square-mile) park is the **Kanyamuia Escarpment.**

Set at an altitude of between 1,200 and 1,600 metres (3,940-5250 feet), Lambwe, which boasts Kenya's only roan antelope, is infested with tsetse fly making it unfit for human occupation. But though the tsetse are fatal to man and his herds, wild game flourishes where they live.

There are no lodges and only one campsite, although camping is allowed in other areas. Consult the warden. Bearing in mind the tsetse, encroaching shambas, and the state of the roads, you may think it wiser to give camping a miss entirely.

The park is about thirty-two (20 miles) south of cluttered and untidy **Homa Bay** town along a rough dirt trail strewn with rocks. Despite its unkempt appearance, Homa Bay is the administrative centre of a large area of Nyanza Province. There is an **airstrip** and one lone **jetty,** but the roads are little more than rough tracks.

The fear in Homa Bay is the Lake Victoria crocodiles, which every now and then haul themselves off the beach to crawl into the downtown area — much to the consternation and alarm of citizens going about their everyday business.

Kenya Railways marine division operates regular scheduled steamer services all along the coast, but the days when it was possible to take a seven-day luxury cruise around Lake Victoria — 1,134 metres (3,720 feet) above sea level — have long gone.

However, the majesty of this coastline — a fascinating mixture of towering bluffs, great peninsulas and islands — remains to be savoured from the deck of the smaller passenger vessels cruising these busy waterways. Fares are low and the timetables, posted at the port jetties — are rigidly followed in fair weather conditions, although strong westerlies at the end of the year sometime delay the outward legs.

Take the steamer out of Homa Bay and you'll enter the **Mbita Passage** at the neck of the **Kavirondo Gulf** — the long inlet that leads to Kisumu, passing between the mainland and **Rusinga Island**, birthplace of the late Tom Mboya, who was brutally assassinated in Nairobi on 5 July, 1969.

One of Kenya's founding fathers, Mboya was also one of the most outstanding and promising politicians of Africa's first generation of Independence statesmen. He lies buried here, on a rocky windswept shore, in a fine **mausoleum**, containing memorabilia and artefacts devoted to his life's work. There's also a **health clinic** dedicated to the politician's memory. His epitaph, like the man and his career, is an inspiration:

Go and fight like this man fought
Who fought for mankind's sake
Who died because he fought
Whose battles are still unwon

The cause to which he dedicated his life may well have had its very earliest beginnings on Rusinga Island for it was here that Mary Leakey uncovered the crumbling skull of *Proconsul Africanus,* a primitive anthropoid ape that lived on Rusinga three million years ago.

Even more outstanding, the earliest fossil remains uncovered on this dusty, bleak, eroded island date back seventeen million years (See "The Dust and the Ashes", Part One).

The road to the island which heads south along the shore and over a causeway is rough. It's easier to travel by boat.

Besides the mausoleum, Rusinga is also a base for visitors flying from Maasai Mara for a day's big-game fishing on the lake waters in search of nile perch and tigerfish.

Neighbouring **Mfangano Island** ruled by a three-man police squad and the local chiefs, is less visited. It is a centre of prehistory, however, with some ancient **rock paintings** — all worth seeing.

The islanders practice their own form of prehistoric fishing — casting kerosine lamps out from the shore after sundown and hauling them slowly inshore, luring squirming shoals of *dagga* (Victoria's freshwater shrimp and a much-loved delicacy) to their nets.

North of Homa Bay rises the gaunt 1,750-metre-high (5,745 feet) crown of **Homa Mountain**, beneath which lime is quarried for Kenya's building industry and other manufacturing processes.

The mountain forms the centrepiece of a great rounded peninsula. Frequent thunderstorms play around its peak, jagged lightning streaking down through indigo-night to play upon Victoria's wind-lashed waters.

The lee of Homa Mountain forms the southern shore of **Kendu Bay,** a charming port village where offshore tugs tow barges along the coastline. When their chimney stacks send pillars of black smoke straight up into the still air you know it heralds the sudden onset of a lake squall.

Just two kilometres from the town is an unusual crater lake, **Simbi**, whose emerald waters are a sea of algae. It has no apparent source so its existence is something of a mystery. You can also visit the **Oriang pottery centre**, a few minutes walk away in the village of the same name. There's also a breeding ground for sacred ibis nearby.

From Kendu Bay it's a short and pleasant cruise across the wide span of the Kavirondo Gulf to **Kisumu.** The ferry passes numerous Luo fishing fleets whose sturdy gaily-decorated canoes and sailing vessels, hand-crafted out of mahogany by the boat builders of the Suba tribe, are a picturesque part of Lake Victoria life.

These dhow-like boats are improvisations of vessels introduced into these waters in the nineteenth-century by Arab traders from the coast. Today some are driven by powerful outboard motors, though this doesn't seem to have diminished Luo skills as watermen.

One of the most colourful sights on these shores are the annual regattas held by the villagers, when muscular oarsmen paddle their high-prowed canoes through the waters, their skins gleaming with spray as waves cream back from the bows.

Most visitors, however, take the tarmac road from Homa Bay to Kendu Bay and then cut east on the Kisumu road to **Oyugis** — famous for its pelicanry. Thousands of the birds nest here in the August-March breeding season.

From Oyugis, the main road cuts through the fertile sugar belt to Sondu, where a **Catholic mission** produces miniature terra-

Above: Kenya Railways' passenger-cargo ferry on Lake Victoria.

cotta sculptures and through **Ahero,** famous for its **heronry** which also lures ibis, cormorant, egrets, and storks.

It finally arrives at Kisumu, capital of western Kenya and home of the populous Luo community. More than three million strong, the Luo range the shores of Victoria from Homa Bay in the south to **Sio Port** on the Uganda border in the north.

Port Florence

Kisumu stands at the mouth of the **Nyando Valley,** close to where the **Nyando River** empties into Lake Victoria's **Winam Gulf** and, like Nairobi, owes its position to the Uganda Railway.

This is where, on 20 December, 1901, Preston triumphantly invited his wife to hammer down the last rail of his five-and-a-half-year engineering odyssey to the great lake.

The railhead was named, briefly, Port Florence — after Florence Whitehouse, wife of the General Manager and Chief Engineer, who had visited the port earlier.

The **rail terminus** is on the jetty where,

until 1977, engines and wagons were loaded on to large, fast-moving rail ferries that crisscrossed and circumnavigated Lake Victoria, carrying goods to Uganda and Tanzania.

As East Africa's major lake port it once flourished with **customs** and **immigration** posts alongside the warehouses. In recent years, however, the collapse of the East African Community has slowed down Kisumu's economic growth.

Today, the ambience in the shadows of the warehouses and industrial plants is remarkably relaxed. But with a population approaching half a million, Kenya's third-largest town is testimony to the dynamic vigour of this still young nation.

The sweltering humidity dictates the easygoing way of life, but when Kisumu's Division One soccer team, Gor Mahia, meet rivals in a league match, there's no shortage of energy, either among players or fans.

The club takes its name from one of the community's mythical heroes of long ago. More relaxed sport includes the **Kisumu Yacht Club** and the **Golf Club** to the north-

Overleaf: Luo fishing boats on Lake Victoria.

Above: Luo with conical fish basket trap on shores of Lake Victoria.

west of town where pythons and hippos are a recognised hazard along the fairways.

Sightseeing

Around Kisumu town, there's plenty to see and do. The colourful **market** by the **bus station** is full of fruit and vegetables as well as household items and, of course, fish in every shape and form, dried and fresh.

Worthwhile buys are the heavy, three-legged Luo stools. The best ones are intricately inlaid with beads, and dark brown from repeated oiling.

The green-and-silver twin minarets of **Jamia mosque** in **Otieno Oyoo Street** were built in 1919, although the women's section on the right was only finished in 1984. The exquisite mats inside come from Saudi Arabia.

There are also some **Hindu temples**, many **Christian churches**, and a **monument** to Archdeacon Owen at the corner of **Kakamega Road** and the road from Kericho.

Many new, white buildings dominate the skyline but the neat administrative buildings — the town is both a provincial and district headquarters — are well-marked. There are **cinemas, banks, post office,** and a 1938 **clocktower** dedicated to the memory of one Kassim Lakha. The **British Council Library** has some useful maps.

The **Kisumu Museum**, open daily, has fascinating exhibits of mammals, birds, primates, amphibians, reptiles, fish, and crustaceans. The **ethnographic exhibits** are also interesting, especially the one devoted to traditional musical instruments, including the fine Nyatiti, the Luo lyre. Outside, the Museum there is a **tortoise pen, snake pit,** and **crocodile pond.** Future plans include an entire compound laid out as a traditional Luo homestead.

Half a kilometre (a third of a mile) beyond the Yacht Club, on the lake shore to the south, past the **Sunset Hotel,** is **Hippo Point,** an ideal place to enjoy one of the lake's spectacular sunsets and watch the hippo splashing just offshore. The **restaurant** serves cold beers and snacks and many a pleasant hour can be spent sipping drinks on the terrace.

Dunga, a small picturesque settlement

Opposite: Traditional Luo dancer.

some two kilometres (just over a mile) further on along the headland, is all that a Luo fishing village should be. If you're keen to spend a night with fishermen on their boats, this is probably the best place to do so, although you can expect some good-humoured bargaining.

Offshore, some thirty kilometres (20 miles) from Kisumu, on the north side of Winam Gulf, is one of Kenya's most recent national parks, the four-square-kilometre (one-and-half-square-mile) **Ndere Island,** which became a sanctuary in 1986.

Way out West

Thirty years after the railhead arrived at Kisumu, the line began to wind out of town again — across the **Equator** at **Maseno** — covering another sixty-five kilometres (40 miles) to the busy market town of **Butere.**

West of this, the road forks left at **Yala,** a small market town with a railway station. The area is dominated by the malarial flatlands and swamps of **Siaya District,** covered only with small villages linked by a few minor roads.

It is largely unvisited by tourists but from **Usengo** on the southern flanks of the large **Yala Swamp,** just a few kilometres from the district capital of **Siaya,** you can climb a nearby hill revered in Luo history as the place where the first of their ancestors arrived to settle after their long trek southwards (See "The People", Part One).

When the Luo first arrived 500 years ago, they clashed with the existing tenants, a Bantu group who they eventually forced into exile. You'll understand why they chose to stay when you gaze upon the island-studded lake and the lagoon below.

On the northern flanks of the Yala swamp is **Sio Port,** once called Port Victoria. It was perhaps a fancy of the early rail planners that the line would one day reach there, but it never did. Sio Port is just a small desultory village that serves principally as a ferry point to carry lakelanders into Uganda by boat or dugout canoe.

Most visitors will take the road north out of Kisumu, up the **Nyando Escarpment** for the seventy-three kilometre (45-mile) journey to **Kakamega,** capital of Kenya's Luyia community.

After **Chavakale,** roughly halfway between the two towns, there's a right turn that climbs up through **Kaimosi** and **Koiprak** to **Kapsabet,** set at a cool and refreshing 2,100 metres (6,400 feet).

Eighteen kilometres (11 miles) away, is the district capital, **Nandi Hills,** a beautiful farm town with **hospital** and **service station.**

Traditional pastoralists, the local Nandi people are skilful cattle farmers. Nandi herds produce more milk than any other district in the country.

Tea and milk are in abundance here and, just a few kilometres away, on the Chemelil-Mumias plains below, grows Kenya's sugarcane, yielding a record 300,000 tons recently. No wonder this western sugarbowl is known as the land of milk and honey.

The contrasts between the two landscapes, separated only by the height of the escarpments, are as sharp and well-defined as the distinctive flavour of Nandi tea.

All is so quiet and peaceful in this rural wonderland it's hard to believe that the Nandi were once fearsome and dedicated warriors (See "The People", Part One). No raiders swarmed down to attack the railway builders as they carved their way to Butere in 1932, but little more than three decades earlier these warriors tormented Preston and his railhead gangs, pillaging the iron tracks for forging weapons, and telegraph wires for crafting copper bracelets.

Dry, scholarly Sir Charles Eliot displayed rare understanding. "One can imagine what thefts would be committed on a European railway if the telegraph wires were pearl necklaces and the rails first-rate sporting guns, and it is not surprising the Nandi yielded to the temptation."

The Nandi also seized the prefabricated sections of the first boat to sail Lake Victoria, the *William Mackinnon,* thus delaying its launch by many months. In 1905 the British exacted sordid vengeance: killing one in every ten warriors, razing villages and seizing the Nandi cattle. Their chief seer, Koitalel, negotiated a temporary truce, but when he went to meet the British for a long-term pow-wow on permanent peace, he was treacherously murdered (see "The Dust and the Ashes", Part One).

Nandi distance runners have earned international renown in Olympic arenas as the world's finest. In one brief spell, Henry Rono accumulated an unprecedented four world records in different events.

Like the Tibetan Abominable Snowman,

Yeti, which roams the Himalaya, the Nandi Bear, *Chemoset*, is said to roam the high forests. Fact or fantasy, it's a story that every so often still makes headlines in the Kenya press.

One of Kenya's most beautiful trees, the Nandi flame tree, takes its name from this region (See "Flora: forests of flame, streets of mauve", Part Three).

If you return to the main road from Kisumu and continue up the north-western base of the Nandi Escarpment, you arrive at Kakamega, where the trail Sergeant Ellis carved with Captain Sclater across Kenya's backbone, from **Fort Smith** in Kikuyuland, finally reached in 1896.

Unique Forest

As you enter town the mission and Christian presence is very visible. The road passes schools and seminaries, before arriving first at the colourful **market** followed by the high-walled prison.

The undistinguished **clocktower** in the town centre was raised in 1935 to commemorate the silver jubilee of King George V's reign.

The town's early fame was as the seat of a "Klondike Gold Rush" in the 1930s, when more than a thousand prospectors staked their claim on what proved to be very sparse veins of the precious ore.

You still find an occasional hardy local prospecting Kakamega's hillside streams, panning for the proverbial alluvial treasure and in Nairobi's streets you may meet a smooth-talking confidence trickster who promises that somewhere out there in the West your fortune can be made.

But **Kakamega Forest** is the town's real treasure, a remnant of unbroken Equatorial jungle that arched west to east across the continent as recently as four centuries ago and can be found nowhere else in Kenya — or East Africa for that matter.

Take the track to the right, just under a kilometre (just over half a mile) after Kakamega's **Approved School**. From the western approach, a sign opposite a **service station** some ten kilometres (six miles) from Kakamega, points right. From here, it's thirteen kilometres (eight miles) to the **Rest House** from the main road, branching right at a large village — Shinyalu — after seven kilometres (four miles) and after a further five kilometres (three miles) left at a **signpost.**

In the reserve there's a **forest Rest House**

with four, first-floor double rooms, and a long verandah facing the wall of tropical greenery a few metres away.

For a modest fee the caretaker, a knowledgeable guide, will take you on a birdwalk through the labyrinth of jungle, spotting birds, monkeys, chameleons and other animals, most of which you would probably miss on your own.

Finally gazetted as a national reserve in 1985, after years of bitter debate, **Kakamega Forest**, covers some forty-five square kilometres (18 square miles) containing Kenya's rarest arboreal, floral, faunal, and avifaunal treasures.

Set at an altitude of between 1,520 and 1,680 metres (4,990-5,512 feet), the hilly terrain is also scattered with seasonal swamps. There are two major rivers, the **Isiukhu** in the north and the **Yala** in the south.

These support the easternmost area of its rain forest, interspersed with grassy glades. More than 125 species of tree, each averaging around thirty-five metres (115 feet) in height, have been identified.

Around twenty per cent of the amphibians, reptiles, birds, and mammals found in this reserve occur nowhere else in Kenya. They include bush-tailed porcupine, giant water shrew, hammer-headed fruit bat, and numerous species of birdlife.

Among the reptiles are some particularly venomous snakes, including the fat and sluggish Gabon viper. And among the primates which include colobus and blue monkey are high-living arboreal pottos — creatures that are only active at night (see "Wildlife: great and small, wild and wonderful", Part Three).

The forest is also home to one of the most fascinating of all Kenya's animals — the scaly-tailed flying squirrel. It belongs to the peculiar group of Anomalurus, rodents, now extinct outside Africa and can "fly" as far as ninety metres (300 feet).

Besides these two rarities, the forest, which is interspersed with open glades and grasslands, hosts abundant monkeys, small antelopes, and a wealth of bird life, including Kenya's only resident parrot population and the great blue turaco, a large, shiny bird the size of a turkey with plumped-up plumage.

From Kakamega the road climbs up through scenic country for about sixty kilometres (37 miles) to **Broderick Falls** to rejoin the 1920s spur of the Uganda Railway, which finally linked Kenya with Uganda.

Above: Broderick — now Webuye — Falls near Bungoma in north-west Kenya.

Until the 1970s, nothing much distinguished this place from the thick forests which cloaked the region except the fifty-two-metre-high (170-feet) cascading **waterfalls** — named after an early European visitor to this region.

A few kilometres above the falls, on the escarpment, stands **Chetambe's Fort,** scene of an 1895 massacre by a British punitive expedition against the Bukusu tribe of the Luyia.

The warriors, dug in behind a 100-metre (330-feet) moat-like rampart, had only shields for defence and spears for weapons against the fire of the British expedition's Maxim machine gun.

In the 1970s, in an Indo-Kenyan partnership organised by the World Bank, this place was chosen as the site of Kenya's paper milling industry. The falls provide an ideal source of water close to one of Kenya's great logging regions.

Today more than 20,000 people depend on this industry for their livelihood. Bustling **Webuye** continues to grow fast as demand for paper increases in education-hungry Kenya.

From here the main Mombasa-Uganda road continues, bumpy and potholed, through boulder-studded hills, open grasslands, small-holdings and sugar fields, to **Bungoma,** a prosperous but dull administrative town.

Marking the end of the road in Kenya is **Malaba** where interminable queues of lorries block both sides of the border. Pedestrians, it appears, can cross without difficulty.

Southwards from Broderick Falls you can follow the course of the track up to the high Uasin Gishu plateau to **Leseru.** This town is famous for its cheeses, and the lovely landscapes of the Uasin Gishu and **Trans Nzoia plateau** of North-Western Kenya.

North-West Kenya: Enchanted Mountains, Unspoilt Vistas

With its high and lovely farmland plateaux, north-west Kenya, the country's most extensive and fertile wheat, grain, and livestock region, is becoming increasingly popular with tourists. The great bulk of 4,321-metre-high (14,178-feet) Mount Elgon, the glorious Cherangani Hills, cresting more than 3,350 metres (11,000 feet), unique pristine forests, and game sanctuaries, make this one of Kenya's most glorious regions.

Exploring its many delights makes several rewarding days for any visitor.

Getting there

From Nakuru the smooth Mombasa-Uganda highway takes you to the village of **Equator** and on through **Timboroa** and its great forest cloak to **Eldoret**, a distance of 156 kilometres (97 miles).

In the cool, dark sanctuary of the forest the railway to Uganda reaches the highest point of any line in the Commonwealth, 2,784 metres (9,135 feet), before crossing the Equator at 2,656 metres (8,716 feet) and down on to the high, level plateau of the **Uasin Gishu** and the **Trans-Nzoia** farmlands. But this journey by road or rail through one monotonous belt of conifer forest after another, is basically flat and boring.

For the most enjoyable route, and to really discover "undiscovered" Kenya, you should turn south-east off the main road, on to the minor roads and dirt trails that lead to the south-eastern edge of the **Elgeyo Marakwet escarpment** of the Rift.

Where to stay

In Eldoret, Sirikwa Hotel (4-star). In Kitale, Kitale Club (pricey and somewhat rundown colonial baroque). In Kaptagat, Kaptagat Hotel (3-star). In Soy, Soy Country Club (not visited). There are others. See Listings for "Hotels".

National Parks

Mount Elgon Lodge (3-star), book through Msafiri Inns, Utali House, Nairobi. There are also three campsites.

Sightseeing

Prosperous farm communities exist in this Kalenjin highland wonderland, with names that snap off the tongue — Kapkut, Kapsabet, and Kaptagat.

The first turning off the highway is the tarmac road east to **Eldama Ravine**, a sprawling town literally pitched on either side of the steep gorge that gives it its name.

It was one of Britain's first administrative centres at the turn of the century and the first District Commissioner was James Martin, the illiterate aide who accompanied Thomson on his epic march of 1883-84 (See "The Dust and the Ashes", Part One).

West of Eldama Ravine a minor road leads around the eastern base of 2,799-metre-high (9,184-feet) **Kapkut** to **Kamwosor**. Here the road forks three ways — west back to the main road, north-west across the railway line (then left to Eldoret) or straight on to **Kapchebelel** and the glittering panorama of **World's End**, one of the most dramatic scarps in the world, and **Nyaru**, where the tarmac ends at the edge of the escarpment.

Great bluffs rise up on either side of the precipitous World's End cliffs. The name is apt. Martial birds and raptors circle on the constant thermals that blast up the face of the cliff and across the plateau.

Before you is a void that stuns the senses and clutches at the stomach: it is awesome and inspiring. Thousands of metres below, beneath the edge of this dizzying drop, unfolds the infinite sweep of the Rift Valley.

Its great eastern wall rises blue-grey in the distance on the other side. Ahead, the valley stretches as far as the eye can see to Lake Bogoria and beyond; through searing heat and dusty desert to Marigat, Baringo, and ultimately to the cataclysmic volcanic cones that mark the southern shores of Lake Turkana.

A road north-east from Kapchebelel leads down below this magnificent cliff to **Chebloch** on the tarmac road from **Kabarnet** to Eldoret.

Another alternative is to take the left turn a few kilometres south of Eldama Ravine to Saos, under the eastern flanks of Kapkuti, and

Above: Kenya's own Grand Canyon — the deep but narrow divide of the Kerio Valley.

on to Kabarnet. There's also a turning west, some kilometres before Kabarnet, that climbs steeply up the scarp through **Cheplembus** and **Kapkalelwa** to Chebloch.

From here, the smooth Kabarnet road twists and winds through the rapidly-growing towns of **Tambach** and **Iten** on the scarp that forms the southern flanks of the Cherangani Hills. Set at an altitude of 1,981 metres (6,500 feet), Tambach is thirty-seven kilometres (23 miles) from Kabarnet, and forty-four kilometres (27 miles) from Eldoret.

Only ten kilometres (six miles) further on, Iten is already pitched another 250 metres (800 feet) higher. Yet despite their development, these towns and the area all around remain unspoilt.

It's hard to imagine twentieth-century civilization amid these tranquil forests and small villages. But the capital of this region, Eldoret, is one of Kenya's most modern towns.

Surrounded by pines and giant blue gums, and rolling fields of grain and meadow pastures, Eldoret is rapidly expanding with textiles, woollen mills, and other industries.

Developed by the South African *voertrekkers* who hauled their caravans through the thick

Mau and Londiani forests across the mud and ruts of the Uasin Gishu in the first twenty years of this century, Eldoret was always regarded as something of an eccentric place.

According to local folklore, the bank was built around the safe where it dropped off the wagon because it was too heavy to move.

But despite its rapid growth, the town is fairly compact and it's worth strolling around the bustling streets to get the feel of highland life.

Today it's the home of Kenya's latest campus, **Moi University,** built on land donated by the Lonrho group, which runs one of the largest agricultural-based industries in the country.

For years, the **East Africa Tanning Extract Company** (EATEC) has tended many thousands of hectares of wattle trees, extracting tannin for the leather industry and using the trunks as telegraph poles. Now EATEC have diversified into mushroom farming and charcoal production. Nothing goes to waste on their farm estates.

The old charcoal kilns have been transformed into mushroom sheds. Cattle dung powers a bio-gas plant which provides fuel and energy for the staff village of 4,000 people — including street lighting.

Eldoret has hotels of varying standards, ranging from top bracket, down to the plain and simple. Lively discos exist at places such as the **New Wagon Wheel,** and there is a thriving **sports club,** and first-class **airport** for domestic and charter operations.

To Kitale

From Eldoret to Kitale is sixty-nine kilometres (43 miles). Leave the Mombasa-Uganda road where it veers west twenty-two kilometres (14 miles) from Eldoret, and continue in a north-westerly direction through Soy, four kilometres (two-and-a-half-miles) after the junction.

Aside from its **country club,** Soy is also noted for its remnant herd of rare Rothschild's giraffe. They became famous in 1974 when Jock and Betty Leslie Melville chose a six-month-old female, Daisy Rothschild, to take to their home in Nairobi's Karen suburb.

From Soy the great mass of **Mount Elgon** dominates the horizon as the road continues, smooth and straight, through **Moi's Bridge,** once known as Hoey's Bridge, and into **Kitale.**

There's an irrepressible feel of the English countryside about the meadowlands around this highland town, which stands 1,890 metres (6,200 feet) above sea level.

Avenues of giant blue gums line either side of the road of this charming rustic farm and market centre. **Kitale Station** is a reflection of the graceful days of the leisurely steam travel which inspired it.

Now noted for its **fruit orchards,** and as headquarters of the giant **Kenya Seed Company,** Kitale's bracing air and relaxed life style, far from the tensions and milieu of metropolitan living, encourage longevity.

It became a boom town briefly during Kenya's 1970s coffee bonanza. Ugandan coffee was smuggled across the border on the back road that cuts high over the shoulders of **Mount Elgon**, the town's magnificent back-drop.

It was originally an old slaving station on the main caravan route between Uganda and Bagamoyo in Tanzania. A circle of stones in the car park of the timbered **Kitale Club** once surrounded the ring to which the slaves were chained.

A century or more later, Kitale's business men and farmers meet in the club's bar and at weekends drive the long, lush fairways of the challenging **golf course**.

But Kitale is primarily the base for visits to the volcanic cone of Mount Elgon, as well as the superb, but completely underrated, surrounding hiking country. It is also the most straightforward departure point for trips into the northern deserts and the only town with a regular bus service to within striking distance of Lake Turkana. Consequently, many travellers merely pass through Kitale.

But unless you are pressed for time, the National Museum, Mount Elgon, Saiwa Swamp National Park, and the Cherangani Hills merit more serious attention.

The Kitale Museum (or Museum of Western Kenya), originally the "Stoneham Museum", was established by an English army officer of that name on his Cherangani farm in 1927.

In 1972, it was transferred to Kitale. The earliest exhibits are on your right as you enter. Other exhibits include those on issues of soil conservation, crop rotation, and land terracing.

Sadly, the famous butterfly collection now consists of a series of fine, empty cases. The Turkana homestead exhibit is interesting. So is the 1916 belt-driven BSA motorcycle in the lobby.

The museum also boasts a **craft shop, laboratories** and a **nature trail,** offering the best place for a picnic in Kitale. Outside the museum is a miniature slope of terraced land with a tortoise pen with both leopard and hinged tortoise inmates.

Next to the main building, the octagonal **Museum Hall** houses some bold murals of Turkana, Maasai, Nandi, and Luo domestic life.

Mount Elgon: Mountain of the Breast

Covering a total of 169 square kilometres (65 square miles) of montane forest and volcanic craters, **Mount Elgon National Park** sits astride Kenya's western border with Uganda. Founded in 1949, the park itself lies on the eastern flank of this massive volcanic cone, its boundaries some distance beneath the summit.

Ancient beyond comprehension, Elgon feels like a link with the beginning of time. It burst out of the Trans-Nzoia plains more than fifteen million years ago. The topmost heights form the Kenya-Uganda border which cuts right across the rim and through the centre of the crater.

Indeed, **Wagagai,** the highest peak at 4,321 metres (14,176 feet), is on the Uganda side of the crater rim, but the variation between one side of the crater and the other is minimal.

Sudek, on the Kenya side, rises to 4,310 metres (14,140 feet), just eleven metres (36 feet) lower. Favourite for many, however, is 4,231-metres-high (13,882-feet) **Koitobos** (Table Rock) a flat-topped basalt peak near the edge of the caldera.

The caldera measures between six and eight kilometres (four-five miles) across while the base of Mount Elgon is tenfold that at between eighty and 100 kilometres (50-60 miles).

At one point the rim is broken by the **Suam Gorge,** a deep rift forming the main outflow from the crater. Farther down, the **Suam river** joins the **Turkwel river** which is spawned in the heights of Uganda's **Kadam** mountain and flows on down through Lodwar to the Jade Sea (See "The Northern Rift: Cradle of Mankind").

Known to the Maasai whose herds once grazed the Trans-Nzoia as Ol Doinyo Igoon (the Mountain of the Breast), Elgon is still home to a remnant group, the il-Kony, who live high up its flanks.

The route to the top is generally easy, and the spectacular cliffs, deep valleys, idyllic tarns, hot springs, and excitement of an excursion into Uganda all make Mount Elgon more than worth the climb.

Getting there

The easiest approach to the mountain is from Kitale. Three gates lead into the park, through the bamboo forest into the giant stands of ancient podocarpus, and on to the moorlands. The most popular is the **Chorlim Gate** off the **Endebess road**, reached along the dirt road that cuts through the rich farmlands below.

The other gates are approached from **Kimilili**, fifty kilometres (31 miles) west of Kitale, and eighty-one kilometres (50 miles) from **Kakamega**. With **Webuye** only twenty kilometres (12 miles) away, and **Bungoma** only sixteen kilometres (10 miles) distance these two towns make a comfortable base for climbs from Kimilili.

If you don't have a 4WD vehicle, you'll have to take a *matatu* to reach **Kapsakwony,** for the Kimilili Track, and **Endebess**. The National Park road turns left up a well-maintained dirt road just a few kilometres beyond Endebess.

Angling enthusiasts who might wish to avoid the mountain heights should motor on towards **Bukwa** on the Uganda border. Some kilometres before this is one of Kenya's best kept secrets — the delightful **Suam fishing camp.**

Mount Elgon is surrounded by forest and you should use the motor track to reach the moorland area, although the one from Mbale in Uganda has not been used for many years.

The main peak, **Wagagai,** offers fantastic views of the crater, **Suam Gorge,** the Ugandan side of the mountain, and the distant landscapes below. It is a seven-to-eight hour round trek from **Lower Elgon Tarn**. There is plenty of water near the summit — in the crater — but no huts.

Set at 4,300 metres (14,110 feet) **Lower Elgon**, is a subsidiary rocky peak with excellent views of the crater and Lower Elgon Tarn. The tarn makes a splendid campsite, twelve hours walk from the **Kimilili Track** roadhead. It is probably the best walk on the mountain.

But from Kitale it's about five hours drive to the Kimilili roadhead — in low-ratio 4WD vehicles — and some initiative, not all entirely dependent on driving skills, to reach the top.

Probably from Kitale the most used trail is along a well-maintained track up through the National Park. In dry weather it's possible to reach the **roadhead** in an ordinary but powerful saloon car.

Although the trail is not as scenically rewarding as the Kimilili trail, the extremely pleasant campsite in the lower parkland of the National Park is an attractive feature of this approach.

When to go

The crater is surprisingly cold and there's usually frost. Snow and hail are common. However, it's possible to climb Elgon at any time of the year, though the rainy seasons of April-May and August-September are best avoided. The best time is between December and March.

Sightseeing

This is one of the loveliest and most unspoilt of all Kenya's national parks. If you are fit and hardy enough to labour up the elephant trails through its glorious forests, you can walk its moorland heights for days without meeting another soul, tramping heaths of tussock

Above: Groundsel on Kenya's high-altitude afro-alpine moorlands.

grass and wild flora, including lobelia and giant groundsel.

Burgeoning under the unique combination of rarefied air, unfiltered ultraviolet rays and freezing nights, these specimens flourish better here than on Mount Kenya or Kilimanjaro.

Different species of game lurk beneath the centuries-old trees that rise thirty metres or so (100 feet) — clean, straight-stemmed, and crowned with evergreen foliage. In the glades and dappled undergrowth beneath, the ever-alert, always nervous buck, duiker, and other small game pause, frozen in the panic of discovery as great herds of buffalo forage for fodder (See "National Parks", In Brief, for wildlife and vegetation).

Lower down are a series of "lava-tube" caves, some of which are more than sixty metres (200 feet) in diameter, set in the high basalt cliffs of the **Endebess Bluffs**.

One of these, **Kitum Cave**, was the inspiration for Rider Haggard's adventure drama, *She*. It's also been the inspiration for a television documentary about Elgon's elephants which "mine" the cave's salt by gouging it out during the night from walls deep inside the mountain, sometimes precipitating a roof fall

that traps one or two of these great pachyderms. The approach from Kitale takes the trekker to Kitum Cave.

Saiwa Swamp

Twenty kilometres (12 miles) south-east of Kitale, in the **Cherangani Hills**, **Saiwa Swamp National Park** whose two square kilometres (less than one square mile) form Kenya's smallest game sanctuary, is five kilometres (three miles) to the right off the main **Kitale-Lodwar road,** near the village of **Kipsain**.

There's also a very smart fishing camp, **Kapolet**, close to the park and from Kipsain another road leads west to the Suam fishing camp.

Set at an altitude of 1,870 metres (6,135 feet), in a basin of the meandering **Koitobos River,** filled with tall bulrushes and sedges, Saiwa Swamp was established principally to protect Kenya's only population of between eighty and 100 sitatunga, a rare amphibious antelope. Other mammals include monkey, nocturnal potto, spotted-necked otter, giant forest squirrel, leopard, and myriad birdlife (See "Wildlife: great and small, wild and wonderful", Part Three).

Above: Mount Elgon's Kitum Cave inspired Rider Haggard's book, *She*.

There is no accommodation nor are vehicles allowed, but there is a **campsite**. Saiwa's rare visitors make their way along a jungle path, where black and white colobus monkeys scamper through the trees, vervets scamper across the ground and you may catch a glimpse of the mandarin-like face of the Brazza monkey, to a wooden **walkway** above the swamp. In the canopy of trees, rare birds flit from perch to perch, including turacos, hornbills, and kingfishers.

Viewing platforms are raised above the waters of the swamp, where visitors can watch for their first sight of the sitatunga. The best times to see these shy creatures are late afternoon and early morning. The furthest platform is less than one kilometre (half-a-mile) from the campsite.

Cherangani Hills: High Peaks and Secret Valleys

The daunting barrier of the dramatic **Cherangani Hills** hides within its forests some of the finest mountain landscapes in the world. It also embraces a place sacred to Kenya nationalists — the small town of **Kapenguria**

where in the 1950s, the colonial government staged the rigged show trial of Mzee Jomo Kenyatta. He was convicted on perjured and fabricated evidence and sentenced to a seven-year incarceration on the burning shores of Lake Turkana.

The schoolroom where the trial was staged is a shrine to the memory of the nation's founding father and the prison compound and cell where he was held opposite the school is a **national monument**.

The Cherangani range rises to 3,517 metres (11,540 feet) at the northern end of the **Elgeyo Marakwet Escarpment** and in places falls 2,400 metres (8,000 feet) to the baking floor of the **Kerio Valley**, gateway to the deserts of Kenya's north.

Kenya's only range of fold mountains, the Cheranganis boast the fourth-highest point in Kenya — and one of the highest points in all Africa — but surprisingly they are rarely visited.

Yet they offer some of the most diverse and splendid mountain landscapes found anywhere — from gently rolling foothills to large and rugged peaks, from thick forest to open moorland with a wealth of afro-alpine flora —

184

and perhaps the deepest and most precipitous escarpment in Africa.

After the highest-point, 3,517-metre-high (11,540-feet) **Nagen,** other major peaks are **Sigogowa,** 3,327 metres (10,915 feet); **Koh,** 2,745 metres (9,000 feet); **Morobus,** 2,269 metres (7,445 feet); **Kaipos,** 2,362 metres (7,750 feet); **Kaibwibich,** 2,689 metres (8,823 feet); **Kalelaigelat,** 3,380 metres (11,090 feet); **Tavach,** 3,298 metres (10,821 feet); **Chepkotet,** 3,370 metres (11,057 feet); **Sondhang,** 3,216 metres (10,543 feet); **Chemnitrot,** 3,355 metres (11,000 feet); **Chesugo,** 3,080 metres (10,110 feet); **Nongwasha,** 3,355 metres (11,000 feet); **Kapsiliat,** 2,604 metres (8,544 feet), and **Kaisungur,** 3,167 metres (10,390 feet).

With the exception of Sigogowa, which stands separate from the main range, you can drive almost all the way to the top of some peaks but others involve strenuous, high-altitude trekking.

Indeed, the Cheranganis offer some of the best walking and trekking in Kenya — neither too hot nor too cold with none of the giant tussock grasses found in the Aberdares, Mount Elgon and Mount Kenya.

The northern end of the range, which is the higher, gives the best walking. In the south the hills are either cloaked in dense forest or thickly populated, and the eastern slopes, near the escarpment, which are the most densely settled, are generally not so appealing.

It's worth noting that the drive to some of the roadheads, especially Nagen, Tavach, Chemnirot, and Sondhang, is extremely long and walking for any distance above 3,000 metres (10,000 feet) without acclimatisation is exhausting (See "Climbing and Trekking Advisory"). A visit to the Cherangani, therefore, may be more tiring than you expect.

Getting there

Kitale in the North and Eldoret in the south are the two main bases from which to explore the Cheranganis. The main northern access to the high peaks is the **Cherangani Highway,** starting near Kapenguria and running through **Labot** to **Iten.**

Matatus ply this route — and from **Cheptongei** to Chesoi (but not beyond) — making it possible to reach the area by public transport. This means long but pleasant walks to the base of the main peaks.

Two rather long and indirect approaches take in some of the finest mountain roads in the country, well worth the travel for their own sake. They both pass through the **Kito Pass,** up the **Tot Escarpment** and off the **Kapenguria-Marich Pass.**

The first, from **Chesongoch** to **Chesoi,** brings you from the Kerio Valley up the Tot Escarpment on a splendid, if extremely rough, mountain road with breathtaking views over the Kerio Valley to the Tugen Hills.

One major attraction is that you can combine a visit to the hot waterfall at **Kapedo,** north of Baringo (See "Great Rift Valley: the land that was Eden") with an excursion through the Kito Pass and across the Kerio Valley.

Suitable **campsites** can be found by leaving **Kapsowar** on the **Cheptongei road** and camping in clearings in the forest, at the bottom of the valley just outside town. The perpendicular slopes above are dotted with distinctive stone-built Marakwet homesteads.

The escarpment itself is the location of an ancient irrigation system some forty kilometres (25 miles) long, feeding water from the Cheranganis into a network of canals, feeder ditches, and aqueducts all along the escarpment and down to its foot (See "The People", Part One). The best place to see this centuries-old system still at work is around **Chesoi** where a metre-wide (three-feet) channel clings to the hillside.

It's a system without parallel in the country and the results are spectacular — intensive, luxuriant *shambas* have grown up between the spurs and down towards the valley's main river.

The second route turns off the **Kapenguria-Marich Pass** road to pass along a valley of Himalayan proportions. Steep in places, this road eventually joins the Cherangani Highway at **Mbanga,** some way north of Labot. There are many good camping spots on the southern section.

It also serves as a first-class shortcut for anyone travelling on to **Lodwar** from Kalelaigelat (See "The North Rift: Cradle of Mankind"). For the road via the Kito Pass and Tot Escarpment, head north from **Baringo** to **Loruk,** where the tarmac ends and the **Maralal road** branches off to the right.

From there, go through **Nginyang** then bear right at the first fork where a sign to the **Post Office** points left. The road now deteriorates and climbs up through the Kito Pass to cross the floor of the Kerio Valley to Tot. At the T-junction, turn left to **Chesongoch.**

Above: Scenic valley floor in the high Cheranganis.

Continue straight through the village and turn right shortly after, on to a steep track that climbs continuously to **Chesoi**, high on the escarpment—one of Kenya's most spectacular roads with views that defy description.

The scenery changes dramatically where the road enters the foothills and forest of the main Cheranganis.

You can bypass Chesoi Centre by continuing straight ahead to **Kapsowar**, a two-hour drive from Tot. Or you can bear right to **Cheptongei,** another two-hour drive. In the middle of the town a right turn takes you on to the Cherangani Highway.

The quickest route to the more southerly peaks, up to Nagen and Chemnirot, is via Eldoret and Iten. The road out of Eldoret, not signposted, begins with a right turn out of the **Sirikwa Hotel** car park followed by a left turn at the first intersection, past the **airport**, and onwards to link up with the tarmac road to Iten.

At Iten, turn left along a dirt road at the **signpost** for thirteen kilometres (eight miles) to **Singore**, where the road swings left.

After just over a kilometre (two-thirds of a mile) take the right turn north — for twenty-two kilometres (14 miles) — to **Cheptongei.** In the middle of the village, there's a left turn on to the Cherangani Highway. Note that some villages are so small, that you miss them if you blink.

The northern approach, via **Kapenguria,** suitable for the northern peaks, is reached from Kitale along the fast tarmac road to Kapenguria. Turn right, beyond Kapenguria on to the Cherangani Highway, signposted **Kaibwibich** and Labot.

The most direct approach to the central Cherangani is via **Cherangani Town**, turning east at **Moi's Bridge** off the Eldoret-Kitale road — or along the road from Kitale to Cherangani Town where a road leads up to the crossroads at **Labot.**

The only petrol stations are at Baringo, Kitale, Eldoret, and Kapenguria and you should allow for increased fuel consumption because of the altitude and the rough state of some tracks.

Apart from one rough section between Kaibwibich and Kapenguria the Cherangani Highway is suitable for two-wheel-drive vehicles. But note that most tracks off the Highway are often completely impassable in wet weather and generally require 4WD.

Other roads have been much improved in the last few years, however, and are in good condition. Some are so rarely used, they are generally grassy and not muddy.

Sightseeing

Sigogowa (or Mtelo Mountain or Sekerr) is an excellent viewpoint. This huge mountain, which stands alone to the north of the Cheranganis, is not representative of the range.

It is best approached from the thornbush scrub of the Turkana plains and up the barren and rugged lower slopes of the mountain to a lush green "lost world" valley inhabited by the Pokot people (See "The People", Part One).

From Kitale follow what is possibly Kenya's most spectacular tarmac road, to **Akeriamet,** at the foot of the Marich pass.

Beyond Akeriamet, several tracks lead off left to meet up at a concrete road that climbs a steep ridge to the **radio relay station.** From the first turnoff you need 4WD.

Continue on a rough dirt track past the relay station to the roadhead at **Mbara.** From Kitale this drive takes between three and four hours.

Situated on a northern spur of the Cheranganis, slightly separate from the main body, **Koh** culminates in **Koh Boss,** a spectacular rock mass which has superb views.

It's reached from a point near the **Weiwei River,** along the Sigor-Tot road, where you take the track south to **Tamkal.** About three kilometres (two miles) before Tamkal, a path leads up to Koh.

Morobus, a small but striking peak close to the Lodwar road between Kapenguria and the Marich Pass, is immediately obvious once you begin the long descent from Kapenguria. Its craggy west face and steep south ridge are stunningly prominent.

From Kitale follow the Lodwar road for about one hour until you reach a convenient stopping point to the north of the hill.

Panoramic

Although it's not particularly impressive as mountains go, **Kaibwibich** does give a spectacular panorama of its distant neighbours **Elgon** and Uganda's **Kadam** — and also the high Cheranganis.

The nearby **rest house,** a little too remote from the main peak to be a good base, is nonetheless in beautiful surroundings. You'll need permission from the DC's office in Kapenguria to use it. The keys are held at the **Chief's office** in Kaibwibich village.

Take the Cherangani Highway south-east from Kapenguria to the village. Turn right up the track signposted "Rest House" and turn left after 400 metres (less than a quarter of a mile) towards the top of the hill.

During the dry season it's usually possible to drive right up to the **trig point** in an ordinary saloon car, but most will find it more convenient to walk the last seventy metres (230 feet) to save opening the gate.

Right in the heart of the high Cheranganis, **Kalelaigelat,** provides considerable sport for drivers, if not walkers, and one approach passes through particularly delightful countryside.

It has a different ambience to most — probably due to its bleak moorlands and surprisingly scanty forest. Sunup from the summit, with views over the Trans-Nzoia, is spectacular.

It makes a convenient and easy peak to climb for those *en route* to **Sondhang** or **Tavach,** and it is worth the detour for those returning from Nagen. The immediate vicinity is too exposed for good camping but there are plenty of spots on the track north to Sondhang.

The first approach is to take the Cherangani Highway to the crossroads before Labot and then the right turn bypassing Labot to **Tangul.** There are several nice campsites in this section. Turn left at Tangul for eight kilometres (five miles) along a well-maintained rural access road to Kalelaigelat. The last section is short but unbelievably steep. Allow about four hours for the drive from Eldoret.

The second approach also starts along the Cherangani Highway, from Kapenguria. After thirty-five kilometres (22 miles), at **Mbanga** there's a left turn on to another rural access road, through beautiful open parkland with several fine camping spots.

After fourteen kilometres (nine miles), turn right on to a poor 4WD track — not only extremely rough but unbelievably steep.

If you continue along the rural access road from this turnoff for another three kilometres (two miles) you arrive at the junction with the first approach. Then continue for another forty-two kilometres (26 miles) along one of Kenya's most spectacular roads to join the Marich Pass tarmac road.

Well-maintained, the road winds up and down through a valley that would not disgrace the foothills of the Himalaya. There are splendid views of Sigogowa and Sondhang.

The other end of this road is forty-three kilometres (27 miles) north of the **Saiwa Swamp National Park** turn off, signposted **Kapchemogon**.

Tavach, a pleasant peak situated on a spur to the west of the main Cheranganis, offers marvellous scenic panoramas.

Camping spots can be found alongside the approach road. The final track, from Kalelaigelat to Sondhang, gives a great feeling of passing through an untravelled world.

From the summit of Kalelaigelat proceed north along the Sondhang track east of a deep valley. (Another of the high peaks, **Chepkotet**, lies to the north-east and is a short walk to the west of the track).

After about ten kilometres (six miles) you come to a small village where a fairly passable track comes in from the left. You can't miss Tavach from this point. It sits on a spur about two kilometres (little more than a mile) distant but if you want to drive you'll definitely need 4WD.

Sondhang, marks the end of the major spur of this part of the Cheranganis, above a steep westerly scarp with another to the east — one of the most memorable of these fine hills.

From the summit of Kalelaigelat, make your way north towards Tavach until you reach the end of the extremely rough track. Although it is only about twenty kilometres (12 miles), allow two hours.

Nagen, highest point in the Cheranganis, is irresistible to all who visit the area and takes you right into the heart of the range through exquisitely varied scenery. At the top you are rewarded with stunning views of the **Weiwei Valley**. If you allow enough time you can also take in Chemnirot — possibly some of the other peaks.

There are two popular routes: one through parkland and woodland with some splendid glades for camping, the other much longer but more sedate as it avoids some fragile bridges.

Drive on to Tangul, as if approaching Kalelaigelat, and then follow the signposted route straight on through Tangul to Kamelogon. In a 4WD, which should also have high clearance, it takes about two hours to the roadhead, which is about thirteen kilometres (eight miles) from Tangul.

A long wheelbase, however, may pose some difficulties on the tight bends higher up. It is easy to loose the track at several points and there is one particularly weak bridge and several other poor ones, although their condition occasionally improves.

However, do note that it can be frustrating and difficult to find the roadhead direct from Chemnirot. For much of the way it is not in view and you have to cross many deep side valleys.

An ascent of **Kaisungur** is easier. It's a relatively simple walk along a high ridge overlooking the central Cheranganis and the Trans-Nzoia farmfields — all heady enough to leave you breathless without fatigue.

Kaisungur can easily be climbed on the approach to Nagen from **Cheptongei**. The area to the north of Kaisungur is much less inhabited than that to the south and offers a refreshing sight to those missing the wilderness.

Follow the Cherangani Highway for twenty-four kilometres (15 miles) from Cheptongei where it skirts the eastern flank of the hill. An obvious rough track leads steeply up to a **radio station.**

Nongwasha, sometimes spelt Longoswa, is a forested mountain six kilometres (four miles) north-west of Chesoi but you'll probably need a local guide to show you the way.

To climb **Kipkunur,** which lies along the west ridge of Kapsowar with a number of impressive cliffs, you have to walk from the road, somewhere between Labot and Kapsowar, and then through thick, well-cultivated smallholdings and forest.

A short walk up one of the most southerly outliers of this range, **Chemurkoi** is rewarded by compelling panoramas in all directions. Follow the Cherangani Highway north-west from Cheptongei past **Kipnai Market** and **school** for twenty kilometres (13 miles) to the start of another rural access road that heads south.

Follow this new road for sixty-two kilometres (39 miles) until, just before a bend to the right, a rough track on the left, bears away over open grassland to a hut about one kilometre (two thirds of a mile) from the road.

Another ingress is a left turn off the Iten road twenty kilometres (13 miles) out of Eldoret to **Moiben** and **Chebororwa.** Opposite the **Chief's office** there's a right turn along a

Above: Tendrils of cloud caress the high points of the lovely Tugen Hills.

steep and winding road through thick forest to the north of the hill.

Neighbouring **Kapsiliat,** north of Iten, also offers splendid panoramas. Twenty-five kilometres (16 miles) after leaving the tarmac at Iten, just before **Chiebiemet,** take the left turn on to a small track for one kilometre (two-thirds of a mile), then cross a bridge and climb for another kilometre (two-thirds of a mile) before taking a right fork followed by a left turn on to a parallel track with a final turn left to a parking spot beyond some estate buildings.

The Great Rift Valley:
The Land that was Eden

The world has many great mountains, lakes, deserts, and oceans. But of its valleys and gorges one alone dwarfs them all in size and dimension. Indeed, after the oceans, the Great Rift Valley is perhaps the single most dramatic feature on earth (see "The Land", Part One).

In Kenya much of the Rift remains an expanse of raw Africa that dazzles the eye with its haunting grandeur. Nowhere is it more apparent, more dramatic, or more picturesque. Entering the country in the north from Ethiopia through the jade waters of Lake Turkana, it slices right through the middle of Kenya like a broad knife-cut to enter Tanzania in the south at Lake Natron.

Incorporating cliffs, escarpments, sand rivers, and arid plains flowing like molten lava from the north down to the low-lying, heat-ridden, soda lakes in the south, in some places this natural divide is up to 100 kilometres (60 miles) wide.

The valley floor rises from little more than 200 metres (650 feet) above sea level at Lake Turkana to reach its highest point around Lake Naivasha at 1,900 metres (6,200 feet), before descending abruptly to enter Tanzania just 580 metres (1,900 feet) above sea level.

Where the valley floor is at its highest so, too, are the valley's precipitous walls, reaching 3,964 metres (13,120 feet) in the Aberdares above Naivasha.

Where the floor is at its lowest, as at Turkana, there is virtually no distinction between the Great Rift and the stark, arid wildernesses that adjoin it. To the east, the featureless semi-desert scrub stretches across hundreds of kilometres to Somalia's Indian Ocean coastline.

Yet in other places, where the floor is not much more than 610 metres (2,000 feet) above sea level its great cliffs rise sheer above it for more than 1,520 metres (5,000 feet).

The power that transformed the face of the world is evident in the Rift's thirty active and semi-active volcanoes and countless boiling springs. They bring sodium carbonate bubbling up from deep beneath the earth, turning many Rift lakes into bitter pans of water or blistering soda flats.

Today the Kenya and Tanzania sections of the Rift are the world's last treasury of cultures, flora, and fauna, both terrestrial and avian, that have continued unchanged for centuries. The valley plains contain the last great assembly of African wildlife and from one end to the other, Kenya's human cultures form a cross-section of the entire African continent's cultural wealth.

Little wonder, perhaps, that many then think of this as Eden.

As a unique geological phenomenon, the Rift was first investigated in 1893 by a young Scot, John Walter Gregory. Marching up to Baringo from Mombasa, he hammered out samples from different rock layers and returned to proclaim his conclusions — that this cataclysmic rent on the face of the earth was formed "by the rock sinking in mass, while the adjacent land remained stationary".

It was Gregory who named it the Great Rift Valley but perhaps the name given by Austrian geologist, Eduard Suess, two years earlier best captures the imagination. He called it *graben*, derived from *grabe*, the grave. In the light of the fossil remains which have since been found on the shores of Lake Turkana no other description could be more exact.

Suess never visited the continent but from a map of Africa he deduced that the Rift Lakes were part of a connected chain created by a series of movements in the earth's surface.

These movements uplifted and exposed sedimentary layers that can be dated precisely, and also preserved prehistoric fossils in a remarkably good state.

All along this majestic flaw, in the walls of its great scarps and close to the surface of its floor, lies evidence of mankind's beginnings. Much still remains to be discovered.

Most of what has already been revealed was found at two of the most significant sites in palaeontological history — **Olduvai Gorge** in the Tanzania Rift and **Koobi Fora** on the eastern shores of Lake Turkana (See "The Dust and the Ashes", Part One).

Where to stay

In Naivasha, Lake Naivasha Hotel (5-star), Safariland Lodge (4-star). In Nakuru, Midland Hotel (3-star); Pivot Hotel (2-star). In Baringo,

Island Camp (4-star), Lake Baringo Club (5-star). In Kabarnet, Kabarnet Hotel (4-star). In Lodwar, New Lodwar Lodge (basic budget). At Lake Turkana, Eliye Springs Lodge (basic), Lake Turkana Fishing Lodge (4-star), Oasis Lodge (basic).

There are others. See Listings for "Hotels".

National Parks

In Lake Nakuru National Park, Lion Hill Camp, book through Sarova Hotels, New Stanley Hotel, Nairobi.

The Southern and Central Rift

From Nairobi take the **Langata Road** from Uhuru Highway to the **Magadi Road**, left, and on through **Ongata Rongai.** Leaving **Kiserian**, and the turnoff to **Ngong Town** on the right, drive on up the south-eastern shoulder of the Ngong Hills at some 2,134 metres (7,000 feet). Here, the ground suddenly drops between 610 and 914 metres (2,000-3,000 feet) to the stunningly stark and dramatic Maasai wilderness of arid thorn and scrub desert studded with volcanic mountains.

This view inspired Isak Dinnesen to begin writing. Today, photographers leap out of their cars with light metre, tripod, and lens ready to capture the scene.

At the scruffy hamlet of **Olepolos** turn right along the dirt road for the circular tour of Ngong Hills (See "The Giant's Knuckles").

From here the Magadi Road takes on a serpentine aspect as it swoops down through a series of exhilarating straights and tortuous hairpins, the temperature increasing by the kilometre. One hour out on a cold winter's day in Nairobi and you're back to full-blooded Equatorial warmth — a swift cure for rheumy bones and muscles.

Just a little over halfway between Nairobi and Lake Magadi you pass through the straggling township of **Oltepesi.** Take the left turn to **Olorgesailie Prehistoric Site,** well signposted, one-and-a-half kilometres (one mile) from the road.

Nothing distinguishes this place as the location of what Dr. Louis Leakey described as "the most significant in the whole world of Aechulian hand axe culture".

Gregory first stumbled over this clearing littered with bones when travelled across the Rift on his approach from the Kapiti Plains,

Overleaf: Soda pans at Lake Magadi.

with the **Meto Hills** — dominated by the **Black Mountain** peak — forming the valley's eastern flank.

At one time this was a lake, fed by the **Keju Nyiro river.** Between 400,000 and 500,000 years ago the lake shores were inhabited by some of our earliest ancestors. The lake disappeared, however, after the river was diverted by one of the many cataclysmic earth movements that shaped the Rift.

When Leakey cleared the site in 1924, on the ground, all around, lay dramatic evidence of the first creature to abandon a four-legged posture and walk upright.

Our earliest ancestor, *Homo erectus*, quickly became an adept pedestrian and groups soon moved south to live around **Olorgesailie.**

The fossils found by Leakey were the broken skeletons of a race of giant baboons, long extinct. They had been slain by rough weapons of chipped stones and crude cobbles that also lay around. These weapons were fashioned from rock that does not occur naturally in this part of the Rift. Man had become a hunter.

Olorgesailie was declared a **National Monument** in 1947 and you can see the fossils *in situ* today — a tenuous thread in the tangled and yet-to-be unravelled tapestry of the story of mankind.

Knowledgeable National Museum guides explain the significance of finds as you visit the site's two square kilometres (less than a square mile). You can spend the night in one of four *bandas*, **guest houses**, or under canvas on the **camping site** — all for a nominal charge.

To reach Lake Magadi you have another forty-five kilometres (28 miles) to travel. The road continues through the **Ol Keju Nyiro valley** (See "The Land", Part One), skirting gaunt and forbidding volcanic outcrops and deep ravines, descending all the time until you crest a final ridge. There, laid out beneath you, is **Lake Magadi,** shimmering with all the fires — cobalt, indigo, reds, crystalline-whites, and pastel-pinks — of Dante's Inferno.

You enter Magadi town across a causeway over the surreal pink saltpans and through a company **police barrier** where all visitors are requested to report their arrival.

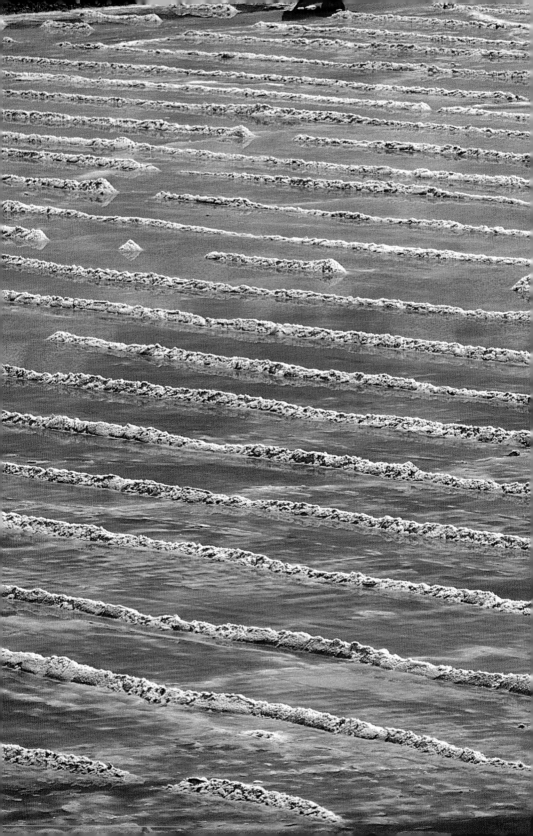

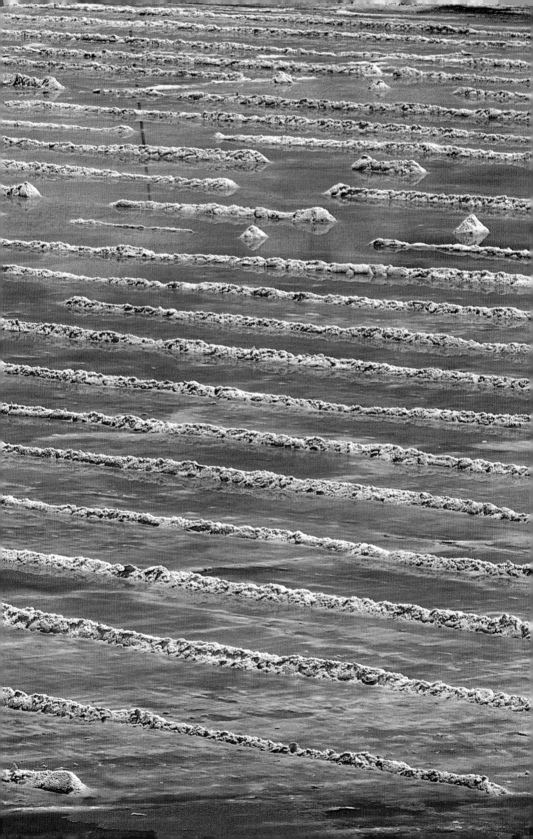

Dante's inferno

Magadi and its close neighbour, **Lake Natron,** just a few kilometres south across the Tanzania border, are the richest of the soda lakes — the others are **Elmenteita, Nakuru,** and **Turkana** — that characterize the East African section of the Rift. Their surface heights vary in altitude from a few hundred metres to more than 1,640 metres (5,000 feet) above sea level.

Lake Magadi, is the world's second-largest single source of trona, *Sodium sesqui carbonate,* after California's Salton Sea. The lake's 100 square kilometres (40 square miles) form a drainage sump without outlet.

Set only 580 metres (1,900 feet) above sea level, the sun's rays funnel mercilessly into this arena, and the intense evaporation creates ideal conditions for excavating the trona. Only after rare rains is the lake covered with water.

Mineral rights were granted to two prospectors, Deacon and Walsh, who staked a claim to Magadi in 1901. In September 1911, the company they established signed a contract with George Pauling to build a 150-kilometre-long (90-mile) railway line from Konza to Magadi. Much of the filming for *Out of Africa* was carried out along this track.

The complications of World War I meant that it wasn't until 1 August 1915 that the line was handed over to the Uganda Railway — now Kenya Railways — which still operates it.

Today, the lake is a prime mover of the Kenya economy and a major foreign currency earner. Each year the company processes between 150,000 and 200,000 tonnes of soda ash for export markets in south-east Asia and the Far East.

Sightseeing

The lake itself is fascinating to walk across — on causeways — but it's important to wear sunglasses and hat. The reflection off the soda surface is searing.

From the air, Magadi's surface is like a covering of crumpled, melted icing mottled with patches of indigo-red where industrial excavators cut through the crust to haul up this naturally recurring source of soda ash — nowhere more than three metres (ten feet) deep — which will never dry up.

Its eastern shores are dominated by the town that the Magadi soda company has developed during the last eighty years —

Above: Young darters on a Rift Lake await the return of their parents with supper.

Opposite: Sundown over the Rift Valley.

complete with elegant residential suburbs, working-class flats, smart **club** with **swimming pool, hospital, schools, mosque, churches,** and a **golf course** with "browns", a mixture of serried sludge and sump oil, instead of greens.

Occasionally millions of flamingos breed here, and the bleak but hauntingly-lovely landscapes around have an astonishing wealth of bird life. Its western shores are beautiful, with hot springs, promontories, and little valleys.

Through the Kedong Valley

The western buttress of the Rift at Magadi is formed by the formidable wall of the **Nkuruman Escarpment** topped by the **Loita Hills.** No road climbs these rugged cliffs but the dirt trails are just about negotiable in 4WD vehicles.

The tracks cut through thick forests to the top where, beyond the Loita Hills, the land levels out in the **Maasai Mara**. Some tour operators arrange individual safaris into these forests and up the escarpment. On your own you could get lost.

The more normal route is to return from Magadi to **Olepolos** and then take the dirt road left along the base of the Ngong Hills through the **Kedong Valley**, past **Susua**, the 2,357-metres-high (7,733-feet) dormant volcano to the west (See "Kenya's Mountains"). Susua has a deep moat in its crater, surrounding an inner plateau like something from Conan Doyle's *Lost World*. Enthusiastic potholers enjoy exploring its many lava tubes.

To get to the plateau you can swing across the giddying drop into the moat over a cable that was put up by the Operation Drake adventure project in the early 1980s. In 1989, the Kenya Speleological Society — an organisation of Kenyan cave explorers — held their annual dinner dance in one of Susua's caves which is known to them as the "Ballroom".

The dirt road links up with the Naivasha-Narok tarmac road. Turn right to the old Nairobi-Naivasha-Nakuru road and then left to where it cuts between the foot of the Rift Escarpment and the 2,776-metre-high (9,108-feet) **Mount Longonot.** With its crumpled crater rim, it is the highest of all Kenya's Rift Valley volcanoes and its sides are lined with lava funnels.

If you wish to climb to the rim — not recommended if you suffer from vertigo — report at the **police station** just outside Longonot Village, where you can leave your car and valuables and ask about a guide.

From the main road a rough track leads seven kilometres (four miles) to the start of the climb. From base to summit all the way around, Longonot's flanks are creased with dozens of the ridges that inspired its Maasai name — *Oloonong'ot*, "mountain of steep ridges" — and studded with parasitic volcanic cones.

Dark clouds often boil over its rim during the rainy season, before rolling on across the gulf and over the facing escarpment, which is almost the same height.

The climb to the top and around the rim is a stiff four to five hours walking. At 3,740 metres (9,000 feet), the air is already beginning to thin and lungs labour, but there's a small plateau on the flanks of the highest point which is ideal for relaxation and a picnic.

On a clear day the views are spectacular. When Thomson climbed it during his 1883 trek he was overcome with vertigo and experienced an irresistible urge to throw himself down into the abyss.

It's easier to circle the rim anti-clockwise — heading towards Naivasha from the top of the climb. From this approach, the ascent to the summit is much quicker since it is neither so difficult or so steep.

The rim is very narrow and extreme caution should be taken as most of the path crosses through unstable, crumbling volcanic lava. The wall inside the crater — the floor is a dead ringer for Conan Doyle's Pleistocene relic of the age of dinosaurs — is a sheer drop of hundreds of metres. One slip could be fatal.

One pilot who flew beneath the level of the rim, to circle inside, dared too much. Caught in the downdrafts that hurtle over its rim, he never emerged.

The crater floor is an unviolated wildlife retreat. Only one precipitous narrow trail zigzags to a small plateau halfway down. From here — if you're feeling suicidal — you can scramble the rest of the way in about ten minutes. But few hazard the further descent through scrub forest and thorn at the bottom where buffalo are thick on the ground.

Until recently, the crater floor and the slopes outside were notable for their steam. Fiery Longonot is only sleeping and the nascent energy beneath its rumbling crown has now been tapped in Africa's only geothermal project.

Above: "Lost World" plateau in crater of volcanic Mount Susua in the Rift Valley.

Several thousand metres beneath the surface, ground waters register an astonishing 304°C (579°F) — one of the hottest temperatures recorded. On the southern slopes, staccato jets of steam from the boreholes rise into the sky.

The railway line passes the eastern base of Longonot, but hundreds of metres above, the **scenic highway** from Limuru rides the escarpment crest at almost 2,743 metres (9,000 feet). This is the main artery that links Uganda and much of eastern and central Africa to the Indian Ocean seaboard.

Nonetheless, the landscape around Longonot's slopes, though close to large population centres, is as wild as any in Kenya.

Despite intensive settlement on its lower flanks, Longonot was declared a fifty-two square-kilometre (20-square-mile) national park in the 1980s along with nearby sixty-eight square kilometre (26-square-mile) **Hell's Gate.**

Also known as **Njorowa Gorge,** Hell's Gate is considered to have one of the most spectacular and exciting walks in Kenya, leading through a gorge lined with sheer, red cliffs (See "National Parks", In Brief, for wildlife and vegetation).

There are many birds of prey and swifts in the area — it's possible to observe between twenty-five and thirty different species in any one day.

The gorge was the ancient outlet for Lake Naivasha. Dominating the scene, the volcanic plug of **Fischer's Tower,** named after the German who explored this region in the nineteenth century, offers a stunning rock climb fraught with peril (See "The Dust and the Ashes", Part One). A similar obelisk, **Ol Basta,** was also exposed when the softer lava surrounding it eroded away.

If you come across fibreglass boulders and rocks among the genuine articles don't be too surprised. In the early 1980s a film crew chose Hell's Gate as one of the locations for *Sheena — Queen of the Jungle* and, in typical Hollywood fashion, decided that nature's handiwork needed an assist from their props department.

From the **Naivasha YMCA** on **Moi South Road** which circles Lake Naivasha, turn left along a trail for the **Park entrance.** Since it's some twenty-six kilometres (16 miles) there and back you'll need an early start to complete the round trip comfortably. Don't forget to

Above: Longonot earth satellite station in Kenya's Rift Valley.
Opposite: Seamed and scarrred profile of Longonot, a sleeping Rift Valley volcano.

carry plenty of water.

There isn't another track so it's easy to follow even when, after two kilometres (little more than a mile) or so, the trail veers suddenly right to reveal Fischer's Tower. It's thought that this volcanic stack was left standing when the water of the prehistoric lake that stretched from Naivasha to Nakuru cut through the gorge in search of an outlet.

The agile rock hyrax and klipspringers have made the gorge's stratified cliffs their own domain and at least one pair of rare Lammergeier eagles breed there. More easily seen are the secretary birds which strut through the grass at the base of the cliffs.

When you reach the southern end of the gorge the second rock tower, Ol Basta, marks its transition into tangled ravine. At this point, you have three options. One is to struggle forward another twelve kilometres (seven miles) to the end of the canyon — with another fifteen-kilometre hike (nine-mile) from there to the Narok road.

If you choose this option, be prepared for a two-day walk — and be sure to take a Survey of Kenya map and compass.

The second option — the most practical —

is to retrace your footsteps to the park gate.

The third, for the adventurous but not the easily tired, is to climb the slope to the right, through thick scrub, to the Olkaria **geothermal station**. From the main building a good track leads on to the lake road just past **Fisherman's Camp**. This leg takes about three hours.

Lake Naivasha: The Pearl In The Rift

It was the German naturalist, Gustav Fischer, who first "discovered" **Lake Naivasha** in 1883 — although the instant the local Maasai discovered him he sensibly turned and fled. The lake's name derives from the Maa word *En-aiposha* ("the lake") and was corrupted forever by early Europeans who recorded the mispronunciation of their Swahili porters.

The English officer who carried out the initial survey for the "Lunatic Line", Captain Macdonald, commented in his diaries that the lake was "full of hippo".

It was here that Gregory paused to make his

first assays of the Rift strata but with the Maasai at that time hostile to strangers, Gregory did not pause long. He picked up his chisels and hammers and marched on another 160 kilometres (100 miles) to Baringo.

Spread out over 110 square kilometres (43 square miles), a pearl in the bosom of the Kenya Rift, the waters of Lake Naivasha glisten silver as the sun slopes swiftly towards the west. It's a popular weekend resort for Nairobi residents.

Purest and highest of all the Rift lakes, Naivasha is also a bird sanctuary without peer. Over 400 species have been recorded here; more than the entire list of birds seen in the British Isles (See "Birdlife", Part Three).

It was on these shores that Joy Adamson fostered Elsa and her cubs, the heroine of her wildlife classic, *Born Free*. Now Adamson's home, **Elsamere,** is a living memorial — a wildlife education centre and museum to the woman brutally murdered at north Kenya's Shaba National Reserve in 1980.

Open to the public during the afternoons, Elsamere is close to the rambling, **Lake Naivasha Hotel** which is framed by yellow fever trees in thirteen hectares (32 acres) of gardens, shrubs, flowers, and verdant lawns which sprawl down to the lake.

Just after the war, this was Kenya's international air terminal when the flying boats of British Overseas Airways flew a leisurely course along the course of the Nile and on down to South Africa. They landed at what is now the hotel, and passengers were ferried ashore before the eighty-four-kilometre (52-mile) journey by road to Nairobi.

Apart from tourism and ornithology, Lake Naivasha is the fount of one of Kenya's great agro-industries. Kenya's fledgling wine industry has taken root here and carefully tended vineyards established since 1980 produce vintage Naivasha wines.

Lake waters irrigate thousands of hectares of fertile volcanic loam which burgeon with vegetables and colourful flowers. During the high season, more than a million stems a night are airlifted to winterbound Europe, taking a hint of the tropical sun to warm thousands of icebound homes with their colour and fragrance.

Naivasha town is some distance from the lake and has little to offer to tourists.

Getting there

Two kilometres (one mile) south of Naivasha, a right turn leads into **Moi South Road**. After a few kilometres you pass the upmarket Lake **Naivasha Hotel,** right and after another eight kilometres (five miles), leaving scrub and farmlands to the left, and vineyards to the right, another right turn leads to **Safariland Lodge**. It's roughly the same distance on round the lake to Carnelly's **Fisherman's Camp.**

Sightseeing

Midway between Lake Naivasha Hotel and Safariland is a **grape farm** which was once a marina. When the lake dries up, a narrow causeway links the farm to **Crescent Island**.

The island takes its name from its shape. It's the visible tip of a volcanic crater rim, forming a bay in the deepest part of the lake.

Lake Naivasha Hotel run regular boat excursions to the island which is a private game sanctuary, home to hundreds of species of birds as well as gazelle, waterbuck, and some large pythons.

It's another rare place where you can wander among the wildlife on foot — in perfect safety. But, if you are on the shoreline, don't go too near the wallowing hippo.

On the nearby mainland the **Naivasha polo club** welcome visitors to watch this "king of games", usually played on Sundays right on the shores of the lake.

Just beyond Fisherman's Camp, a scenic viewpoint overlooks a small lake set in the north-western shores of the main lake.

North of this, some six kilometres (four miles) past the **South Lake police post**, between the shore of the main lake and the road, lie the dark green waters of a third **crater lake** which is something of a bovine health spa. The Maasai claim its alkaline waters offer a cure for sick cattle.

To Gilgil

From Naivasha town, the main street leads out to, left, the major Nairobi-Nakuru road. For twenty-seven kilometres (17 miles) it cuts through thick groves of fever trees — acacia thorn — to bypass, on the right, **Gilgil.**

This sprawling, somewhat scruffy town grew out of a small market centre. Five kilometres (three miles) out of Gilgil, along the **Nyahururu** road, under a narrow railway bridge, **Pembroke College**, right, is an elitist Kenya preparatory school. To the left, **Gilgil**

Club, with its mellow timber buildings, is redolent with colonial ambience.

Sprawling down the moorland salient from the north on the other side of the road is the club's **golf course** — rough fairways, and "browns" instead of greens, but, even so, what a joy a round of golf is in these open highland surroundings.

The **Commonwealth War Cemetery** —one of forty such cemeteries in Kenya maintained immaculately by the Commonwealth War Graves Commission — where about 200 victims of the Second World War are buried, is about two kilometres (little more than a mile) out of town along the same road. Just a little further on is a major military encampment.

Gilgil is also a training base for recruits to Kenya's famous **National Youth Service.** This remarkable institution is not centred on defence but on youth training.

Recruits serve two years, but after basic military training at Gilgil, they are deployed to carry out many large-scale civil projects to help maintain the impetus of national development.

You can also travel north over the high moorlands to Nyahururu through **Ol Kalau,** passing the Wanjohi Valley *en route,* or branch off this road to **Subukia** (See "Heartland of Kenya: magic mountains, moorlands wild").

To Nakuru

Beyond the Gilgil turnoff, the main road sweeps down the eastern wall of the Rift towards **Lake Elmenteita.** There are a number of prehistoric sites in the cliff face and by the road.

One of them, **Kariandus,** is next to the **diatomite mines** of the same name. The site, which has a number of *in situ* Aechulian tool exhibits, about a ten-minute-walk from the road, is open every weekday. It was cleared by Dr. Louis Leakey in 1928 as he rifled through the Rift in search of mankind's origins.

Next door, a mine excavates the Rift's diatomite, a startlingly-white chalky extract. Composed of billions of compressed silica and the skeletons of microscopic sea organisms (diatoms) that flourished here millions of years before mankind evolved, diatomite now serves as a water filter and is used in the brewing industry. It also works as non-toxic insecticide in grain stores and was used

traditionally by the Kikuyu, as *karia andus* ("war-paint").

After half-a-century of excavation the mine has become a deep hole in the ground. A trail leads down its glittering white sides to the bottom where several tunnels are driven into the sides.

Just three kilometres (two miles) beyond the mine, the road cuts above **Elmenteita.** One of the smallest of the Rift lakes, this shallow sump dries up periodically but forms part of the Delamere family's **Soysambu** estate (See "The Dust and the Ashes", Part One).

A dirt road on the left, shortly after Gilgil, skirts the lake shore to follow the old slave trail from Lake Victoria and Uganda. This trail was said to have inspired H. Rider Haggard's *King Solomon's Mines.* Haggard's brother, Captain Jack, served in Lamu for many years as the first British administrative officer and his letters were a great source of inspiration (See "Lamu: Enchanted Islands").

From Elmenteita it's another thirty-seven kilometres (23 miles) to Kenya's fourth-largest town, Nakuru, which takes its name from the Maa word *Enakuro,* "the place of swirling dust".

Nakuru: The Greatest Bird Show on Earth

Photographs taken in 1900 show Nakuru as a desolate empty plain. It appears to begin abruptly at the end of the first railway platform built "as if the bare and mysterious land beyond was forbidden territory", wrote Alastair Matheson in *Railway across the Equator.*

The town that sprang up on this vast, barren plain, with its bleak perspectives soon after the arrival of Uganda Railway came under the patronage of Lord Delamere (See "The Dust and the Ashes", Part One).

The town is perched on the western slopes of the **Menengai Crater,** the second-largest volcanic caldera in the world, overlooking the seasonal Lake Nakuru, which varies in size from five to thirty square kilometres (two-12 square miles), according to the volume of the seasonal rains.

Nakuru is also the farm capital of the country, and the administrative headquarters

Overleaf: Tourists enjoy a pioneer-style ox-wagon trek through the Rift Valley near Lake Naivasha.

of Kenya's sprawling Rift Valley Province which stretches from the Sudanese border to the slopes of Kilimanjaro.

This vibrant, noisy, dusty, entrepôt headquarters of the giant **Kenya Grain Growers Co-operative Union** (KGGCU) and many other large national and multinational enterprises, has grown rapidly in post-Independence Kenya.

It serves as focal point for visits to **Nakuru National Park,** and the nearby, prehistoric settlement site of **Hyrax Hill** on the slopes of Menengai Crater. It also serves as the starting point for trips into Kenya's central Rift Valley.

Sightseeing

Apart from the annual Nakuru Agricultural Society of Kenya show, Kenya's premier farm show, there's not much for visitors to see or do in the town itself. The **Rift Valley Sports Club,** however, with its **cricket ground** and splendid, colonial, solid stone, two-storey **clubhouse,** with residential rooms, is where the elite congregate.

But for tourists, and bird watching buffs, the 188 square kilometres (73 square miles) of **Lake Nakuru National Park** is something of a Mecca. During one of Kenya's cyclical wet spells, ornithologist and artist Peter Scott arrived on these fluctuating shores to marvel at a sight he described as the greatest bird spectacle in the world.

There, wading in the shallows, floating a little way offshore, with more still circling above on the Rift thermals, was a cloud of amorphous blush-pink — two million or more flamingos, one-third of the world's entire population of lesser flamingos.

As a result of Scott's acclaim, the national park flourished. After a drought in the 1980s, a combination of increased rainfall and decreased evaporation lowered the lake's salinity and raised the water level and the flamingos began to disperse.

But there is much more to Lake Nakuru than just flamingo. The national park, small and beautiful, is one of the easiest parks in Kenya to visit. At an altitude of between 1,753 and 2,073 metres (5,350-6,300 feet), the park is bordered to the west by one wall of the Rift Valley and to the east by a salt-dome hill. There is a crater in the north and open plains to the south.

Wooded cliffs and shores surround swamp-fringed water, where sounders of hippo splash by day and graze by night at the northern end. Most of the parkland is covered with light, acacia forest containing well-marked tracks to a variety of hides and lookouts.

The park has more than 450 recorded species of birds, including, many migratory species which leave England during the northern winter. It is one of the few national parks established specifically to protect birds (See "National Parks", In Brief, for wildlife and vegetation).

In recent years it has also become a sanctuary for a group of Rothschild's giraffe and the endangered black rhino. You may be lucky enough to come across the largest of African snakes, the python, which like the boa, squeezes its victims to death.

Menengai Crater and Hyrax Hill

From Nakuru town it is eight kilometres (five miles) to the rim of Menengai. A trail climbs past another of the National Museum's prehistoric sites, **Hyrax Hill,** named after the hyrax that once inhabited this area.

Mankind lived here continuously for at least 3,000 years and the first *in situ* exhibit, from the Neolithic and Iron Age, was discovered by Louis Leakey in 1926. Excavations over an eleven-year period were led by Mary Leakey, with further excavations from 1965-73 by other archaeologists.

On the north side of the museum, baulks have been left in place in one pit-dwelling to show the depth of "fill-in" material removed during the digging. There are thirteen similar dwellings in the **"North East Village"** but it's uncertain whether they were used for animals or humans.

The museum displays village pottery, dating from the fifteenth and sixteenth centuries AD. The villagers are believed to have been semi-nomadic Kalenjin pastoralists.

One hundred metres (300 feet) below the museum, on the slope of Hyrax Hill, are more Iron Age **pits** and a **trench** where an extraordinary collection of some 8,000 stone tools and six Indian coins, aged between sixty and 500 years, were dug up in 1974. How the coins got there remains a mystery.

Nearby is a massive **stone slab** that sealed a Neolithic burial mound. It has been removed to display part of a skull and some bones. Altogether, nineteen Neolithic skeletons and nineteen Iron Age skeletons were discovered at different levels in this mound.

Higher up the hill, an **old fort** overlooking Nakuru is believed to have been the village lookout post. From this post it's something of a scramble up to the dramatic rim of **Menengai** which plunges down 300 metres (1,000 feet) to the bush floor within.

The views are reward enough for the climb. From wall to wall the crater stretches many kilometres and beyond it sweeps the Rift with its fertile wheatlands. Several kilometres away is Lake Nakuru which long ago lapped at the foot of Menengai and turned Hyrax Hill into a peninsula — or even an island.

One of the great Maasai clan battles of the nineteenth century — the Ilpurko versus the Ilaikipiak — was fought here, and the soughing of the wind over the crater rim is said to be the sad and haunted cries of those slain in battle.

Indeed, Menengai still has a sinister reputation today and local people prefer to avoid it.

Lake Bogoria: Fiery Waters, Flaming Colours

From Nakuru, the Rift Valley drops down 900 metres (almost 3,000 feet) on the 118-kilometre (73 mile) descent to the sweltering deserts and semi-deserts that mark **Lake Bogoria, Lake Baringo,** and the **Kerio Valley,** and the **Kamasia** and **Tugen Hills.** All are easy to reach from Nakuru.

The bright, harsh beauty of this region seems quite different from any other part of the Rift which is at its most spectacular here. The wall of the Laikipia escarpment, 2,440 metres (7,000 feet) above sea level, steps down in a series of terrace-like foothills.

With Lake Baringo in between, the great block of the Kamasia and Tugen hills rises thirty-two kilometres (20 miles) away, and another sixteen kilometres (10 miles) beyond that, over the grand canyon of the Kerio Valley, stands the western wall.

The **Elgeyo escarpment** that ends in the 3,350-metre-high (11,000-feet) Cherangani Hills, is probably the most dramatic of all the Rift escarpments. In some places it plunges straight down almost 2,440 metres (8,000 feet) to the Valley floor.

Perhaps the least-visited of all the Kenya Rift lakes, Bogoria lies fifty kilometres (31 miles) from Nakuru at the foot of the sheer **Laikipia Escarpment.** The lake is a glistening sheet of blue and white, tinted by the vivid pink of the flamboyant flamingos wading on its shores. At the eastern edge the **Siracho Cliffs** rise more than 610 metres (2,000 feet).

Bogoria was originally named Lake Hannington after Bishop Hannington who camped around the long, narrow sheet of alkaline water in the 1890s on his way to Uganda, where he was murdered. After Independence it reverted to it's ancient name given long ago by local communities. Gregory, the geologist, thought the lake "the most beautiful sight in all Africa".

Getting there

The broad, smooth Baringo road leaves Nakuru over the north-western shoulder of Menengai, past **Kabarak High School**, founded by President Daniel arap Moi, and on through **Kampi ya Moto.** Drive past the three shops and rail crossing to the left fork for the steep climb up the **Elgeyo Escarpment** to **Eldama Ravine** (See "North-West Kenya: enchanted mountains, unspoilt vistas").

From Kampi ya Moto, the road veers north through **Mogotio,** with a right turn along a dirt trail for twenty kilometres (12 miles) to the entrance to **Lake Bogoria National Reserve.**

An exciting alternative to the main route from Nakuru to Bogoria is to approach the lake across the **Subukia Valley** from Nyahururu in the east (See "Heartland of Kenya").

Where to stay

If you want to camp, **Fig Tree Campsite** with giant fig tree groves that dominate the southern shore, provides cool shelter as well as a few basic provisions. There is plenty of water here: a permanent, crystal-clear, sweet brook runs right through the campsite creating a natural jacuzzi.

Less attractive, however, are the troop of baboons whose favourite haunt — especially between December and February — are the fig trees with their succulent fruits. It's best to be wary of camping directly beneath the trees.

Further west around the lake circuit are

Overleaf: Flamingos on the shores of Lake Nakuru in the Rift Valley

Above: Boiling geysers on the western shores of Lake Bogoria.

two more campsites — **Riverside** and **Acacia Tree** — and a small **picnic area** near the **Hot Springs** at the junction for the track out to the western **Maji ya Moto** gate of the Reserve.

In 1989 a new lodge was being built on the main entrance road in the north. But Bogoria, hidden in its bowl beneath the cliffs, its steep, rocky shores coloured red and green, remains remote and rugged.

Sightseeing

Covering an area of 107 square kilometres (41 square miles), Lake Bogoria National Reserve is at an altitude of between 1,000 and 1,600 metres (3,280-5,250 feet), with thermal **steam jets** and **geysers** boiling out of the rocky ground along its western shores.

It's worth making the springs your first port of call. They erupt from huge, natural cauldrons of super-heated water not far below the surface and drain into steaming rivulets which cut through the crusty ground.

Aside from its hot springs and vast flocks of flamingo, Bogoria is particularly noted for herds of greater kudu, probably the only sanctuary in Kenya where you are virtually

certain to see this unusual, powerful, and handsome antelope with its distinctive lyrate horns (See "Wildlife", Part Three).

To Baringo

Lake Baringo lies between the two walls of the Rift Valley with the dramatic **Kamasia** block in between. Kamasia remained standing when the Valley began to sink and subsequently provided the geologist, John Walter Gregory, with a complete geological history of the Valley.

Leaving Bogoria Reserve by the northern gate, return to the main road which runs another thirty kilometres (17 miles) to **Marigat**. Just before you reach the town a fine new highway on the left, climbs up to **Kabarnet**, administrative headquarters of Baringo district.

Marigat itself is a drab collection of tin huts and administrative buildings. It's another twenty kilometres (12 miles) to the lake itself. Two decades ago this was as remote as any place in Kenya, but now it is only a three-hour drive from Nairobi.

As a result, Lake Baringo has developed

Previous pages: Sundown over a Rift Valley Lake.

210

into one of Kenya's major tourist resorts — particularly for ornithologists, and watersports buffs. Like Lake Naivasha, Baringo's shallow, silt-stained waters, make an odd contrast to the rest of the Rift lakes.

These are the only two freshwater lakes along the length of the Kenya section. Studded with islands, Baringo sustains healthy populations of tilapia fish as well as crocodile and hippo.

Sightseeing

The bird life in this area is phenomenal. Organised bird walks lead along the lowest strata of the Kamasia block on the road outside **Lake Baringo Club**, in the club gardens and on the lake shores. Almost 450 species of bird are resident at Baringo, either permanently or as migrants from the European winter.

Resident ornithologists can be contacted through the club which also organises fascinating lectures on Baringo birds, the indigenous Njemps people, and the area's wildlife. Visits to a Njemps village can be arranged.

Other activities which centre around Lake Baringo Club or **Island Camp** include boat trips around the shores, water skiing, and windsurfing.

The crocodiles are said to be harmless and it's considered safe to swim, but early in the 1980s one attacked and ate a human and was subsequently shot.

From Baringo there are two routes north — both along dirt roads, one of sufficient quality to make the adventure worthwhile.

Some kilometres beyond the northern shore the tarmac ends and a rough trail leads straight down into the heart of the northern Rift. It heads in the general direction of Suguta Valley — one of the hottest places on earth (See "The Northern Rift: Cradle of Mankind") — to **Kapedo,** a small, remote settlement that was abandoned at the end of the 1970s.

Its empty timber-and-tin houses with doors swinging in the breeze, would make an ideal set for a Clint Eastwood western. Close by, a cascading waterfall thunders out of a rock face — at boiling temperatures.

If any road stretched beyond Kapedo, it could be said to be the threshold to Kenya's Northern Rift Valley. But only the sweltering, impenetrable wastes of the Suguta Valley lie ahead and this is the end of the line.

For tourists there is not a great deal to see in this part of the Rift but it does give a lasting impression of the isolation and the scale of the valley as it withers under the scorching heat.

But the road east from Baringo that climbs up the folds of the Laikipia Escarpment, unfolding one magnificent panorama after another, to join the **Nyahururu-Rumuruti-Maralal** road (See "North-East Kenya") — is becoming extremely popular.

And returning south from Lake Baringo, you can explore the **Kamasia** and **Tugen Hills** by taking the magnificent highway, just after Marigat, that climbs the 1,370-metre-high (4,500-feet) western wall of the escarpment. For fifty-seven kilometres (35 miles) this road twists and turns in a series of hairpin bends, from the last of which there is a stunning view of Baringo and the Rift.

The transition from scorched earth to the coolness of these lush green highlands is yet another of those surprises that Kenya suddenly springs forth.

One of Kenya's most beautiful regions, it is at its best after the long rains from March to May. The heat is fiercest in February and early March just before the rains break.

Kabarnet, the administrative headquarters for Baringo District, is a delightful town perched like a saddle on the back of the narrow, but handsome, tree-clad ridge. It looks down on the dramatic **Kerio Valley** — Kenya's own Grand Canyon whose ridge plunges more than 1,000 metres (3,500 feet) in a few kilometres.

The opposite wall rises up equally dramatically and looking down from the wooded ridge, it seems as if you could almost touch the valley floor dappled with sunlight.

Part of Kabarnet straggles down the slopes on either side of the ridge, but most of its development is along the top — giving it a long, slender profile. It's surrounded by prosperous and well-tended farms and small-holdings and makes a delightful away-from-it-all weekend retreat from Nairobi.

Unspoilt hills

Twenty kilometres (12 miles) to the south of the town, along the western ridge of the Kamasia Hills, a new highway leads to President Daniel arap Moi's birthplace high above the Rift, with a panorama that takes in Baringo and Bogoria and the Kerio valley.

To the north lies the rugged saddle of the virtually impenetrable Tugen Hills. Another new road to the west leads down into the Kerio Valley and up to **Tambach**.

Little explored by tourists, the **Kamasia Hills,** the **Kerio Valley,** and the Elgeyo Escarpment are among the most beautiful and unspoilt places of Kenya.

In the Kerio Valley a mining company has established a fluorspar industry which has since run into a recession. Its legacy, however, is the company town of **Kimwarer**, which has developed rapidly as an urban centre. Neat company housing estates make an astonishing counterpoint to the tangled wilderness all around.

The **Kerio Valley Development Authority** has started to encourage fruit orchards and vegetable farms, using the waters of the **Kerio River** for irrigation.

Two new nature sanctuaries — eighty-eight-square-kilometre (34-square-mile) **Kamnarok National Reserve** and the sixty-six square kilometre (25-square-mile) **Kerio Valley National Reserve** have been established along the **Kerio Gorge.** But at the moment you can walk and drive everywhere and many charming Tugen villages — **Kabulwa, Koitilial, Chepkum, Chesetan, Chesongoch** — line the roadside.

One of the most astonishing vistas is the **Elgeyo Escarpment** south of the dreamy village of **Tot**. Below a 2,000-metre (6,560-feet) sheer cliff face spreads a green carpet which blends into the scorching, scrubby, landscape of **Pokot** and **South Turkana.**

The **Elgeyo Escarpment** road is too rocky and too steep for anything less than a 4WD or anyone with less nerve than a very gutsy rally driver!

If you walk from Tot you can climb to the top in one day. Or you can drive twenty-five kilometres (16 miles) up to **Chesoi,** returning from Tot in the direction of Kabarnet and turning right halfway at **Chesongoch** for the main ascent (See "Cherangani Hills: high peaks, secret valleys").

From Tot you can continue along the Rift and join up in the desert with the Lodwar road (not recommended). Alternatively, retrace your route and climb the Kerio hills to Kabarnet — and take the new road from there up the Elgeyo Escarpment to Eldoret.

A third option is to turn east at Tot and drive along the dirt trail through **Kolowa** to **Nginyang** on the Lake Baringo-Kapedo Road.

The Northern Rift: Cradle of Mankind

Nothing could look less like the Biblical Garden of Eden than the desolate, arid badlands of northern Kenya. Yet if historical perspective has any accuracy, the bleak eastern shores of **Lake Turkana** are the one place on earth that might rightly be regarded as Eden.

Lush imagery is nowhere in evidence but the knife-edge lava wastes and petrified forests have both preserved the remnants of the ancient cultures that once lived here and shaped the lifestyles of the contemporary communities — hardy and spartan people who are indifferent to the materialism that has assailed most of the world.

The land yields little. The soil is worn out and the only profit is survival. Simply to stay alive is indicative of both human resourcefulness and dignity (See "The People", Part One).

When the frenzy of the tectonic forces which formed the Great Rift Valley finally abated, Africa endured one last, long-drawn-out tremor. Its spine collapsed, to form the Rift and on either side this great rupture exposed the different strata along its scarps — and the bones and teeth they contained. The grave was open.

All it needed was someone to dig among the bones.

Fate might well have given that honour to Lieutenant Ludwig von Hohnel, Count Samuel Teleki's loyal geographer, biographer, and friend. While Teleki's sole ambition seems to have been to slaughter East Africa's wildlife, von Hohnel diligently recorded the flora, fauna, ecology, geology, geography, and ethnic constituents which formed this part of East Africa and the Rift Valley (See "The Dust and the Ashes", Part One).

At the end of March 1888, Teleki's expedition crossed the shores of Lake Turkana at **Koobi Fora.** Von Hohnel complained on 29 March of the difficulty of walking across Koobi Fora's sandstone rocks, not thinking to look beneath them.

A week later, the tired party approached a Dassenich settlement at what is probably now **Ileret,** where two of the main fossil-bearing areas exist.

Perhaps the two Austrians stumbled across

some fossils for von Hohnel records: "After an hour's walk we issued from the wood which extended in a westerly direction to the side of the lake. Then came a stretch of ground strewn with human skulls and bones."

But learned though he was, von Hohnel failed to recognise the significance of his finds. It was another eighty years, in July 1967, before Richard Leakey flew along the eastern shores of Lake Turkana.

He saw below a tangle of blackened sandstone layers that looked like the slag heaps of a coal pit. Leakey asked the pilot to circle the sand pit off Koobi Fora and fly once more over this weird badland at a height of 300 metres (1,000 feet).

A camera would have recorded this ugly landscape as almost bereft of life. Leakey saw things differently, however, an inspired guess or a vision of the distant past as it might have been.

First, he saw graceful trees and rolling meadowlands where green grasses and vegetables grew. Mischievous monkeys gambolled in the thick foliage. Strange, elephant-like pachyderms with shortened trunks and thick, but smaller tusks browsed quietly.

Nearby some hairy people, small but upright, with squat low foreheads, chattered amicably in one group. In another, workmen banged and chipped stones to fashion new tools.

Now rivers cut through the meadowlands in Leakey's inner eye, waters swift and clear. Eden was spread out before him.

He borrowed a helicopter from the American Omo Valley archaeological team, and returned to the sandstone hills near Alia Bay to check on what his inspired vision had promised.

The helicopter blades had barely stopped whirling before Leakey picked up a Stone Age tool similar to those he had found in Olduvai Gorge when, as a youngster, he joined his famous parents in their excavations.

Within months Richard Leakey had assumed the directorship of Kenya's National Museums to begin the exploration which has confirmed Koobi Fora as the world's richest treasure trove of early hominid fossils.

Fewer than ten years later, he was summoned by his friend, Kamoya Kimeu, to a spot on the outlying edges of the Lake Turkana excavations. Leakey spent weeks piecing together thirty or more fossil fragments to reassemble a skull dating back almost three million years — evidence of *Homo habilis*, handy man, an early tool making ancestor of modern man.

Other discoveries of even greater significance have since been made, including skulls of *Homo erectus*, the first species of man to walk upright. These discoveries confirmed that mankind had been present on earth for at least a million years — 500,000 years longer than was previously believed.

Lake Turkana: The Jade Sea

Formerly known as Lake Rudolf, **Lake Turkana,** covers an area of 6,400 square kilometres (2,500 square miles) along the north-south axis of the Great Rift Valley. Turkana's blue-green waters gave the lake its other name, the **Jade Sea.**

The shores of the lake are mostly desert with occasional groups of ragged palm trees, stripped to ribbons by gales which blow day and night most of the year.

On the western shore two seasonal rivers, the **Turkwel** and the **Kerio,** feed the lake from deltas which spread out like the fingers of a hand. Through the swamps that appear like lurid green oases in this land of rock and sand, the muddy flow of these rivers can be seen right out in the centre of the lake.

To the south, the lake is guarded by an area of black lava boulders, terrible to walk across, that lead up to the crater summit of **Mount Teleki**.

Turkana is fed by the Omo River, Ethiopia's second largest river which is spawned 370 kilometres (600 miles) away on Mount Amara in Ethiopia's western highlands. The Omo cuts a thirty-two-kilometre-wide, (20-mile) swathe through swamp and papyrus to discharge twenty million cubic litres of life-sustaining water each year into East Africa's fourth-largest lake.

The sun remorselessly sucks the water out again by intense evaporation and during the last century the lake has shrunk dramatically. Thousands of years ago it was 150 metres (500 feet) deeper and connected to the White Nile basin by an outlet through the **Lotikipi Plain** beyond **Lokitaung** and the **Murua Rithi Hills.**

Silt from the Omo has built up the lake bed in the north and some parts are now only ten metres (30 feet) deep. Around **Central Island,** however, and in the far south, the water reaches a depth of 140 metres (450 feet).

Turkana is home to some of the world's

most venomous reptiles — saw-scaled vipers, night- and puff-adders, and cobras.

The lake also hosts a rich variety of birds; more than 350 species of resident and migratory birds live on the shores and waters of the lake, feeding on its rich, lacustrine life.

Six ethnic peoples live around the lake shores and hinterland — the warrior-like **Turkana** to the west, the tiny **el-Molo** community around **Loiyangalani** on the south-east shore, the **Samburu** from Loiyangalani all the way up to Rumuruti, and the **Rendille**, **Gabbra**, and **Dassenich** (also known as Merille) to the east (See "The People", Part One).

When to Go

Climatically, Turkana is devastatingly hot and dry throughout the year. When it rains, perhaps once in every ten years around April and May, it can be humid.

Getting there

There are three springboards into the Northern Rift which is considered by many one of the most exciting and adventurous places for independent travel in Africa: from Nanyuki on the shoulders of Mount Kenya to the eastern shore; from Nyahururu-Maralal to the south-eastern lake shores; and from Kitale to the western shore.

However, no road connects the east and west shores which are barred by the virtually impenetrable barrier of volcanic rock that forms the walls of the **Suguta Valley.**

The western approach from **Kitale** is along the new Kenya-Sudan highway for 355 kilometres (220 miles) to **Lodwar,** that winds down through the **Cherangani Hills** (See "High peaks, secret valleys"). It passes **Saiwa Swamp National Park** and through **Kapenguria,** shrine to the memory of Mzee Jomo Kenyatta. Traversing a tributary of the Turkwel River, it cuts through the **Marich Pass,** down to the south Turkana plains and skirts the **South Turkana National Reserve,** 100 kilometres (60 miles) from Kitale.

Set between 900 metres and 2,720 metres (2,950-8,920 feet) above sea level, the reserve's 1,100 square kilometres (425 square miles) are undeveloped. Its arid, thorn-bush plains are dominated by two small mountains with scattered remnant forest on their summit and higher slopes which are a sanctuary for elephant and greater kudu.

The **Kerio River** forms a twenty-five kilometre (15-mile) boundary to the south-east and supports a riverine gallery forest.

To the west of the road, also 100 kilometres (60 miles) from Kitale, is the ninety-two-square-kilometre (35-square-mile) **Nasolot National Reserve,** ranging from 750 to 1,500 metres (2,460-4,920 feet) above sea level.

Harsh and flat, the scorched thornbush plains, crisscrossed with seasonal water-courses, skirt the base of the **Sekerr Mountains.** Here, where it leaves its gorge, the **Turkwel River** is joined by its tributaries, the **Suam** and the **Morun,** and enters the plains, forming the reserve's eastern boundary. In 1989, it was the scene of frenetic activity as constructors finished one of Kenya's largest hydroelectric projects.

Beyond the two reserves the harsh, bleak countryside is roamed by fierce Pokot people, kinsfolk of the Uganda Karamajong nomads and the Turkana, with whom they frequently clash in disputes over cattle.

Some sixty kilometres (40 miles) further on, the road passes through the small town of **Lokichar** and then on through the featureless, Turkana semi-desert to **Lodwar,** some sixty-four kilometres (40 miles) from Lake Turkana's shores.

Set at the foot of the conical **Lodwar Mountain,** fast-growing Lodwar is the administrative centre of the 200,000-square-kilometre (77,220-square-mile) Turkana District.

It was established as a British outpost in the first decade of this century in a not too successful attempt to subdue the independent Turkana.

One of the early administrators was a Scandinavian, Baron Eric von Otter, who could trek through the Turkana desert as swiftly as the nomads and was much respected. He died of skin cancer and was buried, with full British military honours, in Lodwar.

It was also here that Jomo Kenyatta was held for some time under informal house arrest before being moved to Maralal after his release from prison at distant **Lokitaung** (See "The Dust and the Ashes", Part One).

Lodwar is a major crossroad for the region. To the west, a road leads to **Lorukumu** and the Rift escarpment that forms the remote border with Uganda. The main road continues north to **Lokichoggio** and the Sudanese border, and another road leads east to **Ferguson's Gulf,** a dried-up bay of the Jade Sea.

Above: El-Molo, fearless crocodile hunters of the Jade Sea.

Sightseeing

Temperatures are extremely high. Constant winds whip dust around the **mission** buildings and **hospital,** and send it swirling down the mainstreet where small shops and shanties cluster round a ramshackle beer shop.

Lodwar market is colourful and worth a visit, particularly if you want to buy baskets or watch the Turkana women weaving them. The **Diocesan Crafts Shop** sells a large selection of baskets, trays, mats, and other souvenirs.

The town does not boast many comforts although it does have a few places where visitors can stay.

Two resorts

There are two resorts roughly the same distance from Lake Turkana. **Eliye Springs** to the south-east, was once favoured to grow into something of a big game fishing resort and flourished in the late 1960s and early 1970s. Standards have since slipped however and the *bandas* (African-style huts) have become tatty.

Ferguson's Gulf is to the east, near the Turkana village of **Kalokol** where the Norwegians built a massive filleting and freezing plant in the 1970s. Fish catches have fallen since the waters of Ferguson's Gulf, five kilometres (three miles) further on, dried up — leaving **Lake Turkana Fishing Lodge** high and dry.

As the lodge caters mostly for weekend visitors who fly in from Nairobi, accommodation is usually available midweek. There's a campsite nearby and campers can use the lodge bar and water supply.

For a modest sum you can hire fishing rods and hire a boat to go out on Turkana. The game fishing here is rated some of the most exciting and rewarding in the world.

More than forty different species have been recorded including the ferocious, aptly-named tigerfish and man-sized Nile perch, which can weigh in at around 250 kilos (550 lbs).

Should you wish, the lodge will cook your catch for you, while you add your mark to fishing posterity on the walls of the bar.

Central Island National Park

Some fifteen kilometres (nine miles) offshore lie the five square kilometres (two square miles) of **Central Island National Park.**

215

Formed out of three large, still-steaming volcanoes, rising to 240 metres (800 feet) at their highest point, the island is a rare and fragile ecosystem. Its indigenous bushes and wild fruits form a critical link in the migration chain of bird species *en route* from Europe to southern Africa.

The island's three small internal lakes have for aeons been the breeding ground for Turkana's population of Nile crocodile, the largest concentration in the world.

They are survivors of an epoch long before mankind appeared on Turkana's eastern shores and live in perfect harmony with their environment. They feed on the prolific lake fish which sustains a stable population of around 12,000 creatures. Some specimens reach a length of five metres (20 feet) and their form has not changed for 130 million years.

During the April-May hatching season baby crocodiles chirrup in their eggs buried deep beneath the sand to escape the predatory attention of monitor lizards and raptors. Their cries bring the parents scurrying to dig them out and carry them to the water's edge where they will spend their first few months.

Almost at the centre of the lake, on its north-south and east-west axis, Central Island is larger than **North Island** which is sixty-five kilometres (40 miles) away, near the Omo delta.

The only residents on this desolate smudge of rock are snakes which originally drifted down from the delta on floating islands of papyrus.

It is possible to explore the region of Turkana north of Ferguson's Gulf. There is a dirt trail that cuts along the featureless western shore for about ninety kilometres (55 miles) before it links up with the the **Lodwar-Lokitaung-Namuruputh** dirt road.

Turn right on to this road and after twenty kilometres (12 miles) it reaches the Kenya-Ethiopian **border post** of **Todenyang,** probably one of the most remote police and immigration outposts in Kenya's rugged outback.

You can retrace your journey by turning west where the Ferguson's Gulf trail joins the road and visit Lokitaung where there is a deep gorge and a great many fossil trees. Lokitaung also has vital, historic significance to modern Kenyans. It was here that Jomo

Kenyatta and his colleagues served their seven years hard labour.

From Lokitaung the road trails through the featureless scrub desert for 120 kilometres (75 miles) to the new Kenya-Sudan highway. Turn west and its some 160 kilometres (100 miles) to **Lokichoggio** with the Sudanese border some kilometres beyond.

Formerly an administrative centre, Lokichoggio is one of Kenya's most remote townships with a population of around 25,000 and a floating population of aid workers, ICRC officials, and oil exploration teams.

Lokichoggio was in the headlines in 1989 when unknown planes, said to be from Uganda, bombed the town, killing and wounding several Kenyans.

From Maralal: Dustbowls and Oases

The second route to the Northern Rift, on the east shores of Lake Turkana, is through Nyahururu-Maralal. From heartland Kenya, three roads lead to Maralal (See "North-East Kenya: sun-scorched plains of darkness") which marks the end of the first stage of the trip.

Getting there

From **Maralal,** set at 1,490 metres (4,900 feet) above sea level, the rough, rocky 225-kilometre-long (140-mile) road plunges down 1,110 metres (3,650 feet) to the shores of the Jade Sea through a tumultuous landscape which is stunningly dramatic.

Following more or less in the footsteps of Teleki and von Hohnel, and latter-day travelwriters and photographers like John Hillaby (*Journey to the Jade Sea*) and Mohamed Amin (*Cradle of Mankind*), it cuts through some of the toughest terrain in the world.

Skirting the base of 2,583 metres (8,475 feet) high **Poror,** after some thirty kilometres (20 miles) it reaches **Moridjo** on the rim of a vast crescent-shaped escarpment, one of the most dramatic in the Rift Valley.

Plunging down more than 2,000 metres (6,560 feet), it raises the curtain on the magnificent amphitheatre of the Suguta Valley, and then rolls down on to the lethal **El Barta** plains.

After seventy kilometres (45 miles), the trail degenerates into a boulder-strewn track that cuts through the ravine between the **Ndoto Mountains** in the east, where the high point touches 2,640 metres (8,650 feet) and, in the west, the 1,369-metre-high (4,492-feet) **Samburu Hills,** to **Baragoi.**

Another fifty kilometres (30 miles) along a very rough track leads to **South Horr,** where the road enters a gorge of the **Nyiru Mountains,** with 2,752 metres (9,029 feet) high **Mowong Sowang** glowering down from the west and another 2,067 metres (6,782 feet) high peak to the east.

Though it's close to the dustbowl of the **Suguta Valley**, one of the hottest places on earth, South Horr is a veritable oasis, delightfully cool and shaded by stands of verdant trees.

South Horr boasts perhaps one of the loveliest campsites in Kenya which is six kilometres (four miles) beyond the town in the **Kurungu Valley** and surrounded by flowering bushes.

The camp was established by Safari Camp Services who run the budget-priced "Turkana Bus" — converted Bedford trucks which leave for week-long adventure safaris from Nairobi, through Maralal and Kurungu, to the south-east shore of Lake Turkana. Since they started they have never missed a departure and the number of passengers carried by 1989 totalled 30,000.

Recently, rival enterprises have started operating similar services but Safari Camp Services expertise, facilities, and experience give them considerable edge. They also offer luxury safaris.

Showers and cold drinks are available at the Kurungu Valley camp and, considering its location, this amounts to luxury. Furnished *bandas* are available, but camping is the most memorable experience.

The surrounding mountain forest hides myriad wildlife and for a modest fee, local Samburu will take you to the top of Nyiru peak which has stunning views over Lake Turkana (See "Kenya's Mountains").

There is also a *Son et Lumiere* show at the camp featuring displays of traditional Samburu culture.

From South Horr, the track descends another ninety kilometres (60 miles) over cataclysmic rocks and boulders to **Loiyangalani** — the tiny el Molo community's

"place of trees".

Where to stay

Comfortable accommodation is available at **Oasis Lodge** which has a swimming pool but is costly. Safari Camp Services have also established a comfortable base that can fairly claim to be a lodge, and there are several campsites.

Most visitors use the **Sunset Strip** campsite which gives shelter from the wind that lashes down from the summit of 2,295-metre-high (7,530-feet) **Mount Kulal,** to the north-east. Showers, toilets, kitchen, bar, and terrace facilities are available with variable supplies of soda and beer — at double their town price.

Sightseeing

Euphemistically described as the capital of the south-east region around the shores of Lake Turkana, Loiyangalani is a settlement of a few tin shacks, **police post, mission** and **mission school,** campsites, and two lodges. The real measure of its isolation is the fact that the town is often out of beer — and quite unable to replenish stocks.

The only "beach", a grubby stretch of sand several kilometres further on down the main road, is reached over shingles and loose stones that shelter scorpions and carpet vipers. Together, with the resident crocodile and hippo, they deter many visitors from swimming.

If you want to visit **South Island National Park,** it's a thirteen-kilometre (eight-mile) round trip and you need good weather. Sudden 100-kilometre (60-mile) an hour storms whip off Kulal and turn the Jade Sea into a tempest. There are few places to land on the island but the cove in the north is perhaps the best. You'll see the narrow, crescent rim of a submerged volcano just a few kilometres north of here.

Covering a total of thirty-nine square kilometres (15 square miles), South Island is the tip of a volcano, six and a half kilometres (four miles) from the east coast and twenty-four kilometres (15 miles) from the south shore. Its only population is a herd of feral goats.

Volcanic ash covers the island almost end to end and the ghostly glow of its luminous vents at night inspired el-Molo stories of evil spirits.

South Island was also the scene of a mysterious tragedy involving an expedition led by Vivien Fuchs, later knighted for his exploratory work in Antarctica. Three days after landing, in July 1934, he returned to the mainland sending another member of the expedition to join the colleague he had left behind. Neither man was ever seen again.

Few visitors set foot on Turkana's southern shore. It is made up of scorched black lava from two centuries of volcanic eruptions, including, most recently, **Nabuyatom Cone** and **Teleki's Volcano**. Beyond lies the forbidding **Barrier** which blocks the approach to **Suguta Valley**, where the mean yearly temperature is 54°C (130°F).

Thousands of years ago **Lake Logipi** was an extension of Lake Turkana. Now the only water in this enormous dustbowl is alkaline froth. Although the least known of all the Rift's soda lakes, Logipi is a haven for flamingos when the levels of water and algae are right.

To visit this region requires at least two 4WD vehicles, and local guides. You should be absolutely fit and must take sufficient water and fuel with you.

Mount Kulal Biosphere Reserve

Another equally demanding excursion from Loiyangalani can be made to **Mount Kulal**, centrepiece of another of Kenya's four, UNESCO-named Biosphere Reserves which covers an area of 7,000 square kilometres (2,700 square miles) and embraces South Island National Park, most of Lake Turkana, its volcanic southern shores, and the **Chalbi desert,** an ancient lake bed.

The Biosphere Reserve includes many volcanic craters and lava flows. The two most outstanding volcanoes are Teleki's and 2,295-metre-high (7,530 feet) Mount Kulal with its rain and mist forests, box canyons, and deep, volcanic crater. Kulal's two summits are joined by a narrow, steep ridge. The climb itself is straightforward provided you are suitably equipped and use transport to get to the base and back (See "Kenya's Mountains").

Vegetation in the reserve ranges from mountain forest to desert (See "National Parks", In Brief, for wildlife and vegetation).

Mount Kulal and the rest of the Biosphere Reserve have a long but probably discontinuous history of human occupation. Archaeological evidence of pastoral and fishing populations has been found near the old Chalbi Lake.

Today, about 1,000 Samburu live on Mount Kulal, 1,000 Turkana, and 500 el Molo around Loiyangalani on Lake Turkana. Pastoralism continues but the emphasis has shifted from cattle to sheep, goats, and camels.

The alteration of grazing practices, due to the restricted movement of nomadic peoples, has resulted in overgrazing. Perennial grasslands have been generally replaced by annual and ephemeral vegetation and locally by desert.

As the population increases and more trees are felled for fuel, housing, and cattle *bomas*, the forests on Mount Kulal will be reduced. Grass fires started by pastoralists erode the forest edge. Other problems include periodic drought and the concentration of people and livestock into settlements.

The Integrated Project in Arid Lands — IPAL — was set up to study ways of alleviating these problems. Their main considerations have been for the traditional land-user and they have produced guidelines that they hope will conserve this unique corner of the world.

The Garden Of Eden

Sibiloi National Park was gazetted to protect the sites of the many remarkable, hominid fossil finds made by Richard Leakey's team since 1968. It also embraces Central Island National Park.

Situated some 720 kilometres (450 miles) from Nairobi, the park's open, windswept plains, dominated by yellow spear grass and doum palms, are interspersed with luggas, and flanked by volcanic formations, including **Mount Sibiloi,** and the remains of a petrified forest. The climate is hot and windy with fierce and frequent gales (See "National Parks", In Brief, for wildlife).

Covering 1,570 square kilometres (600 square miles) of rock, desert, and arid bush, Sibiloi has proved a unique treasury of mankind's origins. Many important prehistoric fossils were found exposed on the surface, blown clean by the ceaseless wind.

Richard Leakey recounts his discovery of the area's first *Australopithecus* fossil: "There on the sand twenty feet ahead, in full view beside a thorny bush, lay a domed greyish-white object. Halfway to it I sat down stunned, incredulous, staring. For years I had dreamed of such a prize, and now I had found it — the nearly complete skull of an early hominid."

Some of the fossils are displayed *in situ* at a

museum, near the park's headquarters — including part of a one-and-a-half million year old elephant.

To quicken the pace of discovery, Leakey evolved a new approach to palaeontology involving a multi-disciplinary team of scientists. Doors were opened to anyone with the qualities and qualifications to share the work.

Their unique mix of skills, beliefs, and nationalities, has resulted in more profound assessments about early human history than could ever have been achieved by one person (See "The Dust and the Ashes", Part One). The richest discoveries date from between three million and one million years ago.

The precise location of each discovery is marked by a concrete post bearing a reference number. The three most important finds are KNM-ER 1470, which is the skull of *Homo habilis,* and KNM-ER 3733 and 3883, the skulls of *Homo erectus.* Visitors to Sibiloi National Park who want to see these sites require special permission from the National Museums.

It is not just the fossils which have given Sibiloi and Koobi Fora significance. The sedimentary layers in which the fossils were buried have yielded important evidence of the environment three million years ago, and of the animals and plants with which early man and pre-man shared the world.

It's another backbreaking sixty kilometres (40 miles) along the eastern shore to the police and immigration outpost of **Ileret,** "capital" of Kenya's semi-nomadic Dassenich or Merille peoples who occupy the north-eastern area around Lake Turkana and also live across the border in Ethiopia.

Getting there

Sibiloi National Park, incorporating **Koobi Fora's** fossil bearing strata, is only 120 kilometres (75 miles) distant from Loiyangalani. But the only marked trail — if you can call it that — is east through the desert to the outpost of **North Horr** and then north-west to **Alia Bay,** the park headquarters.

The other land route is more than 350 kilometres (220 miles) across the featureless **Chalbi Desert** from **Marsabit** (See "Northeast Kenya: sun-scorched plains of darkness").

In essence, the only two practical ways to arrive at Koobi Fora are either by air from Nairobi or by boat from Ferguson's Gulf.

Right: Crater lake on Lake Turkana's Central Island.

Southern Kenya: Theatres of the Wild

The most popular part of Kenya lies in the southern sector of the country, divided by the canyon of the Great Rift Valley.

Above the **Nkuruman Escarpment** that forms the western wall is the northernmost extremity of the great Serengeti ecosystem, the **Maasai Mara,** for many people incomparably the most breathtaking of all the country's game reserves, perhaps of all Africa.

To the east of the Rift, beyond the Meto Hills that form the Rift's eastern wall, lies celebrated **Amboseli,** at the base of Africa's greatest mountain, **Kilimanjaro,** made famous by countless Hollywood films.

And beyond Amboseli, divided only by a narrow panhandle of wilderness plain and developing smallholdings, lies **Tsavo,** the country's largest national park which is divided by the Nairobi-Mombasa highway.

These arid savannah plains, covered with fragile grasslands and scrub bush, are animal sanctuaries of such magnificence that they have earned Kenya its reputation as the last great treasury of African wildlife.

Few tourist destinations in the world can boast the year-round demand for accommodation experienced by lodge operators in the Maasai Mara, Amboseli, and Tsavo.

Maasai Mara

At the turn of the century, Maasai territory covered more than 150,000 square kilometres (47,000 square miles) — a large portion of the southern uplands of Kenya and what is now northern Tanzania.

Four forested, mountain massifs rose out of this land — the Aberdare Range and Mount Kenya in Kenya, Kilimanjaro and Mount Meru in Tanzania — and it contained two areas outstanding for their wildlife: Amboseli and the Mara.

Through their county councils and a combination of local government by-laws and certain game laws, in 1948 the Maasai turned them into official sanctuaries.

An extension of Tanzania's Serengeti National Park, today the Maasai Mara National Reserve, between 1,500 and 2,170 metres (5,000-7,000 feet) high, covers some 1,672 square kilometres (645 square miles) (See "National Parks", In Brief, for vegetation).

Although often described as the greatest of nature's stages, the Mara adds up to less than four per cent of the whole Serengeti ecosystem. Yet, in 1985, when the migration was at its peak, the reserve held almost 2.5 million large herbivores together with smaller species — 1.4 million wildebeest, 550,000 gazelle, 200,000 zebra, 62,000 buffalo, 64,100 impala, 61,200 topi, 7,500 hartebeest, 7,100 giraffe, 3,000 eland, and 4,000 elephant — plus uncounted antelope, such as dik-dik, grey duiker, klipspringer, steinbok, and hippo, rhino, wart hog, bushpig, and giant forest hog.

In addition there were the predators — lion, leopard, cheetah, hyena, wild dog, jackal — and many small mammals, birds, reptiles, amphibians, and insects.

These creatures crowd into the Mara grasslands for three to four months during the annual migration. In its size and extent, however, the migration is a relatively new phenomenon. When the twentieth century dawned, the animals although abundant did not exist in anything like today's numbers.

There was no link with the Serengeti plains and little, if any, seasonal migration.

But after Independence the Maasai intensified their use of the Loita Hills to the east of the reserve. And in the west, in Tanzania's Musoma District, much of the Serengeti dry weather range was usurped by the Tanzanian Maasai. This also happened on the eastern side of the ecosystem with the expansion of Maasai in Tanzania's Loliondo District.

The result was to turn the animals northwards, more and more into the Mara.

Elephants were another factor. Early this century, there were just a few in the Mara. But they prospered with the rapid spread of woods and thicket, ideal elephant country.

By the 1950s the herds were large enough to open up the woodland and spread across the border into the Serengeti and open up the forests there. The new grasslands that arose suited the grazers, of course.

Thus, in the forty years to 1989, the wildebeest grew from about 100,000 to more than one-and-a-half million. And buffalo, zebra,

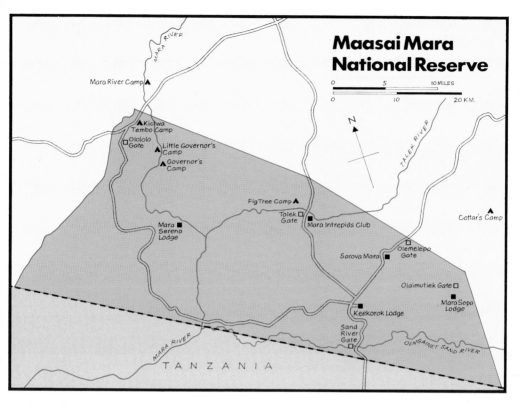

Maasai Mara National Reserve

(Map labels) Mara River · Mara River Camp · Kichwa Tembo Camp · Olololo Gate · Little Governor's Camp · Governor's Camp · Fig Tree Camp · Talek Gate · Mara Intrepids Club · Mara Serena Lodge · Cottar's Camp · Talek River · Olemelepo Gate · Sarova Mara · Olaimutiek Gate · Mara Sopa Lodge · Keekorok Lodge · Sand River Gate · Olngainet Sand River · Mara River · TANZANIA · 0 5 10 MILES · 0 10 20 KM. · N

and gazelles also increased. Their trampling and feeding changed the face of the land.

Although the browsers — impala, giraffe, and elephant — confine themselves to the woodlands and some grazers — buffalo, hartebeest, and topi — remain fairly static, most wildebeest, gazelle, and zebra are migratory.

Now, when the rains bring the first green flush to the short grass plains in southern Serengeti, and the pans and pools fill with water — usually from November to January — these three species crowd the area.

Then, as the dry weather sets in, they pull back north and westwards into the woodlands and longer grasses finally crowding into the golden savannah of the Mara Game in one of the greatest wildlife spectacles ever seen.

Getting there

From the new Nairobi-to-Nakuru road the left turn beyond Rironi takes you onto the old Rift Escarpment road. This is truly atrocious and serves the juggernauts that would otherwise ruin the more recent scenic highway.

The old road was built in the early 1940s by Italian prisoners of war and internees. On the right at the foot of the Escarpment, just before it levels out on the valley floor, is the often vandalised but now restored (1989) **Chapel of St Mary of the Angels** that the road workers built as a thanksgiving. It was consecrated on Christmas Day, 1943.

A few kilometres beyond the chapel there's a turn left along smooth tarmac for 148 kilometres (92 miles) to **Narok** one of the major Maasai administration centres. **Kajiado**, on the south-eastern side of the Rift, is the other.

In 1989, plans were well advanced to tarmac the dirt road that links the tarmac section of the **Kajiado-Ngong Hills road,** taking it over the northern shoulders of these hills, and down the Escarpment past **Susua** in the **Kedong Valley** to join the existing Naivasha-Narok road.

This cuts through the old Maasai grazing grounds which have now become a vast wheat prairie which the Maasai either tend themselves or rent out to large-scale wheat growers and contract farmers. Most of the crop goes to Kenya Breweries and the giant Unga milling conglomerate.

Tall silos on the horizon herald your arrival

Above: Mara Serena Lodge in Maasai Mara game reserve.

at Narok with its acacia and jacaranda trees and the Maasai that stand sentinel at every corner. The town boasts a **club** and has the one and only **petrol station** between the Mara and your return.

While waiting for your tank to be filled you'll be overwhelmed by a veritable mêlée of vendors touting curios — a positive demonstration of Kenya's inherent and dynamic entrepreneurial spirit.

You can also reach Narok from the north — from Nakuru via Njoro along steep roads twisting over the Mau Escarpment, or from the south-west hills (See "Western Kenya: the source of the Nile"). Both roads are rough going.

And even from Narok, the worst is yet to come — after the road crosses the **Engare Narok** river, twenty kilometres (12 miles) beyond Narok at **Ewaso Nyiro** the tarmac ends. Here you turn left for the eastern section of the reserve, where **Keekorok Lodge** and the **reserve headquarters** are located, or right for the western end, including the **Mara river,** and most of the other lodges and camps. These dirt tracks offer some idea of what drivers and vehicles in the annual Safari Rally

undergo each year.

Having travelled once by road, you may well be easily-persuaded to fly next time. Chartered or private planes operate from Nairobi's Wilson Airport and there's also a daily scheduled service by vintage DC-3. It's a forty-five minute flight and, subject to safe landings, you arrive in the Mara without a bruise.

Where to stay

There are three kinds of accommodation: lodges, luxury tented camps, and self-service camping. Among the best lodges are Keekorok, the oldest (built at the spot where hunter Sidney Downey used to base his client's camp); Mara Serena, a five-star Maasai *manyatta;* Kichwa Tembo — "head of the elephants" — (a tented camp at the base of the Olol Escarpment, bathrooms *en suite;* Governor's Camp (on one of Theodore Roosevelt's old campsites at a bend of the Mara River); and Little Governor's — smaller, and more intimate. Cottars Mara, Mara River, Fig Tree, and Mara Sarova camps are all comfortable tented camps.

Campers are restricted to sites outside the

reserve but for one site near Keekorok Lodge (you can buy food from the staff canteen, and drinks from the open bar).

There are also some fine wild campsites — bookable through the National Park headquarters, Nairobi.

Sightseeing

The Serengeti ecosystem covers 40,000 square kilometres (15,500 square miles) between the Rift Valley and Lake Victoria.

Mainly gently rolling country, broken by occasional inselbergs and outcrops, the land slopes east-west from the foot of the Mau, Loita, and Loliondo highlands to Lake Victoria's shore.

Rainfall in the north is virtually double that in the south and it shows. There are fairly extensive woodlands in the north but only light scrub or short-grass savannahs in the south.

The Mara itself is bordered in the east by the **Loita Hills,** south by Tanzania, in the west by the **Soit Ololol Escarpment,** in the north by the **Talek River,** and in the east by **Leganishu,** at 2,191 metres (7,189 feet) the highest peak. The **Nyangores,** and the **Amala,** two large streams draining off the **Central Mau range**, merge downstream as the **Mara River**.

Entering the sanctuary at its northernmost point, the river bisects the reserve from north to south, crosses the Tanzania border and turns westward to Lake Victoria. The altitude gives the region an equable climate even though it is less than two degrees south of the Equator.

From the air, the visual effect of the Mara's thickets and grasslands is not unlike the spots on a leopard's or cheetah's coat. In the *Maa* language Mara has a similar meaning to the English "dappled".

The Mara plains are dominated by *Themeda triandra* (red-oat grass), characteristic of the Serengeti, that furnishes the golden backdrop to many an East African memory.

Most trees in the reserve have no common English names. Of the many species of acacia, two stand out: yellow fever trees, *Acacia xanthoploea*, (See "Flora: forests of flame, streets of mauve", Part Three); and the stunted, shrubby, whistling thorn, *Acacia drepanalobium*, of the open plains, home to a species of ant. They drill their nests in the twigs leaving one or two holes as entrances. When the wind blows across these holes it makes the tinny, whistling sound that gives the tree its common name.

When an animal brushes against the tree, or browses on its leaves, the ants rush out to attack. So, while defending their own nests, the ants also protect the tree. Watch a giraffe browsing on whistling thorn and you will see it take only a few mouthfuls before moving on.

Besides acacia, the Mara's thickets and forest patches contain many other species of tree and shrub. Along water courses several varieties of wild fig attract fruit-eating birds, baboons, monkeys and, at night, fruit-bats.

The Mara's soil is "black cotton" and during the rains they form an almost bottomless morass.

The park is well developed — some say over-developed — and well-served with rough game viewing tracks, passable to most vehicles during dry weather.

Here you can also enjoy the most exotic experience of any safari holiday — dawn flights in a hot air balloon gracefully drifting just a few metres above the game-rich savannah (See "Ballooning in Kenya", Part Three).

Above: Massai warrior.

Amboseli: The Hollywood Image

Long a favourite of Hollywood film makers, **Amboseli National Park's** 392 square kilometres (152 square miles) form the perfect auditorium for scenic views of Africa's highest mountain, 5,895-metre-high (19,340-feet) Kilimanjaro, the highest free-standing mountain in the world.

Ringed by a halo of cumulus, its wedding cake peak floating magically in the incredible blue of the African sky while below herds of giraffe crop the leaves of acacia thorn, Kilimanjaro has become the clichéd symbol of Africa.

But no matter how many times you've seen the movies or the magazine pictures, nothing prepares you for that breathtaking first, real vision of this magic monolith. Seen from the dry bed of the seasonal Amboseli lake, at around 1,200 metres (4,000 feet) above sea level, Kilimanjaro rises another 4,670 metres (15,340 feet) above.

Relatively young by comparison with its neighbouring giants, Mount Kenya and Elgon, Kilimanjaro burst out of the savannah a million years ago, and is covered with one-fifth of all the ice in Africa.

Vegetation ranges from Equatorial tropical rain forest, through savannah, and across true desert — at 4,570 metres (15,000 feet) — to exotic alpine flora.

Besides the mountain, Amboseli is famed for its wildlife spectacle, and the park is one of Kenya's earliest game sanctuaries. It was established in 1948 and in 1961, under a unique agreement, was handed over to Maasai elders of Kajiado District Council — along with an £8,500 a year annuity — for them to run what was then a 3,260 square kilometre (1,260 square mile) national reserve.

Subsequently, in 1973, 392 square kilometres (152 square miles) were excised as a national park.

Once part of the Great Southern Game Reserve, Amboseli's fragile grasslands, like those of the Mara, are under constant attack from the ravaging wheels of tourist minibuses, though it remains virtually as it was when Joseph Thomson marched across it a century ago.

Getting there

It's common these days to fly from the Mara over the Rift and Magadi, to Amboseli or Tsavo. For coastal visitors on a limited up-country game excursion particularly, a short flight of between forty and sixty minutes can save much valuable game-viewing time.

Many people still travel by road however. Take the Mombasa highway east out of Nairobi to **Athi River**, where a smooth road forks right to head south, over the Athi Plains to **Kajiado.** Here, a broad sweep of bleak grasslands, often brooding in the lowering sky of a late afternoon storm, occasionally affords glimpses of the last remnants of its once abundant wildlife — herds of zebra and wildebeest, and maybe a giraffe or two.

Twenty-eight kilometres (17 miles) from Athi River the road runs through the Maasai village of **Isenya** where the Maasai Anglican Church's **Rural Training Centre** is established in an old Mau Mau detention centre. Maasai leatherware is on sale at the tannery.

Twenty-three kilometres (14 miles) beyond Isenya, the road enters Kajiado, the administration headquarters of southern Maasailand at the southern extremity of the **Kaputei Plains.**

Kajiado is all Maasai and cattle. Nearby there's a **marble quarry** that provides the exterior and interior finish for many of Nairobi's new buildings.

The town **cemetery** contains the graves of twenty-four European settlers and Africans killed when General Paul von Lettow-Vorbeck's German army defeated a British force during World War I in a battle at the base of 2,629-metre-high (8,625-feet) **Longido,** just across the border from Namanga, in Tanzania.

Another eighty-eight kilometres (55 miles) on from Kajiado, through unromantic **Bisell** with its **KANU office**, and rolling and broken countryside of red, laterite soil and open, acacia scrub, brings you to **Namanga**.

As you drive, the forested slopes and rugged 2,526-metre-high (8,287-feet) summit of **Ol Doinyo Orok** (the "black" or "Namanga mountain") rise ever higher on the horizon until, just before Namanga, the road skirts its lower slopes. Across the border looms the distant profile of one of Africa's highest mountains, 4,565-metre-high (14,979-feet) **Mount Meru.**

Namanga, a flourishing border town, is

just a short walk through no-man's land from Tanzania, and now abustle again since the reopening of the border in November 1983.

It has a **petrol station** and three hotels of varying standards including the rustic charms of **Namanga River Hotel** which nestles beneath the mountain peak in its well-established gardens and is a useful midway stop on the journey from Nairobi to **Arusha,** 130 kilometres (80 miles) away in Tanzania.

From Namanga it's another seventy kilometres (43 miles) along a dirt road to Amboseli National Park, but the gate is just around the bend from the town. Another route from the gate — the Lake Road — is shorter by some fifteen kilometres (nine miles) but much less predictable because of the flooding of the lake.

The main trail is often rough and heavily corrugated, depending on the amount of rain and whether the Kajiado district council have graded it recently. It runs along a series of ridges on top of the shallow **Ilaingarunyeni Hills,** all pointing towards the dominant feature of the region; snow-capped Kilimanjaro.

Where to Stay

The airstrip built by the National Youth Service in 1973 is surfaced with tarmacadam. Amboseli Serena Lodge (fashioned like a Maasai *manyatta*); Amboseli Lodge (built of sturdy Kenya cedar and local stone); and Kilimanjaro Safari Lodge (built on the site of one of Ernest Hemingway's former camps). There is another luxury lodge outside the park and several tented camps and campsites.

Amboseli's first lodge, Ol Tukai, was built by a Paramount film crew shooting the 1948 epic, *The Snows of Kilimanjaro.*

When shooting was finished, the cottages in which Ava Gardner and the stars lived were handed over to Kajiado district council which turned them into the rustic, self-service lodge that survives today.

Cheap, cheerful, and comfortable, the *bandas* (cottages) come complete with mosquito nets and kitchens, and a well-stocked shop for food and other essentials.

Sightseeing

At first glance, especially in the dry season, **Amboseli National Park** appears a dry, unattractive dustbowl — the result of two decades of tourist erosion. But quell those initial reactions: Amboseli's magic and charm

grow by the second.

Anyone who has sat in a car, windows up, while a pride of seven lion and twelve adolescent young frolic on bonnet and roof, chewing tyres, over the course of a breathlessly long afternoon will not disagree.

Set along the Tanzanian border, beneath the north-west face of Kilimanjaro, a large area of the park is the alluvial dried-up bed of the seasonal soda **Lake Amboseli.** In rare heavy rains this comes into shallow flood.

The soda gives the park its name — Amboseli derives from the Maa for "salt dust". During the dry season the shimmering heat creates a series of mirages over the lake basin.

Most of the park is hot and dry, covered with patches of semi-arid acacias and fragile savannah. However, there are three large **swamps** in the south-east area fed by **underground springs** from the melt waters of Kilimanjaro that filter through its volcanic strata to appear pure and crystal clear.

These springs with their papyrus sedges are the only source of permanent water and the major watering points for the park's wildlife, including fifty-six species of mammal (See "National Parks", In Brief, for wildlife and vegetation).

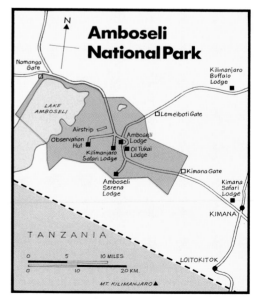

Above: Endangered rhino and elephant graze beneath the distant heights of Kilimanjaro.

From a lookout post on **Observation Hill,** one of the high points of the park, there is a panoramic view of this unique sanctuary and **Enkongo Narok** (Black River) and the **Engone Naibor** and **Loginye swamps** which stand out a brilliant emerald-green.

Excursions from Amboseli

Amboseli is the ideal place from which to visit both the Maasai border town of **Oloitokitok** and the 2,438-metre-high (8,000-feet) **Chyulu Hills** which were recently declared a national park, virtually an extension of Tsavo.

Leaving Amboseli to the south-east the track veers along the southern edge of **Loginye Swamp,** a likely haunt of elephant, hippo, giraffe, and buffalo, and past the incongruous pagoda-style **Kilimanjaro Buffalo Lodge** (this incredible essay in luxury living has its own airstrip). After some twenty kilometres (12 miles) you arrive at the **Emali-Loitokitok** road, also known as the **pipeline road.**

Turn right and then left for Tsavo West, on the road leading to Chyulu Gate and the **Shaitani** lava flow, a relic of the birth of the Chyulus between four and five centuries ago.

Alternatively, after turning right, ignore the left turn and carry straight on to Oloitokitok, directly on the Tanzanian border. The town sits on the lower shoulders of Kilimanjaro beneath the serrated peak of 5,147-metre-high (16,890-feet) **Mawenzi,** some 121 kilometres (75 miles) from Sultan Hamud and virtually the same distance from Namanga.

Oloitokitok, a bustling little town, is well off the beaten track and worth a visit. Market days on Tuesdays and Saturdays are particularly colourful (See "Tastes of Kenya", Part Three) and the panorama over the Amboseli plains to the Chyulus and Tsavo West reward enough for the journey.

A dirt link road crosses the border and runs over the eastern shoulder of Kilimanjaro to the Tanzanian town of Moshi, nestled on the south-east slopes of the mountain.

However, if you wish to tour the Chyulu Hills, turn left on the pipeline road (instead of right for Oloitokitok) and drive straight past Kimana swamp which is rich in wildlife. Nearby Kimana Lodge serves as a flower-strewn haven in the wilderness.

Continue to **Makutano** and turn right along a savagely-dusty track to the northern face of the Chyulu Hills which erupted from the

Above: Delicate veneer of rain flush casts a mantle of green over the Chyulu Hills.

savannah four or five centuries ago.

You can drive up a tortuous 4WD track and along the crest of the hills. This is one of the toughest sections of the famed Safari Rally. The road then leads down into Tsavo.

Among the youngest of the world's mountains, the Chyulus arch their narrow back in an eighty-kilometre-long (50-mile) east-west ridge. Much of this forms the 471-square-kilometre (182-square-mile) **Chyulu Hills National Park.**

The soil is still harsh gritty lava but after the short rains it is coated with a veneer of fragile grass. In such a mantle of green, the Chyulus are supremely beautiful, creating the effect of gentle, grassy moorlands.

Water percolating through the hills forms deep and fast-flowing subterranean rivers that join other underground rivers flowing from Kilimanjaro. These feed the Mzima Springs oasis in arid Tsavo West.

Also deep beneath the hills lies a catacomb of eerie caves, some stretching more than twelve kilometres (seven miles), maybe even longer, but still unexplored.

Tsavo National Park: Last of the Great Tuskers

Tsavo is Kenya's largest national park — and one of the largest wildlife sanctuaries in the world. Among the first to be established in Kenya, in 1948, now combined with the Chyulu Hills National Park, the twin Tsavo West and East national parks cover an area of 21,283 square kilometres (8,217 square miles), more than 400 square kilometres (250 square miles) larger than Wales in Britain.

In all, this adds up to more than four per cent of Kenya's total land area and is a measure of Kenya's concern for its natural heritage that compares favourably with the United States of America, where little more than one per cent of the land is devoted to national parks.

Thirty airfields lie within the combined Tsavo park which is manned by tough and efficient anti-poaching squads. These dedicated wardens and rangers are helping to

Overleaf: Hot air balloon over elephant herd with majestic Kilimanjaro in background.

curb the slaughter of elephant, rhino, and other species that occurred during the 1970s and in the late 1980s. It is not just a heritage they are helping to preserve.

Almost half a million visitors enter Tsavo each year, providing hundreds of thousands of dollars in revenue from gate fees. Its luxury lodges also pay handsome royalties for the privilege of providing five-star comfort in the wilderness.

Located midway between Mombasa and Nairobi at an altitude that ranges from 229 to 2,000 metres (750-6,500 feet), the eastern sector of the park includes part of the 300-kilometre-long (186-mile) **Yatta plateau,** and various volcanic hills. It is otherwise a flat plain, drained by the **Athi, Tive, Tsavo,** and **Voi rivers.**

As unique in character as in size, Tsavo is an outstanding example of how Africa constantly reshapes itself in response to animal and climatic changes. And for a discriminating minority, it is the most fascinating nature sanctuary on the African continent.

More than sixty major mammal species roam its ranges which contain more than 1,000 plant species. In the south these plants are typical of the Maasai grasslands. In the north more arid species survive best (See "National Parks", In Brief, for wildlife and vegetation).

Birdlife is varied and exciting. Crocodile are found in pools, Mzima Springs, and in the rivers of Tsavo East which they share with schools of fish and sounders of hippo.

Once thickly-wooded, Tsavo West was transformed over the years into open grass and bushland by the great elephant herds that roamed endlessly across its red earth.

In the 1960s the Tsavo elephant population was so large — between 50,000 and 60,000 — that a major controversy flared over the need to cull them.

But as the 1980s closed only 5,000 of these creatures were left within the vast confines of the park. Their numbers were decimated not by culling but the random slaughter of ivory-seeking poachers.

But even worse than the elephant massacre has been the decimation of Kenya's — and in particular Tsavo's — rhino population. Nationally, their numbers are down from 70,000 to fewer than 500: Tsavo's from 7,000 to less than fifty.

In such trackless wastes, policing herds

and poachers is an almost impossible task. Ironically the park's name derives from the Akamba for "slaughter".

Another hazard that the park wardens and rangers have to contend with is fire — either started spontaneously during the long, hot, dry summer, or by Akamba honey-hunters guided by the honey-guide bird.

More than 100 of the park tracks, out of 2,000 kilometres (1,250 miles) of dirt trails, are dedicated as fire breaks. Despite the severe reduction in animal numbers, the park's network of well-graded, well-maintained murram roads is one reason why it retains its special magic.

With the reduction in the elephant herds Tsavo West's grasslands are once again reverting to thick scrub woodlands — evident to all who drive through the middle of the park on the Nairobi-Mombasa road (See "Highway to Adventure").

Getting there (Tsavo West)

From Nairobi along the main Mombasa highway there are gates into Tsavo West at **Mtito Andei** and **Kyulu,** between Mtito Andei and **Voi.**

From Amboseli in the south, Tsavo is ninety-one kilometres (56 miles) away — about a two-hour drive. Turn right on to the Oloitokitok road, then left down a corrugated road, through semi-permanent Maasai *manyattas* and homesteads, skirting the base of the Chyulu Hills.

You enter the park itself, as announced by the sudden smoothness of the sandy road, well before arriving at the **Chyulu Gate.**

This road is broken by the coalesced, tar-like waste of the **Shaitani Lava** flow which spewed down from the Chyulus when they erupted out of the plain. The flow takes its name from the Swahili word for "devil". Local lore says that if you clamber to the highest point of this fascinating flow you will vanish forever.

Soon after crossing Shaitani you reach the gate.

Where to stay

Just six kilometres (four miles) from the Chyulu Gate stands Kilaguni Lodge, the first wildlife lodge built in a Kenya national park, opened by the Duke of Gloucester in 1962. Alternatively, you can stay at Ngulia Lodge, on the edge of a high escarpment in the Ngulia Hills. Both merit the definition of "superlative".

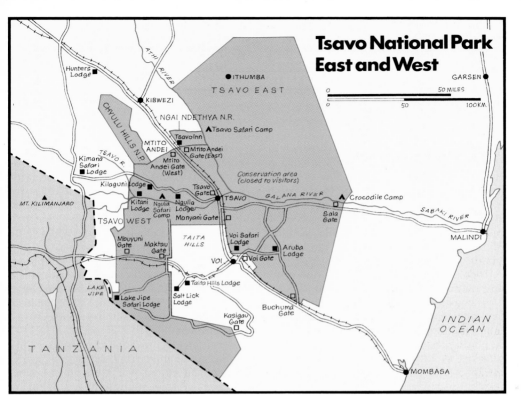

Tsavo National Park East and West

Kitani and Ngulia Safari Camps, two well-equipped, self-service camps, are a few kilometres from the main lodges.

Sightseeing

Tsavo West National Park covers a vast region of 9,065 square kilometres (3,500 square miles) (See "National Parks", In Brief, for wildlife and vegetation). Yet even in the small area around Kilaguni there is so much to see and explore that a single night's stay is insufficient to cover it all.

The lodge itself is a gathering place for myriad game which frequent the two water-holes as enthralled visitors watch from the verandah enjoying the spectacle in comfort. All around superb starlings, hornbills, hyrax, mongoose and squirrels hop and scuttle beneath tables and chairs looking for scraps.

Kilaguni established a concept that linked conservation to tourism. It inspired a host of other lodges that were established in wildlife sanctuaries across the country. Now, in addition, it has a **conference centre**, new **restaurant,** and national park **information centre**.

North of the lodge lie the **Mungai Plains** where the grass is often as high as an elephant's eye. Combined with stunted acacia thorns, it demands a zealous, and tireless, game-spotter to find the animals: but this offers the same sense of excitement as the old hunting safaris.

Tsavo West headquarters, with a well-served, well-maintained campsite for do-it-yourself safari-goers, lie on these plains at **Kamboyo.**

East from the lodge, across the airstrip, the road leads up to the **Roaring Rocks** from which the scarp plunges in a sheer drop of more than 100 metres (300 feet). The place is named after the sound of the cicadas that infest the area, and the wind that whistles over the scarp edge.

It's a notable place for birdwatchers, butterfly enthusiasts, and small-game hunters, with many lizards and other creepie-crawlies.

Another shelter nearby is known as **Poacher's Lookout,** and was built in memory of Jack Hilton, deputy director of Kenya's national parks before Independence.

The biggest attraction in Tsavo West, however, just ten kilometres (six miles) from Kilaguni, is **Mzima Springs,** a fount of cool, clear water.

233

One hundred kilometres (60 miles) away, the Equatorial sun melts the snowcap of Kilimanjaro. The water filters down thousands of metres through the mountain's volcanic strata, to join up with underground rivers flowing from the nearby Chyulu Hills. These burst out in Mzima Springs at a peak rate of almost 500 million litres (110 million gallons) a day.

Years ago a film team constructed an underwater **observation post** in the banks of the Springs. Clamber down a few steps and you enter a new world: hippo move slowly across the bed of the springs rather like moon walkers. Fat tilapia swim by in great schools — only the sudden swirl of a Nile crocodile gliding through the water controls their numbers.

Until the 1980s, the springs were Mombasa's sole source of water, sent gushing down a 150-kilometre-long (95-mile) pipeline, now supplemented by a scheme that draws its supplies from the Sabaki river at Malindi.

During the Great War, the springs were guarded by a fort built by the British. There are trails, and toilets, close to the pools but take care to avoid the wildlife which is numerous and unpredictable.

Areas of Tsavo have also served in various capacities during the last six decades as a refugee camp for Ethiopians who fled the 1930s Italian invasion of their country; a kyanite mine; and a gun emplacement — at Kilaguni, **Kichwa Tembo,** and **"Rhodesian Hill".**

It's thirty kilometres (20 miles) along the main track from Mzima to **Ngulia Hills**, a range of sheer cliffs that rise out of the plains 610 metres (2,000 feet) below.

A detour leads over another fascinating lava flow, **Chaimu,** and down its precipitous side in a series of hairpin bends through Rhino Valley until you come to **Ngulia Safari Camp,** for self-service tourists and visitors.

From here the track climbs up the **Ndawe Escarpment** through thick forest to **Ngulia Safari Lodge**, built atop these cliffs in 1970.

It has created a great avian phenomenon. In October and November during the short rains, when mists are frequent, millions of migrating birds make their passage southward over this region of Kenya.

Disorientated by the shadowy glow of the lodge's artificial moon, they fly down low in their thousands — enabling ornithologists to net and ring them. Many secrets of the immense distances that these birds navigate with uncanny instinct have been revealed.

The lodge is one of the few places in Kenya outside the Mara where there's a possibility of seeing leopard. They haunt the cliffs and forests of these craggy hills. The waterhole draws much big and small game, particularly elephant.

Not far from the lodge there is also a protected **rhino sanctuary.** Three of its residents were stunned with tranquilizing darts on the private Salt Lick game sanctuary to the east and relocated to form a breeding nucleus in the lee of the Ngulia Hills in the hope that in the years ahead their offspring will help to regenerate the rhino population.

The seasonal **Tsavo River** flows around the base of these hills and its scenic valley makes a delightful route for those travelling to Mtito Andei. There are other trails that lead the same way with many interesting diversions off them.

Alternatively, follow the fifty-seven-kilometre (35-mile) trail across the park, through valleys and over hills, to the **Maktau** gate and across the railway line to the main Voi-Taveta road.

Tsavo East: Echoes of a Forgotten Grandeur

Covering an area of 11,747 square kilometres (4,535 square kilometres), much of Tsavo East — the northern sector — is closed to the public. Initially this area served as a corridor and buffer for wildlife populations and today is a strategic battleground in the continuing war against elephant and rhino poachers.

But the areas that are open evoke memories of Africa's former grandeur. Much of this arid landscape is a flat, uninterrupted plain of empty bush, sporadically cluttered with the bizarre shaped "upside down" baobab tree (See "Flora: forests of flame, streets of mauve", Part Three).

Beyond the park border, these same plains are roamed by sparse groups of hunter-gatherers and nomads of Somali stock who eke out a living in countryside where it seems that nothing could survive.

A minority of these nomads are the Wata (See "The People", Part One), Kenya's most

Above: Camel safari in the sprawling reaches of Tsavo East National Park.

renowned trackers and hunters. Hundreds of years before the archers of Plantagenet England faced the French at Agincourt, the Wata were using the long bow.

Though it's strictly illegal, even today they use these weapons to pursue elephants, not as mercenary poachers, but in search of meat both outside and within the long reaches of Tsavo East National Park.

Getting There

There are gates into Tsavo East off the main Nairobi-Mombasa road, at **Mtito Andei, Voi,** and beyond, at **Buchuma**.

Where to stay

Accommodation near Mtito Andei is available at Tsavo Safari Camp on the banks of the Galana, upstream from the Athi and downstream from the Sabaki river.

At Voi, Voi Safari Lodge offers luxurious — and Aruba Lodge self-service — accommodation. The lodge also has a shop selling basic provisions, including firewood on request. It can be noisy at night, depending on which and how many animals decide to pay a visit to the nearby dam.

Half-a-kilometre from Voi, there's a campsite with wooden cottages and running water.

Sightseeing

The entrance at Mtito Andei serves primarily as the gateway to Tsavo Safari Camp on the banks of the **Galana,** which has served for more than two decades as one of the grand African "outback" experiences. It was originally named in honour of Glen Cottar, one of the country's legendary white hunters, whose name is still preserved in Cottar's Camp in the Mara.

The rough road travels through typical Tsavo East *nyika* for twenty-seven kilometres (17 miles) to the river banks. You may, if lucky, come across a herd of Beisa oryx stampeding across the track.

If the crocodile-infested river is in spate, the crossing by rubber dinghy can be both exciting and perilous — but still not as dramatic as a night spent in the camp. Giant tuskers literally walk through the clearing as you eat.

Just inside the Voi gate, on the left, are the **Education Centre, park headquarters** and the **house** where the late David Sheldrick, a

235

dedicated wildlife professional, lived with his wife Daphne. His name is perpetuated in the **Sheldrick Memorial Fund**, dedicated to conservation. Daphne Sheldrick chronicled her husband's life in The *Tsavo Story*, and her own in *Orphans of Tsavo*.

She continues her good work at her home inside Nairobi National Park, and for many years has been the recipient, custodian, and foster-mother of the waifs and strays of Kenya's wildlife — usually orphaned infant elephants, rhinos, and others whose parents were slaughtered by poachers.

From the Voi gate the road to the left climbs up a hill and, just ten kilometres (six miles) into the park, arrives at perhaps the most beautifully-designed of all Kenya's wildlife lodges, Voi Safari Lodge.

Reflecting neither western nor indigenous themes, it is in harmony with its setting, cut into the ledge of a craggy cliff. It offers a taste of both luxury and wildlife; as you swam in the blue-tiled pool, you could, not long ago, look down on herds of elephant and buffalo at the watering hole below.

Climb up the cliff behind (strenuous for the over-40s) to be rewarded by magnificent panoramas to the east and north-east. This amazing landscape seems bereft of any single, outstanding, physical feature.

From the lodge, which seems a million light years from Voi and the hurry-scurry of the Nairobi-Mombasa road, drive twenty-four kilometres (15 miles) past **Irima waterhole,** to a whaleback hump of rock, **Mudanda,** Africa's answer to Australia's Ayers Rock. It towers over a natural dam where Tsavo East's profuse wildlife gather in their thousands during the dry seasons.

From here, retrace your path, then turn along the **Buffalo wallow**, and travel for fifty kilometres (30 miles) to the **Galana river.** Turn right and travel four kilometres (two and a half miles) downstream and you come to **Lugard's Falls,** named after Britain's first proconsul in East Africa, Captain — later Lord — Lugard.

Mighty when in spate, the falls cascade through a narrow rock neck. For the brave or foolhardy only, it's said you can stand astride the top of the falls and watch the waters plunge to the pool below where crocodiles bask motionless in the sun. Do so at your own risk.

From this point, via **Sobo** to the park's **Sala**

Above: Balloon over Salt Lick Game Lodge on the savannah plains south-east of Kilimanjaro.

Gate (and then on to Malindi), is 110 kilometres (68 miles).

Just beyond the Sala Gate, **Galana Game Ranch** was a private, wildlife reserve which provided visitors with several spots to scramble down to the sandy banks. Spread over 250,000 hectares (617,750 acres), the reserve maintained a valuable nucleus of breeding herds of rare species and offered an esoteric, tailor-made safari experience for the wealthy elite. Because of the poaching problem in the area, it has been temporarily closed to tourists.

Galana Ranch lies under the lee of the 300-kilometre-long (186-mile) **Yatta Plateau,** one of the world's longest lava flows. The plateau overshadows the Athi-Galana River, spawned in the Ngong Hills close to Nairobi, for much of the river's course.

Further, along the Galana, at **Crocodile Camp** it is said that you can call the crocodiles by name and they respond. Keep your distance, of course.

If you choose not to journey from Sala through the **Jilore Forest** and **Kakuyuni** to Malindi, you can return to the Mombasa road by passing through the waterless **Taru Desert** and by the **Aruba Dam.**

Staunching the seasonal flow of the **Voi River** off the **Taita Hills** to the south-west, the dam has created an attractive eighty-five-hectare (210-acre) lake some sixty-five kilometres (40 miles) from Sala and forty kilometres (25 miles) from Voi Safari Lodge that provides a large reservoir for elephant and plains game.

Built by the national parks authority, the dam is a popular congregating point for wildlife. Aruba Lodge, a big, shady banda with campsite, offers visitors traditional safari-style life in Africa but with much more comfort and security.

From here you can visit the **Kanderi Swamp** — at junctions 173 and 174 — but remember to keep the windows up as you drive through the tall grass and undergrowth.

Excursions from Voi

Seen from a distance as a bulking mass of blue-grey rock, the rugged **Taita Hills** thrust into the white clouds sailing across the sky. Some forty-three kilometres (27 miles) south of Voi they mark the road to **Taveta,** seventy-one kilometres (44 miles) beyond.

Although craggy and forbidding in appearance, the Hills, in fact, embrace beautiful valleys, bountiful in their harvests of fruit, vegetables, and flowers.

The farmers and their families, the Taita-Taveta people, were among the first inland Kenyans with whom the missionaries and Thomson made contact (See "The People", Part One).

Getting there

From Nairobi take the right turn on the main Nairobi-Mombasa road just before the left turn into Voi Town. The road is tarmacked for forty-three kilometres (27 miles), all the way to **Mwatate, Bura,** and **Wundanyi.** From Bura to **Taveta** is seventy-one kilometres (44 miles) of often corrugated dirt road.

Where to stay

Luxury accommodation is available at both Salt Lick and Taita Hills Lodges, operated by the Hilton International Group. Lake Jipe Lodge is a smart new resort on the shores of reed-fringed **Lake Jipe.**

Sightseeing

Wherever you go in this volcanic landscape covered with savannah grass, scrub, and thorn, the rocky spires, great bluffs and whale-back peaks of the 2,130-metre-high (7,000-feet) Taita Hills dominate the view.

The road to the compact, pleasantly laid-out district capital of **Wundanyi,** on the right off the Taveta road, climbs fifteen kilometres (nine miles) in a series of tortuous hairpin bends. Within twenty minutes tropical Africa seems remote and distant. The smallholdings and neat terraces which step down the steep hillsides could be Mediterranean.

Wundanyi's sense of suspended reality is accentuated by the **Cave of Skulls,** one of many ancestral shrines in the hills. Hidden in a banana grove just below the road, the skulls of thirty-two Taita ancestors, exhumed from their graves, rest in a niche inside the cave.

Above the town, terraced *shambas* (farms) step down the hillside in a profusion of lush greenery.

It was from **Vuria,** the summit of the hills, that the first Christian missionary in Kenya, Johanne Rebmann, saw the snows of Kilimanjaro to the distant north.

The descent is down another precipitous series of hairpin bends past gushing waterfalls to the main road and **Bura,** on the right, where the tarmac ends.

Above: Lake Chala with cloud-capped Kilimanjaro and Mawenzi (right) in background.

Bura was the scene of a climatic World War I battle when the British, under the command of General Jan Smuts, turned the tables on German leader, Lettow von Vorbeck. The battle is commemorated in the Teutonic **Taita Hills Lodge** some few kilometres beyond.

With its sister Salt Lick Lodge, it's part of the privately-owned 11,000 hectare **Salt Lick Game Sanctuary**.

Salt Lick Game Sanctuary

Situated astride the main Voi-Taita road beneath the Taita Hills, and linked by a game corridor to Tsavo West National Park, the sanctuary is some 915 metres (3,000 feet) above sea level.

Abandoned three decades ago as a failed sisal plantation, the land has found new life as one of Africa's most exciting game parks. Predominantly flat-savannah plains, enhanced by a manmade **dam** and **reservoir,** one border of this unfenced, wilderness reserve is marked by a green, riverine forest that follows the course of the **Bura River**.

Since it was established as a reserve, the grasslands and woodlands have drawn an abundance of zebra, buffalo, impala, gazelle, elephant, eland, waterbuck, reed-buck, giraffe, vervet monkey, lion, jackal, and prolific birdlife.

Taita Hills Lodge was built like a German fortress, out of cemented sandbags, to commemorate an epic battle close by. Austere and forbidding from the exterior, although adorned now by a frenzy of climbers and flowering creepers, it is delightfully inviting inside.

It served as a base for James Stewart's 1978 movie, *A Tale of Africa*. Not far from the main building is the timbered chalet built as part of the set and now known as the **James Stewart House.**

Salt Lick Lodge is one of Kenya's finest and consists of rondavels built on stilts along the lines of a typical Taita homestead, connected by overhead walkways. Underneath, large herds of elephant browse undisturbed by intrusive tourists.

Both Salt Lick and Taita Hills Lodges are probably the most unusual conference centres in the world where tycoons, business magnates, and top executives meet, surrounded by lion, elephant, buffalo, and countless other species.

The management employs five wardens and rangers, all national park veterans with immense knowledge of wildlife and conservation. There is an established network of more than 150 kilometres (95 miles) of well-kept, graded roads: off-the-road driving is not allowed.

Taveta

From the Taita Hills sanctuary the road to **Taveta** follows the branch railway line through the southern arm of Tsavo West.

During World War I, when Tanganyika was a German colony, Taveta and the surrounding region was the only theatre of war in Africa.

Taveta fell into German hands when their forces attacked the town on 15 August, 1914 — just eleven days after the outbreak of war.

For the next four years the region was a focal point of the conflict in East Africa. When the Germans retreated, Lettow von Vorbeck and his men continued to harass the much stronger British forces — a drawn out a hit-and-run campaign that later formed the theme of Wilbur Smith's book *Shout at the Devil*, also made into a movie. The main railway line in Kenya was a strategic target and the Germans frequently sent out marauders from Taveta.

The line was later extended across the border to **Moshi** to join up with the Tanzanian Railway system. Later still, it merged with the Uganda and Tanganyika railway systems to form the East African Railways.

Sightseeing

Taveta was linked to the main Mombasa-Nairobi railway line in 1924, and today there's a thrice-weekly train from Voi.

Yet despite its importance as a railway link and border town, Taveta is still waiting to be plugged in to Kenya's national electrical grid and the **bank** near the **border post** is only open on Monday and Friday. The town has a mixed population of Taveta, Akamba, Kikuyu, and Luo.

Twenty kilometres (12 miles) north of the town, an emerald at the throat of Kilimanjaro, four-square-kilometre (one-and-a-half-square-mile) **Lake Chala**, lies close by the dirt road from Taveta to Oloitokitok.

The national boundaries of Tanzania and Kenya slice through the middle of this 100-metre-deep (300-feet) crater lake fed by the melting snows of Kilimanjaro. No one quite knows how its family of resident Nile croco-dile came to live there.

You can camp in a number of places on the crater rim and a rather precarious precipitous path leads down to the water's edge. Kenya's aqualung divers often go diving at weekends — despite the crocs.

When ice-capped Kilimanjaro is visible, the setting is magnificent and well worth the effort of getting there. But you must take everything you need — there is no tourist infrastructure.

South-east of Taveta is **Lake Jipe,** equally worthwhile, especially for bird lovers. There are a number of routes down to the shore from the Taveta-Voi road. The easiest is to turn right roughly ten kilometres (six miles) east of the town where a signboard reads "Jipe Sisal Estate".

Twenty-five kilometres (16 miles) along this track you come to Tsavo West national park's **Jipe Gate** and you can park right on the lake shore. Both simple *bandas* and camping facilities are available.

The reed beds and dappled waters of Lake Jipe are set against the background of Tanzania's **North Pare Mountains** where, from small villages, slender spirals of smoke climb unwavering into the still air.

Just as at Chala, the national borders slice right through the middle of the lake. To explore the waters, hire a punt from the national park office on the shore.

Floating on the lake — perhaps in Tanzanian waters, since nothing marks the division between one nation and the other — watching the sudden swoop of a cormorant as it dives for a fish beneath the surface, is euphoric.

A baroque monument near the lake shores testifies to the brevity of life and the strength of man's conceit. This many-bedroomed castle, with the dimensions and perspectives of a medieval European fortress, is known as **Grogan's Folly.**

It was built by Ewart Grogan, who walked from the Cape to Cairo for the love of a woman and settled in Kenya, like a latter-day Rhodes, to make his fortune, often without scruple. The castle is in the grounds of the sisal plantation he established.

Nairobi - Mombasa: A Highway to Adventure

The 500 kilometre (300 mile) Nairobi-Mombasa road, the first leg of a planned Trans-African Highway, stretching from the Indian Ocean to Lagos and the Atlantic, was completed as recently as until 1969.

But today parts of it resemble an ante-diluvian fossil and there are some car-breaking, bone-rattling stretches that will knock the breath from your body.

Getting there

Most people detour via **Namanga** through **Amboseli** and **Tsavo National Parks** (see "Southern Kenya: theatres of the wild"). Alternatively, a longer route leads via Namanga, through Arusha in Tanzania, around the southern face of Kilimanjaro to Moshi, and then on to Taveta and Voi, the route pioneered by L. Galton Fenzi, founder of Kenya's Automobile Association.

But for visitors interested only in seeing the coast, travel operators offer air options. Mombasa is only forty-five minutes from Nairobi by jet, or ninety minutes by Fokker Friendship.

The final travel option is ideal for those who prefer to relive the splendour and romance of pioneer days. The grand-sounding Kenya Railways overnight "Express" train takes thirteen hours to complete the journey, in either direction. In 1901 it took as long as a week.

But in spite of the often appalling condition of some stretches, the road remains the most obvious route, indispensable to those who wish to travel down in their own cars or on one of the many, frequent express coaches which cover the journey in about six hours at knockdown rates in more ways than one: in 1989 the one-way ticket cost the equivalent of seven US dollars.

Certainly, if you've time to stop and take in the many interesting attractions along the way, the first journey along the road is an exhilarating experience.

Where to stay

In Makindu, Hunter's Lodge (4-star); in Mtito Andei, Tsavo Inn (3-star); in Voi, Voi Safari Lodge (5-star). There are others. See Listings for "Hotels".

Sightseeing

Out of Nairobi **Uhuru Highway** leads straight on to the **Mombasa Road.** This dual carriage-way leads past drive-in cinemas, night clubs, sprawling low-cost and urban housing estates, until it bears off the **Jomo Kenyatta Airport** road. The final twenty-seven kilometres (17 miles) go past junk heaps, a Ministry of Transport **public weighbridge** and broiler, textile, and distillery plants to Athi River.

Ninety years ago this was as romantic and interesting as any place in Kenya. When the railhead arrived here it was part of the 25,000-square-kilometre (9,650-square-mile) Great Southern Game reserve of which the Nairobi National Park's **Athi River gate** is the sole heritage.

Less romantically, Athi River is now the base for the Kenya Meat Commission **abattoirs** — you'll know you're there by the **toll station** and the smell — and the giant Athi River Portland **Cement works.** With many other up and coming industrial plants, this region is beginning to look like Thika.

The Athi river, that gave the town its name, rides down from the Ngong Hills through Nairobi game park and still supports a crocodile or two. It continues flowing on down through Tsavo East — where it becomes the **Galana River** — and on to Malindi where it enters the Indian Ocean as the **Sabaki River.**

The Mombasa Road climbs out of the shallow river valley on a wide bend, past the **Small World Country Club,** and the vast game-rich ranching country of the **Athi Plains.** To the south, David Hopcraft, son of a famous settler family, runs a ranch which domesticates Africa's antelope and gazelles.

On the left, just past the club, is the great rock bluff of **Lukenia,** much frequented by the Mountain Club of Kenya (See "Kenya's Mountains"). The road then dips down before climbing up a few kilometres to the left fork to **Machakos** (See "Hills and orchards").

The remains of the old toll station are just after this fork. Approach slowly — the road bumps which remain are gigantic. From this point the road rises towards the undulating "cotton soil" escarpment and reflects its foundations with great depressions where the soil has subsided.

The panoramas on either side are handsome — mainly large-scale ranches where domestic bovines mingle with herds of gazelle and antelope on the **Kaputei Plains.** The views to the south-west are particularly stunning examples of endless sunbaked plains with the backdrop of the Ngong Hills now far distant.

This fairly long, straight stretch of switch-back road ends where there's a right turn to **Konza,** leading to Konza station, a few kilometres down the dirt trail, the junction for the railway line to **Kajiado** and **Magadi**.

Here the Mombasa road veers left on to firm, smooth, bedrock, through semi-arid country dotted with euphorbia and cacti, and climbs slightly before descending off the Kaputei escarpment through **Salama** where scores of exhausted juggernauts park after their laborious climb up the long, steep slope of the **Ukambani Hills.** Over the years their slow progress and extreme weight has gouged deep ruts in the up slow lane.

When you swoop down to the base of the hills and the gentle incline of the long inland steppe that ends beyond Voi, you pass **Kima**, on the right, which was the stage for one of the grand dramas enacted during the building of the Lunatic Line.

In 1899, Charles Ryall, twenty-five, had been engaged as an Assistant Superintendent of the newly-formed Kenya Police, on attachment from the Punjab Police in India.

A few days before his twenty-sixth birthday he and two colleagues set up an ambush at Kima for a maneating lion that had been attacking passengers and railway staff.

Ryall left a window open in a railway carriage and offered himself as bait to tempt the creature. Unfortunately, however, he fell asleep and the diseased and ageing lion jumped into the coach and dragged him out, the two Europeans powerless to help.

Ryall's remains are buried in Nairobi's first cemetery, behind the Railway Golf Course, overlooking the Nyayo National Stadium (See "Nairobi: city in the sun").

Kima is Kiswahili for mincemeat and may reflect the gruesome sense of humour of the railway management of the day.

Right: The Nairobi-Mombasa lifelines — road and railway — in the lee of the 300-kilometre-long Yatta Plateau in background.

After Kima, the road leaves bedrock and deteriorates to slump bed as it passes the gaunt outcrop above **Sultan Hamud.** This town arose out of an 1899 railhead at Mile 250, 114 kilometres (70 miles) from Nairobi where, with some pomp and circumstance, the ruler of Zanzibar arrived to inspect the progress of this curious British enterprise. The town already springing up around the railhead was duly christened Sultan Hamud in his honour, and so it remains.

The original Sultan Hamud remains, untouched by progress, much as it must have been in the first decade of this century. A newer Sultan Hamud, with **bars, mosque, board** and **lodgings**, is springing up alongside the road on the left.

Road to Amboseli

To the south-east lie the dusty alluvial **Maasai Plains**. A spur line branched out into this wilderness to a dot on the map called **Kibini** where rail engineers sank a borehole for water for the steam locomotives. Much later the line was upgraded for wagons to move rock quarried for the cement factory at Athi River.

A gravel road leads south to **Loitokitok** on the slopes of Kilimanjaro, and to **Ol Tukai**, in the heart of **Amboseli National Park** (See "The Hollywood image").

All this area was a natural wonderland. Greater kudu inhabited the rock outcrops and hills around here until the 1930s. The plains beyond were named *Simba* (lion) after the many prides that roamed there.

Emali, just a few kilometres on from Sultan Hamud, rests on the north-western edge of the Simba plains, surrounded by well-tended *shambas* (farms) and an unusually long bridge, over the railroad, on the eastern edge of town. In the days when there was no tarmac to **Namanga**, Emali was the popular turnoff point for people from upcountry Kenya heading to **Amboseli.**

Immediately to the right of the bridge is the turning along the **water pipeline road** that leads to the foot of the **Chyulu Hills** and on to **Kimana Lodge**, eighty kilometres (50 miles) away.

Otherwise Emali is just a typical Kenya roadside town and from here to **Hunter's Lodge** is all Maasai country — fairly featureless and remote.

Hunter's Lodge at **Kiboko** (which in Kiswahili, means "whip") is named after J. J.

Hunter, a Scottish-born hunter who killed more than 1,000 rhinoceros in this area alone on a government contract.

Hunter's Lodge is about one-third of the way from Nairobi to Mombasa and a good place to pause for refreshment in the **landscaped gardens** that offer sanctuary to more than 250 species of birds.

From here it's only a few kilometres to **Makindu**, with its ornate and embellished Good Samaritan Sikh temple, strung with fairy lights and quite unmissable, which marks Mile 200 on the Lunatic Line. The temple offers free food and accommodation for the weary traveller — a living example of the tenets of the Guru Nanak faith.

Thirteen kilometres (eight miles) further on from Makindu is an **Akamba Handicrafts Co-operative,** which now provides work for over fifty members. A percentage of takings goes to run the operation and buy wood: the remainder is divided equally among the carvers. Visitors are allowed to watch and photograph.

Now the vegetation on either side of the road becomes a profusion of lush undergrowth, a reversion of grasslands to woodlands, where grotesque baobabs proliferate, as the road sweeps on to **Kibwezi**, a small dark and sombre Akamba trading centre just off the main road at the **Kitui** junction.

It was here that some of the first inland missions — and Kenya's first but unsuccessful coffee and successful sisal plantations — were established in the early 1900s. Malaria, blackwater fever, and tsetse fly were so endemic, however, that the coffee and the missions — but not the German sisal — were uprooted and moved to the healthier environment of the Kikuyu uplands around Nairobi.

The sisal was uprooted much later in the 1970s for an ambitious floriculture venture. But it failed. Replanted in the 1980s, it is now once again Kenya's premier sisal plantation.

Kamba beekeepers at the side of the road proffer jars of pure honey — but sample it before you buy. Taste buds differ and some of it is not 100 per cent. Some unscrupulous sellers have watered the honey down with sugar solution — and still float a few bees on top to make it look like the real thing!

The road north from here takes you on through the **Kibwezi Forest** to remote and arid Kitui. Off this road you could take either the first fork, right after some kilometres, to **Kanziko** and then **Mutha**, close to **South Kitui National Reserve,** or take the sharp right turn at **Mutomo,** further on which also leads to Mutha.

Covering 1,833 square kilometres (707 square miles) of arid, infertile land, the reserve embraces the seasonal **Thua River** and its floodplain, surrounded by dense bushland with low hills.

Also in this vicinity but further east along the main road and not yet marked on any map of Kenya, is the 212-square-kilometre (81-square-mile) **Ngai Ndethya National Reserve** which protects a migration corridor between Tsavo East and West.

Forest of Vultures

From Kibwezi the road pushes on through fairly densely-cultivated countryside, with new towns developing swiftly on the north side, to **Mtito Andei** ("Forest of Vultures").

Mtito Andei is almost geometrically the halfway stage between Mombasa and Nairobi, and marks the arid boundary of the land of the Wakamba (See "The People", Part Three).

It is still little more than a sleepy halt in the desert, despite the **mosque, AA post, curio shop, main gate** to Tsavo West, "Greasy Joe" **restaurants, service stations,** the now rundown **Tsavo Inn,** and the original **rail station.**

The first establishment of any note after the station was a Great War **airstrip,** still there just off the road at the east end of town.

From Mtito Andei the road runs for ninety-eight kilometres (60 miles) through the heart of the Tsavo parks, alongside the railway, to Voi. There's an element of poignancy in the signs warning: "Elephants Have Right of Way". Old Kenya hands can remember days, even in the 1960s and 1970s when they had to wait hours for elephant herds to clear off before they could get out of their cars to change tyres after a puncture.

Now the grasslands that the elephants opened up are reverting to thicket and scrub woodlands and soon the tsetse fly may re-establish itself. Giant baobabs, with the gouged-out trunks that the elephant used as scratching posts, still stand here.

Further along the road, gaunt, forbidding mountains begin to punctuate the *nyika* (comiphora-acacia woodland). The seasonal Tsavo ("Blood") **River** flows around the base of the impressive **Ngulia** massif (See "Southern Kenya").

A few kilometres north-eastward, just after the park's **Tsavo River gate,** on the right, a relatively new road bridge crosses the main Mombasa-Nairobi railway line. The road is usually a heaving mass of baboons so reduce speed.

On the eastern bank there's an incongruously-modern motel called **The Maneaters.** Only its name indicates that this was the location of one of the epic dramas of Victorian railroad construction.

When R. O. Preston established the railhead on this spot in mid-1898 he thought it would only be a matter of days before moving on. The resident wildlife thought differently.

Two lions held several thousand Indian and more than 1,300 African workers at bay in a siege that lasted for weeks. Several Africans and almost thirty Indians were killed by these shadowy maneaters in a stranger-than-fiction scenario that was later related by Colonel J. H. Patterson in his book, *Maneaters of Tsavo.*

This military martinet, self-appointed saviour of the fear-crazed rail gangs, bungled ambush after ambush, before finally despatching the two killers. He then glorified his role by writing a melodramatic best-seller that captured the imagination of Victorian Britain.

The stuffed skins of the two killers are exhibits at Chicago's Field Museum in America.

The bridge over the railway was a strategic German target during World War I — but the maps the Germans captured from the British were inaccurate and led them astray.

The **Manyani Gate** to the left, a few kilometres beyond Maneaters, leads into Tsavo East and just beyond that, on the right, is **Mbololo Hills Prison,** formerly **Manyani Detention Camp,** where the colonial authorities held what they termed "hard-core" Mau Mau freedom fighters during the bitter struggle for Independence.

Now the **Prison Industries showroom** displays beautifully-crafted furniture, and the lush **prison farm** shows that, properly watered and tended, even Tsavo's marginal soil can bloom with crops.

Continue to head towards the mass of **Voi Mountain** where, in 1948 Bob Astles, who later earned notoriety as Uganda dictator Idi

Overleaf: Following the course of the "Lunatic Line" built between 1895-1901, a modern locomotive cuts through farming country.

Amin's henchman in the 1970s, crashed his plane in thick cloud. He walked away alive although his passenger was less fortunate and was killed instantly.

A bit further and a sign announces **Voi airstrip** — near to the spot where Karen Blixen's lover, Denys Finch Hatton, crashed and died. From then on the road travels downward, past the **service station** on the left, and the **Taita Hills** and **Taveta junction** to the right, and round the outside of the rapidly developing industrial and commercial entrepôt of **Voi,** on towards Mombasa.

Voi, the capital of this region, was the first main upcountry railhead on the Uganda Railway where passengers enjoyed the first of many overnight stops. Until recently, the *dak* bungalow built to accommodate passengers still provided dinner, bed, and breakfast before the onward journey.

Mackinnon Road

From Voi the road winds on another 150 kilometres (95 miles) across the treacherous **Taru Desert,** a scorched wilderness, entirely without water, to Mombasa. The main settlement in the Taru is **Mackinnon Road,** another memorial to the unfulfilled sense of mission of that prudent Victorian. It is distinguished by the silver dome of the **Sayyid Baghali Shah Mosque**, on the right, by the railway track.

Thirty kilometres (19 miles) later comes **Samburu** with, right, a dirt road that leads to the western foot of the **Shimba Hills** (See "The South Coast: pearls upon a string"). To the left, the road passes through **Silanoni** and **Mbongo** along the lip of the plateau that looks down on the coast littoral.

Another thirty kilometres (19 miles) or so beyond Samburu the first palm groves, at **Mariakani**, named after the Kamba arrows used against the Maasai, announce your entry into a world quite different from upcountry Kenya.

A busy market centre, with **co-operative dairy processing plant, service station,** and always milling crowds, Mariakani marks the junction, to the left, for **Kaloleni**, twenty-two kilometres (14 miles) away, famous for its palm wine.

Continue along the road to **Mazeras**, with its untidy, dilapidated tin-and-timber **shanty shops** and the left turn to **Rabai** and **Ribe.** Johann Krapf, the missionary, established Kenya's first church and permanent mission at Rabai in 1846. Within the year he lost his wife and daughter to fever.

The church has long since vanished but next door to the **cottage** where Krapf's colleague, Johanne Rebmann, lived stands **St Paul's,** built in 1887, and, hung with a litany of the previous church and mission's troubled existence, is still in use.

Two years before it was built, Bishop Hannington bade farewell to his fellow missionaries from Rabai, before starting out for the interior and Uganda where he met his death.

Later Krapf offered to help some Methodist missionaries from Britain build a mission at nearby Ribe. There is still a **Methodist mission** and **school** atop Ribe's hill but jungle has now grown over the hillside ruins of the first mission and its **graveyard.**

At Mazeras, beyond the Rabai junction on the main road, is another Methodist venture, the **Mazeras Craft Training Centre.** It is located opposite Mombasa's **Mazeras Botanical Gardens** where lily-ponds are crossed by willow-pattern bridges, and coarse lawns have been planted with bamboo and palms — a cool green place for a picnic away from the humid heat. The gardens have official opening hours but since there is neither gate nor guardian you can enter at any time.

Soon after this, the road drops down the final escarpment and enters the slums of hinterland Mombasa, marked by oil refineries, factories, rusty litter, shantytowns, and milling crowds, where palms and mangoes grow incongruously against the detritus of industrial enterprise.

Do not linger. The heat is overwhelming but beyond the everlasting flares of the oil refinery, the palm-fringed silver beaches and blue waters of the Indian Ocean await you.

The Coast: The Coral Strand

For more than half of Kenya's three-quarters of a million visitors a year, the coast is where the safari begins and ends. It stretches some 480 kilometres (300 miles) from Tanzania in the south to Somalia in the north. At intervals it is broken by ancient river mouths, now become tidal creeks, and the deltas of Kenya's two biggest rivers, the **Sabaki** and the **Tana**.

Lush contrast to the deserts, plateaux, and mountains upcountry, it is a world removed from the primordial wildlife which roam the diminishing wildernesses inland. After hours of nonstop driving tiredness vanishes at the sight of the *makuti* (palm-thatch) roof of your hotel and the caress of an evening breeze off the Indian Ocean.

More than half of Kenya's 100 international-class hotels — five of which are listed in the register of the world's 300 greatest hotels — are beach hotels.

As luminous, tropical night descends, fire-flies perform their incandescent dance among the bougainvillaea and succulents, and a pale moon strides across the lagoon. The air is scented with the sweetness of the frangipani which seem to bloom, even in the silver glimmer of night.

Early in the morning, while it is still dark, the echoing calls of *muezzins* from the minarets summon the faithful to prayer as they did centuries ago when the first Arab trader came to seek profit, and stayed to settle.

They gave birth to a new culture, Swahili, and a new *lingua franca*, Kiswahili (See "The Dust and the Ashes", Part One).

For much of its length — from **Vanga** in the south, 230 kilometres (150 miles) to Malindi in the north — the shore is protected by a fascinating coral reef.

Inside its protective arms, in sheltered lagoons grow magical marine plants and vividly-coloured fish and marine creatures. Dying generations of coral polyps build up these incredible submarine ridges and precipices — and new coral continues to extend the reefs seaward.

National marine parks off **Watamu, Malindi, Mombasa,** and **Shimoni**, now protect these reefs and the waters they embrace.

Overleaf: Mombasa Island and its Kilindini port.

Holiday playground

All this has become one of the world's great holiday playgrounds. Early morning sees the first pink blush of dawn on the far horizon and sandals of cloud stepping across the sky glow briefly before fading. The incoming tide raps the reef and floods the lagoon. Sailboards are pushed out from the shore and suddenly heel into the breeze, lithe helmsmen tacking by inclination of hip and knee.

The water is always warm, ranging from 27° to 35°C (80°-95°F) and is never ruffled by storms. Kenya's climate reflects the kindness of its tropic shores. Shade temperatures rarely rise above 35°C (95°F): although the sun shines clear almost every day — even during the rainy seasons — the heat is usually tempered by a cooling breeze.

Swimming is safe on almost every beach, though at low tide it's best to wear some footwear to avoid injuries from stonefish, coral, and other hazards.

Visitors unaccustomed to the direct, vertical rays of an Equatorial sun should wear a T-shirt at first when swimming or walking. Prolonged exposures for more than an hour have resulted in severe sunburn with the victims in hospital — no place to spend a Kenyan holiday.

Most people come simply to enjoy sun, sea, and sand but for those inclined to snorkel and scuba dive, Kenya's reefs, coral gardens, and lagoons are among the most beautiful in the world, filled with more than 200 species of fish.

The reef is broken in only a few places, by river mouths or creeks. Of these, the deepest, most sheltered, with a safe channel through the protecting reef, are those on either side of **Mombasa Island.**

These anchorages gave the town an important strategic role to play in the coast's turbulent history (See "The Dust and the Ashes", Part One). It came into being as an entrepôt because it was one of the finest natural harbours along the East African coast. Mombasa's natural advantage makes it Kenya's second largest city and premier trading port.

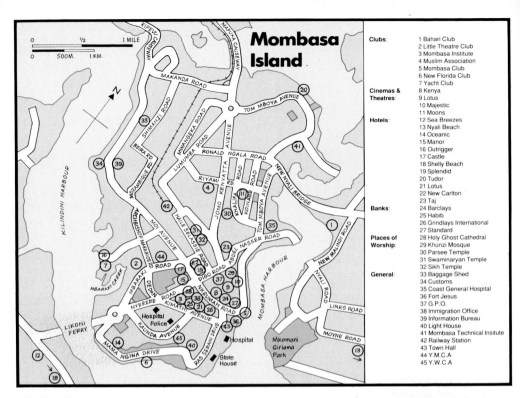

Mombasa Island

Clubs:	1 Bahari Club
	2 Little Theatre Club
	3 Mombasa Institute
	4 Muslim Association
	5 Mombasa Club
	6 New Florida Club
	7 Yacht Club
Cinemas &	8 Kenya
Theatres:	9 Lotus
	10 Majestic
	11 Moons
Hotels:	12 Sea Breezes
	13 Nyali Beach
	14 Oceanic
	15 Manor
	16 Outrigger
	17 Castle
	18 Shelly Beach
	19 Splendid
	20 Tudor
	21 Lotus
	22 New Carlton
	23 Taj
Banks:	24 Barclays
	25 Habib
	26 Grindlays International
	27 Standard
Places of	28 Holy Ghost Cathedral
Worship:	29 Khunzi Mosque
	30 Parsee Temple
	31 Swaminaryan Temple
	32 Sikh Temple
General:	33 Baggage Shed
	34 Customs
	35 Coast General Hospital
	36 Fort Jesus
	37 G.P.O.
	38 Immigration Office
	39 Information Bureau
	40 Light House
	41 Mombasa Technical Insitute
	42 Railway Station
	43 Town Hall
	44 Y.M.C.A
	45 Y.W.C.A

Getting there

Mombasa is served by air, sea, rail, and road. By road from Nairobi the 485-kilometre journey (300-mile) takes between five and seven hours. There are many express bus services.

By air, the frequent domestic flights take either forty-five or ninety minutes, depending on the aircraft.

By overnight train, the journey takes thirteen hours.

Though passenger ships no longer ply to and from the port it might be possible to find a berth on one of the many cargo ships that sail from Europe through the Red Sea and south down the coast, or round the Cape from the Atlantic and north up the coast. For this you must allow several weeks of sea travel.

Where to stay

Castle Hotel (3-star), Oceanic (4-star), Outrigger (4-star), Hotel Splendid (2-star), Lotus Hotel (2-star), Manor Hotel (4-star), New Carlton (3-star). There are many others. See Listings for "Hotels".

Sightseeing

Measuring little more than fourteen square kilometres (less than five square miles),

Mombasa island is grossly overcrowded. The original, narrow-streeted town, built from coral-rock in shades of buff, rose, and ochre, was designed for another, more leisurely age and only one-third of its current population.

This coral island is connected to the mainland in the west by causeway, north by bridge, and south by old-fashioned ferry.

Arriving by air you'll land at **Moi International Airport,** officially opened by President Moi in August 1979. On the drive into town the road passes through **Port Reitz,** named after the nineteenth-century British naval lieutenant who, in 1824, established a one-man "British Protectorate" in Mombasa, some sixty years before the actual fact. His protection was short-lived — as was he. Reitz died of malaria aged only twenty-three (See "The Dust and the Ashes", Part One).

Four kilometres (two and a half miles) from the airport you join the road from Nairobi, then cross the **Makupa causeway** following the railway.

The road diverges from the railtrack as it arrives on the island to head another four kilometres (two and a half miles) through the suburbs, straight down **Jomo Kenyatta Avenue,** to the town centre. This is marked by the **roundabout,** just over seven kilometres (four miles) from the airport where the **Elim Pentecostal Church's** garden once hosted two **palm trees** planted by Princess Margaret in 1956 and Queen Elizabeth, the Queen Mother, in 1959.

Jomo Kenyatta Avenue is bisected by the junction that leads to the Japanese-built **Nyali Bridge** linking the island to the northern mainland.

Drive past a police station, the **Tom Mboya Memorial Hall,** a **baptist** church and an odd-looking **mosque,** and finally you arrive at what was, until 1989, Mombasa's traditional market place, **Mwembe Tayari.** Here in the 1880s, the young Mr Ainsworth inspected his safari caravan of porters before setting off for his long walk upcountry to become Britain's inland representative in Machakos.

Mwembe Tayari is no longer a market place and is now a congested bus station and snack bar area.

The big street market is **Makupa market,** off Mwembe Tayari in the heart of **Majengo,** the island's low-income housing district. A colourful, multi-purpose market with a lively atmosphere, it is well worth a visit. Drive along **Jomo Kenyatta Avenue,** then turn left into **Salim Mwa Ngunga Road.**

Mombasa is a good place to buy cheap fabrics — the Kenya coast is famous for these and **Biashara Street** offers the latest in *kanga* (printed cotton wrap-arounds) designs. It's worth comparing prices before buying or bargaining for bulk buys. Beyond the **Kwavi Road intersection,** Biashara shifts from textiles to a section of household goods.

Next to the Mwembe Tayari bus station is a sombre **war memorial,** guarded by four bronze sentinels of the King's African Rifles. It was raised, two years before the memorial in Nairobi, to honour the Kenyans who fell for an alien Empire in World War I. Opposite is the **Bohra cemetery.**

Go straight ahead at the roundabout, to where Kenyatta Avenue joins the main street, **Digo Road,** then turn right. To the right of Mwembe Tayari, opposite another **mosque,** Kenyatta Avenue cuts into **Mwembe Tayari Road.** You'll pass a succession of typical Mombasa eating houses and hostelries — signposted by their utilitarian decor and vivacious customers — a **Khoja cemetery,** and a **Hindu temple** guarded by two blue,

plaster sentinels that portray Krishna's reincarnations.

Continue along this road to Mombasa's functional **Central Railway Station,** built in 1932 when the terminus was moved from the dockside.

From the station, it is one straight kilometre (two-thirds of a mile) along **Haile Selassie Road** (formerly Station Road) to Digo Road, where the main post office for Post Restante and other services is open Monday-Friday 08.00-16.30 and 08.00-12.00 on Saturday.

Follow Digo Road south past **Gusii Street,** on the right, with its magnificent **mosque** and the comfortable **Splendid Hotel,** and **Meru Road** on the left where there's a **Shiva temple,** past the old "Theatre Royal", now the **Regal cinema,** to **Moi Avenue** (formerly Kilindini Road) otherwise Kenya's "costa del sol".

Strolling and people watching are the time-honoured occupations. Curio sellers, conmen, ladies of the night, sailors, tourists, and taximen patrol the long, straight dual-carriageway which leads to the docks.

Moi Avenue is the best place to hire cars and change money: Barclays Bank's **bureau de change** is open Monday-Saturday 08.00-12.30 and 14.00-17.00. Car hire tends to be cheaper (though still expensive) than in Nairobi and most of the major outlets have branches here or in neighbouring **Nkrumah Road.**

After the intersection continue past the passageway on the left, to the **Fontanella bistro,** curio stands and **Castle Hotel,** famous as a pick-up point in all senses of the word. Immediately visible, round a gentle bend, are the Avenue's famous "elephant" tusks, erected in honour of Britain's Queen Elizabeth II on her 1952 coronation.

The aluminium tusks arch over Moi Avenue close to the **Information Bureau** — open Monday-Friday 08.00-12.00, 14.00-16.30; Saturday 08.00-12.00, which is well administered with a number of leaflets and maps available.

On your right, before you reach the tusks is the **New Carlton Hotel** which is nowhere near as grand as its name implies. Opposite is **Uhuru Park,** now totally hidden by the curio stalls, but with an **Uhuru Fountain** that displays an outline of Africa.

There's also the **Bella Vista** service station and restaurant, unchanged since they were built, and then a little further down on the left,

Above: Mombasa's bustling Biashara Street.

the **Sunshine Day and Night Club.** After this you pass under the **railway bridge** into the docks.

East of Digo Road is Mombasa's original "Arabian Nights" **Old Town.** Almost inevitably, visitors first make for the red-buffed **fortress** whose fifteen-metre-high (50-feet), two-and-a-half-metre-thick (nine-feet) battlements tower over the old town's alleyways.

Constructed by the Portuguese who "colonised" the East African coast in the sixteenth century, **Fort Jesus** was designed by an Italian architect as a huge pentagon.

As with all classic European fortresses of its age, this ensured that assailants were met from all its walls by crossfire. Surrounded by a twelve-metre-deep (40-feet) moat and guarded at each corner by four towers, the fort has a gruesome and bloody history.

Building first began in 1593 and was finished five years later. The fort, which retains much of its original character, was restored between 1958 and 1960 with a £30,000 donation from the Gulbenkian Foundation and re-opened in October 1960 — fittingly — by a Portuguese envoy.

Opposite: Mombasa's "Old Town".

Relics from the seventeenth-century wreck of the Portuguese ship, *Santa Antonio de Tanna*, which sank in the harbour, were recovered in the early 1980s and are on display in the museum inside.

The ship arrived from Goa on 15 September, 1697, and was immediately bombarded by Mombasa's Arab defenders. She dragged her anchor and drifted on to the reef where she was holed. Hauled off, she sank at once.

Rusting nineteenth-century **cannon** and more modern armament from the British ship the *Pegasus*, with the guns from the German battleship *Konigsberg*, which sank the *Pegasus* in Zanzibar harbour before she was destroyed as she hid up the Rufiji delta in Tanganyika, stand outside the walls. Nearby is the **monument** that honours Muslim Major Wavell who commanded the Arab Rifles in World War I.

The massive ramparts of this bastion slope gently down to the wide, but ruined steps, now overgrown with bushes and trees, that lead to the old **slave harbour** from which spices and slaves were shipped.

Slaves were imprisoned in a cave with a freshwater well — now foul and odiferous.

The port is used, less frequently each year, by the few dhows that continue the 3,000-year-old tradition of trade with the Gulf and Asia.

Leaving the fort by the **Water Gate** you enter the Old Town, keeping the Mombasa club, *circa* 1885, Kenya's oldest gentlemen's club to your right, down **Mbarak Hinaway Road**, formerly Vasco da Gama road. It was renamed in honour of the last of the Sultan of Zanzibar's Mombasa governors.

The narrow lanes are lined with wooden, "Juliet" balconied houses, reminiscent of Elizabethan tudor, which are authentic Arab *mashrabia*. Studded between the maze of buildings are twenty-odd mosques, where the faithful are summoned to prayer by the *muezzin*.

On **Bachawy Road** stands the **Mandhry mosque,** officially the oldest, founded in 1570. It's rarely open to visitors, but you can still admire its outstanding minaret.

Just around the corner from the mosque, in **Government Square**, is one of the many galleries that sell art, Arabian carpets, carved doors, and more mundane curios.

The **Jain Temple,** in **Langoni Road,** with it's dome topped by a spire of gold, and heavy doors carved from solid silver, is worth a visit. Other religious architecture is found in the **Baluchi Mosque** in **Makadara Road,** a green-, white- and pink-coloured 1964 successor to the original built in 1875 by the Baluchis who migrated from the Makran coast of what is now Pakistan.

Adjacent to **Jamhuri Park** is a **Shiva temple** guarded by two plaster lions and the elephant-headed god, Ganesh, and a remarkable pantheon of animal gods and devils. The temple spire is adorned by a crock of gold.

The **Dawoodi Bohra,** *circa* 1902, is near Mombasa's own **Thirty-nine Steps**. These take you up to a clifftop of scrub wasteland and litter, overlooking the old harbour.

Mombasa's early buildings contrast sharply with the 1980s high-rises beginning to spring up in the city centre, particularly around **Treasury Square**. Here law courts and banks — architectural remembrances of Britain's tenure in Kenya — used to stand near to the **Catholic Memorial Cathedral.**

Treasury Square was also the site of the first station built for Mackinnon's narrow-gauge, grandiose-sounding Central African Railway. Only eleven kilometres (seven miles) of track were ever laid and it ended up as Mombasa's one and only tram service (See "The Dust and the Ashes").

Drive up to the roundabout that intersects Moi Avenue and Digo Road and turn left into what now becomes **Nyerere Avenue**, past the British Council library and the **Manor Hotel,** almost a century old. It stands opposite the **Anglican Cathedral** that commemorates Archbishop Hannington who was murdered in Uganda in the last century.

After the roundabout marking the intersection with **Dedan Kimathi Avenue,** formerly Ayub Khan Avenue, the road follows the line of Mackinnon's Central African Railway track.

Further along is a left turn into **Kaunda Avenue,** which leads to the entrance of the **Oceanic Hotel** with its commanding panoramic views of **Likoni Creek** and the deepwater entrance of **Kilindini Docks**.

After the left turn into Nyerere Avenue at the roundabout, a right turn leads to **Likoni Ferry.** Here the road become **Mama Ngina Drive,** Mombasa's grand, essentially unspoilt, marine esplanade which leads past the **New Florida nightclub,** right, and **Fort St Joseph,** whose baobab forest has now been partly uprooted for estate development, though not without controversy.

After this the drive cuts through the middle of **Mombasa Golf Club's** nine-hole course, established in 1911, and then on along by the wall of **State House,** and back into Treasury Square.

Alternatively, you can turn right at the Likoni Ferry roundabout into **Mbaraki Road,** and past the baobabs that shelter the intriguing **Mbaraki Pillar,** a phallic pillar tomb of coral-rag which is believed to have been the eighteenth-century burial place of the Sheikh of Changamwe. He was head of one of the twelve original tribes of Mombasa Island.

Further along are some **cemeteries** containing fifty-two Commonwealth military graves from World War I and 146 from World War II.

By the **Little Theatre Club** on the left, Mbaraki Road becomes **Mnazi Moja Road** and runs into Moi Avenue. The club is sometimes the venue for the Shangari players

Opposite: 15th-century pillar tomb outside Malindi's Juma "Friday" mosque.

Above: Youngsters enjoy the warmth of the Indian Ocean.

who put on works by African playwrights but more often it is an outlet for amateur dramatics by the expatriate community.

First left off Mnazi Moja Road is **Archbishop Makarios Road** which takes you to the excellent **Outrigger Hotel** and **Mombasa Yacht Club.**

Nearby stands **Kilindini Mosque,** built in the 1970s replacing the monument established by three tribes who migrated to Kilindini from the hinterland in the sixteenth century. The original ruins of this seventeenth- or eighteenth-century mosque were intertwined with vast parasitical trees and creepers.

The north side of the Island around **Tudor Creek,** which you can explore by dhow or power boat, is mainly modern and residential. It's the anchorpoint for the splendid Japanese-built **toll bridge** that connects the island to the north mainland.

Abdel Nasser Road, the continuation of **Digo Road,** leads past the **municipal** (formerly Mackinnon) **market,** right, and the Sunni mosque, **Masjid Nur,** across what the Portuguese in the sixteenth century christened *Cidade dos Mouros*. Probably Mombasa's first settlement, from around the eleventh

century, it was sacked and razed to the ground in 1505. Behind the **Institute of Islamic Culture** on the right, are the ruined remains of a **mosque** that may have existed at that time.

The ruins are close to the 1918 **Alidina Visram High School,** formerly the Aga Khan Boys School, and the **Coast General Hospital,** which is on the left.

Excavations in 1976, on a site set aside for proposed hospital extensions revealed massive ruined walls, and shards of Islamic and Chinese pottery of the Ming era, dating from long before the Portuguese arrived.

Beyond is the **Lady Grigg Maternity Hospital**, built in honour of a colonial notable, and a **lighthouse**. Here, the old **Nyali Bridge,** a pontoon on floats, used to bridge Tudor Creek.

Mombasa's nearest beaches are **Shelly Beach** on the south coast. Take the Likoni ferry over the creek then turn first left and continue for three kilometres (two miles). **Nyali Beach** on the north coast, over Nyali Bridge, is also close by: turn first right after the bridge and drive for four kilometres (two and a half miles).

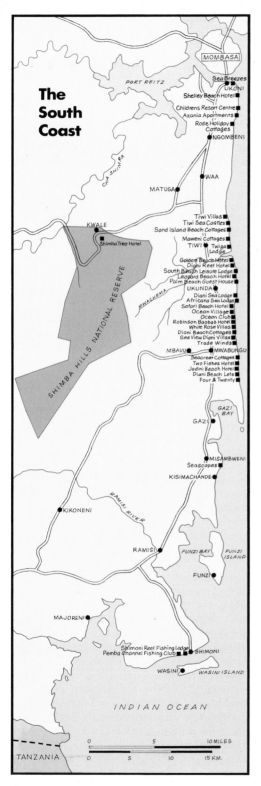

The South Coast

The
South
Coast

MOMBASA
PORT REITZ
Sea Breezes
UKONI
Shelley Beach Hotel
Childrens Resort Centre
Azania Apartments
Rose Holiday
Cottages
NGOMBENI
CHASHIMBA
WAA
MATUGA
KWALE
Tiwi Villas
Tiwi Sea Castles
Sand Island Beach Cottages
Shimba Tree Hotel
Maweni Cottages
TIWI   Twiga
Lodge
Golden Beach Hotel
Diani Reef Hotel
South Beach Leisure Lodge
Leopard Beach Hotel
Palm Beach Guest House
UKUNDA
MWACHEMA
SHIMBA HILLS NATIONAL RESERVE
Diani Sea Lodge
Africana Sea Lodge
Safari Beach Hotel
Ocean Village
Ocean Club
Robinson Baobab Hotel
White Rose Villas
Diani Beach Cottages
Sea View Diani Villas
Trade Winds
MBAVU   MWABUNGU
Seacrest Cottages
Two Fishes Hotel
Jadini Beach Hotel
Diani Beach Lets
Four & Twenty
GAZI
BAY
GAZI
MISAMBWENI
Seascapes
KISIMACHANDE
RAMISI RIVER
KIKONENI
RAMISI   FUNZI BAY   FUNZI
ISLAND
FUNZI
MAJORENI
Shimoni Reef Fishing Lodge
Pemba Channel Fishing Club   SHIMONI
WASINI   WASINI ISLAND
INDIAN OCEAN
0   5   10 MILES
TANZANIA   0   5   10   15 KM.

The South Coast: Pearls upon a String

South of Mombasa, across Likoni Creek, lies a ribbon of lagoons and beaches strung together like pearls upon a string. From Mombasa to the Tanzanian border they are generally quieter than those to the north. But **Diani Beach** is the equivalent of California's Sunset Strip.

Down at the far end of the southern coastal strip is unspoilt **Shimoni** with its relics of the slave trade and unspoilt coral gardens.

For most of the way the road runs parallel to the shore, about two or three kilometres (one and a half miles) inland and, in most cases, when you leave the road you'll find untrodden paths and beaches.

Getting there

A new suspension bridge to link **Kilindini Creek** to the southern mainland is on the drawing board in Tokyo but, for the present, the way to this tropical paradise is by old-fashioned **motor ferry**.

The usually long wait on the ferry ramp acclimatizes visitors to the essence of what passes for pace at the coast. *Haraka Haraka Haina Baraka* goes the old Swahili, saying in effect: "Don't do today what you can put off until tomorrow and hopefully longer".

The actual crossing takes four minutes, but allow at least an hour on either side. Wear a hat and suntan lotion if you have to wait in the middle of the day: it gets very hot.

Where to stay

In Likoni, Shelley Beach Hotel (4-star); In Tiwi, Tiwi Sea Castles (self-service), Tiwi Villas (self-service), Twiga Lodge (budget). There are others. See Listings for "Hotels".

Sightseeing

There's not much to do in **Likoni** itself, which is little more than an untidy afterthought to Mombasa town. From the ferry ramp a road runs off around the headland to the east, but there's no beach to speak of — just weed-covered coral at low tide.

But the pleasantly-comfortable **Shelley Beach Hotel** has a fine swimming pool and the ambience is all coastal. The hotel's charm derives from its antiquity; it's the oldest of the

Above: Dinner aboard a dhow in Mombasa's Tudor Creek.

south coast hotels and has lost none of its character.

The main road southwards for thirteen kilometres (eight miles) to **Waa** is based on the old, single-lane tarmac track which then degenerated into dirt track.

After leaving Likoni, whose southern limits are marked by the right turn for the **Kenya Naval headquarters** at **Mtwonge**, on the south shore of Kilindini Creek, the roads runs through one of the least spoilt areas of the Kenya coast.

Prolific trees and undergrowth line the road, interspersed with scattered coral-rag and thatch villages and women as undulating as the surface of the road.

Just outside Waa, where the tarmac used to end, begins one of Kenya's finest highways, a smooth, broad strip of tarmac that runs all the way south to **Lunga Lunga,** the border town with Tanzania.

Almost immediately to the right is a turning on to a two-lane highway that climbs twelve kilometres (seven and a half miles) to **Kwale,** the administrative, tree-shaded district capital, set in the cool heights of the Shimba Hills. The transition from languid, tropical shore to hilly reserve takes no more than twenty minutes.

Kwale, where the elephant and the buffalo frequently roam, takes its name from the Swahili word for the many endemic spurfowl of the area. In 1988, customers at the one-street town's most popular bar were kept indoors long after closing hours because elephant and buffalo were grazing on the grass outside the front door.

Shimba Hills National Reserve

Three kilometres (two miles) south of Kwale, along a corrugated, elephant-dunged, murram track, the 192-square-kilometre (74-square-mile) **Shimba Hills National Reserve** lies some twenty kilometres (12 miles) directly inland from the beach strip, ranging in height from between 120 and 450 metres (400-1,500 feet).

Basically a dissected forested plateau of conical hills, steep ridges and ravines, where many of the surviving trees are thousands of years old, the hills are a major water catchment area. But because of its porous soils little remains on the plateau itself. Instead, the water filters down to the base of the hills.

Above: Young crocodiles bask on rock at coastal crocodile farm.

Constantly fanned by strong sea breezes and frequently shrouded by early morning cloud and mist, the hills are much cooler than the rest of the coast.

The forested slopes and undulating grasslands of the scarp are surrounded by a forest reserve covering almost 200 square kilometres (77 square miles).

It is the only place in Kenya where you can see sable antelope. Roan antelope, translocated here at the beginning of the 1970s, did not thrive as expected. Although closely related to sable, sharing much the same range, the herd is now extinct.

The one luxury lodge, sister to upcountry Treetops, is rated as the finest of Kenya's forest lodges. Other facilities offered include two first-class campsites, picnic site, and nature trail.

The roads are well-graded and signposted, to places such as **Makadara** and **Longomwagandi** forests, perhaps the only authentic African jungle at the coast, where lianas — parasitic climbers — are locked in deadly embrace with their ancient and gigantic hosts: all in perpetual gloom, with borussa fruit (which make the elephant tipsy)

and butterflies, and, of course, leopard.

You can visit the open areas and vantage spots such as **Giriama Point** and **Pengo Hill Lookout,** which is the highest point.

Still unspoilt, the rolling downs and thick, ancient rain forests offer occasional glimpses of the reserve's elusive wildlife populations, especially on early morning game drives. The seemingly infinite expanse of grassy plains and cloud-flecked hills recall the olden days of Africa. Truly magnificent.

Back on the main coast road, the first resort after the Kwale turnoff and, after Likoni, the oldest on the south coast, is **Tiwi.** Located six kilometres (four miles) from Waa, turn left down a coral sand road for another two kilometres (little more than a mile). Tiwi has many self-catering bungalow resorts.

You can also reach Tiwi Beach from another turn one-and-a-half kilometres (one mile) beyond the first turn. Go left again, then follow the road for three kilometres (two miles) down to the estuary of the seasonal **Mwachema River**. At low tide you can wade across to the northernmost extremity of fabulous **Diani Beach**, the south coast's matchless resort.

Diani: An Original Tropical Paradise

Diani is Kenya's original tropical paradise; palm-fringed beaches, caster-sugar sands and translucent, cornflower-blue sea. The offshore reef that stretches the length of the south coast is a twenty-minute swim away, and has been proposed as a marine national park and reserve.

Even at low tide, the water is deep enough for swimming and snorkeling with shallow pools elsewhere for wading and paddling.

Beneath the sea's placid surface, an inner universe of strange rock formations, swaying weeds, and sculptured corals are dazzlingly lit by shoals of angel, jewel, lion, zebra, and parrot fish.

Every resort hotel hires out snorkeling equipment and many offer aqualung facilities for those who wish to swim up to fifty metres (150 feet) down. Diani is also a mecca for windsurfing, water-skiing, and paragliding fanatics.

Getting there

From Tiwi you cross to Diani at **Kongo**, on a sweep of the estuary guarded by giant sentinel baobabs, where the magnificent and well-preserved fifteenth-century **Mwana Mosque** still stands. The vaulted roof of its prayer-room is intact and worshippers still come to recite their prayers to Allah the Merciful.

The estuary was the focal point of a now-abandoned scheme to make Diani into one of the most glittering resorts in the world. Designers and landscape planners devised a dam which would have turned the estuary into a manmade lagoon. But you'll probably agree that it's far better left as nature intended it.

From Kongo, however, it's a long and tiring walk to the main drag of Diani Beach so most will opt to return to the main road to continue another five kilometres (three miles) to what by coast standards is the bustling little town of **Ukunda.** It sprawls between the shopping centre along the hinterland main road — with **bank, post office** and **dukas** — and the Diani Beach strip, with two shopping centres and **airfield**. Turn left at the main road to get down to what is now universally known as Kenya's Sunset Strip.

Where to stay

Africana Sea Lodge, Diani Reef, Diani Sea Lodge, Golden Beach, Jadini Beach, Leisure Lodge, Leopard Beach, Nomad Beach Bandas, Robinson's Baobab, Trade Winds, Two Fishes. A mixture of five and four star hotels with a comfortable beachcomber-style alternative in Nomad Beach Bandas. There are many other options including self-service chalets, cottages, and camping sites. See Listings for "Hotels".

In Shimoni, Pemba Channel Fishing Club (4-star) and Shimoni Reef Fishing Lodge (4-star). There are others. See Listings for "Hotels".

National Reserves

Shimba Tree Hotel (5-star), Kwale, book through Block Hotels, Rehema House, Nairobi, and Nyali Beach Hotel, Mombasa.

Sightseeing

The strip is divided into north and south. Turn left, off the slip road from Ukunda, to go north; right to go south. The north end is a johnny-come-lately but has some magnificent hotels with equally magnificent beaches.

But south is where Diani started years ago. Dan Trench, a now ancient scion of one of Kenya's settler families, built the original Jadini Beach hotel. He still lives nearby though it's doubtful if he recognises the hotel today.

Although its architecture is admittedly impressive, it's not much compensation for those who remember the good old days when Diani Beach was all the more delightful.

The first hotel along this road, on the left (as are all hotels here), is **Trade Winds,** which retains all its original atmosphere. Mellow, sociable, and offering bar games, it aims at the middle market and is something like a good, English village pub.

Directly opposite the track down to Trade Winds is a monolithic **baobab tree** with a twenty-two-metre girth (72-feet), so ancient that it is protected by Presidential decree.

It's a survivor of the impenetrable **Jadini Forest** that used to clothe all this section of the Coast. As you head south you'll come across the forest remnant along any of the tracks, right, that lead into magnificent stands of hardwood trees where birds, butterflies, baboon, colobus, and vervet monkeys make their home.

At night, myriad eyes glitter in the dark. They are probably bushbabies, though locals like to recount tales of leopard.

Above: Ancient Kongo Mosque marks the Mwachema Estuary between Tiwi and Diani Beaches.

The most atmospheric spot along Sunset Strip is **Nomad**'s, usually fully occupied by locals looking more for ambience and *cordon bleu* cuisine than air-conditioning and plush menus.

Nomad's also run the only beach bar along the whole coast — set in the cemented remains of a wrecked dhow.

Diani's night-time entertainment takes the form of discotheques and live bands at all the hotels — lively and exhausting. There's also traditional Giriama dancing, which is fun and different.

The **Bushbaby,** an open-air nightclub opposite the **Two Fishes Hotel,** attracts locals as well as tourists in search of local colour.

But be careful about walking on the beach at night. Romantic it may be, but mugging has become more common in recent years.

To Shimoni

From Ukunda the main road runs south through palm plantations, swamps, and sugar, a still virtually undeveloped area, little affected by the swift growth of Kenya's tourist industry, to **Shimoni,** the first permanent British settlement on the Kenya mainland.

Along the way, delightful side trails invite you to discover a stretch of beach or remnant jungle all to yourself for a day.

Ten kilometres (six miles) out of Ukunda is another turning on the right, up to the back door of the Shimba Hills. A left turn to **Kinondo** leads to a jungle-shrouded peninsula. Offshore, **Chale Island** awaits exploration. If you hire a boat to take you there, be warned that the seaward side is a mass of sand flies which bite perniciously.

Another ten kilometres (six miles) brings you to the sleepy little village of **Gazu** where the **primary school** was once the home — and headquarters — of Sheikh Mbaruk ("Baruka") bin Rashid, a rebellious Mazrui leader who allegedly tortured opposition supporters before suffocating them with the smoke of burning chillies.

Ask a local person for directions. There's no signboard and the village is on the edge of a deep, mangrove-infested bay.

Two-and-a-half kilometres beyond (one and a half miles) is East Africa's largest **coconut factory** which processes millions of nuts a year, the flesh laid out to dry for three or four days to turn into copra.

A once neglected fishing village, **Msambweni,** twenty-five kilometres (15 miles) from Ukunda, has recently grown in popularity, particularly amongst hedonistic local residents. Its name derives from the Kiswahili for "Place of the Antelope".

But Msambweni's seventeenth-century old slave pen testifies to the thousands who endured incarceration and lifelong servitude. The anti-slave crusade finally brought an end to the evil trade at the close of the nineteenth century.

Walk along the beach, negotiating difficult coral impediments, and eventually you'll reach **Funzi Island** separated from the mainland by a narrow, high-water channel that you can wade across at low tide.

A de luxe fishing resort was in the throes of being built in 1989 (the island offers superb deep-sea fishing opportunities). It is also possible to camp. There are beaches and sections of reef scattered close to the forested shore on both sides of the island.

Return to the main road and head on another thirteen kilometres (eight miles) to the **Ramisi River** where the land on either side of the road and river was once cultivated as one of Kenya's biggest sugar plantations.

Lying on the shore, just before you reach **Ramisi,** is the old hamlet of **Shirazi,** also

Above: Moray eel and underwater photographer in coral lagoon at Kenya coast.

Opposite top: Angel fish in one of Kenya's coral gardens.

Below: Starfish in a marine national park.

Opposite: Underwater marine garden off Kenya's south coast.

known as **Kifunzi**. Any track, left, through the old sugar fields takes you to this tiny settlement, a backwater in every sense of the word.

Now the people spend their days cutting mangrove poles, catching fish, and market gardening, though their efforts are all too often demolished by greedy monkeys. But the setting is exotic — a modern *Jamaica Inn,* and worth the short walk off the main road.

From Ramisi the main road runs another thirty-five kilometres (21 miles) to the **Lunga Lunga** border post. But to get to the definitive end of the south coast, as far as visitors are concerned, turn left to **Shimoni**, just three kilometres (two miles) beyond Ramisi where a cluster of battered signs mark the turning for the old headquarters of Sir William Mackinnon's enterprise, IBEA.

Shimoni long established as a settler's resort is famous for its deep-sea, big game fishing in the unparalleled reaches of **Pemba Channel** which divides the coast from Tanzania's **Pemba Island**, some forty kilometres (25 miles) offshore.

Shimoni is the Swahili word for "Place of the Hole" — which refers to the gloomy fifteen-kilometre-long (nine-mile) cave where slaves were penned before being shipped north-westward.

The path to this coral cave winds into the jungle from a point directly opposite the jetty. You descend by ladder through a jagged hole. Sunlight glimmers from holes in the forest floor, illuminating stalactites and dangling lianas.

But Shimoni's greatest attractions lie off-shore. For this is the home of one of Kenya's great marine national parks, twenty-eight-square-kilometre (10-square-mile) **Kisite Marine National Park** and the adjacent eleven-square-kilometre (four-square-mile) **Mpunguti Marine National Reserve**.

Wasini Island

Located in the coral gardens about one kilometre (half-a-mile) south of **Wasini Island**, this trapezoid section of the Indian Ocean encompasses four small, arid coral islands and a considerable area of fringing reefs and surrounding sand. It's said to provide the best goggling on the East African coast (see "National Parks", In Brief).

You can walk around seventeen-square-kilometre (six-and-a-half-square-mile) **Wasini** — just five kilometres (three miles) long and one kilometre (half-a-mile) wide — in a couple of hours.

The island boasts a small pillar tomb set with many shards of Chinese pottery and its shores are a beachcomber's delight. Your many finds will include pieces of glass, and a variety of shells, both natural and manmade. The scrap metal is detritus from World War I when Wasini was used as a firing range. For collectors of *bric-a-brac*, it is a veritable Mecca.

At the end of the 1970s the **Wasini Island restaurant** was established at the southern tip of the island, **Ras Mondini** with a liquor licence for customers only — lest offence be given to the Muslim villagers of **Wasini** and **Kifundi.**

The restaurant management also arrange snorkeling trips to the fabulous reefs around Kisite island. You travel in a large dhow and a mammoth-size seafood lunch is included.

Behind Wasini village lies an extraordinary area of long-dead coral gardens now land-locked but occasionally flooded by spring tides. Covered in a mass of lemon grass, this coral offers the odd sensation of snorkeling over dry land.

Seventeen kilometres (ten and a half miles) south of Shimoni across the bay from the peninsula is **Vanga,** which can also be reached by a murram road off the main road just before Lunga Lunga.

Untouched at present by Kenya's tourist industry, Vanga lies in a tangle of mangrove swamps. A **causeway**, flooded every so often by spring tides, leads over one of the swamps to the town. If you want to explore the mangroves, you can hire one of the precarious local dugouts.

Mombasa to Malindi: Sun, Sand, Sailing and Surfing

For years, the northern springboard from Mombasa was a toll bridge floating on pontoons that rose and fell with the tide. Today an elegant new Japanese single-span bridge arches over **Tudor Creek**, dramatic evidence of the transformation that Independence and package tourism have wrought. This route takes you out along a trail that incorporates tarmac, gravel, dirt road, ferry and boat, and stretches 386 kilometres (240 miles) to the Somalia border.

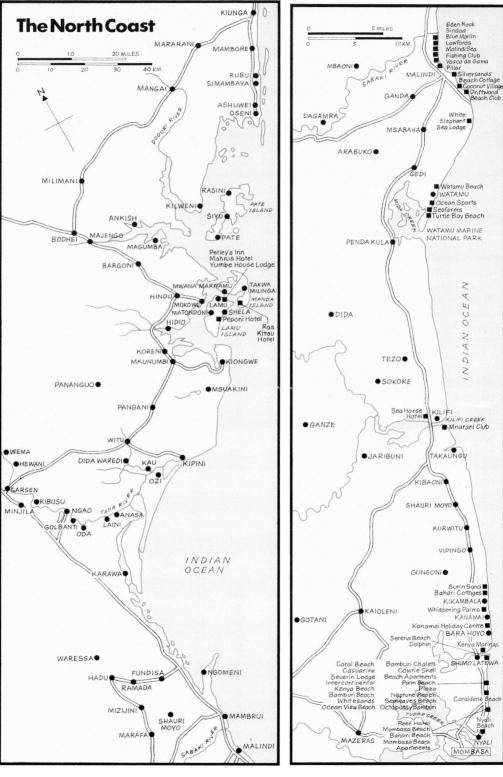

The North Coast

KIUNGA
MARARANI
MAMBORE
RUBU
SIMAMBAYA
MANGAI
ASHUWEI
OSENI
MILIMANI
RASINI
KILWENI
SIYU
PATE ISLAND
ANKISH
BODHEI   MAJENGO
MAGUMBA
BARGONI
Petley's Inn
Mahrus Hotel
Yumbe House Lodge
MWANA MARIYAMU   TAKWA
MILINGA
HINDU   MANDA ISLAND
MOKOWE   LAMU
MATONDONI   SHELA
HIDIO   Peponi Hotel
LAMU ISLAND   Ras Kitau Hotel
KORENI
MKUNUMBI   KIONGWE
PANANGUO
MSUAKINI
PANGANI
WITU
WEMA
HEWANI
DIDA WAREDI   KAU   KIPINI
OZI
GARSEN
KIBUSU
MINJILA   NGAO   ANASA
GOLBANTI   LAINI
ODA
TANA RIVER
KARAWA
INDIAN OCEAN
GOTANI
WARESSA
FUNDISA
HADU   NGOMENI
RAMADA
MIZIJINI
SHAURI MOYO   MAMBRUI
MARAFA
SABAKI RIVER   MALINDI
DODORI RIVER
N

MBAONI
SABAKI RIVER   MALINDI
DAGAMRA
GANDA
GEDI   Eden Rock
Sindad
Blue Marlin
Lowfords
Malindi Sea
Fishing Club
Vasco da Gama
Pillar
Silversands
Beach Cottage
Coconut Village
Driftwood
Beach Club
White Elephant
Sea Lodge
MSABAHA
ARABUKO
GEDI
Watamu Beach
WATAMU
Ocean Sports
Seafarers
Turtle Bay Beach
WATAMU MARINE NATIONAL PARK
PENDA KULA
MIDA CREEK
DIDA
INDIAN OCEAN
TEZO
SOKOKE
GANZE
Sea Horse Hotel   KILIFI
KILIFI CREEK
Mnarani Club
JARIBUNI   TAKAUNGU
KIBAONI
SHAURI MOYO
KURWITU
VIPINGO
GONGONI
Sun'n Sand
Bahari Cottages
KIKAMBALA
Whispering Palms
KANAMAI
KAIOLENI   Kanamai Holiday Centre
BARA HOYO
Serena Beach
Dolphin   Kenya Marinas
SHIMO LATEWA
Coral Beach   Bamburi Chalets
Casuarina   Cowrie Shell
Severin Lodge   Beach Apartments
Intercontinental   Palm Beach
Kenya Beach   Plaza
Bamburi Beach   Neptune Beach
Whitesands   Seawaves Beach
Ocean View Beach   Octopussy Bamburi
Coraldene Beach
Reef Hotel   Nyali Beach
Mombasa Beach
MAZERAS   Bahari Beach   NYALI
Mombasa Beach
Apartments
TUDOR CREEK
MOMBASA

267

Getting there

From Kenyatta Avenue, travelling inland, take the intersection, right, clearly marked **Nyali toll bridge.**

Where to stay

Just a small cross-selection of hotels on the north Mombasa mainland covering Nyali, Bamburi, and Shanzu beaches: Bahari Cottages (self-service), Bamburi Beach Hotel (4-star), Bamburi Chalets (self-service), Casuarina Hotel (4-star), Coral Beach Hotel (4-star), Dolphin Hotel (5-star), Mombasa Inter-Continental (5-star), Kenya Beach Hotel (4-star), Mombasa Beach Apartments (self-service), Mombasa Beach Hotel (5-star), Neptune Beach Hotel (5-star), Nyali beach Hotel (5-star), Reef Hotel (5-star), Seawaves Beach Hotel (not visited), Serena Beach Hotel (5-star), Severin Sea Lodge (4-star), Whitesands (4-star). In Kikambala, Sun and Sand Beach Hotel (4-star), Whispering Palms (4-star), Kanamai Holiday Centre (not visited), Kenya Marinas (not visited). There are others. In Kilifi, Mnarani Club Hotel (5-star), Sea Horse Hotel (Budget).

There are others. See Listings for "Hotels".

Sightseeing

Leaving the bridge, turn right on to the **Kisauni headland** which accommodates more five-star hotels along its Nyali, **Bamburi,** and **Shanzu** strip than any other area of the country.

Almost immediately you'll come to a right turn which takes you through **Freretown,** Kenya's first colony for liberated slaves. It was established in the last century by Sir Bartle Frere, a former governor of Sind in India.

Continue along to **Cement Road** for the **Tamarind,** perhaps Kenya's most upmarket restaurant. With attractive Moorish decor, the Tamarind overlooks Tudor Creek and the jetty below where you board the Tamarind dhow to dine afloat, under the stars and tropical moon, to the music of the resident ensemble.

The road goes on to **English Point** past the **Krapf Memorial** that records the sad fate of the wife and child of the coast's first Christian missionary — and marks their graves. It also records the spot where he made his pledge to attempt the conversion of the African continent (See "The Dust and the Ashes", Part One).

Nearby is the 1910 **Mombasa Swimming Club** and on the left, **Moi Park,** formerly Princes Park, which was presented to the city by the Dukes of Windsor and Gloucester and is the site of the annual **Mombasa Show**.

The park borders the private residential estate of Nyali (Kiswahili for "clearing"). It was cleared in the first decade of the century when it was developed as a sisal estate. Later a group of investors brought the land to turn into a kind of coastal Muthaiga.

Now spacious, gracious houses, an eighteen-hole golf course, and smart hotels, of which the oldest—and arguably most splendid — is Nyali Beach, adorn this stretch of coastline and spin on into the neighbouring beaches.

Just a kilometre (half a mile) inland from Nyali Beach hotel is **Bamburi cement factory,** once the tenth-largest in the world, sprawled over hectares of coral that has been extensively quarried.

It has since been rehabilitated, in one of the most exciting environmental successes ever achieved, by Swiss ecologist Rene Haller. He transformed the gaping sores and scars of the quarries into a forest-clad wonderland of nature trails, fish ponds, and wildlife and birdlife sanctuary that now constitutes a major tourist attraction as well as profit-making farm.

One of Kenya's latest national marine parks lies off the Nyali headland. Ten-square-kilometre (four-square-mile) **Mombasa Marine National Park** is surrounded by a 200-square-kilometre (77-square-mile) marine national reserve and was established in 1986.

At the far end of the Nyali-Bamburi beach strip, on the link road that runs along the back of the hotels, **Mamba Crocodile Village** earns substantial money from the sale of crocodile skins as well as drawing thousands of visitors daily to see the reptiles, and other attractions.

The road runs past **Kipepeo Aquarium,** with its splendid display of tropical marine life, a **German beer garden,** and on through **Kenyatta** and **Shanzu Beaches.** Kenyatta Beach is where the late President Kenyatta had his old coast home and today there are many graceful hotels. There are more hotels along the strip at Shanzu, ending in the African Safari Club's **Palm Beach Hotel,** twelve kilometres (seven miles) off the main road.

Turn left, inland, past the maximum security Shimo la Tewa **gaol** and after three kilometres (two miles) you'll come to another of the club's enterprises, the **Shimo la Tewa Sports Centre.**

After another two kilometres (one and a third miles) or so a signboard reading "Danger" announces your arrival at the south bank of **Mtwapa Creek** where, for many years, a hand-hauled rope ferry was manoeuvred by a crew singing ballads in the style of Paul Robeson. It was the only way north.

Now, however, a Japanese-built **toll suspension bridge** leaps across the mirror surface of the creek. The shores on either side are lined with marinas and water sport centres since the creek's deep waters are ideal for scuba diving and water skiing. Rarely ruffled by a breeze, they are protected on either side by the cliffs topped by elegant bungalows with sweet-scented gardens.

On the far bank, turn right along a sand road for one-and-a-half kilometres (one mile), to **Kenya Marineland and Snake Park.** Here you'll find turtles, sting rays, small but colourful fry, hand-fed sharks — and a writhing mass of deadly mambas and less poisonous species in the serpentarium. In the same grounds a Belgian couple have transformed the old snackbar into **Le Pichet**, a true gourmet experience.

From Mtwapa Creek up to Malindi the scenery is a collage of rolling baobab country, sisal plantations, cashew trees, thick jungle and swamp.

Some sixteen kilometres (10 miles) beyond the bridge is one of Kenya's national monuments, the lost city of **Jumba la Mtwana** (Kiswahili for the "House of Slaves"). To get there turn right again off the main road. Like the better-known lost city of Gede, it was abandoned sometime between the fourteenth and fifteenth centuries and was swiftly shrouded in jungle.

It lay for more than 400 years until it was discovered in the late 1960s and the jungle was hacked away in the early 1970s. The revealed city was smaller than Gede but still fascinating with four **mosques,** a **cemetery,** and **houses**.

Five kilometres (three miles) beyond this turn off, go right again and continue for two kilometres (little more than a mile) to **Kikambala Beach** with the **Whispering Palms** and, further north, the Sun 'n Sand. This was one of Kenya's earliest coast resorts. Apart from the **Sun 'n Sand** the original, airy, high-pitched, *makuti*-thatched hotels favoured for their simplicity and coolness have been replaced with massive blocks of concrete annexes for rooms, service areas, and entertainment — to most people's regret.

From Kikambala, the coast remains commercially unspoilt and undeveloped until Kilifi, the midway point between Mombasa and Malindi. The only exception is the sprawling **Vipingo sisal estate.**

One of the earliest cash crops introduced to Kenya, sisal is now a speculative and often ruinous proposition thanks to the advent of manmade fibres.

Vipingo was established more than half a century ago on 8,100 hectares (20,000 acres). This massive enterprise has its own town, factories, and narrow-gauge railway but today much of the plantation has gone to seed.

Forty-four kilometres (27 miles) from Mombasa, a right turn leads five kilometres (three miles) to **Takaungu**, a charming Arabic village of whitewashed houses. Close by, overlooking a mangrove creek, is the forgotten grave of an Omani sultan, who died here in the nineteenth century. A traditional wood-carving industry thrives here, turning out intricately-carved doors with Arabic inscriptions.

Above: Dugout *ngalwa*, canoe, in coast lagoon.

Kilifi Creek

Ten kilometres (six miles) along the main road from the turnoff the tarmac arrives at **Mnarani,** at the southern headland of **Kilifi Creek**, a kind of tropical Dartmouth that stretches inland some fifteen kilometres (nine miles).

On the brow of the headland to the right, along a snaking trail, stands the former **Mnarani Club,** complete with **airstrip,** swimming pool, and **jetty** for yachts and power boats. Still famous for its big game fishing competitions it has now become a more formal hotel.

To the left of the brow is another **serpentarium** and, close behind, some seventeenth-century **ruins,** including a **mosque,** and several **pillar tombs.** These were despoiled by the savage Galla warriors who came down from the hinterland to raid all along the coast. The ruins were cleared in the early 1970s.

In 1989, crossing Kilifi Creek was a protracted affair — the antiquated **vehicle ferries** often create traffic jams kilometres long. It is nonetheless a beautiful location.

High cliffs line the entrance to this natural deep water harbour and only the entrance through the reef limits the draught of vessels capable of mooring within. Gracious Mediterranean-style houses step down the cliffs overlooking the ocean-going yachts which bob at their moorings below.

In 1989 Japanese bridge builders were well on the way to completing construction of an elegant bridge, a boon to motorists, but a sad defacement of the creek's peaceful and unspoilt tranquillity.

Kilifi serves as a natural water sports arena with windsurfing, water-skiing, powerboat racing, and sailing among its prime attractions. It lures other *aficionados,* too, including bird lovers.

Millions of carmine bee-eaters make their nests in the mangrove swamps at the far end of the creek. With their long beaks, tapering bodies, and elongated tails, they swoop at dusk in great clouds, cutting out the light like a darkening storm.

After capturing the insect, bee-eaters carefully remove its venomous sting before swallowing it. The sound of their wings fills the air with a vibrant humming noise (See "Birdlife: an avian spectacle without equal".

Opposite: 17th-century Mnarani ruins at Kilifi.

Kilifi town spreads along the north side of the creek to the right of the main road. Although the best beaches are found on the open coast to the north-east, most are accessible only through private property.

Kilifi also boasts a **cashew-nut processing factory** where over 1,500 workers process sixty tonnes of nuts a day — kernels for eating, and juice for brake linings.

Nature reserve

Just out of the town, to the left, lies **Arabuko-Sokoke Forest** an ornithological treasure house and an area rich in rare fauna. It is the last of the great indigenous coastal forests and although under threat, offers protection to some rare trees. It was established as a forest nature reserve in 1943 and with the addition of sixteen square kilometres (six square miles) in 1977 now covers 417 square kilometres (161 square miles).

One of the most important nature conservation sites in East Africa, the forest is the only surviving lowland coastal forest of any size with many important and threatened plant species.

Mammals include Ader's duiker, blue duiker, golden-rumped elephant shrew, bristle-tailed elephant shrew, and coastal races of the bushbaby.

Threatened birds include the Sokoke Scops owl and Clarke's weaver, both endemic to this forest, east coast akalat, Amani sunbird, and Sokoke pipit. Migratory visitors include pitta, and spotted ground thrush.

Sokoke Scops owl is grey-white in colour with a tonal "tonk, tonk" call that one forester imitates so well he can usually lure an owl close enough for nocturnal visitors to see.

Aders', or Zanzibar duiker, all of thirty-five centimetres (14 inches) high, now feared extinct on that island, is found only here, around the Gede ruins, and in the Boni National Reserve.

Another rare creature is the astonishing golden-rumped elephant shrew. Bushbabies are endemic. The forest also has a prolific variety of rare, brilliantly-coloured butterflies, and the *Leptopelis flavomaculatus* frog is only known from this forest and the Shimba Hills.

Forest clearance outside the boundary is a threat as the Forest Reserve is basically too small to support viable breeding populations

of many threatened birds.

Sadly some trees have been cut down by sawmillers, but most hardwood forest and many rubber trees remain untouched. These have been fenced off and the gates kept firmly locked.

If you inquire at the **Forestry office** you may be allowed to wander in the nature sanctuary. In the thick tangle of undergrowth and gloom of the forest floor you'll find a compass useful if not essential.

Back on the main road northwards to the lost city of Gede, the next forty kilometres (25 miles), is through thatched villages that slumber drowsily, offering glimpses of life styles that have changed little over the years. Unaffected by increasing numbers of tourists, and birthplace of Kiswahili, the *lingua-franca* of eastern Africa, some of these villages have been here 1,000 years or more (See "The Dust and the Ashes", Part One).

One of the world's great living languages, initially Kiswahili was a fusion of Arabic and indigenous vernaculars. Like all great languages it continues to borrow freely from others. Urdu words, like *gari* for "vehicle", have an intrinsic place in this fusion — as do English words. When the British arrived there was no word for Commissioner so it was adapted phonetically as *Komishona.*

The language grew and developed in cities like **Gede** — turn right at the **signpost** marked Watamu — whose mystery has never been solved. Gede vanished inexplicably in the sixteenth century, swallowed by voracious trees and lianas, to lie undiscovered until late this century.

The eighteen hectares (45 acres) of ruins show that it was inhabited by a cultured and gracious community, but no records survive to reveal its history or why it was abandoned, virtually overnight.

Walking through the relics of these old buildings, including the **Dated Tomb,** *circa* 1399, it's not difficult to sense the brooding spirits that remain. In the old mosques and houses, bats swoop through the dank air and snakes slither silently out of sight under the crumbling walls.

In the ruins and the adjacent jungle, the Sokoke's golden-rumped elephant shrew has found a second home. You'll see it nowhere else but in these two places.

Gede was gazetted as a **national monument** in the 1920s. The National Museum runs a small on-site **museum** with evidence showing that Gede once traded actively with Arabia and Asia although it is now five kilometres (three miles) from the sea and two kilometres (one and a third miles) from **Mida creek.**

In contrast to the ruins, Gede's Giriama **folk village**, by the main entrance and car park, pulsates with life and the exotic rhythms of traditional Giriama music.

Watamu

From modern Gede village the road runs another six kilometres (four miles) to a fork left for one and a half kilometres (one mile) to **Watamu**. Set around **Turtle Bay,** a curve of aquamarine water, Watamu's coral gardens and atolls sweep inland into the recesses of **Mida Creek.**

Watamu's somnolent days have long since gone. Upcountry Europeans, package tourists from Germany and Italy, Samburu and Maasai *morani* dominate the waterfront.

The village has a **post office, mosque,** *dukas*, and **serpentarium**, all overhung with coconut palms and proliferating tropical creepers, succulents, and plants.

Covering ten square kilometres (four square miles), **Watamu National Park** is surrounded by a thirty-two-square-kilometre (12-square-mile) national marine reserve — embracing a thirty-kilometre-long (19-mile), five-kilometre-wide (three-mile) strip of coast and sea, including Mida Creek.

At the northern end of the marine reserve is the six-square-kilometre (two-square-mile) **Malindi Marine National Park,** surrounded by another 213-square-kilometre (82-square-mile) national marine reserve some twenty kilometres (12 miles) further north. Together these ocean sanctuaries became one of Kenya's four Biosphere Reserves in May 1979.

The park and reserve contain a remarkable marine ecosystem of rock platforms, cliffs, coral reefs, lagoons, and sandy beaches which offer three major habitats: intertidal rock, intertidal sand and mud, and the sublittoral area.

There is no continental shelf and the coastline is bordered by fringing reefs on the seaward side plunging down vertically many hundreds of metres within a short distance of the reef.

Between the limestone cliffs are stretches of

Above: Catamaran racing off the Kenya coast.

beautiful sandy beach. **Mida Creek** contains tidal mudflats with fringing mangrove swamp. Between March and May, waders particularly are thick on the mudflats as they halt to rest and hunt food on their long migratory journey (See "Birdlife: an avian spectacle without equal").

Watamu's central motif, **Whale Island**, a humpbacked piece of coral opposite the entrance to the creek, is also something of a bird sanctuary. Between June and September it is an important nesting ground for roseate and bridled tern and many shore birds, including sanderling, curlew sandpiper, whimbrel, grey plover, greater sand plover, and Mongolian plover. Non-breeding visitors include lesser crested tern, Saunder's little tern, and sooty gull.

Both national parks and reserves initially were established in 1968 to stop the depradation of coral and cowrie by tourists and locals, although some poaching still persists. The most significant effect on the area is the silt from the Sabaki River which carries a heavy load during the rainy seasons as a result of uncontrolled cultivation in the Ukambani hills.

The effects of tourism on this sensitive ecosystem have yet to be investigated. However, only traditional fishing is now permitted. But watersports are allowed throughout the year.

The **coral gardens** are breathtaking, and scuba divers, for their part, delight in the discoveries deep below where brilliantly-coloured fish swarm to eat out of their hands. For non-divers, glass-bottomed boats give a splendid view.

At high water divers can visit an underwater cave where tewa (giant rock cod), weighing up to 400 kilos (880 lbs), hang suspended upside down, disorientated by the glimmering ceiling. But the swift undercurrents are unpredictable so it's not a trip for the novice.

Malindi: Swell for Surfers

Malindi was where Vasco da Gama first set foot in East Africa in 1498, having veered away from Mombasa when his anchor ropes were cut (See "The Dust and the Ashes", Part One).

His monument now stands on the headland

where he stepped ashore. Immediately he arrived, da Gama made friends with the Sultan, who by all accounts, was sociable and cultured. His welcome was memorable. "For nine days we had fêtes, sham fights and musical performances."

Finally, loaded with fruit and provisions, the Sultan saw the Portuguese mariners off, sending along with them his own pilot who knew the sea route to Calcutta. Thus was the sea passage from Portugal to India pioneered.

In the middle of the last century the missionary Krapf found Malindi derelict but when the Sultan of Zanzibar reinvigorated trade in 1860 he resettled the town with slaves and traders.

After that, apart from a few settler retirement homes and its **golf club,** Malindi remained virtually unchanged from the limbo it was thrown into in the sixteenth century when the Portuguese moved their "colonial" headquarters to Mombasa.

But from the 1930s, ever since author Ernest Hemingway arrived to game-fish, only to spend more time tippling gin in the bar of the Blue Marlin than out on the water, Malindi has been the locale for most of Kenya's big game fishing tournaments.

And in the 1960s and 1970s it became the spearhead of the package tour set and beach hotels sprang up almost overnight.

From all over the world deep sea sports anglers fly in to joust with the giants for which the Kenya coast is renowned. Now, along with Kiswahili and English, German and Italian dialects echo in the colourful markets.

Established in the thirteenth century, Malindi stands around the panoramic sweep of a wide bay — one of the few places along the coast where the Indian Ocean swell over the broken reef makes surfing possible the year round.

However, the best months are between late June and early September when the seasonal monsoon sweeps in truly magnificent rollers. Most hotels rent out surfboards.

Watersports are undoubtedly Malindi's prime tourist attraction with sailboarding, water-skiing, and diving also available.

Where to stay

Blue Marlin (4-star), Club Che Shale (4-star), Coconut Village (not visited), Driftwood Beach Club (Upmarket beachcombing), Eden Roc (3-star), Lawford (3-star), Silversands Beach Cottage (self-service), Sindbad (3-star), White Elephant Sea Lodge (not visited). There are others. See Listings for "Hotels".

Sightseeing

Malindi Airport on the main Mombasa-Malindi road, thirteen kilometres (eight miles) from the Gede turnoff, is marked by a curious injunction to drivers to dim their lights to avoid dazzling oncoming aircraft. The town itself lies two kilometres (little more than a mile) beyond.

Its entrance is marked by churches on the left and a flower-strewn **roundabout** with bypass, right, leading to the national park and the beach strip of **Silversands**.

Further on, on a headland overlooking the marine park, stands the **Vasco da Gama Pillar,** a cross fashioned from Lisbon stone, which the navigator raised next to what was the Sultan of Malindi's palace, in January 1499.

Subsequently, it was torn down but restored by the Portuguese in the sixteenth century, and saved from collapse in 1873 by the crew of a British naval ship who protected it with a cone of concrete. More rescue work had to be undertaken in the 1930s and 1940s — not to save the monument but to shore up the cliffs on which it stands.

South of this, the road leads to **Silversands,** shaded by a swaying backdrop of casuarina, tamarisk, and whispering palms with many campsites, ending at the **Driftwood Club.**

Nearby is the **Birdland aviary** which contains about 1,000 birds covering some 230 species including carmine bee-eaters, hornbills, and a tame ostrich, and other wildlife such as baboons, monkeys, and mongoose.

Closer to the **marine park headquarters** the **serpentarium** contains only species endemic to the Malindi area — including deadly black and green mamba — in coral snake pits where they live an almost wild existence.

The headquarters of Malindi Marine National Park is at **Casuarina Point.** In the coral heads and grass-shrouded hollows of these underwater gardens, snorkelers and scuba divers swim alongside rainbow coloured fish, over potato, staghorn, and mushroom coral. Off **Barracuda Reef,** the deeps of **Stork Passage** teem with big game fish. **Tewa Reef** and the caves by **Sail Rock** are other attractions.

In Malindi itself there is the "**old town**" of the 1930s to 1950s. It is an interesting Swahili quarter, with a large and busy market (where buses and *matatus* arrive), shops, and hotels, stretching down to what the pre-war European retirees thought of as the village green, now the town's **Uhuru Gardens,** with its Second World War **memorial.**

To the right is the **Bohra Mosque** built in 1928, close to the monument to Vasco da Gama — single cross, stone sail, and image of the navigator — unveiled by a Portuguese envoy in 1960. The **brass plaque** was subsequently removed by thieves.

Beyond this, the **offices** of the Malindi local authority, marked by four ancient **cannons** and a **bell,** were originally built by the IBEA in 1890 (See "The Dust and the Ashes", Part One).

On the main road is **Lawford's Hotel,** established in 1934 by Leo Lawford, a retired upcountry colonial district officer.

In the genuinely old town, there are close to a dozen mosques including the elegant **Juma'a Mosque** on the spot where slaves were auctioned off once a week until the trade was banned in 1873. After this, only Giriama people could be sold as slaves.

Alongside is the fifteenth century, phallic **Pillar Tomb** containing the mortal remains of Sheikh Abdul Hassan. Next to it stands a much-abbreviated nineteenth-century **tomb.**

Offshore, out in the Indian Ocean, are found some of the finest and largest fighting fish in the world — barracuda, wahoo, tunny (longtail, yellowfin, and skipjack), bonito, kingfish, sailfish, dorado, and marlin (Pacific blue, black and striped). There are also shark (tiger, mako and hammerhead), and rainbow runner.

Kenya has claimed six world records and thirty-six of seventy-nine all-Africa records. In the peak season, between October and February, many classic international fishing contests are held. These are usually run from the Malindi **Sea Fishing Club,** along the seafront, to the right, close to the **fish market.**

Some distance beyond these, right, is what might well have been the first **church** in East Africa. Dedicated to Vasco da Gama, it forms part of a sixteenth-century chapel near the spot where St Francis Xavier paused to bury two soldiers on his 1542 journey to Goa.

When the church was refurbished in 1933, decorators stripping off the ancient plaster discovered a painting of the crucifixion underneath.

In the north of the town there is the **Malindi Snake Park** which also has cages of monkeys and tortoises including a large and venerable specimen from the Seychelles that is at least 200 years old.

The nearby **Blue Marlin** — built in 1931 as the Palm Beach Hotel — is where Hemingway once stayed and caroused over split gins instead of deep sea fishing.

Habari Night Club and **St Anthony's Catholic Church** stand cheek-by-jowl along this strip of beach where Karen Blixen once picnicked with Denys Finch Hatton. Italian, Swahili, and German restaurants are interspersed with **Lutheran** and **St Andrew's Churches** and a number of hotels including the **Sindbad, Eden Roc, Malindi Safari Club,** and **Malindi Chalets.**

At the north end of the strip there's a left fork to the **Suli Suli Sporting Club,** and a sand track straight on to **Malindi Golf Club,** where visitors can either play tennis or nine holes of golf on payment of a green fee.

At the left fork, where the tarmac ends between the Suli Suli and the Palm Tree Club, **Kiswani Dairy Farm,** left again, was founded in the 1930s by Commander Lawford with a herd of Jersey and Guernsey cattle which thrived.

Speed bumps on the approach to the bridge across the **Sabaki River** herald the scenic, if bruising, road to Lamu and Kenya's remote north — a journey through still unspoilt forests and sleepy coastal villages.

The river was the northern border of Zanzibar's sixteen-kilometre-wide (10-mile) coastal strip. Runaway slaves used to settle in safety on the far bank — only to discover the only market for their crops was in Malindi.

The Road to Lamu: Mad Dogs, Eccentric English

For many people the essence of Kenya's coast is best savoured in the 222 kilometre (138 miles) stretch north of Malindi.

From Malindi, the Tana River, Tawaka, and Malindi Taxi services send their buses rumbling north on a journey which takes anything from half a day to possibly two days, depending on whether the **Tana** is in flood and the state of the track.

You can also sail by dhow from Mombasa's

Old Port, which means at least one full day spent wallowing in the Indian Ocean swell. Or you can drive from the other side of the **Sabaki** suspension **bridge** through a succession of sunny Giriama villages set in baobab and fruit groves where the traditional dress of the coast still prevails (See "The People", Part One).

Sightseeing

Some little distance from Malindi there's a right fork to **Marafa village,** then a right turn again for half-a-kilometre (a third of a mile) to a strikingly-coloured lunar landscape of eroded pinnacles and cliffs, dubbed by locals **Hell's Kitchen.** Dating geologically from the Pliocene era these thirty-metre-high (100-feet) pillars of buff, russet, pink, and maroon sandstone are known as "demoiselles".

Steep paths take you through this odd and tortured landscape where different layers of rock have been exposed by wind and rain.

Returning to the Lamu road, you travel on another thirteen kilometres (eight miles) to **Mambrui,** thought to have been surveyed in the fifteenth century by the Portuguese. The old cotton plantations worked by slaves still flourished in the 1930s.

Near the decaying **cemetery** is a **pillar tomb** inset with Ming dynasty porcelain bowls. The 1962 **Riadha Mosque,** which overlooks the village from the only high point, has a lime-green dome inscribed with quotations from the Qur'an. Similar inscriptions have been carved on the **school** next to it.

After Mambrui the road reaches **Gongoni,** with a **signpost** marking a track on the right to the Italian **space research centre.** The ancient Bajun settlement is indicated by an interesting ruin that marks the harbour. This was an anchorage superior even to those at Mombasa and Malindi. Folklore suggests that Gongoni was destroyed by a thirteenth-century flood — a divine act of retribution against the womenfolk of that time who persisted in bathing in milk.

Some distance from the village at the end of the peninsula is **Ngomeni** where the Arabian Nights ambience of the village — minarets, castellated mosques and discreet maidens dressed in veils — are juxtaposed with twentieth-century technology.

Out at sea, in the wide sweep of **Formosa Bay,** stands the **San Marco satellite launching pad,** and its sister platform, built by the Italians in the late 1960s. To get there, follow a track through the marshy estuary, past some manmade lagoons built to trap the incoming tide to recover salt by evaporation.

Further north along the Lamu Road is **Fundi Issa,** some thirty-three kilometres (21 miles) from Malindi where a right turn leads along four kilometres (two and a half miles) of sand trail to **Robinson Island.** Waist-deep, local Giriama women make the crossing balancing gourds and calabashes of water on their head.

Both Fundi Issa village and the island take their name from a local shipbuilder who is said to have gone into seclusion there in the 1920s. His were the only water wells in the area but the womenfolk could only draw water after they shaved their heads — which led them to name the place *Kinya'ole,* (Barber's Island).

A descendant of one of Kenya's old European settler families, David Hurd, has turned the sandbank into an idyllic, castaway island, complete with *cordon-bleu* seafood and watersports. At low tide you can walk across from the mainland to this desert *pied-a-terre* in ankle-deep water.

Hurd's success inspired another desert-island resort, only five (three miles) kilometres further on along the Lamu road. Known to the locals as the *Mto wa Mawe,* (River of Rocks), **Giriama Village Island** has a restaurant and bar, four *makuti*-thatched huts and serves seafood lunches and dinners of crab and other crustacea.

Another thirteen kilometres (eight miles) beyond Fundi Issa there's a right turn to **Karawa** on the magnificent sweep of **Formosa Bay** which is unprotected by a reef and pounded by breakers that make for enthralling surfing.

From the turn off, the Lamu road cuts through the delta of the Tana river where its many fingers treble and quadruple back on themselves. Then from a final ridge with, the broad green delta spread out below, the track drops gently down past the left turn to **Hola** and **Baomo Lodge** and on to **Garsen,** some thirty kilometres (19 miles) inland from the sea, and exactly 111 kilometres (69 miles) between Malindi and Lamu. The narrow **causeway** ends on the south bank of the Tana.

Garsen is the capital of the heartland of the Orma and Pokomo people. No tourist resort, it has only one-street of desultory *dukas,* often dry petrol pumps, and not a single hotel.

The **ferry** tends to be unpredictable and travellers have been stranded there for days. In the dry season, it is easy enough to cross, but during exceptional rains when the Tana is in spate, often spilling out on either side of its banks for ten kilometres (six miles) or more, the "main" road to Lamu vanishes under water or becomes a sea of glutinous mud.

With the current too swift to risk the perilous passage, the antiquated ferry comes to a standstill on one bank or the other. At such times, Pokomo boatman use their *ngwalas* (dugout canoes), to ferry waiting tourists, backpackers and local itinerants across to the other side (See "The People", Part One). There, if you're lucky, you may find a bus waiting to take you on to **Mokowe** and the ferry to **Lamu Island.**

The forty-eight kilometres (30 miles) along the dyke track to the next major village, **Witu,** is notable only for the green thread of the jungle, flooded plantations and smallholdings, borassus palms, ibis, and egret.

But hidden in the delta's tangle of mangrove swamps are the remnants of the rubber plantations and other ventures initiated by the Europeans and locals who settled here around the turn of the century.

In the 1860s the Sultan of Witu cut a canal across the swamps between the Tana and the small stream **Ozi** to exploit the Tana waters. Two decades later, in 1892, it engulfed his plantations and the flooded Tana adopted the canal as its avenue and changed course permanently.

The main channel still pours into the Indian Ocean at **Kipini**, twenty-one kilometres (13 miles) east of Witu along a jungle-lined track.

Now somewhat subdued, Witu, with its abundant mango plantations, once prospered. It was once proclaimed the state of Swahililand by the former Sultan of Pate who fled the northern island in 1862 after offending the much more powerful Sultan of Zanzibar.

Calling himself Simba — "the Lion" — he even produced his own currency and issued his own Swahililand stamps. The end came after the "Sultan" signed an 1888 alliance with the Dendhart brothers from Germany.

The Berlin treaty of 1890 swept aside this puny alliance, and when nine Germans stayed on to establish a sawmill in the princedom it angered his successor, his son, who saw them as a threat. During an argument, one of the Germans shot the "Sultan's" guard and was killed in return, along with the others.

The "Sultan" refused to discuss this matter with the new administration, so a British expeditionary force of almost 1,000 razed the town and surrounding plantations.

There must be something that induces madness in the air of this region. At least three early colonial officers are reputed to have committed suicide while based at Kipini, where the wreck of the launch *Pelican* — in which one District Commissioner flew the British flag as far upstream as Garissa — lay rusting on a mudbank for years.

Before World War I another European settler, Charlie "Coconut" Winton, decided to set up a new plantation. When it failed he retired to his house in Lamu, closed its doors and never set foot outside them for forty years.

His contemporary, Percy Petley, also experimented disastrously with Witu agriculture. He went bankrupt before setting up **Petley's Inn** in Lamu. It acquired a reputation as a most eccentric hostelry. Surprised guests were often told to cook their own food and, if they objected, were ordered to leave the premises.

Today, all that remains in Witu of this and subsequent history is a **plinth** and **flagstaff** (*circa* 1949) guarded by two **cannon** brought from Lamu by the British. One is dedicated to Khalifa, the "Sultan's" son, and other displays a **plaque** recording its manufacture in Cossipore, India, in 1852. The town mosque, **Masjid al-Nur** (the House of Light) built in the 1900s, was refurbished in 1968. Another mosque is the **Jami Witu Mosque.**

Near Witu, around one of the largest of the delta's lakes, **Kenyatta,** a settlement scheme for Kenyans expelled from Tanzania after the breakup of the East African Community in the 1970s, has become a self-sufficient township of some 20,000 people.

From Witu it's another thirty-two kilometres (20 miles) to **Mkununumbi** where you turn right for **Kiongwe** on the **Ras Tenewe** headland that protects the Lamu archipelago.

A large area of the headland between Kipini in the south and Kiongwe, facing Lamu, is scheduled to become Kenya's latest wildlife sanctuary, the **Ras Tenewe Coastal Zone National Park.**

Back on the main road it's another twenty-five kilometres (16 miles) from Mkununumbi to **Hindi** and then right for eleven kilometres (seven miles) to **Mokowe** where a motor boat takes you out around the creek for the thirty-minute voyage to **Lamu Island**.

If you're driving yourself, you have to leave your vehicle in the car park where you pay the *askari* (watchmen) to guard it.

From Mokowe

From Hindi it's forty kilometres (25 miles) through **Bargoni** and **Majengo** to the hamlet of **Bodhei** where a barely discernible trail, right, leads to Kenya's three most remote reserves — **Dodori, Boni**, and **Kiunga National Marine Reserves.**

Alternatively, you can drive on east another forty kilometres (25 miles) to **Ijara** beyond which there's a left turn on to the **Bura** road, past the **Tana River Primate Reserve.** The road to Bura continues along another forty-four kilometres (27 miles) skirting the **Arawale National Reserve**, sanctuary for Kenya's only herd of Hunter's hartebeest with their lyre-shaped horns. For both reserves there is an entrance charge but for Arawale it is only a token gesture. There is no entrance into the park.

Dodori National Reserve ranges from sea level to 100 metres (300 feet) high and covers 877 square kilometres (339 square miles) in the coastal zone of north-eastern Lamu District, extending north towards the Somalia border.

It's bisected by the **Dodori River** which flows along an alluvial valley of short-grass flood plains where Pleistocene sand dunes run parallel to the coast (See "National Parks", In Brief, for wildlife and vegetation).

The reserve's creeks and inlets also serve as a substantial breeding ground for the rare mermaid-like dugong and green turtle.

It is a buffer zone between Kiunga Marine National Reserve and the increasing human activities on the mainland.

There is one **campsite** but with the incursion of ruthless, armed Somali poachers throughout this territory in the late 1980s it would be advisable to check with police and park authorities on the potential dangers.

The nearby Boni National Reserve, covering some 1,339 square kilometres (517 square miles) of Garissa District flush alongside the Somalia border, separated from the sea by a narrow coastal strip, is the only coastal, lowland, groundwater forest in Kenya with dry lowland bush and grassland in the drier areas (See "National Parks", In Brief, for wildlife and vegetation).

And the whole of the neighbouring sixty-kilometre-long (37-mile) coastal reef and lagoon, from the Somalia **border** in the north to **Oseni** in the south forms the 250-square-kilometre (37-square-mile) Kiunga Marine National Reserve, rising from sea level to thirty metres (100 feet) high.

It contains more than fifty offshore islands, sandy beaches, mangrove swamps, coral reefs, mainland sand dunes, and forest and became one of Kenya's four Biosphere Reserves in 1980 — an important breeding ground for the dugong, a strange aquatic mammal that gave rise to the legends of the mermaid.

Poaching of green turtle and its eggs has been reduced by the efforts of the Game Warden, Lamu, but there is still some poaching of dugong.

Pounding surf undercuts the seaward side of the uninhabited offshore islands where, astonishingly, lesser kudu, bushbuck, monkeys, porcupines, and wild pig roam; and wild birds nest in the cliffs — particularly in the breeding season between June and August. These include sooty gulls, roseate terns, and white-cheeked and bridled terns.

The extensive **coral gardens** offer sanctuary to an abundant population of reef fish.

Kiunga is the least developed of the marine reserves. The Government built a fully-equipped **marine research station** but there are no scientists locally available. Basic research and scientific training, in the initial phases, will require international support and co-operation.

Swimming, sailing, water-skiing, and diving are all allowed. And on **Kiwaiyu Island,** a thatched **tourist village** is truly the most "away-from-it-all" retreat of any in Kenya.

The camp, developed in 1979 out of the ten beach-tents of the older Kiwaiyu Safari Village, sleeps no more than twelve at a time in chalets and six-berth cruisers.

The administrative centre for this area is **Kiunga,** a remote and idyllic unspoilt village about 150 kilometres (95 miles) by road from Lamu, and about 100 kilometres (60 miles) by air. An old colonial officer's **house** is sole evidence of Britain's far-reaching imperial ambitions.

Lamu: Enchanted Islands

The islands of the **Lamu Archipelago** are the last survivors of a 1,000-year-old civilization that developed between the ninth and nineteenth centuries (See "The Dust and the Ashes", Part One).

Lamu, some 100 kilometres (60 miles) south of the Somali border, was one of the trading ports from which ivory, rhino horn, and slaves were exported for centuries.

The Swahili *Lamu Chronicle* claimed that the town was founded by Arabs in the seventh century but the **Pumwani Mosque** dates from 1370 and there is no mention of Lamu itself until 1402.

Like Mombasa and Malindi, Lamu was a thriving port and sultanate during the eighteenth and nineteenth centuries when it was frequently at ritualized war with its neighbours — **Pate, Siyu** and **Faza** — all island kingdoms of this northern archipelago.

Every so often boats would sail across, pennants flying, richly-uniformed soldiers orchestrating their battle cries with style and dignity, to taunt their rivals. Actual conflict was rare but when the armies did meet the end was often bloody.

In 1813, the Nabhani of Pate fatally miscalculated the ebb of the tide when his fleet sailed into Shela, a Lamu beach, to fling down what was probably meant to be a metaphoric gauntlet at the Sultan's feet.

Enraged, the Sultan ordered an advance and the Pate battalions retreated swiftly to their boats — now left high and dry by the retreating tide. The result was a grisly massacre from which Lamu emerged the golden winner.

For sixty years Lamu controlled all trade until the British forced Zanzibar to sign an anti-slaving pact. British naval patrols along the coast blockaded slave ships and brought missionaries and crusaders, such as Stanley, who asserted authority over this island kingdom.

The first resident agent, a Frenchman, arrived in the nineteenth century followed later by Americans coming to trade, and Germans to colonize.

Since then Britons have contributed much to Lamu's idiosyncratic traditions. The Freelanders, a group who intended to reach Mount Kenya and set up a "socialist Utopia" never went any further — and appalled the islanders by their drinking and immorality.

Although rapidly-decaying, the town today is a living monument to its past. The old houses, built with walls of coral two-thirds of a metre (two feet) thick, have a series of alcoves, about three metres (ten feet) wide, rather than rooms.

Their width is decided by the length of the mangrove poles used for for floorings and ceilings. Many are three stories high, with precipitous staircases that end on a flat roof where much of the life of the community goes on.

Lamu town turns its back to the open sea and looks across at **Manda Island.**

With its seaboard obscured in mangrove swamps, Lamu is still a busy port, mangrove poles being the major export. The creeks around the island and on the mainland constitute 450 square kilometres (174 square miles) of gazetted forest reserve with strict controls on felling and exporting.

Lamu's appeal derives from the unique character of the people who live there. Their culture is very old, and of mixed origin.

Although based on the Islamic religion, most customs derive solely from the Swahili culture, a people of mixed Bantu and Arab blood who many centuries ago were prosperous and politically powerful (See "The Dust and the Ashes", Part One).

Outwardly, little has changed in this strictly Islamic enclave, where the only motor car belongs to the District Officer who can travel little more than two kilometres — none of it in the built-up area.

Lamu retains its air of slumbering mystery. The elegant centuries-old houses with their fountains in flower-filled *cortiles* (courtyards) reflect a heritage that had running water, plumbing, and simple air-conditioning while Europe was still in bondage to the dark ages.

In the alleyways walk women, clad in the *bui-bui* (the all-embracing black robe that denotes the modesty of their faith), with only their eyes revealed to public gaze.

By turning its back on the modern Western world, Lamu perversely attracted its attention. Kenya's tourist authorities advertise Lamu widely. **Jetties** and **airstrip** have been improved, the Lamu Society formed, and *pro rata* the ratio of guide books is Kenya's highest.

Getting there

The **Makowe Jetty** serves not only Lamu but Manda, and Pate. The airstrip on Manda, however, serves air passengers, who are taken by a motorised dhow to Lamu.

When to go

Lamu is pleasant at any time of the year but the tourist class hotels are closed between May and June for renovation and staff holidays.

Where to stay

Mahrus Hotel (Budget), Peponi Hotel (one of the world's 200 great *little* hotels), Petley's Inn (4-star), Ras Kitau Club, Manda Island (4-star).

Above: Dhow drifts gracefully on the mirror surface of a Lamu backwater.

Opposite: Launching hand-crafted dhow at Lamu.

Sightseeing

There's no shortage of things to see and do in Lamu. Wherever you decide to go, your main form of transport, apart from walking, will be donkey — or dhow.

Only nineteen kilometres (12 miles) long, by eight kilometres (five miles) wide, Lamu island consists mainly of high sand dunes and waving palm trees. At the northern end the two towns, **Lamu** and **Shela**, are separated by more than two kilometres (one and a half miles) of beach.

On the **quayside** where you land there's a **notice** ordering visitors to report to the police, also **Petley's Inn** (founded by Percy Petley who hunted, it is said, with a fist that felled leopards, and acquired in 1957 by a former British consular officer in Ethiopia and Djibouti), and Lamu **National Museum**.

Much of the museum, which opened in 1971, was established by James de Vere Allen who collected many outstanding examples of local arts and crafts, including carved doors that rival those of Zanzibar, made of wood from the mahogany bean tree; ebony thrones inlaid with bone and ivory; "Arab" chests made from Tanzanian teak; scale-model dhows, and jewellery fashioned by Lamu's few surviving silversmiths.

You'll also find a reconstruction of an *mtepe* (large canoe) which Lamu invented with the British Navy's help. The last genuine *mtepe* vanished in the 1930s.

These twelve-metre-long (40-feet) canoes had planks sewn with coir because the Sultan mistrusted metal. The museum also houses siwas (great horns of ivory or brass) jealously-guarded symbols of kingship which were usually blown only on State occasions.

All these and much more you can see in the exemplary museum, opened in 1971. However, the museum does not have Charles — "Coconut Charlie" — Witton's art collection which he bequeathed to Fort Jesus Museum, Mombasa.

The Museum was once the British DC's house and its architecture is redolent of those imperial days. The first British proconsul in Lamu was Rider Haggard's brother, Captain Jack Haggard, whose letters inspired the author (See North-west Kenya: "Enchanted mountains, unspoilt vistas"). He caught two legendary three-metre-long (ten-feet), 230-kilo (500-lb) dugong, "mermaids", now displayed in London's Natural History Museum.

Above: Ritual sword fight marks Lamu's yearly Maulidi festival.

The **brass cannon** which the British used to subdue Witu's Swahililand stand in front of the museum. To the right is the **Riyadha Mosque** and to the left the **Catholic church** of Mary the Mother of Jesus. Before it was built Catholics, mostly visitors, used the **Presbyterian kirk.**

The church is set discreetly back from the street. All this land about the Museum was reclaimed from the sea by dumping garbage. Before that, according to one of East Africa's first British administrators, Sir Frederick Jackson, the shore was a "public, very public latrine".

To the left of the church is Petley's Inn which was bought by two Americans in the 1970s. Expensively restored, it is now managed by a Kenyan hotel company.

Beyond this, the waterfront — **Kenyatta Road** — is dominated by administrative offices and the **Customs** compound. In the town itself a colourful **market** is held each morning in front of the old **Sultan's Fort** which was begun by the Omanis in 1808. Completed some twelve years later it was restored in 1857 and again in 1987. It's now the island **prison** (photography forbidden).

Lamu's main street — formerly *Usita wa Mui,* now **Harambee Road** — used to be the waterfront before last century's reclamation. Alleys run off it in an uphill east-west direction which ensure that the yearly monsoons sweep away the weeks of dust and odiferous droppings cleanly.

These alleys are extremely labyrinthine so make sure you have a map (the Museum sells a very good one) to guide you through them.

The other national monument in Lamu is the fluted fourteenth-century **pillar tomb** behind the **Riyadha Mosque** on the town's upper slopes. It was built in 1900-1901 and is perhaps the most senior of the town's forty-two mosques, all of which are involved in the Island's famous **Maulidi celebrations,** a major festival in the international Muslim calendar.

This was established by Sheikh Habib Salih, who settled in Lamu after leaving the Hadhramaut in the 1880s and became Lamu's patron. He made Lamu famous for its Qur'anic college and for Maulidi, the Prophet's birthday celebration.

For a week, religious festivities, feasting, and dancing draw Muslim pilgrims from all over East Africa and the Indian Ocean. It's the best time to be in Lamu; but you'll need to arrive at least a week in advance to secure a room.

Next to the Riyadha is the Sheikh's **Muslim Academy** which, like much of Lamu today, is heavily under Saudi patronage.

There's another interesting fifteenth-century **tomb** in Lamu, which contains the remains of Mwana Haddie Famau, a local woman. Located near to a betel plantation, the tomb is now walled up and the porcelain-embedded pillars which stood at each corner have long since vanished.

For those still keen on reliving Lamu's past, eight eighteenth-century town-houses have been restored by the Lamu Society which uses the rents for further restoration.

History and Lamu's Arabian Nights ambience are the main reasons for visiting the island. As you might expect, the town's night-life wouldn't exactly shatter the coterie that inhabit the Champs Elysées.

Most restaurants and hotels are Muslim so if you like your evening tot or beer and the flesh of the swine you may be disappointed.

But, that apart, Lamu cuisine is a subtle blend of Arabian, Asian, European, and Swahili menus, and eating out can be extremely esoteric.

The walk from Lamu to Shela Beach takes between forty and sixty minutes. Once thriving, **Shela's** most notable landmark is the 1829 **Friday Mosque** with its rocket-shaped minaret — the first of six built during Shela's heyday. Fifty-eight steps, each one of a different height, take you to the top where there is a marvellous panorama of the Shela sand dunes, which are said to cover **Hadibu**, the island's first seventh-century Arab settlement, and the scene of the eighteenth-century massacre.

In the scrub above the beach lie the neglected **graves** of a former IBEA officer, Mr. Sandys, and Lt. Col. Pink who took over Petley's Hotel.

The beach beyond Shela, unprotected by a reef, is one of the few places on the coast where you can surfboard. And the beaches on **Manda**, opposite Shela, are equally idyllic, enhanced by the mysterious weather-scarred cannon that lie scattered around.

Manda's **Ras Kitau Club** stands on a promontory near the ruins of **Takwa**, an ancient city razed between the sixteenth and seven-teenth centuries. The five hectares (twelve and a half acres) of ruins cleared by Kirkman in 1951 were documented between 1977 and 1979 by Thomas Wilson.

You can only reach Manda by dhow — either from Lamu or Shela. On the journey through the mangrove swamps you can re-live the days of Humphrey Bogart in the *African Queen* but spared the leeches. You wade the last few metres and then walk through the baobab groves to the **Takwa National Monument**.

Takwa's doors all face north to Mecca as does the main street with the **mosque** at the end of it. Overall, the town has extremely ancient significance and still attracts an occasional pilgrim from Shela, some of whom claim descent from Takwa, come to pray for rain.

On the left there's a seventeenth-century seven-metre-high (22-feet) **tomb** with corner pinnacles and, in the centre of the north wall, a ruined **mosque** with a lofty column and a restored *mihrab* (pulpit).

For guide books on these subjects Esmond and Chryssee Bradley Martins' *Quest for the Past* is well-illustrated and James Allen's more costly *Lamu Town* contains the essence of most contemporary research — including town wards, mosques, carved doors, and an account of local handicrafts.

Apart from this, Manda and its somewhat distant neighbour, **Pate Island**, can boast at least twelve major and fourteen minor historical sites including Pate's fascinating **Siyu fort**. Access is by sea only and you'll need a guide.

Pate

Pate is two hours by boat from Lamu. A *matatu* boat service — one of three plying the route — leaves daily from the municipal jetty. On Pate they call at **Mtangawanda** (for Pate town; about two hours) and **Faza** (up to four hours) in the north of the island.

By air, a grass **landing strip** carved out of tropical forest is all that denotes Pate's place in the twentieth century. But the island has some of the most impressive ruins anywhere in Kenya.

Pate has to be explored by foot and the most popular route is to start in Pate Town and walk, via **Siyu**, to Faza returning to Lamu

Overleaf: Local regatta between inshore dhows at Lamu.

from there. If you're worried about accommodation bring a tent. Normally, however, you'll be besieged by generous islanders inviting you to stay as soon as you arrive.

Carry water and food with you since supplies are unpredictable. The island *dukas* don't offer much choice so it's also a good idea to carry your own rations.

From the **dock** an hour-long jungle trail leads through mango and coconut plantations and dense bush to Pate Town. The **Nabhani ruins** outside Pate Town are rich with walls, buildings, tombs, mosques, and mysterious edifices.

Most impressive are the **mosque** with two mihrabs, a nearby **house** which still has a facing of beautiful **niches**, and the remains of a sizable **mansion**. Many of the interiors are so entangled by jungle that exploration is difficult. But persevere — you'll experience a great sense of personal adventure.

According to its Arabian history, recorded in the *Chronicles of Pate*, the town was founded by Arab immigrants in the early years of Islam. In the thirteenth century, however, a dispossessed group of Arab rulers, the Nabhani, arrived to take over. Archaeological evidence supports these claims showing the existence of a flourishing port on the present site of Pate as early as the tenth century.

In the seventeenth century the Portuguese exerted some influence on the island but to little avail. In the late eighteenth century, Pate underwent a cultural rebirth with a tide of creative activity similar to Lamu's, although the two towns were permanently at war. But the 1813 massacre marked the end of Pate as a city state.

Siyu, facing north-west in the middle of the island, is not so well-documented. But during the seventeenth and eighteenth centuries it flourished as a centre of Islamic scholarship — and hideaway for Muslim intellectuals and craftsmen.

Unlike the other towns, Siyu showed little or no interest in trade and so passed the avaricious eyes of the Portuguese unnoticed, although later the British Vice Consul in Zanzibar described it as "the pulse of the whole district".

Instead of trading, Siyu's inhabitants occupied themselves with producing copies of the the Qur'an, bookmaking, text illumination, and cottage industries like woodwork and leatherwork — for which Siyu is still famous.

Indeed, Siyu carved doors are among the most exquisite of all Swahili doors, with distinctive *guilloche* patterns and inlays of ground shell.

In 1847, Siyu lost its independence to the Sultan of Zanzibar. Today the town's stout nineteenth-century **fort** and its rusting **cannon**, its mirror image reflected in the still waters of the mangrove creek, is Siyu's most striking building, giving no indication of its mysterious builder.

The surrounding houses each stand alone with no real streets to connect them so, although larger than Pate, Siyu radiates much more of a village ambience.

Pate island's greatest historical site, far out on the south-eastern shore, is the 1,200-year-old city-state of **Shanga**. Donkeys carry the few visitors from the grass airstrip along a jungle trail of mango and coconut plantations, across the unspoilt hinterland, pausing briefly in their passage through thatched villages, to the recently uncovered ruins of the oldest-known settlement on the coast.

First settled between the eighth and ninth centuries, Shanga vanished almost overnight. In the mid-fifties the indefatigable James Kirkman landed on the island shores and stumbled upon its ancient ruins, overgrown in a thick jumble of creeper, baobab, bush, and weed.

But serious excavation did not begin until 1980 when an Operation Drake team, led by archaeologist Mark Horton, dug down through several layers of houses and streets to its ninth-century level.

The dry fossils and ancient ruins they found reveal the bare bones of a fascinating drama covering several centuries. High-class merchants and their women lived lives of splendour in this busy port-state until, centuries after it was established, the retreating sea left it high and dry.

Now only echoes of the past haunt the eight hectares (20 acres) of ruins, some with recesses where ceramics and works of art were displayed. The mosque, with its **kiblah** pointing to Mecca, denotes the prevailing faith, but as the inhabitants slowly left, only the legacy of a graceful age remains.

The ruins are a vivid contrast to the cultures inland on the mainland, which they plundered for slaves and artefacts as the source of their wealth.

North-Eastern Kenya: Sun-scorched Plains of Darkness

The desolate, arid badlands of north-eastern Kenya are a vast, magnificent, and still largely-unexplored wilderness. Although they constitute more than one-third of Kenya, fewer than five per cent of Kenya's twenty-three million people live in the region.

Once patrolled by scouts on camelback during the 1960s, it was the scene of a bitter guerilla war between Somali *Shifta* (bandits) who claimed this land for Somalia.

After Independence, the area was closed to visitors for many years although work continued on vital projects such as oil exploration and water drilling. Most of the few who do inhabit this region are hardy nomads, Kenya ethnic Somali, and the Gabbra. The Gabbra call it *Dida Galgalu* (Plains of Darkness) and if you walk anywhere in this area you'll wonder how anyone or anything could possibly survive.

Featureless to all but those who roam its hidden trails, it's easy to get lost in what was once romantically known as Kenya's Northern Frontier District (NFD).

Where to stay

In Maralal, Maralal Safari Lodge is three kilometres (two miles) out of town on the Lake Turkana Road — costly but attractive, comfortable but under-utilized. Maralal Campsite is just past the lodge.

National Parks

In Marsabit National Park, Marsabit Lodge (about three kilometres — two miles — from the main park gates, in a superb location) (4-star). Marsabit campsite, is near the main gate. The rangers will let you camp in their compound if wild animals worry you.

National Reserves

Samburu Lodge (on the north bank of the Ewaso Nyiro with riverside bars and restaurant) (5-star); Samburu River Lodge, (5-star). In Buffalo Springs Reserve, Buffalo Springs Lodge (3-star). In Shaba Reserve, Sarova Shaba (opened in 1989 and arguably the last word in safari comfort) (5-star).

Larsen's Camp in Samburu NR is the latest of the small, personal, permanent camps and evokes the old days of affluent safari camps. Champagne Ridge Campsite (Buffalo Springs NR) is not far from first gate. There are also three campsites in Shaba NR.

Getting there

There are two gateways into this featureless terrain — from Nanyuki on the shoulders of Mount Kenya, and from Nyahururu above the Marmanet Forest. The road from Nyahururu sweeps down through the forest to dusty **Rumuruti** (See "Heartland of Kenya", Part Two), southernmost border of Samburuland.

From Rumuruti the gravel road roughly follows the course of the **Ewaso Narok River**, for the first half of the 145-kilometre (90-mile) journey to **Maralal**, past **Colcheccio**, a large ranch which offers facilities to tourists and has been used, more than once, as a film location.

At roughly the halfway stage, a left turn leads to a well-graded track — with fabulous views over the Rift Valley — that leads down to Lake Baringo (See "Great Rift Valley: the land that was Eden").

Further on, at **Kisima** just a few kilometres before Maralal, there is a sharp right turn to **Archer's Post** and **Isiolo**, which offers magnificent views over the northern badlands.

Maralal

Maralal, the Samburu administrative centre and district capital, is an exciting town nestling in the western bosom of the **Ol Doinyo Lenkiyo** mountains. It offers all the ambience of a frontier town. In fact, even the climate is appropriate — swirling dust with log fires a necessity at night.

Two dusty main streets, a few *dukas*, a bank, and a hotel or two are the major facilities. Maralal is a good place to study the Samburu, particularly on Christian holidays. Many of the younger generations have converted to catholicism and their Palm Sunday procession, with women in their thousands, gaily-adorned and waving branches and leaves, is a kaleidoscope of colour and a frenzy of excitement.

Remember that if you are heading north, to Lake Turkana, or east through **Wamba**, and the Great North Road to Marsabit and Moyale,

Above: Sundown over the Ewaso Nyiro in Samburu National Reserve.

Maralal is the last place where you can change money at either the lodge or the bank.

It also has the last post office and is the last place where you can be sure of getting petrol for thousands of kilometres around. And if you're particularly partial to a beer in the middle of the forthcoming desert, be sure to stock up.

Maralal is also home to one of Kenya's most significant national monuments, **Kenyatta House**, the bungalow where Kenyatta was detained prior to his final release in 1961.

There's not much else, apart from the **Samburu Rural Development Centre**, outside the town, some local soothsayers and blacksmiths, and an authentic **Turkana** village.

To venture into the Northern Frontier District proper, retrace your footsteps to Kisima and take the dirt road through **Wamba**, a truly authentic Samburu town that lies at the foot of **Warges**, the southernmost and highest summit of the **Ol Doinyo Lenkiyo** mountains. Martial eagles circle on the strong thermals and hunt for prey in the sheer ravines below.

Another summit in this range, 2,375-metre-high (7,790-feet) **Matthews Peak**, was named by the Teleki expedition in appreciation of the

help they received from Sir Lloyd Matthews, commander in chief of the Sultan of Zanzibar's army.

From here the road continues to the Great North Road, joining it north of Archer's Post, at the foot of the **Lololokwe Mesa**. You can, obviously, reach Maralal and Rumuruti in reverse order — through Nanyuki and Isiolo.

From Nanyuki

From Nanyuki, the road climbs through the crisp mountain air, past wheatfields and verdant smallholdings to **Timau**, and then on up over the shoulders of Mount Kenya before the dramatic descent to the scorching, brown-baked, semi-desert of the Northern Frontier District.

The modern road plunges down more than 2,135 metres (7,000 feet) from 3,050 metres (10,000 feet) in fewer than forty kilometres (25 miles).

If you travel by night, you'll see **Isiolo** long before you arrive — the town a glittering necklace of light on the distant plain far below.

Beyond the **mosque** on the outskirts, the tin roofs of the town close in on either side.

For all its squat, nondescript, single-storey main street — reminiscent of the Wild West — Isiolo is gateway, if not capital, to a good third of Kenya.

The tarmac peters out at the **checkpoint** on the northern boundary of the town, where the road becomes the **Great North Highway**. This sea of corrugations heads to Addis Ababa, the Ethiopian capital, and a dirt road leads eastward into the trackless wastes of this desert. All travellers must record their departure from Isiolo — and an expedition into the vast wilderness beyond soon convinces you why.

Sightseeing

In Isiolo you'll find many local souvenir vendors selling "traditional" copper, brass, and aluminium Samburu bangles, plastic elephant "hair" bracelets, short "Somali swords" in red leather scabbards, and other trinkets.

Apart from its mosques and one main street, with typical basic but comfortable boarding and lodging (try an early morning bucket shower in the backyard looking up at Mount Kenya's silhouette against the blush of dawn for a real sense of adventure), there's not a great deal to see in Isiolo — but there's plenty of atmosphere.

The frontier ambience — Kikuyu mamas selling fresh produce from their highland shambas, Somali and Boran cattlemen arguing the price with cattle dealers, and the itinerant Samburu, Gabbra, Turkana, and resident Meru — makes this town a real melting-pot of diverse cultures.

Isiolo is the main departure point for the four major destinations of this vast desert area — **Marsabit, Moyale, Wajir**, and **Mandera**. The journey to Marsabit takes between five and six hours, and five-six hours more from Marsabit to Moyale, and nine hours to Wajir with four more hours to Mandera. These times assume that there are no hold-ups both literally — bandits are still rife in the remote areas — and in the mechanical sense.

The roads could also be out of action because of rains and floods. However, in 1989 there were definite plans to tarmac the Great North Road from Isiolo to the Ethiopian border at Moyale by 1992. This will provide a first-class all weather road between Nairobi and Addis Ababa. This plan was first launched in the 1960s but has been stymied on this last leg by financial restraints.

For most tourists, the first destination, forty-five kilometres (38 miles) out of Isiolo into the badlands, is **Samburu National Reserve**. This covers 165 square kilometres (64 square miles) on the north bank of the **Ewaso Nyiro River**, ninety kilometres (56 miles) north of Mount Kenya.

Set at an altitude of between 800 and 1,230 metres (2,625-4,036 feet), the reserve is a lava plain with steep-sided gullies and rounded basement hills. The Ewaso Nyiro river forms thirty-two kilometres (20 miles) of the southern boundary and is Samburu's central feature.

Upstream, the same river plummets over Thomson's Falls. In spate its waters quickly swell and become a raging torrent. Early in 1986, and again in 1987, it dried up during a prolonged drought that came to an abrupt end when a flash flood sent a wall of water three metres (10 feet) deep rolling down its dry bed, sweeping away all before it.

In this landscape, battlements made of scarps and fallen boulders rise up out of the thorn scrub, and where the stone and dirt road lurches down a dip and over a *wadi* (dried-up river) the rugged hills to the northwest vanish from view. Vegetation consists of acacia woodland with bush, grass, and shrubland with a narrow, riverine woodland of doum palm along the Ewaso Nyiro river.

Samburu is one of the few sanctuaries in Kenya which is home to Grevy's zebra, whose bat-like ears and single-direction stripe, are notably different from the Burchell's (common) zebra. Rare, beisa oryx, and blue-shanked Somali ostrich can also be seen (See "National Parks", In Brief, for other wildlife).

Adjoining the reserve, more or less a contiguous southward extension of the same environment, is **Buffalo Springs National Reserve**, covering some 131 square kilometres (51 square miles) of gently rolling, lowland plains interspersed by seasonally dry luggas and the Ewaso Nyiro river — the reserve's northern boundary.

Unlike most rivers, these waters never reach the sea. They bury themselves in the **Lorien Swamp** near the desert town of **Habaswein** in the east. The vegetation and wildlife are the same as Samburu.

Shaba National Reserve

A few kilometres to the east, across the rutted surface of the Marsabit road, lies **Shaba National Reserve**, the third of the Samburu

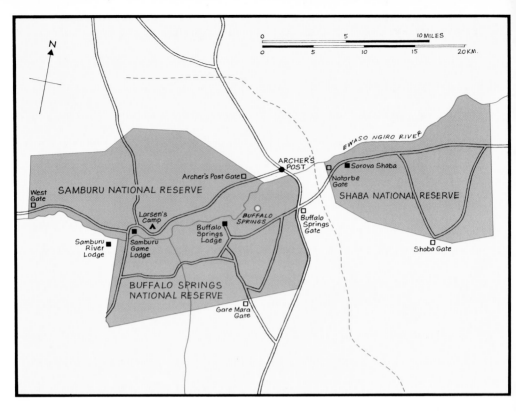

reserves. It is less popular than the other two but beloved by the late Joy Adamson who made a camp here to continue her work on rehabilitating leopard to the wild.

Still relatively undeveloped, although a new luxury lodge opened in 1989, Shaba is one of Kenya's most pristine game reserves, with untouched vistas and other unspoilt splendours.

Covering an area of 239 square kilometres (92 square miles), the reserve is set at the base of the Mount Kenya foothills, seventy kilometres (43 miles) north of the main massif, at an altitude of between 700 and 1,500 metres (2,300-4,920 feet).

Beyond the foothills, the reserve covers a lava plain with ridges dominated by the **Shaba Massif**. The northern boundary includes thirty-four kilometres (20 miles) of the **Ewaso Nyiro river** and there are numerous springs and a large swamp. Vegetation and wildlife are the same as Samburu.

Great North Road

The Great North Road that divides Shaba from Buffalo Springs and Samburu now thrusts northward through **Archer's Post**, forty-eight kilometres (30 miles) from Isiolo, some 320 kilometres (200 miles) from Nairobi, into a stark, dramatic wilderness of desert and mountain.

Built in the 1960s by Kenya's National Youth Service the broad road is pitted with giant corrugations, extremely difficult to drive over even at speed because they are spaced so far apart.

After Archer's Post — named after an early English settler who made his camp here and which is now a military training ground — the roads heads for the brooding, sugarloaf profile of 1,980-metre-high (6,500 feet) high **Lololokwe** (See "Kenya's Mountains"). From the summit, Somali *shifta* used to pin down with gunfire the construction teams of the youth service.

Lololokwe is something of a challenge to climbers. The Mountain Club of Kenya handbook suggests some routes — with a warning to beware the rhino that are said to roam the mountain.

Just before you reach the base of this rocky hump, a dirt road veers west, through **Wamba**, into Samburu country and the lush forest lands of the **Lorogi Plateau** in the **Karisia**

Hills, then continues on to Maralal.

After Lololokwe the road heads directly north through a severe ravaged landscape to **Seredupi** and **Lodosoit** after which it cuts through the eastern extremities of Kenya's least known game sanctuary, **Losai National Reserve**, located in the mountains that rise up out of the **Kaisut Desert**.

Losai National Reserve

Situated 175 kilometres (110 miles) north of Mount Kenya at an altitude of between 625 and 1,750 metres (2,050-5,740 feet), the 1,807-square-kilometre (698-square-mile) reserve is a lava plateau dissected by dry luggas with scattered volcanic plugs and cones covered with thorny bushland. Its wildlife used to include elephant and black rhino.

It is virtually impenetrable, even by 4WD vehicle, although in the middle is the medical mission of **Ngoronet** with its airstrip. The reserve touches the fringes of both the **Ndoto** and **Ol Doinyo Lenkiyo** mountains, visible to the west. The Ndoto range is home to the Ndoto Forest, one of Kenya's biggest with almost 1,000 square kilometres (390 square miles) of indigenous, virgin timber (See "Kenya's Mountains").

Set on the Great North Road, at the northern edge of the reserve, is the mission town of **Laisamis**. Before the World War I an English aristocrat making a hunting trip in this region with Colonel J. H. Patterson, the martinet of the *Maneaters of Tsavo* melodrama, pitched camp near here. Returning from a foray into the Kaisut desert he found his wife locked in the Colonel's arms, *inflagrante*, and returned to the desert where he shot himself.

Another lurching 100 kilometres (60 miles) across the Kaisut Desert, a tumultuous landscape of raddled lava and rocks resembling lumps of rusted cannon ball and shot, that is home to the Rendille and Gabbra people, will take you to **Logologo**.

This neat little mission town, its two-storey houses strangely incongruous in the desert wilderness, has grown up around the airstrip.

The **Milgis Lugga** passes under one of the bridges built by the youth service. Before it was built, flash floods tumbling down from the mountains delayed travellers for days.

Shortly after Logologo, the road crosses the border of the **Marsabit National Reserve** and begins to climb up the slopes of the volcanic mountain that rises abruptly out of the desert, to **Marsabit**, a bleached, brown monochrome of a town. Astonishingly, Marsabit boasts a microwave telephone link with the outside world.

Capital of a sprawling administrative region, Marsabit is where Gabbra, Rendille, and Borana people meet on common ground — usually in the utilitarian bars where the atmosphere is more appealing than the decor. They are attractive but uncompromising pastoralists with fascinating cultures (See "The People", Part One).

There is a **bank**, **Post Office**, **service station** and workshop, although the petrol pumps sometimes run dry which means waiting until the next tanker arrives.

The town is as hot as the surrounding desert — the grass brown, parched and patchy. Two kilometres (little more than a mile) away, the dirt track halts at the gate of the 2,088-square-kilometre (806-square-mile) Marsabit National Reserve.

Marsabit National Reserve

Situated 560 kilometres (348 miles) north of Nairobi, **Marsabit National Reserve** is a forested mountain oasis with several volcanic craters, many filled with freshwater lakes. Lower down, the forest merges into acacia grasslands which in turn give way to arid, thorny bushland on the lower slopes.

Once through the gate and round the first bend, you enter another world where the forest closes in and is reflected in two magic crater lakes. Born out of volcanic fire, Marsabit is often swathed in mists. Each night, as the desert air cools, clouds take form and an hour or two before dawn, clamp their clammy fingers around the western peak. The mist rarely releases its grip before early afternoon.

The forests, watered by the mists, sustain elephant which are famous for their giant tusks.

The reserve is also renowned for its herds of greater kudu that were once rare in Kenya, but have made a comeback from the ravages of the rinderpest epidemic which almost wiped them out at the turn of the century (See "National Parks", In Brief, for wildlife).

At least fifty-two species of eagle, hawk, and falcon nest in the sheer 200 to 215 (650-700 feet) high cliffs, amid stands of juniper and podocarpus, which give the reserve's craters a green fur lining. Altogether there are 350 recorded bird species. Rare lammergeier eagles nest on the sheer cliffs of Gof Bongole — the largest crater — which has a ten kilometre (six mile) rim.

Higher up Marsabit mountain, another amphitheatre called **Lake Paradise** lies at the bottom of the bowl, below an old 150-metre-high (500-feet) caldera rimmed with forest trees laced with Spanish moss. On one side, however, the caldera descends almost to lake level, and from the air it looks like an eye.

Here, American film makers, Martin and Olsa Johnson, made their home for four years in the early 1920s, producing some of the world's first wildlife movies.

There are some walking trips you can make from Marsabit in a few hours. **Gof Redo** is a sizable crater about five kilometres (three miles) north of the town where the road to the **Chalbi desert** and **North Horr** forks left off the main Moyale road.

The crater lies another three kilometres (two miles) along the Chalbi road. A right turn along a dirt track for about one kilometre (a third of a mile) leads to the crater, a favoured haunt of the rare greater kudu. You can scramble down the crater wall if you wish.

You can also walk to the **Singing Wells** at **Ulanula** which are owned by the Borana. The wells plunge vertically, some four to fifteen metres (15-50 feet) down. Each morning, the well masons work in mud and water to fashion a trough in the quick-drying sun.

Four men form a human ladder, with the lowest one standing chest-deep in the water below, the second perched on a rocky ledge, the third balanced expertly on two slender poles, and the fourth at the top.

They swing three buckets of stitched giraffe hide up and down in harmonic rhythm, singing a hymn-like song as they work.

The trough fills quickly and Borana women hurry to take home the day's water supplies as their livestock drink eagerly (See "The People", Part One).

Desert people hold their animals in high esteem. Rather than risk them dying in Marsabit's chill night air, they opt to walk up to seventy kilometres (45 miles) to the warmth of the desert floor before returning in a day or two to water them again.

If you continue along the Chalbi road for 350 kilometres (220 miles) across the pitiless glare of the Chalbi Desert you will come to **North Horr** and from there you can drive to

Koobi Fora and the **"Cradle of Mankind"** (See "The Northern Rift").

The signpost at the edge of Marsabit town gives the distance to the eastern shores of Lake Turkana as more than 350 kilometres (220 miles) but, unless you are fully-equipped for a hazardous expedition in searing heat across trackless desert, it's best to ignore the temptation to make the journey.

Chalbi, a vast salt desert, in fact used to be the bed of an ancient lake. Even now, during extraordinary rains which fall perhaps once every fifty years (as in the early 1960s) Chalbi floods and becomes a shallow inland sea covering several thousand square kilometres.

From Marsabit the Great North Road continues north across the inhospitable wastes of the *Dida Galgalu* ("Plain of Darkness") and then veers east over the **Ngaso Plain** to Moyale. It takes between five and six hours of rugged travel to cover the 245 kilometres (150 miles) from Marsabit in a 4WD vehicle.

Sightseeing

Moyale consists of a small and delicate **mosque**, one main street, a few sandy side streets, a row of *dukas*, the ubiquitous **bar**, a **camel corral, post office, police station, small market** and two abandoned petrol stations.

It is attractive for its **Burji architecture** — mud-and-dung on a framework of withies and wood, with a flat or slightly tilted roof that projects to form a porch, supported by sturdy posts and tree trunks.

The roof, often as much as half-a-metre thick (two-feet), is a conglomeration of dried mud, sticks, scrap, and vegetation. Chicken and goats live on this, improving the roof's fertility which in turn adds another layer of insulating herbage every time it rains.

Consequently, while the outside temperature hovers above 30°C (86°F) the interiors are always comfortably cool.

A most exciting excursion is to cross the valley into **Ethiopia** to spend a few hours or even a night on the other side. The border is open to Kenyans and Ethiopians, but other nationals require visas.

At the Ethiopian post, you'll be asked for your entry visa. If you have one, your passage is straightforward. If not, explain you are just visiting briefly and go to see the customs and immigration officials.

After a short delay here, you should be allowed in. Nonetheless, custom searches are

Above: Forbidding volcanic mountains guard the approach to Suguta Valley.

thorough and cameras have to be left behind.

You climb a wide stretch of tarred road into **Ethiopian Moyale** which is larger than its Kenyan counterpart and more prosperous with power supplies and piped water. Like many Ethiopian towns it has a distinctly Italian ambience. Two kilometres (little more than two miles) into Ethiopia there's an excellent state-run hotel, the **Bekele Molla**. In the town itself, there are many bars and bistros.

But these aside, life is much the same. Nonetheless, you can sample traditional Ethiopian *njera* (unleavened millet bread) and *wat*, their spicy stew. And guaranteed to make you feel light-headed is *tej*, a powerful mead brewed from honey and as alcoholic as full-proof whisky.

Northern Frontier: The Harshest Desert

From Ethiopian Moyale, there is a smooth tarmac road all the way to the capital of Addis Ababa. If you wish to make this journey you must obtain a visa in advance. Most, however, will opt to continue their exploration of north-eastern Kenya by returning, via Marsabit, to Isiolo.

If you have incredible stamina and a penchant for risks, you may consider taking the desert trail from Moyale east to **Mandera** and **Wajir**.

But remember that although the route is clearly shown on all maps you may have to carve your own trail to Mandera, set snug against the Ethiopian and Somalia border. This track has long been abandoned and since the route to Wajir has hardly ever been used you may have to forge a new trail there, too. On rare occasions Kenya police or army vehicles go this way but otherwise there is nothing apart from camel trains on the move. At the end of the 1980s the *shifta* had once again become active in this region so you would be better advised to make the long journey back to Isiolo and start your exploration of the north-eastern desert from there.

Getting there

From Isiolo, the route to the north-east is one of the most remote trails in the country — crossing a sizzling, flat-as-a-pancake desert of sand and scrub. As you drive, the horizon appears to melt continuously in front of your eyes. So flat, monotonous, and spotted with thorn bush, is the landscape that if you stray just a few metres from the trail you become disorientated and hopelessly lost within minutes.

Sightseeing

The trail drives through this featureless plain, past the village of **Kula Mawe**, and the right fork through **Garba Tula** to **Garissa**, and on to **Mado Gashi**. Here is the meeting point for Eastern and North-Eastern provinces. Many of the buses that ply this long-distance desert road use Mado Gashi as a convenient night-stop.

In the late 1960s American teams swept across this desert with drilling rigs to sink boreholes for local townsfolk and nomadic communities. But more often than not the water was too alkaline to use. In the waddies around town you'll see Boran and Somali camel herders digging deep into the sand to tap the residue of the last rains, hidden well below the surface.

From this dusty shantytown with its two provincial **police headquarters**, it's another bumpy, sandy, scorching fifty kilometres (30 miles), past the western extremity of the **Lorien Swamp** where the desert finally sucks the Ewaso Nyiro dry, and across the **Sabena Desert** to the French Foreign Legion town of **Habaswein**, which looms in the distance like a Hollywood set for *Beau Geste*.

From Habaswein, with its castellated, fortress-like buildings, it's another 110 kilometres (70 miles) to **Wajir**, some fifty kilometres (30 miles) from the Somali border.

Bristling thorn bushes grow out of the grey sand that stretches away to an ill-defined horizon. There is no surface water for hundreds of kilometres in any direction but around Wajir more than 100 wells are scattered across seventy square kilometres (30 square miles) of desert.

These wells, only about six metres (20 feet) deep, have been in use for centuries. Indeed, legend has it that some 3,000 years ago the Queen of Sheba watered her camels here.

White buildings, with little minarets rising above the flat-roofed houses, endow Wajir with all the ambience of Arabia. Set at 900 metres (2,950 feet) above see level, Wajir is a major administrative centre for thousands of square kilometres of north-eastern Kenya, with a **DC's office**, **police station**, **hospital**, and **army camp**.

A plaque on the wall behind the DC's desk records the names of illustrious predecessors from both before and after Independence.

On the outskirts of the town there is an odd-looking building that houses the **Royal Wajir Yacht Club**, even though the nearest water is 500 kilometres (310 miles) away. The club was given the Royal prefix after entertaining a member of Britain's royalty but is now used as a residence for civil servants.

Wajir's sandy streets see few vehicles but a circle of whitewashed stones at one end of the main street serves as a roundabout.

There are a few all-purpose *dukas* selling canned groceries and other goods, a butcher's shop, and a confectioner who specialises in producing the sweet, syrupy cakes favoured by Somalis.

Hidden behind a low stone wall, overgrown by weeds and encroached on by the desert sands, is the **town cemetery**.

There's little of inspiration, save perhaps for the colourful **market** — a maze of grass and stick huts, and wooden kiosks on the west side of town which sell domestic ware including pottery incense burners to scent clothing.

Sunrise bestows a special magic on this desert capital. The sky fills with birds and the sound of wings. Huge flocks of sand grouse come in from the desert to drink in the pools around the wells, doves flutter across the roof tops, and scavenging maribou storks gather like hunched soldiers around the town garbage pit.

Mandera

From Wajir to Mandera it is another 185 kilometres (115 miles) across the trackless wastes of the **Gora Dudu Plains**. The route veers east at the fork just after **Tarba** to the dusty settlement of **El Wak** — in Somali it means "the Wells of God" — which used to be an outpost for a camel police patrol. Just beyond the town a right turn loops back and across the Somalia border.

From here it's about another 100 kilometres (70 miles) along what is ostensibly the main road to **Ramu**. It was tarmac at one time but the desert has worn away most of this.

Ramu, on the Ethiopian border by the seasonal **Daua River**, boasts a **National**

Christian Council of Kenya shelter. You can spend the night here if a room is available. There is also a Kenya Army garrison plus the most virulent mosquitoes you'll find anywhere in the country.

From Ramu, the tarmac is surprisingly continuous all the way along the last stretch east to **Mandera**, tucked in against the Somalia-Ethiopian borders. Straight as an arrow, walled in the north by an unnamed range of gaunt and forbidding Ethiopian mountains, the road offers plenty of excitement, crossing a series of precipitous switchback north-south ridges without regard for gradient or safety. The roadside is littered with the wrecks of lorries and other vehicles that failed to negotiate these lethal bends.

Sightseeing

Almost 1,000 kilometres (620 miles) from Nairobi, Mandera's contact with the capital is tenuous. A light plane flies in daily with mail and other supplies but the townsfolk rely mostly on Somalia for their staples.

As at Moyale, the border between Kenya and Somalia is freely open for the local people. Indeed, Somali currency is also widely accepted in the town which lacks Wajir's sense of permanence and makes its southerly neighbour look positively urbane.

Aside from a cluster of Somali hamlets, the town is little more than a collection of dilapidated administrative buildings. Nevertheless, it is interesting to stroll around.

The main focus is the **market**, a bustling maze of huts and shelters with a happy hour from 21.00-22.00 when the *miraa* arrives. If you're lucky, the **Mandera Club**, member's only, may allow you in to buy a beer. The only licensed premises in town, the Club opens at 16.00.

But Mandera is a thriving black market entrepôt. Essentials such as detergents, tea, coffee, and *miraa* cross into Somalia in exchange for electronic goods, cameras, and other luxuries from the duty-free Arabian Gulf.

The only school for an area of 25,000 square kilometres (9,650 square miles), **Mandera Secondary Girls School**, still has few students.

For those seeking onward travel into Somalia, head for Mandera's cross-border counterpart, **Bula Hawa**. There doesn't appear to be a formal Kenya border post and there's no need for a visa, but you'll need your passport. You'd be well advised to leave any valuables behind in Mandera.

At the Somalia border post it's more than likely that you'll be waved in through the bustle and told to report to the police station.

Bula Hawa ("Eve's Village") is a small town whose exotic main street has been described as a Bedouin "Harrods"!

Colourful kiosk owners relax on brilliantly-coloured Sindbad carpets, drinking endless cups of tea, surrounded by an Alladin's Cave of high-tech wealth and luxury goods. You can buy almost anything, from the most expensive French perfumes, personal stereos, colour TVs, videos, tape recorders, chinaware, cut glass, cosmetics, cameras — *ad infinitum*. You name it and this original duty-free bazaar will probably have it!

If you have a visa, you can continue through the bullet-ridden streets of Bula Hawa to the Somalia capital of **Mogadishu**, many hundreds of kilometres away, or return to Nairobi by plane. Be prepared to fight for your seat.

The only certain flights are chartered by local entrepreneurs and there's always a desperate scramble at the air strip as the charterer touts the seat to the highest bidder.

From Garissa

The other gateway to the north-east is **Garissa**, on the Tana River, only 380 kilometres (235 miles) from Nairobi either through Thika or Machakos and Kitui.

A fairly good road will deliver you to this dusty administrative centre so long as there is no bandit ambush *en route*. Garissa is located just 400 metres (1,310 feet) above sea level, at the lowest bridging point across the Tana river.

It is the hottest town in Kenya and rather dull, despite the many **bars**, **banks**, and **petrol stations**. It is a bit of a no-man's-land, hovering between coast, upcountry, and desert.

Sightseeing

Garissa is the base from which to explore the Tana basin as it rolls down to the sea beyond **Garsen**. And a thrice-weekly bus service to Wajir and Mandera follows the road that joins the Isiolo-Wajir road at Mado Gashi.

The road to Garsen leads straight along the southern bank of the Tana for 150 kilometres (90 miles) through **Tula** to **Hola** passing both the extensive **Bura settlement scheme** and the 533 square kilometres (206 square miles) of the remote **Arawale National Reserve** to the north.

You can cross the Tana at Hola by ferry and then turn back, westwards for a few kilometres, to the reserve which is set on a flat plain dissected by sandy-bedded rivers and covered with thorny bushland (See "The Road to Lamu: mad dogs, eccentric English").

Hola, which falls within the Coastal province of Kenya, is the administrative headquarters of the Tana River District with a **post office, hospital, police station**, and **petrol station**.

It's another eighty-seven kilometres (55 miles) downstream, all along the south bank, to **Garsen**. Roughly halfway between the two is one of Kenya's most unique wildlife sanctuaries, the **Tana River Primate Reserve** which covers 169 square kilometres (65 square miles) of flood plains, sand levees, old river channels, oxbow lakes, and ponds in a fifty-kilometre (30-mile) riverine belt along the Tana's north bank.

This highly diversified range of riverine forest with patches of bush and grasslands provides cover and food for almost 300 species and is the last sanctuary for the endemic red colobus and mangabey monkeys found nowhere else in eastern and central Africa. They are survivors of a time when rain forest used to stretch in a broad swathe from east to west across Africa.

There are five other primates including Sykes monkey and yellow baboon (See "National Parks", In Brief, for wildlife). More than 240 bird species have been recorded as well as twenty-two species of fish. There is one **luxury lodge** and one **tented camp**.

From here it's another forty kilometres (25 miles) or so to Garsen which marks the ferry-crossing point for those travelling to Lamu, and the capital of the Pokomo people who are agriculturists and renowned boatmen.

Right: Sunup over the Kenya wilderness.

PART THREE: SPECIAL FEATURES

Above: Lush harvest of Kenya's tropical orchards.
Opposite: Lone acacia and rhino on a deserted Kenyan savannah plain.

Wildlife: Great and Small, Wild and Wonderful

Kenya boasts one of the greatest wildlife populations in the world: some truly unique, much of it rare, and a few whose lineage goes back long before the first ancestors of mankind evolved on the shores of Lake Turkana, northern Kenya's remote inland sea.

A large area on its eastern shores forms one of more than fifty nature sanctuaries established to preserve for future generations a wildlife, marine, and prehistoric heritage which has few equals.

Kenya's first national park, Nairobi, opened its gates in 1946. By Independence in 1963 there was a network of twelve parks and reserves. Expansion was swift.

Within the next twenty-five years their number increased to more than fifty. They range from the combined area of the twin Tsavo parks, which cover more than 21,200 square kilometres (8,200 square miles), to the Saiwa Swamp National Park which covers two square kilometres (less than one square mile) (See "National Parks", In Brief).

Kenya has more than eighty major animal species — from the "Big Five", the most cherished trophies among the old hunting fraternity, to tiny antelope, such as the dik-dik which is no bigger than a rabbit.

The Big Five: Elephant

The **African elephant** weighs anything from three-and-a-half to six-and-a-half tonnes. It eats between ninety and 270 kilos (200-600 lbs) of fodder and drinks between 200 and 300 litres (44-66 gallons) of water a day. It depends almost entirely on its trunk for scent and communication, washing and cleaning, carrying and clearing, and for drinking and eating.

The tusks, upper incisors, are simply secondary — but important — lifting, carrying, and clearing tools.

An elephant's life span depends on its lower teeth, which are highly adapted to its mode of living. As one is worn away, the next one moves down the jaw to push it out.

When the last one has come forward and is worn down, at anywhere between fifty to seventy years old, the elephant will eventually die of starvation.

It takes close to two years from conception to deliver the young, which weighs between 120 and 135 kilos (265-300 lbs). During labour the mother is attended by two other females — "midwives" — which accompany her when she withdraws from the herd to give birth in discreet privacy.

Although their sight is poor, elephants have an excellent sense of smell and well-developed hearing, with a brain that weighs three times that of a human brain — between three and a half and five kilos (8-11 lbs).

Rhinoceros

The **black rhinoceros**, the smaller of the two rhino species, weighs around 907 to 1,364 kilos (2,000-3,000 lbs). The average size of its horns varies between fifty and ninety centimetres (one and a half-three feet) for the front horn and just over fifty centimetres (almost two feet) for the rear horn.

With its relatively small feet, three-toed hoofs and pointed prehensile upper lip, the black rhinoceros is a browser that used to be found anywhere from sea level up to 3,500 metres (1,150 feet), in vegetation ranging from savannah to montane forest. In the last twenty years its numbers have been decimated by poachers — reduced virtually to the point of no return.

The **white rhinoceros** derive their name from the Afrikaans "weit", meaning wide-mouthed. With their square lips, white rhinos are grazers, not browsers and even more sedentary, docile, and gregarious than black rhino. They move in families and groups of between two and five.

The white rhinoceros, much more solid than the black, is normally a good fifteen centimetres (six inches) higher at the shoulder and weighs between 2,000 and 4,000 kilos (4,400-8,900 lbs), making it the biggest of all land animals after the elephant.

Buffalo

The **African buffalo** needs plenty of fodder to maintain its strength and stamina. They are voracious eaters, browsing and grazing on a variety of grasses, leaves, twigs, and young

Above: Endangered white rhino in one of Kenya's wildlife sanctuaries.

shoots for most of their fifteen to twenty years.

Gregarious, they frequently form herds of 500 up to 2,000. Buffalo are found everywhere in Kenya, from sea level to mountain forests above 3,000 metres (9,840 feet), always close to water. They are particularly dangerous with unpredictable and volatile tempers.

Lion

The **lion**, largest of Kenya's three big cats, weighs up to 280 kilos (620 lbs). It's amber-coloured eyes, like those of the leopard, differ from those of most cats in that they are circular, not oval.

Inherently lazy, the lion nevertheless is extremely powerful. At one leap it can clear a barrier almost four metres (13 feet) high or a chasm up to twelve metres (30 feet) wide.

Lion hunt communally by running down their preferred prey — zebra, hartebeest, wildebeest, and other gazelles — at a top speed of around sixty-four kilometres (40 miles) an hour. Their favourite method is to pounce at the victim's back, dragging it to the ground and seizing it by the throat. Another

method is suffocation by holding the victim's muzzle in its mouth.

On average, in an ordinary year, a lion or lioness accounts for nineteen head of game at a weight of about 115 kilos (250 lbs) for each kill.

Prides, which number up to thirty animals, mostly females and young, mark their range — up to 160 square kilometres (525 square miles) — by urination.

The lion's roar, rarely heard during daytime, carries as far as eight kilometres (five miles) and signals territorial ownership. So powerful is this roar it stirs the dust two metres (six and a half feet) away.

Leopard

The **leopard** is much smaller than the lion and weighs between thirty and eighty kilos (65-180 lbs). Its sandy fur is exquisitely-patterned with dark rosettes.

Leopard move mainly at night and are rarely seen during the day when they rest up in the branches of a shady tree. Superb hunters, they prefer to kill by leaping from the branches and seizing the neck or throat of their

Overleaf: Majestic elephant — their future in peril.

Above: Crested crane stalks in front of a Cape buffalo.

prey. Leopard kills last longer.

What they cannot eat immediately, they haul up a tree, out of reach of scavengers. In this way leopards monopolize their kill — even if towards the end it become rancid. Leopard kill anything from small rodents to fairly large gazelle and antelope. They even eat fish and come readily to carrion.

Cheetah

Cheetah are the most slender of the three big cats and weigh between forty-five and sixty-five kilos (95-140 lbs).

With their deep chest, slender body and long thin legs, cheetah are built for speed. They are the fastest animal in the world and have recorded speeds of more than 112 kilometres (70 miles) an hour. But the burst of energy is brief and always leaves the cheetah gasping for breath.

Sometimes cheetah are so short of air that their victims escape the capture hold — a slashing, claw-raking blow to the flank — and make off. At other times, a more dominant killer or scavenger — lion or hyena — will move in and steal the kill from the panting cheetah.

Giraffe

Nature has given the **giraffe**, the world's tallest creature, several systems to help it cope with life as the "skyscraper of the bush". These include a prehensile upper lip and a forty-five-centimetre (eighteen-inch) tongue — the longest in the world.

They also have a complex and unique system of canals and valves that maintain constant blood pressure whether the giraffe is standing tall — or bending down to drink.

Giraffe, more closely related to the deer family than any other living creature, run in a curious and fascinating loping gallop at speeds of up to fifty-six kilometres (35 miles) an hour.

Measuring anything from four and a half to five and a half metres (15-18 feet) from the tip of their toe to the top of their head, giraffe can weigh up to 1,270 kilos (2,280 lbs).

Already more than one and a half metres (five feet) high at birth and around seventy kilos (150 lbs) in weight, the young continue to grow for the first seven to ten of their twenty-five years.

There are two races of common giraffe in Kenya. Maasai giraffe are found mainly to the

Above: Lion cub.

Above: Mating lion and lioness.

Above: Leopard lazes in a Maasai Mara tree.

south-west of Athi River: Rothschild giraffe with their distinctive white "stockinged" fore-legs are now found only in Lake Nakuru National Park.

The much less-common reticulated giraffe, found north of the Tana River, is undoubtedly the most handsome.

Hippopotamus

Weighing up to four tonnes, **hippo** are the third-largest land animal. But they can stay submerged for up to six minutes.

True amphibians, they eat, mate, and give birth under water and spend most of the day sleeping and resting, usually in the water, coming up frequently to blow air and recharge their lungs.

Around sundown the schools (or "sounders") leave the water, adult bulls at the back, to spend the night within the limits of their "home-range". This is a pear-shaped area marked by well-defined pathways. Here, they search for grass and other vegetation, each animal eating around sixty kilos (130 lbs) of fodder nightly.

Opposite: Cheetah on an Amboseli acacia thorn.

Usually born in the water, the young are suckled at first on land. Hippo mothers are stern disciplinarians. Disobedient young are chastised, sometimes with a savage bite, with the youngster made to cower in submission.

Crocodile

For all its sinister-looking teeth, the **crocodile** is unable to chew. When it eats large prey, this reptile clamps on to its victim's legs and threshes around in the water, often rotating several times until the limb is wrenched from the trunk.

To swallow, it raises its head and lets the food fall to the back of its throat. Digestion is slow. Bodies recovered from dead crocodiles fifteen hours after the reptile has made a kill have been virtually unmarked. Crocodiles kill with a blow of either the head or tail.

These cold-blooded saurians depend entirely on external temperatures to maintain their own, and regulate their body heat according to the time of day.

They leave the water early in the morning to warm up in the sun, return to the water to

Above: Gregarious hippos in a Mara waterhole.

escape the excessive heat of high noon, and return later in the cooler part of the day to bask in the sun once more until around sundown, when they return to the water for the night. They can stay submerged for up to one hour.

Other cats

The **serval** has long legs, large oval ears, a medium build, and weighs between thirteen and fifteen kilos (30-35 lbs). It's main food is rodents but it also eats lizards, fish, vegetables, birds, and small antelope, depending on what is available. To catch birds it leaps high into the air as the victim takes off.

Serval cats can be found throughout Kenya — from lowland savannah to high mountain moorland.

Caracal

The **caracal**'s flat head, long legs, and powerful shoulders give it the proportions of a lynx. With hind legs longer than the forelegs, the caracal can suddenly spring into the air and pull down a bird in mid-flight, sometimes as high as three metres (10 feet) which, for its size, is a phenomenal distance. Few cats can emulate this feat.

Copy cats

Civets are long-legged, dog-like creatures, and the largest of the viverrid family, weighing between nine and twenty kilos (20-45 lbs). Their long coarse body has a varied pattern of black spots.

Civets are found in savannah and sometimes dense forest though they hide during the day in old burrows. They have a low-pitched cough and growl. Another species, the **palm** (or two-spotted) **civet**, spends most of its life in trees or vines and mews like a cat.

Small-spotted (or **Neumann's**) **genet** are widespread through Kenya's savannah country. Mainly solitary and nocturnal, they are equally at home on the ground or in trees. So slender and flexible is the genet's body that it can follow its head through any opening.

Large spotted (or **bush**) **genets** are longer than the more common small-spotted genet, and lack a dorsal crest. They have shorter fur and larger body spots. Widespread throughout Kenya, they favour woodland and forest.

Opposite: Hippo and young thunder into the Mara river.

Although a member of the viverrid family, when angry or threatened genet spit and growl like cats. Their normal call is a clear, metallic note.

Mongooses

Kenya's **dwarf mongoose**, smallest of Kenya's six or seven species, is active during the day looking for grubs, insects, larvae, spiders, small rodents, reptiles, eggs, and young birds for food. They roam in packs of up to fifteen and attack live prey *en masse*, swooping down on the victims with a savage growl.

Stockily-built, with a short snout and speckled brown or reddish-brown coat, mongoose live in dry savannah woodlands, taking refuge in old termite hills, rock crevices, or hollow trees. These nomadic creatures show little concern for their own safety and are frequently seen. They communicate with a wide vocabulary of bird-like chirrups and whistles.

The largest of Kenya's mongooses is the **large grey mongoose**. Another species, the slender (**black-tipped**) **mongoose** is often mistaken for a ground squirrel when running because of the similar way it holds its tail up straight.

The **white-tailed mongoose** varies its behaviour according to its habitat. They favour almost any kind of environment from wooded areas, bush, even open plains, to locations close to water where they add molluscs and crabs to their universal diet.

The **banded mongoose** moves around in packs of up to a dozen. Highly social animals, their groups often grow to number between thirty and fifty gregarious and appealing creatures.

Hyrax

The beguiling **tree hyrax** is perhaps best known both as the elephant's closest relative and for its scream.

Delivered in the dead of night its searing, anguished cry sounds like the Devil incarnate. In fact, it serves as a territorial call much like the lion's roar.

Tree hyrax are nocturnal and well adapted for climbing trees. The soles of their feet are kept continuously sticky by a substance secreted from a gland. Tree hyrax can be found at almost any altitude in almost any forest from sea level to around 4,000 metres (13,125 feet).

Lighter in colour, **rock hyrax** have evolved

Top: Greater kudu.
Above: Rock hyrax.

Top: Reticulated giraffe.
Above: Bat-eared Fox.

feet that enable them to move with agility among boulders and precipices. Their soles have semi-elastic, "rubber" pads which provide a sure grip on all inclines in all conditions.

Dogs and Jackals

Wild dog are social animals that live and hunt in packs of as few as ten to as many as 100. They can sustain a speed of fifty kilometres (30 miles) an hour for almost two kilometres (just over a mile).

When one dog is exhausted another takes its place at the front of the chase. The pack eats on the run, tearing the flesh off the prey while it is in flight, often ripping out its entrails until the luckless victim drops exhausted. A pack of twelve dogs can consume a full-grown impala within ten minutes.

The pack hunts only at sunup and sundown, between 06.30 and 07.30 in the morning and 18.00-19.00 evening. A pack's kill averages just under two kilos (four and a half lbs) of flesh a day for each animal.

Lame and sick dogs which trail after the hunt are well cared for. When they come upon the kill they are made welcome to the feast. Colleagues will regurgitate semi-digested meat for them to eat, as they do for their young.

Black-backed (or **silver-backed**) **jackal**, the most common of Kenyan jackals are distinguished by the broad black band, similar to that of a German shepherd (Alsatian) dog, that runs along the back, and their white underbelly.

These resourceful animals hunt and scavenge, in packs of as many as thirty, on small antelope up to the size of a Thomson's gazelle.

The most elusive of the three, the **side-striped jackal**, gets its name from the indistinct light stripe along its flank.

Golden jackal are very adaptable to changing circumstances and environment, and have been found living close to villages, large towns, and even in the suburbs of Nairobi, where they scavenge on garbage dumps at night.

The **bat-eared fox**'s enormous ears provide acutely-tuned antennae for picking up the location of the insects on which it feeds, and also help in defence. Ever alert, its ears twitch left or right only to be flattened close against the side of its face when danger threatens.

Bat-eared foxes are active at night and spend the day drowsing outside the burrow. They mate for life and are the only one of the seven African foxes to be found in Kenya.

Although dog-like in appearance and behaviour — males cock their legs to urinate — **hyena** are probably more closely related to the mongoose. For many years they were considered scavengers, but they are, in fact, ruthless killers.

Spotted hyena hunt in packs of up to thirty. Their range of prey is varied and their appetite indiscriminate. They cut down wildebeest, zebra, and gazelle at speeds of up to sixty-four kilometres (40 miles) an hour.

These voracious killers follow pregnant female prey, snatching their new-born as they are delivered. Strong teeth and powerful jaws allow hyena to crack bones easily to suck out what is, to them, the delectable marrow. Given the opportunity, spotted hyena attack humans and, not infrequently, their own kind.

The **aardwolf**'s sandy-brown coat, marked by dark vertical stripes, makes it look like a more elegant miniature of the striped hyena, to which it may be distantly related. Some experts think the aardwolf is a unique species, but others suggest it is a form of hyena which, through a changing diet over the centuries, has degenerated into a family by itself.

Baboons and Monkeys

Unlike most other primates, Kenya's two species of baboon display many canine characteristics including barking, walking on all four limbs, and carnivorous habits.

The larger **olive baboon**, the most common, is found everywhere in Kenya except the east where the **yellow baboon**, smaller in height, is dominant.

They cover up to eighteen kilometres (10 miles) a day in a constant search for food — shoots, roots, seeds, bushes, flowers, insects, and an occasional kill. They prey on timid mammals — hares and young gazelle — whose defence is to "freeze" to the ground. They also snatch up fledgling birds.

Baboon normally use trees only to escape danger and to sleep. They are extremely social, living in well-organised groups, known as troops, that average between forty and eighty animals.

Each troop is permanent, ruled by a dominant male which assumes authority by force. When it becomes senile, a younger leader usurps its place in a vicious battle for power.

Baboon are fierce fighters and predators regard them with respect. They are well-equipped for defence, with acute hearing and eyesight allied to extremely effective teeth. They often inflict severe, sometimes fatal, wounds on their enemy.

Colobus

Black and white colobus monkeys differ from most other monkeys in two respects. They have no thumb and only four digits on either hand, and they spend virtually their entire lives above ground, in the highest levels of the forest.

Rarely, if ever, do they come down to earth. Few creatures can equal their climbing ability or their leap — as much as thirty metres (100 feet). They differ, too, from most other monkeys in their capacity to remain silent, often for hours on end.

Colobus live in troops of up to twenty-five animals made up of several family groups.

Vervet

Vervet are the guenon group of tree-dwelling, daytime monkeys confined to tropical forest. The one exception is **black-faced vervet** (or green) monkey which lives down on the savannah.

The only monkey of its kind, they use the gallery forests and thick bush for refuge and sleep, but forage widely on open ground, often over long distances of up to 400-500 metres (1,310-1,640 feet), in troops of between six to twenty, although groups of up to l00 have been observed.

Vervets have acute vision and excellent hearing but a poor sense of smell. They communicate with a wide range of facial expressions, lowering their eyebrows, raising and jerking their heads, and make threatening gestures with bared teeth and wide open mouth.

Patas

The **patas monkey**, also known as the red hussar, is the only primate that does not mix with other monkeys. Large, tall and long-legged, it lives almost exclusively on the ground and can stand fully erect and walk on its hind legs.

The patas weighs up to ten kilos (22 lbs) and is known as the "greyhound of the apes". They have been clocked at fifty-six kilometres (35 miles) an hour. Patas use trees and termite hills as vantage points.

Sykes

Sykes monkey have a distinct white throat and chest patch, although they are members of the blue monkey races which are larger and rather stout. They hold their thick long tails, with a slightly curved tip, higher than the body when walking.

Sykes have narrow, elongated purplish-black faces, no beards, but dense, bristly tufts of hair on their foreheads, earning them also the name of "diadem". Moving their black legs in a distinctive, gentle, trotting gait, these monkeys are found wherever there are forests.

Sykes are related to the extremely-rare and beautiful **golden monkey**, distinguished by its greenish-gold back merging to orange on its flanks. Golden monkeys live in limited numbers in isolated pockets of western Kenya.

Above: Rare mandarin-faced de Brazza monkey, found in Saiwa Swamp National Park.

Bushbaby

The **lesser galago** is a nocturnal primate better known as the **bushbaby**. This endearing creature is small, slimly-built with thick, woolly fur, and has a conspicuous white stripe down its nose. Widespread — and common — throughout Kenya they hide in coastal bush, acacia woodlands, and forests.

Bushbabies are well-adapted to life in the trees. Their tail acts as a counterweight and they use their hind legs for grasping branches before leaping from one to another. They sometimes come down to the ground where they walk upright or in a crouch. They can jump an incredible three metres (10 feet) on their extremely powerful, kangaroo-like hind legs.

Zebra

The zebra's vivid and eye-catching stripes are unique. No two animals are alike. Just as a fingerprint distinguishes one human from another, so the zebra's stripes mark each creature as a distinct individual.

Of the two species, **Grevy's zebra** are considered the more beautiful. Larger, heavier and taller than the common (or **Burchell's**) **zebra**, its stripes are more numerous and much narrower, in black or dark brown on a cream white background. Burchell's zebra is smaller, more like a pony, with fewer, broader stripes, especially on the rump and hind-quarters.

Zebra stallions fight ferociously for mates and dominance. These clashes are spectacular affairs with rival stallions rearing and plunging, lashing out with both hind and forelegs, and neck wrestling. Occasionally, they will suddenly go down on their forelegs and slash savagely at each other's neck with bared teeth.

The Antelopes

Eland are the heavyweights of Kenya's fragile pastures and weigh close to a tonne. But they can leap, virtually from standing position, to a height of more than two metres (six and a half feet).

Between 170 and 180 centimetres (five and a half-six feet) at the shoulder, they are the largest of Kenya's antelope. Their large, twisted horns average around eighty centimetres (two and a half feet) long — the record length being more than one metre (three feet). These horns are important for feeding.

Above: Wildebeest and zebra on the annual migration from Serengeti to Maasai Mara.

To collect twigs, they grasp them between their two horn pedicles (or stalks), breaking them loose with a shake of their head and powerful neck.

Kudu

Weighing between 280 and 320 kilos (600-700 lbs), **greater kudu** can easily clear two metres (six and a half feet) at a jump despite their impressive weight.

Distinguished by what are among the most magnificent horns in the antelope kingdom, their spiral antlers average around 130 centimetres (over four feet) long, with the record length a fraction under 180 centimetres.

Their acute hearing is accentuated by their ability to turn their large rounded ears in almost any direction. These large, slender, and elegant antelopes, grey in colour with six to eight prominent vertical white stripes on either flank, raise their tail when alarmed — the white underside serving as a warning.

The **lesser kudu,** a smaller, more graceful version of the greater, displays more stripes — between eleven and fifteen — down the flank. They prefer much drier country and can go without water for a long time.

Bongo

The **bongo** is the largest of Kenya's forest antelopes, with twelve to fourteen vertical white stripes — fewer than its west African counterpart — down the flanks of its bright chestnut coat. With age, the coat darkens.

Unwilling jumpers, bongo are shy and easily disturbed. They live in pairs and groups of up to thirty to thirty-five, but old bulls leave the herd to live out the end of their twelve- to fourteen-year life span alone.

Sitatunga

The **sitatunga**, or **marshbuck,** is unique among antelopes and is easily distinguished. It has evolved two-toed, elongated hooves on either foot that spread widely to dissipate its weight, which enables it to move about on mats of floating weeds, and appear to walk on water.

When alarmed, they bark and sink into the water until only the tip of their nostrils shows. Sitatunga swim adeptly.

The only place they can be seen in Kenya is in the tiny Saiwa Swamp National Park (See "North-west Kenya: enchanted mountains, unspoilt vistas", Part Two).

Above: Bongo, a rare nocturnal mountain antelope

Waterbuck

Waterbuck have scent glands that give off an unpleasant musky smell so powerful that, long after they have left, it serves as a tell-tale indication of their previous presence.

Their majestic horns are unmistakable. Around an average of seventy centimetres (little more than two feet) long, the record length is a fraction over one metre (three feet). With a short, glossy, brown to greyish-brown coat, the **common waterbuck** is distinct from the **Defassa waterbuck**, by the white crescent across its rump — the Defassa having pure white buttocks.

Oryx

Oryx wield their long horns with dexterity in the savage cut and thrust of the wild, often impaling their victims with such force that the horns pass through the body. These horns average about seventy centimetres (just over two feet), with a record length of more than a metre (three feet).

Some experts suggest that the oryx's distinctive black and white facial markings serve as a warning to predators.

Beisa oryx are found north of the Tana.

Fringe-eared oryx, marked by the distinctive tassel on the end of their ears, and heavier and darker brown coats, are found south of the Tana.

Topi

The **topi,** familiar sentinel in Kenya's Maasai Mara, is prime flesh for all the predators which follow the migration. Large and robust, the topi's shoulders are noticeably higher than their rump, giving them the familiar hartebeest look.

An overall reddish-brown to purplish-red colour, they have distinct dark patches on their face, upper forehead, legs, hips, and thighs.

Jousting males, each of which has its own territory, drop to their knees and clash horns. Rutting males mark out their territory with dung heaps and by rubbing facial and foot glands on the ground. They then take guard on the nearest high ground, usually an old termite mound.

Topi are found in the Mara, north of the Tana River, and east of Lake Turkana. The related species, **tiang**, live on Lake Turkana's north-westernmost shores.

Hartebeest

Much topi behaviour also characterizes the **hartebeest.** Males keep watch from knolls or high ground after defining their territory and winning the courtship battle for a harem.

But for a good part of their twelve to fifteen years, hartebeest bulls are celibate. The losers form bachelor herds but old bulls are cast out to live a solitary existence until they die.

The most common, **Coke's hartebeest,** is around 120 centimetres (four feet) high at the shoulder, and weighs between sixty-two and ninety kilos (132-198 lbs). **Jackson's hartebeest** are larger, and **Hunter's** smaller. Hunter's are unmistakable because of the shape of their horns and the white chevron between their eyes.

Coke's are widespread in southern Kenya; Jackson's are found only in the extreme north-west; and Hunter's occur between the Tana River and Somalia. One small group has been translocated to Tsavo National Park.

Wildebeest

The **wildebeest** is the star of the world's greatest animal spectacular — the annual migration from Serengeti to the Maasai Mara.

More than a million of these strange-looking creatures are joined by zebra and topi to march from the lush grasslands of southern Serengeti to the northernmost corner of the Mara's rolling grasslands.

Thousands swarm into the swollen rivers behind their leaders in such numbers that many hundreds die. Their bloated carcasses sustain abundant numbers of crocodile.

On the hoof, wildebeest move in a single-file formation that is unique among plains game. They provide a veritable banquet for predators which grow fat on the abundant pickings of the migration. Not surprisingly. With a weight of between 160 and 220 kilos (350-720 lbs), the wildebeest is a meal on its own (See "Southern Kenya: theatres of the wild", Part Two).

Roan

Roan antelope are the third-largest of Kenya's antelopes and aggressive animals, with weapons to match. The male's horns, on average, are seventy centimetres (just over two feet) long.

The roan depends almost entirely on grass throughout its fifteen-year life span, living in herds of up to twenty. Rutting males joust with rivals by going down on their knees and making sweeping movements of the horns. In Kenya they are found only on the shores of Lake Victoria at Lambwe Valley, and in the trans-Mara region.

In the Shimba Hills are Kenya's only remaining **sable antelope**, similar to the roan but slightly smaller. The sable is one of the most beautiful of large antelopes: the male's satin-like coat appears almost pure black, the female's dark reddish-brown.

Gazelles

Both grazers and browsers, **Grant's gazelles** can endure extreme heat and go without water for long periods during their ten to twelve years of life.

Moving about throughout most of an active day, rarely seeking shade, they form herds varying in size from six to thirty, usually with a male in charge of a harem of about a dozen does. Their call is an alarmed grunt or bleat.

Thomson's gazelles are their smaller look-alikes and they are often found together on the Maasai plains. The only certain way of telling them apart is that the white on the buttocks reaches above the tail in the Grant's and in the Thomson's it ends below the root of the tail.

Their short stumpy tails rotating in perpetual motion, Thomson's gazelles are flesh for almost every predator. They have no alarm call: instead, they signal danger by rippling or flexing the muscles in their flanks.

They can leap incredibly high in a stiff-legged, standing-still jump known as "stotting" or "pronking".

Impala

Emblem of the East African Wildlife Society, the **impala** is also food for almost every large predator, yet it continues to maintain itself in large populations.

One reason is its habit of breaking into prodigious leaps when threatened. In a series of spectacular soaring bounds, it leaps over obstacles up to three metres (10 feet) above the ground or jumps ditches up to ten metres (33 feet) wide. Changing direction upon each landing, their zigzag course disconcerts any predator.

Bushbuck

The **bushbuck's** dappled white markings are

Above: Python swallows a young gazelle

a perfect example of natural camouflage. Blending into rock and bush, this shy, mainly nocturnal creature of forest and thicket flits elusively in and out of cover. Bushbuck need this camouflage to avoid their principal enemy, the leopard.

When cornered or wounded they defend themselves and their young with considerable courage. Their short bushy tails are white underneath. Raised on the run, this serves as a warning beacon for others.

Reedbuck

The **bohor reedbuck** is an elusive antelope, shy and easily startled, which is normally seen at sunup and sundown.

During the day these small, graceful antelope lie up in reed beds or tall grasses, shaping the stems around them into a shelter. Alarmed, they squat down on the ground, only bolting at the last moment. They run with a peculiar gait — like animated rocking horses suddenly brought to life. Reedbuck are hunted by all the large predators.

The bohor reedbuck is widespread in southern Kenya, west of the Tana River.

The similar but slightly larger **Chanler's mountain reedbuck** is found in central and western Kenya on open, grass slopes up to 4,000 metres (13,125 feet).

Dik-dik

The **dik-dik** is a gentle, greyish fawn which darts through the thickets in shy and elusive flight around twilight. They live in pairs, or occasional family groups, and establish middens, up to a metre (three feet) in diameter to mark the boundaries of their territory.

Kirk's dik-diks have hindquarters taller than their front shoulders and long, thin legs and a sloping back. They look permanently startled.

In flight, they run in a series of zig-zag bounds. Their alarm call is a shrill whistle, a bit like a bird call — or a zik-zik cry — hence their name. **Guenther's long-snouted dik-dik** is found in northern Kenya.

Klipspringer

The **klipspringer** measures around fifty to fifty-five centimetres (one and a half-two feet) high from hoof to shoulder, and weighs between eleven and eighteen kilos (25-40 lbs). It is a phenomenal jumper.

It bounces on the tips of its rubbery hooves as it walks, and this tip-toe effect

Below: Kirk's dik-dik.

Above: Gerenuk, the giraffe-necked gazelle.

makes its exceptionally strong legs look even longer.

Unlike the coat of any other African antelope, the klipspringer's olive-yellow coat, speckled with grey, is stiff and brittle, serving as a cushion to ward off the shocks of hitting rock walls when they jump.

Living only in rocky hills, klipspringer, like most other antelope, mark their territories with a secretion from their scent glands.

Oribi

The **oribi** is another of Kenya's beautiful small antelopes, with a long slender neck and silky coat, varying from pale fawn grey to bright reddish-brown.

Oribi live in pairs or small parties and, when alarmed, give loud shrill whistles or sneezes. They leap straight up in the air in a stiff-legged, standing-still jump before bounding off. Some experts suggest they do this to scan a larger area of bush for signs of predators.

Steinbok

Steinbok (or Steenbok) often elude their predators by suddenly darting down an old aardvark burrow in which, in more placid times, the females may also raise their young.

Living alone, pairing only during the mating season, steinbok avoid hilly country and are often found in sand dunes along the Kenya Coast.

Gerenuk

In the Somali language **Gerenuk** means "giraffe-necked". This unique antelope's neck has evolved through the milleniums to become longer, making it easier for the gerenuk to feed. It has also learned to use its rear legs for standing so as to reach the lush leaves higher up on acacia thorns and the other desert shrubs on which it survives.

These elegant creatures are fascinating to watch in motion. Extremely swift, they bring their long necks down in line with their slender backs making them suddenly appear to have shrunk to about half their height.

Gerenuks were only "discovered" as a species in 1878.

Suni

Suni, a forest antelope, are only thirty centimetres (one foot) tall and eight kilos (18 lbs) in weight. They are rarely seen and move mostly at sunup and sundown.

But suni leave one tell-tale clue to their presence — a strong, musky scent which lingers, like that of the waterbuck, long after it has left a location. Their specific Latin name, *moschatus*, derives from the large gland below their eyes which gives off the pungent odour.

Duiker

The bush (or grey) **duiker** stands around sixty centimetres (two feet) from hoof to shoulder and weighs between eleven and thirteen kilos (25-29 lbs). They are widespread throughout the country, though there are many local variations in the size of body, horns, colour, and thickness of the coat. In mountain regions this is unusually shaggy.

Mountain duiker, the only duiker found in open range, are the most universal. They live from sea level desert to snowline, although almost never in bamboo or dense forest.

They are also the most adaptable of the duiker and have survived where others have become extinct. They are often found on farms — even in small vegetable gardens.

Forest duikers are red in colour and move in a characteristically hunched posture, with their head close to the ground. This enables them to move more easily through thick and often tangled undergrowth, using their regular, well-marked trails and passages.

When alarmed, all duiker plunge into thick cover. Their name, given them by the early Afrikaans settlers in Africa, is Dutch — meaning "diver".

Below: Red-headed agana with striped sand snake.

Above: Chameleon, cleverest of nature's camouflage artists.

Left: Klipspringer, tiny antelope of rocks and cliffs.

319

Birdlife: An Avian Spectacle without Equal

Of the world's estimated 8,600 bird species, Africa south of the Sahara can boast about 1,750, of which East Africa can claim 1,294, and Kenya 1,054 species, making Kenya the greatest country in Africa for bird watching.

Indeed, the number of bird species is surpassed only in the Latin American countries of Columbia, Venezuela, and Peru, where most of the forest birds are not easily seen.

Birdwatchers in Kenya stand a good chance of seeing at least sixty per cent of all African avifauna — within a tiny radius of Nairobi more than fifty per cent of Kenya's birds have been recorded. To see more than 100 species in a day is quite common.

With its vast deserts, rolling grasslands, massive mountains, and tropical coast Kenya encompasses many habitats which serve as home or resting place to great numbers of endemic and migrant species.

Waterbirds

Kenya's Rift Valley lakes support an immense number of waterbirds and many other species abound in the grasslands and acacia woodlands that surround them.

Apart from Baringo and Naivasha, all the Rift Valley lakes are alkaline because of the intense volcanic activity of the last twenty million years. Lake Magadi has the greatest concentration of salts.

Except for algae, no vegetation grows on these alkaline lakes. But freshwater Naivasha and Baringo encourage a proliferation of waterplants and fish, some close inshore, supporting a large number of fish-eating birds. Another freshwater lake in Kenya besides Naivasha and Baringo is the shallow Lake Jipe along the south-eastern border with Tanzania. Also there are the swamplands of Amboseli National Park and Mzima Springs.

Freshwater Lakes

More than 400 species — greater than the total bird species of the British Isles — have been recorded at freshwater Lake Naivasha alone.

Here, you are likely to see Kenya's two species of cormorant. The **greater cormorant**, is black with white on the foreneck and breast: the **long-tailed cormorant**, also black, usually rests on rocks or tree trunks in the water, wings outstretched.

Cormorant dive and swim beneath the water for their prey, bringing it to the surface where it is tossed in the air, caught, and swallowed. After this, when perched, they stretch out their wings to dry out in the sun.

The **African darter** behaves in a similar fashion, but it's distinguished by its much longer neck which assumes an S-shape at rest. This neck enables the bird to dart its bill forward, rather like an arrow, and pierce the fish.

Other large waterbirds readily visible, either standing at the water's edge or wading in the shallows waiting to catch fish, are different species of **heron**, **ibis**, and **stork**.

The most outstanding, the **Goliath heron**, largest of all herons. You can tell the smaller **black-headed heron**, which also feeds onshore off insects and rats, by its grey, white and black colour.

Even smaller is the thickset, biscuit-coloured **squacco heron** whose wings turn white during the breeding season. When searching for food, this characteristically stealthy heron stands stock still, neck held back as it waits for prey to come within distance, then strikes in a flash.

You may see some herons moving their head from side to side when fishing. This enables them to get a proper fix on the target before they strike.

Ibises are readily identified by their downcurved bills. The loud shriek of the **hadada ibis** can be heard just around sundown and sunup — and during bright, moonlit nights. This sociable bird has olive-brown feathers with bright metallic-green reflections.

The **sacred ibis** is seen more frequently. Flocks of them often gather on waste ground in Nairobi, at the lakes, and in lagoons and estuaries at the coast. They are easily identified by their white feathers, bare black head and neck, and long downcurved bill.

Ducks and Geese

The freshwater lakes also play host to a great many ducks, some resident, others migrant, of many different sizes. Because their flight feathers all moult at once, ducks and geese are unable to fly for some weeks after the breeding season, making them extremely vulnerable to predators.

The biggest, a tree duck, is known somewhat misleadingly as the **spurwing goose**. It has a dark-red bill, glossy metallic black upper parts, and white belly.

The much smaller, white-faced **whistling duck**, also a tree duck, has a distinctive clear whistling call and is easily identified by its white face, reddish plumage, and barred flanks.

Of the geese, the **Egyptian goose**, with its predominantly brown plumage, white shoulders, and honking call is very common in Kenya and easily recognized.

Although of similar size, the **knob-billed** goose is almost silent. Readily identifiable by its black and white plumage, during the breeding season the male develops a distinctive knob at the base of its bill.

One of the most beautiful of the large African birds, and the national symbol of Uganda, the **crowned crane**, with its straw-coloured crest and black crown, is also one of the most distinctive.

The **hammerkop**, which has a wide range in tropical Africa, is the only member of its family in Kenya. It has a conspicuously long, backward-pointing crest, resembling a hammer, hence its name.

The hammerkop's nest is an astonishing work of sticks and vegetation, lined with mud or dung, usually balanced in the fork of a tree near a river or swamp. Between ninety centimetres and one metre in diameter (two and a half-three feet) it has a side entrance leading to an enclosed chamber.

Hammerkop will return to the old nest and add to it year after year until eventually it collapses under its own weight. Hammerkop feed off frogs and tadpoles, caught sometimes from the back of a hippopotamus.

Birds of prey

Three birds of prey are common on the Rift lake shores. The **fish eagle**, with its striking white head, chest, back and tail, chestnut belly, and black wings is the most frequently seen, usually perched on the limb of some tall tree on the shoreline.

Fish eagles leave this perch with astonishing suddenness to swoop down to the surface where their talons grasp the wriggling prey with consummate ease. Their echoing, haunting cry is one of the most dramatic and familiar bird sounds in Kenya. Fish eagles are found wherever there is water.

Also seen close inshore as it darts and flashes among the reeds and papyrus, the diminutive **malachite kingfisher**, lives extensively off Naivasha's abundant tree frogs and fish.

Its exquisite colouring — cobalt-blue crown barred with black, bright ultramarine blue on the back, with reddish underparts — is glittering contrast to the black-and-white pied kingfisher often seen in characteristic hovering flight over creeks and estuaries.

Immediately its prey is spotted, the **pied kingfisher** plunges blindly into the water, eyes closed, giving it a success ratio of about one-in-ten.

Top: Pied kingfisher.
Above: Abyssinian ground hornbill.

Kenya's waters attract many different gulls. The **grey-headed gull**, found almost exclusively on the lakes, is easily identified by its grey head, generally white and pale grey colours, and red bill and legs.

The **red-knobbed coot** is another familiar resident of Kenya's lakes. Its very plain, slate-black colour is distinguished by the red knob on its forehead. Feeding off plants just beneath the surface, they perform a valuable service for the ecosystem — keeping water free of weeds.

Another bird, the curious **African jacana** appears to walk on water because its widely-splayed feet and long legs enable it to walk and feed, on water-lilies and other water grasses.

Jacanas have diminished with the introduction of the beaver-like coypu which, with their voracious appetite, have all but destroyed Naivasha's water-lilies.

Alkaline lakes

Lake Nakuru is world-famous for its hordes of **lesser** and **greater flamingo**. Of the world's six and a half million flamingos, the lesser is most numerous. About four million live in the alkaline lakes of the East African Rift Valley — in Ethiopia, Kenya, and Tanzania.

Greater flamingo, outnumbered almost 100 to one, are readily distinguished by height. Males reach an impressive 180 centimetres (six feet), twice that of the lesser flamingo. In each species the female is smaller.

Both species are pink with red legs, webbed feet, a long sinuous neck and a unique bill, especially adapted for their food needs. The inside of the mouth serves as an efficient filter.

Lake Nakuru sustains both flamingos and substantial numbers of **white pelican**.

The white pelican, almost entirely white with black flight feathers, is often seen with the **pink-backed pelican**, distinguished by its smaller size, pale grey plumage, and head crest.

Besides pelicans and flamingos, a number of other attractive smaller species live at Nakuru, among them the **avocet**, easily recognized by its black and white plumage, long grey-blue legs, and upturned bill.

Left: Bateleur eagle – one of Kenya's great raptors.

Another black-and-white species, with a straight long bill, and extraordinary vermilion-red legs, is the **black-winged stilt**. It is the only other bird, apart from flamingo, whose legs are longer in proportion to its body. When breeding parents are disturbed they play a decoy — walking away from the nest, dragging an open wing on the ground as if injured.

Two species of stork are frequently seen on Kenya's lakes and waterways. The distinctive **yellow-billed stork**, with black and delicately-hued pink-white plumage, red legs, and downcurved orange bill, catches fish and frogs with astonishing speed as it stands in the water, its open bill half-submerged.

The ugly, unmistakable **marabou stork**, perhaps the most common in Africa and often associated with town tips because of its scavenging habits, hunts flamingo chicks by stampeding a flock and picking up stragglers.

Of the the migrant **waders** and **plovers** by far the most common is the **ruff**. Their breeding plumage is extremely spectacular and elegant but they are seen in Kenya in their rather dull, non-breeding colours.

The resident **blacksmith plover**, commonly found inland near water surrounded by short grass and muddy shores, has a distinctive black, white and grey plumage, and conspicuous white crown.

Normally silent, it becomes extremely noisy during breeding when it flies fearlessly at any enemy, uttering the characteristic metallic cry — like metal on metal — that gave it its name.

Coastal areas

European visitors find many migrant species difficult to identify because their summer, or breeding, plumage differs considerably. Identification is further complicated between April and May when some waders begin to change into their summer plumage ready for the flight back to their northern breeding grounds.

Although the **greenshank**, a sizable wader with a slightly upcurved bill, is common to all Kenya's wetlands, the largest numbers are found at the coast.

The **little stint**, the smallest of the wintering shorebirds, arrives from its breeding grounds in the USSR early in August after making its way along the eastern Mediterranean.

Running at breakneck speed as it feeds along the water's edge, the **sanderling**, a small, dumpy bird from eastern Greenland, Siberia, and Arctic America, always seems in a hurry.

Among the visiting birds, the **great white egret**, a member of the heron family, is readily distinguished from its close relatives, the **yellow-billed egret** and **little egret**, by its all-white plumage, all-black legs, and long black or yellow bill.

Another bird with all-white plumage, bare red legs and face, the **African spoonbill** takes its name from its long, spatulate bill.

With its large head and big yellow eyes, the **water thicknee**, an unusual looking bird with large eyes that help it to see at night, is widespread along the creeks and islands of the Kenya coast.

The bushy grassland hosts many **bee-eaters**, attractive, fearless birds with long bills and brilliant plumage, which hunt bees, wasps, hornets, and similar insects.

Back on the perch, the bee-eater knocks the insect briskly against a branch until the venom is discharged and the bee can be swallowed.

The **white-fronted bee-eater** is readily identified by its brilliantly-coloured plumage.

The **carmine bee-eater**, the most eye-catching with greenish and cobalt-blue head, neck and rump, breed in the Lake Turkana basin in the north and travel to the coastal lowlands between November and the end of March. They can be seen in their thousands roosting in the mangroves north of Mombasa, particularly at the inland edge of Kilifi Creek.

The **little bee-eater** in sharp contrast, is mostly green with a yellow throat.

Woodland birds

The **golden palm weaver** is another common bird found in trees, bushes and reeds, along coastal rivers or streams. Almost entirely yellow, this bird has a bright orange head and black eyes. Its look-alike, the **golden weaver**, has a chestnut head and pale red eyes.

The **secretary bird**, the sole member of its family, found only in Africa from sea level to 3,000 metres (10,000 feet), is usually seen in pairs. This terrestrial bird of prey stands almost one metre (three feet) high and has a wingspan of more than two metres (seven feet).

It's easily recognised by its grey and black

plumage, long legs with black "plus-fours", and a conspicuous crest which can be raised like a halo.

It spends most of its life strutting on the ground, looking for snakes, insects, and rats. It pounds the snakes to death with sledgehammer blows of its feet.

Perhaps the most frequently seen bird of prey in Kenya is the **augur buzzard** which chooses particularly high vantage points in the branches of tree, on top of high rocks, or even telegraph posts where it sits a long time scouting for prey.

As you drive through Kenya, you will see this bird — readily recognized by its slate-grey upper parts and generally entirely white underparts — on these high perches.

Not long ago the **helmeted guinea-fowl** could be seen in flocks numbering as many as 2,000. But in recent years they have been killed extensively for the pot. Perhaps their last stronghold is the Maasai area. Generally black, thickly-freckled all over with white, the bird sports a bony crest or horn on its crown.

Another game bird, the **yellow-necked spurfowl**, which frequents open bush country, is plentiful, particularly along the edges of forest and woodland. About the size of a domestic fowl, its most conspicuous feature is its yellow throat.

There are sixteen species of pigeon in Kenya of which the **speckled pigeon** is the largest. Extremely widespread, it is found between 500 and 3,000 metres (1,600-10,000 feet) in acacia woodlands, on cliffs, and sometimes around houses. With its brownish-back and wings, grey underparts, and marked "dominoes" round its eye, it's easy to identify.

Attractive birds

Kingfishers, hoopoes, bee-eaters, and hornbills are distant kin to the **rollers** which run kingfishers close for beauty.

Perhaps the most eye-catching of all, the **lilac-breasted roller** is tawny-brown on top, rich lilac on the throat and breast, with the remaining plumage various shades of bright- and greenish-blue. But the birds earned them their name from the brilliant aerobatics they perform when courting.

A large, unusual downcurved prominent bill with a large masque is the most noticeable feature of **hornbills**. When indigenous trees are in fruit in the thickly-wooded coastline, raucous brayings and grunts betray the presence of the **silvery-checked hornbill**.

The plumage of the largest member of the family, the **ground hornbill**, is generally black with a red face and throat in the male and usually blue in the female.

When breeding, the female **red-billed hornbill** finds a suitable hole or hollow in a tree and walls herself in with mud, dung, and saliva, regurgitated by the male. The female puts these into the entrance hole until the opening narrows to a slit and she cannot leave the nest. As she settles down to lay three to six eggs, the male feeds her through the opening.

Top: Saddlebill stork.
Above: Great white egret.

When the eggs hatch the male works hard to feed his vociferous and demanding family until the female grows new feathers and breaks out. By this time the young are still only half-grown.

The chicks repair the damaged exit by re-plastering as soon as the mother has left. Now both parents feed them until the young are ready to break out of the nest.

Woodpeckers

Among the woodpeckers, the **Nubian wood-pecker,** has short legs and strong feet. With these, and its stiff, wedge-shaped tail, it climbs trees easily. Its extraordinarily long tongue, coated with mucous is projected to catch ants, sap from trees, or to "spear" large insects. It uses its strong, chisel-like bill to drill into wood for larvae, and to excavate nest holes.

There is a large family of **flycatchers**. The male **paradise flycatcher**, with its glossy-black chest, neck and head, blue eye-ring and bill, and black flight feathers, is probably the most attractive. It is more common in its white phase, when the tail, back and wings are white, particularly along the coast.

It uses cobwebs to bind together and anchor its nest of twigs, grass, and lichen.

Although the blue-eared **glossy starling** is seen less often than the more common **superb starling**, it glitters with a metallic, iridescent-green sheen in bright sunshine. In other light, it sometimes seems bluish, violet, or even golden. The yellow-orange eye is characteristic.

Desert birds

Found in dry-bush and semi-desert country, the **pale chanting goshawk** was named for its melodious call — repeated hour on hour at the start of the breeding season.

The chant is also made on the wing when the pair soar together in circles.

Pale-grey, with bright reddish-orange legs, finely-barred belly and a white rump, the bird spends much of its time on the ground unlike other hawks.

Bustards, their strong legs adapted to life on the ground, are well-suited to desert life. The **kori bustard**, the biggest member of the family in Kenya, is easily identified by its size and broad wings. Though its flight is laboured, it is powerful and rapid.

The ornamental plumes of loose feathers on the head, nape, and long neck are used in remarkable breeding displays. When threatened they hide by crouching low. These birds are omnivorous.

The **spotted thicknee** — once known as the spotted stone curlew — is the dry country counterpart of the water thicknee, with the same large eyes.

Habitually watchful, thicknees spend the day standing or sitting still in shade where their cryptic appearance makes them virtually invisible. When approached they flatten themselves on the ground, head and neck outstretched.

Living in hot, arid lands and eating grain, **sandgrouse** need to drink at least once a day. The young must rely on the male parent which often flies up to eighty kilometres (50 miles) in search of water. It crouches down in the water and thoroughly soaks its belly feathers before the long journey back to the nest.

There it fluffs out its feathers as the chicks crouch beneath it and draw the water out of its plumage with their beaks. The belly feathers hold three times as much water as any other bird.

The **chestnut-bellied sandgrouse**, living in arid bush and plains, is the most common species in Kenya.

If you visit the dry country of the southern Rift Valley you may well hear a remarkable and unmistakable birdsong — the call of the **red** and **yellow barbet** whose song, in fact, is a duet, sometimes even a chorus.

During this performance, observed Sir Frederick Jackson, an early British administrator, the birds "seem to work themselves up into a great state of excitement and perform many curious antics".

One of the most photographed birds in Kenya, the **superb starling**, is notable for its metallic greenish-blue back, black head, and narrow white band across the breast separating the metallic-blue upper parts from the bright chestnut belly.

Another common family, the **weavers**, all share the ability to tie knots and build completely enclosed woven nests.

Taking a long piece of grass and placing at the tip of a branch, weavers hold one end down with a claw and use their beak to weave the other end in, out and over, until it forms a suspended ring.

With the bird in the middle of the ring, it fashions more and more strands, meticulously working each piece of grass, until a hollow ball is made.

Inhabiting wooded grassland below 1,400 metres (4,500 feet), the **white-headed buffalo weaver** is seen often. Its nest, an untidy structure hanging from the branch of a thorn tree, with an entrance from below, is made of thorn twigs for protection, and lined with grass or feathers.

The entrance to the elaborate hanging nest of the vitelline **masked weaver** is also at the bottom but it contains a partition to stop the eggs from falling out. And, as it is suspended from the end of a slim branch, its occupants are safe from monkeys, snakes, and other predators.

Other weavers build even more elaborate nests, with long vertical entrance tunnels hanging at the side. Other safely measures include building nests close to the hives of stinging insects, large birds, or even people.

The white-browed **sparrow weaver,** whose rather loose and untidy nests are seen on acacia trees, is extremely common in dry country.

Another member of the family, the **red-naped widowbird** male, in its striking breeding plumage, has an entirely black body with a scarlet crown and nape. The female is a nondescript tawny buff colour.

After breeding, the male loses its handsome tail feathers and scarlet colouring and you can no longer tell it from the female.

The female **Holub's golden weaver,** golden yellow in colour, is extremely demanding. The male may build as many as six large, rough and loosely woven nests, before she is satisfied — and sometimes she refuses all.

Quelea and **mousebird** are agricultural pests which destroy and damage grain and fruit. The **red-billed quelea**, a member of the weaver family, often found in flocks of more than a million, is a menace to small grain crops. But in spite of large-scale slaughter the plague continues.

The **speckled mousebird**, member of a small family peculiar to Africa, is no bigger than a sparrow, but its long tail, made up of ten stiff, graduated feathers, gives it an overall length of thirty centimetres (one foot). Its head is topped by a marked crest.

They have extremely strong feet with sharp claws and outer toes that move forwards or backwards, enabling them to climb easily and perch or cling in all kinds of positions.

Grassland birds

The majestic **ostrich**, measuring between two to three metres (six and a half-10 feet) high from the tip of its two-toed claw to the crest of its bald head, is the largest living bird but cannot fly. However, its strides of four metres (13 feet) are enough to leave all but the swiftest of hunters behind.

Ostrich can maintain speeds of fifty kilometres (30 miles) an hour for up to thirty minutes. On the run, however, they often vanish abruptly from view. They stop in full stride and drop suddenly into a squatting position, extending their neck along the ground.

In full stride they can bound up to a height of one and a half metres (five feet) and their lethal kick can bend an iron bar at right angles. They share the distinction of being a flightless, running bird with the South American rhea, and the emu and cassowaries of the antipodes.

Millions of years ago there were nine species of ostrich, but now only the African ostrich survives, characterized by its height, half of which is made up of its neck, and its two-toed foot, legs, and thighs.

Females are shabby brown with pale edgings to their feathers. Males are much more

Above: Ostrich.

dandy with vivid black and white plumes on the wings and tail. The adult male stands two and a half metres (eight feet) and weighs more than 130 kilos (300 lbs).

Eggs average fifteen to sixteen centimetres (six inches) long and weigh up to one and a half kilos (three lbs). One is equal to two or three dozen domestic eggs and tastes the same.

Chicks can run almost as soon as they hatch. After only a month — they grow like weeds at a rate of six to eight centimetres (one and a half-two inches) a week — they can reach a speed of fifty-five kilometres (35 miles) an hour.

Ostrich have tough gullets and voracious appetites and have been known to swallow coins, nails, horseshoes, and other metal objects. Reared from the young, they make faithful pets.

On the plains among the herds of wild or domestic animals flocks of large, white birds are a familiar sight. **Cattle egrets** are one of the few bird species which benefit from mankind. They prey on the insects disturbed by the movements of the herds.

Above: Secretary bird.

Vultures

Circling slowly, gliding on the rising thermals **vultures** remain aloft all day watching herds of animals and the movements of jackals and hyenas.

When a vulture sees a corpse it planes down swiftly and is soon joined by others. They can eat up to six kilos (13 lbs) of food at one sitting and become so bloated, they cannot take off. They find a secluded spot to rest until the meal is digested.

The largest African vulture, the **lappet-faced vulture**, with its massive bill and a pinkish bald head, is most frequently seen in the national parks. But the smaller **Ruppell's vulture** with its dark-brown plumage and creamy white edges that give it a spotted appearance, is much more common.

The **black-shouldered kite**, a member of the hawk family, is thickset, pale grey above and white below, with black shoulders, a short, white square tail and striking red eyes. This beautiful bird of prey hovers like a kestrel.

The **black kite**, one of the most familiar and obvious, is seen near human habitations in Kenya up to 3,000 metres (10,000 feet). It is readily recognizable by its dark brown plumage, yellow bill and markedly forked tail.

Plovers

Although most plovers are found near the sea, lakes, rivers, mudflats, and swamps, the **crowned plover** is a wanderer of grass bushlands up to 3,000 metres (10,000 feet) above sea level.

Notable for its black head with white ring on the crown, this handsome bird has a white abdomen, pale greyish-brown back, red legs, and red bill with a black tip.

But its nest, like that of all plovers, is built in a shallow, quite often unlined, indentation on the ground.

The chicks' marking is perfect camouflage. When warned by the parent they crouch down as the adult bird diverts attention by spreading one of its wings wide as if injured — a form of distraction display common among plovers.

Ground-living larks are usually softly-coloured but their exquisite song, serving as both courtship and territorial defence, more than compensates. They prefer open country and normally sing from a perch.

On the open grasslands in Kenya larks and

pipits predominate but although somewhat alike in appearance, the two are not closely related. The pipit family consists of graceful and slender birds, with an upright stance.

Rhinoceros, giraffe, zebra, buffalo, various antelope, even wart hog, and most domestic stock are visited by **oxpeckers**, known as tickbirds. These belong to the starling family.

The **red-billed oxpecker** walks about on buffalo like a woodpecker, its stiffened tail and sharp, curved claws, enabling it to move about with ease.

It feeds mainly on bloated ticks, but also flies, scar tissue, blood, living tissue, and the discharge from open wounds, making it unpopular with cattle breeders.

Garden birds

Strikingly beautiful, the unmistakable **hoopoe**'s main body plumage is bright pinkish-cinnamon with wings and tail having alternate black and white bars. The erectile crest feathers are pinkish with black tips, and the black bill has a slight downward curve.

Hoopoes nest in holes, either in trees, rocks, banks, or even buildings. Pairs are often seen on lawns hunting for large insects, larvae, worms, and lizards. Their monotonous call of "hoop, hoop, hoop" is low and penetrating.

Looking rather like thrushes to whom they are related, **babblers** keep up a continuous chatter as they move around on bushes or on the ground searching mainly for insects.

The **robin chat**, with its reddish-orange throat and chest, well-marked white eye-stripe, and a grey belly, is an excellent mimic of other birds and often gives a full concert repertoire. Its natural song seems to have territorial and advertising functions. Robin chats feed mainly on the ground and, although shy, can be relatively tame in gardens.

Chats are often parasitized by the **red-chested cuckoo**. The potential host is kept under close observation by the female cuckoo when building its nest. She sneaks in to lay her egg when the nest is unattended, sometimes removing one of the robin chat eggs.

The cuckoo egg hatches first and the chick's first instinct is to eject any other object in the nest. Either the eggs or the young of the robin chat are manoeuvred to the edge and pushed out, leaving the cuckoo chick in sole possession.

The host parents seem unconcerned and feed the large, demanding interloper until it leaves the nest. Even then, the foster parents continue to feed the growing cuckoo until it is independent.

Perhaps the most spectacular of Kenya's brilliantly-coloured starlings, with their metallic gloss, is the male **violet-backed starling**, which has white underparts and an iridescent purple back and head. In some light it appears plum-coloured, even crimson.

When the wild fig trees come into fruit, flocks of these starlings feast themselves for three to four days. When the fruit is gone the birds also disappear.

In many respects sunbirds are similar to humming birds but they are not related. Both groups have long curved beaks, brilliant plumage, and draw nectar from flowers which helps pollination.

Sunbirds are a distinct family of small birds, with slender, pointed, downcurved bills. In most species the male has brilliantly-coloured plumage, most of it with an iridescent metallic sheen. The females are generally drab.

The **waxbill** family of small to very small seed-eaters includes the **red-billed firefinch**, perhaps, the most familiar bird in Africa.

The female is dull brown with a tinge of red on the tail, but the male plumage is entirely pinkish-red with a few whitish spots on the breast.

The nest, with its side entrance, is an untidy ball of dry grass, lined with feathers and placed low down in bushes. The bird is known to be parasitized by the **purple indigobird**, a member of the parasitic division of the vast weaver family.

Flora: Forests of Flame, Streets of Mauve

Myriad and marvellous botanical glories adorn Kenya. To a great extent, from rare orchids to precious hardwood forests, the beauty of its flowers, shrubs, and trees characterizes the country.

After the rainy seasons flowers burst into riotous colour everywhere — even in semi-desert and desert regions.

And throughout the year, rivers in drier areas are lined with doum palms and large acacias; mountain foothills are clothed in majestic forests; and plains of the great game parks are dotted with baobab and thorn.

Besides trees, there are many saplings, shrubs, herbs, grasses, seedlings, ferns, mosses, orchids, lianas, fungi, and lichen (See "Mount Kenya", Part Two).

One general feature of Kenya's indigenous forests is the diversity of their tree species. Where forests in Europe and North America have no more than twenty-five species, Kenya's forests have no less than fifty and some a good deal more — the forest on Mount Elgon, for example, contains sixty-two tree species.

Other completely indigenous forests grow in vital watershed areas such as Mount Kenya, the Aberdares, Shimba Hills, Nandi Hills, the Mau Range, and Kakamega.

But although Kenya's indigenous baobab, fig, camphor, and high-altitude hagenia, among others, create unique woodlands they can take up to 200 years to mature.

Consequently, many logged areas have been replanted with faster-growing exotics, some from as far away as Australia or South America.

Kenya's forests can be divided into several categories. The lowland forests are small patches, mainly confined to local hill ranges, such as the Taita Hills and Mount Kasigau.

Set less than 330 metres (1,080 feet) above sea level, these patches consist of mixed evergreen forest with much *afzelia* and *trachylobium*, and *brachylaena* in drier areas.

Higher up, between 800 and 1,600 metres (2,625-5,250 feet) above sea level there are *ocotea* and *Newtonia buchananii*.

Upland forests are predominant in Kenya, beginning with plateaux forests that lie between 1,300 and 2,000 metres (4,265-6,560 feet) in places where the annual rainfall is 875-1,000 millimetres (34-40 inches), such as Nairobi, Ngong, Nyeri, and Kiambu. Here, where the climate is equable and cool, and mixed evergreen forests of *brachylaena* and *croton* flourish.

Above 2,000 metres (6,560 feet) on Mount Kenya, Mount Elgon, the Aberdares, the Kikuyu-Laikipia Escarpment, and the Mau-Elgeyo-Cherangani mountain ranges, mixed evergreen forests are of *ocotea*, *juniperus*, *hagenia*, and bamboo.

Along the coast, particularly in the sheltered estuaries of Mida Creek and the Tana River, and on the leeward side of the Lamu Archipelago, mangrove swamp forests flourish. These have great commercial value since mangrove timber is used for building poles, charcoal, and leather tanning.

Mangrove swamps also play a critical ecological role in filtering the organically-rich material carried down to the sea by rivers, and serve as an important breeding ground for various forms of marine life.

In Kenya's exotic, non-indigenous forest plantations, **conifers** are cropped for paper manufacture, furniture, packaging, and particle and building board.

The non-indigenous hardwood **eucalypts** are cropped for building and woodfuel. None of these forests have as much diversity of species as the indigenous forests, nor are they as rich in fauna.

Finally, there is the ubiquitous **coconut** whose original home is a mystery. Some authorities consider it to be Polynesia, while other maintain that the first nut came from South America and then journeyed westwards thousands of years ago, drifting in ocean currents across the Pacific to reach the shores of Africa.

The coconut palm furnishes almost everything that man needs for survival and shelter — food and drink through its nut, while husk fibres make ropes and mats and are used to stuff mattresses. The nut shell is turned into charcoal. The leaves are used to thatch houses or woven into baskets and mats. And the trunk is used to build houses.

The major economic product is dried nut flesh, copra. It is processed to yield coconut oil for cooking, and coconut meal, a valuable high-protein livestock food.

The indigenous **doum palm** is the only member of its family which grows branches. Its long slender stems divide regularly into two, giving the tree its distinctive appearance. It often grows to a height of more than fifteen metres (50 feet).

The three-cornered orange-brown fruit have edible skin, but are not very tasty. Elephants often eat them and consequently disperse its seeds far and wide in their dung. Traditionally, the fruit is used to make buttons and necklaces and the leaves for weaving baskets and mats.

Wild **date palms** are also widespread throughout Kenya, particularly in hot, dry areas alongside streams and swamps where there is a high water table.

Although edible, its fruit is disappointing to taste and the commercially-cultivated variety has a bigger, fleshier, and more tasty fruit.

Date palms have served as a staple for the people of the Middle East and North African deserts for many centuries. Arab traders introduced the tree to Kenya long ago but although it has great potential as a food in Kenya's dry marginal northern areas, it has been little exploited. However, its leaves are used for basketwork and making sleeping mats.

The exotic **golden wattle**, a member of the acacia family, was introduced from Australia. It is widespread in Kenya and has light, greyish-green foliage and beautiful yellow flowers.

But exotic acacias apart, Kenya boasts more than forty indigenous species, including flat-topped **red thorn acacia**, which grows in many parts of the Great Rift Valley and in other areas.

Its extremely heavy and durable hardwood is used for building bridges, as fence posts, pulley blocks, and rough farm buildings.

One of the most beautiful of Kenya's acacias, found besides streams and lakes throughout the Rift, is the distinctive **fever tree**. With its widespread, flat-topped crown and yellow bark, the tree is easily recognised.

Early travellers who camped in its shade linked the tree with their bouts of malaria and gave it its common name.

Acacia trees serve many functions. They are used to feed goats, and as fencing posts and fuel. Where they grow on river banks, they anchor the soil: where they drop their nutrient-rich leaves at the beginning of the

rainy season, they add nitrogen to the ground.

Acacia hardwood timber is also a lasting building material and is used for carving. It also supplies the leather industry with tannin. One species yields a high-quality gum used in industry.

The **baobab**, with its "upside-down" look, central to many African legends and superstitions, is revered. The rotund, glossy trunk sprouts a crown of thick branches which look more like roots since they are bare of leaves for most of the dry season. Found in many parts of Kenya less than 1,300 metres (4,000 feet) above sea level, baobabs which grow to a diameter of between five and seven metres (15-20 feet), and not much more than that in height, live for many centuries.

The tree is a ubiquitous gift of nature. Its hollowed-out trunk can store water or be split lengthways to make canoes. Bark fibres are twisted into ropes and baskets. Leaves and fruit-pulp are used medicinally and the seeds and leaves are edible.

Above: White and pale yellow-flowered frangipani — the scent of angels.

The attractive **camel's foot tree** takes its name from its two-lobed foliage which bears some resemblance to a camel's hoof. A native of Asia, its many branches are adorned with fragile, delicate-pink flowers, strikingly like some orchids. It is also known as the orchid tree.

Glorious **Australian flame trees** rise more than thirty-three metres (100 feet) high, and their crimson mass of blooms are visible for a considerable distance. However, it flowers all too rarely.

Native to Madagascar, the magnificent **flamboyant flame tree** was first discovered in 1824. Since then it has been introduced to tropical areas all over the world including Kenya where it thrives best at heights beneath 1,370 metres (4,500 feet), especially where it is warm and dry.

With its canopy of scarlet flowers, the flamboyant is truly well-named. Its blossoms cast a warm glow over Mombasa's streets and gardens.

One of the most memorable and striking of all Kenya trees is the **Nandi flame tree**, also known as the African tulip tree, spectacular when it blooms with large orange-red flowers fringed in gold.

Its buds are filled with water which spurts out if punctured, hence its other name, as "fountain tree".

In the West African jungle, where it was discovered in 1757, the tree was thought to possess supernatural powers. The flowers were used in voodoo ceremonies and the wood was made into tribal drums by witch doctors.

Another Australian exotic, the **bottlebrush**, owes its name to the beautiful red or white flowers that drape around its stem like a bottlebrush.

The pink blossoms of the **Cape chestnut** make it one of the most beautiful of Kenya's indigenous deciduous trees. It fills the mountain forest homelands with sweet-scented fragrance and vibrant colour and is also cultivated in many gardens and parks.

Introduced from tropical America, the fast-growing deciduous **cassia** readily took root in Kenya where its yellow blossoms warm the streets, parks, and gardens with their bright colour. It grows about nine metres (30 feet) high.

An exotic from Brazil, the **chorisia** or (floss-silk) tree, reaches close to fifteen metres (50 feet) and is often confused with its bombax lookalike. The seed of the fruit is protected by kapok, a cushion of fine cotton-like material used to stuff cushions, mattresses, and toys.

Its smooth, green trunk is covered with spines and its flowers, which vary in colour from vivid-red to pink, have five petals.

One of the more easily recognised of Kenya's native trees, even when it is not in bloom, is the **red-hot poker tree**, or the Kaffir Boom.

This attractive deciduous tree with its bright red upright lowers is extremely widespread in Kenya, and reaches a height of around fourteen metres (45 feet). Its red and black seeds were once used to weigh gold and jewellery.

Unlike other members of Australia's eucalyptus family, the **red flowering gum** does not grow to great heights but is much admired for the ornamental beauty of its pink and red flowers.

Another widespread member of the Australian eucalyptus family, the familiar **blue gum tree** which lines the streets of almost every town, can be recognised by its habit of continuously shedding bark from the trunk and branches.

Blue gums produce more firewood, at a faster rate, than any other tree in Kenya. Some reach heights of more than 100 metres (320 feet).

The delicate, bell-shaped flowers of the **jacaranda**, an exotic from Brazil, blossom sometime between September and November, when Nairobi and other Kenyan towns are strewn with a thick carpet of blue-violet petals.

The quick-growing, well-shaped, deciduous *Himalayan Prunus* (**bird cherry tree**), blossoms twice a year — at the beginning of the rainy season. Its delicate pink flowers can be seen in many gardens and residential streets.

The drooping branches of the **pepper tree** from Peru look like those of the weeping willow. Its round red-ripe berries hang in loose clusters. It produces a strong resin.

The **tipu** (Pride of Bolivia) is a, beautiful tree, with a splendid crown of light, small-leaved foliage, and plentiful clusters of yellow, pea-shaped flowers.

Opposite: Bougainvillaea — emblem of Kenya's gardens.

Shrubs

More than 200 species of *Acalypha* shrubs, flourish in Kenya. They have markedly varied foliage, ranging from deep-pink, red, brown, greenish-brown, to various shades of green. One species **copperleaf**, is a native of the South Sea Islands.

Despite its name and pretty pink flowers, the **desert rose**, (mock azalea), found in Kenya's semi-desert lands, is highly lethal. Its milky sap, a potent toxin, is used as arrow poison.

Yesterday, today and tomorrow takes its name from its dark purple-blue blossoms, which change to mauve, cream and white, as they age. An evergreen from Brazil, during the night it gives off one of nature's sweetest fragrances.

Candle bush, a wild indigenous shrub of grassland, scrub, and forest edge is most obvious along country roads during the flowering season. Its bright yellow flowers form dense clusters of upright spikes like candelabra.

The fast-growing, soft-wood shrub, **moonflower**, (devil's trumpet), bears large, trumpet-shaped, extremely sweet-scented white flowers. But the fragrance conceals the kiss of death: the flower of this common garden plant is extremely poisonous.

From Guatemala, **snow on the mountain** is reminiscent of a miniature poinsettia. Its tiny cream bracts, sometimes tinted rose, completely cover the one- to three-metre-high (three-10 feet) compact bushes and make an arresting sight.

As characteristic of tropical Christmas as is holly in northern latitudes, **poinsettia**, (Christmas star), is widely-used as decoration and on Christmas cards and calenders but in Kenya it only blooms during July.

A native of tropical America, the extremely beautiful rosette-shaped coloured bracts range from scarlet to pink to pale yellow but with insignificant flowers.

Hibiscus, (Chinese rose), from China, is probably the world's best-known tropical flower. Now widespread at the Kenya coast it produces a host of beautiful flowers of various colours, all with prominent yellow stamens and red stigmas — blooms that Hawaiian maidens weave into traditional garlands to greet visitors.

Although Kenya has a number of indigenous hibiscus species, the Chinese exotic occurs in many colours and forms, including double-headed flowers.

Christ thorn, (the crown of Thorns), imported from Madagascar, is perhaps the best-known member of the euphorbias. With its formidable thorns, it makes an excellent hedge that grows to about two metres (six feet) high. It can also be clipped back to edge flower-beds or allowed to grow into a large, attractive bush covered in red flowers.

Found particularly along the coast and in upcountry Kenya, the nostalgic fragrance of **frangipani** (the temple tree), makes it, perhaps, the loveliest of Kenya's exotic shrubs.

The shrub takes its name from the twelfth-century perfume developed from its flowers by the Italian nobleman, Frangipani. The white variety is a native of the West Indies. The pink-flowered frangipani comes from Central America.

The **bird of paradise** shrub from South Africa, also known as the crane flower, was endowed with both names because of the uncanny resemblance of its flowers to a bird's head. Once seen, it can never be forgotten.

A much-branched evergreen shrub from Columbia, the **fire bush**, carries a great profusion of bright orange-yellow flowers, hence its alternative name, oranges and lemons.

Cape honeysuckle, as its name suggests, originates from South Africa. In full sun and dry conditions, it produces wonderful orange-red spikes of flowers in terminal clusters.

Thevetia, (yellow oleander), from tropical America, has shiny, elongated leaves reminiscent of oleander. The attractive lemon-yellow blossoms, with their sweet, delicate fragrance, flower for most of the year. But the milky sap is dangerously poisonous.

Climbers

If any flower is symbolic of colourful Kenya, it has to be that of the **bougainvillaea**. Found everywhere, this thorny shrub climbs to the tops of the tallest trees by its long, spiny tendrils.

The scores of different forms and colours of commonly-cultivated bougainvillaea create a fantastic mosaic of colours, ranging from deep magenta-purple, through crimson and soft-pink, to brick-red and bronzy-gold, even white.

A native of Brazil, it was first brought to Europe by an eighteenth-century French navigator, Louis de Bouganville, who found specimens in Rio de Janeiro.

One of the most beautiful climbers, with large tresses of deep-violet flowers, is **petrea**, known as purple wreath. It, too is a native of Latin America.

Golden shower, perhaps the best-known of the begonia family, which grows freely and blooms in profusion in full sun is a native of Brazil, its gorgeous clusters of orange-coloured flowers catch the eye everywhere. Drought-resistant, it flowers most of the year.

Succulents

Aloes are African members of the lily family, and Kenya has many species which flower after the rains.

The sap of the spiny, sharp-pointed leaves has long been used to relieve burns, insect bites, and other inflammations. Today aloes are grown commercially for use in cosmetics, shampoos, and suntan lotions.

The **giant cactus** is a sturdy, tall-growing, branched species from South America. Its five- and seven-sided branches, covered in spines, develop large, whitish, trumpet-shaped flowers on their edges, which only blossom at night.

The **candelabra tree**, a succulent cactus-like euphorbia grows as high as fifteen metres (50 feet). From its relatively short, thick trunk a number of spiny branches spread in candelabra fashion. It is usually seen in savannah country, sometimes on a termite mound, and is extremely common in parts of the Rift Valley where Lake Nakuru National Park's euphorbia forest is one of the largest in Africa.

A plant which often reaches five metres (15 feet), the prickly pear is also a member of the cactus family. The "leaves", in fact, are really stems and branches: the real leaves have been transformed into spines and bristles.

Its yellow to orange flowers turn into pear-shaped fruits which, once the spines have been removed, are edible.

Another member of the African lily family and a native of southern Africa, the many tubular flowers of **Agapanthus** may be blue or white. It grows easily in most areas.

Feathery bamboo, a vigorous-growing bamboo, is used to make fences and scaffolding, and for a variety of other building purposes. Where there is enough rain it grows as high as fifteen metres (50 feet), with green stems. One handsome variety of this treelike grass from South America, known as **golden bamboo**, has yellow stems.

Many types of tropical American **canna** grow in Kenya and provide an infinite variety of strikingly-coloured flowers. Foliage may be tall or dwarf, green or bronze.

Epidendrum, an attractive and easily-grown orchid from South America, has erect, relatively thin, single, or few branched stems with numerous white aerial roots at the base. Many varieties with different-coloured flowers have been cultivated.

The **water-lily** family is well distributed in freshwater lakes and ponds throughout most of the world, including the tropics. The long stalks arising from the rootstock end in circular, oval, or heart-shaped blades which float on the surface of the water. The strikingly-lovely flowers, blue, yellow, or pink, rise above it.

Above: Euphorbia of the arid lands.

Tastes of Kenya: A Culinary Safari

It has been conjectured that a New Yorker, put on the traditional diet of a Samburu, Turkana, Kalenjin, or Maasai nomad would very soon die of an overdose of cholesterol. These pastoralists live almost exclusively off milk and meat. Unusually active, they often walk many miles every day and are exceptionally fit, so all this exercise, together with a salt-free regime, keeps heart disease at bay.

Most of Kenya's other, traditional diets are high in fibre, protein, iron, fructose, and complex carbohydrates. They're mainly vegetable-orientated, although the array of ethnic dishes reflects the country's culinary diversity.

Flavours range from the rather bland dishes from upcountry, through exotic recipes from Arabia and the subcontinent to those brought in from Europe.

Most Kenyans breakfast on sweet, milky tea and bread, followed by lunch and dinner of *sukuma wiki, irio, githeri, matoke,* or *ugali,* served with stew or roast meat.

Ugali is Kenya's equivalent of western bread, potatoes, or pasta. Together with potatoes, it is the basic food of many peoples and apart from milk, the only staple available in some poorer areas.

It is a thick "porridge" made from ground maize flour, and it's best to try it for the first time outside Nairobi where packet "instant" ugali is sometimes served instead of the real thing.

Kenyans eat ugali by rolling it into a small ball in their right hand and using this to scoop up the accompanying side dish of meat or fish stew or vegetables. It is also delicious with *maziwa lala* (a cross between yoghurt and sour cream) or gravy. Black or brown finger millet or cassava are sometimes used to make different, stickier versions of ugali.

Spinach

Sukuma wiki (kale) was introduced to Kenya by Europeans as cattle fodder. It was gradually adopted into ethnic diets by people throughout the country and now it is eaten everywhere. Less bitter than spinach, chopped fine and stir-fried with onions and tomatoes, it is particularly delicious.

There are two other common kinds of spinach: one introduced by immigrant Italians and the other, *mchicha,* native to Kenya. It has a chartreuse coloured leaf. Cooks often add a pinch of bicarbonate of soda to turn the leaves darker green.

Githeri, mataha, njahi, and *irio* are Kikuyu dishes that are served in ethnic restaurants and cafes nationwide.

Githeri is a simple red beans and maize mixture to which potatoes, carrots, spinach, tomatoes, onions and, occasionally, diced meat are added.

Mataha is *githeri* with potatoes and pumpkin leaves instead of spinach.

Njahi made with black beans is generally served only at celebrations, is is a beautiful pale, purplish-pink colour, often garnished with raw banana slices.

Irio, the most popular dish, is made with green peas soaked overnight, then cooked for two hours or more until tender. Fresh maize kernels and potatoes, sometimes sweet potatoes, are added and it is cooked again until the maize is soft. Then the mixture is sprinkled with salt and mashed together.

Irio is served with meat stew in gravy or tomato-based sauce. It is eaten in the same manner as *ugali,* though it is also delicious served cold the next day, cut into slices and dabbed with spicy mustard.

Irio can be any colour from pale green to pale lavender and has the double advantage of being filling, cheap — and nutritious.

Meat, fish and poultry are generally served as accompanying side dishes. How they're prepared depends on the people and the region.

Maasai nomads enjoy boiled goat soup flavoured with roots, with the meat eaten separately afterwards. Other people slaughter and roast or boil beef for celebrations, reserving certain portions for specific age and gender groups with the *mzee* (elders) usually receiving the choicest cuts.

The Luos eat boiled or roast beef and goat in tomato-based sauces.

Kikuyu are traditionally supposed to prefer stewed, boiled, or roast mutton and beef to poultry or fish, which are widely eaten elsewhere. They make a passable haggis and

Above: Some traditional Kenya dishes — githeri, irio, and others.

sausages of blood and intestines called *Mutura*. It's close to the black pudding enjoyed in Britain. They also enjoy sheep or goat brains and ox and sheep's tongue.

Chicken is a favourite among the highland peoples who serve it curried or cooked in oil, tomatoes, and onions.

Fish

Fish is most popular in coastal areas, where sea-perch, parrotfish, red snapper, kingfish, giant crayfish, jumbo prawns, crabs, oysters, and sailfish are cheap and readily available.

In the lake regions, Nile perch, tilapia, and trout are the main catches. Nile perch is a favourite throughout Kenya, mainly because its firm texture and mild taste make it a versatile ingredient in many recipes.

It can be roasted or baked in its skin over charcoal and served with vegetables. On the coast, the Swahili simmer it in lime juice and coconut milk with ginger, garlic, tomatoes, and onion.

Asians eat it with small hot rings of green pepper. And at Muthaiga Club in Nairobi, it is served smothered in seaweed and orange sauce.

Europeans often consider it most delicious of all when it is steamed and served with a few herbs and butter or with fresh slivers of green onion and ginger.

Thinly-cut, smoked sailfish, battered sea

337

Above: Harvest of the Indian ocean: choice fish and crustacea.

perch, trout, parrotfish, and tilapia are also popular.

Tilapia is often gutted, deboned, laid out like paper and left to dry in the sun. Dried Nile perch and *omena*, a tiny iridescent fish, are also sold to be rehydrated as fish stew with onions, spices, and other vegetables. Although they smell rather pungent, once soaked and cooked, these dried fish are quite palatable.

Dried foods apart, absolute freshness and simplicity of ingredients are the key to Kenyan cuisine.

Although the same ingredients are used, recipes vary from region to region; the Boran of Marsabit cook with curry; Somali people add *jira* (cumin), cardamom, cinnamon, cloves, and ginger; the coastal Swahili add coconut; the Luo around Lake Victoria prefer *dhania* (coriander) to eastern spices, and the Kikuyu, traditionally, do not use any herbs at all.

Most traditional dishes are mild, salt-free, and have a subtle blend of flavours. As ethnic groups move and resettle, however, and European and Asian influences continue to spread, so African tastes are slowly changing. Spices, peppers, wine, coconut, and other condiments are increasingly used and add a new range of flavours to the traditional Kenyan menu.

But traditions persist — even in urban areas. Most Kenyans come from rural back-grounds and many people still have a smallholding or well-tended vegetable garden that produces most of what they eat.

Even in Nairobi, *sukuma wiki*, *mchicha*, tomatoes, *dhania*, and some type of pumpkin are found in virtually every garden — often at the expense of flower beds and lawns.

Maize, the most popular crop of all, grows on every spare piece of land, not only in farms, but along the roadside, in the median strips of dual carriageways, and even in flower-pots.

Kenyans nibble fresh, charcoal-roasted corn much as westerners eat French fries or chips. Vendors can be seen roasting the maize ears on black stoves and, at the coast, they also fry hot cassava chips and boil strong coffee served in small cups without handles. These are Kenya's traditional "fast foods", sold in dusty lanes, along main thoroughfares, and in markets everywhere.

Fresh foodstuffs

Market days are colourful and noisy — a time to gossip, socialise, sell and buy foodstuffs not grown at home.

Most large towns have a central market, either indoor or out in the open. But these markets differ greatly in character between towns and regions.

At Oloitokitok, a small, busy trading town in the far south on Mount Kilimanjaro's north-eastern slopes near Tanzania, the market appears an almost perfect square of colour on the dusty landscape.

Informal, kanga-clad highland women are joined by nomadic Maasai women from the plains below who are festooned like Christmas trees, with beads circling their foreheads, wreathed around their necks, and hanging off their ears like tinsel.

On the ground, on brown burlap sacks, colourful stacks of tomatoes, carrots, potatoes, *sukuma wiki*, small hot green peppers, ginger root, and plump, purple eggplants, are laid out for inspection. Peanuts are hawked around by small children to be sold by the cupful, handful, or in small paper cones.

All this is vivid contrast to Lodwar market on the flat, white-hard desert sand of Turkana in the north-west of Kenya.

The dark, graceful Turkana women dress entirely in brown goat skins, relieved only by mounds of opaque red, green, blue, yellow, and black beads, whose effect is as muted as Loitokitok dress is vibrant.

But Lodwar market, the most exotic in Kenya, is cleverly organised and absolutely spotless. The central section is reserved for cattle sales and is the exclusive domain of men.

For its extensive display of fresh vegetables and fruit, Kisumu market is not easily forgotten. Lake Victoria spreads out beyond the town in the sparking sunshine, making Kisumu appear like a miniature San Francisco. In summer it is exceedingly hot and humid, but in the African winter the weather is mild and the large market is packed with an abundance of food.

Green or purple-black avocados, the size of small footballs, are ranged alongside pine-apples so sweet and non-fibrous they taste like candy.

Red onions are sold in fifteen-kilo (30-lb) sacks and garlic by the bunch. All manner of pumpkins and peppers are on display, to-gether with many varieties of rice, corn meal, flour, brown and finger millet, red beans, chick peas, and dried corn kernels.

Different again is Mombasa market whose sights and smells are flavoured by Indian and Arab spices, giving it the feel of a bazaar.

And largest of all is the City Market in Nairobi, where fresh dill, watercress, *dhania*, parsley, fennel, and basil are usually available.

Most produce is bought daily to market from nearby farms, especially pineapples, passion fruit, pawpaw, mangoes, melon, strawberries, and the ubiquitous bananas.

With some thirty varieties, bananas are always available. In season, these vary from tiny, sweet, "baby" bananas, through large yellow and green bananas, to fat red bananas with their distinctive tangy lemon flavour.

Bananas are used in both sweet and sa-voury dishes. In restaurants they're often sauteed in butter, honey, brandy or rum, or deep-fried in light batter, or served as condiments to fish or meat curries.

Even outside the markets, hawkers can often be seen along the roadside selling their surplus produce. In the central highlands, potatoes, cabbages, carrots, onions, oranges, pawpaw, and mangoes are particularly abundant.

Live chickens, rabbits, honey, plums, and pears can be bought on the escarpment road over the edge of the Rift Valley, only a few kilometres from Nairobi.

Many different varieties of potatoes, cassava, yams, and an array of peppers are widely grown. Other vegetables include radishes, Brussels sprouts, mushrooms, asparagus, cauliflowers, zucchini, and cucumber.

Sporting Kenya: Third World Superstars

For most people, the mention of Kenyan sport conjures up images of athletes powering their way to success at the Olympics, or all the drama and spectacle of the Safari Rally. But it would be a mistake to think that these are what Kenyan sport is all about.

With its diversity of environments and mostly fine, predictable weather, Kenya is a veritable playground in the sun. For resident and visitor, player and spectator, Kenya offers the enthusiast a virtually unlimited choice of sports.

Although the sports played in Kenya were once the preserve of the Europeans and Asians who introduced them, they have since become an African success story. Today's sportsmen produce world-class performances and use facilities that are second to none. Considering the financial constraints that face all developing nations, Kenya's many triumphs in the twenty-five short years since Independence is all the more remarkable.

Participatory sports

Kenya's reputation as a sports haven is best illustrated by the host of participation sports available to resident and visitor alike. From a sedate game of bowls or croquet to something a little more strenuous, such as tennis, squash, rugby, cricket, or watersports, Kenya has something for everyone.

Golf

Golfers who visit Kenya will not be disappointed by either the courses or the facilities. There are many scenic courses to choose from, where green fees are inexpensive and caddies are always available. The first class course at Muthaiga Golf Club plays host each year to the Kenya Open Golf Championship, which is part of the African Safari Circuit. Though the prize money may not be as much as it is elsewhere, the Kenya Open is an important stepping stone for those wishing to play on the European PGA Circuit.

Modern players who have gone on to bigger and better things include Seve Ballesteros, Nick Faldo, Ian Woosnam, Sandy Lyle, and Tony Jacklin — all of whom have played at Muthaiga.

And Kenya is probably the only country in the world with the following rule: "If a ball comes to rest dangerously close to a hippopotamus or crocodile, another ball may be dropped at a safe distance, but no nearer the hole, without penalty."

Tennis, squash and table tennis

Like golf, tennis and squash were exclusively played by Europeans until Independence. Since then fitness- and status-conscious Africans and Asians have taken up these sports with considerable enthusiasm and limited success. Kenya won the East and Central African Squash Championship in 1984 and Paul Wekessa is the first Kenyan to play the men's professional tennis circuit. Although Kenyan tennis is not highly ranked internationally — the best result came in 1987 when Kenya won two gold and one silver medal at the Fourth All Africa Games — Kenyans compete in the Davis Cup and host the Kenyan Open (an Association of Tennis Professionals ranking tournament) each year. Table Tennis enjoys considerable popularity and Kenya hosted the 1989 World Cup. Visitors wishing to play tennis, squash, and table tennis will find first class facilities and traditional Kenyan hospitality at any of Kenya's sports clubs or international hotels along the coast.

Bowls and croquet

Those wishing to indulge in more leisurely pursuits such as lawn bowls and croquet will find world class facilities and standards at a select number of sports clubs. Kenya regularly competes in major international tournaments such as the Commonwealth Games. Those wishing to play should bring their own kit.

Darts

Those preferring to smoke and drink while playing their "sport" will find Kenya is a nation of darts lovers. Keenly contested competitions are held all over the country. Linked as they are to bars, cigarette and drink manufacturers are pouring large amounts of money into developing both the popularity and the standard of the game.

Table-top games such as billiards, pool, and snooker are almost exclusively found in sports clubs, though there is a pool table on

Above: Bowls competition at Nairobi Club.

the mezzanine floor of Nairobi's Cameo cinema.

Gym and health clubs

Body-builders and weight-watchers needn't worry that all their hard work will turn to flab on their Kenyan safari. All sorts of stainless steel instruments of torture await them in one of Kenya's health and fitness clinics and gymnasia. Saunas and masseurs are also available to those who need them. Costs are fairly high but compare well to prices at home. Some of the international hotels provide these facilities.

Swimming

Those looking for some exercise and relief from the heat will find swimming pools at all international hotels. Guests are admitted free of charge. If these shallow short-length pools aren't your cup of tea, there is an Olympic-length swimming pool at Nyayo Stadium.

Action and Adventure

Many people come to Kenya for the sports they can't watch or play at home: gliding, ballooning, scuba diving, sailing, sailboard-ing, surfboarding, water-skiing, climbing, trek-king, freshwater and marine fishing.

Along the edge of the Rift Valley powerful thermals thrust upward carrying all who dare to soar like an eagle. Hang-glider enthusiasts will find dozens of places to jump off into space although conventional glider pilots will have to go to Nakuru for their pleasure.

The Rift Valley's almost continuous ther-mals make it possible for gliders to stay aloft for hours and to travel considerable distances, hundreds of feet above some of the most spectacular scenery on earth.

You will need to bring your own hang-glider but conventional gliders can be hired at Nakuru. Joy flights are also available to those wishing to savour the delights of powerless flight.

If all that sounds a bit too wimpish, you can always go to Wilson Airport to do a spot of parachuting. Or on the coast, paraglide — hanging from a parachute while being pulled along by a speedboat.

When the British came to Kenya, they sought to impose a little bit of England on the land-scape. Besides building mock-tudor mansions and stately parks and gardens, they filled the streams with trout. Today, serious fly-fishermen will find some of the gamest fish in the world in the streams of the Aberdares, the Cheranganis, and Mau Plateau. Fly-fishermen should also note that Kenya manufactures flies and lures for a growing international market at a fraction of the cost elsewhere.

For those who haven't mastered the art of fly-fishing, Kenya's lakes may provide more successful hunting grounds. Large-mouth bass, fighting tiger fish, sweet-tasting tilapia, and huge Nile perch await the angler in Lake Victoria, Lake Turkana, and the Rift Valley lakes.

Freshwater fishermen will need to bring their own equipment and pay a nominal fee for a fishing licence. In all, fishermen are well catered to, with access roads and simple huts provided for their convenience. However, they should always exercise caution with regard to the weather and wildlife.

Kenya offers some of the world's best deepwater, off-shore fishing with marlin, sailfish, shark, swordfish, tuna, and wahoo luring all those who see themselves in the Hemingway mould. The main bases for this sport are Shimoni, Mombasa, Kilifi, Watamu, and Malindi. Here, anything from small outboard dinghies to fully-crewed luxury yachts with every conceivable convenience and the most up-to-date equipment can be hired for a relatively small outlay.

The season lasts between November and March when the gentler northeast monsoon blows. At the same time, the Somali current runs along the Kenya coast bringing with it nutrients from the Arabian sea which, in turn, attracts the fish.

Kenya's palm-fringed coastline is much more than a place to lie in the sun and paddle in the almost tepid waters of the Indian Ocean. Just off-shore lie Kenya's coral gardens — a magnet for snorkelers and scuba-divers the world over.

Those wishing to explore the shark-free reefs will find many outfits — all professionally run and offering top quality equipment for hire — catering to every level of experience. Scuba divers will be required to produce a certificate of competence, though there are plenty of scuba schools for the beginner.

Sailing and wind-surfing are boom sports on the coast with most hotels and independent operators providing equipment and training, if required. Standards have rapidly improved to the point where Kenyans have started winning international regattas, some of which are now being held in Kenya. The sport is mostly conducted on an informal basis with wind-surfers simply trying to master the techniques or sailors trying beat their friends in point-to-point races.

More conventional sailors will find opportunities to tack, reach, and run with the wind on lakes Naivasha, Victoria and, as improbable as it sounds, Nairobi Dam. Water-skiiers will be able to indulge their passion at the coast, Lake Naivasha, and Lake Baringo.

The Safari Rally

As with athletics, the Safari Rally has become synonymous with Kenya. Each Easter, the excitement and thrills of the world's toughest rally are broadcast to millions of homes around the world.

For over 4,500 kilometres (2,500 miles) the world's best rally drivers hurtle, day and night, through the Kenyan outback, battling with thick mud, blinding dust, unpredictable wildlife, the clock, and each other for the coveted winner's laurel. Most never finish — in fact, there have been only three occasions when more than half the starters got home safely.

The first Safari Rally (then known as the Coronation Rally) was held in 1953. On that occasion, fifty-seven local drivers wound their way through East Africa. Despite the organisers' attempts to keep the rally a strictly amateur event, it stirred the imagination of the world's media and the interest of the international racing fraternity.

Once it gained international status in 1957, the rally (then known as the East Africa Safari Rally) was soon contested by drivers and major works teams from overseas. Owing to problems in neighbouring Tanzania and Uganda, the Safari Rally was confined to Kenyan roads in 1974.

Today, the Safari Rally is an important event on the international racing calendar with successful drivers and works teams being awarded valuable points in the World Rally Championship. But foreign drivers with their formidable reputations and multinational backing are not, surprisingly, the most successful.

Now in its fourth decade, the rally has been won by locals on all but nine occasions.

Above: Frontrunner in the gruelling 4,000-kilometre-long Safari Rally.

Above: Kenyan athletes — the cream of the world's middle and long-distance runners.

Above: Soccer is Kenya's national sport.

Of the local drivers, Shekhar Mehta is the only man to have won the rally five times. His international record is more than respectable with consistently high placings around the globe.

One reason for Kenyan drivers' success is explained by their knowledge of local conditions. A full programme of events that are used to determine "Motorsportsman of the Year" is held throughout the year. They include road safety, training, economy-run, fun, and national rallies, and even go-cart races which are held at Nairobi's Embakasi racetrack.

Athletics

Few countries have ever done so well in any one sport as Kenya in athletics. By the late-1980s Kenya's dominance of middle and long-distance running had been established beyond all doubt.

Yet Kenyan athletes didn't compete in their first international meet until 1952. And their first gold medal came ten years later in the Perth Commonwealth Games.

The phenomenal ability of Kenya's athletes first came to international attention with superlative performances by the legendary Kipchoge ("Kip") Keino and Naftali Temu. In 1965 Keino claimed his first gold medal when he won the 1,500 metres at the First All Africa Games in Brazzaville. The following year he won two gold medals in the Jamaica Commonwealth Games for the one mile and three mile events. At the same games, Temu won gold for the six mile and followed that success by winning the 5,000 metres in the 1967 Helsinki World Games.

In the 1968 Mexico Olympics Temu got the ball rolling by winning the 10,000 metres. Amos Biwott won Kenya's second gold in the 3,000 metres steeplechase. And Keino put the icing on the cake when he won the 1,500 metres. The Kenyans returned home to a heroes welcome with three gold, four silver, and one bronze medal.

At the 1970 Edinburgh Commonwealth Games, Keino again won gold in the 1,500 metres. Robert Ouko (800 metres), Charles Asati (400 metres), and the men's 4 x 400 metres relay team also proved Mexico was no fluke and, in all, Kenya won four gold, one silver, and four bronze.

Keino reappeared at the 1972 Munich Olympics but was unable to retain his 1,500 metres crown. He made up for that, however, by winning the 3,000 metres steeplechase. The men's 4 x 400 metre relay team surprised everyone when they snatched Kenya's second gold.

And Kenya consolidated her authority on the track by adding two silver and one bronze to the medal tally. Not only was this Keino's last Olympic Games, it was also to be Kenya's last until 1984 as Kenya chose to boycott both the Montreal and Moscow Olympics.

With five gold, one silver, and six bronze medals Kenya literally ran away with the 1974 Commonwealth Games in Christchurch. Mike Boit and Benjamin Jipcho emerged as Kenya's new stars although their moment of glory was short-lived. In 1978 their compatriot, Henry Rono, burst on the scene by setting world records in the 3,000 metres, 5,000 metres, 10,000 metres, and 3,000 metres steeplechase.

In the 1978 Commonwealth Games in Edmonton, Kenyan athletes continued their winning ways with five gold, four silver, and two bronze medals. Mike Boit won the 800 metres gold, and Rono came home with both the 5,000 metres and 3,000 metres steeplechase titles — a result considered average back in Kenya.

Kenya's non-appearance in the 1976 and 1980 Olympics saw Kenyan standards fall dramatically in the early 1980s. One gold, one silver, and three bronze medals at the 1982 Brisbane Commonwealth Games were followed with a medal-less World Championship in 1983 and only a two-medal haul at the 1984 Los Angeles Olympics. At least Kenya could take comfort from Julius Korir's gold-medal winning performances in the Brisbane and Los Angeles games in the 3,000 metres steeplechase.

Not until 1987 was Kenyan pride fully restored when their athletes won the 800 metres (Billy Konchellah), 10,000 metres (Paul Kipkoech), and marathon (Douglas Wakiihuri) at the World Championships in Rome. The following year they won the 5,000 metres (John Ngugi), 3,000 metres steeplechase (Julius Kariuki), 1,500 metres (Paul Rono), and 800 metres (Paul Ereng) at the Seoul Olympics.

In 1989 Kenya continued to amaze the world when the remarkable Ngugi won the World Cross Country Championships an unprecedented fourth consecutive time. In 1988 and 1989 Kenyans also won the famous London, New York, Honululu, and Boston marathons — 1989 also saw Paul Koech break the longest-standing world record in men's athletics, fellow Kenyan Henry Rono's 3,000 metres steeplechase.

Boxing

After athletics, boxing is the number two sport to have brought international fame to Kenya. Kenyan boxers have consistently performed well at international levels in both the Commonwealth Games — their best performance was in Brisbane in, 1982 when they won five gold, one silver, and one bronze medal — and the King's Cup, where they were runners-up in 1982.

Following the 1987 All Africa Games, Kenya were undisputed African champions with eight gold and two bronze medals. The next year, Robert Wangila won Kenya's first Olympic gold medal in Seoul. Wangila later turned professional.

Kenya's other international successes include Stephen Muchoki who won the Second World Amateur Boxing Championships in 1978 in addition to his gold medals in the 1974 and 1978 Commonwealth Games; and Philip Wariunge who won gold medals in the 1966 and 1970 Commonwealth Games, and bronze and silver medals in the 1968 and 1972 Olympic Games respectively.

Despite the success of individuals such as Wangila, Muchoki, and Wariunge, boxing in Kenya remains very much a team sport with several teams competing in a national league.

Kenya has yet to make the same sort of impact in other martial arts — judo, karate, tae-kwan-doh, and wrestling. Enthusiastic

Above: Trekkers on Mount Kenya's alpine crags and moorlands.

clubs are doing their level best to rectify that with keenly contested tournaments being held throughout the country. Limited continental success augurs well for their future.

Football

To the hundreds of thousands of football fans in Kenya who cram the stadiums each weekend, nothing is more exciting than watching their favourite team in action. As in most most countries, passions run high and occasionally tempers flare. Yet for all its popularity, Kenya footballers have still to perform well at the highest levels.

International success for the Kenyan national team — Harambee Stars — has been confined to the regional East and Central African Championship which they have won eight times since 1967. The closest they came to a major tournament victory was in 1987 when they were runners up to Eygpt in the Fourth All Africa Games.

At club level, Kenya has much the same sort of record, winning nine East and Central African Championships since 1974. Gor Mahia,

however, went on to win the Nelson Mandela Cup in the Africa Cup Winners Tournament in 1987.

At the domestic level, Gor Mahia's main rivals are AFC Leopards. Between them they have won the National Football League seventeen times since 1963. A match between these two rivals is always colourful and entertaining with bands and eccentric cheerleaders urging on their team.

Hockey

Kenya's Asian community has proved the backbone of Kenyan hockey. From the 1950s until the early 1970s, hockey grew from strength to strength as Kenya performed well in the international arena.

After the 1956 Olympics Kenya was ranked tenth in the world: following the 1964 Olympics this had improved to sixth.

But the highpoint of Kenyan hockey came in 1971 when the Kenyan team came fourth in the first World Cup and won the East Africa Hockey Championships for the sixth consecutive year.

Opposite top: Basketball stars in action.
Opposite: Rugged sport of kings on polo field near Nairobi.

Since then, Kenyan hockey has slipped into the doldrums. The odd win or draw against more highly-fancied teams, coupled with Kenya's gold medal in the 1987 All Africa Games, has gone some way to restoring lost pride.

Cricket

Like hockey, cricket is largely an Asian affair, though Africans are beginning to make their mark felt. In 1986 the captain of the national team's tour of the UK was an African. Unlike hockey, Kenyan cricket has never made much of an impact in the international arena, though Kenya was represented in the 1975 World Cup as members of a composite East African side. Kenyan born-and-bred cricketers, however, have gone on to play at the highest level — Derek Pringle for England, Qasim Omar for Pakistan, and Dilip Patel for New Zealand.

As an associate member of the International Cricket Conference, Kenya competes in a preliminary series to determine the vacant spot in each World Cup.

Other spectator sports

Even though Kenyan teams enjoy limited international success in basketball, handball, netball, volleyball, and rugby, they are played with considerable enthusiasm on a regular basis throughout Kenya.

For those who enjoy the "sport of kings", Nairobi's Ngong Road Racecourse offers an eight-race card almost every Sunday afternoon, except through August-September, and on most public holidays. The racing is well patronised and professionally-run with stipendary stewards, a qualified handicapper, bookmakers, and Tote facilities. With the excellent amenities and catering, an afternoon at one of the world's prettiest courses is surprisingly inexpensive and utterly enjoyable.

Polo is a sport enjoyed by a small but dedicated group of Kenyans and expatriates wealthy enough to maintain a couple of ponies. Polo matches are played at Jamhuri Park, with an international tournament featuring some of the world's best players sealing the season.

Ballooning: Loads of Hot Air

Tanned nut-brown by his years under the African sun, Dudley Chignall stands in the wicker and willow basket suspended beneath the canopy of his hot air balloon and cons the slowly moving craft through the stillness of early morning.

One hundred metres (300 feet) below, the grotesquely enlarged shadow of the thirty-metre-tall (100-feet) ovoid waltzes in slow time across the golden grasslands of Kenya's Maasai Mara game reserve.

Warm air spills into the chill morning sky as Chignall opens the vent in the nylon canopy to send his ethereal craft circling one way and the other — its dark image on the ground flushing antelope and other game from the cover of thicket and thorn.

Gas burners roar into action and a three-metre-long (10 feet) spear of incandescent flame surges into the envelope as the craft climbs another 100 metres (328 feet) higher.

The balloon's lift comes because the hot air is slightly lighter than the surrounding cold atmosphere. The hotter the balloon, the faster it rises. As the air cools, it slowly descends. The pilot can control the balloon to brush the grass or the tops of trees, but if he wishes he can go as high as 4,500 metres (15,000 feet) without difficulty.

In 1976, Chignall's partner and colleague, world-renowned wildlife film maker, Alan Root, launched Kenya's — and Africa's — first commercial balloon service above the wonderland of the Maasai Mara, the northern-most extension of the famous Serengeti ecosystem.

Now Kenya boasts the greatest number of passenger balloon flights in the world. Most mornings, the skies above the Mara are filled with as many as fifteen of these strange and graceful craft. The larger balloons carry up to ten passengers and pilot. Ground crew vary between four and six personnel. Not yet 08.00, the gentle breeze that now blows is the first of the day's many thermals, and still carries a chill in its breath.

Distances travelled vary according to the wind speed but tend to average between ten and fifteen kilometres (six-nine miles). In Kenya balloons never fly in winds of more than twenty-five kilometres (15 miles) an hour.

Flights last about sixty minutes and end when the balloon lands in whichever location wind and fate have taken it.

Near the basket, Chignall's ground crew have set up a camp dining table and after disembarking, the passengers sit down on the gas cylinders for what may well be the second grandest experience of a lifetime: a *cordon bleu*, champagne breakfast in the wild, surrounded only by the bleating, roaring cacophony of the Mara's teeming wildlife.

This safari adventure without equal has become one of the most sought after experiences in Kenya.

Apart from the many competing balloon services in the Mara, Chignall and Root's company, Balloon Safaris, have now launched the first commercial passenger service in Salt Lick, a private game reserve run by Hilton International.

So big has the demand grown that Kenya now issues its own balloon pilot licences. It requires at least thirty-five hours of flying before a pilot becomes eligible for a commercial licence. Kenya's Directorate of Civil Aviation imposes controls and regulations as stringent and demanding as those in Europe.

Services have operated occasionally in Samburu National Reserve in Kenya's north. But balloons require flat, clear spaces on which to land, so many game parks are not suitable.

Opposite: Champagne breakfast after an early morning balloon flight.

Overleaf: Hot air balloons drift silently over the Mara's rolling grasslands.

Following page: Flaming dawn heralds another day's birth at the Kenya coast.

Kenya's Mountains

All Kenya's mountains have been mapped and photographed and all but some remote peaks in the remote north have been climbed.

The narratives of the ascents of some of the major peaks, found in archives and diaries, are interesting. Most smaller mountains, however, were climbed only for some scientific or administrative pursuit — and the record is scattered in obscure works.

Although not particularly high, some of the hills along the Nairobi-Mombasa road are spectacular. These and the Taita Hills were visited by many early travellers including the three Germans Baron von der Decken, Johan Krapf, and Johanne Rebmann, and the two Britons, Charles New and Joseph Thomson. Indeed, Rebmann travelled by the Sagala Hills as early as 1847.

That October he was refused permission to climb Kisigau because he was wearing shoes. Perhaps, the real reason is that he was suspected of being a spy. It was in the Taita hills that he first saw Kilimanjaro's snowclad summit.

New, who climbed the 1,640-metres-high (5,383 feet) south-west shoulder of Kisigau in July 1863, remembered, "Never did I perform a harder three hours' task. . . ."

Surrounded by perpendicular cliffs, Kisigau reminded him of St Paul's Cathedral. New also visited the Taita Hills, climbed a spur of Vuria and reached the 1,146-metre-high crest (3,760-feet) of Marimba south of the Voi-Taveta road.

Twenty years later Joseph Thomson took three hours to reach the summit of Ndara and journeyed to a valley running deep into Bura mountain where "the stupidity of our guide who took us the wrong road" landed him at the bottom of a steep precipice — "1,000 feet from the top".

The North

The area offers a surprising variety of mountains ranging from dramatic steep isolated peaks such as Baio to the extensive podocarpus forest of the Matthews Range.

The hills, which all create their own climate, rise out of semi-desert, but many are forested on top.

Guides: Because of the thick vegetation and forest, a guide is essential on most peaks.

Logistics: These mountains are fairly remote and care must be taken. When planning a visit, many prefer to travel in convoy to obtain some security against breakdown.

Water is rare and, whether travelling by car or on foot, you should not only carry adequate supplies but also fill up at all the sources listed.

Camping: Generally camping is possible anywhere in the area. But care should be taken to achieve some privacy. Along the route travelled by the various Turkana "buses", there are a number of organised campsites, with water, showers, and toilets. They are usually full of Turkana Bus passengers, however, and you are likely to be pestered by trinket-sellers and professional photograph-posers.

Public Transport: For most areas there is virtually no transport, let alone public transport. It should be possible, however to reach Wamba from Isiolo by hitch-hiking or *matatu*, and from there make an attempt on Warges.

Security: Security in the area is generally quite good, except for Losiolo. Although there have been *shifta* (bandits) reported in the gap between the Matthews and the Ndotos range and on the El Barta Plains around Baragoi they are not a cause for concern. They do not seem to have troubled vehicles passing through the area.

FOROLE 2,007 metres (6,584 feet)

Forole lies on the Ethiopian border to the north of the **Huri Hills**. A long craggy ridge, steep on both the Kenyan and Ethiopian sides, it is covered and surrounded by thicker bush.

Although **Forole** is a dramatic mountain and the views are good, many other peaks give intrinsically nicer walks. But undoubtedly Forole's attraction is that you can stand with one foot in Ethiopia while reflecting on the inevitable excitements of the long and arduous journey to the top.

A series of small springs on the Kenyan side have paths running to them, penetrating the thicker lower bush. It is essential to use these paths and is probably best to obtain a guide from the **village** at the foot of the mountain, although this can be extremely expensive.

JABISA 1,544 metres (5,065 feet)

Views like those from the top of Jabisa don't come any grander. You can see **Lake Stephanie**, **North Island**, the **Lapurr Range**, **Forole**, **Mount Kulal**, and the **Mega Escarpment** in Ethiopia.

The area is particularly hot, and for the traverse of the main peaks you should carry at least five litres of water. The nearest sources are at **Sabarei** and **El Sardu**. Guides are not necessary.

PORR 668 metres (2,191 feet)

This mountain forms a perfect pyramid on the north side of **El Molo Bay** on **Lake Turkana**. Rising 300 metres (1,000 feet) above the lake, it is more of an enjoyable trek for hill-walkers than for serious mountaineering.

The approach track passes through a number of dry luggas bordered by thorn trees and other bushes. They provide a break from the winds coming off Mount Kulal that rise very suddenly as the sun sets.

KULAL 2,285 metres (7,498 feet)

Covered by thick and ancient green forests, Kulal, like **Marsabit**, is an incredible and almost unbelievable contrast to the lava wastes around Lake Turkana. The exciting approach and spectacular views over the lake and into the deep mountain gorges make it one of Kenya's most rewarding mountains.

The highest point lies to the north on a narrow ridge near the **Arabel** end. **Ladarabach** to the south is easier to reach.

The ridge between Ladarabach and the **summit** has been crossed only two or three times. It's very challenging, with long traverses across loose soil above steep drops and sections of extremely severe climbing grades.

The eastern side of the ridge forms the head of the **El Kajarta Gorge**, the most spectacular on the mountain. With difficulty you can reach it from the road to the east of the mountain — and it's worth the effort.

The spectacular drive up Ladarabach is rough. Just short of the **roadhead** is **Gatab Mission** where you can hire guides and obtain water. At the roadhead a splendid **campsite** perched at the edge of the mountain offers magnificent panoramas of Lake Turkana.

From here a day's easy walking through lush forest and over attractive meadowlands takes you to another fine viewpoint overlooking the lake — and yet another overlooking the El Kajarta Gorge to Arabel.

The drive up Arabel, which is less spectacular with few views of the lake, is also very rough and there is little traffic — no more than two or three vehicles each year.

NYIRU 2,829 metres (9,283 feet)

Rising out of thorn scrub, this impressive, large and bulky mountain with stunning views of the scorching **Suguta Valley**, **Lake Turkana**, and the northern deserts, shares with Marsabit and Kulal, the blessing of thick, cool forests and pleasant meadowlands which shroud its summit.

During the long dry seasons the Samburu pastoralists take their cattle up **Nyiru** for grazing and some live there permanently, creating a bewildering array of cattle trails which means you will need a guide.

Water is always available near the **summit** and there are plenty of campsites if you want to spend a night or two at the top. Again, you'll need to find shelter from the strong early night wind.

The most common approach, via **Tum**, gives the shortest ascent with easy access to the most spectacular of the peaks and a pleasantly cool early morning ascent in the mountain's shadow.

This approach also allows you a detour down the mountainside into the **Suguta Valley**, a real Dante's inferno where temperatures rarely drop below 38°C (100°F). Turn left twelve kilometres (seven and a half

miles) before Tum and follow the track past Pakati **mission post** down into the valley. Bear right at an obvious fork for the trail to **Lake Logipi**.

Be prepared. Thousands of years ago Suguta was the bed of the the the southern extension of Lake Turkana. It is rarely visited and the boulder-strewn track is steep and incredibly rough — you'll drive most of it in low-ratio first gear so allow a full day for the sixty kilometres (40 miles) to Lake Logipi and back.

SUPUKO 2,067 metres (6,780 feet)

This highest point on the spectacular eastern ridge of the **South Horr Valley** is generally neglected in favour of its bigger neighbour on the other side.

But a circuit of the two main peaks, **Porale**, 1,990 metres (6,530 feet), and **Supuko**, 2,066 metres (6,780 feet), offers some fascinating, if difficult, ridge walking with marvellous views of **Nyiru**, the **South Horr Valley**, and the northern deserts. The best place to start from is **Kurungu Camp** using guides.

Two obvious rock faces that lead up to summits can be seen above Kurungu Camp: one in the north, **Porak**; the other in the south, **Mumusia**.

Hidden by a subsidiary north-west peak, Supuko is three kilometres (almost two miles) to the north of Porak and not too obvious from the road.

Ndoto Range

ALIMISION 2,637 metres (8,650 feet)

Located in the centre of the range, an extremely narrow ridge which forms the highest part of Alimision offers splendid scenic landscapes.

The climb is mainly along cattle trails and not much obscures the views. The last leg is an enjoyable airy scramble but quite daunting for those who suffer from vertigo. A **spring** near the summit is sometimes dry.

Much bigger than it looks, **Alimision** towers 1,676 metres (5,500 feet) above the roadhead at **Arsim**. It is possible to approach it via **Lesirikan** but this means an extremely long and tiring walk.

POI

Climbers rate **Poi** in the northern **Ndoto Range** the most challenging climb in the country after Mount Kenya — and almost as technically demanding. The easiest route is a Grade V climb.

Poi is surrounded on three sides by almost sheer cliffs between 300 and 610 metres (1,000-2,000 feet) high — a rock climbing paradise that amounts to five kilometres (three miles) of cliffs.

The fourth side forms a ridge which creates a barrier between **Arsim** and **Ngurunit**.dramatic 600-

BAIO 1,751 metres (5,746 feet)

Baio rises almost sheer out of the desert for 1,219 metres (4,000 feet) some thirty kilometres (20 miles) from the main **Ndoto range**. Its southern face is a dramatic 600 metre-high (2,000-feet) overhanging precipice, invisible until you reach the **summit**.

The reasonably short climb means you can stay on the summit for some time to enjoy the stupendous scenery — Baio itself, **Holilugum Nder**, the **Ndoto range**, **Poi**, the **Matthews Range**, **Marsabit**, and the **Kaisut Desert**.

If lucky you may see some of the greater kudu that live on the mountain. Another attraction of climbing Baio is the pleasure of camping at Ngurunit and bathing in the **rock pools**.

Although not essential, it is worth hiring a guide and also an *askari* to guard your vehicle. These can be arranged through the local chief.

There are two routes: The first, which is extremely steep and direct, avoids most of the thorn bush but involves some airy scrambling, which is avoided by the second route, although this is much longer and through dense bush.

From **Ngurunit** drive for forty kilometres (25 miles) along the **Laisamis road** to where a track on the right leads to a **UNESCO research station**. You can't miss it because of the large herds of camels all around it.

Continue past the station for another four kilometres (two and a half miles) to the foot of the mountain and park just west of a large and obvious gully which faces north-east and marks the northern flank.

Matthews Range

OL DOINYO LENKIYO 2,286 metres (7,505 feet)

This remote and rarely visited mountain is at the northern end of the **Matthews Range**.

From **Isiolo** you drive 119 kilometres (74 miles) along the **Great North Road** towards **Marsabit** to a left turn on to a track to **Lodosoit**. Five kilometres (three miles) along this take the left fork and drive another fifteen kilometres (ten miles) to a vermiculite **mine**.

From the mine it's a another twenty kilometres (12 miles) to a col between **Il Bision** and the main range.

MATTHEWS PEAK 2,375 metres (7,792 feet)

Covered in lush and beautiful podocarpus forest, this is the highest mountain in the main part of the **Matthews Range** with delightful walks through the cool of the forest.

You can stay at the splendid **Kitich Camp**, an expensive luxury tourist camp at the **roadhead**, or camp at the Wildlife Department's **campsites** lower down the valley. Water is available everywhere and the **Ngeng River** has some marvellous large **rock pools** that are ideal for swimming.

You can either hire guides from Kitich Camp or one of the rangers from the **game post**.

From Isiolo you follow the Marsabit road to the **Wamba turnoff** of the left, twenty kilometres (12

miles) beyond **Archer's Post**. Follow this road for forty kilometres (25 miles) to the next turnoff on the, right, signposted Wamba, and immediately left onto the **Barsaloi road**.

Drive along this road for eighteen kilometres (11 miles) to a right fork that leads on fifteen kilometres (ten miles) to **Ngalai**. Just before Ngalai bear right along a rough track for ten kilometres (six miles) to **Kishishi Game Post** where you sign in. Follow the trail back for half-a-kilometre a third of a mile and then turn north across several difficult luggas to Kitich Camp.

MATTHEWS SOUTH PEAK 2,285 metres (7,497) feet

Much easier to climb than **Matthews**, which takes the form of a U-shaped ridge, the south peak is notable for the excellent viewpoint on **Londoma** in the south-west. **Ukut**, the forested high point, is in the south-east corner.

Kishishi Game Post lies at the head of the U-shaped ridge, the outside of which is made up of many steep and rocky faces.

You'll need a guide as the inside of the ridge is shrouded with thick forest and it is easy to lose your way. There is also a great deal of confusion over names and you may be taken to the wrong place.

WARGES 2,688 metres (8,820 feet)

This extremely large and attractive mountain with its magnificent panoramas lies to the south-east of the Matthews Range. The **campsite** in the **Wamba Valley** is a delightful place to stay before setting off.

The lower parts of the mountain are covered with thick and sometimes impenetrable bush. Its crest sports another of the many lush and ancient podocarpus forests of these northern mountains.

How much you enjoy the first part of the climb through the bush depends on how easily you find a decent game trail to follow. They are becoming rarer as the game diminishes and after the rains, when the wildlife spreads out, they often don't exist. So what should take between four and five hours can sometimes involve up to two days.

You'll definitely need a guide and you should rely on his judgement.

From **Wamba**, bear right at the end of the main street to take the extreme right fork to the **Forestry house** where you can hire a guide.

LOLOLOKWE 1,853 metres (6,080 feet)

Surrounded on three sides by sheer 300-metre-high (1,000-feet) cliffs, this spectacular mountain is a distinctive landmark for travellers on the **Great North Road**. Its main attraction is the walk round the top of its massive bluff. To the north, the smaller hill with a microwave **relay station** also offers splendid views.

From **Isiolo** drive north on the **Marsabit** road past the Wamba turn off and past the main wall of **Lololokwe** until you can see a valley to the north of the main mountain. Turn off here and drive up the valley to the **roadhead**.

You should take an *askari* to guard your vehicle. The journey from Isiolo is about one hour.

LOSIOLO 2,470 metres (8,104 feet)

On a clear day from the **summit** of Losiolo, one of Kenya's finest viewpoints, you can take in one of the most spectacular panoramas Kenya offers — the **Ndoto Range**, the **Cherangani Hills** (including **Sekerr**), **Mount Nyiru**, **Lake Baringo**, and **Tiati** in the **Tugen Hills**.

The **roadhead**, one of two in Kenya known as **World's End**, is an extremely popular **viewpoint**.

From Maralal drive north for eighteen kilometres (11 miles) along the **Baragoi road** to the **Poror turnoff** of the left, and follow this track through Poror **village** for three kilometres (just over two miles) to a **T-junction**.

Take the left turn for just over seven kilometres (four miles) to reach World's End. It takes about forty-five minutes from Maralal.

The Tugen Hills

The Tugen Hills offer many delightful and relatively short walks, all with magnificent and varied views. They make an extremely pleasant excursion from Nairobi.

Kabarnet, the administrative capital of the region, has a good, reasonably-priced hotel. A few kilometres east of Kabarnet the road to **Tenges** is one of the most scenic roads in Kenya with incredible views of the Rift. A third tarmac road heads north from Kabarnet to **Kabartonjo** and a fourth to Iten across the floor of the Kerio Valley.

TIATI 2,351 metres (7,713 feet)

Tiati, a large northern outlier of the **Tugens**, is separated from them by the **Kito Pass**. It's a long hot climb through rugged scenery to an extremely good viewpoint.

A small forest below the summit makes a pleasant **campsite** but you need to carry your own water. The nearest water is at **Barpello mission**. A guide is essential.

You drive through the Kito Pass from the Cheranganis. After a long flat straight section near the top of the pass the road turns right and drops steeply. From this point Barpello mission, where you hire guides and askaris, is about one kilometre (two-thirds of a mile) off the main road some seven kilometres (four miles) from the summit of the pass.

From the mission turnoff continue along the main road another two kilometres (just over a mile) towards **Tot** to the right turn signposted "Freedom from Hunger" and follow this for eleven kilometres (seven miles) to the campsite at the roadhead. You'll need a 4WD vehicle.

SAIMO 2,501 metres (8,207 feet)

Rising out of heavily cultivated farmland, the summit of this pleasant forested peak consists of three peaks, the highest being the middle one. The forest is host to some brilliant butterflies and many orchids.

There are splendid views over **Baringo**. The approach road also gives good views of the **Cheranganis**, the northern part of the **Kerio Valley**, **Tiati**, and **Saimo** itself. There are many tracks through the farms and forest and plenty of volunteer guides. Saimo is an enjoyable morning's outing from Kabarnet.

From **Kabarnet** drive nineteen kilometres (12 miles) north to **Kabartonjo** and then continue along a rough dirt road — that gets rougher — to **Bartalimo**. It takes an hour.

MAROP 2,306 metres (7,567 feet)

This mountain, with panoramic views of the Rift Valley and the Tugen Hills, is a short excursion from Kabarnet.

Drive from **Kabarnet** along the **Marigat road** to the point where it passes the southern end of an obvious ridge leading south from **Marop**. There is a track, signposted to **Kasare** and **Kapkomoi Primary Schools**, along the west side of the ridge. Leave the car by the main road, or drive along the track for some way. It becomes increasingly rough.

From the main road, follow the track for about three kilometres (just over two miles) to a fork which you ignore and continue north for one more kilometre (two-thirds of a mile). This brings you north-west of the summit to a point where an old motor track, to the right, zigzags up the hill to the col below the summit. From here it's a short scramble to the summit.

KIBIMJOR 2,347 metres (7,699 feet)

With its impressive knife-edge ridge leading to the summit of this handsomely shaped mountain, the climber is rewarded with mind-boggling views, both from the top and the approach roads.

The first approach is suitable for saloon cars. The second, though slower and rougher, is much more scenic, circuiting **Eldama Ravine**.

From Kabarnet drive to **Tenges** and continue south for three kilometres (almost two miles) to the road, opposite an old forest station, leading west to a quarry.

KAPKUT 2,800 metres (9,185 feet)

With its spectacular viewpoint overlooking the southern end of the **Kerio Valley**, **Kapkut** is reached by a long drive through rolling farmland followed by a short walk.

Densely-populated and intensely cultivated, camping is only possible at the roadhead.

Follow the **Nyaru** road from Eldama Ravine for about twenty kilometres (12 miles) to **Kipsaos**. Just before village take the right turn to a good dirt road that runs east along the rim of the Kerio Valley with splendid views. Continue to the **roadhead**.

A gentle fifteen-minute walk, past a school and through forest, brings you to the grassy **summit**. From the roadhead you can also walk to Kaisamu, 2,726 metres (8,943 feet) high, opposite Kapkut.

The Mau

The **Mau Escarpment** forms the western wall of the Great Rift Valley with a north-western extension as far as **Tinderet** which overlooks **Lake Victoria**.

Although within easy reach of **Nairobi**, the hills are rarely explored and have suffered severe deforestation and dense settlement.

But the craters on the volcanic outliers of **Buru** and **Loldiani** make extremely pleasant excursions.

TINDERET 2,640 metres (8,663 feet)

This impressive mountain, overlooking the eastern shores of Lake Victoria, is clearly visible from the **Nakuru-Kericho road**, with some splendid scenic approach roads. Thick bamboo and forest on the **summit** severely limit the views.

Follow the **Londiani-Fort Ternan road** towards Londiani to a left turn to **Tinderet Tea Estate** and follow this road for eight kilometres (five miles). here you come to a road heading north across the range and returning in a large semi-circle to a **roadhead** near a ridge running north of the peak. It's between thirty and thirty-five kilometres (19-22 miles) from **Kipkelion**.

There is an old disused footpath to the **summit** which you will need to locate.

LOLDIANI 3,011 metre (9,878 feet)

You can reach the summit by road and the twin craters of this large forested volcano are fascinating. Follow the **Eldoret** road from Nakuru to a right turn signposted **Molo Forest Station** just before Molo. Follow this road past the forest station for five kilometres (three miles) to a **crossroads** at the start of a **village**.

Take the right turn and drive for ten kilometres (six miles) to the forest where the road continues for another two kilometres (just over a mile) to the crater rim and the roadhead.

There's a rough track for three kilometres (almost two miles) down into the crater, to a lovely campsite in a clearing by a stream. There are also some campsites on the inner crater rim and in the inner crater.

For the summit which is densely forested with bamboo, follow the main Eldoret road from Nakuru for fifty kilometres (30 miles) where it veers left and another road continues straight on. Take this road for twelve kilometres (seven miles) to a right turn on to a murram road.

Follow this for twelve kilometres (seven miles) to a fork and keep left. Continue for another twelve kilometres (seven miles) to a turn right which leads six kilometres (almost four miles) to the **police** station and **post office** on the summit.

MELILI 3,098 metres (10,165 feet)

The road passes close to the highest point of the **Mau**, but the approach roads are extremely rough.

From **Njoro** take the **Narok** road past **Egerton College** for forty-four kilometres (27 miles) and through **Mau Narok** to a left turn.

Follow this past some **sawmills** for another twenty-one kilometres (13 miles) then sharp left for the last nine kilometres (six miles) to the **summit**.

BURU 2,854 metres (9,365 feet)

Isolated from the **Mau** range, this fascinating volcanic peak with many craters stands between **Naivasha** and **Elementeita** in the Rift Valley. Although the mountain is settled on its lower and middle slopes, you will spend most of the walk in forest with tantalising glimpses of **Mount Longonot** and **Lakes Elementeita**, and **Nakuru**.

From Naivasha follow the new **Nakuru road**. Turn left, on to the **Moi South Lake Road**, continue for almost nine kilometres (six miles) to a **three-way junction** where the road branches left.

Take the road on the right bearing towards **Eburru** for fourteen kilometres (almost nine miles) until you come to a fork. Take the track on the left for two kilometres (just over a mile) to another left fork which leads to **Eburru** village. After passing **Eburru Harambee Secondary School**, bear sharp right on to the road that climbs the hill behind the village.

Follow this for three kilometres (almost two miles) to the crest of a slope past a triangular fork where roads lead right and left, and a private track goes half right. Continue straight on into the floor of a large crater and a large levelled apron where the road starts to bear left.

From the **parking spot**, the summit is very evident and from the corner of the apron a wide footpath climbs parallel to its right hand side.

Follow this to the rim of the large crater, passing a much smaller crater on the right.

After about two hours, the track bears right across level ground and descends steeply to a level section with an ill-defined path to the left. Follow this, keeping a large steep sided crater on your right, to the bamboo-covered summit. The climb takes about an hour.

The Aberdares

The third highest mountain range in Kenya after Mount Kenya and Mount Elgon, there is much to enjoy — and to frustrate — in the Aberdares (See "Magic mountains, moorlands wild", Part Two).

There is a well-maintained network of roads running on the broad moorland plateau in the central part of the range between **Naivasha** and **Nyeri** which allow you to visit most waterfalls. There is one approach to **Satima** and the northern moorlands, and some rarely-used approaches to

Kinangop. It's advisable whatever the time of year or weather to use 4WD.

Where to stay

There is a small **fishing lodge** offering bunkhouse accommodation where you can also camp. For weekends in January, February and March, book at the Mountain National Park HQ, Mweiga. At other times, it is hardly ever used.

KIPIPIRI 3,349 metres (10,987 feet)

Standing to the west of the range and divided from it by the deep cleft of the Wanjohi ("Happy") Valley, Kipipiri is an outlier with a flat topped dome offering fine views to the west over the Rift. It is much less covered by cloud than the peaks in the main range.

It is quite possible to climb it in a long day from Nairobi. The foot of the mountain is densely-populated and heavily-cultivated, making camping less than ideal, but by no means impossible. The schoolmaster at **Geta** allows parties to camp on his **playing field**.

It is possible to climb Kipipiri from any direction, but the approach from the north is easiest. Carry all your water.

From **Gilgil** follow the **Nyahururu road** for twenty-five kilometres (15.5 miles) to the first stretch of the wheatfields of this highland plateau and a right turn, signposted **Wanjohi**.

Drive south through Wanjohi towards Geta, taking the first major dirt road on the right. From this climb a track up an evident spur running north. The journey takes about three hours from Nairobi.

Follow the ridge, which is covered in bamboo in places, to many of the false summits. The climb takes between two and three hours.

SATIMA 3,999 metres (13,120 feet)

The highest point of the Aberdares is nothing more than a strenuous high-altitude walk but with splendid views over the **Laikipia** and **Mount Kenya**.

There are two approaches. Both require a 4WD vehicle and the walks are entirely on the high moorland ground. Carry all your water.

From Naivasha

From Nairobi, just before the Naivasha turn-off on the **Nairobi-Nakuru road**, there is a turn right signposted **North Kinangop**. Follow this until the tarmac ends with a left turn on a rough track to Aberdare National Park. Follow this to the **Mutubio Gate**. The final leg before the gate, astonishingly, is tarmac. From the gate it's three kilometres (almost two miles) to a crossroads. The left hand track is no longer used.

The right hand track heads to the 300-metre-deep (1,000-feet) **Karuru Falls** and the **fishing lodge.** Continue straight across for another three kilometres (almost two miles) to a second crossroads

where the disused track rejoins from the left and the right track leads to the fishing lodge and the **Kiandongoro Gate.**

Continue straight across again for another nine kilometres (almost six miles) then bear left at a fork. The right fork goes to the **Ruhuruini Park Gate.** Another ten kilometres (six miles) on, you come to the **Wandares track** on the left, marked by the fire tower on the hill beyond.

From Nyeri

From Nyeri follow the **Nyahururu** road for thirteen kilometres (eight miles) through **Mweiga** to a left turn clearly signposted **Wandares Park Gate**, and the start of the **Wandares track.**

Follow the Wandares track to a small timber cabin and continue along the extremely rough trail to the roadhead. Camping at the roadhead exposes you to strong winds. Camping lower down exposes you to strong lions. Stay in the cabin. Either approach takes about four hours from Nairobi.

Follow the track from the roadhead north-west, following the southern contours, beneath the high points of the ridge, along the game trails until you reach the last col below Satima.

From here you can climb straight up to the lower north peak or bear south-west to the true **summit**. Most of the walk is on gentle gradients but you'll certainly feel the altitude on the final climb. It takes about three hours.

From Nyahururu

From Nyahururu follow the **Nyeri road** for six kilometres (almost four miles) to a signposted right turn through **Kaheho** to the **Shamata gate**.

There is a more direct but much rougher approach to this gate via **Ol Kalau**. After the gate ignore the signs to the campsite and continue for six kilometres (almost four miles) to the junction with the disused **Virgin's Lane** and continue another three kilometres (almost two miles) to a fork.

Bear right (left here, and left again, brings you to **Chebuswa Hut**; left but then right takes you down **Elephant Entry Road** to the **Ngobit Gate**). Continue to the roadhead. The last two kilometres (just over a mile) is usually extremely muddy and soggy.

Follow the track from the roadhead and then bear south on the game trails to a ridge that overlooks the **Dragon's Teeth** — unmistakable volcanic cones — and other outcrops.

Walk down into the basin keeping the Teeth to the west and you will eventually reach some ridges where the going is better and which you can follow up to Satima. The walk takes between three and four hours.

TABLE MOUNTAIN 3,971 metres (12,438 feet)

South-west of **Satima**, right on the edge of the main escarpment, **Table Mountain** is the end of a ridge which is mostly higher than the peak. Two approaches are possible.

The first, rarely if ever used, climbs the escarpment above **Wanjohi** through various bands of vegetation. The second approach is along the rarely travelled ridges south of Satima.

From the summit of Satima continue south along the main ridge of the Aberdares. After an initial steep descent, you'll reach a small water pool.

Fill up here for the night's camp then climb the next peak on the ridge, and rather lower one that follows after this, to descend to a col which has reasonable camping nearby and can be reached conveniently in a day from Nairobi. From Satima it takes between one and two hours.

From here continue up to the next high point and then turn sharp right to the rock castle (mentioned in route one), down into a valley and straight up the side of the ridge leading to Table Mountain. Alternatively, continue straight on before bearing half right to follow a subsidiary ridge leading into the basin at the head of the valley.

From here you climb straight up the side of the ridge and follow it to the summit. It takes between two and three hours from the campsite. The round trip from Nairobi is perfectly feasible in a weekend.

THE ELEPHANT 3,590 metre (11,780 feet)

This distinctive peak, which takes its name because of its shape when seen from South Kinangop, offers fine views of the **Kinangop** and over the Kinangop Plateau. It is normally tackled *en route* for the Kinangop.

From **South Kinangop** village drive east along the winding **Thika road** to **Kiburu forest station** where you may be obliged to pay fees, or hire a guide in lieu.

Turn left here and drive north for twenty-two kilometres (14 miles) to a T-junction where you take right turn on to the **Fort Hall** (Muranga) **track**. From here continue straight past all junctions for another two kilometres, (just over a mile) leaving your vehicle just before a steepish downhill slope to avoid having to drive it back up if it rains.

Continue on foot along the Fort Hall Track past a small landslide and the crest of the ridge. Descend for a short section in a south-easterly direction into a clearing on your left. The climb to the Elephant starts at the top of the clearing.

Follow the path along the main ridge to a small clearing on a grassy knoll with views of the steep ridge ahead.

Avoid the game trails to the east and continue straight up the ridge through some bamboo after which the going becomes much easier. There is a **derelict hut** about three hours walk from the **roadhead** with some possible camping spots nearby — or you can sleep in the hut.

From here you continue in a northerly direction for about another hour to the Elephant which has four summits, lying along a transverse ridge, all of equal height. To climb all four takes about an hour.

THE KINANGOP 3,906 metres (12,816 feet)

Perhaps the grandest and most impressive peak in the Aberdare massif, **Kinangop** stands tall among an array of large ridges, in complete contrast to the rolling moorland of the northern Aberdares.

The true **summit** is reached by an airy scramble up a volcanic outcrop.

From the **Elephant**, climb down the col between the two westernmost summits heading west and down the gullies to reach the relatively flat ground at the foot of a ridge leading to the Kinangop, a subsidiary of the main ridge.

Follow this along the crest to avoid tussocks. In spite of appearances, it does not involve a great deal of switchbacking. Where the ridge merges into the mountain, strike straight up the side, and then follow the crest to the summit, the third of the volcanic outcrops.

Mountains of Maasailand

This large group of very different mountains is spread widely over southern Kenya.

SUSUA 2,357 metres (7,732 feet)

Susua is much neglected in favour of its neighbouring volcano, **Longonot** (See "The Land that was Eden", Part Two). This is probably because the mountain appears unimpressive from a distance, due to the relatively gentle angle of its outer slopes — although it makes for a much more pleasant walk.

It is also possible to drive up into the floor of the outer of its two craters where you encounter an extraordinary sense of isolation.

The **inner crater** is a concealed until you reach its very lip, with large central plug, shaping the crater like a ring.

Susua also has some fascinating **lava caves**. The outer crater is occupied by Maasai, who may ask for water. Take all water with you.

Cars should not be left unattended in secluded spots by the caves, though they are probably safe when left in prominent positions by the summit roadhead.

You may be able to climb Susua from the main **Narok road**, which can be reached by public transport, but it's a long hot walk to the base.

Camp either by the caves for seclusion and shade, or by the road head for better views.

Leave **Ngong town** on the right turn at the T-junction and then bear right at an offset roundabout. Follow this road down into the Rift.

At a small group of *dukas* turn right, signposted **"Rifle Range"**: Follow the road, ignoring both a frequently used left turn to the rifle range and a second minor left turn, to head north past the rock faces of **Ndeiya**, and a large drop in the Rift Valley floor. Follow the road down this and head towards the east side of Susua.

At the base of the eastern flanks, the main track

forks right, but take the left branch which to a small group of *dukas* and *manyattas*.

From here a rough track, with deep water runnels at the side, heads straight up for seven kilometres (four miles). Turn left for the cave area or right to follow the track for eight meandering kilometres (five miles) to reach the edge of the inner crater.

From the roadhead follow game tracks anti-clockwise around the rim, staying close to the rim. It takes between one and two hours to reach the summit and the complete circuit takes between six and eight hours. It can be extremely unpleasant because of the sharp lava fields.

NGONG 2,461 metres (8,074 feet)

On a clear day from this is pleasant undulating ridge perched on the edge of the Rift Valley, you can see some of the best views in the country — with vistas over **Sabuk**, **Mount Kenya**, the **Aberdares**, **Longonot**, **Suswa**, **Shambole**, the **Nkuruman Escarpment**, **Lengai**, **Mount Meru**, **Kilimanjaro**, and many others, all visible from **Lamwia**, the highest point.

About twenty-five kilometres (16 miles) south-west of **Nairobi**, the four peaks of the Ngong Hills, resembling knuckles, are commonly numbered one to four from north to south. The southernmost, Lamwia, is number four. The traverse of the ridge an enjoyable short excursion, mostly on grassy tracks.

ESAKUT

A delightful mountain in the Rift Valley behind the Ngong Hills. Although only two hours from Nairobi, it is hardly ever climbed. It gives a delightful ridge walk and good views.

You are advised to wear boots as the ground is very stony. Watch out for ticks — the hill is notorious for them. Take all your water.

At Ngong town turn right at the T-junction and then bear right at an offset roundabout. Follow this road, the Ngong circular road, for eight kilometres (five miles) from Ngong.

At this point the road to Ndeiya and Susua branches off right. Continue for another eight kilometres (five miles) and then turn right on to a rocky track carry on for a few hundred metres to the fork left. Follow the road for about four kilometres (two and a half miles) until it suddenly heads north. Just after the sudden right hand bend is a left turn.

Take this rough track which heads initially west and then south, over a ridge of Esayeti into the basin between the two mountains. Park at any convenient point. It takes two hours from Nairobi.

OLOOLKISAILI 1,760 metres (5,774 feet)

This prominent hill lies just to the south of the Magadi Road, and offers good ridge walking, but it's a long hot climb. The hill is a roughly north-south ridge that curves round the remains of a crater to the east.

Of the two summits at both ends of the ridge, the northern one is highest by about one metre (three feet). There are three approaches. The first two give access to the north and south summits respectively, the third to the centre of the main ridge from where either summit can be tackled.

In all cases, just follow the best looking line, but be prepared for some steep ground. Take plenty of water. Boots are recommended.

It is possible to stay at the *bandas* at **Olorgesailie Prehistoric Site** (convenient for the first ascent) or camp at the foot of the climb to get a suitably early start.

SUBUGO 2,683 (8,802 feet)

This is the highest point of the rolling, grassy **Loita Hills**, a pleasant range to the west of the **Nkuruman escarpment**. The easy-going underfoot and the wide open spaces make an enjoyable walk.

The area is sparsely inhabited by Maasai, some of whom have settled. For rock climbers, **Lost Aloe Crag** is worthwhile.

Drive west From **Narok**, turn left on to the **Keekorok road**, and after a few metres fork left again on to the **Narosura road**.

Follow this through Narosura to climb the Loita escarpment, the top of which is about eighty kilometres (50 miles) from Narok. From here a rough 4WD track used to lead up to Subugo, although the first part is very steep.

Alternatively about three kilometres (almost two miles) from where the road finally levels off completely is a deep valley on the right. It is possible to drive some way into here to find a suitable campsite.

The campsite is at 2,133 metres (7,000 feet) and is extremely cold at night. Lost Aloe Crag lies on the north east side of the valley, about one and a half kilometres (almost one mile) from the road.

CHYULU 4,430 metres (7,134 feet)

The highest point of a very lovely range of hills running parallel to the Nairobi-Mombasa road offers a scope for hill walking and very good views of Kilimanjaro.

The hills are mostly grass covered with extensive stands of forest. Conditions vary with the rains and the grass is either very high or very short. Fires occur frequently and destroy much of the vegetation.

There is no water. *Miraa* grows in places and you'll probably see people gathering it for sale. There is a lot of game, but the elephant and buffalo are extremely shy.

4WD is recommended for all routes.

NZAUI 1,830 metres (6,003 feet)

This dramatic-looking peak, described by Lugard as "the massive sentinel that guards the gate to the heart of Africa", is obvious to those driving to Nairobi from Mombasa. **Nzaui** is now best known for the rock climb, **"The Nose"**. The summit is covered in forest but there is a good viewpoint nearby.

There is a small network of roads on the mountain, and a **forest station** with a pleasant **rest house**, recently repaired by the Mountain Club of Kenya. There is a water supply at the rest house which also has excellent camping nearby.

Nzaui makes a pleasant, if long, day trip, or a good lazy weekend. Drive down the Mombasa road to Emali and turn left along a murram road for several kilometres, through **Matiliku market**, continuing north with the rock face to your right.

A little before **Nziu village** a track turns right on the crest of the hill. A battered **signpost** facing the other way is marked "Nzaui Forest, Kyense Highway, eight miles".

Follow the track, crossing a wide sandy **river bed** and soon after turn right and follow the track, which is very stony in places and can be impassable after heavy rains.

It is usually passable by 4WD or, high clearance cars. After traversing horizontally for a kilometre or two (about a mile) it gradually climbs to the summit. Near the top the track divides: the left branch leads to the Rest House, and the right to the view point by the **summit**.

Taita Hills

The Taitas are surprisingly green, lush, rugged, and give good views. Except for their highest peaks they are densely-inhabited by the friendly Taita people. There are no security problems.

VURIA 2,209 metres (7,248 feet)

The highest point in the Taitas, this excellent viewpoint looks out over **Kasigau, Mawenzi, Kibo, Ngulia**, and the **Chyulus**. The plains of **Tsavo** seem to be vertically below.

From **Voi** take the **Taveta road** past **Bura**. About one kilometre after the Bura turn off go right to follow a good murram road up a dramatic but pretty valley.

Yala is the rock peak to the right of the valley head: **Vuria**, the highest point, is to the left. Over fifteen kilometres (nine miles) from the main road, some *dukas* mark the col at the head of the valley. Turn left to drive right round the northern flank of Vuria.

After just over three kilometres (two miles) a track goes off left. It is generally good, but steep and leads three kilometres (almost two miles) to the **radio station** on the summit.

It is pleasant to camp right by the track on the last but one bend just below the top, though it can be extremely cold. The best views are not from the summit, but directly away from it, from the last bend. This takes you to an open clearing.

KASIGAU 1,641 metres (5,383 feet)

Standing completely alone in the plains south of

Voi, this impressive mountain is steep on all sides and features a number of large precipices.

Guides are advisable and can be obtained from the Chief's Office or possibly the forest post. The best camping can be found by driving a few kilometres up the **Mwatate-Rukanga** road, and pulling off into clearings in the bush. The drive round **Kasigau** is recommended.

The walk starts in **Rukanga village**. Either drive down the **Mombasa road** thirty kilometres (20 miles) south of the Voi to **Maungu** turn off and turn right. Alternatively, if coming from the Taitas, turn south off the **Voi-Taveta** road onto an unlikely looking track five hundred metres (a third of a mile) east of the Wundanyi turn off.

After five kilometres (three miles) turn left then right through some estate buildings, and then look for signs to **"Kasigau Road"** to avoid getting lost in the **sisal estate**.

From the main road, walk along the branch going into the town centre, then bear right to follow a water pipe into a forested gully to the right of a large castle-like buttress. Water is available at the head of the pipe.

Climb steeply through the forest to the main ridge. At this point you may find you have circled round behind the ridge without realising it, so turn right, not left as you might expect.

Follow the ridge through the forest, until a final steep ascent brings you to the summit. It is worth reaching the tops of some of the buttresses for more extensive views.

Climbing and Trekking Advisory

Any reasonably fit person can trek, but the fitter you are, the more you will enjoy it. Do as much walking and exercise as possible to prepare yourself for Kenya's highland trails.

The best time for climbing or trekking is in the two dry seasons — January to March, and July to October. You can organise your expedition through one of Kenya's specialised tour operators or by consulting the Mountain Club of Kenya (See Listings).

Trekking demands that you wear strong, comfortable boots with good soles although, at low altitudes, tennis shoes or running shoes are adequate.

Higher up, good boots are essential, and in snow or ice these should be large enough to allow for one or two layers of heavy woollen or cotton — never nylon — socks. Bring several pairs. Wearing light shoes or sneakers after the day's walk will help to relax your feet.

Loose fitting trousers, hiking shorts or, for women, wrap-around skirts are ideal. It is better to wear two light layers of clothing than a single thick one. If you get too hot, you can always peel the top layer off. At very high altitudes wear thermal underwear.

Your pack should be as small as possible, light, and easy to open. The following gear is recommended:

Two pairs of woollen or corduroy trousers or skirts; two warm sweaters; three drip-dry shirts or T-shirts; ski or thermal underwear; at least half-a-dozen pairs of woollen socks; one pair of walking shoes; one extra pair of sandals; light casual shoes or sneakers; woollen hat; gloves or mittens; strong, warm sleeping bag with hood; a thin sheet of foam rubber for a mattress; padded anorak or parka; plastic raincoat; sunglasses and sun lotion; toilet gear; towels; medical kit; water bottle; and a light day pack. It is better to carry too many clothes than not enough. Drip-dry fabrics are best.

Your medical kit should include pain killers (for high-altitude headaches); mild sleeping pills (for high-altitude insomnia); streptomycin (for diarrhoea); septram (for bacillary dysentery); tinidozole (for amoebic dysentery); throat lozenges and cough drops; ophthalmic ointment or drops; one broad spectrum antibiotic; alcohol (for massaging feet to prevent blisters); blister pads; bandages and elastic plasters; antiseptic and cotton; a good sun block; and a transparent lip salve.

In addition to these, you should carry food, a torch, candles, lighter, pocket knife, scissors, spare shoelaces, string, safety pins, toilet paper, and plastic bags to protect food, wrap up wet or dirty clothes, and carry your litter. Much of this can be bought in Kenya. You can probably buy your tent and photographic equipment more cheaply at home. It is also wise to carry high-energy food such as chocolate, dried fruit nuts, and whisky, brandy, or vodka for a warming nightcap.

Cooking and eating utensils are normally provided by the trekking agency and are carried by the porters.

Lock your bag against theft or accidental loss. And make sure you have plenty of small currency for minor expenses along the way.

Water is most likely to be contaminated below 2,900 metres (9,500 feet) so do not drink from streams no matter how clear or sparkling they look. Chlorine is not effective against amoebic cysts. All water should be well boiled or treated with iodine: add four drops per litre and leave for twenty minutes before drinking.

Walk at your own pace. Drink as much liquid as possible to combat high altitude and heat dehydration. Never wait for blisters to develop but pamper tender feet with an alcohol massage.

Mountain Sickness

Both trekkers and climbers are at risk of mountain sickness. Sudden ascents to heights of 3,600 metres (12,000 feet) and more, without acclimatization, can lead to an accumulation of water, either on the lungs or brain. If this occurs it is *essential* to descend immediately to seek prompt medical attention. If left untreated, mountain sickness can be fatal.

Early mountain sickness acts as a warning. It can develop into pulmonary oedema (waterlogged lungs) or cerebral oedema (waterlogged brain). The symptoms are headache, nausea, loss of appetite, sleeplessness, fluid retention, and swelling of the body.

Mountain sickness develops slowly, manifesting itself two or three days after reaching high altitudes. The cure is to climb no higher until the symptoms have disappeared.

Pulmonary oedema is characterized by breathlessness and a persistent cough, even when resting, accompanied by congestion of the chest. If these symptoms appear, descend at once.

Cerebral oedema is less common. Its symptoms are extreme tiredness, vomiting, severe headaches, staggering when walking, abnormal speech and behaviour, drowsiness, and even coma. Victims must return at once to a lower altitude and abandon all thoughts of their trek.

There have been more recorded cases of mountain sickness on Mount Kenya than any other mountain, mainly because of the quick ascent to extreme heights. Youth, strength, and fitness make no difference. Above 3,000 metres (9,840 feet) the air becomes noticeably thinner and those who climb too high, too fast, are exposing themselves to risk.

You should plan frequent rest days between 3,700 and 4,300 metres (12,000-14,000 feet), sleeping at the same altitude for at least two nights. Climb higher during the day but always descend to the same level to sleep.

Never pitch camp more than 450 metres (1,500 feet) higher in any one day, even if you feel fit enough for a climb twice that height. At 4,300 metres (14,108 feet), the body requires three to four litres (five-seven pints) of liquid a day. At low altitude try to drink at least a litre (two pints) a day.

If you begin to suffer early mountain sickness, go no higher until the symptoms have disappeared. If more serious symptoms appear, descend immediately to a lower elevation. Mild symptoms should clear between one and two days. If a doctor is available the symptoms can be treated but in severe cases the patient must descend.

Some victims are incapable of making correct decisions and you may have to force them to go down against their will. The victim must always be accompanied.

If the victim is unable to walk he should be carried down at once. No matter what the reason, never delay, even at night.

Mount Kenya National Park runs a highly-skilled Mountain Rescue Team.

Kenya's Mountain Ranges

Mount Kenya:

Batian, 5,199m, **Nelion** 5,188m, **Lenana** 4,985m.

Mount Elgon:

Wagagai 4,322m, **Sudek** 4,310m, **Koitobos** 4,231m.

Aberdare Range:

Lesatima 3,994m, **Kinangop** 3,906m, **Kipipiri** 3,349m.

Cherangani Hills:

Chemnirot 3,505m, **Kalelaigelat** 3,380m, **Chepkotet** 3,370m, **Kaisungur** 3,167m

Sekerr Range:

Mtelo 3,325m.

Mau Range:

Melili 3,099m.

Ndoto Mountains:

Bokhol 2,534m.
Nyambeni Range:
Itiani 2,513m.

Ngong Hills:

Ol Lernoya 2,461m.

Taita Hills:

Vuria 2,209m.

Individual peaks

Nyiru 2,805m.
Longonot 2,777m.
Subugo 2,683m.
Ol Doinyo Orok 2,553m.
Chyulu Hills 2,175m.
Ol Doinyo Sapuk 2,146 m.

Kenya's major rivers

Tana 708 kms; Athi-Galana-Sabaki 547 kms; Mara 290 kms; Nzoia 258 kms; Turkwel-Suam 354 kms; Arror-Kerio 350 kms; Ewaso Ngiro (North) 330 kms; Voi 210 kms; Yala 180 kms; Ewaso Ngiro (South) 140 kms; Melawa 110 kms; Sondu 110 kms; Kuja 90 kms.

Kenya's major lakes

Victoria, 67,493 sq kms; Turkana, 6,405 sq kms; Baringo, 129 sq kms; Magadi, 104 sq kms; Naivasha, 114-991 sq kms; Amboseli, 0-114 sq kms; Jipe, 40 sq kms; Bogoria, 34 sq kms; Nakuru, 5-30 sq kms; Elementeita, 18 sq kms.

Kenya's major waterfalls

Gura 273 m; Seven Forks (Kindaruma) 135 m; Nyahururu (Thomson's) 73 m; Swift-Rutherford 67 m; Broderick 52 m; Yala 40 m; Selby 35 m; Chania 25 m; Thika 25 m.

PART FOUR: BUSINESS KENYA

The Economy

Kenya's economy rests firmly on the pillar of agriculture which accounts for over one-third of GDP and approximately two-thirds of exports. Agriculture is supplemented by three other major income-generating sectors — manufacturing, commerce, and tourism — which collectively account for an additional one quarter of GDP. A fifth important sector is Government services, accounting for about seventeen per cent of GDP.

Sound economic management coupled with significant inflows of foreign capital have allowed Kenya to weather a series of challenges during the 1980s. These include the 1980-1983 global recession and a sharp fall-off in food production due to prolonged regional drought.

In the four years to 1988 economic growth averaged over four per cent. Inflation was kept below ten per cent a year.

Since Independence, Kenya's economic policies have been guided by pragmatism rather than ideology. The Government's basic economic philosophy has been to create a mixed economy in which private and public sectors play complementary roles.

Local and foreign private investment is encouraged through legal safeguards and monetary and fiscal incentives.

Opportunities

Agriculture

For centuries the agricultural sector has been the mainstay of Kenya's economy and remains one of the country's chief sources of income, employment, and foreign exchange.

Kenya's most important export crops, coffee and tea, are recognised worldwide for their quality. Other important traditional export crops are pyrethrum, pineapples, and sisal.

Expansion is expected largely from intensification of smallholdings leading to better yields and crop diversification. A new Ministry to bring marginal arid and semi-arid lands into use was created in 1989. But because of constraints on land-ownership most direct investors in agriculture face one of two choices.

The first, and most promising, choice is to organise small farmers to supply agriculture produce. Several "outgrower" schemes in Kenya have proved highly successful. Investors capable of organising domestic supply from small farmers can reap rich rewards. Secondly, large landowners may

wish to enter joint ventures with foreign investors. Opportunities also exist in the supply of agricultural inputs and services, seed production, pest control, small dam construction, irrigation systems, and specialized services for such crops as oil seeds, barley, tobacco, sugar cane, and ground nuts.

New opportunities have also arisen in non-traditional agricultural exports. Kenya's fertile land, diverse agro-ecological zones, resourceful small farmers, and well-developed physical infrastructure provide ample support for a wide variety of alternative crops.

Exports of flowers, fresh fruits, and vegetables have grown rapidly, particularly such crops as strawberries and passion fruit.

The new refrigerated container handling facility at Mombasa port should also help to spur the growth of horticultural exports.

Many investment opportunities also exist in agro-processing. Multinational companies such as Del Monte and BAT Industries have been processing agro products in Kenya for many years, strong testament to the potential of crop processing.

Mangoes, passion fruit, papaya and other tropical fruits all lend themselves to processing into juice or concentrate; beans and carrots to canning; ginger, garlic, and onions to dehydration; eucalyptus, jojoba, and castor oil to extraction; and mangrove forests to charcoal production.

Along with many rivers and lakes, the Indian Ocean and Lake Victoria, offer many opportunities for fish farming, particularly prawns, trout, and crocodiles, as well as the processing (filleting and fish-meal production) of offshore fish.

Another item with considerable potential is the production of tanned hides and leather goods for export. Kenya produces approximately 1.5 million hides and five million skins a year, most of which are processed only as far as the wet-blue stage for export.

Manufacturing

Since Independence, Kenya's manufacturing sector has grown at twice the rate of the economy as a whole. Much of this is the result of a successful policy of import substitution. Many consumer products once imported are now produced nationally.

But opportunities still exist for product innovation and import substitution, particularly for intermediate goods and products with high local-value-added content. The greatest potential, however, lies in export-orientated manufacturing.

The introduction of an in-bond manufacturing programme has created considerable opportunity for light manufacturing and assembly operations for export. Given the well-developed nature of the garment and textile industries in Kenya, the ready-to-wear clothing sector, in particular, offers strong potential.

There are currently forty-five textile operations and more than 400 garment workshops. Firms establishing export-orientated textile and garment assembly operations can draw upon an available pool of trained and experienced labour, including technical and supervisory personnel.

The supporting infrastructure is also well-developed with reliable maintenance and repair services readily available.

Opportunities also exist in other light assembly export operations — such as electronic equipment and components, toys, houseware, and footwear.

And there are both national and regional markets for locally-assembled vehicles and agricultural machinery, for chemicals, fertilizers, and mineral products.

These include the production of PVC granules from ethyl alcohol; formaldehyde from ethanol; caustic soda and chlorine-based products; tallow for soap; the mixing and granulating of fertilizers; the extraction of caffeine from tea waste; sheet glass and ceramics; and the mining and processing of marble.

Tourism

Tourism is Kenya's largest source of foreign exchange earnings. In 1987, almost 700,000 tourists visited Kenya. The country hopes to attract one million foreign tourists a year by the year 2000. To achieve this, the Government is committed to upgrading and expanding the infrastructure, including roads and international and domestic airports with a firm commitment to preserve wildlife and other natural resources.

Private investment is welcomed in hotels, restaurants, and other facilities. Kenya's Indian Ocean coast, rapidly becoming a top choice for sun and sand-seeking vacationers from Europe and farther afield, offers particularly attractive opportunities for development.

The potential for new investment in hotels on the coast is estimated at 1,000 beds a year — until 1993 at least.

Small enterprises

Increased agricultural incomes, along with renewed emphasis on development of industries which utilize local resources, provide increasing opportunities for small businesses.

Among the many that have been identified are honey processing, oil milling, small dehydration plants, rice bran oil, animal feeds, surgical cotton gauze, surgical dressings, sanitary towels, biscuits, confectionery, potato crisps, bakeries, ice creams, dairy products, hosiery, industrial clothing, school uniforms, low-cost footware (from PVC, cloth, and leather), umbrellas, raincoats, school equipment, stationery, soaps, stoves, door handles, gate valves, electrical fittings, bricks, roof tiles, agricultural implements — such as animal-driven ploughs and pangas (machetes) — picture frames, sporting goods, toys, dry cleaning services, production of speciality paper from textile waste, and many others.

The Workforce

Kenya's 1987 population was around twenty-one million and, with an estimated growth rate of 3.7 per cent a year, it will be thirty-five million by the year 2000.

The major population centres are the capital, Nairobi, Mombasa, Kisumu, Nakuru, Eldoret, and Thika. Kenyan labour is plentiful, educated, young, mobile, willing to learn, and English-speaking. But only fifteen per cent of a potential work force of about eight million are formally employed although a significant number earn their living in the informal, entrepreneurial (*jua kali*) sector.

With 300,000 Kenyans entering the job market annually, absenteeism and turnover rates are low whether the employee is unskilled, semi-skilled, skilled, or at management level.

Education

Anticipating an increased demand for skilled and semi-skilled labour, the Government reorganised the education system in 1984 to provide eight years of primary and four years of secondary schooling. Another four years of higher education emphasizes vocational training.

The country has four public universities in addition to a number of private universities and institutions offering professional skills.

Technical artisans of extremely high-calibre graduate from the country's three polytechnics, seventeen institutes of technology, and twelve technical training institutes.

Management personnel are recruited from university through advertisements or employment agencies. Many companies identify potential employees by hiring university students as summer interns during university holidays.

Investment

Kenya has followed a mixed economic development model since Independence. Although the respective roles of public and private sectors have evolved over time, the country has experienced remarkable continuity in its economic development strategy.

This strategy is to promote rapid economic growth through public investment while simultaneously providing incentives for local and foreign private investment in key economic sectors.

Kenya's guiding economic philosophy is pragmatic rather than idealistic. The key elements include:

- Maintenance of a flexible exchange rate to ensure sufficient rewards for exports in which Kenya enjoys true competitive advantages, and for efficient import substitution.
- Maintenance of farm prices to ensure adequate returns for both small and large producers, thus helping to generate food production and promote a more even rural-urban balance.
- Liberal import policies that rely more on tariffs and less on licensing to improve the efficiency and competitiveness of domestic industries.
- Wage policies that contribute to price stability, encourage job-creation, and limit disparities between wages in the formal and informal sectors.
- Interest rate policies to provide positive incentives to savers and promote efficient allocation of credit among borrowers.
- Liberalization of price controls so that prices reflect market forces, real scarcities of finished goods, and production costs.

Private Sector

Kenya's economic strategy confirms a general move in favour of an increased private sector role in the economy. In general, private sector development has enjoyed consistent support since Independence.

Recently, however, the Government has begun to recognize that constraints on public sector financial and managerial resources makes an even broader private sector role imperative.

Under an appropriate incentive system, private investors can make attractive profits and contribute to the broad-based development of Kenya. Such incentives should remain stable over a long period.

The Government wants to use fiscal and monetary policies, as well as market-based incentives, to ensure a flourishing private sector.

Government investment in industrial and commercial activities will be highly selective and the privatization of some existing parastatal enterprises is anticipated.

There is no equivalent in Kenya of the UK Restrictive Trade Practices Act. Similarly, there is no anti-trust legislation.

Foreign Investment

The Government welcomes foreign investment and offers investors a number of incentives and guarantees. All sectors of the economy are open to foreign investment, although there are restrictions in small-scale retail operations and on foreign ownership of agricultural land.

Unless highly beneficial, foreign investments below K£500,000 are also discouraged.

Finally, both local and foreign private investment in the production and distribution of arms and ammunition, and involvement in basic infrastructure, such as roads and communications, is forbidden.

Incentives

Performance Requirements

No formal performance requirements are required from local or foreign investors. The only specific performance-type requirement is for the manufacture-in-bond programme which is open only to firms that export 100 per cent of their output. Except in the case of vehicle assembly, there are no minimum requirements for employing a local workforce.

Investment Priorities

Kenya has none of the restrictive industrial licensing found in many other developing countries. Investments are regulated by specific legal provisions such as the Exchange Control Act, Foreign Investment Protection Act, Customs and Excise Act, and by specific sector laws such as the Industrial Registration Act, Banking Act, Hotel and Restaurants Act, Trade Licensing Act, etc.

The highest priority is given to new investment proposals which contribute to the overall economic objectives — job creation, rural development, and foreign exchange generation.

Three general activities are strongly encouraged: export-orientated manufacturing and agro-industry; efficient import substitution; and small-scale, labour-intensive enterprises, especially those owned by indigenous entrepreneurs. Priority is given to:
- Investments which utilize domestic raw materials, intermediate goods, and components.
- Local resource-based activities such as agro-processing, mining, and leather production.
- Export-orientated operations that generate net foreign exchange earnings. Manufacturing operations based on import substitution, which provide little or no net foreign exchange savings are give a low priority.
- Projects which introduce new skills and technology.
- Agricultural outgrower schemes involving small indigenous farmers as subcontractors or suppliers.
- Local private investment in small-scale, labour-intensive projects.

In promoting foreign investment, Kenya looks for large capital transfers; investments which make major contributions to food security through investment in irrigation, or introduction of new crops and technology which improve small-farmer output.

Although foreign ownership of agricultural land is not normally allowed, the Government may relax this for investments which meet these criteria.

Foreign investments below £500,000 are discouraged — unless they make special contributions in those areas noted above.

Similarly, foreign investments that involve minimal capital transfers and rely heavily on local borrowing are also given a low priority.

Guarantees to Investors

Additional investment incentives are under consideration. In addition to its pro-private sector investment climate, under the Foreign Investment Protection Act (FIPA) Kenya offers manifold guarantees with regard to repatriation of profits, dividends, interest, and capital.

To be eligible for FIPA guarantees, investors must obtain a Certificate of Approved Enterprise from the Ministry of Finance. This allows after-tax profits to be transferred out of Kenya including retained profits which have not been capitalized; the original equity investment, plus retained profits which have been capitalized; and principal of foreign loans and interest as specified.

If permission for the transfer of capital gains arising from the sale of foreign assets is refused, they must be invested in Government Securities at market rates. The interest income from these securities, however, may be transferred out of Kenya. In addition, at the end of five years the capital gains may be repatriated in the same manner as the original equity investment.

Kenya belongs to the World Bank-affiliated Multilateral Investment Guarantee Agency (MIGA) which gives guarantees against commercial risk to enterprises that invest in member countries.

Kenya is also a member of the International Centre for the Settlement of Investment Disputes (ICSID): any disputes with the Government may be referred to this neutral organisation for arbitration.

Finally, United States' firms or citizens who invest in Kenya are eligible for insurance against expropriation, war, revolution, and insurrection from the Overseas Private Insurance Corporation (OPIC).

Kenya has an unblemished record for meeting its international commitments. Its Constitution guarantees that no property can be compulsorily acquired by the Government except in accordance with the law. And in the event of acquisition in the public interest, the Government is obliged make full and prompt compensation. Affected parties have direct access to the High Court.

Market Access

As a signatory to the Lome Convention, Kenya's products receive preferential access to 320 million consumers in the European Economic Community (EEC). Preferences include:
• Duty-free entry for all Kenyan industrial products.
• Highly favourable treatment for a wide range of farm produce including beef, fish, dairy products, cereals, and fresh and processed fruit and vegetables.
• Kenyan products are free of quotas or other restrictions.

Kenya also enjoys preferential market access under the Generalized System of Preferences (GSP) which allows manufactured and semi-manufactured goods duty-free access to selected markets.

Under this scheme a wide range of Kenya's manufactured products are entitled to preferential treatment in the United States, Japan, Canada, Switzerland, Norway, Sweden, Finland, Australia, Austria, New Zealand, and most East European countries.

Kenya is also a member of the Preferential Trade Area (PTA) with exports and imports between eighteen countries in eastern and southern Africa entitled to preferential tariff rates under the PTA rules of origin. Only companies that are more than fifty-one per cent locally-owned are eligible for reductions in tariffs that can amount to as much as sixty-five per cent — a major incentive for investors wishing to export or import within the PTA markets.

Manufacturing under bond

To encourage manufacturing in Kenya for world markets, a manufacturing — under — bond programme is open to both local and foreign investors.

As all goods produced under the programme are exempt from Customs duties and sales taxes on plant, machinery and equipment, raw materials, components, and other imported inputs, it allows manufacturers to compete effectively in world markets.

Goods produced under bond are also exempt from all export taxes and levies. Finally, manufacturers receive top priority for import licences and other required approvals.

Only manufacturers who produce solely for export and not for local and export markets can take part. Firms exporting goods worth less than K£500,000 a year or employing less than fifty people do not qualify.

Eventually the programme will be open to production facilities anywhere in the country, but initially licences will be granted only to operations located in Nairobi, Mombasa, and Kisumu, or their environs.

Management must provide offices for the exclusive use of customs, as well as weighing and measuring equipment, and may have to reimburse the labour costs of customs personnel.

Export Compensation

Kenya also offers export compensation to firms which sell all or part of their output abroad. Manufacturers of most goods are eligible for a refund equivalent to twenty per cent of the Free On Board (FOB) value of their exports, provided that these goods have a local value added component of at least thirty per cent, and that duties paid on major imported raw materials or components account for at least twenty per cent of the CIF value of the imports.

Firms manufacturing under bond do not qualify for export compensation.

Capital Investment Allowance

To encourage industries in rural areas, investors outside Nairobi and Mombasa qualify for an investment allowance of seventy-five per cent on plant, machinery, buildings, and equipment.

But in Nairobi and Mombasa new investments qualify for the lower rate of twenty-five per cent. For manufacturers under bond in all locations, the rate is 100 per cent. These allowances take the form of a tax deduction applied through accelerated depreciation of capital assets.

Investment allowance applies to industrial buildings for manufacturing and any new fixed plant and machinery but not replacement machinery.

The investment allowance for hotels is based only on the cost of construction — and does not include the cost of fixtures and fittings.

Import Duty and Sales Tax Waivers

In certain circumstances manufacturers may apply for import duty drawbacks or sales tax remission through the Industrial Protection Committee. Most consideration is given to applications where the items are for export but export compensation not claimed.

Where the Government wishes to encourage or protect a new industry sales tax and import duty waivers are also available. This is also common to contracts financed by overseas aid agencies so that the contractor does not have pay import duty or sales tax on his equipment — provided it is re-exported at the end of the contract.

Imported plant and equipment up to a maximum CIF value of K£500,000, intended for small-scale industries located outside major cities, may be exempt from Custom duties and sales tax. A fifty per cent remission of duties and tax is granted to industries established more than twenty kilometres (12 miles) outside the limits of Nairobi and Mombasa and within a ten-kilometre-radius (six-mile) of towns with a population of more than 20,000 (according to the 1979 census).

Industries in places where the population is less than 20,000 are given 100 per cent duty exemption. Investors should apply to the Ministry of Finance for these exemptions.

Getting Started

The principal forms of business enterprise in Kenya are registered companies (private and public); branch offices of companies registered outside Kenya; partnerships; sole proprietorship; and co-operatives. Most large scale businesses are conducted through limited liability companies regulated by the Companies Act.

Company Registration

The first step to forming a Kenyan company is the approval and reservation of a company name by the Registrar of Companies (PO Box 40112, Nairobi). All registered company names, private or public, must have "limited" as the last word. Next, the company must draft a memorandum and articles of association stating the company's name, its domicile, original share capital, the number of shares each subscriber holds, its objects, location, and postal address.

The articles, concerning matters such as directors' powers, share issue and allotment, transfers, and shareholders' rights, set out regulations for the company's operation.

Foreign shareholders must have approval from the Central Bank of Kenya (PO Box 6000, Nairobi) to appoint non-resident directors, allot shares to non-resident shareholders; subscribe to the memorandum and articles of association for, or on behalf of, non-residents; and have permission from the Ministry of Finance to issue shares to any corporate body which is not a company formed or registered under the Companies Act of Kenya.

The company should submit the memorandum and articles of association to the Registrar of Companies for registration, together with required fees, statutory forms, written consent of each director to act as such, and each director's particulars, including the names and addresses of other companies of which he or she is a director, and approvals of the Central Bank, where applicable.

On registration, the Registrar General issues a certificate of incorporation, and the company becomes a legal entity. The company then meets to appoint directors, the secretary, auditors and bankers, and to approve the company seal.

A private company usually commences trading upon receipt of its Certificate of Incorporation. A public company must comply with certain other requirements, principally the filing of a prospectus or a statement in lieu of a prospectus.

If there is any alteration in the above particulars, the company must deliver particulars of the alteration to the Registrar within sixty days.

A foreign company so registered has the power to hold land in Kenya as though it were incorporated under the Kenya Companies Act.

A foreign company must exhibit its name and state the country in which it is incorporated on any prospectus, at every place where it carries on business, and on its bills, letterheads, etc. Particulars of directors must be shown on all trade circulars, letters, etc., as for a company incorporated in Kenya.

Every foreign company shall prepare a yearly balance sheet and profit and loss account and, if it is a holding company, group accounts.

These accounts must comply with the provisions of the Act as though the company was incorporated in Kenya and a copy must be sent to the Registrar of Companies for registration. A foreign company need not comply with this section of the Act if:
• It is incorporated in the Commonwealth.
• It is a private company (except where one of the shareholders is a company that is not a private company); and
• In every calendar year, a certificate signed by a director and the secretary of the company, verifying the conditions. requisite for such exemption, is delivered to the Registrar.

There are no legal requirements for the audit of a branch company's accounts, but the tax authorities place greater reliance on audited accounts.

A foreign company wishing to issue a prospectus in Kenya must have Central Bank approval.

When a foreign company ceases to operate a branch in Kenya it must file a return with the Registrar of Companies.

Partnership

The partnership act in Kenya lays down, in general terms, relationships between partners and between partnerships and the public.

The relationship between the partners can be modified by a partnership agreement. If carrying on business in the names other than those of the partners a partnership must be registered with the Registrar General under the Registration of Business Names Act.

Partnerships are not subject to income tax, since the partners are taxed on each individual's share of the income. Nevertheless, partnerships are obliged to file a tax return.

Acquisition and Takeover

The Capital Issues Committee must be consulted whenever a foreign interest is involved in a proposed acquisition or takeover.

The Committee, which operates under the Ministry of Finance, is made up of representatives from the Ministries of Finance, Commerce, Industry and the Central Bank. The Capital Issues Committee also grants permission to companies that wish to be quoted on the Nairobi Stock Exchange.

A merger between two or more independent enterprises engaged in manufacturing or distributing substantially similar commodities, or engaged in supplying substantially similar services, or a takeover of one or more such enterprises, or by a person who controls another such enterprise, requires the authority of the Ministry of Finance

under the Restrictive Trade, Monopolies, and Price Control Bill, 1988.

Registration of Foreign Capital

Foreign capital is acknowledged in a Certificate of Approved Enterprise issued by the Treasury. The Certificate states the amount of the equity investment and, if applicable, loan capital. It also shows the currency of any loan capital and the allowable rate of interest. In the case of a branch company, the amount of fixed capital is normally shown under the Certificate of Approved Enterprise.

If no Certificate of Approved Enterprise is given, then the Central Bank can be asked for a written acknowledgement of the foreign funds invested. Such investments do not carry the specific rights given in the Foreign Investment Protection Act (FIPA). The remittance of dividends largely depends on Kenya's foreign exchange position at the time of asking.

Technology agreements between an investor and a local organisation need Central Bank approval if foreign exchange remittances are involved.

But it is increasingly difficult to obtain exchange control approval for royalty or management agreements. Many have been withdrawn — or renegotiated — since 1982.

Effect on Foreign Investment

At times these complex and lengthy approval procedures have deterred potential investors. Existing investors have learned to operate within the controls, but the current shortage of foreign exchange often leads to delays in payments to non-residents.

Restrictions of Foreign Ownership

A Certificate of Approved Enterprise is not usally given to foreign investors for speculative investments that have no economic value. A change of ownership in an existing business from local to foreign would not qualify — unless it could be proved that the business was being purchased for expansion.

Approval may also be withheld where a new investment competes with local enterprises that already meet local market needs. The main sectors of the economy affected by this restriction are tourism, agriculture, and the distributive trades.

There are no percentage restrictions on foreign ownership of local enterprises and joint ventures. But if foreign participation is more than fifteen per cent of the equity, for the purpose of borrowing foreign exchange from Kenyan banks, the enterprise is regarded as non-resident.

Non-resident enterprises in the agricultural, manufacturing, exporting, and tourism industries enjoy certain local borrowing facilities without Central Bank approval. These facilities vary, depending on the level of local participation.

Trends

Although the Government continues to encourage foreign investors, the allocation of foreign exchange is strictly controlled and all applications for foreign exchange are closely scrutinised.

On the other hand, as the Government looks towards the growth of the gross national product (GNP), especially in the export sector, it recognizes that such expansion entails foreign exchange cost.

Trade Licensing

Trade licensing in Kenya is regulated by the Trade Licensing Act.

Any business in Kenya can only be conducted in accordance with the terms of a current licence (the term "business" is defined as "carrying on the occupation of regulated trade").

In addition, non-citizens may not conduct a business in any place that is not a general business area, or in any specified goods, unless their licence specifically authorizes it.

Miscellaneous

A licence from Kenya Post and Telecommunications is required for radio telephones.

All factories must be registered with the Chief Inspector of Factories, who must certify that the premises conform to the provisions of the Factories Act in regard to health, safety, and welfare of employees.

A licence from the Transport Licensing Board will be required to operate any goods or passenger vehicles. Special movement permits are required for the transport of specified farm produce, such as cereals.

If the land on which a project is to be located is bought or leased from an existing owner, and the title allows it to be used for the purpose contemplated, no further approval is required.

But any change of land use must be approved by the Commissioner of Lands. Farmland cannot be transferred without the approval of the local Land Control Board — or Presidential exemption. Government permission is also required for the transfer of any Coast property.

New buildings must be zoned accordingly, and planning permission obtained from the relevant city or local authority, or from the Director of Physical Planning in the Ministry of Local Government and Physical Planning.

If the Kenya Power and Lighting Company cannot supply power permission to generate electricity may be needed from the Ministry of Energy and Regional Development, depending on the capacity required.

If an existing authority, such as a city or municipal council, cannot supply water then permission to extract, store, and use water from any source is needed from the Ministry of Water Development.

Import Procedures

Imports are subject to the Ministry of Commerce's licensing requirements. Approval is dependent on the availability of foreign exchange and the priority given in the import schedule.

Firms can import urgent spare parts and accessories with an FOB value up to K£250 without a licence.

Every year the items on these schedules are revised. Import Licensing Schedules are available from the Government Printer.

All imports worth more than K£2,000 are subject to quality and quantity inspection, carried out by SGS Kenya, Bureau Veritas, or Cotecna, depending upon the origin of the imports.

Customs clearance is issued at the port of entry after duty and sales tax have been paid.

All applications for import licences must be accompanied by a banker's cheque equal to one and a half per cent of the value of the imports. Payments for imports can only be made after the Central Bank is satisfied that all formalities have been fulfilled.

Export Procedures

The Central Bank and the Commissioner of Customs and Excise control export procedures. The government's main concern is that all foreign exchange is paid in Kenya.

Exporters offering more than ninety days credit need specific approval and a certificate from the Customs and Excise Department to claim export compensation.

Exporters who wish to take advantage of PTA's concessional tariffs need a certificate of compliance with rules of origin from the Ministry of Commerce.

The External Trade Authority of the Ministry of Commerce (KETA), advises the Government on policy and helps exporters.

Price Controls

Under the Price Control Act the Ministry of Finance can impose a maximum charge for any service. From time to time, the type of goods and the prices are amended by the Ministry.

The Act gives the Price Controller wide powers, such as the right to enter premises, inspect books and accounts, prohibit or regulate the movement of price-controlled goods, and impose fines for offences. There are also regulations in the Act concerning proper marking and labelling of goods and the making out of detailed invoices.

Kenyanization

Kenyans naturally aspire to control their own economy. They want their country's resources to be used for national development and the betterment of the lives of all citizens.

Excessive unemployment, aggravated by urban drift, has led to increasing government pressure on the private sector to Kenyanize personnel, to use labour-intensive methods, and to increase the worker payroll. It also provides a ready supply of unskilled labour.

Kenyanization, however, does not conflict with the Government policy of encouraging foreign investment. By increasing the level of investment, and in contributing to the Government goal of maintaining a rapidly-growing and stable mixed economy in which equal opportunities are assured, the two policies in fact complement each other.

Work Permits

The Government is pragmatic about granting work permits to expatriates. It recognizes that every investor requires specific expertise to run a business, particularly at the start.

Kenya's work permit policy allows investors to meet their genuine needs for expatriate management and technical personnel. Over time wherever possible, however, the Government does expect investors to replace expatriate with local personnel and a time-phased programme for training Kenyan replacements must accompany each work permit application.

Normally, technical experts employed by industry are allowed work permits without undue delay.

Foreign investors, approved under the Foreign Investment Protection Act, are allowed to employ at least one person of their choice to oversee their operations in Kenya.

But in 1989, the work permit policy was under revision. The new policy may link the number of work permits to the size of investment and actual job creation.

If qualified Kenyans are available for a job, however, it is in the investors's own interests to employ such personnel.

Visitors cannot take up work (paid or unpaid), or live in Kenya without the authority of the Principal Immigration Officer.

Patents

Patents are administered by the Registrar of Patents in the Office of the Attorney General. The Patent Registration Act provides for registration in Kenya of patents granted in the United Kingdom.

Applications must include a certified copy of the specifications of the United Kingdom Patent, along with a certificate from the Comptroller of Patents, Designs, and Trademarks of the United Kingdom.

Application in Kenya for patents granted in the United Kingdom must be made within three years of receipt of the original patent and registration in Kenya is parallel with the original grant.

Trademarks

Trademarks in Kenya are regulated by the Trademarks Act administered by the Registrar of Trademarks in the Office of the Attorney General.

Application to register trademarks must be made by the owner or their legal representative.

Applications are examined and advertised in the Kenya Gazette.

If no objection is received within sixty days, the trademark is then registered. The duration of trademarks is seven years from the date of filing and fourteen years on renewal.

Finance

Kenya has a well-developed financial system consisting of the Central Bank, twenty-four commercial banks, including Kenya Commercial Bank, Barclays Bank, Citicorp, Standard Chartered Bank, National Bank of Kenya, and about fifty non-bank financial institutions.

The commercial banks have more than 400 service centres throughout the country. In addition there are six development finance institutions, forty-seven insurance companies, a number of building societies, and more than 900 savings and credit institutions.

The Central Bank of Kenya administers the Exchange Control Act and also supervises the commercial bank and non-bank financial institutions.

The commercial banks offer a wide range of services, including short-term working capital loans, short-term roll-over financing and letters of credit. They normally provide only short-term, working capital, and only consider long-term finance of three to seven years on a case-by-case basis.

Limitations on local borrowing by foreign investors are relatively relaxed. There is no restriction whatsoever on local borrowing by firms with foreign ownership of less than fifteen per cent.

Firms with fifty to sixty per cent foreign ownership are now entitled to borrow locally up to forty per cent of their net worth, plus foreign loans. Firms with foreign ownership in excess of eighty-five per cent may borrow up to twenty per cent of their net worth.

However, where the shareholding in the hands of Kenya nationals exceeds fifty per cent, but it is less than eighty-five per cent, the firm can borrow up to sixty per cent of net worth, plus foreign loans. Foreign companies are also allowed to borrow locally for payment of customs duties and sales taxes on imported machinery.

In addition, investors can borrow local funds equal to the amount payable as duty and sales-tax on imported machinery and equipment. The Central Bank may consider relaxing of the limits on local borrowing on a case-by-case basis.

The criteria used in evaluating requests for increased local borrowing are the size of the investment, its exchange-generating potential, and its overall economic contribution to the country.

The six development banks operating in Kenya provide long-term finance for business projects of all sizes. And project finance for private sector ventures is available from international lending institutions, such as the East African Development Bank (EADB), International Finance Corporation (IFC), and other international development finance institutions created by industrialised countries to finance projects in developing countries.

There are also a number of donor-aided term finance windows and offshore lines of credit to support project finance now available through commercial banks.

Kenya's capital market is still relatively new. Secondary trading in long-term securities is carried out by a group of six Nairobi-based brokerage firms on the Nairobi Stock Exchange, formed in 1954. Brokers act purely on an agency basis. Currently, fifty-seven securities, including common shares, preferred shares, and debt securities, are listed on the stock exchange.

New issues of long-term private-sector securities in Kenya must be approved by the Capital Issues Committee of the Ministry of Finance.

This committee approves the issue price, timing of sales, and the allotment plan for shares. Two recent issues, one by Barclays Bank of Kenya Ltd, and one by Jubilee Insurance Co Ltd, were over-subscribed.

A large number of small shareholders own shares and the Government has created a Capital Market Development Council to further strengthen the capital market.

Private insurance and pension funds are important mobilizers of long-term savings in Kenya. These institutions, which normally invest their funds in real estate (ownership and property loans) and listed securities, have become an important source of financing for commercial and industrial construction

Taxation

The Income Tax Act distinguishes between companies that are resident and those that are non-resident for Kenyan income tax purposes.

A company is considered resident if it is managed and controlled by the board of directors in Kenya.

A company incorporated in Kenya is also considered resident in Kenya. A company may also be deemed resident in Kenya by a notice given in the Official Gazette.

Companies resident in Kenya are taxable on their worldwide profits. Any profits from trade carried on partly within Kenya and partly without Kenya are deemed to be incurred wholly in Kenya and taxable accordingly.

Income earned by a branch of a resident company that carries on business outside Kenya is subject to tax in Kenya, regardless of whether or not it is subject to tax in that country. Profits and losses are computed under normal Kenyan income tax rules, including wear and tear (depreciation) allowances.

Income from the foreign subsidiary of a resident company is not taxable if this income is remitted in the form of dividends or interest. Service fees received would probably be considered as taxable. The rules and practices in the area of taxation of foreign subsidiaries are not highly developed because there is very little outward investment.

There is no provision under Kenyan income tax for credits to be given against the Kenyan tax payable on income from foreign operations.

The only basis under which foreign taxes may be eligible for credit is if a tax treaty exists with the country in which the profits are earned. In these circumstances, the credit given is restricted to the amount of Kenyan tax on the profits of the foreign branch as computed for Kenyan income tax purposes.

Foreign taxes actually paid in excess of the amount credited cannot be carried forward or back for credit against liabilities for other years of income.

Where foreign tax is not eligible for credit, it is allowed as a deduction in computing profits subject to Kenyan income tax.

Taxation of non-resident companies

A non-resident company carrying on business in Kenya is subject to Kenyan income tax on the results of the business carried on in Kenya, unless specifically exempt.

Business income is computed for a branch company in the manner applicable to a resident company. The only exceptions are that payments of interest, royalties, and professional or management fees paid by the branch company to its head office abroad are not deductible for the purpose of Kenyan income tax, nor, in the case of insurance companies, are reinsurance premiums deductible when paid to head office.

Capital gains tax is also payable by a branch company in respect of the disposal of assets and property owned by the branch company, or used by it in connection with its permanent establishment in Kenya. Tax is withheld from the gross proceeds at the rate of two and a half per cent as a payment, on account, of any liability to capital gains tax.

A branch of a non-resident company subject to tax in Kenya will pay tax at the special rate of 52.5 per cent on its profits, as opposed to the normal rate for resident companies of forty-five per cent. However, there is no further withholding tax on any transfers of profit remitted by the branch company to its head office.

Representation Offices

A large number of representative offices in Kenya monitor the activities of a group either throughout Central and East Africa or, in some cases, throughout the whole of Africa.

Those companies not doing business in Kenya

are exempt from Kenyan income tax. If the head office function, however, is carried on in conjunction with an operation in Kenya that is subject to Kenyan income tax, then the expenses incurred in maintaining the administrative office will not normally be deductible.

Royalties

Tax is withheld from royalties paid to non-residents at the rate of twenty per cent, subject to treaty relief. The definition of a royalty is extremely wide and includes not only patent royalties, but also a right to use any literary, artistic or scientific work, or to payments for information concerning industrial, commercial, or scientific equipment or experience.

Rent

A resident who rents land in Kenya from a non-resident owner must deduct withholding tax on the payment at the rate of twenty per cent.

Management Fees

Where a resident company makes a payment to a non-resident in respect of management or professional fees, it should withhold tax at the rate of twenty per cent, subject to treaty relief.

Tax is not withheld for general and administrative expenses incurred by a non-resident parent company and invoiced to a Kenyan resident subsidiary, since these expenses are non-deductible.

There are also provisions whereby management and professional fees paid to a non-resident might be exempt from tax, generally when the Government or a local authority are party to the agreement for the provision of services, and the Minister of Finance agrees that the payment should be exempted from withholding tax.

Entertainers

Tax at the rate of twenty per cent is also withheld from any payment to a non-resident in connection with any entertainment or sporting event, or any other event that provides diversion to an audience. This provision also applies to any other non-resident person who assists, promotes or otherwise supports the staging of such an event.

Dividends, Interest, Pensions, & Annuities.

No special rules exist for other income of a passive nature derived by non-residents from sources within Kenya. The withholding tax rates outlined above apply in exactly the same situation to any dividends, which are taxed at fifteen per cent, interest at 12.5 per cent, and pensions and annuities at five per cent.

Investment Vehicles

There are no commonly used investment vehicles that allow non-residents to hold any interest or equity in Kenyan concerns. Any such companies would be subject to tax in the normal way in Kenya,

and withholding taxes would apply in exactly the same manner to any payment or distributions made by the vehicle to its non-resident owner.

Corporate Tax

Locally registered and incorporated companies, both foreign and local, pay corporate tax at the rate of forty-five per cent of taxable income. Branches of foreign companies pay income tax at the rate of 52.5 per cent, which is a corporate tax burden comparable to European levels.

There are no provincial or municipal income taxes, but local authorities may levy property taxes. No other corporate income taxes or surtaxes exist.

Businesses which suffer losses can carry forward such assessed tax losses to be set off against subsequent taxable profits. Losses may be carried forward until adequate profits have accrued to absorb them.

Income Tax

Income tax is charged on income earned in Kenya by any resident. A wife's income is assessed independently of the husband, and is taxed at the same rates.

Expatriates working in regional offices located in Nairobi are exempted from income tax on one-third of their earnings, if such earnings are paid from offshore sources. Expatriates employed in Kenya are also allowed to remit part of their earnings in foreign currency.

Sales Tax

Sales tax is levied on all manufactured goods produced or imported, into Kenya. The *ad valorem* rate is seventy per cent on most goods, with higher rates levied on drinks, cigarettes, and luxury items.

Tax treaties

Comprehensive tax treaties are in force with Canada, Denmark, the Federal Republic of Germany, Malawi, Norway, Sweden, the United Kingdom, and Zambia.

These tax treaties generally help to avoid double taxation and reduce or waive the withholding taxes outlined above.

PART FIVE: FACTS AT YOUR FINGERTIPS

Visas and immigration regulations

Citizens of Denmark, Eire, Ethiopia, Finland, Germany (Federal Republic), Holland, Italy, Norway, Spain, Sweden, Turkey, and Uruguay do not need visas. Neither do Commonwealth citizens unless they are nationals of Australia, Nigeria, or Sri Lanka.

All other nationalities require visas — as do all arrivals from South Africa, regardless of nationality. British nationals of Bangladesh, Indian, or Pakistan origin all require visas issued (or approved) beforehand by Kenya's immigration authorities.

Visitors not requiring a visa and holding an onward or return ticket normally obtain a "Visitors Pass" on arrival at any Kenya port of entry, free of charge. These are usually valid for three months.

No visitor can take up work or residence without the authority of the Principal Immigration Officer.

Since visa regulations are subject to change it is advisable to double-check visa requirements with airline offices, tour operators, or Kenya Government offices abroad well ahead of your intended visit. Visa applications normally take six weeks to process and usually allow a maximum stay of three months (in certain circumstances this can be extended).

Health requirements

All visitors must produce a yellow fever vaccination certificate. As a precaution, visitors arriving from places where there is cholera should also bring evidence of recent inoculation.

Malaria is endemic the year round throughout Kenya in all areas below 2,000 metres (6,500 feet) and intending visitors should begin to take a recommended prophylactic two weeks before their arrival and for six weeks after their departure.

International flights

Kenya is well served by international flights from all round the world. Thirty-two international airlines provide scheduled services to and from the country. The approximate flying time to Nairobi from Europe is eight hours; from North America sixteen hours; from India six hours; from the Gulf four hours; from the Far East and Australasia sixteen hours.

Kenya has two main points of entry by air: Jomo Kenyatta International Airport, Nairobi, and Moi International Airport, Mombasa. Both are among the most modern in Africa, with full passenger facilities — including twenty-four-hour currency exchange facilities, post-office, shops, restaurants,

snack bars, and bars. A porter service is available both inside and outside the customs area. For arrivals without health certificates, a vaccination service is also available.

For transport into town Kenya Airways provide regular bus services; taxis and self-drive hire-cars are available; and for those on a group tour, mini-buses are provided by tour operators. Additionally, there is a Kenya Bus Service (KBS) into Nairobi.

Air fares

The usual range of fares is available: business and economy class; excursion fares, bookable anytime for stays of between fourteen and forty-five days; and Advance Purchase Excursion (APEX) fares bookable one calendar month in advance, allowing for stays of between nineteen and ninety days. The price of the cheaper APEX fare varies according to the season, with June to September and December to January considered the "high" seasons. You can make stopovers *en route* with all fares except APEX. Reductions are available for children.

Departure tax

In 1989 the airport departure tax was US$20 a person, payable only in US dollars or UK Sterling. For internal flights there is a departure tax of Kshs 50/-.

Arrival by sea

Kilindini Port, Mombasa, is one of the busiest docks on Africa's eastern seaboard. Regular passenger services were suspended early in the 1970s but there is a full range of customs and immigration posts for arriving passengers. Some cargo liners offer limited passenger berths and cruise liners make occasional calls for short stopovers.

Arrival by rail and lake steamer

There are two points of entry into Kenya by rail — at Malaba on the Kenya-Uganda border, and at Taveta on the Kenya-Tanzania border. Arrivals undergo full customs and immigration checks.

Kisumu also serves as an entry point by inland waterway with full customs and immigration stations at Kisumu docks. International passenger services on Lake Victoria, however, have been suspended since 1977.

Arrival by road

Kenya is bordered by Somalia in the north-east, Ethiopia in the north, Sudan in the north-west,

Uganda in the west, and Tanzania in the south. There are many land entry points.

There are customs and immigration check posts at two or three places on the Somali border. The main one is at Mandera. The border posts between Kenya and Ethiopia are Moyale, Fort Banya (Ileret), and Todenyang.

Between Kenya and Sudan, Lokichoggio, and between Kenya and Uganda, Oropol, Katikekile, Bukwa, Malaba, and Busia.

The border posts between Kenya and Tanzania are Sirari (Migori) in the south-west, Namanga and Oloitokitok in the south, and Taveta and Lunga Lunga in the south-east.

Customs

Customs formalities are kept to a minimum. Unused personal effects, unexposed film, cameras, and accessories (except cine and slide projectors) may be temporarily imported duty free.

Visitors are also permitted to carry in two hundred cigarettes or fifty cigars duty free, one litre of alcohol, and a quarter litre of perfume.

Refundable deposits may be required for the import of radios, tape-recorders, musical instruments, and similar equipment.

A visitor wishing to bring in home video equipment in the form of cameras and recorders should consult the nearest Kenya Tourist Office, Consulate or High Commission, as a customs bond is normally required for the time the equipment is in the country.

The import of firearms, agricultural and horticultural produce, and pet animals, is forbidden.

Road services

There are regular bus services between all major towns in Kenya. It is advisable to book ahead. The services run by reputable companies are swift and economic in well-maintained vehicles.

In addition, many bus companies and transport operators, Rift Valley Peugeot Services (RVPS) for example, run express passenger saloon car services on the same routes. There are also many other, less reliable, bus services available.

Taxi services

There are taxi services in Nairobi, Mombasa, and most large towns. They can be found at designated taxi ranks and outside the larger hotels. The biggest taxi operator is Kenatco which operates a large fleet of Mercedes-Benz saloon cars in Nairobi and Mombasa.

Car hire

There are many car-hire companies in Kenya, offering everything from small two-door sedans to spacious 4WD vehicles. While some offer a flat weekly rate, most charge a daily rate, plus mileage and insurance. Vehicles can be hired on a self-drive

basis or with driver.

Driving

Drivers require a valid International Driving Licence. Visitors may use their domestic licences for up to ninety days providing they are endorsed at the Road Transport Office, Nyayo House, Nairobi.

Those with their own vehicles require a *Carnet de passage* and *Triptique* and International Certificate of Insurance.

Petrol is sold in litres and driving is on the left, as in Britain.

Rail and ferry services

Kenya Railways operates a total network of 2,733 route kilometres (1,698 miles) of railway track, consisting of the main lines from Mombasa to Kisumu and from Nakuru to Malaba. Branch lines are from Nairobi-Thika-Kiganjo-Nanyuki, Voi-Taveta, Konza-Kajiado-Magadi, Gilgil-Ol Kalau-Nyahururu, Rongai-Solai, Leseru-Kitale, and Kisumu-Butere.

There are 137 stations, more than 200 diesel locomotives, more than 500 coaches, and 6,500 freight wagons. The workforce is more than 23,000 people.

Kenya Railways also operate the inland marine services — passenger and cargo — between Kisumu, Kendu Bay, Mbita, Kuwour, Karungu, and Mfangano in Kenya. Services between Port Bell, in Uganda, and Mwanza, in Tanzania, were suspended in 1977. There are four ships (three in service and one yet to be commissioned), two tugs, and nine lighters.

Climate

Temperatures rarely fall below 24° Centigrade during the day and 10° Centigrade at night. Warm woollens are advised for late evenings. Warmer clothing should be worn in upcountry areas. Kenya has two rainy seasons — the short rains usually fall between October and December and the long rains from March to early June.

Currency

The Kenya shilling is divided into 100 cents. Notes are issued in denominations of 500, 200, 100, 50, 20, and 10 shillings. There are five and one shilling coins and 50, 10, and five cent coins.

Currency Regulations

The import or export of Kenya currency is not allowed. Foreign currency must be changed at banks or through licensed exchange dealers such as the main hotels.

There are no restrictions on the amount of foreign cash or travellers' cheques brought into the country which is noted on a currency declaration form issued on arrival. Whatever remains can be freely taken out so long all foreign exchange transactions are entered by the authorized dealers. Before the record is finally inspected by customs on departure, any surplus Kenya currency can be reconverted into foreign currency at banks at the two international airports which maintain a twenty-four-hour service.

Banks

Barclays Bank operate "Bureaux de Change" in Nairobi and Mombasa. These are open longer than the normal banking hours of 09.00 to 14.00 Monday to Friday. Some banks open between 09.00 and 11.00 on the first and last Saturday of each month. Banks at Kenya's international airports are open twenty-four hours a day.

Credit cards

American Express, Diners Club, Visa, Access, Barclaycard, and MasterCard are widely accepted throughout Kenya. American Express, Diners Club, Visa, and MasterCard all have local offices or agents in Nairobi and Mombasa should you need to contact them for any services, cash advances, or to report a lost or stolen card.

Government

Kenya is an Independent Republic within the Commonwealth, a member of the United Nations Organization and the Organization of African Unity. It covers 582,644 square kilometres (225,000 square miles) astride the Equator. The population is about 20 million. The capital is Nairobi which covers an area of 690 square kilometres (266 square miles) with a population of about one million. It was incorporated as a city by Royal Charter in March 1950. Other major towns include Mombasa (pop: about 420,000), Kisumu (pop: about 420,000), Nakuru, Meru, and Eldoret.

The government operates under an executive President who is also Commander in Chief of the Armed Forces and the President of the sole political party, the Kenya African National Union (KANU). He is assisted by a Vice-President and a Cabinet chosen from the legislature, the National Assembly.

In addition to the 188 members who are elected to Parliament every five years, there are twelve nominated MPs, a Speaker, and the Attorney-General. In 1989 the executive wing of the government consisted of twenty-eight ministries, each headed by a minister and two assistant ministers, and administered by a permanent secretary.

The judiciary consisted of the High Court, presided over by a chief justice, magistrate's courts, and a court of appeal.

Kenya's eight provinces are each headed by a provincial commissioner and each of the forty-one districts by a district commissioner who is assisted by several district officers. In addition, there are chiefs and assistant chiefs who work at sub-district level.

The provision of various services and utilities is undertaken by County Councils, municipal local authorities and, in the case of Nairobi, the Nairobi City Commission.

Language

The official language in Kenya is English. The national language is Kiswahili. English is taught in all schools and is well understood, particularly by the younger generation. There are more than eighty vernaculars. At the coast many of the people involved in tourism speak German, French, or Italian, or all three.

Religion

All major faiths are represented in Kenya. There are more than 1,700 registered religious organisations. The majority (about seventy per cent) are Christian, worshipping in mainstream churches (Anglican, Baptist, Catholic, Coptic, Orthodox, Pentecostal, and Presbyterian) and numerous Afro-Christian sects. The largest minority faith (about twenty per cent) is Islam. The remainder are Sikhs, Hindus, or belong to traditional animist religions. Services in Christian churches are conducted in English or Kiswahili.

Time

Kenya is three hours ahead of Greenwich Mean Time (GMT).

Daylight

The swift sunup and sundown at around 06.30 and 18.45 — varying only by thirty minutes the year round — maintains an almost constant twelve hours of daylight through the year.

Business hours

Businesses operate 08.00 to 17.00, Monday to Friday, and 08.30 to 13.00 on Saturday. They remain closed on Sundays. Some general stores or *dukas* (shops) stay open well into the evening and over most of the weekend. In Mombasa, trade may start as early as 07.00 with a long siesta break between 12.30 to 16.00, re-opening until well after dark.

Security

Kenya is a friendly country and well-policed. Walking alone at night, however, is inadvisable. Preferably use taxis which are found outside most hotels. Do not leave valuables in hotel rooms and do not carry large sums of cash. If you have valuables, use a safe deposit box.

Communications

A first rate communications system links every corner of Kenya to every country of the world. Kenya Post and Telecommunications Corporation provides international direct dialling and subscriber trunk dialling services to all major cities. The KPT's external telecommunications department offers telex, facsimile, data communication, and related services through the Longonot Communications Satellite earth station.

In 1989 overseas calls to Europe and the United States cost about three US dollars a minute and to the Far East about four US dollars a minute. Cheap rates apply from Monday to Friday between 18.00 and 07.00, and at weekends from 14.00 Saturday to 07.00 Monday. The charge is about sixty per cent of the normal.

International telegraph, telex, and facsimile services are available, and telex and facsimile rental services are provided by most major hotels. Costs range from one and a half US dollars a minute to the United Kingdom, and two US dollars a minute to the United States — plus a fifteen per cent communication tax.

Media

Kenya is among those developing countries where freedom of expression and the press is guaranteed by the constitution. In addition to five daily and Sunday newspapers (three English-language and two Kiswahili), Kenyans have a wide choice of many weeklies and monthlies.

Large country areas are served by fortnightly "rural" newspapers, and in more remote rural areas where people have difficulty in obtaining access to these media, Ministry of Information offices organised along provincial, district, and sub-district lines. Gathering and disseminating national news is the responsibility of the Kenya News Agency.

Radio and television programmes are broadcast in English, Kiswahili, and in the case of radio, vernacular languages, by the parastatal Kenya Broadcasting Corporation (KBC). Radio broadcasts for eighteen hours and, during the day, is used extensively for educational purposes. Television broadcasts for six hours each evening during the week, ten hours at weekends.

To make documentary and feature films in Kenya, producers require a licence from the Ministry of Broadcasting and Information.

Energy

The electricity supply is 240 volts (50 cycles AC) although in some hotels wall sockets are provided for 110-volt American appliances. US visitors should, however, still bring a small step-down voltage converter.

Medical services

Overall, medical facilities are better in Kenya than in most other African countries. There are one or two first-rate hospitals in Nairobi and at the coast and a surprising number of specialist physicians and surgeons, some with international reputations, and some fine dentists and opticians.

Medical insurance

Cover can be bought in Kenya at reasonable cost from indigenous and locally based multi-national insurance firms but it is usually cheaper in your own country. Another option is to buy inexpensive insurance from the famous Flying Doctor Service in Kenya. In the event of serious illness or accident on safari, the doctors fly out from their headquarters at Wilson Airport and either treat the casualties themselves or fly them back to Nairobi for hospital treatment.

Chemists/Drugstores

There is no shortage of chemists or drugstores in Kenya, all staffed by qualified pharmacists. Most drugs are available, although sometimes under unfamiliar brand names. If a visitor's specific prescription is not available, the pharmacist will often be able to prescribe a suitable alternative without the need to visit a doctor. Advice and treatment for minor ailments is always generously available.

Most chemists close on Saturday afternoon, Sundays, and public holidays. When closed, the name and location of the duty chemist is usually posted on the shop door, or may be obtained at the nearest hospital. Weekend chemist opening times are published by the local newspapers.

Liquor

Licensing hours are liberal. Local spirits and wines as well as well as imported brands are available. Beer is price controlled, wines and spirits are not. Kenya beer is a frequent winner of international brewing awards for light lagers.

Tipping

In the better restaurants and hotels a service charge is included in the tariff. If you should want to tip someone who has been especially helpful, ten per cent is reasonable. Otherwise, do as you see fit — remembering that while not to tip can result in poor service, too large a tip can make it difficult for the next customer.

Clubs

Clubs are a prominent feature of Kenya social life. Some are organised around sport; others are religious, cultural, and philanthropic. Most have excellent facilities and are happy to welcome visitors, especially members of international clubs and societies that are represented in Kenya. Others charge a temporary membership fee.

English-Kiswahili Dictionary

Hello	Jambo
How are you?	Habari
I am well (good, fine, etc.)	Mzuri
Thank you	Asante
(verymuch)	(sana)
Goodbye	Kwaheri
Hotel	Hoteli
Room	Chumba
Bed	Kitanda
Food	Chakula
Coffee	Kahawa
Beer	Pombe
Cold	Baridi
Hot	Moto
Tea	Chai
Meat	Nyama
Fish	Samaki
Bread	Mkate
Butter	Siagi
Sugar	Sukari
Salt	Chumvi
Bad	Mbaya
Today	Leo
Tomorrow	Kesho
Now	Sasa
Quickly	Haraka
Slowly	Pole-pole
Hospital	Hospitali
Police	Polici

MORE WORDS

Mr	Bwana
Mrs	Bibi
Miss	Bi
I	Mimi
You	Wewe
He, She	Yeye
We	Sisi
They	Wao
What?	Nini?
Who	Nani?
Where? (Place)	Mahali gani?
Where? (Direction)	Wapi?
When?	Hini?
How?	Vipi?
Why?	Kwanini?
Which?	Ipi?
Yes	Ndiyo
No	Hapana

To eat	Kukula
To drink	Kukunywa
To sleep	Kulala
To bathe	Kuoga
To come	Ijayo
To go	Kwenda
To stop	Kusimama
to buy	Kununua
To sell	Kuuza
Street/road	Bara bara
Airport	Uwanja wa Ndege
Shop	Duka
Money	Pesa
Cent	Senti
One	Moja
Two	Mbili
Three	Tatu
Four	Ine

Five	Tano
Six	Sita
Seven	Saba
Eight	Nane
Nine	Tisa
Ten	Kumi
Eleven	Kumi na moja
Twelve	Kumi na mbili
Thirteen	Kumi na tatu
Twenty	Ishirini
Twenty-one	Ishirini na moja
Twenty-two	Ishirini na mbili
Twenty-three	Ishirini na tatu
Thirty	Thelathini
Forty	Arobaini
Fifty	Hamsini
One hundred	Mia moja
One thousand	Elfu moja

Phrases

Where is the hotel?	Hoteli iko wapi?
Good morning	Habara ya asubuhi
Good afternoon	Habari yamehana
Good evening	Habari ya jioni
Please come in	Karibu ndani tafadhali
Please sit down	Keti tafadhali
You're welcome	Una karibishwa
Where do you come from?	Ume kuja kutoka wapi?
I come from...	Nime toka...
What is your name?	Jinalakonani?
My name is...	Jina langu ni....
Can you speak Swahili?	Waweza kuongea kiswahili?
Only a little	Kidogo tu
I want to learn more	Nataka kujifunza zaidi
How do you find Kenya?	Waonaje Kenya?
I like it here	Hapa napenda
The weather is hot isn't it?	Hewa hapa in joto sivyo?
Yes, a little	Ndiyo kidogo
Where are you going?	Una kwenda wapi?
I am going to...	Nakwenda...
Turn right	Geuka Kulia
Turn left	Geuka kushoto
Go straight	Enda moja kwa moja
Please stop here	Simama hapa tafadhali
How much?	Ngapi?
Wait a minute	Ngoja kidogo
I have to get change	Ni badilishe pesa kwanza
Excuse me	Samahani
Where is the toilet?	Wapi choo?
In the back	Upande wa nyuma
Where may I get something to drink?	Naweza kupata wapi kinywaji?
One cup of coffee	Kikombe kimoja cha kahawa
How much does this cost?	Inagharimu pesa ngapi?
That's quite expensive	Waweza kupunguzu

In Brief

Kenya National Parks

Kenya's national parks are wildlife and botanical sanctuaries set aside to conserve their unique species and for educational and recreational enjoyment by Kenyans and overseas visitors. National parks form the mainstay of Kenya's tourist industry.

Parks and Reserves Legislation

The original National Parks administration, established in 1945, was combined with the former Game Department under the Wildlife (Conservation and Management) Act of 1976. It regained an independent status when it became a self-funding and semi-independent parastatal in July 1989.

National Parks and National Reserves may be established on any type of land with the consent of the appropriate district authority or the National Assembly.

Under certain conditions, within National Reserves, the land may be used for other purposes than nature conservation.

Within Marine National Parks and Reserves swimming, sailing, and water-skiing are allowed but permission is required for the passage and anchorage of boats.

All fishing is prohibited, except for traditional methods that have permission to continue.

Forest Reserves and Nature Reserves, for the protection of forest, coastal, and watershed resources, are declared under the Forest Act.

Biosphere Reserves

In 1989 there were 271 dedicated Biosphere Reserves throughout the world ... four of them in Kenya.

Biosphere Reserves are protected environments that contain unique landforms, landscapes, and systems of land use.

While National Parks may not serve scientific research, Biosphere Reserves do. Their management is undertaken by the host government, with different ministries responsible for each different land use.

Funds for specific research projects and scientific and administrative training are provided through UNESCO.

The major research project at Mount Kulal Biosphere Reserve is International Protection of Arid Lands (IPAL). Mount Kenya Biosphere Reserve is to have one devoted to research on African mountains.

World Heritage Sites

There are little more than 100 World Heritage Sites which are more strictly protected under international law than Biosphere Reserves. They are either unique cultural sites — the Pyramids, Acropolis, Taj Mahal — or unique natural sites, such as Australia's Great Barrier Reef, or Tanzania's Selous National Park.

In Kenya, which was due to sign the convention in 1989, probable cultural sites include Fort Jesus, the Gede ruins, and the Koobi Fora fossil beds. Natural sites under consideration are Mount Kenya, Hell's Gate, and Maasai Mara national reserve.

Parks and Reserves Administration

National Parks, National Reserves, and all other wildlife areas are the responsibility of the Director of the Wildlife Conservation and Management Department (WCMD).

National Reserves are administered by the local authority, but staffed by National Parks staff, the exception being Shimba Hills which is managed by WCMD.

Kenya's total wildlife conservation area is 44,359 square kilometres (17,127 square miles), or 7.6 per cent of Kenya's 582,644 square kilometres (225,000 square miles).

Nature and Forest Reserves

Nature Reserves and Forest Reserves are managed by forestry staff of the Forest Department within the Ministry of Environment and Natural Resources. Those of most interest are often given additional protection under National Parks and National Reserve legislation, which in turn makes them more accessible than many other forests.

In 1988 there were 210 gazetted forest reserves in Kenya (eighty-three under Government administration and 126 under trust, or local government administration). This means that 16,916 square kilometres (6,531 square miles), or 2.97 per cent of Kenya's total land area is devoted to forests.

There were also 130 non-gazetted forests (eleven under government protection and 119 under trust protection), giving Kenya another 5,034 square kilometres (1,944 square miles) devoted to forestry.

Biosphere Reserves

Kiunga Biosphere Reserve
Size: 250 sq kms
Province: Coast
District: Lamu
Geographical location: North-eastern coastal border of mainland Kenya and Pate Islands, Indian Ocean
Altitude: Sea level-30m

Vegetation: Microscopic marine plants, marine angiosperms, and dugong grass. On the mainland there are coastal scrublands and mangroves

Fauna: Dugong and green turtle are common. There are extensive coral formations and an abundant population of reef fish

Bird life: The offshore islands are rich in marine birds with large nesting colonies of various gulls and terns

Visitor facilities: Swimming, sailing, waterskiing, and diving are all permitted

Mount Kulal Biosphere Reserve

Size: 7,000 sq kms (South Island National Park 39 sq kms)

Province: Eastern

District: Marsabit

Geographical location: South-east of Lake Turkana

Altitude: 378-2,416m

Vegetation: Ranges from mountain forest to desert with rainforest, mistforest, grasslands, dry evergreen forest, woodlands, bushlands, and saltbush scrublands

Fauna: Greater kudu, oryx, gerenuk, giraffe, zebra, dikdik, gazelle, elephant, cheetah, lion, black rhino, leopard, ostrich, and crocodile

Cultural heritage: Long but probably discontinuous history of human occupation with archaeological evidence of pastoral and fishing populations near the old Chalbi Lake

Visitor facilities: No information

Malindi/Watamu Biosphere Reserve

Size: 261 sq kms (Malindi Marine National Park 6; Watamu Marine National Park 10; Malindi Marine National Reserve 213; and Watamu Marine National Reserve 32 sq kms)

Province: Coast

District: Kilifi

Geographical location: A strip of coast and sea 30kms long and 5kms wide, including Mida Creek; south of Malindi and 88kms north of Mombasa

Altitude: Sea level

Vegetation: Algae, microscopic marine plants, marine angiosperms, mangroves, palms, and casuarina

Fauna: Various crabs, corals, molluscs, cowrie, and marine worms

Bird life: Whale Island is a nesting ground for roseate and bridled tern and there are numerous shore birds

Visitor facilities: Boat trips, water-sports, and coral viewing

Mount Kenya Biosphere Reserve

Size: 715 sq kms (Mount Kenya National Park 580 sq kms)

Province: Central/Eastern

District: Nyeri/Meru

Geographical location: Mount Kenya straddles the equator, 193kms north-east of Nairobi and 480kms from the Kenya coast

Altitude: 1,600-5,199m

Vegetation: Rich alpine and sub-alpine flora with montane and bamboo forests, moorlands, and tundra. Between 3,800 and 4,500m many bizarre species flourish, notably giant rosette plants of which 13 species are endemic to Mount Kenya

Fauna: In the lower forest and bamboo zone there are giant forest hog, tree hyrax, white-tailed mongoose, elephant, black rhino, suni, duiker, and leopard. Moorland mammals include the Mount Kenya mouse shrew, hyrax, and duiker. At higher altitudes the endemic mole-rat is common and there have been rare sightings of the golden cat

Special features: Several mountain peaks with isolated glaciers. The highest peaks are Batian 5,199m and Nelion 5,188m There are about 20 glacial tarns (small lakes) and numerous glacial moraine features

Visitor facilities: One lodge, several climbing huts, and three campsites

National Parks

Aberdare National Park

Size: 766 sq kms

Province: Central

District: Nyeri/Muranga

Geographical location: Central highlands, west of Mount Kenya

Altitude: 1,829-3,994m

Vegetation: Rich alpine and sub-alpine flora giving way at lower altitudes to bamboo forests and montane forest

Fauna: Mammals of the forest zone include blue monkey, colobus, leopard, elephant, warthog, black rhino, giant forest hog, bushbuck, buffalo, red duiker, and suni. The open moorlands have serval, eland, several species of duiker, and the rare bongo

Bird life: More than 200 recorded species

Special features: Trout can be caught in the moorland streams

Visitor facilities: Two lodges, two self-help fishing lodges, and five campsites

Amboseli National Park

Size: 392 sq kms

Province: Rift Valley

District: Kajiado

Geographical location: On the Tanzanian border, north-west of Mount Kilimanjaro

Altitude: Up to 1,155m

Vegetation: Semi-arid acacias and grasses with papyrus sedges in the swamplands

Fauna: Fifty-six species of mammal including baboon, vervet monkey, lion, cheetah, leopard, elephant, zebra, hippo, black rhino, Maasai giraffe, oryx, wildebeest, gerenuk, impala, and Grant's gazelle

Bird life: More than 425 recorded species
Visitor facilities: Four lodges and several campsites

Central Island National Park ... see **Sibiloi National Park**

Chyulu National Park ... see **Tsavo National Park**

Hell's Gate National Park
Size: 68 sq kms
Province: Rift Valley
District: Nakuru
Geographical location: South of Lake Naivasha in the Rift Valley
Altitude: 2,777m
Vegetation: A wide variety of succulents
Fauna: Plains game include eland, giraffe, zebra, impala, Grant's, and Thompson's gazelle. Other wildlife includes klipspringer, hyrax, and mountain reedbuck
Bird life: Many birds of prey and swifts. It is possible to observe 25-30 species in any one day
Visitor facilities: None

Lake Nakuru National Park
Size: 188 sq kms
Province: Rift Valley
District: Nakuru
Geographical location: Central Kenya, 140kms north-west of Nairobi
Altitude: 1,753-2,073m
Vegetation: The lake is fringed by swamps and the surrounding areas support a dry transitional savannah with dry forest occupying the more elevated areas
Fauna: Mammals include the rare long-eared leaf-nosed bat, colobus, spring hare, clawless otter, rock hyrax, hippo, leopard, waterbuck, impala, Thompson's gazelle, striped hyena, hunting dog, bat-eared fox, wild cat, and golden cat. Rothschild's giraffe and endangered black rhino have been recently introduced
Bird life: More than 450 recorded bird species. One of the few parks established specifically for the protection of birds, flamingo in particular
Visitor facilities: One lodge, one luxury camp, and three campsites

Meru National Park
Size: 870 sq kms
Province: Eastern
District: Meru
Geographical location: East-north-east of Mount Kenya
Altitude: 366-914m
Vegetation: Mainly thorny bushland in the north, wooded grasslands in the west, and open grasslands elsewhere. Dense riverine forests of doum and raffia palm grow along the watercourses, and sedges occupy riverine swamps
Fauna: Large mammals include lion, leopard, cheetah, elephant, zebra, black rhino, reticulated giraffe, hippo, lesser kudu, oryx, gerenuk, hartebeest, and Grant's gazelle
Bird life: There are 277 recorded species including the Somali ostrich
Visitor facilities: One luxury lodge, one self-help lodge, and several campsites

Mount Elgon National Park
Size: 169 sq kms
Province: Rift Valley
District: Trans Nzoia
Geographical location: On the western border with Uganda
Altitude: 2,336-4,321m
Vegetation: There are several zones ranging from wet montane and bamboo forests to afro-alpine moorlands and tundra
Fauna: Colobus, elephant, leopard, giant forest hog, bushbuck, eland, buffalo, duiker, and golden cat
Special features: A flat-topped basalt column known as Koitobos (Table Rock) and the "lava-tube" caves, some over 60m in diameter, which are visited by elephants in search of salt
Visitor facilities: Three campsites

Mount Kenya National Park ... see **Mount Kenya Biosphere Reserve**

Mount Longonot National Park
Size: 52 sq kms
Province: Rift Valley
District: Nakuru
Geographical location: South of Lake Naivasha, in the Rift Valley
Recently gazetted. No further information

Nairobi National Park
Size: 117 sq kms
Province: Nairobi
District: Nairobi
Geographical location: About 8kms south of Nairobi
Altitude: 1,533-1,760m
Vegetation: Dry transitional savannah on the plain with gallery forests in the valleys
Fauna: The close proximity of forest cover, pasture and permanent water makes this the centre of an animal migration area, particularly in drought years. Concentrations of larger mammals with over 80 recorded species, except elephant. Hippo and crocodile can be found in various ponds, water-holes, and the Athi river
Bird life: There are some 500 species
Visitor facilities: Being a mere 15 minutes from Nairobi, there is no accommodation nor are there any campsites

Ol Doinyo Sapuk National Park
Size: 18 sq kms
Province: Eastern
District: Machakos
Geographical location: East-south-east of Thika, 50kms north-east of Nairobi
Altitude: 1,524-2,146m
Vegetation: Montane forest
Fauna: Colobus, monkey, leopard, black rhino, bushbuck, buffalo, duiker, and impala
Visitor facilities: Two campsites

Ndere Island National Park
Size: 4.2 sq kms
Province: Nyanza
District: Kisumu
Geographical Location: Lake Victoria
Gazetted 1986. No further information

Ruma (Lambwe Valley) National Park
Size: 120 sq kms
Province: Nyanza
District: South Nyanza
Geographical location: 10kms east of Lake Victoria in western Kenya
Altitude: 1,200-1,600m
Vegetation: A mixture of tall grassland and woodlands with extensive acacia thickets
Fauna: Roan antelope, leopard, buffalo, and topi. Giraffe, zebra, and ostrich have been recently introduced
Visitor facilities: Camping is allowed

Saiwa Swamp National Park
Size: 2 sq kms
Province: Rift Valley
District: Trans Nzoia
Geographical location: Situated below the Cherangani Hills, 20kms north-east of Kitale in western Kenya
Altitude: 1,860-1,880m
Vegetation: Swamp vegetation of tall bulrushes and sedges
Fauna: Primarily established for the protection of 80-100 sitatunga. Other mammals include monkey, nocturnal potto, spotted-necked otter, giant forest squirrel, and leopard
Visitor facilities: None

Sibiloi National Park
Size: 1,575 sq kms (Sibiloi National Park 1,570; and Central Island National Park 5 sq kms)
Province: Eastern
District: Marsabit
Geographical location: Situated on the eastern shores of Lake Turkana, 720kms from Nairobi
Vegetation: Grassy plains with yellow spear grass and doum palms. Scrubby salvadora bush is found on Central Island
Fauna: Mammals include zebra, gazelle, oryx, hartebeest, topi, lion, and cheetah. The world's largest crocodile population (12,000) breeds on Central Island

Bird life: More than 350 recorded species
Special features: Koobi Fora palaeontological site
Visitor facilities: Several campsites are available but visitors must bring their own supplies, including petrol. Due to this park's remote location, prospective visitors are advised to consult the relevant authorities beforehand

South Island National Park ... see Mount Kulal Biosphere Reserve

Tsavo National Park
Size: 21,283 sq kms (Tsavo East National Park 11,747; Tsavo West National Park 9,065; and Chyulu National Park 471 sq kms)
Province: Eastern/Coast
District: Kitui/Machakos/Taita-Taveta
Geographical location: South-east Kenya, inland from Mombasa
Altitude: 229-2,438m
Vegetation: Bush grasslands and acacia woodlands, dotted with baobab and ivory palm, with saltbush, doum palm, tamarind, and fig trees by riversides and the Mzima Springs
Fauna: Larger mammals include lion, leopard, cheetah, elephant, black rhino, hippo, giraffe, lesser kudu, eland, oryx, cape buffalo, zebra, yellow baboon, waterbuck, gemsbok, Coke's hartebeest, gerenuk, and gazelle. Crocodile can be found in pools while various fish live in the Mzima Springs
Visitor facilities: Several lodges and campsites

Marine National Parks

Kisite Marine National Park/Mpunguti Marine National Reserve
Size: 39 sq kms (Kisite Marine National Park 28; and Mpunguti Marine National Reserve 11 sq kms)
Province: Coast
District: Kwale
Geographical location: South of Wasini Island off Shimoni, on the south coast near the Tanzanian border
Altitude: Sea level to about 5m
Vegetation: Sea grasses and marine algae
Fauna: Corals, sea urchins, cowrie, starfish, various crabs, sergeant-major fish, parrot fish, and butterfly fish
Visitor facilities: None

Malindi/Watamu Marine National Park ... see Malindi/Watamu Biosphere Reserve

Mombasa Marine National Park
Size: 10 sq kms
Province: Coast
District: Mombasa
Geographical location: Offshore from Mombasa
Gazetted 1986. No further information

National Reserves

Arawale National Reserve
Size: 533 sq kms
Province: North Eastern
District: Garissa
Geographical location: 5kms from Tana River and 130kms north of Malindi
Altitude: 85-100m
Vegetation: Thorny bushland
Fauna: This reserve is the only area in Kenya where Hunter's hartebeest can be found. Also includes zebra, elephant, lesser kudu, buffalo, hippo, and crocodile
Visitor facilities: None

Bisanadi National Reserve
Size: 606 sq kms
Province: Eastern
District: Isiolo
Geographical location: Adjacent to north-east boundary of Meru National Park
Altitude: 320-660m
Vegetation: Mainly thorny bushland and thicket merging into wooded grasslands. Dense riverine forests of doum and raffia palm occur along watercourses, with various sedges in riverine swamps
Fauna: In the wet season, this is the dispersal area for wildlife from Meru National Park, primarily elephant and buffalo
Visitor facilities: None

Boni National Reserve
Size: 1,339 sq kms
Province: North Eastern
District: Garissa
Geographical location: North-east coast
Altitude: 0-100m
Vegetation: The only coastal lowland groundwater forest in Kenya. Lowland dry bushlands and grasslands in drier areas
Fauna: Large concentrations of elephant in the dry season. Other mammals include Harvey's and Ader's duiker
Visitor facilities: None

Buffalo Springs National Reserve
Size: 131 sq kms
Province: Eastern
District: Isiolo
Geographical location: 85kms north of Mount Kenya
Altitude: 900-1,000m
Vegetation: Riverine forest of acacia and doum palm, acacia woodlands, bush, grass, and scrublands
Fauna: Elephant, zebra, reticulated giraffe, oryx, cheetah, and crocodile
Birdlife: There are 320 recorded species
Visitor facilities: Two lodges and five campsites

Dodori National Reserve
Size: 877 sq kms
Province: Coast
District: Lamu
Geographical location: North-east coast
Altitude: 0-100m
Vegetation: Mangrove swamp, lowland dry forest, marshy glades, and groundwater forest
Fauna: Major breeding ground for topi. Larger mammals include elephant and lesser kudu. The reserve also has substantial breeding grounds of dugong and green turtle along the shoreline
Bird life: Prolific birdlife, especially pelican
Visitor facilities: One campsite

Kakamega Forest National Reserve
Size: 45 sq kms
Province: Western
District: Kakamega
Geographical location: Western Kenya, north of Kisumu
Altitude: 1,520-1,680m
Vegetation: This is the easternmost area of the Congo-West African equatorial rainforest. The fairly dense forest is interspersed with grassy glades. At least 125 tree species with an average height of 35m
Fauna: Some 10-20% of the amphibians, reptiles, birds and mammals found here occur nowhere else in Kenya. They include bush-tailed porcupine, giant water shrew, and hammer-headed fruit bat. The forest also supports numerous species of primates including colobus and blue monkey
Visitor facilities: None

Kamnarok National Reserve
Size: 88 sq kms
Province: Rift Valley
District: Baringo
Recently gazetted. No further information

Kora National Reserve
Size: 1,787
Province: Coast
District: Tana River
Geographical location: On the Tana River, 125kms east of Mount Kenya
Altitude: 250-440m
Vegetation: Mostly acacia bushland with riverine forests of doum palm, acacia, and Tana River poplar
Fauna: Elephant, black rhino, hippo, lion, leopard, cheetah, serval, caracal, wildcat, genet, spotted and striped hyena, and several species of antelope. The rivers support a wide range of amphibians, lizards, snakes, tortoise, and crocodile
Visitors facilities: None

Lake Bogoria National Reserve
Size: 107 sq kms
Province: Rift Valley
District: Baringo
Geographical location: 50kms north of Nakuru in

the Rift Valley
Altitude: 1,000-1,600m
Vegetation: Mainly thorny bushland with small patches of riverine forest. Grasslands along shoreline
Fauna: Greater kudu
Birdlife: Flamingo
Special features: Thermal areas with steam jets and geysers
Visitor facilities: Two campsites

Losai National Reserve
Size: 1,806 sq kms
Province: Eastern
District: Marsabit
Geographical location: Situated in the Losai Mountains south-west of Marsabit National Reserve in northern Kenya, 175kms north of Mount Kenya
Altitude: 625-1,750m
Vegetation: Thorny bushland
Fauna: Former habitat of elephant and black rhino
Visitor facilities: No tourism allowed

Maasai Mara National Reserve
Size: 1,672 sq kms
Province: Rift Valley
District: Narok
Geographical location: South-western Kenya bordering Serengeti National Park, on the Tanzanian border
Altitude: 1,500-2,170m
Vegetation: Open grasslands with patches of acacia woodland, thickets, and riverine forests
Fauna: In the dry season (July-October) the reserve is a major concentration area of migratory herbivores including approximately 250,000 zebra and 1.3 million wildebeest. There are also gazelle, elephant, topi, buffalo, lion (Kenya's largest population), black rhino, hippo, hyena, giraffe, leopard, and mongoose
Bird life: Prolific, including 53 birds of prey
Visitor facilities: Several lodges and campsites

Marsabit National Reserve
Size: 2,088 sq kms
Province: Eastern
District: Marsabit
Geographical location: Northern Kenya, 560kms north of Nairobi
Altitude: 420-1,700m
Vegetation: Higher altitude forest merges into acacia grasslands in the middle altitudes. Arid thorny bushland dominates the lower zone
Fauna: Elephant, greater kudu, monkey, baboon, hyaena, aardwolf, caracal, cheetah, lion, klipspringer, gazelle, oryx, and reticulated giraffe. There are 13 recorded species of bat
Bird life: More than 350 species, including 52 birds of prey
Special features: Volcanic craters, several containing fresh water lakes

Visitor facilities: One lodge and three campsites

Mwea National Reserve
Size: 68 sq kms
Province: Eastern
District: Embu
Geographical location: 100kms north-east of Nairobi
Altitude: 1,000-1,100m
Vegetation: Mainly thorny bushland with patches of woodland. Scattered baobab.
Fauna: Small numbers of elephant, buffalo, lesser kudu, crocodile, and hippo
Visitor facilities: None

Nasolot National Reserve
Size: 92 sq kms
Province: Rift Valley
District: West Pokot
Geographical location: Situated 100kms north of Kitale in western Kenya, near the Uganda border
Altitude: 750-1,500m
Vegetation: Mainly thorny bushland
Fauna: Elephant, black rhino, and lesser kudu
Visitor facilities: No information

Ngai Ndethya National Reserve
Size: 212 sq kms
Province: Eastern
District: Machakos
Geographical location: South-east Kenya between Tsavo East and Tsavo West National Parks
Altitude: 650-750m
Vegetation: Thornbush and thicket with scattered baobab
Fauna: Migration corridor between Tsavo East and Tsavo West
Visitor facilities: None

North Kitui National Reserve
Size: 745 sq kms
Province: Eastern
District: Kitui
Geographical location: Adjacent to Meru National Park
Altitude: 428-675m
Vegetation: Bushland and riverine forest
Fauna: Crocodile and hippo along the Tana river
Visitor facilities: None

Rahole National Reserve
Size: 1,270 sq kms
Province: North Eastern
District: Garissa
Geographical location: 150kms east-north-east of Mount Kenya.
Altitude: 250-480 metres
Vegetation: Dry thorny bushland
Fauna: Elephant, Grevy's zebra, and beisa oryx
Visitor facilities: None

Rimo (Kerio Valley) National Reserve
Size: 66 sq kms

Province: Rift Valley
District: Elgeyo Marakwet
Recently gazetted. No further information

Samburu National Reserve
Size: 165 sq kms
Province: Rift Valley
District: Samburu
Geographical location: 90kms north of Mount Kenya.
Altitude: 800-1,230m
Vegetation: Narrow riverine woodland of doum palm. Otherwise acacia woodland with bushland, grassland, and shrubland
Fauna: Elephant, cheetah, reticulated giraffe, oryx, vervet monkey, zebra, and crocodile.
Visitor facilities: Two lodges, one luxury tented camp, and three campsites.

Shaba National Reserve
Size: 239 sq kms
Province: Eastern
District: Isiolo
Geographical location: 70kms north of Mount Kenya
Altitude: 700-1,500m
Vegetation: Acacia woodlands, bushlands, and grasslands. Riverine communities dominated by acacia and doum palm
Fauna: Gerenuk, gazelle, oryx, zebra, giraffe, cheetah, leopard, and lion
Visitor facilities: One luxury lodge and three campsites

Shimba Hills National Reserve
Size: 192 sq kms
Province: Coast
District: Kwale
Geographical location: 30kms south-west of Mombasa
Altitude: 120-450m
Vegetation: Forests and grasslands interspersed with woodlands, riverine forests, coastal bushland, and scrubland
Fauna: Antelope, buffalo, waterbuck, reedbuck, hyaena, warthog, giraffe, elephant, leopard, baboon, and bush pig
Visitor facilities: One luxury lodge, two campsites, a picnic site, and nature trail

South Kitui National Reserve
Size: 1,833 sq kms
Province: Eastern
District: Kitui
Geographical location: Adjacent to the north boundary of Tsavo East National Park
Vegetation: Bush grasslands and acacia woodlands, dotted with baobab, ivory palm, and saltbush
Fauna: Larger mammals include lion, leopard, cheetah, elephant, black rhino, hippopotamus, giraffe, lesser kudu, eland, oryx, cape buffalo, zebra, yellow baboon, waterbuck, gemsbok, Coke's hartebeest, gerenuk, and gazelle
Visitor facilities: No tourism allowed

South Turkana National Reserve
Size: 1,091 sq kms
Province: Rift Valley
District: Turkana
Geographical location: North-west Kenya, 100kms north of Kitale
Altitude: 900-2,270m
Vegetation: Dense thorn bush, riverine forest, and scattered forest
Fauna: Elephant and greater kudu
Visitor facilities: None

Tana River Primate Reserve
Size: 169 sq kms
Province: Coast
District: Tana River
Geographical location: Inland from the Indian Ocean, 120kms north of Malindi on the Tana River between Hola and Garsen
Altitude: 40-70m
Vegetation: Highly diversified riverine forest with nearly 300 species. Some bush and grasslands
Fauna: The seven primates include endemic red colobus, mangabey, monkey, and baboon. Also elephant, hippo, gazelle, duiker, river hog, giraffe, lion, waterbuck, bush squirrel, and crocodile
Bird life: 248 bird species have been recorded
Visitor facilities: One lodge and one tented camp. Boat trips available

Marine National Reserves

Kiunga Marine National Reserve … see Kiunga Biosphere Reserve

Malindi/Watamu Marine National Reserve … see Malindi/Watamu Biosphere Reserve

Mombasa Marine National Reserve
Size: 200 sq kms
Province: Coast
District: Mombasa
Geographical location: Offshore from Mombasa
Gazetted 1986. No further information

Game Sanctuaries

Taita Hills Game Sanctuary
Size: 113 sq kms
Province: Coast
District: Taita-Taveta
Geographical location: South-eastern Kenya, next to Tsavo West National Park
Altitude: Up to 914m
Vegetation: Savannah grasslands and woodlands
Fauna: Zebra, buffalo, impala, gazelle, elephant, eland, waterbuck, reedbuck, giraffe, vervet monkey, lion, and jackal
Visitor facilities: Two lodges

Nature Reserves

Arabuko Sokoke
Cheptugen-Kapchemutwa
Kaimosi Forest
Karura
Katimok-Kabarnet
Langata
Mau South West
Mbololo
Nandi North
Uaso Narok

Addresses

Wildlife
Conservation and
Management
Ministry of
Tourism and
Wildlife
Langata Road
PO Box 40241
Nairobi

Provincial
Wildlife Officer
(Marine National
Parks)
PO Box 82144
Mombasa

Gazetted Forests

Aberdare
Size: 1,030 sq kms
Province: Central
District:
Nyandarua
Nyeri
Muranga

Arabuko-Sokoke
Size: 418 sq kms
Province: Coast
District: Kilifi

Bahati
Size: 102 sq kms
Province: Rift
Valley
District: Nakuru

Buda
Size: 7 sq kms
Province: Coast
District: Kwale

Dagoretti
Size: 8 sq kms
Province: Central
District: Kiambu

East Ngambeni
Size: 107 sq kms
Province: Eastern
District: Kitui

Eastern Mau
Size: 650 sq kms
Province: Rift
Valley
District: Nakuru

Eburru
Size: 87 sq kms
Province: Rift
Valley
District: Nakuru

Eldoret
Size: 1.5 sq kms
Province: Rift
Valley
District: Uasin
Gishu

Escarpment
Size: 0.7 sq kms
Province: Central
District: Kiambu

Gongoni
Size: 8 sq kms
Province: Coast
District: Kwale

Gonja
Size: 8 sq kms
Province: Coast
District: Kwale

Kamiti
Size: 2 sq kms
Province: Central
District: Kiambu

Kapolet
Size: 16 sq kms
Province: Rift
Valley
District: Trans
Nzoia

Kapsaret
Size: 12 sq kms
Province: Rift
Valley
District: Uasin
Gishu

Kaptagat
Size: 130 sq kms
Province: Rift
Valley
District: Uasin
Gishu

Karura
Size: 10 sq kms
Province: Nairobi
District: Nairobi

Kiambu
Size: 1.3 sq kms
Province: Central
District: Kiambu

Kibwezi
Size: 59 sq kms
Province: Eastern
District: Machakos

Kiganjo
Size: 3 sq kms
Province: Central
District: Nyeri

Kijabe Hill
Size: 7 sq kms
Province: Rift
Valley
District: Nakuru

Kikuyu Escarpment
Size: 419 sq kms
Province: Central
District: Kiambu

Kilombe Hill
Size: 16 sq kms
Province: Rift
Valley
District: Baringo

Kipkabus
Size: 57 sq kms
Province: Rift
Valley
District: Uasin
Gishu

Kipipiri
Size: 50 sq kms
Province: Central
District:
Nyandarua

Kitale
Size: 24 sq kms
Province: Rift
Valley

Lusoi
Size: 3 sq kms
Province: Rift
Valley
District: Laikipia

Loriak
Size: 50 sq kms
Province: Rift
Valley

District: Laikipia

Lerogi
Size: 910 sq kms
Province: Rift
Valley
District: Samburu

Leshau
Size: 2 sq kms
Province: Central
District:
Nyandarua

Londiani
Size: 1 sq kms
Province: Rift
Valley
District: Kericho

Lugori
Size: 22 sq kms
Province: Rift
Valley
District: Samburu

Loitokitok
Size: 8 sq kms
Province: Rift
Valley
District: Kajiado

Mailuganji
Size: 17 sq kms
Province: Coast
District: Kwale

Maji Maztri
Size: 77 sq kms
Province: Rift
Valley
District: Baringo

Mangrove forests
(5)
Size: 450 sq kms
Province: Coast
District: Kilifi
Kwale
Lamu
Mombasa
Tana River

Marmanet
Size: 233 sq kms
Province: Rift
Valley
District: Laikipia

Marsabit
Size: 153 sq kms
Province: Eastern
District: Marsabit

Matthews Range
Size: 938 sq kms

Province: Rift
Valley
District: Samburu

Mau Narok
Size: 8 sq kms
Province: Rift
Valley
District: Nakuru

Menengai
Size: 60 sq kms
Province: Rift
Valley
District: Nakuru

Molo
Size: 9 sq kms
Province: Rift
Valley
District: Nakuru

Mount Elgon
Size: 733 sq kms
Province: Rift
Valley
District: Trans
Nzoia

Mount Kenya
Size: 2,009 sq kms
Province: Central
Eastern District:
Kirinyaga
Nyer Meru
Embu

Mount Londiani
Size: 297 sq kms
Province: Rift
Valley
District: Baringo/
Nakuru

Mount Nyiru
Size: 459 sq kms
Province: Rift
Valley
District: Samburu

Mugaga
Size: 2 sq kms
Province: Central
District: Kiambu

Mukagado
Size: 302 sq kms
Province: Rift
Valley
District: Laikipia

Muringato Nursery
Size: 0.3 sq kms
Province: Central
District: Nyeri

Mwachi
Size: 4 sq kms
Province: Coast
District: Kwale

Magumo North
Size: 2 sq kms
Province: Central
District:
Nyandarua

Magumo South
Size: 4 sq kms
Province: Central
District:
Nyandarua

Namanga Hill
Size: 118 sq kms
Province: Rift
Valley
District: Kajiado

Nabkoi
Size: 30 sq kms
Province: Rift
Valley
District: Uasin
Gishu

**Nairobi
Arboretum**
Size: 0.3 sq kms
Province: Nairobi
District: Nairobi

Nakuru
Size: 7 sq kms
Province: Rift
Valley
District: Nakuru

Ndare
Size: 56 sq kms
Province: Eastern
Rift Valley

District: Meru
Laikipia

Ndotos Range
Size: 972 sq kms
Province: Rift
Valley
District: Samburu

Ngong Road
Size: 13 sq kms
Province: Nairobi
District: Nairobi

Ngong Hills
Size: 31 sq kms
Province: Rift
Valley
District: Kajiado

North Tinderet
Size: 262 sq kms
Province: Rift
Valley
District: Uasin
Gishu

Nyamweru
Size: 8 sq kms
Province: Central
District: Kiambu

Nyeri
Size: 11 sq kms
Province: Central
District: Nyeri

Ol Arabel
Size: 94 sq kms
Province: Rift
Valley
District: Laikipia

Ol Bolossat
Size: 33 sq kms
Province: Central
District:

Nyandarua

Rumuruti
Size: 64 sq kms
Province: Rift
Valley
District: Laikipia

Shimba
Size: 192 sq kms
Province: Coast
District: Kwale

South Laikipia
Size: 35 sq kms
Province: Central
District: Nyeri

**South Western
Mau**
Size: 869 sq kms
Province: Rift
Valley
District: Kericho
Nakuru

Sekhendu
Size: 8 sq kms
Province: Rift
Valley
District: Trans
Nzoia

Timau
Size: 3 sq kms
Province: Eastern
District: Meru

Timboroa
Size: 60 sq kms
Province: Rift
Valley
District: Baringo
Uasin Gishu

Tinderet
Size: 279 sq kms
Province: Rift

Valley
District: Kericho
Nandi

Tumeya
Size: 2 sq kms
Province: Rift
Valley
Western District:
Uasin Gishu
Kakamega

Uaso Narok
Size: 21 sq kms
Province: Rift
Valley
District: Laikipia

Western Mau
Size: 198 sq kms
Province: Rift
Valley
District: Kericho/
Nakuru

West Molo
Size: 3 sq kms
Province: Rift
Valley
District: Nakuru

Witu
Size: 39 sq kms
Province: Coast
District: Lamu

**Non-gazetted
Forests**

Boni
Size: 185 sq kms
Province: Coast
District: Lamu

Hewani
Size: 27 sq kms
Province: Coast
District: Tana

River

Kazuki Hill
Size: 2 sq kms
Province: Central
District: Muranga

Kokani
Size: 62 sq kms
Province: Coast
District: Tana
River

Kingatua
Size: 0.6 sq kms
Province: Central
District: Kiambu

Mangrove forests
(4)
Size: 267 sq kms
Province: Coast
District: Kilifi
Kwale
Mombasa
Tana River

Mwina
Size: 34 sq kms
Province: Coast
District: Tana
River

Wayu
Size: 420 sq kms
Province: Coast
District: Tana
River

Address

Forest Department
Ministry of
Environment
and Natural
Resources
PO Box 30513
Nairobi

Wildlife Profile

Eastern Africa's open plains, particularly in Kenya, nourish the last great herds of wildlife left in the world. They hold a greater number and diversity of species than any other continent.

There are almost 100 species of grazers (ungulates) whereas the whole of Asia can claim only seventy, South and Central America only sixteen, Europe only thirteen, and North America only eleven.

Together with predators and scavengers, the rich birdlife — third in the world in its number of species — reptiles, insects, and oddities, this abundant wildlife gives Kenya rightful claim to be called the Last Eden.

In fact, of the whole range of fauna, only the major primates — chimpanzee and gorilla — are missing.

Mammals

(Swahili names, if any, in brackets):

Elephant, *Loxodonta africana* (Tembo/Ndovu): Widely distributed. Rain forests, secondary forests, highland forests, open woodlands, savannah, dry bush, and swamps. Tsavo, Mount Kenya, the Aberdares, and Meru National Park, Amboseli, Samburu, and Maasai Mara.

Rock hyrax, *Heterohyrax brucei* (Pimbi): Widely distributed. Cliffs, rocky hills, and stony mountain slopes. Usually seen on Hyrax Rock, Nairobi National Park.

Tree hyrax, *Dendrohyrax arboreous* (Perere): Widely distributed. Forests. Nocturnal. More often heard than seen.

Black rhinoceros, *Diceros bicornis* (Kifaru): Widely distributed but few remaining. Bush, savannah light forests, highland forest, and high altitude moorlands. Tsavo, Nairobi National Park, Amboseli, Samburu, Maasai Mara, Mount Kenya, and the Aberdares.

White rhinoceros, *Diceros simus* (Kifaru): Introduced. Meru National Park.

Burchell's zebra, *Equus burchelli* (Punda milia): Widely distributed in grasslands, open savannah, and grassy flats surrounded by bush. Large numbers seen at Amboseli and Maasai Mara.

Grevy's zebra, *Equus grevi* (Punda milia): Dry grassy bush country. Seen in Samburu, Marsabit, also in Meru National Park. Northern Kenya, east of Lake Turkana and north of Tana River.

Buffalo, *Syncerus caffer* (Nyati or mbogo): Widely distributed. Rain forests, secondary forests, highland forests, open woodlands, savannah, bush, and swamps. Large numbers in Tsavo, Meru National Park, Samburu, Amboseli, Maasai Mara, and mountain national parks.

Wildebeest, *Connochaetes taurinus* (Nyumbu): Widely distributed. Grassland, savannah, and open woodlands. Southern Kenya, north to Mau Forest and Thika River. Their mass migrations in Maasai Mara are considered one of nature's greatest spectacles.

Coke's hartebeest, *Alcelaphus buselaphus cokii* (Kongoni): Widely distributed. Grasslands and open grassy savannah. Southern Kenya, north to Lake Naivasha, upper Tana and Galana Rivers. Nairobi National Park, Amboseli, and Maasai Mara.

Lelwel hartebeest, *Alcelaphus buselaphus lelwel* (Kongoni): Savannah. North-western Kenya. A hartebeest resembling the Lelwel lives in the Lambwe Valley of western Kenya, another on Laikipia, north of Mount Kenya.

Hunter's hartebeest, *Damaliscus hunteri* (Kongoni): Restricted to an area of sansevieria bush with grassy clearings extending from the Tana River to southern Somalia. Some have been transferred to Tsavo Park.

Topi, *Damaliscus korrigum jimela* (Nyamera): Grasslands and open savannah. Western Kenya, along Kenya coast from the Sabaki River to the Somalia border. Numerous in Maasai Mara.

Harvey's duiker, *Cephalophus harveyi* (Funo): Widely distributed in forests, bush, and high grass jungles. Being secretive in their habits, duikers are only encountered accidentally.

Blue duiker, *Cephalophus monticola* (Paa): Widely distributed in forests, gallery forest, and bushlands.

Yellow-backed duiker, *Cephalophus sylvicultor* (Paa): Forests with plenty of undergrowth, gallery forest, and dense savannah. Mau Forest.

Grey duiker, *Sylvicapra grimmia* (Nsua): Widely distributed. Bush, forest edges, cultivations, and high grass.

Suni, *Nesotragus moschatus* (Paa): Locally in highland forests, coastal forests, and dense bushlands.

Steinbok, *Raphicerus campestris* (Dondoro): Widely distributed. Grasslands, with a certain amount of scattered bush. As far north as Laikipia, and the foot of Mount Elgon.

Klipspringer, *Oreotragus oreotragus* (Mbusi mawe): Widely distributed but confined to rocky hills and mountain ranges. Hell's Gate and Tsavo.

Oribi, *Ourebia ourebia* (Taya): Widely distributed. Grasslands, open savannah woodlands, and hilly country, scrubby bush.

Kirk's dikdik, *Rhynchotragus kirkii* (Dikidiki or

suguya): Widely distributed in dry bush country. Often seen in Tsavo, Amboseli, and Maasai Mara.

Guenther's dikdik, *Rhynchotragus guentheri* (Dikdik or suguya): Northern Kenya. Samburu.

Waterbuck, *Kobus ellipsiprymnus* (Kuro): Widely distributed. Savannah, bush, and gallery forests. Eastern Kenya. Tsavo, Amboseli, and Nairobi National Park which has a mixed population of common and defassa waterbuck.

Defassa waterbuck, *Kobus defassa* (Kuro): Widely distributed in western Kenya, east of Nairobi National Park to the Maasai Mara. Laikipia Plateau, and Nakuru National Park.

Uganda kob, *Adenota kob thomasi*. Grasslands, savannah, and never far from water. Western Kenya, where it is now rare.

Bohor reedbuck, *Redunca redunca* (Tohe): Widely distributed in grassy areas with patches of bush, and reedbeds, never far from water. Can be seen especially well in Nairobi and Nakuru National Parks.

Chanler's mountain reedbuck, *Redunca fulvorufula chanleri* (Tohe): Rocky slopes, escarpments, and stony ridges. Central and western Kenya. Seen in Nairobi National Park.

Impala, *Aepyceros melampus* (swara pala): Widely distributed in Kenya north to Wamba and northern Uaso Nyiro (Samburu). Can be seen in large numbers in Tsavo, Nairobi National Park, Amboseli, and Maasai Mara.

Thomson's gazelle, *Gazella thomsoni* (Swara tomi): Grasslands and savannah. Laikipia Plateau, southern Kenya, west to Lake Victoria, east to Tsavo West. Common in Nairobi National Park, Amboseli, and Maasai Mara.

Grant's gazelle, *Gazella granti* (Swara granti): Grasslands, open savannah, and dry bush. Widely distributed in Kenya, east almost to Indian Ocean, west to Lake Victoria. Can be seen in Tsavo, Nairobi National Park, Amboseli, Maasai Mara, and Samburu. The Grant's gazelle of northwestern Kenya is known as Bright's gazelle.

Gerenuk, *Litocranius walleri* (Swara twiga): Dry bush country. Northern and eastern Kenya, Lake Magadi region. Tsavo, Meru, Samburu, and Amboseli are good places to see this species.

Beisa oryx, *Oryx beisa* (Choroa): Desert scrub, dry bush, and grasslands with scattered trees. Northern Kenya, south to Laikipia Plateau and Tana River. Can be seen in Samburu, Marsabit, and Meru National Park.

Fringe-eared oryx, *Oryx beisa callotis* (Choroa): Dry bush country and grasslands. From Tana River south to Kilimanjaro area and west of Lake Magadi. Can be seen in Tsavo and Amboseli.

Sable antelope, *Hippotragus niger* (Palahala, mbarapi): Rare in Kenya. Savannah with patches of bush and open meadow, especially of the miombo forest type. Coastal areas north to Bamba, inland from Kilifi. Shimba Hills National Reserve near Mombasa.

Roan antelope, *Hippotragus equinus* (Korongo): Fairly rare in Kenya. Savannah interspersed with grassy patches, rolling uplands with bush and open forest. Small herds. Maasai Mara, and Lambwe Valley. Introduced into the Shimba Hills.

Eland, *Taurotragus oryx* (Pofu or mbunja): Widely distributed, through numbers much reduced in densely settled areas. Grasslands, savannah, and mountain moorlands. Nairobi National Park, Tsavo, and Maasai Mara.

Bushbuck, *Tragelaphus scriptus* (Mbawala or pongo): Widely distributed, wherever bush and undergrowth offer good cover. Nairobi National Parks and mountain national parks are good places to see this species.

Greater kudu, *Strepsiceros strepsiceros* (Tandala mkubwa): Rare and local in southern Kenya, more common on the mountains of the northern regions. Dense savannah, especially of the miombo forest type, rocky hills covered with forests, and thorn thicket belts of dense bush along rivers. Can be seen at Marsabit and Lake Bogoria.

Lesser kudu, *Strepsiceros imberbis* (Tandala ndogo): Northern Kenya, south through eastern part of country to Kilimanjaro region and southern Uaso Nyiro. Tsavo, Amboseli, and Meru National Park.

Bongo, *Boocercus euryceros*, Highland forests of Kenya, usually between 2,100 and 3,300 metres (6,890-10,830 feet). Mount Kenya, the Aberdares, Mau Forest, and Cherangani Hills.

Sitatunga, *Limnotragus spekei*, (Nzohe): Swamps. Western Kenya. Can be observed in the Saiwa Swamp near Kitale.

Maasai giraffe, *Giraffa camelopardalis* (Twiga): Dry thorn country, acacia grasslands, savannah, bushlands, andhighland forest. Widely distributed in southern Kenya, north to the Tana River. Tsavo, Nairobi National Parks, Maasai Mara, Amboseli, and many other places.

Reticulated giraffe, *Giraffa camelopardalis reticulata* (Twiga): Northern Kenya. Meru National Park, Samburu, and Marsabit. A sub-species is known as **Rothschild's Giraffe**, *Giraffa camelopardalis rothschildi*.

Bush pig, *Potamochoerus porcus* (Nguruwemwitu): Widely distributed. Forests, gallery forests, and bushy savannah. Crepuscular and nocturnal. Rarely seen.

Giant forest hog, *Hylochoerus meinertzhageni*: Rain forests, gallery forests, and highland forest. Mount Elgon, Cherangani Hills, Mau Forest, Mara River, the Aberdares, and Mount Kenya.

Wart hog, *Phacochoerus aethiopicus* (Ngiri): Widely distributed. Savannah and bushy grasslands. Common in Nairobi National Park and many other reserves.

Hippopotamus, *Hippopotamus amphibius* (Kiboko): Widely distributed. Rivers, lakes, and swamps. Good places to see this species are the Mzima Springs (Tsavo West), the Hippo Pools of Nairobi National Park, and the Mara River.

Carnivores

Lion, *Panthera leo* (Simba): Still widely distributed. Grasslands, savannah, open woodlands, bush, and semi-deserts. Nairobi National Park, Maasai Mara. Tsavo West, Amboseli, and Samburu are good places to see and study lions.

Leopard, *Panthera pardus* (Chui): Widely distributed. Forests of every type, savannah, bush, grasslands, semi-deserts, and rocky mountain areas. Usually very secretive and rarely seen.

African wild cat, *Felis sylvestris lybica* (Paka pori): Widely distributed. Nocturnal.

Cheetah, *Acinonyx jubatus* (Duma): Fairly widely distributed in grasslands and open savannah. Can usually be seen in Nairobi National Park. Amboseli, Samburu, and Maasai Mara.

Serval cat, *Leptailurus serval* (Mondo): Widely distributed, but rarely seen. Dry bush country and savannah. Shy, solitary, and mainly nocturnal.

Spotted hyena, *Crocuta crocuta* (Fisi): Widely distributed. Mainly nocturnal, but sometimes encountered in daytime.

Striped hyena, *Hyaena hyaena* (Fisi): Nocturnal and rarely seen.

Aardwolf, *Proteles cristatus* (Fisi ndogo): Looks like a small striped hyena and is sometimes encountered in daytime.

Spotted-necked otter, *Lutra maculicollis* (Fisi maji): Widely distributed. Rivers, lake shores, papyrus marshes, reed beds, and quiet backwaters. Especially common around Lake Victoria.

Clawless otter, *Aonyx capensis* (Fisi maji) is found in rivers, streams, and swamps up to 3,000 metres (9,843 feet).

Honey badger, *Mellivora ratel* (Nyegere): Nocturnal. Can be seen regularly near several lodges and do-it-yourself camps.

Grey or golden jackal, *Canis aureus* (Mbweha): Grasslands and savannah. Amboseli.

Black-backed jackal, *Canis mesomelas* (Mbweha): Widely distributed. Savannah and grasslands. It is most commonly seen in Nairobi National Park, Amboseli, Maasai Mara, and many other places.

Side-striped jackal, *Canis adustus* (Mbweha): Very nocturnal, rarely seen.

Hunting dog, *Lycaon pictus* (Mbwa mwitu): Widely distributed, though much reduced in numbers. Bush, light forest, savannah, and grasslands. Can be seen in Tsavo, Maasai Mara, Samburu, and occasionally Nairobi National Park and the Laikipia Plateau.

Bat-eared fox, *Otocyon megalotis* (Mbwela masikia): Widely distributed. Grasslands and open woodlands. Can often be seen in Amboseli, occasionally in Nairobi National Park.

White-tailed mongoose, *Ichneumia albicauda* (Nguchiro): Widely distributed. Nocturnal. Often seen in car lights.

Black-tipped mongoose, *Herpestes sanguineus* (Nguchiro): Widely distributed. Diurnal. Often seen crossing road.

Dwarf mongoose, *Helogale parvula* (Nguchiro): Widely distributed. Diurnal and gregarious. Often seen on termite hills.

Banded mongoose, *Mungos mungos* (Nguchiro): Grasslands. Diurnal and gregarious. Often seen in Maasai Mara.

Genet, *Genetta spp.* (Kanu): Widely distributed. Nocturnal. Have become very tame at several lodges.

Primates

Bushbaby, or **greater galago,** *Galago crassicaudatus* (Komba): Widely distributed. Gallery highland forests and bamboo thickets. Nocturnal. Can often be heard wailing and screaming. **Senegal galago,** *Galago senegalensis*, are found in savannah and woodlands.

Potto, *Perodicticus potto* Western Kenya: Nocturnal and rarely seen. Found in Kakamega, Kaimosi, and Mau Forests.

Olive Baboon, *Papio anubis* (Nyani): Savannah, gallery forests, bush, rocky mountains. Most of Kenya, particularly Nairobi National Park, and the Aberdares.

Yellow baboon, *Papio cynocephalus* (Nyani): South-eastern Kenya, Amboseli, and Tsavo West.

Crested mangabey, *Cercocebus galeritus*: Lower Tana, Witu, and Lamu hinterland.

Red colobus, *Colobus badius*: Tana River and Sokoke-Arabuko Forest near Malindi.

Black-and-white colobus, *Colobus abyssinicus* (Mbega): Forests, especially highland forest of Mount Kenya, the Aberdares, Mount Elgon, and Nakuru National Park.

Vervet monkey, *Ceropithecus aethiops* (Tumbiri or tumbili): Widely distributed. Savannah, woodlands, mountain, forests, and gallery forest.

Blue or Sykes monkey, *Ceropithecus mitis* (Kima): Favours denser and more extensive forests. Larger and very variable in colour.

Red-tailed monkey, *Ceropithecus nictitans*: Evergreen and gallery forests. Western Kenya.

Brazza monkey, *Cercopithecus neglectus*: Forests, especially along rivers and swamps. Western Kenya, particularly Mount Elgon and Kitale.

Patas monkey, *Erythrocebus patas*: Savannah, acacia scrub. North-western Kenya, Uasin Gishu, and Laikipia districts.

Bird Checklist

With its many contrasts of landscape from glacial mountains and alpine moorlands, through close-canopy forest and mangrove swamp, to savannah and semi-desert, and with many freshwater and alkaline lakes, and a tremendous variety of botanical species, Kenya hosts some 1,500 bird species. Some of the more common or spectacular species — excluding the many migrants from the north, are:

Ostrich: Two subspecies: **Maasai Ostrich**, *Struthio camelus massaicus*: Widely distributed in grasslands and open savannah. North to Tana River; **Somali** or **blue-shanked ostrich**, *Struthio camelus molybdophanes*: Dry bush country in northeastern Kenya. Samburu.

Pelicans: **Grey pelican**, *Pelecanus rufescens*: White, greyish on wings, head and belly, tinged pinkish on back and rump. Inland lakes. **White pelican**, *Pelecanus onocrotalus*: Somewhat larger, white, tinged with pink during breeding season. Common on Lakes Naivasha and Nakuru.

Cormorants: **White-necked cormorant**, *Phalacrocorax carbo*, and **pigmy cormorant**, *Phalacrocorax africanus*: Common on Lakes Naivasha and Nakuru. **Darter**, *Anhinga rufa*: Related to cormorants. Widespread on lakes and rivers. Long, thin neck.

Herons: **Blackheaded heron**, *Ardea melancocephala*: Common and widely distributed. Lake shores, river banks, and swamps; often quite far from water. **Goliath heron**, *Ardea goliath*: Largest African heron. Never far from water. Can be seen at Lake Naivasha. **Night heron**, *Nycticorax nycticorax*: Lakes, rivers, and marshes. Can be seen at Lakes Nakuru and Naivasha.

Egrets: **Yellow-billed egret**, *Mesophoyx intermedius*: Swamps, rivers, and lakes. Locally numerous. **Little egret** *Egretta garzetta*: Smaller with black bill. **Cattle egret**, *Bubulcus ibis*: Widely distributed, usually in flocks, often accompanying game or domestic stock. Feeds on insects disturbed by grazing animals.

Storks: **Saddle-billed stork**, *Ephippiorhynchus senegalensis*: Swamps, marshes, and reedy lake shores. Singly or in couples. Seen fairly regularly in Buffalo Springs, also Amboseli and Maasai Mara. **Yellow-billed stork**, *Ibis ibis*. Widely distributed. Flat shores and sandbanks of shallow lakes and rivers. Often in small parties. **Open-billed Stork**, *Anastomus lamelligrus*: Lakes, marshes, and large lagoons. Sometimes in large flocks. Often seen on the Galana River and Aruba Dam (Tsavo East). **Marabou**, *Leptoptilus cruminiferus*: Widely distributed. Open savannah, often in big flocks. A stork with the habits of a vulture. **Hammerkop**, *Scopus umbretta*: Rivers, pools, and shallow lake shores. Big spherical nest can be seen in riverine forests. **Abdim's stork**, *Sphenorynchus abdimi*. Visits East Africa from Sudan, often in large flocks.

African Spoonbill, *Platalea alba*: Shallow lakes, lagoons, and dams. Can be seen in Rift Valley lakes.

Ibises: **Sacred ibis**, *Threskiornis aethiopicus*: Widely distributed. Lakes, rivers, and marshes. Often in flocks.

Hadada, *Hagedashia hagedash*: Well-watered and well-wooded areas. Usually singly or in pairs. Can be seen in Nairobi National Park and at Lake Naivasha.

Flamingos: **Lesser flamingo**, *Phoenicopterus minor*: Bill dark red, tipped black. Common at Lakes Magadi, Elementeita, Nakuru, and Bogoria. **Greater flamingo**, *Phoenicopterus ruber*: Bill pink and black. Recorded breeding at Lakes Magadi, Elementeita, and Nakuru. Often in close association with smaller species.

Geese: **Egyptian goose**, *Alopochen aegyptiaca*: Common and widely distributed. Lakes, ponds, dams, rivers, and marshes. In pairs and family parties. Outside breeding season also in flocks. **Spurwing goose**, *Plectropterus gambiense*: Lakes and rivers, often in big flocks. **Knob-billed goose**, *Sarkidiornis melanotos*: In small flocks on lakes, pools, and wooded swamps. Can be seen at Lake Naivasha.

Ducks: **African pochard**, *Aythia erythrophthalmus*: Common on lakes, often in flocks of fifty or more. **Yellow-billed duck**, *Anas undulata*: Open waters, reedy ponds, and rivers. Gregarious. **Red-billed**

duck, *Anas erythrorhyncha*: Common in swamps, reedy pools, and inlets of lakes. **Hottentot teal**, *Anas punctata*: Shallow saline and freshwater pools with mud banks, shallow grassy coves. Can be seen at Lake Nakuru. **Cape wigeon**, *Anas capensis*: Large and small sheets of saline water and marshes. **White-faced tree-duck**: *Dendrocygna viduata*: River flats, swamps, saltwater lagoons, estuaries, pools, and rivers. Often in large flocks. **Fulvous tree-duck**, *Dendrocygna bicolor*: Inland lakes and marshes.

Secretary bird, *Sagittarius serpentarius*: Often seen in grasslands, savannah, and light bush. Forages on ground.

Vultures: Animal carcasses very quickly attract vultures of several species, especially **hooded vultures**, *Necrosyrtes monachus*; **white-backed vultures**, *Pseudogyps africanus*; and **Rueppell's griffon vultures**, *Gyps rueppellii*. They all give way to the large **Lappet-faced vulture**, *Torgos tracheliotus*. The **Egyptian vulture**, *Neophron percnopterus*, uses stones to break ostrich eggs. **Lammergeier** or **bearded vulture**, *Gypaetus barbatus*: Rather scarce, but can be seen around Elgon, Rift Valley (Hell's Gate), Mount Kenya.

Kites and buzzards: **Black-shouldered kite**, *Elaus caeruleus*: Savannah, dry grasslands, and cultivated areas. Often seen Nairobi National Park. **Yellow-billed kite**, *Milvus migrans*: A subspecies of the European black kite. Common in savannah, along lakes, rivers, and also in towns. **Augur buzzard**, *Buteo rufofuscus*: Very common in mountains, open savannah, and cultivated areas.

Eagles: **Verreaux's eagle**, *Aquila verreauxi*: Rocky hills, mountains, and gorges. Has bred in Nairobi National Park. **Tawny eagle**, *Aquila rapax*. Widely distributed. Common in open savannah, cultivated areas, bush, and semi-deserts. **Martial eagle**, *Polemaetus bellicosus*: Widely distributed. Woodlands, savannah, and thornbush. Can be seen in Nairobi National Park. **Long-crested hawk eagle**, *Lophaetus occipitalis*: Fairly common in riverine forests, bush, wooded, and cultivated areas. Can often be seen perched on telegraph poles. **Bateleur eagle**, *Terathopius ecaudatus*: Fairly common in open savannah and thornbush country. Flight is swift and rocking. **African fish eagle**, *Cuncuma vocifer*: Common along rivers, lakes, estuaries, and seashore. Loud, ringing call.

Falcons: Many different species can be seen. **Peregrine**, *Falco peregrinus*: A small race of the well-known cosmopolitan species. The **African hobby**, *Falco cuvieri*: A distinct species. Savannah and thornbush country. **Lanner**, *Falco biarmicus*: Seen fairly often in savannah and in dry country, usually near rocks. The shrike-sized **pigmy falcon**, *Poliohierax semitorquatus*: Thornbush and semi-desert areas. Especially common in northern Kenya (Samburu). Smallest of African raptors.

Hawks: There are several species of goshawks and sparrow-hawks. **Pale chanting goshawk**, *Melierax metabates*: often seen in acacia and bush country.

Goshawk, *Melierax mitrata*: often seen in acacia and bush country.

Guineafowl: **Helmeted guineafowl**, *Numida mitrata*: Widely distributed and often seen in big flocks. **Vulturine guineafowl**, *Acryllum vulturinum*. Dry bush. Northern and eastern Kenya. Especially common in Samburu.

Francolins: **Yellow-necked spurfowl**, *Francolinus leucoscepus*: Widespread and common in dry open bush and grasslands, in the vicinity of cultivated areas. **Jackson's francolin**, *Francolinus jacksoni*: Mountain forests. Can be seen in the Aberdares and Mount Kenya National Park.

Rails: **Black crake**, *Limnocorax flavirostra*: Common and often seen. Marshes, swamps, river banks, and lake shores. Will walk around on a hippo's back. **Red-crested coot**, *Fulica cristata*: Lakes, dams, and swamps. Very common at Lake Naivasha. **Purple gallinule**, *Porphyrio porphyrio*. Swamps and papyrus marshes. Can often be seen at Lake Naivasha.

Crowned crane, *Balearica regulorum*: Widely distributed. Swamps, lake shores, and grasslands. In pairs, small parties, or flocks.

Bustards: **kori bustard**, *Ardeotis kori*: Open savannah, thornbush, and grasslands. Nairobi National Park, Amboseli, Samburu. and Maasai Mara. **Black-bellied bustard**, *Lissotis melanogaster*: Fairly common in open grasslands and cultivated areas. Maasai Mara, Tsavo National Park. **White-bellied bustard**. *Eupodotis senegalensis*.

Stone curlews: *Burhinus* spp: Of the three species of stone curlews, two are mostly found near water, one in dry scrub, bush and open woodlands.

Jacana, or **lily trotter**, *Actophilornis africanus*: Walks on floating vegetation. Common at Lake Naivasha and Amboseli.

Plovers and related species: **Crowned plover**, *Stephanibyx coronatus*: Not bound to the vicinity of water. Very common on grasslands, especially in short grassy areas. **Blacksmith plover**, *Haplopterus armatus*: Common near rivers, swamps, and lakes. **Spurwinged plover**, *Haplopterus spinosus*: Along rivers and lakes. Can be seen in Rift Valley lakes and Samburu. **Wattled plover**, *Afribyx senegallus*: Swamps and damp areas with short grass. Western Kenya. Of the smaller species, **Kittlitz's plover**, *Charadrius pecuarius*, and the **three-banded plover**, *Charadrius tricollaris*, are widely distributed on sand banks and mud flats along lakes, rivers, and dams. **Chestnut-banded plover**, *Charadrius pallidus venustus*: Found at Lake Magadi only. **Black-winged stilt**, *Himantopus himantopus*: Marshes and salt lakes. Very common at Lakes Magadi and Nakuru. **Avocet**, *Recurvirostra avocetta*: Mud flats, estuaries, and lagoons. Can be seen at Lakes Nakuru and Magadi.

Coursers: Several species on grasslands and dry bush country. **Temminck's courser**, *Cursorius temmincki*: Can often be seen on recently burnt ground. **Heuglin's courser**, *Hemerodromues cinctus*: Occurs in Tsavo National Park.

Gulls:Grey-headed gull, *Larus cirrhocephalus*: Most common gull on East African inland waters. **Sooty gull**, *Larus hemprichii*: Occurs on the coast.

Sandgrouse: Several species. **Yellow-throated sand-grouse**, *Eremialector gutturalis*: One of the most common and widely distributed. At Amboseli and in many other places it can be seen coming to water holes in large flocks.

Pigeons and doves: Numerous in species and numbers. **Speckled pigeon**, *Columba guinea*: One of the most handsome. **Ring-necked dove**, *Streptopelia capicola*: Widely distributed. Very common in savannah, bush, and cultivated areas. **Namaqua dove**, *Oena capensis*: Dry bush and semi-desert areas. Very pretty.

Cuckoos: Well represented in East Africa. **Red-chested cuckoo**, *Cuculus solitarius*: Calls "tit-tit-whoo" **White-browed coucal**, or **waterbottle-bird**, *Centropus superciliosus*: Skulks in dense bush, especially near rivers, and in reed beds. Has a bubbling call, like water being poured out of a bottle. **Emerald cuckoo**, *Chrysococcyx cupreus*, **didric cuckoo**, *Chrysococcyx caprinus*, and **Klaas' cuckoo**, *Chrysococcyx klaas*: Distinguished by the metallic colouration of their upperparts.

Parrots: **Grey parrot**, *Psittacus erithacus*: Largest African parrot. A renowned "talker". Found locally in western Kenya. **Red-headed parrot**, *Polocephalus guilelmi*: Mountain forests. Seen quite regularly along the Naro Moru River.

Turacos: Several species of *Green red-winged turacos*, *Touraco* spp: Coastal highland and mountain forests. **Grey touracos** or "go-away" birds are partial to savannah and dry bush. **White-bellied go-away bird**, *Corythaixoides leucogaster*: Common at Samburu.

Rollers: Represented by several species. **Lilac-breasted roller**, *Coracias caudata*: Commonly seen in savannah and bush country. **Broad-billed roller**, *Eurystomus glaucurus*: Forests, savannah, riverine forests, and mountain areas, going up into the bamboo zone.

Bee-eater, *Melittophagus*: Represented by a number of species. **Little bee-eater**, *Melittophagus pusillus*: Widely distributed. **White-fronted bee-eater**, *Merops bullockoides*: Often seen in the Lake Naivasha region, including Hell's Gate. **Cinnamon-chested bee-eater**, *Melittophagus oreobatus*: Often seen at the Naro Moru River. **Carmine bee-eater**, *Merops nubicus*: Common in coastal areas from November to April.

Kingfishers: Some kingfishers are always found close to water. **Giant kingfisher**, *Megaceryle maxima*, and **Pied kingfisher**, *Ceryle rudis*: Large rivers and lakes. **Malachite kingfisher**, *Corythornis cristata*: Along streams, rivers, and lake shores fringed with reeds, papyrus, and other dense vegetation. Very pretty **grey-headed kingfisher**, *Halcyon leucocephala*: Seen far away from water. **Brown-hooded kingfisher**, *Halcyon albiventris*, and **striped kingfisher**, *Halcyhon chelicuti*: Mainly birds of savannah and woodlands.

Hornbills: The **tokos**, *Tockus erythrorhynchus*, and others: Widely distributed. Savannah and bush country. **Large forest hornbills**, such as **Trumpeter hornbills**, *Bycanistes bucinator*, and the

Silvery-cheeked hornbill, *Bycanistes brevis*: Coastal, riverine and mountain forests. **Ground horn-bill**, *Bucorvus leadbeateri*: Grasslands and savannah. Forages on the ground.

Hoopoes and **wood hoopoes**: The **African hoopoes** *Upupa* spp: closely resemble the European species. Wood hoopoes are long-tailed, iridescent green, black, or blue in colour. **Green wood hoopoe** or **kakelaar**, *Phoeniculus purpureusi*: Woodlands and riverine forests. Usually met with in small, noisy flocks.

Nightjars: Some nightjars have distinctive calls, but when seen flitting at night, or sitting on a road in car lights, the many different species are not easy to distinguish from each other.

Owls: **African marsh owl**, *Asio capensis*: Quite frequently flushed out of high grass. **Verreaux's eagle owl**, *Bubo lacteus*: Often discovered sitting on an acacia tree in riverine forest or savannah country.

Mousebirds: **Speckled mousebird**, *Colius striatus*: Common and widespread along forest edges, bushy savannah, thick scrub, and cultivated areas. **Blue-necked mousebird**, *Colias macrourus*: Dry bush.

Trogons: **Narina's trogon**, *Apoloderma narina*: Highland and mountain forests. One of the most beautiful of East African birds.

Barbets: Many species. **Red-and-yellow barbet**, *Trachyphonus erythrocephalus*: Often seen perched on termite hills in dry bush country. Samburu and Tsavo National Parks. One of the most striking, **D'Arnaud's barbet**, *Trachyponus darnaudii*: Less colourful, but worth watching for its interesting mating behaviour. Male and female sing and posture together, bobbing, bowing, and wagging their tails.

Honey guides: Greater or **black-throated honey guide**, *Indicator indicator*: So named because they guide humans or honey badgers to bee's nest.

Woodpeckers: Many species. One of the most common and widely distributed is the **Nubian woodpecker**, *Campethera nubica*. All types of savannah country.

Swifts: Various species. Seen practically everywhere, from the streets of Nairobi (**Little Swift**, *Apus affinis*) to the crags of Mount Kenya (**Alpine Swift**, *Apus melba*).

Passerines: Too many species to mention. Among the more colourful are glossy starlings. **Superb glossy starling**, *spreo superbus*: Very tame around lodges and picnic sites. **Golden-breasted starling**, *Cosmopsarius regius*: Can be observed and photographed at Kilaguni Lodge at close range. **Sunbirds**: Small, often colourful birds which dip their beaks into flowers. Not to be mistaken for humming birds. **Scarlet-chested sunbird**, *Nectarinia senegalensis*: Very striking and often seen. **Weaver birds**: Make beautifully woven nests, often arranged in such large colonies they can't be missed. Yellow, or a combination of yellow and black. **Sparrow weaver**, *Plocepasser mahali*: One of most common and widespread. Brown and white plumage. **Dine-melli's buffalo weaver**, *Dinemellia dinemelli*: Common and very characteristic of dry bush country. Black, white, and red. **Common buffalo weaver**, *Bubalornis albirostris*: Male is black. The enormously long-tailed **wydahs** and **widow birds** are related to the weavers. **Pintailed wydah**, *Vidua macroura*: Black and white. **Long-tailed widow bird**, *Euplectes progne*: Black with some red and white on the wings. Seen between Nanyuki and Nyeri. At mating time, widow birds perform interesting courtship dances. Among the **finches**, there are many small and colourful species, especially **Cordon bleu**, *Uraeginthus bengalus*; **Purple grenadier**, *Uraeginthus ianthinogaster*; and **Fire-finch**, *Logonosticta rubricata*.

Shrikes: No traveller in East Africa can miss the black and white **Fiscal shrike**, *Lanius collurio*, of which in some places there seems to be two to every bush. The shrike family, as a whole, is very well represented, but many species are shy and less easily seen than the fiscal and its close relations.

Oxpeckers: Game watchers will soon become aware of two oxpeckers: **Red-billed oxpecker**, *Buphagus erythrorhynchus*, and **Yellow-billed oxpecker**, *Buphagus africanus*. They climb around on rhinos, buffaloes, giraffes, and other animals in search of ticks.

Reptile and Amphibian Profile

Nile Crocodile, *Crocodylus niloticus*: Widely distributed in rivers, lakes, and swamps, but much reduced through uncontrolled shooting and trapping. There is often a spectacular concentration at Crocodile Point, below the Lugard Falls of the Galana River in Tsavo East. During the last few years crocodiles have been on the increase in Samburu's Uaso Nyiro river and a few can usually be seen at Mzima Springs, the Hippo Pools of Nairobi National Park, and on the Mara and Tana Rivers. One of the last great sanctuaries for crocodiles is Lake Turkana.

Lizards: Monitor lizards: Can attain a length of two metres (six feet) or even more. **Nile Monitor**, *Varanus niloticus*: Mainly found along rivers. Known to dig up crocodile's nests and to eat the eggs. **Spotted Monitor**, *Varanus occelatus*: Dry bush and savannah country, at a considerable distance from any water. **Small geckos** have established themselves in human habitations. The adhesive pads on their toes allow them to run up and down walls and even to walk on ceilings. **Rock agama**, or **rainbow lizard**, *Agama agama*: Very beautiful. Can be seen around many of the lodges and do-it-yourself camps. Males are blue, with red heads. Fascinating to watch their colours become more intense or fade away, according to their state of agitation.

Chameleons are represented by a number of species, some of which are armed with horns.

Turtles are common in streams, rivers, and the sea.

Tortoises — especially the **Leopard tortoise**, *Testudo pardalis* — can often be found in grasslands and savannah.

Snakes: Visitors are usually surprised at the apparent lack of snakes. However, these reptiles are shy and secretive, and some have predominantly nocturnal habits. Only on rare occasions will the tourist travelling by car catch a brief glimpse of one as it slithers across the road. But in the country, moving about on foot, you soon come to realize that snakes are not uncommon. Most venomous species tend to get out of the way of any human being, warned of his approach by the vibration of the ground. **Black mamba**, *Dendroaspis polylepis*: Has a sinister reputation of occasionally attacking without provocation, but this usually happens when it finds itself cut off from its hiding place. Not common in Kenya. **Puff adder**, *Bitis arietans*:

Widespread and fairly numerous. The most dangerous of Kenya's snakes. Relying on its wonderful camouflage, it usually does not take evasive action but remains motionless. A person walking through scrub or high grass can easily put his foot close enough to make it strike with lighting speed. **Black-necked** or **spitting cobra**, *Naja nigricollis*: When cornered accidentally, it ejaculates its venom, aiming, if possible, at the face of its presumed enemy. **Green tree snake** or **boomslang**, *Dispholidus typus*: May be seen slithering along a branch. It carries its poison fangs so far back in its jaws that to be bitten, a human being would have to put a finger into its mouth. **Rock python**, *Python sebae*: Widely distributed and not uncommon in some places but not often seen. A truly magnificent snake that quite often attains a length of up to five metres (16 feet). There are records of pythons over eleven metres (37 feet) long. **Amphibians** are represented in East Africa by **caecilians**, **toads**, and **frogs**. There are no newts or salamanders. Frogs are especially numerous, ranging from tiny **Tree frogs** with adhesive pads on their toes, to the huge **Bullfrog**, *Pyxicephalus adspersus*: Up to twenty-five centimetres (10 inches) in length and able to dig itself into the earth, vanishing from sight within about twenty minutes. **Clawed frog**, *Xenopus laevus*: Only rarely leaves the water. Has a flattened body, small forelimbs, large hind-limbs, and carries sharp, black claws on the first, second, and third toe. Males make rattling calls which can be heard a considerable distance away. The legless, worm-shaped **caecilians** spend most of their time underground or under stones, fallen leaves, in rotten tree trunks, or termite hills, and are rarely seen.

Insects and Arachnids

Most tourists who come to Kenya to collect insects are looking for **butterflies**, **moths**, or **beetles**. These groups occur all over Kenya, with some species only in confined areas.

Around 600 species of butterflies are found, with closely defined limits for the coastal, dry-country, upland species, and those which occur in western Kenya. Only a very few common species are found over the entire country.

Along the coastal belt, from the Tanzania border northwards to Malindi, there are several interesting species. *Euphaedra neophron*, a purplish-brown butterfly, is to be found in the forests and under the cashew-nut and coconut plantations. A browner form of the same butterfly is also found at Taveta Forest, around Meru, and near Mount Kenya. Quite a number of coastal butterflies can be found as far inland as Meru, having made their way across the dry semi-desert plains along the Tana River. Also occasionally found in this area is *Papilio ophidicephalus*, a magnificent, large, black and yellow butterfly whose long tail has a brilliant blue and red patch at its base. This butterfly is sometimes quite common in Kibwezi Forest, between the town and where the railway line crosses the road.

Between the coastal belt and just short of Nairobi are the great grassy plains of Kenya, which also cover the Rift Valley. Generally speaking, there is not enough rain to allow trees to grow, and a special group of butterflies has evolved to cover this vegetation, *Colotis* are white butterflies with brilliant red or orange tips and are common. So are the blue and yellow panisies, *Precis* spp, which can be seen settled on their territories of dry earth among the grass. Where the forest has been cut down, for example for housing in the Nairobi area, these butterflies are also to be found. The northern deserts of Kenya are a major extension of this area which is poor in species even during the infrequent rains.

Small mountains and hills are much more interesting. On the Taita Hills live a blue and black swallowtail, *Papilio taita* and *Cymothoe taita*, a creamy-white and black butterfly. Both of these are also found in Mbololo Forest on the top of the hills close to Voi on the Mombasa-Nairobi Road.

The Kakamega Forest in western Kenya, contains the same richness of fauna as the great rain forests of the Congo Basin and attracts a similar butterfly population. A large number of species can be seen and caught in any one day.

The best butterfly areas are also good for moths, particularly during the rains. The first night of the rains is always the most productive. It is advisable to use either a black-white or an ordinary pressure lamp and a white sheet for collecting, or the moths will be badly damaged by large beetles in some areas.

If it starts raining, or is raining in a normally dry area, any light will produce magical results. Great clouds of moths, along with millions of termites, will always come in the wet weather, even in the centre of Nairobi.

The best areas for **beetles** are the same as for butterflies, except that during the first nights of the rains, the area around Voi is very good for **dung-beetles**, *Scarabaeidae* spp.

A spectacular manifestation of insect life are the **termite hills** dotted all over the countryside. Up to three metres (10 feet) in height, they're often crowned by a series of turrets containing air-shafts, or running straight up in one single hollow tower that resembles a miniature factory chimney.

Termites are often referred to as "white ants" but, in fact, they are related to cockroaches. They may have been the first creatures on earth to establish a social organisation. Deep in the centre of the termite castle lies the strongly cemented royal cell where the gigantic queen spends her life tended by an army of workers and well-armed soldiers, and produces eggs at a rate of about one every two seconds.

During the wet weather columns of **soldier ants**, also known as "safari ants" or "siafu", meander in thick black bands for hundreds of yards through bush and forest. These bands are formed by a two-way stream of bush ants and guarded on both flanks by aggressive, large-pincered "soldiers".

If you look closely where the column fans out, you'll see a wholesale massacre of spiders, cockroaches, crickets, caterpillars, even of frogs, lizards, and small snakes.

An arthropod not classified among the insects is the **giant millipede**, popularly known as "Tanganyika Railway". This glossy black creature with reddish-brown legs, up to thirty centimetres (12 inches) in length is perfectly harmless.

However, the big **centipedes** that lurk under tree trunks and fallen leaves have a venomous bite.

There are a number of species of **scorpions** in Kenya. Most of them are small with disagreeable but harmless stings. In hot, dry, bush country, however, there are scorpions up to twenty centimetres (eight inches) long, which are as dangerous as they look.

Scorpions are related to **spiders**, among which are some striking and beautiful species. The huge, yellow and black *Nephilia spiders*, construct amazingly tough, golden yellow webs. They are harmless, as are practically all other East African spiders. The one known exception is an uncommon species related to the black widow, *Latrodectes*, of America. It is black with dark red markings and a globular body. Its bite is quite venomous, though not necessarily fatal.

Animal Checklist

Mammals

INSECTIVORES
Rufous Spectacled Elephant Shrew
Yellow-Rumped Elephant Shrew
Rwenzori Golden Mole
East African Hedgehog
Otter Shrew
Giant White-Toothed Shrew

BATS
Straw-Coloured Fruit Bat
Epauletted Fruit Bat
Hammer-Headed Fruit Bat
Mouse-Tailed Bat
White-Bellied Tomb Bat
Hollow-Faced Bat
False Vampire Bat
Yellow-Winged Bat
Lander's Horseshoe Bat
Lesser Leaf-Nosed Bat
Giant Leaf-Nosed Bat
Long-Eared Leaf-Nosed Bat
African Mouse-Eared Bat
Banana Bat, or African Pipistrelle

Yellow-Bellied Bat
Angola Free-Tailed Bat
White-Bellied Free-Tailed Bat
Flat-Headed Free-Tailed Bat
Giant Free-Tailed Bat

POTTOS, GALAGOS and MONKEYS,
Potto
Greater Galago
Bush Baby
Tana Manabey
Black-Faced Vervet Monkey
Blue, or Sykes' Monkey
Brazza Monkey
Red-Tailed, or White-Nosed Monkey
Patas Monkey
Olive Baboon
Yellow Baboon
Black and White Colobus
Red Colobus

PANGOLINS
Lesser Ground Pangolin

CARNIVORES
Hunting Dog
Golden Jackal
Black-Backed, or Silver-Backed Jackal
Side-Striped Jackal

Bat-Eared Fox
Zorilla
Ratel, or Honey Badger
Clawless Otter
African Civet
Neumann's, or Small-Spotted Genet
Bush, or Large-Spotted Genet
African Palm Civet
Marsh Mongoose
Dwarf Mongoose
Large Grey Mongoose
Slender, or Black-Tipped Mongoose
White-Tailed Mongoose
Banded Mongoose
Aardwolf
Spotted Hyena
Striped Hyena
Cheetah
Caracal
African Wild Cat
Serval
Golden Cat
Lion
Leopard

ANT BEARS
Ant Bear, or Aardvark

HYRAXES
Tree Hyrax
Rock Hyrax

ELEPHANTS
African Elephant

ODD-TOED UNGULATES
Black Rhinocerous
Square-Lipped, or White Rhinocerous
Grevy's Zebra
Burchell's, or Common Zebra

EVEN-TOED UNGULATES
Hippopotamus
Giant Forest Hog
Wart Hog
Bush Pig
Common Giraffe
Reticulated Giraffe
Coke's Hartebeest, or Kongoni
Jackson's Hartebeest
White-Bearded Gnu, or Wildebeest
Hunter's Hartebeest, or Hirola
Topi
Zanzibar, or Ader's Duiker
Yellow-Backed Duiker
Blue Duiker
Bush Duiker
Klipspringer
Suni
Oribi
Steinbok
Kirk's Dikdik
Guenther's Dikdik

Common Waterbuck
Bohor Reedbuck
Chanler's Mountain Reedbuck
Impala
Thomson's Gazelle
Grant's Gazelle
Gerenuk
Roan Antelope
Sable Antelope
Oryx
Bongo
Sitatunga
Bushbuck
Greater Kudu
Lesser Kudu
Eland
African Buffalo

HARES and RABBITS
African Hare
Spring Hare

RODENTS
Cane Rat
Porcupine
Striped Ground Squirrel
Unstriped Ground Squirrel
Bush Squirrel
Giant Forest Squirrel
Scaly-Tailed Spring Hare
African Dormouse
Crested Rat
Giant Rat
Kenya Mole Rat
Naked Mole Rat

Birds

OSTRICH
Ostrich

GREBES
Little Grebe

PELICANS
White Pelican
Pink-Backed Pelican

CORMORANTS
White-Necked Cormorant
Long-Tailed Cormorant

DARTERS
African Darter

HERONS and EGRETS
Cattle Egret
Black-Headed Heron
Goliath Heron

HAMERKOP
Hamerkop

STORKS
Marabou Stork
Yellow-Billed Stork

IBISES and SPOONBILLS
Sacred Ibis
Hadada Ibis
African Spoonbill

FLAMINGOS
Greater Flamingo
Lesser Flamingo

DUCKS and GEESE
Eygptian Goose

BIRDS OF PREY
Secretary Bird
White-Backed Vulture
Bateleur
Pale Chanting Goshawk
Augur Buzzard
Long-Crested Eagle
Tawny Eagle
Fish Eagle
Black Kite
Black-Shouldered Kite

GAME BIRDS
Crested Francolin
Yellow-Necked Spurfowl
Helmeted Guinea-Fowl
Vulturine Guinea-Fowl

CRANES
Crowned Crane

CRAKES, RAILS, and COOTS
Black Crake
Red-Knobbed Coot

BUSTARDS
Kori Bustard

JACANAS, or LILLY-TROTTERS
African Jacana

PLOVERS and ALLIES
Blacksmith Plover
Crowned Plover
Black-Winged Stilt

GULLS and TERNS
Grey-Headed Gull

SANDGROUSE
Chestnut-Bellied Sandgrouse
Black-Faced Sandgrouse

DOVES and PIGEONS
Speckled Pigeon
Red-Eyed Dove
Ring-Necked Dove
Laughing Dove
Namaqua Dove

TURACOS
Schalow's Turaco
Hartlaub's Turaco
White-Bellied Go-Away-Bird

CUCKOOS and COUCALS
Red-Chested Cuckoo
White-Browed Coucal

OWLS
Pearl-Spotted Owl

SWIFTS
Little Swift

MOUSEBIRDS
Speckled Mousebird
Blue-Naped Mousebird

KINGFISHERS
Pied Kingfisher
Malachite Kingfisher
Grey-Headed Kingfisher

BEE-EATERS
Little Bee-Eater

ROLLERS
Lilac-Breasted Roller
Rufous-Crowned Roller

HOOPOES
African Hoopoe

WOOD HOOPOES
Green Wood Hoopoe

HORNBILLS
Red-Billed Hornbill
Yellow-Billed Hornbill

BARBETS
Red-Fronted Barbet
Red-Fronted Tinkerbird
Golden-Rumped Tinkerbird
D'Arnaud's Barbet
Red and Yellow Barbet

WOODPECKERS
Nubian Woodpecker

LARKS
Rufous-Naped Lark
Fischer's Sparrow Lark

SWALLOWS and MARTINS
Wire-Tailed Swallow
Red-Rumped Swallow
Striped Swallow

WAGTAILS and PIPITS
African Pied Wagtail
Golden Pipit
Yellow-Throated Longclaw

BULBULS
Yellow-Vented Bulbul

SHRIKES
White-Crowned Shrike
Black-Headed Tchagra
Tropical Boubou
Black-Headed Gonolek
Slate-Coloured Boubou
Fiscal Shrike

THRUSHES and ALLIES
Stonechat
Capped Wheatear
Anteater Chat
Spotted Morning Warbler
White-Starred Bush Robin
Robin Chat
White-Browed Robin Chat

Olive Thrush

BABBLERS and CHATTERERS
Rufous Chatterer

WARBLERS
Hunter's Cisticola
Rattling Cisticola
Tawny-Flanked Prinia
Black-Breasted Apalis
Grey-Backed Camaroptera
Crombec

FLYCATCHERS
White-Eyed Slaty Flycatcher
Silver Bird
Chin-Spot Puffback
Blue Flycatcher
Paradise Flycatcher

TITS
White-Breasted Tit

SUNBIRDS
Amethyst Sunbird
Scarlet-Chested Sunbird
Variable Sunbird
Eastern Double-Collared Sunbird
Mariqua Sunbird
Tacazze Sunbird
Red-Chested Sunbird
Beautiful Sunbird
Malachite Sunbird
Bronze Sunbird
Golden-Winged Sunbird
Kenya Violet-Backed Sunbird
Collared Sunbird

WHITE-EYES
Kikuyu White-Eye

BUNTINGS
Golden-Breasted Bunting

FINCHES
Yellow-Rumped Seed-Eater
Brimstone Canary
Streaky Seed-Eater

WAXBILLS and ALLIES
Green-Winged Pytilia
Yellow-Bellied Waxbill
Common Waxbill
Purple Grenadier
Red-Cheeked Cordon-Bleu
Red-Billed Firefinch

Cut-Throat
Bronze Mannikin
Pin-Tailed Wydah
Paradise Wydah

WEAVERS and ALLIES
Reichenow's Weaver
Golden Palm Weaver
Taveta Golden Weaver
Masked Weaver
Vitelline Masked Weaver
Speke's Weaver
Black-Headed Weaver
Chestnut Weaver
Spectacled Weaver
Red-Headed Weaver
Cardinal Quelea
Red-Billed Quelea
White-Winged Widow-Bird
Red-Collared Widow-Bird
Yellow Bishop
Black-Winged Bishop
Red Bishop
West Nile Red Bishop
Long-Tailed Widow-Bird
Jackson's Widow-Bird
Red-Billed Buffalo Weaver
White-Headed Buffalo Weaver
White-Browed Sparrow Weaver
Grey-Capped Social Weaver

STARLINGS
Blue-Eared Starling
Ruppell's Long-Tailed Starling
Violet-Backed Starling
Hilderbrandt's Starling
Superb Starling
Golden-Breasted Starling
Wattled Starling
Red-Billed Starling

ORIOLES
Black-Headed Oriole

DRONGOS
Drongo

CROWS
Pied Crow
Indian House Crow
Cape Rook
Fan-Tailed Raven
White-Naped Raven

A Demographic Profile

Kenya is inhabited by all three of the great language families of Africa.

With the exception recent immigrant communities, Kenyans can be divided into three distinct generic groupings: Bantu, Nilotic, and Cushitic. Each group belongs to a different language family — the Bantu to the Niger-Kordofanian family, Nilotic to the Nilo-Saharan family and Cushitic to the Hamito-Semitic family of Afro-Asiatic origin.

Within Kenya the Bantu languages are further classified geographically into Western, Central, and Eastern. The Nilotic languages are divided into Western, Eastern, and Southern although Maa, an Eastern Nilotic language, is spoken far south of any Southern Nilotic language.

The Cushitic language is represented in Kenya by two different branches, the Eastern and Southern Cushitic. Dahalo is the sole example of the latter still spoken in Kenya.

Although it is not easy to determine the boundary between a language and a dialect, on the foregoing classification it can be said that some thirty languages are spoken in Kenya.

Many languages may be mutually intelligible and decisions as to their status are only arbitrary and made with many reservations. Two-thirds of Kenya's people speak a Bantu language as their mother tongue; thirty per cent are Nilotic speakers and only three per cent speak Cushitic languages. However, the mainly nomadic people of this group range across forty per cent of the 582,644 square kilometres (224,500 square miles) of Kenya's territory.

One effect of the colonial regime was to make divisions between tribes more rigid, more distinctive and, therefore, more closely associated with vested interests, rights, and privileges. Most early European administrators too readily identified tribes as time-honoured units. But, as linguistic and anthropological studies are continuing to reveal, this was far from the truth and remains so.

The names of the ethnic groups are those in common usage. However, the Kiswahili plural prefix "Wa" is frequently used by Kenyans when referring to these groups, as in Wakikuyu, Wakamba, Wataita, Wamaasai, Wanandi, and so on. The Western Bantu groups incorporate their own plural prefix "Aba", as in Abaluyia, Abagusii, Abasuba, and Abakuria.

Population By Tribe/Ethnic grouping

Burji: number unknown, North-east Kenya, Moyale and Marsabit districts.
Dassenich: 20,000, Todenyang area of Turkana, the northern tip of Lake Turkana at Ileret, and Marsabit district.

El Molo: 500, Loiyangalani, south-east shores of Lake Turkana.
Embu: 180,000, Embu district.
Gabbra: 30,500, Marsabit district.
Gusii: 994,000, Kisii and South Nyanza districts.
Ilchamus: 7,500, Lake Baringo.
Iteso: 132,500, Busia and Bungoma districts.
Kamba: 1.7 million, Machakos and Kitui districts.
Keijo: number unknown, Elgeyo Escarpment.
Kikuyu: 3.2 million, Nyeri, Muranga, Kiambu, and Kirinyaga districts.
Kipsigis: 1.6 million, Kericho district.
Kuria: 89,000, south of Kisii on either side of the Kenya-Tanzania border.
Luo: 1.9 million, Kisumu district.
Luyia: 2.1 million, Kakamega district.
Maasai: 241,500, Narok and Kajiado districts.
Marakwet: number unknown, Kerio Valley and Cherangani Hills of Elgeyo-Marakwet district.
Mbeere: 1,600, lowlands south-east of Embu district.
Meru: 840,000, Meru district.
Mijikenda: 733,000, coastal hinterland, especially Kilifi district.
Nandi: number unknown, Nandi district.
Okiek: 7,200, highland forests, including the Mau and Ol Doinyo Lenkiyo Ranges, Cherangani, and Kamasia Hills.
Orma: 32,000, north-east Kenya, around the Tana River.
Pokomo: 40,000, Tana River district.
Pokot: number unknown, West Pokot district.
Rendille: 22,000, Marsabit district.
Sabaot: number unknown, either side of the Bungoma-Trans Nzoia district boundary.
Sakuye: 1,800, along Ewaso Ngiro River, Isiolo district.
Samburu: 73,400, Samburu and Marsabit districts.
Segeju: 200, Kidumu and Shimoni villages, Kwale district.
Somali: 381,000, Mandera, Wajir and Garissa districts.
Suba: 59,500, Rusinga and Mfangano islands of Lake Victoria and coastal locations of South Nyanza district.
Taita/Taveta: 168,000, Taita-Taveta district.
Tharaka: 9,750, lowlands east of Mount Kenya.
Tuken: number unknown, Tugen and Kamisia Hills.
Turkana: 207,250, Turkana district.

Kenyan Population by sex and age

	0-14	15-49	50+	TOTAL
MALE	3,720,044	3,185,981	685,436	7,707,113
FEMALE	3,689,973	3,348,711	667,431	7,719,948
TOTAL	7,410,017	6,534,692	1,352,861	5,327,061

Population by province

Nairobi: 684 sq kms, 827,775 (1,201 to the sq km)
Coast: 83,040 sq kms, 1,342,794 (16 to the sq km)
Central: 13,173 sq kms, 2,345,833 (178 to the sq km)

Eastern: 155,759 sq kms, 2,719,851, (17 to the sq km)
North Eastern: 126,902 sq kms, 373,787 (2 to the sq km)
Nyanza: 12,525 sq kms, 2,643,956, (211 to the sq km)
Rift Valley: 163,883 sq kms, 3,240,402, (19 to the sq km)
Western: 8,196 sq kms, 1,832,663, (223 to the sq km)
Total
Kenya: 564,162 sq kms, 15,327,061, (27 to the sq km)

Population by Race

Kenyan Africans	15,029,720
Kenyan Asian	32,554
Kenyan European	4,445
Kenyan Arab	18,861
Other Kenyans	57,318
Africans	71,818
Asians	46,046
Europeans	35,456
Arabs	20,285
Others	10,213
Not Stated	343
Total	15,327,061

All figures from the 1979 Kenyan national census. The Kenyan birthrate in 1989 was 3.9%.

GAZETTEER
(First line indicates kilometre distance between major towns)

ARCHER'S POST
Nairobi 323, Isiolo 48, Nanyuki 123, Marsabit 239, Wamba 56, Maralal 110.
Alt: 790m (2,600ft). Post Office. Police post. Pop: 807. Samburu District, Rift Valley Province. Archer's Post Dispensary (Mission). Nearest hospital: Isiolo. Petrol and diesel usually available.

ATHI RIVER
Nairobi 27, Machakos 38, Mtito Andei 209, Namanga 138, Mombasa 458.
Alt: 1,520m (5,000ft). Post Office. Police Tel: 20222. Pop: 9,760. Machakos District, Eastern Province. Athi River Health Centre (Govt) Tel: 20368. Nearest hospital: Nairobi. Petrol and diesel.

BARAGOI
Nairobi 441, Nyahururu 243, Loiyangalani 225, Maralal 97
Alt: 1,520m (5,000ft). Police Tel: 4. Pop: 2,592. Samburu District, Rift Valley Province. Baragoi Health Centre (Govt). Nearest hospital: Maralal. No petrol or diesel.

BARINGO (see Lake Baringo)

BUNA
Nairobi 793, Wajir 156, Moyale 101.
Alt: 940m (3,100ft). Police. Pop: 500. Wajir District, North Eastern Province. Buna Dispensary (Govt). Nearest hospital: Moyale. No petrol.

BUNGOMA
Nairobi 402, Eldoret 90, Kakamega 74, Kitale 127, Kisumu 127, Webuye 35.
Alt: 1,430m (4,700ft). Post Office. Police Tel: 20847. Pop: 25,161. HQ Bungoma District, Western Province. Bungoma District Hospital (Govt) Tel: 20345. Petrol and diesel usually available.

BUSIA
Nairobi 479, Bungoma 65, Eldoret 155, Kakamega 92, Kisumu 130.
Alt: 1,190m (3,900ft). Post Office. Police Tel: 2ll0. Customs Tel: 2038. Immigration Tel: 2027. Pop: 24,857. HQ Busia District, Western Province. Busia District Hospital (Govt) Tel: 2720. Border post with Uganda. Petrol and diesel.

BUTERE
Nairobi 408, Bungoma 43, Busia 71, Kakamega 53, Kisumu 59.
Alt: 1,370m (4,500ft). Post Office. Police Tel: 4. Pop: 1,044. Kakamega District, Western Province. Butere Health Centre (Govt) Tel: 28. Nearest hospital: Mumias Mission Hospital. Petrol.

CHIEBIEMET
Nairobi 372, Eldoret 60, Iten 25,
Alt: 2,590m (8,500ft). Police Post. Pop: 1,000. Elgeyo Marakwet District, Rift Valley Province. Chiebiemet Dispensary (Govt). Nearest hospital: Kapsowar Mission Hospital. Petrol.

CHEPKORIO
Nairobi 313, Eldoret 39, Nakuru 157, Eldama Ravine 57.
Alt: 2,500m (8,200ft). Police Tel: 2Y6. Pop: 500. Elgeyo Marakwet District, Rift Valley Province. Chepkorio Health Centre (Govt) Tel: 1Y2. Nearest hospital: Plateau Reformed Church Hospital. No petrol.

ELBURGON
Nairobi 194, Molo 13, Nakuru 38, Njoro 20.
Alt: 2,410m (7,900ft). Post Office. Police Tel: 5. Pop: 5,343. Nakuru District, Rift Valley Province. Elburgon Health Centre (Govt) Tel: 33. Nearest hospital: Molo. Petrol.

ELDORET
Nairobi 312, Nakuru 156, Kitale 69, Bungoma 90.
Alt: 2,100m (6,900ft). Post Office. Police Tel: 32223. Pop:. 50,503. HQ Uasin Gishu District, Rift Valley Province. Eldoret District Hospital (Govt) Tel: 33472; Uasin Gishu Hospital (Private) Tel: 32720. Petrol and diesel.

ELIYE SPRINGS
Nairobi 799, Kitale 418, Lodwar 63.
Alt: 375m (1,230ft). Pop: 500. Turkana District, Rift Valley Province. Nearest hospital: Lodwar. Nearest petrol: Lodwar.

ELDAMA RAVINE
Nairobi 216, Eldoret 96, Nakuru 60.
Alt: 2,130m (7,000ft). Post Office. Police Tel: 3.
Pop: 2,692. Baringo District, Rift Valley Province.
Eldama Ravine Health Centre (Govt) Tel: l2;
Mercy Mission Hospital Tel: 16. Petrol.

EL WAK
Nairobi 822, Wajir 185, Mandera 177.
Alt: 427m (1,410ft). Post Office. Police Tel: 2002.
Pop: 500. Mandera district, North Eastern
Province. El Wak Sub Health Centre (Govt).
Nearest hospital: Wajir or Mandera. Petrol
sometimes available.

EMBU
Nairobi 139, Meru 137, Muranga 52, Nyeri 96,
Sagana 40.
Alt: l,372m (4,500ft). Post Office. Police Tel: 20l02.
Pop: 16,155. HQ Embu District and HQ Eastern
Province. Embu District Hospital (Govt) Tel:
20487. Petrol and diesel.

FERGUSON'S GULF
Nairobi 800, Kitale 419, Lodwar 64.
Alt: 375m (1,230ft). Pop: 500. Turkana District, Rift
Valley Province. Nearest hospital: Lodwar. Petrol.

GARISSA
Nairobi 380, Mombasa 468, Wajir 321 (via Modo
Gashi), Mwingi 202, Modo Gashi 161.
Alt: 100m (320ft). Post Office. Police Tel: 2005.
Pop: 14,076. HQ Garissa District and HQ North
Eastern Province. Garissa Provincial Hospital
(Govt) Tel: 2284. Petrol and diesel.

GARSEN
Nairobi 715 (via Mombasa), Mombasa 230,
Malindi 111, Garissa 238, Lamu 111.
Alt: 30m (100ft). Police Tel: 44. Pop: 1,007. Tana
River District, Coast Province. Garsen Health
Centre (Govt) Tel: 35. Nearest hospital: Ngao
Mission Hospital. Ferry across Tana River from 6
am to 6 pm only. Petrol.

GILGIL
Nairobi 116, Nakuru 40, Naivasha 27, Nyahururu
82.
Alt: 2,010m (6,600ft). Post Office. Police Tel: 2222.
Pop: 9,103. Nakuru District, Rift Valley Province.
Gilgil Health Centre (Govt) Tel: 2214. Nearest
hospital: Naivasha. Petrol.

HABASWEIN
Nairobi 527, Wajir 110, Modo Gashi 50, Isiolo 242.
Alt: 275m (900ft). Police Tel: 4. Pop: 500. Wajir
District, North Eastern Province.
Habaswein Dispensary (Govt) Tel: 9. Nearest
hospital: Wajir. Petrol.

HOLA
Nairobi 802 (via Mombasa), 531 (via Garissa),
Mombasa 317, Garissa 151, Garsen 87, Malindi
208.
Alt: 60m (200ft). Post Office. Police Tel: 2009. Pop:

5,352. HQ Tana River District, Coast Province.
Hola District Hospital (Govt) Tel: 2025. Petrol.

HOMA BAY
Nairobi 423, Kericho 157, Kisii 59, Kisumu 104
(115 via Kendu Bay), Mbita 35.
Alt: l,145m (3,750ft). Post Office. Police Tel: 22626.
Pop: 7,489. HQ South Nyanza District, Nyanza
Province. Homa Bay District Hospital (Govt) Tel:
22004. Petrol.

ISIOLO
Nairobi 285, Marsabit 277, Meru 57, Nanyuki 85,
Modo Gashi 192. Archer's Post 38, Garba Tula 125.
Alt: 1,220m (4,000ft). Post Office. Police Tel: 2008.
Pop: 11,331. HQ Isiolo District, Eastern Province.
Isiolo District Hospital (Govt) Tel: 2031. Petrol.

ITEN
Nairobi 346, Eldoret 34, Tambach 10, Kabarnet 60,
Kaptarakwa 27, Tot 108, Kapkerop 33.
Alt: 2,225m (7,300ft). Police Tel: 2063. Pop: 743.
HQ Elgeyo Marakwet District, Rift Valley
Province. Iten District Hospital (Govt) Tel: 2014.
Petrol and diesel.

KABARNET
Nairobi 282, Marigat 42, Nakuru 146, Tambach 37,
Eldoret 88, Mogotio 104.
Alt: 2,060m (6,750ft). Post Office. Police Tel: 2333.
Pop: 3,621. HQ Baringo District, Rift Valley
Province. Kabarnet District Hospital (Govt) Tel:
2064. Petrol.

KAHAWA
Nairobi 12, Thika 30, Nanyuki 188.
Alt: 1,555m (5,100ft). Pop: 30,958. Nairobi Area.
Kahawa Health Centre (City Council). Nearest
hospital: Nairobi. Petrol and diesel.

KAJIADO
Nairobi 76, Namanga 88, Athi River 51.
Alt: 1,740m (3,520ft). Post Office. Police Tel: 21222.
Pop: 3,520. HQ Kajiado District, Rift Valley
Province. Kajiado District Hospital (Govt) Tel:
21021. Petrol and diesel.

KAKAMEGA
Nairobi 402, Bungoma 74, Kisumu 73.
Alt: 1,525m (5,000ft). Post Office. Police Tel: 20222.
Pop: 32,025. HQ Kakamega District and HQ
Western Province. Kakamega General Hospital
(Govt) Tel: 20020. Petrol and diesel.

KALOLENI
Nairobi 473, Mombasa 52 (via Mariakani),
Mariakani 20, Kilifi 35, Mazeras 22.
Alt: 210m (700ft). Pop: 1,171. Kilifi District, Coast
Province. Saint Luke's Kaloleni Mission Hospital
Tel: 16. Petrol and diesel.

KAPENGURIA
Nairobi 413, Eldoret 101, Kitale 32, Lodwar 323.
Alt: 2,135m (7,000ft). Post Office. Police Tel: 2622.
Pop: 2,752. HQ West Pokot District, Rift Valley

Province. Kapenguria District Hospital (Govt) Tel: 2621. Petrol and diesel.

KAPSABET
Nairobi 325, Eldoret 48, Kakamega 68, Kisumu 85, Nandi Hills 18.
Alt: 1,950m (6,400ft). Post Office. Police Tel: 2004. Pop: 2,945. HQ Nandi District, Rift Valley Province. Kapsabet District Hospital (Govt) Tel: 2005. Petrol and diesel.

KAPTAGAT
Nairobi 320, Eldoret 34, Nakuru 164, Eldama Ravine 61.
Alt: 2,380m (7,800ft). Post Office. Police Tel: 9. Pop: 500. Uasin Gishu District, Rift Valley Province. Kaptagat Dispensary (Govt). Nearest hospital: Plateau Reformed Church Hospital (22 kms). Petrol.

KARATINA
Nairobi 128, Muranga 41, Nanyuki 72, Nyeri 27.
Alt: 1,770m (5,800ft). Post Office. Police Tel: 71222. Pop: 2,980. Nyeri District, Central Province. Karatina Health Centre (Govt) Tel: 71358. Nearest hospital: Nyeri. Petrol and diesel.

KEDOWA (Lumbwa)
Nairobi 240, Nakuru 84, Kericho 73, Kisumu 156, Kipkelion 38.
Alt: 1,920m (6,300ft). Post Office. Police Post. Pop: 4,875. Kericho District, Rift Valley Province. Lumbwa Health Centre (Govt). Nearest hospital: Londiani. Petrol.

KERICHO
Nairobi 266, Kisii 98, Kisumu 83, Nakuru 110, Molo 52.
Alt: 2,010m (6,600ft). Post Office. Police Tel: 20222. Pop: 19,192. HQ Kericho District, Rift Valley Province. Kericho District Hospital (Govt) Tel: 20116; Kericho Nursing Home (Private) Tel: 20270. Petrol and diesel.

KERUGOYA
Nairobi 132, Embu 31, Nyeri 41.
Alt: 1,555m (5,100ft). Post Office. Police Tel: 21002. Pop: 3,552. HQ Kirinyaga District, Central Province. Kerugoya District Hospital (Govt) Tel: 21058. Petrol.

KIAMBU
Nairobi 16, Ruiru 16, Limuru 27.
Alt: 1,675m (5,500ft). Post Office. Police Tel: 22221. Pop: 3,669. HQ Kiambu District, Central Province. Kiambu District Hospital (Govt) Tel: 22333. Petrol and diesel.

KIBOKO
Nairobi 160, Mombasa 325, Mtito Andei 76.
Alt: 900m (3,000ft). Pop: 500. Machakos District, Eastern Province. Nearest hospital: Makindu (Govt) Tel: 8. Petrol and diesel.

KIGANJO
Nairobi 147, Nanyuki 50, Nyeri 7.
Alt: 1,740m (5,700ft). Post Office. Police Tel: 86022. Pop: 2,234. Nyeri District, Central Province. Kiganjo Dispensary (Mission). Nearest hospital: Nyeri. Petrol.

KILIFI
Nairobi 543 (via Mombasa), Mombasa 58, Malindi 61, Kaloleni 40.
Alt: Sea level. Post Office. Police Tel: 2109. Pop: 5,866. HQ Kilifi District, Coast Province. Kilifi District Hospital (Govt) Tel: 2525. Petrol and diesel.

KIMILILI
Nairobi 409, Eldoret 97, Kakamega 81, Kitale 50, Bungoma 16, Webuye 20.
Alt: 1,675m (5,500ft). Post Office. Police Tel: 18. Pop: 2,143. Bungoma District, Western Province. Kimilili Health Centre (Govt). Nearest hospital: Misikhu Mission. Petrol.

KINANGO
Nairobi 490, Mombasa 58, Mariakani 37, Mazeras 46, Samburu 55.
Alt: 215m (700ft). Pop: 1,691. Kwale District, Coast Province. Kinango Hospital (Govt) Tel: 4. Petrol and diesel.

KISII
Nairobi 364 (via Nakuru), Kericho 98, Kisumu 121, Nakuru 208.
Alt: 1,675m (3,750ft). Post Office. Police Tel: 20222. Pop: 29,661. HQ Kisii District, Nyanza Province. Kisii District Hospital (Govt) Tel: 20473; Kisii Nursing Home (Private) Tel: 20034. Petrol and diesel.

KISUMU
Nairobi 349, Kakamega 53, Kericho 83, Kisii 121, Homa Bay 142.
Alt: 1,145m (3,750ft). Police Tel: 44444. Pop: 152,643. HQ Kisumu District and HQ Nyanza Province. Nyanza Provincial General Hospital (Govt) Tel: 40152: Victoria Hospital (Govt) Tel: 2563. Petrol and diesel. Main part of entry on Lake Victoria.

KITALE
Nairobi 381, Eldoret 69, Kapenguria 32, Nakuru 225.
Alt: 1,890m (6,200ft). Post Office. Police Tel: 20895. Pop: 28,320. HQ Trans Nzoia District, Rift Valley Province. Kitale District Hospital (Govt) Tel: 20951; Mount Elgon Hospital (Private) Tel: 20025. Petrol and diesel.

KITUI
Nairobi 195, Garissa 269, Mtito Andei 184, Thika 153.
Alt: 1,160m (3,800ft). Post Office. Police Tel: 22804. Pop: 4,402. HQ Kitui District, Eastern Province. Kitui District Hospital (Govt) Tel: 22206. Petrol and diesel.

KWALE
Nairobi 516, Mombasa 31, Mariakani 64, Kinango 30, Ukunda 20.
Alt: 370m (2,200ft). Post Office. Police Tel: 4014.
Pop: 2,200. HQ Kwale District, Coast Province.
Kwale Hospital (Govt) Tel: 4024. Petrol and diesel.

LAKE BARINGO
Nairobi 274, Nakuru 118, Marigat 15, Kabarnet 57, Eldoret 145.
Alt: 975m (3,200ft). Pop: 500. Baringo District, Rift Valley Province. Kampi ya Samaki Health Centre (Govt). Nearest hospital: Kabarnet.

LAKE TURKANA
See separate entries for Eliye Springs, Ferguson's Gulf, and Loiyangalani.

LAMU
Nairobi 826 (via Mombasa), Mombasa 341, Malindi 222, Garsen 111, Witu 66.
Alt: Sea level. Post Office. Police Tel: 3217, Customs Tel: 3039, Immigration Tel: 3032. Lamu District, Coast Province. Lamu District Hospital (Govt) Tel: 3012. Access to Lamu is by way of two ferries: the Garsen ferry operates from 6 am to 6 pm only and the Mokowe ferry until 7 pm. Cars can be left on the mainland at a guarded car park. Secondary port of entry by sea.

LIMURU
Nairobi 35, Naivasha 54, Nakuru 121.
Alt: 2,225m (7,300ft). Post Office. Police Tel: 40222. Pop: 1,728. Kiambu District, Central Province. Limuru Health Centre (Govt) Tel: 41274. Nearest hospital: Tigoni. Petrol and diesel.

LODWAR
Nairobi 736, Kitale 355.
Alt: 460m (1,500ft). Post Office. Police Tel: 21071. Pop: 500. HQ Turkana District, Rift Valley Province. Turkana
District Hospital (Govt) Tel: 21622. Petrol and diesel.

LOITOKITOK (see Oloitokitok)

LOIYANGALANI
Nairobi 569, Nyahururu 371, Maralal 225, North Horr 88, Marsabit 276 (via North Horr).
Alt: 380m (1,250ft). Police Post. Pop: 1,060. Marsabit District, Eastern Province. Loiyangalani Dispensary (Mission). Nearest hospital: Maralal. Petrol sometimes available from Mission.

LOKITAUNG
Nairobi 944, Kitale 563, Lodwar 208.
Alt: 730m (2,400ft). Post Office. Police Post. Pop: 500. Turkana District, Rift Valley Province. Lokitaung Hospital (Govt).

LONDIANI
Nairobi 219, Nakuru 63, Kericho 52, Kisumu 135.
Alt: 2,285m (7,500ft). Post Office. Police Tel: 4.
Pop: 2,994. Kericho District, Rift Valley Province.

Londiani Hospital (Govt) Tel: 19. No Petrol.

LUNGA LUNGA
Nairobi 604, Mombasa 119, Msambweni 50.
Alt: 60m (200ft). Pop: 1,671. Police Tel: Kwale 400l, Customs Tel: l4, Immigration Tel: l20. Kwale District, Coast Province. Lunga Lunga Dispensary (Govt) Tel: 30. Nearest hospital: Msambweni. Border with Tanzania. Petrol.

MACHAKOS
Nairobi 65, Athi River 38, Mtito Andei 209.
Alt: 1,615m (5,300ft). Post Office. Police Tel: 21221. Pop: 84,320. HQ Machakos District, Eastern Province. General Hospital (Govt) Tel: 21911; Machakos Nursing Home (Private) Tel: 21168. Petrol and diesel.

MAGADI
Nairobi 107.
Alt: 610m (2,200ft). Post Office. Police Tel: 9. Pop: 2,515. Kajiado District, Rift Valley Province. Magadi Soda Company Hospital (Private) Tel: 78. Petrol and diesel.

MALINDI
Nairobi 604 (via Mombasa), Mombasa 119, Garsen 111, Lamu 222, Kilifi 64, Mambrui 16.
Alt: Sea level. Post Office. Police. Tel: 20485. Customs Tel: 20165. Immigration Tel: 20149. Pop: 23,275. Kilifi District, Coast Province. Malindi District Hospital (Govt) Tel: 20490. Secondary port of entry by sea. Petrol and diesel.

MAMBRUI
Nairobi 618 (via Mombasa), Mombasa 133, Malindi 14.
Alt: Sea level. Pop: 1,256. Kilifi District, Coast Province. Mambrui Dispensary (Govt). Nearest hospital: Malindi. No petrol.

MANDERA
Nairobi 999, Wajir 362, Isiolo 714, El Wak 177, Garissa 683.
Alt: 305m (1,00ft). Post Office. Police Tel: 2003. Customs. Immigration. Pop: 946. HQ Mandera District, North Eastern Province. Mandera District Hospital (Govt) Tel: 2004. Border post with Ethiopia and Somalia. Petrol.

MARALAL
Nairobi 344, Nyahururu 146, Loiyangalani 225, Baragoi 97.
Alt: 1,495m (4,900ft). Police Tel: 2622. Pop: 10,230. HQ Samburu District, Rift Valley Province. Maralal District Hospital (Govt) Tel: 2623. Petrol sometimes available.

MARIGAT
Nairobi 253, Nakuru 97, Kabarnet 29, Lake Baringo 21, Eldoret 130, Mogotio 62.
Alt: 1,070m (3,500ft). Police Tel: 9. Pop: 865. Baringo District, Rift Valley Province. Marigat Health Centre (Govt). Nearest hospital: Kabarnet. Petrol.

MARSABIT

Nairobi 562, Isiolo 277, Moyale 245, North Horr 188, Loiyangalani 276 (via North Horr), Archer's Post 239.
Alt: 1,675m (5,500ft). Post Office. Police Tel: 2022. Pop: 8,739. HQ Marsabit District, Eastern Province. Marsabit District Hospital (Govt) Tel: 2006. Petrol sometimes available.

MASENO

Nairobi 372, Kisumu 23, Butere 36, Bungoma 79, Kisii 110, Kericho 84, Homa Bay 142, Kakamega 42.
Alt: 1,435m (4,700ft). Post Office. Police Tel: 150. Pop: 1,639. Kisumu District, Nyanza Province. Maseno Mission Hospital Tel 6. Petrol and diesel.

MAUA

Nairobi 338, Meru 48, Nanyuki 133, Isiolo 105.
Alt: 1,615m (5,300ft). Post Office. Police Tel: 22. Pop: 1,805. Meru District, Eastern Province. Maua Mission Hospital Tel 2. Petrol.

MERU

Nairobi 290 (via Nanyuki), Nanyuki 90, Isiolo 57, Embu 137.
Alt: 1,220m (4,000ft). Post Office. Police Tel: 20223. Pop: 72,049. HQ Meru District, Eastern Province. Meru District Hospital (Govt) Tel: 20370. Petrol and diesel.

MIGORI

Nairobi 435 (via Nakuru), 350 (via Narok), Kericho 169, Kisumu 192, Kisii 71, Homa Bay 78. Alt: 1,370m (4,500ft). Police Tel: Suna 28. Pop: 6,135. South Nyanza District, Nyanza Province. Migori Health Centre (Govt) Tel: 58. Nearest hospital: Rapogi Hospital (Mission). Petrol and diesel.

MODO GASHI

Nairobi 477, Isiolo 192, Wajir 160, Habaswein 50, Garissa 161.
Alt: 300m (1,000ft). Police Post. Pop: 500. Isiolo District, Eastern Province. Modo Gashi Dispensary (Govt). Nearest hospital: Wajir.

MOLO

Nairobi 207, Nakuru 51, Elburgon 13, Kisumu 156. Alt: 2,470m (8,100ft). Post Office. Police Tel: 21006. Pop: 5,350. Nakuru District, Rift Valley Province. Molo Hospital (Govt) Tel: 21112. Petrol.

MOMBASA

Nairobi 485, Malindi 119, Lamu 341, Mtito Andei 249, Lunga Lunga 119.
Alt: Sea level. Post Office. Central Police Station Tel: 25501. Customs Tel: 314044. Immigration Tel: 311745. Pop: 341,148. HQ Mombasa District and HQ Coast Province. Coast Provincial General Hospital (Govt) Tel: 314201; Aga Khan Hospital (Private) Tel: 312953; Mombasa Hospital (Private) Tel: 312190. Main port of entry by sea. Petrol and diesel.

MOYALE

Nairobi 807, Marsabit 245, Wajir 257.
Alt: 1,070m (3,500ft). Post Office. Police Tel: 2014. Customs. Immigrations. Pop: 7,478. Marsabit District, Eastern Province. Moyale Sub-district Hospital (Govt) Tel: 2022. Border post with Ethiopia. Petrol sometimes available.

MTITO ANDEI

Nairobi 236, Mombasa 249, Voi 98.
Alt: 730m (2,400ft). Post Office. Pop: 2,067. Machakos District, Eastern Province. Nearest Hospital Makindu. Petrol.

MURANGA

Nairobi 87, Nanyuki 113, Nyeri 68.
Alt: 1,280m (4,200ft). Post Office. Police Tel: 22600. Pop: 15,343. HQ Muranga District, Central Province. Muranga District Hospital (Govt) Tel: 22780. Petrol and diesel.

MUTOMO

Nairobi 274 (via Kibwezi), Kitui 68, Mtito Andei 116.
Alt: 1,010m (3,300ft). Police Tel: 2. Pop: 500. Kitui District, Eastern Province. Mutomo Mission Hospital Tel: 16. Petrol.

MWEIGA

Nairobi 167, Nyeri 12.
Alt: 1,890m (6,200ft). Post Office. Police Tel: 2. Pop: 500. Nyeri District, Central Province. Mweiga Dispensary (Mission). Nearest hospital: Nyeri. Petrol.

MWINGI

Nairobi 178, Thika 136, Garissa 202, Kitui 78.
Alt: 1,070m (3,500ft). Police Tel: 32. Pop: 2,303. Kitui District, Eastern Province. Mwingi Dispensary (Govt). Nearest hospital: Kitui. Petrol.

NAIROBI

Mombasa 485, Malindi 604, Nakuru 156, Eldoret 312, Kitale 381, Kisumu 349.
Alt: 1,645m (5,400ft). Head Post Office. Central Police Station Tel 22222. Pop: 827,775. Kenyatta National Hospital (Govt) Tel: 726300; Aga Khan Hospital (Private) Tel: 72451; Nairobi Hospital (Private) Tel: 722160, and MP Shah Hospital (Private) Tel: 742763. Petrol and diesel.

NAIVASHA

Nairobi 89, Nakuru 67, Gilgil 27.
Alt: 1,890m (6,200ft). Post Office. Police Tel: 20199. Pop: 11,491. Nakuru District, Rift Valley Province. Naivasha Hospital (Govt) Tel. 20052; Naivasha Nursing Home (Private). Petrol and diesel.

NAKURU

Nairobi 156, Eldoret 156, Kisumu 193, Kitale 225. Alt: 1,830m (6,000ft). Post Office. Police Tel: 42222. Pop: 92,851. HQ Nakuru District and HQ Rift Valley Province. Nakuru Provincial General Hospital (Govt) Tel: 42563; Nakuru War Memorial Hospital (Private) Tel: 43444. Petrol and diesel.

NAMANGA
Nairobi 164, Kajiado 88.
Alt: 1,295m (4,250ft). Post Office. Police Tel: 2.
Customs Tel: 9. Immigration Tel: 19. Pop: 2,017.
Border post with Tanzania. Namanga Hospital
(Govt) Tel: 15. Border post with Tanzania. Petrol.

NANDI HILLS
Nairobi 307, Eldoret 66, Kakamega 86, Kisumu
103, Kapsabet 18.
Alt: 1,980m (6,500ft). Post Office. Police Tel: 43005.
Pop: 1,419. Nandi District, Rift Valley Province.
Nandi Hills Hospital (Govt) Tel: 43024. Petrol.

NANYUKI
Nairobi 200, Isiolo 85, Meru 90, Nyahururu 97.
Alt: 1,850m (6,400ft). Post Office. Police Tel: 22222.
Pop: 18,986. HQ Laikipia District, Rift Valley
Province. Nanyuki District Hospital (Govt) Tel:
22033; Nanyuki Cottage Hospital (Private) Tel:
22684. Petrol and diesel.

NARO MORU
Nairobi 177, Nanyuki 23, Nyeri 33.
Alt: 1,980m (6,500ft). Post Office. Police Tel: 3.
Pop: 500. Nyeri District, Central Province. Naro
Moru Health Centre (Govt) Tel: 9. Nearest
hospital: Nanyuki. Petrol.

NAROK
Nairobi 148, Nakuru 188 (via Naivasha), Kisii 157.
Alt: 1,980m (6,500ft). Post Office. Police Tel: 2367.
Pop: 5,690. HQ Narok District, Rift Valley
Province. Narok District Hospital Tel: 2300. Petrol
and diesel.

NGONG
Nairobi 26.
Alt: 1,980m (6,500ft). Police Tel: Karen 564055.
Pop: 4,004. Kajiado District, Rift Valley Province.
Ngong Health Centre (Govt). Nearest hospital:
Nairobi. Petrol and diesel.

NORTH HORR
Nairobi 657, Loiyangalani 88, Marsabit 188.
Alt: 550m (1,800ft). Police Post. Pop: 1,325.
Marsabit District, Eastern Province. North Horr
Dispensary (Mission). Nearest hospital: Marsabit.

NYAHURURU (Thomson's Falls)
Nairobi 198, Gilgil 82, Nanyuki 97, Maralal 146,
Nyeri 100, Nakuru 72, Rumuruti 48.
Alt: 2,350m (7,700ft). Post Office. Police Tel: 22333.
Pop: 11,277. HQ Nyandarua District, Central
Province. Nyahururu District Hospital (Govt) Tel:
22114. Petrol and diesel.

NYERI
Nairobi 155, Nanyuki 57, Muranga 68, Embu 96.
Alt: 1,770m (5,800ft). Post Office. Police Tel: 2222.
Pop: 35,753. HQ Nyeri District and HQ Central
Province. Central Province General Hospital
(Govt) Tel: 2480. Mount Kenya Hospital (Govt)
Tel: 2033. Petrol and diesel.

OL KALAU
Nairobi 146, Nakuru 70, Gilgil 30, Nyahururu 52.
Alt: 2,380m (7,800ft). Post Office. Police Tel: 3.
Pop: 1,911. Nyandarua District, Central Province.
Ol Kalau Hospital (Govt) Tel: 33. Petrol and
diesel.

OLOITOKITOK (Loitokitok)
Nairobi 235 (via Emali), Namanga 123.
Alt: 1,680m (5,500ft). Post Office. Police Tel: 7.
Customs Tel: 6. Immigration Tel: 3. Pop: 2,071.
Kajiado District, Rift Valley Province. Loitokitok
Hospital Tel: 40. Border post with Tanzania. Petrol
and diesel.

RONGAI
Nairobi 189, Nakuru 33, Eldoret 131.
Alt: 1,890m (6,200ft). Post Office. Police Tel: 11.
Pop: 583. Nakuru District, Rift Valley Province.
Rongai Health Centre (Govt) Tel: 23. Nearest
hospital: Nakuru. Petrol and diesel.

RUIRU
Nairobi 23, Thika 19, Nanyuki 177.
Alt: 1,525m (5,000ft). Post Office. Police Tel: 22222.
Pop: 1,718. Kiambu District, Central Province.
Ruiru Health Centre (Govt) Tel: 22545. Nearest
hospital: Thika or Nairobi, Petrol and diesel.

RUMURUTI
Nairobi 232, Nyahururu 34, Nanyuki 131, Maralal
112.
Alt: 2,130m (7,000ft). Post Office. Police Tel: 3.
Pop: 1,487. Laikipia District, Rift Valley Province.
Rumuruti Hospital (Govt) Tel: 6. Petrol.

SAGANA
Nairobi 99, Nanyuki 101, Thika 57, Nyeri 56,
Embu 40, Muranga 12.
Alt: 1,190m (3,900ft). Post Office. Police Tel: 2.
Pop: 2,098. Kirinyaga District, Central Province.
Sagana Rural
Health centre (Govt) Tel: 20. Nearest hospital:
Muranga. Petrol and diesel.

SIAYA
Nairobi 418, Kisumu 69, Butere 46, Bungoma 89,
Busia 70, Kakamega 85.
Alt: 1,280m (4,200ft). Post Office. Police Tel: 21428.
Pop: 4,022. HQ Siaya District, Nyanza Province.
Siaya District Hospital (Govt) Tel: 10. Petrol and
diesel.

SOTIK
Nairobi 319 (via Nakuru), 260 (via Narok),
Kericho 53, Kisii 45, Narok 112.
Alt: 1,830m (6,000ft). Post Office. Police Tel: 8.
Pop: 1,334. Kericho District, Rift Valley Province.
Sotik Dispensary; Kapkatet Hospital (Govt) Tel:
Litein 63. Petrol.

SOY
Nairobi 338, Eldoret 26, Kitale 43, Nakuru 182.
Alt: 1,950m (6,400ft). Police Tel: 9. Pop: 500. Uasin
Gishu District, Rift Valley Province. Soy Health

Centre (Govt) Tel: 14. Nearest hospital: Eldoret.

SULTAN HAMUD
Nairobi 114, Mombasa 371, Kiboko 46, Mtito Andei 122.
Alt: 1,250m (4,100ft). Post Office. Police Tel: 5. Pop: 1,360. Machakos District, Eastern Province. Sultan Hamud Health Centre (Govt) Tel: 7. Nearest hospital: Makindu Tel: 8. Petrol and diesel.

TAMBACH
Nairobi 356, Eldoret 44, Kabarnet 37, Iten 10.
Alt: 1,980m (6,500ft). Police Post. Pop: 654. HQ Elgeyo Marakwet District, Rift Valley Province. Tambach District Hospital (Govt) Radiocall Nairobi 3772. Petrol.

TAVETA
Nairobi 448, Mombasa 265, Voi 114.
Alt: 760m (2,500ft). Post Office. Police Tel: 4. Customs Tel: 18. Immigration Tel: 24. Pop: 1,812. Taita-Taveta District, Coast Province. Taveta Hospital (Govt) Tel: 6. Border post with Tanzania. Petrol.

THIKA
Nairobi 42, Nanyuki 158, Muranga 45, Kitui 153, Mwingi 136, Garissa 338.
Alt: 1,495m (4,900ft). Post Office. Police Tel: 21999. Pop: 41,328. Kiambu District, Central Province. Thika Hospital (Govt) Tel: 21621. Petrol and diesel.

THOMSON'S FALLS (see Nyahururu)

TIGONI
Nairobi 26, Nakuru 127, Limuru 6.
Alt: 2,135m (7,000ft). Post Office. Police Tel: 40222. Pop: 500. Kiambu District, Central Province. Tigoni Hospital (Govt). Petrol.

VOI
Nairobi 334, Mombasa 151, Mtito Andei 98.
Alt: 550m (1,800ft). Post Office. Police Tel: 2106. Pop: 7,397. Taita District, Coast Province. Voi Hospital (Govt) Tel: 7. Petrol and diesel.

WAJIR
Nairobi 637, Garissa 321 (via Modo Gashi), Moyale 257, Mandera 362, Isiolo 352, Modo Gashi 160.
Alt: 240m (800ft). Post Office. Police Tel: 21002. Pop: 6384. HQ Wajir District, North Eastern Province. Wajir District Hospital (Govt) Tel: 21031. Petrol.

WAMBA
Nairobi 389, Isiolo 104, Nanyuki 189, Meru 161.
Alt: 1,675m (5,500ft). Post Office. Police Tel: 4. Pop: 2,256. Samburu District, Rift Valley Province. Wamba Hospital (Mission).

WITU
Nairobi 760 (via Mombasa), Mombasa 275, Garsen 45, Lamu 66.

Alt: Sea level. Post Office. Police Tel: 7. Pop: 2,288. Lamu District, Coast Province. Witu Health Centre (Govt) Tel: 9. Nearest hospital: Kipini Hospital (Govt).

WUNDANYI
Nairobi 377, Mombasa 194, Voi 43.
Alt: 1,250m (4,100ft). Post Office. Police Tel: 2002. Pop: 500. HQ Taita-Taveta District, Coast Province. Taita District Health Centre (Govt) Tel: 2041. Nearest hospital: Wesu (Govt) Tel: 5. Petrol.

Kenyan Administrative Areas

Province	District
Coast	Kilifi
	Kwale
	Lamu
	Mombasa
	Taita-Taveta
	Tana River
Eastern	Embu
	Isiolo
	Kitui
	Machakos
	Marsabit
	Meru
North Eastern	Garissa
	Mandera
	Wajir
Central	Kiambu
	Kirinyaga
	Muranga
	Nyandarua
	Nyeri
Nairobi	Nairobi
Rift Valley	Baringo
	Elgeyo Marakwet
	Kajiado
	Kericho
	Laikipia
	Nakuru
	Nandi
	Narok
	Samburu
	Trans Nzoia
	Turkana
	Uasin Gishu
	West Pokot
Nyanza	Kisumu
	Kisii
	Siaya
	South Nyanza
Western	Bungoma
	Busia
	Kakamega

Museums

From prehistoric fossils to the origins of man to the more recent past, more than 400 historical sites illustrate Kenya's rich and diverse history.

Established by Kenya's National Museum, most of these sites are the subject of ongoing scientific research — archaeological and palaeontological.

Most of these sites are restricted to the public because of their size, inaccessibility, or vulnerability to damage and pilfering. In many cases, they are of little apparent interest to the non-scientific community.

There are, however, twenty-four sites which are open to the public. Accessible and well documented, these sites are of immediate interest to the most casual observer.

National Museums

In addition to the National Museum headquarters in Nairobi, there are also branch museums in Kisumu, Kitale, Lamu, Meru, and Mombasa.

Historic Sites

Chetambe Fort
Province: Western
District: Bungoma
Features: Palaeontological site

Diani
Province: Coast
District: Kwale
Features: Ancient mosque, still in use

Fort Jesus, Mombasa
Province: Coast
District: Mombasa
Features: Seventeenth century Portuguese fort, overlooking the Indian Ocean. The museum illustrates the ancient culture of the coast

Fort Ternan
Province: Rift Valley
District: Kericho
Features: Palaeontological site, described as Africa's richest known source of animal fossils dating back fourteen million years

Gede
Province: Coast
District: Kilifi
Features: Ruined city of Islamic origin dating from the thirteenth century

Hyrax Hill
Province: Rift Valley
District: Nakuru
Features: Prehistoric site, including artifacts, Iron Age settlement, hill fort and Neolithic cemetery

Kariandus
Province: Rift Valley
District: Nakuru
Features: Prehistoric site, including artifacts and fossils

Kenyatta House, Maralal
Province: Rift Valley
District: Samburu
Features: Kenyatta's place of detention during Kenyan struggle for Independence

Kijabe
Province: Central
District: Kiambu
Features: Church built by Italian Prisoners of War

Kiunga
Province: Coast
District: Lamu
Features: Islamic ruins, including mosques and tombs

Koobi Fora
Province: Eastern
District: Marsabit
Features: Palaeontological site, including evidence of the existence of a relatively intelligent hominid two million years ago. There is a museum and campsite for visitors

Malindi
Province: Coast
District: Kilifi
Features: Vasco da Gama's pillar, erected 1499

Mambrui
Province: Coast
District: Kilifi
Features: Pillar tomb decorated with late-Ming bowls

Mbaraki
Province: Coast
District: Kwale
Features: Portuguese pillar

Mnarani
Province: Coast
District: Kilifi
Features: Sixteenth century mosque and tombs

Mtwapa
Province: Coast
District: Mombasa
Features: Ruins of a fourteenth-fifteenth century slave-trading settlement

Muhanda Fort
Province: Western
District: Bungoma
Features: Palaeontological site

Olorgesailie
Province: Rift Valley
District: Kajiado
Features: Prehistoric site, hand axes and other stone tools preserved in situ, together with fossils of extinct mammals

Selangai
Province: Rift Valley
District: Kajiado
Features: Maasai circumcision stones and Maasai water wells

Shanga
Province: Coast
District: Lamu
Features: Seven acres of Islamic ruins dating from the tenth century

Sibiloi
Province: Eastern
District: Marsabit
Features: Petrified Forest

Songhor
Province: Rift Valley
District: Kericho
Features: Palaeontological site

Takwa
Province: Coast
District: Lamu
Features: Fifty hectares (125 acres) of Islamic ruins dating from the sixteenth and seventeenth century

Thim Lich
Province: Nyanza
District: South Nyanza
Features: Stone structures and ancient fortress

The Museum also acquires new land and initiates new projects. Local residents and visitors can now enjoy the **Ololua Forest Recreation Area** near Karen, Nairobi which provides a safe, peaceful atmosphere for family outings, nature walks, picnics, and horse riding.

Here school children learn forest appreciation through lectures and guided walks. Eventually the Museum hopes to develop a proper Visitor's Centre offering information and refreshments.

Public Holidays

January 1	New Year's Day
March/April	Good Friday
	Easter Monday
May 1	Labour Day
June 1	Madaraka Day (anniversary of Self-Government)
October 10	Nyayo Day (anniversary of President Moi's inauguration)
October 20	Kenyatta Day (anniversary of Jomo Kenyatta's release from prison)
December 12	Jamhuri/Uhuru Day (anniversary of Independence and formation of Republic)
December 25	Christmas Day
December 26	Boxing Day
Variable	Idd-ul-Fitr (Muslim holiday celebrating the end of Ramadan, in 1989 this occurred in early May)

Calendar of Annual Events

January	International Bill Fishing Competition, Malindi
February	Mombasa Fishing Festival
March	Kenya Open Golf Championship
Easter	Safari Rally
Mid-June	Nakuru Agriculture Show
End-August	Mombasa Agricultural Show
End-September	Nairobi Agricultural Show
November	Malindi Fishing Festival

Airlines

Nairobi offices

Aeroflot
International House
PO Box 44375
20746

Air France
Hilton Hotel
PO Box 30159
726265-67/726268

Air India
Jeevan Bharati House
Harambee Avenue
PO Box 43006
334788/340925

Air Madagascar
City Hall Way
PO Box 41723
25286/26494

Air Malawi
City Hall Way
PO Box 52676
333683/340212

Air Mauritius
Union Towers
Moi Avenue
PO Box 45270
29166-7

Air Tanzania
Chester House
Koinange Street
PO Box 20077
336224/33637

Air Zaire
Shretta House
Kimathi Street
PO Box 46282
24786/25626

Air Zimbabwe
Chester House
Koinange Street
PO Box 14515
339522

Alitalia
Mama Ngina Street
PO Box 72651
24361-3/822351

British Airways
International House
PO Box 45050
334400/822555

Cameroon Airlines
Riani House
Kenyatta Avenue
PO Box 45749
337788

EgyptAir
Hilton Hotel
PO Box 44953
26821-2

El Al (Israel Airlines)
KCS House
Mama Ngina Street
PO Box 49316
28123/330935

Ethiopian Airlines
Bruce House
Muindi Mbingu St.
PO Box 42901
330837/330857

Gulf Air
International House
PO Box 44417
728402/4

KLM
Fedha Towers
PO Box 49239
822376/332673-4

Kenya Airways
Nationwide House
Koinange Street
PO Box 19002
29291/332750

Lufthansa
IPS Building
Kimathi Street
PO Box 30320
335819/335846

Nigeria Airways
Hilton Hotel
PO Box 57058
336555/336436

Olympic Airways
Hilton Hotel
PO Box 42536
338026/822259

PIA
ICEA Building
Banda Street
PO 47365
822386/333900-1

Pan American World Airways
Hilton Hotel
PO Box 30544
23581/822313

Royal Swazi
Reinsurance Plaza
Taifa Road
PO Box 58716
339300-3

Sabena
International House
Mama Ngina Street
PO Box 43706
22185/333198

Saudia
Jamia Mosque
PO Box 58452
334270/335612

Somali Airlines
Bruce House
PO Box 53463
335738/335409

Sudan Airways
UTC Building
General Kago Street
PO Box 48492
25129

Swissair
Corner House
Mama Ngina Street
PO Box 44549
331012/822250

TWA
New Stanley Hotel
PO Box 30493
24036/20265/331400

Uganda Airlines
Uganda House
Kenyatta Avenue
PO Box 59732
21354/28668

Zambia Airways
Kaunda Street
PO Box 42479
24722/21007

The following airlines have offices in Nairobi but do not operate services:

Air Canada
Rehema House,
Standard Street
PO Box 30601
339755-57

Japan Airlines
International House
Mama Ngina Street
PO Box 42430
20591/333277

Varig
Eagle House
Kimathi Street
PO Box 48997
20961/337097

Air Charter

A-D Aviation
Wilson Airport
PO Box 47906
Nairobi
891180

AfricAir
Wilson Airport
PO Box 45646
Nairobi
501219/501210

Afro Aviation
Wilson Airport
PO Box 39422
Nairobi
26944

Aim Air
Wilson Airport
PO Box 21099
Nairobi
501612/501610

Air Kenya
Wilson Airport
PO Box 30357
Nairobi
501601-4

Air Mara
Lamu Road
PO Box 146
Malindi
20287

CMC Aviation
Wilson Airport
PO Box 44580
Nairobi
501221

Cassman Brown
Wilson Airport
PO Box 46247
Nairobi
501421

Executive Aviation
Wilson Airport
PO Box 17152
Nairobi
332382/822655

Falconair
Wilson Airport
PO Box 30603
Nairobi
501523

Pioneers Airlines
Wilson Airport
PO Box 43356
Nairobi
501399

Rent-A-Plane
Wilson Airport
PO Box 42730
Nairobi
500506/501431

Safari Air Services
Wilson Airport
PO Box 41951
Nairobi
501211-3

Skymaster
Wilson Airport
PO Box 20042
Nairobi
501608

Sunbird Aviation
Wilson Airport
PO Box 46247
Nairobi
501421-4

Sunbird Aviation (Coast Air)
Moi International Airport
PO Box 84700
Mombasa
433320/433332

Tradewinds Airways
Bruce House
Standard Street
PO Box 42474
Nairobi
23071

Airports

Jomo Kenyatta
International Airport
Off Mombasa Road
PO Box 19001
Nairobi
822111

Wilson Airport
Langata Road
PO Box 19011
Nairobi
501941

Kisumu Airport
Nyerere Road
PO Box 12
Kisumu
40125/40729

Malindi Airport
Mombasa Road
PO Box 67
Malindi
20981/20060

Moi International
Airport
PO Box 98498
Mombasa
433211

Nanyuki Airport
PO Box 54
Nanyuki
21116

Foreign Diplomatic Missions

Nairobi

Algeria
Matungulu House
Mamlaka Road
PO Box 53902
334227/334178

Argentina
Town House
Kaunda Street
PO Box 30283
335242

Australia
Development House
Moi Avenue
PO Box 30360
334666/334672

Austria
City House
Wabera Street
PO Box 30560
333272/28281-2

Bangladesh
Lenana Road
Hurlingham
PO Box 49866
723160-1

Belgium
Silopark House
Mama Ngina Street
PO Box 30461
20501/25143/23879

Brazil
Jeevan Bharati Bldg.
Harambee Avenue
PO Box 30754
338975/337722-3

Bulgaria
Kabarnet Road
PO Box 44778
567308

Burundi
Development House
Moi Avenue
PO Box 44439
338721/338735

Canada
Comcraft House
Haile Selassie Ave.
PO Box 30481
334033-6

Chile
International House
Mama Ngina Street
PO Box 45554
337987/337934

China
Woodlands Road
PO Box 30508
722559

Colombia
Tchui House
Muthaiga Road
PO Box 48494
765911

Costa Rica
Westwood Road
Karen
PO Box 30750
501501

Cyprus
Eagle House
Kimathi Street
PO Box 30739
20881

Czechoslovakia
Milimani Road
PO Box 30204
721896-8

Denmark
HFCK Building

Corner Kenyatta Ave
PO Box 40412
331088/331098

Djibouti
Comcraft House
Haile Selassie Ave.
PO Box 59528
339633/339640

Eygpt
Harambee Plaza
PO Box 30285
25990-2

Ethiopia
State House Road
PO Box 45198
723027/723035

Finland
International House
Mama Ngina Street
PO Box 30379
336717/334777-8

France
Embassy House
Harambee Avenue
PO Box 41784
339783-4/339973-4

Gabon
Othaya Road
Lavington
PO Box 42551
569429

Germany (Federal
Republic of)
Embassy House
Harambee Avenue
PO Box 30180
21316/27069

Greece
IPS Building
Kimathi Street
PO Box 30543
Telex: 22008
340722/340744

Holy See (The
Vatican)
Mnyani Road
PO Box 14326
48468/48583/48370

Hungary
Mtundu Road
Muthaiga
PO Box 30275
763427/763263

Iceland
Norwich Union
House
Mama Ngina Street
PO Box 45000
338522

India
Jeevan Bharati
Building
Harambee Avenue
PO Box 30074
24500/22566-7

Indonesia
Utalii House
Uhuru Highway
PO Box 48868
Telex: 23171
330797

Iran
Corner State House
Road & Dennis Pritt
Road
PO Box 49170
720343/720796

Iraq
Lower Kabete Road
PO Box 49213
725510/725587/
724866

Ireland
Maendeleo House
Monrovia Street
PO Box 30659
26771-4

Italy
Prudential Assurance
Building
Wabera Street
PO Box 30107
337356-7/337016-7

Japan
ICEA Building
Kenyatta Avenue
PO Box 60202
332955-9

Korea (South)
Kencom House
City Hall Way
PO Box 30455
322839/333581-3

Kuwait
IPS Building
Kimathi Street
PO Box 42353
338558/330901

Lebanon
Maendeleo House
Monrovia Street
PO Box 55303
23708

Lesotho
International House
Mama Ngina Street
PO Box 44096
337493/24876-7

Liberia
Bruce House
Standard Street
PO Box 30546
22604-5

Libya
Jamhiriya House
Loita Street
PO Box 60149
29884/29857

Luxembourg
International House

Mama Ngina Street
PO Box 30610
26183/24318

Madagascar
Koinange Street
PO Box 30793
26494

Malawi
Bruce House
Standard Street
PO Box 30453
21174/20435/335363

Mauritius
Union Towers
PO Box 45270
330215

Malaysia
Eagle House
Kimathi Street
PO Box 48916
29724-5

Mexico
Kibagare Way
Loresho Ridge
PO Box 41139
582850/582579

Morocco
Diamond Trust
Building
Moi Avenue
PO Box 61098
22361/22264

Netherlands
Uchumi House
Nkrumah Avenue
PO Box 41537
332420/27111-2

Nigeria
Lenana Road
Hurlingham
PO Box 30516
564116-8

Norway
Rehani Building
Koinange Street
PO Box 46363
337121/22/24

Oman
Matundu Road
Muthaiga
PO Box 43458
65674/93/94

Pakistan
St Michaels Road
Westlands
PO Box 30045
61666-9

Peru
Enterprise Road
PO Box 59446
554317/555744

Philippines
State House Road
PO Box 47941

725897/721791

Poland
Kabarnet Road
PO Box 30086
566288

Portugal
Reinsurance Plaza
Taifa Road
PO Box 34020
38990/339853

Romania
Norfolk Towers
Kijabe Street
PO Box 48412
27515

Rwanda
International House
Mama Ngina Street
PO Box 48579
334341/336365

Saudi Arabia
Muthaiga Road
PO Box 58297
762781-4

Somalia
International House
Mama Ngina Street
PO Box 30769
24301

Spain
Bruce House
Standard Street
PO Box 45503
336330/335711

Sri Lanka
International House
Mama Ngina Street
PO Box 48145
27577-78

Sudan
Minet ICDC House
Mamlaka Road
PO Box 62577
720883/720889

Swaziland
Silopark House
Mama Ngina Street
PO Box 41887
339231-3

Sweden
International House
Mama Ngina Street
PO Box 30600
29042-5

Switzerland
International House
Mama Ngina Street
PO Box 30752
28735-6

Tanzania
Continental House
PO Box 47790
331093/331104

Thailand .
Grevillea Grove
Westlands
PO Box 58349
62742-4

Turkey
Gigiri Road
PO Box 30785
520404

Uganda
Uganda House
Kenyatta Avenue
PO Box 60853
3308801/330834

United Kingdom
Bruce House
Standard Street
PO Box 30465
335944-60

Union of Soviet
Socialist Republics
Lenana Road
Hurlingham
PO Box 30049
722462

United States of
America
Moi Avenue
PO Box 30137
334141-50

Venezuela
International House
Mama Ngina Street
PO Box 34477
332300/340167

Yemen (Peoples'
Democratic Republic
of)
Lenana Road
Hurlingham
PO Box 44642
564379

Yugoslavia
State House Road
PO Box 30504
720670-1

Zaire
Electricity House
Harambee Avenue
PO Box 48106
29771-2

Zambia
Nyerere Road
PO Box 48741
24796/724799

Zimbabwe
Minet ICDC House
Mamlaka Road
PO Box 30806
721045/49/71

Mombasa

Denmark
PO Box 99543
316051

Finland
PO Box 99543
20501/20229

France
PO Box 90262
21141/25380

Germany
PO Box 90171
24938/39

India
PO Box 90614
24433/311051

Italy
PO Box 84958
311532/26955

Netherlands
PO Box 90230
311434-5

Norway
PO Box 83058
485494/471771

Switzerland
PO Box 85722
316684-5

United States of
America
PO Box 88079
31510

Kenyan Missions Abroad

Australia
PO Box 1990
Canberra
ACT 2600
474788

Belgium
1-5 Avenue De La
Joyeuse Entrée
1040 Brussels
2303065/2303100

Canada
Gillin Building
141 Laurier Ave
West Ottawa
Ontario KIP 5J3
613563

China
No 4 Xi Liu Jie
San Li Tun
Beijing
523381

Ethiopia
PO Box 3301
Addis Ababa
180033/180136

Eygpt
20 Boulos Hanna St
Dokki

PO Box 362
Cairo
704455-6

France
3 Rue Cimaros
75016 Paris
5533500

Germany (Federal
Republic of)
Villichgasse 17
5300 Bonn-Bad
Godesberg 2
Micael Plaza
353066/356041

India
66 Vasant Marg
Vasant Vihar
New Delhi
672280/672053

Italy
Via Del Circo
Massimo
Rome 00153
5781192/5780995

Japan
24-20 Nishi-Azobu
3 Chome
Minato-Ku
Tokyo
794006

The Netherlands
The Hague
636175

Nigeria
52 Queen's Drive
Ikiyi
PO Box 6464
Lagos
682768/685531

Pakistan
8 Street 88
PO Box 2097
Islamabad
823819

Rwanda
PO Box 1215
Kigali
2774

Saudi Arabia
Baladia St
PO Box 6347
Jeddah
6656718/6601885

Somalia
PO Box 618
Mogadishu
80857/80858

Sudan
Opposite Dolly Hotel
PO Box 8242
Khartoum
940386

Sweden
2TR Birger

Jarilsgatan 37
71145
Stockholm
218399/04/09

Switzerland
80 Rue De Lausanna
1202 Geneva
327272/327038

Tanzania
NIC Investment
House
Samora Ave
PO Box 5231
Dar es Salaam
31526

Uganda
60 Kira Rd
PO Box 5220
Kampala
231861/233146

United Arab
Emirates
PO Box 3854
Abu Dhabi
366300

United Kingdom
45 Portland Place
London WIN 4AS
01-362371-5

Union of Soviet
Socialist Republics
Bolshyaya Ordinka
Dom 70
Moscow
2373462/2374702

United States of
America
2249 R Street NW
Washington DC
20008
440215

United States of
America
866 United Nations
Plaza
New York 10017
4214740

Zaire
5002 Avenue de 1
Ouganda
Zone de Gombe
PO Box 9667
Kinshasa
30117

Zambia
5207 United Nations
Ave
PO Box 50298
Lusaka
212531/212361

Zimbabwe
5 Park Lane
PO Box 4069
Harare
790847

Kenya Tourist Offices

France
2 rue Volney
Paris 75002
260-66-88

Germany
6000 Frankfurt
A Main 1
Hosch-strasse 53
282551/282552

Hong Kong
1309 Liu Chong Hing
Bank Building
24 Des Voeux Road
Central
PO Box 5280
5-236053/4

Japan
Yurakucho Building
1-10 Yurakucho
Chome
Chiyoda-Ku
Tokyo
214-3595

Sweden
Birger Jarlsgatan 37
2TR
PO Box 7692
Stockholm 11145
218300/04/09

Switzerland
Bleicherweg 30
PO Box 770
8039 Zurich
01-202-22-43/44/46

United Kingdom
25/25 New Bond
Street
London W14 9HD
01-355-3144

United States of
America
424 Madison Avenue
New York
NY 10017
486-1300
and

Suite 111-12 Doheny
Plaza
9100 Wilshire
Boulevard
Beverly Hills
California 90121
274-6635

Hotels

NAIROBI

CRAZE HOTEL
Ngong Road
PO Box 48471
564173

DEVON HOTEL
Uhuru Highway
PO Box 41123
742813

ESPERIA HOTEL
Parklands Road
PO Box 14642
742818

FAIRVIEW HOTEL
Bishops Road
PO Box 40842
723210/1

GREENVIEW
LODGE
Nyerere Road
PO Box 42246
720908/723280

FIG TREE HOTEL
Ngara Road
PO Box 31938
743697

GROSVENOR
Ralph Bunche Road
PO Box 41038
722080/1/720002

HERON COURT
Milimani Road
PO Box 41848
720740/1/2/3

HILLCREST HOTEL
Waiyaki Way
PO Box 14284
60060

HILTON
INTERNATIONAL
Mama Ngina Street
PO Box 30624
334000

HOTEL
AMBASSADEUR
Moi Avenue
PO Box 30399
336803

HOTEL
BOULEVARD
Harry Thuku Road
PO Box 42831
337221/27567-8

HOTEL CHIROMO
Chiromo Road
PO Box 44677
745085

HOTEL COMFY
Keiya Road
PO Box 20320
743969/743959

HOTEL COUNTY
Corner Uhuru
Highway & Haile
Selasie Avenue
PO Box 41924
26190/22341

HOTEL EMBASSY
Tubman Road
PO Box 47247
24087/24533/24534

HOTEL EMSLEY
Tsavo Road
PO Box 49860
23437

HOTEL GLOB
Kirinyaga Road
PO Box 32087
27845

HOTEL GLORIA
Tom Mboya Street
PO Box 32087
28916

HOTEL HERMES
Cnr Haile Selassie
Avenue & Tom
Mboya Street
PO Box 62997
727911/2/3/4

HOTEL INTER-
CONTINENTAL
City Hall Way
PO Box 30353
335550

HOTEL MERCURY
Tom Mboya Street
PO Box 13083
20068/338063

HOTEL SALAMA
Tom Mboya Street
PO Box 28675
25898

HOTEL WINDSOR
Keiyo Road
PO Box 20350
25753

HURLINGHAM
Arwings Kodhek
Road
PO Box 43158
721920/723001

IMPALA HOTEL
Parklands Road
PO Box 14144
742346/740631

JACARANDA
Westlands
PO Box 14287
742272

KENYA
CONTINENTAL
HOTEL
Rhapta Road
PO Box 73893
60321

KENYA
INTERNATIONAL
Murang'a Road
PO Box 22411
742825

KWALITY HOTEL
Arwings Kodhek
Road
PO Box 44275
721285

MERIDIEN COURT
Murang'a Road
PO Box 30278
333916

MILIMANI HOTEL
Milimani Road
PO Box 30715
720760

NAIROBI SAFARI
CLUB
Cnr Koinange Street
& University Way
PO Box 43564
330621

NAIROBI SERENA
HOTEL
Cnr Nyerere Road &
Kenyatta Avenue
PO Box 46302
725111

NEW GARDEN
Monrovia Street
PO Box 40836
21317

NEW STANLEY
Kimathi Street
PO Box 30680
333233

NORFOLK HOTEL
Harry Thuku Road
PO Box 40064
335422

OAKWOOD HOTEL
Kimathi Street
PO Box 40683
22229/26234

PANAFRIC HOTEL
Kenyatta Avenue
PO Box 30486
720822

PARKLANDS
SHADE HOTEL
Ojijo Road
PO Box 33003
749042

PARKSIDE HOTEL
PO Box 53104
333445

PLUMS HOTEL
Ojijo Road
PO Box 40747
745222

SAFARI PARK
Thika Road
PO Box 45038
802493

SAGRET HOTEL
Milimani Road
PO Box 18324
333395/720933

SIDAI HOTEL
PO Box 43750

SILVER SPRINGS
HOTEL
Arwings Kodhek
Road
PO Box 61362
722451

SIMARY SAFARI
HOTEL
PO Box 31166
750623

SIXEIGHTY HOTEL
Cnr Kenyatta
Avenue & Muindi
Mbingu Street
PO Box 43436
332680

SOLACE HOTEL
Tom Mboya Street
PO Box 48867
331277

SUNCOURT INN
University Way
PO Box 51454
21418/21413/21458

TERMINAL HOTEL
Moktar Daddah
Street
PO Box 43229
28817/8

UTALI HOTEL
Thika Road
PO Box 31067
802540

WESTVIEW HOTEL
Rhapta Road
Westlands
PO Box 14680
60294

YOUTH HOSTEL
Ralph Bunche Road

YMCA HOSTEL
State House Road
PO Box 30330
724116

YWCA HOSTEL
Mamlaka Road
PO Box 40710
724699

MOMBASA

CASTLE HOTEL
Moi Avenue
PO Box 84231
23403

HOTEL BAVARIA
Ronald Ngala Road
PO Box 99261
491839

HOTEL
EXCELLENT
PO Box 98888
25154

HOTEL FORTUNA
Haile Selassie Road
PO Box 81914
20594

HOTEL HERMES
Msanifu Kombo
Street
PO Box 98419
313599

HOTEL SEA
BREEZES
Likoni Road
PO Box 960222
451218

HOTEL SKYWAY
Moi Avenue
PO Box 83933
313536

HOTEL SPLENDID
PO Box 90482
20967/20817

HUNTER'S HOTEL
Jomo Kenyatta
Avenue
PO Box 98583
490500

HYDRO HOTEL
Digo Road
PO Box 85360
23784

KILINDINI HOTEL
Moi Avenue
PO Box 81259
23166

LOTUS HOTEL
Cathedral Road
PO Box 90193
313207/313234

MANOR HOTEL
Nyerere Avenue
PO Box 84851
314643

NEW CARLTON
Moi Avenue
PO Box 86779
315116

NEW MERMAID
Moi Avenue
PO Box 84899
313082

NEW PALM TREE
HOTEL
Nkrumah Road
PO Box 90013
311756/312169

OCEANIC HOTEL
PO Box 90371
311191/2
OUTRIGGER
Ras Liwatoni
PO Box 82345
Mombasa
20822/3

TAJ HOTEL
Digo Road
PO Box 82923
23198/313545

SOUTH COAST

AFRICANA SEA
LODGE
PO Box 84616
(01261) 2052

AZANIA
APARTMENTS
PO Box 85965
Mombasa
451548

CHILDREN'S
RESORT CENTRE
PO Box 96048
Mombasa
451417

DIANI BEACH
COTTAGES
PO Box 14
(01261) 2113/2628

DIANI BEACH LETS
PO Box 26
Ukunda
(01261) 2113

DIANI REEF HOTEL
PO Box 35
Ukunda
(01261) 2602

DIANI SEA LODGE
PO Box 37
Ukunda
(01261) 2060/2114

FOUR 'N' TWENTY
PO Box 90270
Mombasa
312449

GOLDEN BEACH
PO Box 31
Ukunda
(01261) 2054

JADINI BEACH
PO Box 84616
Mombasa
(01261) 2021-2

LEISURE LODGE
PO Box 84383
Mombasa
(01261) 2011-2

LEOPARD BEACH
PO Box 34
Ukunda
(01261) 2110-1

MAWENI
COTTAGES
PO Box 96024
Mombasa
(0127) 4064

NOMAD BEACH
BANDAS
PO Box 1
Ukunda
(01261) 2155

OCEAN CLUB
PO Box 88
Ukunda
(01261) 2003/2188

OCEAN VILLAGE
PO Box 88
Ukunda
(01261) 2725

PALM BEACH
GUEST HOUSE
PO Box 66
Ukunda
(01261) 2171

ROBINSON'S
BAOBAB HOTEL
PO Box 84792
Mombasa
(01261) 2026

ROSE HOLIDAY
COTTAGES
PO Box 96051
Mombasa
451600

SAFARI BEACH
PO Box 90690
Mombasa
(01261) 2726

SAND ISLAND
BEACH COTTAGES
PO Box 96009
(0127) 4065

SEA CREST
COTTAGES
PO Box 44053
Nairobi
22728-9 (Nbi
booking)

SEASCAPES
PO Box 45541
Mombasa
334996/20486 (Nbi
booking)

SEA VIEW DIANI
VILLAS
PO Box 45626
(01261) 2138/2089

SHELLEY BEACH
PO Box 82345
Mombasa
451001-4

SOUTH BEACH
LEISURE LODGE
PO Box 84383
Mombasa
(01261) 2011-2

TIWI SEA CASTLES
PO Box 49110
Mombasa
803158/802336-7
(Nbi booking)

TIWI VILLAS
PO Box 24752
Nairobi
(0127) 4080/4065

TRADE WINDS
PO Box 8
Ukunda
(01261) 2016

TWIGA LODGE
PO Box 80820
Mombasa
Tiwi 2Y2

TWO FISHES
PO Box 23
Ukunda
(01261) 2101

WARRANDALE
COTTAGES
PO Box 11
Ukunda
(01261) 2186

WHITE ROSE
VILLAS
PO Box 42200
Nairobi
(01261) 2064/2236
29898 (Nbi booking)

SHIMONI

PEMBA CHANNEL
FISHING CLUB
PO Box 44
Msambweni
5Y2

SHIMONI REEF
FISHING LODGE
PO Box 82234
Mombasa
471771

NORTH COAST

BAHARI BEACH
HOTEL
Bamburi Road
PO Box 81443
Mombasa
471073

BAHARI
COTTAGES
PO Box 80929
Mombasa
485633

BAMBURI BEACH
Malindi Road
PO Box 83996
Mombasa
485611

BAMBURI
CHALETS
PO Box 84114
Mombasa
485706

CASUARINA
Malindi Road
PO Box 82792
Mombasa
485076

CORAL BEACH
Malindi Road
PO Box 84231
Mombasa
23403

CORALDENE
BEACH HOTEL
Malindi Road
PO Box 80940
Mombasa
485421

COWRIE SHELL
BEACH
APARTMENTS
Bamburi Road
PO Box 806
Mombasa
485971

DOLPHIN HOTEL
PO Box 81443
Mombasa
485801

HOTEL INTER-
CONTINENTAL
PO Box 83492
Mombasa
485811

KANAMAI
HOLIDAY CENTRE
PO Box Kikambela
46/101

KENYA BEACH
HOTEL
Bamburi Road
PO Box 95748
Mombasa
485821

KENYA MARINAS
PO Box 15070
Kikambela
485738/485866

MOMBASA BEACH
APARTMENTS
PO Box 89362
Mombasa
472255

MOMBASA BEACH
PO Box 90414
Mombasa
471861

NEPTUNE BEACH
PO Box 83125
Mombasa
485701

NYALI BEACH
Book through:

Block Hotels
PO Box 47557
Nairobi
335807

OCEAN VIEW
BEACH HOTEL
Malindi Road
PO Box 81127
Mombasa
485601

OCTOPUSSY
BAMBURI
Malindi Road
PO Box 83135
Mombasa
472215
25277/312578/
315430 (Nbi booking)

PALM BEACH
Malindi Road
PO Box 81443
Mombasa
485408

PLAZA HOTEL
Bamburi Road
PO Box 88299
Mombasa
485321/485325

POLLMAN BEACH
COTTAGES
Bamburi Road
PO Box 81117
Mombasa
485632

REEF HOTEL
PO Box 82234
Mombasa
471771

SEAWAVES BEACH
Malindi Road
PO Box 80940
Mombasa
485492

SILVER BEACH
PO Box 81443
Mombasa
471471

SERENA BEACH
PO Box 90352
Mombasa
485721

SEVERIN SEA
LODGE
Bamburi Road
PO Box 82169
Mombasa
485001

SUN & SAND
BEACH HOTEL
Kikambala
PO Box 2
8/55

WASON BEACH
COTTAGES
Malindi Road
PO Box 81219
Mombasa
485216

WHISPERING
PALMS HOTEL
Kikambala
PO Box 5
3/4/5/6

WHITESANDS
Malindi Road
PO Box 90173
Mombasa
485926

KILIFI

MNARANI CLUB
HOTEL
PO Box 81443
Mombasa
(01252) 18/26
336858 (Nbi booking)

SEA HORSE HOTEL
PO Box 70
(01252) 90/64
20592 (Nbi booking)

WATAMU

OCEAN SPORTS
PO Box 340
(01233) 32008

SEAFARERS
Lamu Road
PO Box 182
(01223) 6/52

TURTLE BAY
BEACH HOTEL
PO Box 457
(01223) 3

WATAMU BEACH
PO Box 300
(01223) 1/10

MALINDI

BLUE MARLIN
PO Box 20
(0123) 20441

CLUB CHE SHALE
Off Garsen Road
PO Box 492
(0123) 20063

COCONUT
VILLAGE
PO Box 868
(0123) 20928

DRIFTWOOD
BEACH CLUB
PO Box 63
(0123) 20155

EDEN ROC HOTEL
Lamu Road
PO Box 350
(0123) 20480

LAWFORD'S
Lamu Road
PO Box 20
Telex: 21410
(0123) 20440/1

MALINDI SEA
FISHING CLUB
PO Box 364
(0123) 20410

OZI'S BED &
BREAKFAST
Seafront Road
PO Box 60
(0123) 20218

PALM TREE CLUB
Lamu Road
PO Box 180
(0123) 20397

SILVERSANDS
BEACH COTTAGE
Tourist Road
PO Box 91
(0123) 20385/20842

SINDBAD HOTEL
Lamu Road
PO Box 30
(0123) 21175

WHITE ELEPHANT
SEA LODGE
Casaurina Point
PO Box 553
(0123) 20528

LAMU

MAHRUS HOTEL
Harambee Road
PO Box 25
(0121) 1

PEPONI HOTEL
Shela
PO Box 24
(0121) 3029/3154

PETLEY'S INN
Kenyatta Road
PO Box 4
(0121) 48107
29612 (Nbi booking)

RAS KITAU HOTEL
Manda Island

YUMBE HOUSE
LODGE
Next to Museum
PO Box 81
(0121) 3101/3280

**UP-COUNTRY
ACCOMODATION**

BUNGOMA

BUNGOMA
TOURIST HOTEL
PO Box 972
(0337) 126

BUNGOMA SIMBA
PO Box 663
20804

EGRET HOTEL
PO Box 1100
(0337) 41241

ELDORET

SIRIKWA HOTEL
Oloo Street
PO Box 3361
Telex: 35010
(0321) 31655

EMBU

IZAAK WALTON
INN
PO Box 46527
Nairobi
27828 (Nbi booking)

GILGIL

GILGIL
MAKUTANO
PO Box 255
2075

HOMA BAY

HOMA BAY HOTEL
PO Box 42013
29751/23488/330820
(Nbi booking)

ISIOLO

LEWA DOWNS
TENTED CAMP
Book through:
Wildlife Trails
Hilton Hotel
PO Box 42562
Nairobi
27048

KABARNET

KABARNET HOTEL
PO Box 42013
Nairobi
29751/23488/339820
(Nbi booking)

KAKAMEGA

GOLF HOTEL
PO Box 118
459
29751/23488/330821
(Nbi booking)

KAPTAGAT

KAPTAGAT HOTEL
PO Box 46527
Nairobi
27828 (Nbi booking)

KARATINA

ELEPHANT
CASTLE
PO Box 370
29615

KARATINA
TOURIST LODGE
Private Bag
71522/71772

NEW KARATINA
LAMU LODGE
PO Box 918
71629

KAPSABET

KAPSABET HOTEL
PO Box 449
2176

KERICHO

TEA HOTEL
PO Box 75
(0361)

KISII

KISII HOTEL
PO Box 26
48
RIVERSIDE
TOURIST RESORT
PO Box 2401
(0381) 21646

KISUMU

GET IN HOTEL
Johana Ouko Road
PO Box 807
(035) 42682

HOTEL BEOGRADA
Omino Crescent
PO Box 920
(035) 3424

HOTEL
CASSANOVA
Kibos Road
PO Box 920
Kisumu
(035) 2201

HOTEL DARARILE
Kibos Road
PO Box 240
(035) 3395

IMPERIAL HOTEL
Jomo Kenyatta
Highway
PO Box 1866
(035) 41485

LAKE VIEW HOTEL
Alego Street
PO Box 1216
(035) 3141

NEW KISUMU
Kenyatta Highway
PO Box 1690
(035) 40336-7

NEW VICTORIA
Gor Mahia Road
PO Box 276
(035) 2909/41849

SUNSET HOTEL
Aput Lane
PO Box 215
Telex: 31177
(035) 41100

KITALE

KITALE CLUB
PO Box 30
30

KWALE

SUGAR TREE
HOTEL

SHIMBA TREE
HOTEL

LAKE BARINGO

ISLAND CAMP
Book through:
PO Box 42475
Nairobi
25941/25641

LAKE BARINGO
CLUB
Book through:
Block Hotels
Rehema House
PO Box 47557
Nairobi
335807

LAKE NAIVASHA

FISHERMAN'S
CAMP
Book through:
Lets's Go Travel
Caxton House
Standard Street
PO Box 60342
Nairobi
340331/29539-40

LAKE NAIVASHA
HOTEL
Book through:
Block Hotels
Rehema House
PO Box 47557
Nairobi
335807

SAFARILAND
LODGE
South Lake Road
PO Box 72
(0311) 20241

LAKE TURKANA

ELIYE SPRINGS
LODGE
PO Lodwar
Radiocall Nairobi
2064

LAKE TURKANA
FISHING LODGE
Book through:
PO Box 41078
Nairobi
26623/26808

415

OASIS LODGE
Book through:
PO Box 56707
Nairobi
25255

LODWAR
NEW LODWAR
LODGE
PO Box 123
21223/21231

MAKINDU
HUNTERS LODGE
PO Box 77
21439/20592 (Nbi
booking)

MARALAL
MARALAL SAFARI
LODGE
Book through:
Thorn Tree Safaris
Standard Street
PO Box 42475
Nairobi
25641/25941/28981

MERU
MERU COUNTY
PO Box 1386
20427/20432

PIG AND WHISTLE
PO Box 99
14

MOLO
HIGHLANDS
PO Box 142
50

MTITO ANDEI
TSAVO INN
PO Box 30139
Nairobi
27136 (Nbi booking)

MWEIGA
ABERDARE
COUNTRY CLUB
PO Box 449
723776 (Nbi booking)

NAKURU
MAU VIEW LODGE
PO Box 1620
44926

MIDLAND HOTEL
Geoffrey Way
PO Box 908
(037) 41277/43958

NAKURU WEST
LODGE
PO Box 497
41452

PIVOT HOTEL
PO Box 1369
(037) 40822/42473

NAMANGA
NAMANGA RIVER
HOTEL
PO Box 30471
Nairobi
336858 (Nbi booking)

NANYUKI
EL KARAMA
RANCH
Book Through:
AA Travel
PO Box 14982
742926

MOUNT KENYA
SAFARI CLUB
PO Box 35
Telex: 22016
(0171) 2141

SPORTSMAN'S
ARMS HOTEL
PO Box 3
(0171) 2057

SWEETWATERS
TENTED CAMP
Book through:
Lonhro Hotels
Bruce House
PO Box 58581
Nairobi
723776

NARO MORU
NARO MORU
RIVER LODGE
PO Box 18
23

**NYAHURURU
(Thomson's Falls)**
THOMSON'S FALLS
LODGE
PO Box 38
6

NYERI
GREENHILLS
HOTEL
Mumbi Road
PO Box 31326
(0171) 2017/2687/
2688

OUTSPAN HOTEL
Book through:
Block Hotels
Rehema House
PO Box 47557
Nairobi
335807

WHITE RHINO
HOTEL
Kenyatta Road
PO Box 30
(0171) 2189/2031

SOY
SOY COUNTRY
CLUB
PO Box 2
Soy 1Y1

THIKA
BLUE POSTS
HOTEL
Murang'a Road
PO Box 42
(0151) 22241

WHITELINE HOTEL
Stadium Road
PO Box 290
(0151) 22857

TIGONI
KENTMERE CLUB
PO Box 49666
Kiambaa 253

National Parks and Reserves

ABERDARE
THE ARK
Book through:
Lonhro Hotels
Bruce House
PO Box 58581
Nairobi
723776

TREETOPS
Book through:
Block Hotels
Rehema House
PO Box 47557
Nairobi
335807

AMBOSELI
AMBOSELI LODGE
and
KILIMANJARO
SAFARI LODGE
and
KIMANA LODGE
Book through:
Kilimanjaro Safari
Lodge
Grindlays Building
PO Box 30138
Nairobi
Telex: 22371
332334/337510/
338888

AMBOSELI SERENA
Book through:
Serena Lodges
Kimathi Street
PO Box 48690
Nairobi
339800

**KILIMANJARO
BUFFALO LODGE**
Book through:
PO Box 72630
Nairobi
336088/336724/
337410

OL TUKAI LODGE
Book through:
Aardvark Safaris
IPS Building
PO Box 49718
Nairobi
331718/334863

**BUFFALO
SPRINGS**
BUFFALO SPRINGS
TENTED LODGE
Book through:
African Tours &
Hotels
Utalii House
PO Box 30471
Nairobi
336858

LAKE NAKURU
LION HILL CAMP
Book through:
Sarova Hotels
New Stanley Hotel
PO Box 30680
Nairobi
333233

MARSABIT
MARSABIT LODGE
Book through:
Msafiri Inns
Utalii Hse
PO Box 42013
Nairobi
29751/23488/330820

MAASAI MARA
COTTARS CAMP
Book through:
Nairobi Travel
Centre
Kaunda Street
PO Box 41178
Nairobi
27930/27939/331960

FIG TREE CAMP
Book through:
PO Box 40693,
Nairobi
21439/20592/332170

GOVERNORS
CAMP
and
LITTLE
GOVERNOR'S
CAMP
Book through:
PO Box 48217
Nairobi
331871/331041

KEEKOROK LODGE
Book through:
Block Hotels
Rehema House
PO Box 47557
Nairobi
335807

KICHWA TEMBO
CAMP
Book through:
Lonhro Hotels
Bruce House
PO Box 58581
Nairobi
723776

MARA INTREPIDS
CLUB
Book through:
Talek Limited
Chester House
PO Box 14040
Nairobi
335208/331688

MARA SERENA
LODGE
Book through:
Serena Lodges
Kimathi House
PO Box 48690
Nairobi
339800

MARA SOPA
LODGE
Book through:
PO Box 72630
Nairobi
336088/336724

MAASAI MARA
RIVER CAMP
Book through:
PO Box 48019
Nairobi
331191/29009

SAROVA MARA
Book through:
Sarova Hotels
New Stanley Hotel
PO Box 30680
Nairobi
333233

**MERU NATIONAL
PARK**
LEOPARD ROCK
SAFARI LODGE
Book through:
AA Travel
Union Towers
PO Box 14982
Nairobi
337900

MERU MULIKA
LODGE
Book through:
Msafiri Inns
Utalii House
PO Box 42013
Nairobi
29751/23488/330820

MOUNT ELGON

MOUNT ELGON
LODGE
Book through:
Msafiri Inns
Utalii House
PO Box 42013
Nairobi
29751/23488/330820

MOUNT KENYA

MOUNTAIN
LODGE
Book through:
African Tours &
Hotels
Utalii House
PO Box 30471
Nairobi
336858

NAIROBI

MASAI LODGE
Book through:
Thorn Tree Safaris
Standard Street
PO Box 42475
Nairobi
25641/25941/28981

SALT LICK

SALT LICK LODGE
Book through:
Hilton International
Watalii Street
PO Box 30624
Nairobi
334000

TAITA HILLS
LODGE
Book through:
Hilton International
Watalii Street
PO Box 30624,
Nairobi
334000

SAMBURU

LARSENS TENTED
CAMP
and
SAMBURU LODGE
Book through:
Block Hotels
Rehema House
PO Box 47557
Nairobi
335807

SAMBURU RIVER
LODGE
Book through:
Serena Lodges &
Hotels
Kimathi House
Kimathi Street
PO Box 48690
Nairobi
339800

SHABA NATIONAL RESERVE

SAROVA SHABA
Book through:
Sarova Hotels
New Stanley Hotel
PO Box 30680
Nairobi
333233

TSAVO EAST

ARUBA LODGE
Book through:
AA Travel
Union Towers
PO Box 14892
Nairobi
337900

CROCODILE
TENTED CAMP
Book through:
Repotel
Caltex House
Koinange Street
PO Box 46527
Nairobi
27828

TSAVO SAFARI
CAMP
and
VOI SAFARI LODGE
Book through:
African Tours &
Hotels
Utali House
PO Box 30471
Nairobi
336858

TSAVO WEST

KILAGUNI LODGE
and
NGULIA SAFARI
LODGE
Book through:
African Tours &
Hotels
Utali House
PO Box 30471
Nairobi
336858

KITANI LODGE
and
NGULIA SAFARI
CAMP
Book through:
Let's Go Travel
Caxton Hse
Standard Street
PO Box 60342
Nairobi
29539/29540/340331

LAKE JIPE SAFARI
LODGE
Book through:
PO Box 31092
Nairobi
27623

SHIMBA HILLS

SHIMBA HILLS
TREE HOTEL
Book through:
Block Hotels
Rehema House
PO Box 47557
Nairobi
335807

Business Associations

Agricultural Society
Of Kenya
PO Box 30176
Nairobi
566655

Architectural
Association of Kenya
Professional Centre
Parliament Road
PO Box 44258
Nairobi
20582

Association of
Accountants in East
Africa
PO Box 20716
Nairobi
338446

Association of Civil
Engineering
Surveyors of Africa
PO Box 40915
Nairobi
332195

Association of
Consulting Engineers
of Kenya
PO Box 72643
Nairobi
22543

Association of
Professional Societies
in East Africa
PO Box 72643
Nairobi

Automobile
Association Of
Kenya
Argwings Kodhek
Road
PO Box 40087
Nairobi
720382/723195

Automobile
Association of Kenya
Nkurumah Road
PO Box 86250
Mombasa
26778

Brewers Association
of East Africa

Ronald Ngala Street
PO Box 30161
Nairobi
20962

Cotton and Lint Seed
Marketing Board
Uchumi House
PO Box 30477
Nairobi
331006

Commonwealth
Parliamentary
Association
PO Box 41842
Nairobi
21291

East African Tea
Trade Association
Nkrumah Avenue
PO Box 42281
Nairobi
337521

Federation of Kenya
Employers
Oginga Odinga Road
PO Box 1449
Kisumu
41504

Federation of Kenya
Employers
Nyerere Avenue
PO Box 84115
Mombasa
311112

Federation of Kenya
Employers
Arwings Kodhek
Road
PO Box 48311
Nairobi
721929/721948

Institute of Certified
Public Accountants
of Kenya
Red Cross Building
Paliament Road
PO Box 59963
Nairobi
24629

Insurance
Association of
Eastern Africa
Silopark House
Mama Ngina Street
PO Box 45338
Nairobi
20212

Inter-Governmental
Standing Committee
on Shipping
Digo Road
PO Box 99329
Mombasa
20160

Kenya Association of
Hotel Keepers &
Caterers

Wabera Street
Nairobi
330868

Kenya Association of
Manufacturers
Kenyatta Avenue
PO Box 30225
Nairobi
21452/21602

Kenya Association of
Tour Operators
Kaunda Street
PO Box 48461
Nairobi
25570/25103

Kenya Bankers
Association
PO Box 73100
Nairobi
336681/21704

Kenya Clearing
Forwarding &
Warehousing
Association
Ambalal House
PO Box 87227
Nairobi
311778

Kenya Coffee
Growers Association
Haile Selassie
Avenue
PO Box 72832
Nairobi
21725

Kenya Film
Corporation
Uchumi House
PO Box 30674
Nairobi
26651/331745

Kenya Grain
Growers Co-
operative Union
PO Box 50
Nakuru
41800-8

Kenya Hospital
Association
Nairobi Hospital
PO Box 30026
Nairobi
722160

Kenya Medical
Association
Professional Centre
Parliament Road
PO Box 48502
Nairobi
25434

Kenya Medical
Research Institute
Mbagathi Road
PO Box 54840
Nairobi
722541/722672

Kenya National
Chamber of
Commerce &
Industry
Ufanisi House
PO Box 47024
Nairobi
20866/20867/334413

(Branches in: Busia,
Kisumu, Kakamega,
Mombasa, Kilifi,
Nakuru, Nyahururu,
Thika, Nyeri, and
Muranga)

Kenya Pilots
Association
Kimathi Street
PO Box 46041
Nairobi
27055

Kenya Regiment
Association
PO Box 42216
Nairobi
724135

Kenya Sisal Board
Inspectorate
Mozambique Road
PO Box 81764
Mombasa
24325

Kenya Tea
Development
Authority
Rahimtullah Trust
Tower
Moi Avenue
PO Box 30213
21441/25086

Kenya Tourist
Development
Corporation
Utalii House
Uhuru Highway
PO Box 42013
29751/23488

Kenya Transport
Association
Lunga Lunga Road
PO Box 78198
541876

Law Society of Kenya
Parliament Road
PO Box 72219
Nairobi
25558

Mombasa & Coast
Tourist Association
Tom Mboya Street
PO Box 99596
Mombasa
22391

National Nurses
Association of Kenya
PO Box 49422
29083

Clubs

Sporting clubs and associations

NAIROBI

Aero Club
Wilson Aerodrome
PO Box 40813
501772

Aga Khan
5th Avenue
Parklands
PO Box 10843
742890

Amateur Boxing
Association of Kenya
PO Box 47769
802701/28919

Barclays Sports Club
Thika Road
PO Box 30120
802847

Caltex Sports Club
Koinange Street
PO Box 49693
22104

County Sports Club
PO Box 53407
60065

East Africa Kennel
Club
Nyerere Road
PO Box 14223
724766

East Africa Motor
Sports Club
Mombasa Road
PO Box 42786
822843

Globe Eleven Sports
Club
Muthangari
PO Box 43876
49383

Harlequin (Rugby)
Football Club
Ngong Road
PO Box 42999
568565

Impala Club
Ngong Road
PO Box 41516
565684/560638

Jockey Club of Kenya
PO Box 40373
566108-9

Karen Country Club
PO Box 24816
882801/2

Kenya Amateur
Athletic Association
Nyayo Stadium
Uhuru Highway
PO Box 46722
29301/337406

Kenya Football
Federation
Nyayo Stadium
Uhuru Highway
PO Box 40234
26138

Kenya Golf Union
Muthaiga
PO Box 49609
763898

Kenya Karate
Association
PO Box 32184
553226

Kenya Lawn Tennis
Association
Hospital Road
PO Box 43184
725084

Kenya Olympic
Association
Caltex House
Koinange Street
PO Box 40872
331355

Kenya Rugby
Football Union
PO Box 48322
Nairobi
340936

Kenya Taekwondo
Association
Koinange Street
PO Box 61002
336389

Muthaiga Country
Club
Muthaiga Road
PO Box 30181
767754

Nairobi Club
Ngong Road
PO Box 30171
725726

Nairobi Gymkhana
Forest Road
PO Box 40895
742804/742882

Nairobi Sailing & Sub
Aqua Club
PO Box 49973
501250

Ngara Sports Club
PO Box 42804
501631

Parklands
Ojijo Road
PO Box 40116
742938/745164

Premier Club
Forest Road
PO Box 40143
767606

Public Service Club
Hospital Road
PO Box 41185
724031

Railway Club
Haile Selassie
Avenue
PO Box 40476
729820

Railway Golf Club
Haile Selassie
Avenue
PO Box 40476
724084

Rugby Football
Union of East Africa
Ngong Road
PO Box 45766
568565

Royal Nairobi Golf
Club
Ngong Road
PO Box 40221
725768/9

Shell & BP
Gigiri Road
PO Box 41221
749462

Shimba Union Club
Forest Road
PO Box 40114
764069

Sir Ali Muslim Club
Park Road
PO Box 41284
767613

Sir Yusufali Sports
Club
Thika Road
PO Box 45318
802932

Vet/Lab Sports Club
Kabete
PO Box 29105
592214/592108

MOMBASA

Aga Khan
Aga Khan Road
PO Box 82289
313710

Bahari Club
PO Box 90413
Mombasa
471316

Coast Gymkhana
PO Box 84895
313343

Coast Province
Sports Council
Mama Ngina Drv
PO Box 82573
20909

Ghaze Social &
Sports Club
Haile Selassie Road
PO Box 80299
21281/749619

Jaffery Sports Club
Nyerere Avenue
PO Box 81452
313093

Mombasa Club
PO Box 90270
312449/316545

Mombasa Sports
Club
PO Box 90241
24705

Mombasa Golf Club
PO Box 90164
313352

Mombasa Deep Sea
Fishing Club
PO Box 84958
311532

Mombasa Sea
Angling Club
Ras Liwatoni
PO Box 82345
Mombasa
20823

Mombasa Water
Sports Club
Rassini Road
PO Box 81315
20008

Mombasa Yacht Club
Liwatoni Road
PO Box 90391
313350

Nyali Golf & Country
Club
PO Box 95678
471038

United Sports Club
Nyerere Avenue
PO Box 81607
313546

UPCOUNTRY

Eldoret Club
PO Box 78
(0321) 2385/31395

Kericho Club
PO Box 82
(0361) 20860

Kitale Club
PO Box 30
(0325) 20030

Limuru Country
Club
PO Box 10
40721/41351

Nakuru Golf Club
PO Box 652
(037) 40803

Nyanza Club
PO Box 29
Kisumu
(035) 40575

Nyeri Club
PO Box 74
(0171) 4515

Sigona Golf Club
PO Box 10
Kikuyu
(0154) 32431

Thika Sports Club
PO Box 257
(0151) 21321

Service clubs

Kiwanis Club of
Olive Branch
PO Box 45259
Nairobi
333056/332500

Lions International
District 411
PO Box 41981
Nairobi
554098

Rotary International
District 920
PO Box 41910
Nairobi
24128

Round Table
Association
PO Box 41504
Nairobi
336858

United Kenya Club
PO Box 42220
Nairobi
728346/728348

Tour
Operators

NAIROBI

Aardvark Safaris
IPS Building
Kimathi Street
PO Box 69496
331718/334863

Abercrombie & Kent
Mama Ngina Street
PO Box 59749
334955/334943

Across Africa Safaris
Bruce House
Standard Street
PO Box 49420
338230

African Tours &
Hotels
Utalii House
Uhuru Highway
PO Box 30471
336858

Airland Tours &
Travel
Reinsurance Plaza
PO Box 70509
338869

Afro Aviation
Services
Rahimtulla Trust
Building
PO Box 39422
26944

Alfaraj
Rehema House
Standard Street
PO Box 44444
27989

Alick Roberts Safaris
Karen
PO Box 24405
891338

Andrew James
Karen
PO Box 24874
882147

Archer's Tours
Nanak House
Kimathi Street
PO Box 40097
331825/23131

Adventureland
Safaris
PO Box 44899
28961

African Alpine
Safaris
PO Box 20224
334955

African Adventure
Safaris
Ridgeways Road
PO Box 40414
512328

African Travel &
Safaris
Standard Street
PO Box 47839
338080

Afrikan Cultural
Safaris
Hilton Hotel Arcade
PO Box 42468
335581

Ahmedi Expeditions
NCM House
Tom Mboya Street
PO Box 22129
338840

Andrew Holberg
Safaris
Ridgeway Road
PO Box 30328
512558/512289

Balloon Safaris
Westminster House
Kenyatta Avenue
PO Box 43747
338041

Banko Tours Travel
& Car Hire
Latema Road
PO Box 11536
26736

Baringo Bird & Game
Safaris
PO Box 1375
Nakuru
Molo 51Y4

Bateleur Safaris
Hilton Hotel
PO Box 42562
27048/891007

Best Camping Tours
Nanak House
Kimathi Street
PO Box 40223
28091/29667/763469

Big Five Tours &
Safaris
Kenyatta Avenue
PO Box 10367
29803

Bill Winter Safaris
Karen
PO Box 24871
882526

Blacklines Tours
Finlay House
PO Box 55304
331424

Blue Bird Tours &
Travels
Kenyatta Avenue
PO Box 42350
337337-8

Bookings Ltd
New Stanley Hotel
Standard Street
PO Box 56707
25255

Bongo Tours &
Safaris
Silopark House
PO Box 59487
29696

Bruce Travel
Koinange Street
PO Box 40809
26794

Bruce Safaris
Caxton House
Kenyatta Avenue
PO Box 40662
27311

Bushbuck
Adventures
Hughes Building
Muindi Mbingu
Street
PO Box 67449
60437

Bunson Travel
Service
Pan Africa House
PO Box 45456
21992

Centrex Tours
Hughes Building
Muindi Mbingu
Street
PO Box 41830
332267

Cheli & Peackock
PO Box 39806
(0154) 22170

Crossway Car Hire,
Tours & Travel
Postal Chambers
Banda Street
PO Box 10228
20848

David Read Safaris
PO Box 183
Kitale
Dosojin
Standard Building
Wabera Street
PO Box 74612
339780

Dik Dik Safaris
Hilton Hotel
PO Box 43004
23268

Duma Tours &
Safaris
Songoot Walk
PO Box 48167
764518

Ebra Tours & Safaris
Standard Building
PO Box 43457
334937/331494

Eclipse Safari
Services
Heron Court Hotel
PO Box 59863
720640

EA Ornithological
Safaris
Ndoto Road
Lavington
PO Box 48019
48772

EA Wildlife Safaris
Fedha Towers
PO Box 43747
27217

El Tome Safaris
City Hall Annex
PO Box 10243
23133

EMM International
Reinsurance Plaza
PO Box 48017
331801/27883/20541

Eric Risley Tours
Ndege Road
Langata
PO Box 24751
891370

Flamingo Tours
Kencom House
PO Box 44899
28961

Four by Four Safaris
PO Box 24397
21065

Flamingo Travel
Hilton Hotel
PO Box 45070
27927

Frontier Safari
Riara Road
PO Box 21090
558093

Franz Lang Safaris
Langata South Road
PO Box 42026
62670

Funga Safaris
Caltex House
Koinange Street
PO Box 41558
337751

Furaha Travel
Mamujee Building
Tom Mboya Street
PO Box 41641
333696

Gametrackers
Finance House
Banda/Loita Streets
PO Box 62042
338927/22703

General Tours &
Safaris
Norwich Union
House
Kimathi Street
PO Box 30585
22303/331325

Gateway Travel
Utalii House
PO Box 22522
23449

Greyline Safaris
Mama Ngina Street
PO Box 22450

Global Tours
Kimathi Street
PO Box 56986
338788

Glory Car Hire Tours
Reinsurance Plaza
PO Box 66969
25024/24428/331523

Glen Cottar Safaris
Kaunda Street
PO Box 44626
558331/558122

HAT
PO Box 55182
24079/728002

Homeland Travel
Utalii House
Uhuru Highway
PO Box 57571
339151/22125

Haidery Tours Travel
Impala House
Tom Mboya Street
PO Box 45728
336201

Holiday Tours
Panafric Hotel
PO Box 72171
720418

Inside Africa Safaris
Haile Selassie
Avenue
PO Box 59767
337154/23304

Intasun Holidays
Kenwood House
Kimathi Street
PO Box 42977
340161/24037

Intercontinental
Tours & Travels
Texcal House
Koinange Street
PO Box 49473
339518

Intra Safaris
College House
University Way
PO Box 50096
29961

Ivory Safaris Tours
Mama Ngina St
PO Box 74609
26623/26808

Jet Travel
Rehani House
Banda Street
PO Box 58805
332544

JH Safaris
University Way
PO Box 42238
28168

Jambo Tours
Scandinavia
Corner House
PO Box 34187
336767

Kenebco Tours &
Travel
Nanak House
Kimathi Street
PO Box 20640
27203

Kenya Mystery Tours
Phoenix House
Standard St
PO Box 30442
336876

Kenya Wildlife Trails
Kimathi House
Kimathi Street
PO Box 44687
28960/28942

Ker & Downey
Safaris
Enterprise Road
PO Box 41822
556466

Kimbia Kenya
Chester House
Koinange Street
PO Box 40089
337892

Kenya Photographic
Safaris
Rattansi Trust
Building
Wilson Airport
PO Box 25253
569870/566223

Ken Travel
Ghale House
Moi Avenue
PO Box 30537
330708

Kenyafonic Touring
Muindi Mbingu
Street
PO Box 51239
332292

Kimbia Kenya
Chester House
Koinange Street
PO Box 40089
337892

Low Budget Car Hire
& Tours
Tubman Road
PO Box 20393
29488

Lucky Cabs Tours &
Safaris
Nyerere Road
PO Box 49461
725857

Let's Go Travel
Caxton House
Standard Street
PO Box 60342
340332/29539-40

Mashariki Tour
Mashariki Motor
House
PO Box 30179
558144

Mathews & Roberts
Safaris
Miotoni Lane
Karen
PO Box 47448
882559

Menno Travel Service
Jubilee Building
PO Box 40444
Telex: 22119
332375/332439

Micato Safaris
Rahimtulla Trust
House
Moi Avenue
PO Box 43374
336138

Michaelides Safaris
New Waumani Hse.
Westlands
PO Box 48010
740074/748442

Mountain Travel
Centre
Mama Ngina Street
PO Box 20115
334574

Mountain Travel
Mama Ngina Street
PO Box 57341
23649

Mongoose Tour Co.
Ambassadeur Hotel
Moi Avenue
PO Box 70192
20048/336803

Mumbiastros Safaris
Donyo Sabuk
Avenue
PO Box 11366
21171

New Horizon Travel
Agency
International House
PO Box 40193
338837

Nilestar Safari Centre
Hilton Hotel
PO Box 42291
28941/24885/337392

Njambi Tours
Hotel
Intercontinental
PO Box 30618
331762

Nairobi Travel
Centre
Fedha Towers
PO Box 41178
27930

Nyati Tours
City Hall Way
PO Box 46841
26896

Oak Tours & Travel
Gilfillan House
Kenyatta Avenue
PO Box 32846
21399

Orbit Travel
Gilfillan House
Kenyatta Avenue
PO Box 18509
21498

Pan African Travel
Organization
Tunmaini House
Nkrumah Avenue
PO Box 44209
333281

Pelizzoli Safaris
Nanak House
Kimathi Street
PO Box 48287
331231

Percival Tours
IPS Building
Kimathi Street
PO Box 43987
331667

Perry Mason Safaris
Jubilee House
Kimathi Street
PO Box 49655
882249

Pollman's Tours
Cannon House
Haile Selassie Ave.
PO Box 45895
27250/29792

Private Safaris
Caxton House
Kenyatta Avenue
PO Box 45205
337104/337115

Pelican Tours
Moi Avenue
PO Box 18755
339897

Resident's Travel
Den
Centro House
Westlands
PO Box 14960
743415-4

Rhino Safaris
PO Box 48023
Telex: 22081
28102/25419/332372

Richard Bonham
Safaris
PO Box 24133
882521

Robin Hurt Safaris
Dagoretti Road
Karen
PO Box 24988
882826/882086

Safari Bookings
Woodvale Grove
Westlands
PO Box 600006
747555

Safari Camp Services
Nginyo House
Koinange Street
PO Box 44801
28936

Safari Travel Kenya
KCS House
Mama Ngina Street
PO Box 31120
23141/22290-1

Safaris Unlimited
PO Box 20138
332132

Safariworld Kenya
Hilton Hotel
PO Box 56803
20940

Sapieha Tours
PO Box 48682
512283

Scenic Safaris
Westminster House
Kenyatta Avenue
PO Box 49188
26526/29092/25833

Sea Sports & Safaris
Mutero Estate
Karen
PO Box 24959
882766

Senator Travel
Service
Rehama House
Standard Street
PO Box 46654
22855/24410/336529

Shimba Tourist
Service
Langata Road
PO Box 41942
501366/501488

Silver Spear Tours
Consolidated House
PO Box 40433
334722

Somak Travel
Corner House
PO Box 48495
332346/20557

Southerncross Safaris
Pan Africa House
Standard Street
PO Box 48362
26069/21030

Special Camping
Safaris
Gilfillan House
Kenyatta Avenue
PO Box 51512
338325

Star Travel and Tours
New Stanley Hotel
Standard Street
PO Box 48225
26996/20165

Sunbelt Safaris
Kencom House
Moi Avenue
PO Box 49492
25383/22491

Sunny Safaris
Portal Place
Banda Street
PO Box 74495
27659

Suntrek Tours
Monrovia Street
PO Box 48146
24967

Thorn Tree Safaris
Jubilee Building
Kaunda Street
PO Box 42475
25641/25941/28981

Thru The Lens
Camping Safaris
Jubilee House
PO Box 34777
Telex: 25745
726820

Tippett's Safaris
Uhuru Highway
PO Box 43806
332132

Tour Africa Safaris
Corner House
PO Box 34187
336767-9

Tor Allan Safaris
Chester House
Koinange Street
PO Box 41959
891190

Trans-African Guides
Koitobas Road
Karen
PO Box 49583
891172

Transworld Safaris
Corner House
PO Box 44690
333129

Travel Brokers
Salama House
Mama Ngina Street
PO Box 44082
26808

Travel Mart
Nanak House
Kimathi Street
PO Box 46085
22508/27637

Travelour
Longonot Place
Kijabe Street
PO Box 12547
22942

Travel Promoters
Sarit Centre
Westlands
PO Box 56457
749473-7

Tropical Ice
Jubilee Exchange
Building
Kaunda Street
PO Box 57341
23649

Tropical Land Tours
and Safaris
Westlands Road
PO Box 14874
749259

Ulf Aschan
Wilson Airport
PO Box 44715
337312/330590

United Touring
Company
Fedha Towers
PO Box 42196
331960

Unlimited Travel
New Stanley Hotel
Standard St
PO Box 30722
23752/334664

Universal Safari
Tours
Cotts House
PO Box 49312
21446/339818

Vacational Tours
Cnr Kenyatta
Avenue & Muindi
Mbingu Street
PO Box 44401
29470/29942/23312

Visit Africa
Queensway House
Kaunda Street
PO Box 59565
23257

Waku Waku Safaris
PO Box 58989
725151

Westminster Safaris
Westminster House
Kenyatta Avenue
PO Box 57046
338041-45

Yare Safaris
Westlands Road
PO Box 63006
337392

Zirkuli Expeditions
Postal Chambers
Banda Street
PO Box 34548
23949/20848

Zodiac Travel
Hughes Building
PO Box 46851
23148/22789

MOMBASA

Archer's Mombasa
Ambalal House
PO Box 84618
311884

African Hunting
Safaris
Nkrumah Road
PO Box 80627
312448

Diamond Car Hire
Tours & Safaris
PO Box 87898
311672

Express Safaris
Moi Avenue
PO Box 86031
25699

Galu Safaris
Nkurumah Road
PO Box 99456
314174

Gupta's Car Hire
Moi Avenue
PO Box 83451
311182/20728

Highways Tours
Moi Avenue
PO Box 84787
26886/20383

Jumbo Tours
Moi Avenue
PO Box 80717
20418

Ketty Tours Safaris
PO Box 82391
312204/311355

Kuldips Touring Co
Moi Avenue
PO Box 82662
25928/24067/26407

Leisure Car Hire
Tours & Safaris
Moi Avenue
PO Box 84902
24704/314846

Lofty Safaris
Hassanali Building
Nkrumah Road
PO Box 80629
314397/20241

Leisure Car Hire
Moi Avenue
PO Box 84902
24704/314846

Marajani Tours
Moi Avenue
PO Box 86103
314935/315099

Nile Star Tours
Nkurumah Road
PO Box 90090
315926

Pollman's Tours
Moi Avenue
PO Box 84198
20703/312565-7

Southerncross Safaris
PO Box 90653
20737/26765

Turkana Safaris
Castle Hotel
Moi Avenue
PO Box 99300
21065

NANYUKI

Flame Tree Safaris
PO Box 9
Nanyuki
Nanyuki 2053

Olechugu Safaris
Ol Donyo Farm
PO Box 295
Nanyuki
Timau 24

Car Hire Companies

NAIROBI

Across Africa Safaris
Bruce House
Standard Street
PO Box 49420
332744/23013

Avenue Service
Station
Kenyatta Avenue
PO Box 14673
332166/7

Avis
Union Towers
PO Box 49795
Moi Avenue
336794/334317-8

Kenyatta Avenue
336703/4
Hilton Hotel
29576

Jomo Kenyatta
Airport
822186

Budget
Utali House
Uhuru Highway
PO Box 48555
23098/9
23074

Central Rent-A-Car
Fedha Towers
Standard Street
PO Box 49439
22888/332296

Coast Car Hire
New Stanley Hotel
PO Box 56707
20365/336570/25255

Crossways Car Hire
Tours and Travel
Portal Chambers
Banda Street
PO Box 10228
23949/20848

Europcar
Bruce House
Standard Street
PO Box 49420
332744

Jomo Kenyatta
Airport
335290

Gametrackers
Finance House
PO Box 62042
338927/22703

Glory Car Hire
Reinsurance Plaza
PO Box 66969
25024/24428/331533

Habib's Car Hire
Agip House
Haile Selassie
Avenue
PO Box 48095
20463/23816

Hertz
Muindi Mbingu
Street
PO Box 42196
331960/27847/8

Inside Africa Safaris
Haile Selassie
Avenue
PO Box 59767
23304/337154/
740869

Intasun Holidays
Kenwood House
Kimathi Street
PO Box 42977
340161/334438

Kenya Wildlife Trails
Kimathi House
Kimathi Street
PO Box 44687
28960/28942

Lets Go Travel
Caxton House
Standard Street
PO Box 60342
340331

Market Car Hire
Koinange Street
PO Box 49713
25797/335735

Scenic Safaris
Westminster House
Kenyatta Avenue
PO Box 49188
26526/29092/25833

Texcal House Service
Station
Koinange Street
PO Box 49473
331327/330787

Vacational Tours
Kenyatta Avenue
PO Box 44401
23312/29470/29942

Wheels Car Hire
Jubilee Exchange
Building
Kaunda Street
PO Box 47173
336038/25103

MOMBASA

Avis
Moi Avenue
PO Box 84868

23048/20465
Two Fishes Hotel
(01261) 2101

Moi International
Airport
433211

Mombassa Beach
Hotel
471861

Glory Car Hire
Trans Ocean House
Moi Avenue
PO Box 85527
21159/313561

MALINDI

Avis
Sitawi House
PO Box 197
20513

Lawfords Hotel
20440

Watamu Beach Hotel
Watamu 1

Bus Companies

NAIROBI

Akamba
Lagos Road
PO Box 40322
22027

Coast Bus Services
Accra Road
PO Box 16030
29494

OTC
Racecourse Road
PO Box 30475
23476

Goldline
Crossroads
PO Box 28016
25279/21963/553172

Karim Bus Co
Kirinyaga Road
PO Box 43802
338515

Kirima Bus Service
New Pumwani Road
PO Box 28470
29136

MPS (Kenya)
Duruma Road
PO Box 43940
334431

Malindi Taxis
Kirinyaga Road
PO Box 47960
24315

Mawingo Bus
Services
Cnr Landhies and
Cross Road
29411

Merali Bus Services
Racecourse Road
24812

Nairobi Bus Union
Lagos Road
PO Box 10219
21642

Nairobi Delux
Services
335421

Rift Valley Peugeot
Service
Latema Road
PO Box 458817
26374

United Peugeot
Service
Duruma Road
PO Box 43940
27739

Shore Line Coach
Service
PO Box 45274
557218

MOMBASA

Ambiance Bus
Service
Jomo Kenyatta
Avenue
PO Box 82199
494693

Goldline
Mwembe Tayari
Road
PO Box 83542
20027/26757

Ivenya Bus Service
Jomo Kenyatta
Avenue
PO Box 81664
491544

MPS
Haile Selassie Road
PO Box 83614
20368

Malindi Taxis
Jomo Kenyatta
Avenue
PO Box 83857
25441

Mawingo Bus
Services
Jomo Kenyatta
Avenue
314318

Nairobi Deluxe
Jomo Kenyatta
Avenue
PO Box 83857
492431

Tawakal
Jomo Kenyatta
Avenue
PO Box 87630
491960

Taxis

NAIROBI

Airporter
Jomo Kenyatta
Airport
PO Box 19027
822348

Archers Cabs
Koinange Street
PO Box 40097
20289/21935

Jambo Taxis
PO Box 75057
Jomo Kenyatta
Airport Branch
822011
University Way
Branch
27377

Kenatco Taxis
Uchumi Hse
PO Box 46991
21561/25123/338611

Kenya Taxi Cabs
Association
PO Box 74526
Excelsior Hotel
Branch
726047
Koinange Street
Branch
726330
Lilian Towers Branch
332416
Muindi Mbingu
Street Branch
726048
Utalii Street Branch
726241

MOMBASA

Archers
PO Box 84618
25362

Kenatco Taxis
PO Box 93179
20340/331456
Taxi Service Voda
PO Box 81030
23701

Major Hospitals

NAIROBI

Nairobi Hospital
Arwings Kodhek Rd
722160-6

Aga Khan Hospital
Corner 3rd Parklands
Avenue & Limuru
Road
742531

Mater Misericordia
(Maternity)
Dagenham Road
Nairobi south 'B'
556878

Gertrude's Garden
Children's Hospital
Muthaiga Road
65305/6

MP Shah Hospital
Corner Shivachi Rd
& Parklands Rd
742763

MOMBASA

Aga Khan Hospital
Vanga Road
312953

Coast Provincial
General Hospital
Kisauni Road
24111

Katherine Bibby
Hospital
Makadara Rd
312190

Lady Grigg
Maternity Hospital
Abdel Nasser Road
314201

**For all emergency
services: Dial 999.**

Banks

African
Development Bank

Algemene Bank of
Africa

Bank of Baroda

Bank of India

Bank of Credit &
Commerce
International
Overseas Ltd

Bank of Nova Scotia

Bank of Oman

Bank of Tokyo Ltd

Barclays Bank of
Kenya Ltd

Biashara Bank of
Kenya

Central Bank of
Kenya

Chase Manhattan
O'seas Corp

Citibank N.A.

Commercial Bank of
Africa

Continental Illinios
National Bank &
Trust Co of Chicago

Co-operative Bank of
Kenya

East African
Development Bank

First American Bank
of Kenya

Grindlays Bank
International (Kenya)

Habib Bank

Habib AG Zurich

Industrial
Development Bank
Ltd

Kenya Commercial
Bank

Kenya Post Office
Savings Bank

Middle East Bank
Kenya

National Bank of
Kenya

Pan African Bank

Standard Chartered
Bank Africa

Trade Bank

**Credit Card
Representatives**

American Express
Bruce House
Standard Street
PO Box 40433
Nairobi
334722

Diners Club
International House
PO Box 30403
Nairobi
727243-8

Visa/Barclaycard
Barclays Bank
Moi Avenue
PO Box 30120
Nairobi
26386

Casinos

NAIROBI

International Casino
Museum Hill

Safari Park Hotel &
Casino De Paradise
Thika Road

Inter-Continental
Hotel Casino
Cnr Uhuru Highway
& City Hall Way

MOMBASA

International Casino
Leisure Lodge
Diani Beach

International Casino
Oceanic Hotel
Light House Road
Nightclubs

Night Clubs

NAIROBI

Annabells
Moi Avenue

Bubbles
(International
Casino)
Museum Hill

Beat House
Kimathi Street

Bedouin Complex
Mombasa Road

Bombax Club
Ngong Road

Brilliant
Murang'a Road

Cantina
(Wilson Airport)
Langata Road

Carnivore
Langata Road

Club Boomerang
Westlands Road

Club le Chalet
(Chiromo Hotel)
Chiromo Road

Florida 2000
Moi Avenue

Garden Square
City Hall Way

Hollywood
Moktar Daddah
Street

Hillock
Enterprise Road

Imani Night Club
Ronald Ngala Street

JKA Resort Club
Mombasa Road

Lost World
Mombasa Road

New Florida Night
Club
Koinange Street

Visions
Kimathi Street

MOMBASA

Bora Bora
Malindi Road

Bird
Behind PO next to
Bristol Hotel

Banda Disco
(Africana Sea Lodge)
Diani Beach

Breakers
(Bamburi Beach
Hotel)
Malindi Road

Club Jade
(Neptune Beach)
Bamburi

Discongoma
(Diani Reef Hotel)
Diani

Kasbah
Digo Road

Le Club
(Hotel Inter-
Continental)
Shanzu Beach

New Florida
Mama Ngina Drive

New Star Day &
Night Club
Nkurumah Road

Rainbow
Mnazi Moja Road

Sunshine Day &
Night Club
Moi Avenue

Tiffanys
Ambalal House

The Pitt
(Robinson Baobab
Hotel)
Diani Beach

Cinemas

NAIROBI

ABC
Yatta Road

Bellevue Drive-In
Mombasa Road

Cameo
Kenyatta Avenue

Casino
Ndumberi Road

Embassy
Latema Road

Fox Drive-In
Thika Road

Kenya
Moi Avenue

Metropole
Adams Arcade

Nairobi
Uchumi House
Aga Khan Walk

Odeon
Latema Road

Rainbow
Biringo Square

Sun City
2nd Avenue
Eastleigh

20th Century
(Duplex)
Mama Ngina Street

MOMBASA

Kenya
Nkrumah Road

Lotus
Makadara Road

Majestic
Nehru Road

Moons
Khalifa Road

Theatres

NAIROBI

Braeburn Theatre
Litanga Road
PO Box 45112
567901

Kenya National
Theatre
Harry Thuku Road
PO Box 43031
20536

Phoenix Players
Parliament Road
PO Box 52383
25506

MOMBASA

Little Theatre Club
Mnazi Moja Road
PO Box 81143
312101/35497

Art Galleries

NAIROBI

Africa Cultural
Gallery
Mama Ngina Street
PO Box 10320
3334044

African Heritage
Kenprop Bldg
Kenyatta Ave
PO Box 17871
554378/555501

Gallery Watatu
Standard Street
PO Box 41855
28737

Handcarvers Gallery
City Hall Way
PO Box 41133
28903

Paa Ya Paa Gallery
Ridgeways Road
PO Box 49646
512257

Tazama Art
Rehema House
Standard Street
PO Box 21130
335597

The Art Gallery
Corner House
Mama Ngina Street
PO Box 48725
337159

Wood & Stone
Gallery
Bruce House
Kaunda Street
PO Box 21558
22505/25648

Kenya Media Directory

Magazines

Africa Economic
Digest
PO Box 74248
Nairobi
27055

Afro Love
PO Box 11302
Nairobi
28251

Autonews
PO Box 30339
Nairobi
25502

Beyond
PO Box 22027
Nairobi
338211

Business Contact
PO Box 72732
Nairobi
21044

Consumers Digest
PO Box 50795
Nairobi
333322/330557

Drum
PO Box 43372
Nairobi
23684/23690

East African
Computer News
PO Box 67335
Nairobi
332219

Executive
PO Box 47186
Nairobi
555811/557868

Finance
PO Box 44094
Nairobi
21581/331457

Golf News
PO Box 31283
Nairobi
339738

Health Digest
PO Box 60481
Nairobi
26556

Inside Kenya Today
PO Box 30025
Nairobi
23201

Kenya Farmer
PO Box 47186
Nairobi
555811/557868

Mashambani
PO Box 43350
Nairobi
338869

Mother & Care
PO Box 57640
Nairobi
338462

Parents
Stellan Consult Ltd
PO Box 50795
Nairobi
21431/333222

Personal Secretary
PO Box 56795
Nairobi
330541

Presence
PO Box 10988
Nairobi
20196

Rainbow
PO Box 42271
Nairobi
724166

Safari
PO Box 30339
Nairobi
25502/22470

Signature
PO Box 46319
Nairobi
335210

Step Magazine
PO Box 58070
Nairobi
802281

Swara
PO Box 20110
Nairobi
27047/331888

Student's Tribune
PO Box 30344
Nairobi
334244

The Kenya Builders
PO Box 72732
Nairobi
21044

The Nairobi Observer
PO Box 67791
Nairobi
20758

The Service Guide
PO Box 12697
Nairobi
337027

Trade & Industry
PO Box 30339
Nairobi
25502

Trade Guide
PO Box 61356
Nairobi
20853

Tradeways
PO Box 70287
Nairobi
25445

Transport
PO Box 44094
Nairobi
340482

True Love
PO Box 43372
Nairobi
23684

Viva Magazine
PO Box 46319
Nairobi
340530

Weekly Review
PO Box 42271
Nairobi
27596

Woman's Voice
PO Box 44659
Nairobi
22095/27033

YMCA
PO Box 30330
Nairobi
724116

Youth
PO Box 45245
Nairobi
23641

Newspapers

Coastweek
Nkrumah Road
PO Box 87270
Mombasa
313767

Kenya Times and
Kenya Leo
Muindi Mbingu
Street
PO Box 30958
Nairobi
24251

Daily Nation
Tom Mboya Street
PO Box 49010
Nairobi
27651/27166

The Standard
Likoni Road
PO Box 81649
Nairobi
540280

Foreign newspapers
are also available,
usually two days
after publication.

Radio

Kenya Broadcasting
Corporation

Three services —
English, Kiswahili,
and vernacular.

Hours of
transmission: 5.00am
to 11.00pm (midnight
on Saturdays)

Broadcasting House
Harry Thuku Road
PO Box 30456
Nairobi
334567

Television

Kenya Broadcasting
Corporation

One service —
broadcast to western
Kenya (band 1,
channel 2), Nairobi
area (band 1, channel
4), coastal area (band
3, channel 6), and
Mount Kenya area
(band 3, channel 10).
English and
Kiswahili
programmes.

Hours of
transmission: 5.00pm
to 11.00pm and
2.00pm to 11.00pm
(Saturdays).

Broadcasting House
Harry Thuku Road
PO Box 30456
Nairobi
334567

International News Services

Foreign
Correspondents'
Association
Press Centre
Chester House
Koinange Street
PO Box 44598
Nairobi
Telex: 22758/25101/
25151
48948/330261/23143

Cultural Centres, Libraries, and Museums

NAIROBI

Alliance Francaise
ICEA Building
Kenyatta Avenue
340054/340079

American Cultural
Centre
National Bank
Building
Harambee Avenue
337877

Bomas of Kenya
Forest Edge Road
891802

British Council
ICEA Building
Kenyatta Avenue
334855

French Cultural Centre
Loita Street
336263

Goethe Institute
German Cultural
Centre
Maendeleo House
24640

Italian Cultural
Institute
Wabera Street
20278/340966

Kenya National
Archives
Moi Avenue
28959/28020

Japan Information
Centre
Post Bank House
Market Lane
331196

Kenya National
Library Service
Ngong Road
27871/29186

McMillan Memorial
Library
Banda Street
21844

National Museum of
Kenya
Museum Hill Road
742161

Railway Museum
Moi Avenue
21211

KITALE
Kitale Museum
20670/20311

KISUMU
British Council
Oginga Odinga Road
2957

Kisumu Museum
40804

LAMU
Lamu Museum
3073

MARALAL
Kenyatta House
2092

MERU
Meru Museum
20482

MOMBASA
Alliance Francaise
Freed Building
Moi Avenue
25048

British Council
City House
Nyerere Avenue
23076

Fort Jesus Museum
312839/312246

National Library
Service
Moi Avenue
26380

Bibliography

The African Letters (1988), edited by G. F. V. Kleen, published by St. Martin's Press, New York.

Africa's Rift Valley (1975), by Colin Willock, published by Time-Life Books, New York.

The Beautiful Birds of Kenya (1985), by John Karmali, published by Westlands Sundries, Nairobi.

The Beautiful People of Kenya (1989), by Mohamed Amin, Duncan Willetts, and Brian Tetley, published by Westlands Sundries, Nairobi.

The Beautiful Plants of Kenya (1986) by John Karamali, published by Westlands Sundries, Nairobi.

The Beauty of Kenya (1984), by Mohamed Amin and Duncan Willetts, published by Westlands Sundries, Nairobi.

The Beauty of the Kenya Coast (1986), by Mohamed Amin and Duncan Willetts, published by Westlands Sundries, Nairobi.

The Book of Kenya (1980), by Gerald Cubitt and Eric Robbins, published by Collins and Harvill Press, London.

Cradle of Mankind (1981), by Mohamed Amin and Brian Tetley, published by Chatto & Windus, London.

Faces of Kenya (1977), by David Keith Jones, published by Hamish Hamilton, London.

Facing Mount Kenya (1965), by Jomo Kenyatta, published by Mercury Books, London.

A Far Off Place (1978), by Laurens Van Der Post, published by Harcourt Brace Jovanovich, Inc., New York.

A Field Guide to the Birds of East Africa (1967), by J. G. Williams, published by Collins, London.

A Field Guide to the Butterflies of Africa (1969), by J. G. Williams, published by Collins, London.

A Field Guide to the National Parks of East Africa (1967), by J. G. Williams, published by Collins, London.

Flame Trees of Thika (1987), by Elspeth Huxley, published by Penguin Books, Inc., New York.

Fodor's Kenya (1987), Random House, New York.

A Guide to Kenya and Northern Tanzania (1971), by David F. Hoorobin, published by East African Publishing House, Nairobi.

Guide Book to Mount Kenya and Kilimanjaro (1971), by John Mitchell. Mountain Club of Kenya, Nairobi.

Harambee Country (1970), by Kenneth Bolton, published by Geoffrey Bles Ltd, London.

Ivory Crisis (1983), by Mohamed Amin and Ian Parker, Published by Chatto & Windus, London.

Journey through Kenya (1982), by Mohamed Amin, Duncan Willetts, and Brian Tetley. Bodley Head, London.

Journey to the Jade Sea, by John Hillaby, published by Paladin, London.

Kenya (Insider's Guide series) (1989), Hunter Publishing, New York.

Kenya: The Magic Land (1968), by Mohamed Amin, Duncan Willetts, and Brian Tetley, published by Bodley Head, London.

Kenya Travel Guide (1988), (Berlitz Travel Guides series), Macmillan Publishing Co., New York.

Kenya: A Visitor's Guide (1987), by Arnold Curtis, published by Hunter Publishing, Inc., New York.

The Kenya Pioneers (1985), by Errol Trzebinski, published by W. W. Horton & Co., New York.

The Last of the Maasai (1987), by Mohamed Amin, Duncan Willetts, and John Eames, published by Bodley Head, London.

Maasai (1980), by Carol Beckwith and Tepilit Ole Saitoti, published by Elm Tree Books, London.

The Maasai: Herders of East Africa (1964), by Sonia Bleeker, published by Dobson Books, London.

Malindi (1975), by Esmond Bradely Martin, published by East African Literature Bureau, Nairobi.

The Marsh Lions (1982), by Jonathan Scott and Brian Jackman, published by Elm Tree Books, London.

My Pride and Joy (1987), by George Adamson, published by Simon & Schuster Inc., New York.

The Orphans of Tsavo (1966), by Daphne Sheldrick, published by Collins & Harvill Press, London.

Out of Africa (1981), by Isak Dinesen (Karen Blixen), published by Modern Library, New York.

Out in the Midday Sun: My Kenya (1987), by Elspeth Huxley, published by Viking Penguin, New York.

People of Kenya (1967), by Joy Adamson, published by Collins & Harvill Press, London.

Portraits in the Wild: Animal Behaviour in East Africa (1975), by Cynthia Moss, published by Elm Tree Books, London.

Portraits of Africa (1983), by Mohamed Amin and Peter Moll, published by Collins & Harvill Press, London.

Railway Across the Equator (1986), by Mohamed Amin, Duncan Willetts and Alastair Matheson, published by Bodley Head, London.

Rhinos: Endangered Species (1988), by Malcolm Penny, published by Facts On File, New York.

Run Rhino Run (1983), by Esmond and Chryssee Bradley Martin, published by Chatto & Windus, London.

Shepherds of the Desert (1984), by David Keith Jones, published by Elm Tree Books, London.

A Story like the Wind (1978), by Laurens Van Der Post, published by Harcourt Brace Jovanovich, New york.

Treetops Hotel (1969), by Eric Sherbrooke Walker, published by Robert Hale & Co, London.

The Tree where Man was Born (1972), by Peter Matthiessen, published by E. P. Dutton, New York.

An Unfinished Journey (1987), by Shiva Naipul, published by Viking Penguin, New York.

The Tsavo Story (1973), by Daphne Sheldrick, published by Collins & Harvill Press, London.

White Man's Country: Lord Delamare and the Making of Kenya (1935), by Elspeth Huxley, published by MacMillan & Co, London.

White Mischief (1984), by James Fox, published by Random House, New York.

The White Nile (1967), by Alan Moorhead, published by Penguin, London.

INDEX